Command Decisions

COMMAND

Prepared by
the Office of the Chief
of Military History,
Department of the Army

Kent Roberts Greenfield
GENERAL EDITOR

Martin Blumenson

Robert W. Coakley

Stetson Conn

Richard M. Leighton

Charles V. P. von Luttichau

Charles B. MacDonald

Sidney T. Mathews

Maurice Matloff

Ralph S. Mavrogordato

Leo J. Meyer

John Miller, Jr.

Louis Morton

Forrest C. Pogue

Roland G. Ruppenthal

Robert Ross Smith

Earl F. Ziemke

DECISIONS

With an
Introduction by
HANSON W. BALDWIN

Harcourt, Brace and Company
NEW YORK

first edition

"Japan's Decision for War" by Louis Morton appeared as "The Japanese Decision for War" in *United States Naval Institute Proceedings,* December, 1954. Copyright, 1954 by the United States Naval Institute and reprinted by permission.

"The ANVIL Decision: Crossroads of Strategy" by Maurice Matloff appeared in different form as "Was the Invasion of Southern France Necessary?" in *United States Naval Institute Proceedings,* July, 1958. © 1958 by the United States Naval Institute and reprinted by permission.

"The Decision to Halt at the Elbe" by Forrest C. Pogue appeared as "Why Eisenhower's Forces Stopped at the Elbe" in *World Politics,* April, 1952. Copyright, 1952 by *World Politics* and reprinted by permission.

"The Decision to Use the Atomic Bomb" by Louis Morton appeared in *Foreign Affairs,* January, 1957. Copyright 1957 by The Council on Foreign Relations, Inc., New York and reprinted by permission.

Library of Congress Catalog Card Number: 59-10247
Printed in the United States of America

Contents

v

List of Maps

Introduction
by Hanson W. Baldwin

"History," said Voltaire, "can be well written only in a free country."

This book strikingly illuminates the truth of Voltaire's epigram.

Its twenty chapters—each dealing with a major decision of World War II—represent a distillation of the most comprehensive and painstakingly documented historical project of all time. During and since the war, a unique team of historians, researchers, writers, and secretaries has been filing, culling, collating, studying, and compiling the history of the United States Army's participation in the world's greatest conflict. Millions of documents in miles of filing cabinets—our own records, the records of our enemies, the records of our Allies—have been consulted and the whole supplemented by war and postwar interviews with generals and buck privates and on-the-spot observations.

These Herculean labors have resulted in the publication of scores of thick, fat detailed volumes; others are still to be published. The grand total will include almost one hundred books—factual, precise, let-the-chips-fall-where-they-may type of history.

This gigantic project, unequaled in scope, detail or in the impartial, objective thoroughness of its coverage, has been described as a "history for historians." It was, in a sense, so intended.

The distinguished historians who contribute to this volume are, like Homer, recorders of a modern Iliad—our Army's efforts in the greatest war the nation ever has fought. They have had one aim—to let the facts speak for themselves, to present the "truth, the whole truth and nothing but the truth."

To do this is never an easy task, least of all in such a crowded and global panorama as was World War II. Someone has said of military history that "facts are naked on the battlefield; tomorrow they are generally dressed up." This is the dilemma of all military historians. Combat history must be recorded while it is still hot, before the blood dries and the bullets stop singing. But battlefield facts are never enough. The platoon leader, the company commander, even the general never sees the "Big Picture"; he, each in his way, is the executor of grand strategy but not its author. To know what really happened, it is not enough to consult the men who were there or even to be there yourself. One must also learn why it happened, how the decision was born and shaped, the factors that went into it, the various personalities that influenced it.

Then, too, if one is to write a "history for historians," one cannot indulge in either subjective interpretations or in fatalistic analysis. History is *both* men and events and how one influences the other; the actors in the great dramas here presented helped to shape and fashion those dramas, unlike the characters in *War and Peace,* who, in Tolstoy's concept, were chips caught up on a tidal wave of circumstance. One will find in this volume little interpretation and no opinion except that which is inherent in the marshaled facts.

This, then, is the approach, and it is the triumph of these historians that they have proved what many once doubted: that an officially sponsored government history project can, in a free society, present the facts without fear or favor and with no ax to grind.

Such an approach as this is, indeed, only possible in a free country; it stands in strong contrast to the "double-think" and "double-talk" of Communism. The historians who contribute to these pages write frankly and objectively of the mistakes and faulty planning that marred the record of victory in World War II. But in Soviet history one will find few acknowledgments of error, no record of Vlasoff, the renegade general—chief of staff of the armies in front of Moscow, later captured and a puppet of the Germans. Vlasoff's role in history, as far as the Kremlin is concerned, has been blanked out; he never existed. Soviet military history (except that small portion of it privately written for restricted military use) is, like all Communist writing, a glorification of the Soviet state, a dramatic though unintentional, affirmation of Voltaire's words.

The substance of this book is almost as broad as the war of which it treats—a war in which more than 16,000,000 Americans served in uniform and almost 300,000 lost their lives in combat on battlefields ranging from the tangled rain forests of New Guinea and the sands of the great deserts of the Middle East to the *bocage* country of Normandy and the mountain tundra of the Aleutians.

The great decisions here recounted deal with many of the echelons of command—the decisions of chiefs of state on grand strategy; the decisions of theater commanders; the decisions of general staffs and combined chiefs of staff; the decisions of corps commanders.

They were decisions made by Americans and decisions made by our enemies; they were decisions that channeled the torrent of history, altered the lives of millions, destroyed empires, changed the map, dictated the course of campaigns and battles. They include compound decisions—"politico-military"—purely military judgments, and decisions influenced by personality and prestige factors. One will find in the pages of this book all the complex motivations and factors that influence the life of man and make war an art rather than a science. One will read of the long chance and the great gamble, of weary caution, of how a famous general turned, like Nelson, a blind eye to his orders, of the complex interplay of politics and personalities, of the importance of supply—"for want of a nail the battle was lost."

Command Decisions—a selection from the great Army history project of which it is a part—reflects the high lights of World War II. It is not, and is not intended to be, a comprehensive history of the war; naval campaigns and air battles play only an incidental part in these pages. It is bound to leave unanswered questions; it poses some of the might-have-beens of the past; it whets the appetite for history. Above all, this book probably sheds more light on the intricate process of military decision-making—a process that varies in methodology from the haphazard "by-guess-and-by-God" to infinitely detailed calculation and analysis—than any work yet published.

There are four great lessons that emerge from these pages.

The first is that grand strategy in modern war—at least in democratic states and among allied coalitions—is the product of many minds. Napoleon, with his hand thrust in his coat, could no longer survey the modern battlefield and choose the opportune moment to order a cavalry charge. War today is a management process; most decisions, at least at or above the general officer level, emerge from group or committee discussions and consultations. One-man generalship—though still a factor—is far less important than it was in the days when the range of weapons was a few thousand yards and there was nothing more lethal than bullets, shells, and sabers. (There are, of course, exceptions to the current practice of "war by committee"; Hitler's dictatorial decisions were sweeping and absolute.)

The second lesson—in some ways seemingly contradictory to the first—is that man is still the ultimate arbiter of battle. In the Napoleonic era, God, it was said, was on the side of the Big Battalions. After the Industrial Revolution, God was on the side of the Big Factories. In the Atomic Age, God might be said to be on the side of the Big Bang. World War II was won by the Allies primarily because of overwhelming material superiority—essentially a product of American industry. Yet time and again in these pages one can see the course of history changed by the actions of one strong man, by his will, his conviction, his courage, his "guts," his determination, his *élan*. Man—not machines—makes war. Man without machines is doomed on the modern battlefield. But man without courage, toughness, will to win is also doomed, no matter how powerful his machines. Man, this book really tells us, is still the soul of battle.

The third great lesson implicit in these pages is the importance of land power to decision in war. It is fashionable in the era of jet planes, missiles, and nuclear arms to consign "GI Joe" to the limbo of the past; there are even some pseudo-historians who claim that victory in World War II was primarily the product of sea and air power. This book effectively gives the lie—though this is not its purpose—to such contentions. But perhaps more important, from its pages can be projected some idea of the shape of things to come. Military force of today and tomorrow is indivisible (as indeed it was in World War II); all technical and tactical developments clearly attest to the unity of sea and land and air. But man is a land animal; the objectives of all wars are land objectives—the defense or the attack of nations, cities, terrain. Warriors now leap into the skies, cruise deep beneath the seas, are starting the conquest of space, but the objectives for which they fight all lie upon the good earth. Ground armies—though far different in character from the triangular infantry divisions of World War II—still possess their ancient validity.

And finally, perhaps the greatest truth that future generations may cull from this book is that war, if it is to have any meaning, must have a compound objective. Victory alone is never enough; the painful postwar years have demonstrated that American military victory in World War II—sweeping and complete though it was—did not win a political peace.

As Kent Roberts Greenfield, for years Chief Historian of the Army's Office of Military History and wise guide and mentor to all those who have contributed to this volume, has written: "As far as the United States was concerned, military strategy conceived in terms of . . . [unconditional surrender] became national policy for the duration of the war."

Unlike Britain, the United States had no clear-cut, specific political objective in World War II; we aimed to win—period.

But victory in conflict, as the bloody painful history of man has emphasized aeon after aeon, is never enough. War, if it is to have any logical meaning, must have a political, not merely a military, objective. It *must not* result merely in the substitution of one enemy for another; it *must* result in a more stable and a more secure world. War without political objectives represents senseless slaughter. More than ever today, in the age of the atom, grand strategy represents the enduring marriage of military and political factors.

Command Decisions

Louis Morton

1

Germany First:
The Basic Concept of Allied Strategy
in World War II

Behind all the critical decisions of World War II was a preponderance of judgment among those responsible for American strategy that the main effort of the United States in a war with the Axis Powers of Europe and Asia should be made in the European theater and that Germany must be defeated first. This view coincided, naturally enough, with the interests of the European members of the coalition but was based entirely on the estimate that such a course of action would best serve the interests of the United States. It was an American consensus, arrived at only after a long sequence of discussions and decisions which reflect a reorientation of American views, interests, and plans going back to World War I. Made before American entry into World War II, in the context of a world threatened by Axis aggression in Europe and Asia, the judgment that Germany must be defeated first stands as the most important single strategic concept of the war. From it and the painful deliberations that preceded the decision, the war plan known as RAINBOW 5 was finally crystallized; the plan was put into effect when the Japanese struck at Pearl Harbor and the Philippines on that "day of infamy" in December 1941. The present essay is a review of this vitally important process of crystallization.[1]

American strategical planning in the period immediately following World War I was largely conditioned by the postwar political system and by the wide popular reaction against war. The Versailles Treaty, the Washington Treaties of 1921-1922, and the League of Nations (to which Germany was admitted in 1925) gave promise to

3

the war-weary peoples of the world of an international order in which war would be forever banished. That promise seemed to many to have been fulfilled in 1928 when representatives from most of the nations in the world met at Paris to sign the Kellogg-Briand Pact renouncing war as an instrument of national policy. Though the United States was not a member of the League, American policy was closely and consciously designed to support the actions of the League in its efforts to further world peace.

During these years of disillusion with war, isolationism, and Congressional economy, military planning in the United States was largely theoretical. Germany had just been defeated and stripped of military power. Russia was preoccupied with internal problems and, though Communism was recognized as a menace, the Bolshevik regime was in no position to engage in military adventures beyond its frontiers. Neither France nor Italy had sufficient naval force to attempt any major operation in the Western Hemisphere and had no reason to do so in any case.

Of all the powers in Europe, only Great Britain was theoretically in a position to engage the United States in war with any prospect of success. The British had extensive holdings in the Western Hemisphere from which to launch attacks on American territory and they had enough dreadnoughts and battle cruisers to obtain naval supremacy in the Atlantic. But the possibility of a contest with Britain was extremely remote, for there was no sentiment for war on either side of the Atlantic.

In the Pacific and Far East, the situation was different. Between Japan and the United States there were a number of unresolved differences and a reservoir of misunderstanding and ill will that made the possibility of conflict much more likely in that area than in the Atlantic. Moreover, Japan's position had been greatly strengthened as a result of the war and the treaties that followed. In the view of the planners, the most probable enemy in the foreseeable future was Japan. Thus, U.S. strategic thought in the years from 1919 to 1938 was largely concentrated on the problems presented by a conflict arising out of Japanese aggression against American interests or territory in the Far East.

The preparation of strategic war plans involving joint (*i.e.,* Army and Navy) forces—and for all practical purposes this meant most of the plans prepared by the American staff—was the responsibility of the Joint Board, predecessor of the Joint Chiefs of Staff. Reorganized in 1919 to correct defects that had become apparent since its establishment in 1903, the Board consisted of six members, the Army Chief of Staff and the Chief of Naval Operations, their deputies, and the chiefs of the War Plans Divisions of each of the services. To it came all matters that required cooperation between the two services, either by referral or on the initiative of the Board itself. It had no executive functions nor command authority and until 1939 reported to the War and Navy Secretaries. Its recommendations were purely advisory, and became effective only upon approval by both Secretaries, and, in some cases, by the President himself.

The most notable improvement of the 1919 reorganization was the formation of a Joint Planning Committee to assist the Board. Consisting of eight officers, four each from the War Plans Division of the Army and of the Navy, this committee performed the detailed investigation and study required for policy decisions, preparation of war plans, and all other matters involving joint actions of the Army and Navy. It was, in effect, a working group for the Joint Board and made its reports and recommendations directly to that body.

The problems considered by the Joint Board after World War I varied widely, but the development of joint war plans constituted, as it had from 1903 to 1913, the major work of the Board, with most attention being given to plans for a possible war with Japan—called ORANGE in accordance with the system in effect between 1904 and 1939 of designating war plans by colors, each color corresponding to a specific situation or nation. The mandate to Japan of the German islands in the Central Pacific had given that nation numerous bases astride the U.S. Fleet's line of communication with the Philippines and made American defense of the islands in the war with Japan virtually impossible. Moreover, in the Five Power Naval Treaty of 1922, the United States, Great Britain, France, and Italy had promised not to fortify their Far Eastern possessions in return for a pledge by the Japanese to restrain themselves similarly. By this agreement Japan was virtually assured that the Philippines, Guam, and Hong Kong would not become formidable fortresses threatening its home islands. And although Japan had to accept British and American superiority in capital ships at the Washington Conference of 1922, its naval position in the Pacific improved greatly as a result. In the years that followed, while the United States scrapped ships and Japan built them, the strength of the U.S. Fleet relative to that of Japan so declined that it is doubtful if during the 1920's and 1930's it could have met the latter on equal terms in the western Pacific.

The first postwar plan for war in the Pacific, developed between

1921 and 1924, reviewed America's unfavorable strategic position and recognized Japan as the probable enemy. The strategic concept adopted by the planners in the event of hostilities was to fight "an offensive war, primarily naval" with the objective of establishing "at the earliest date American sea power in the western Pacific in strength superior to that of Japan." To do this, the United States would require a base in that area capable of serving the entire U.S. Fleet. Since the only base west of Pearl Harbor large enough for this purpose was in Manila Bay, it would be essential, said the planners, to hold the bay in case of war and be ready to rush reinforcements, under naval protection, to the Philippines in time to prevent their capture. To the Army fell the vital task of holding the base in Manila Bay until the arrival of the Fleet, but the major role in any war with Japan would be played by the Navy, for success in the final analysis depended on sea power.

War Plan ORANGE made no provision for a landing on the Japanese home islands. Japan was to be defeated by "isolation and harassment," by the disruption of its vital sea communications, and by "offensive sea and air operations against her naval forces and economic life." Presumably it would not be necessary to invade Japan, but the planners recognized that if they could not bring Japan to her knees by these means, they would have to take "such further action as may be required to win the war." [2]

For about fifteen years, the strategic concepts embodied in the ORANGE plan formed the basis for most American war planning. Variations of the plan were prepared and discussed at length. Every conceivable situation that might involve the United States in a war with Japan, including a surprise air attack on Pearl Harbor, was carefully considered and appropriate measures of defense were adopted. At least half a dozen times between 1924 and 1938, the plan was revised, sometimes in response to military changes and sometimes as a result of Congressional sentiment, or because of the international situation. Each time, all the implementing plans had to be changed. The Army and Navy had their separate ORANGE plans, based on the joint plans and complete with concentration tables, mobilization schedules, and the like. In addition, U.S. forces in the Philippines, Hawaii, Panama, and other overseas bases had their joint and service plans, as did the defense sector and continental commands within the United States. Rarely have plans for a war been so comprehensive and detailed, so complete on every echelon, and so long in preparation.

But the United States never fought this war, for ORANGE was based on a situation that never came to pass. The ORANGE war envisaged by the planners was a war between the United States and Japan alone. Neither side, it was assumed, would have allies or attack the territory of a third power. It was a war that was to be fought entirely in the Pacific, with the decisive action to take place in the waters off the Asiatic coast.

These assumptions by the military strategists of the Army and Navy were entirely justified by the international situation and reflected a reasonable estimate of the most probable threat to American interests, an estimate that was shared by most responsible officials during these years. But the planners did not—indeed, could not—ignore other possibilities, no matter how remote. Thus, during the same years in which they labored on ORANGE, the joint planners considered a variety of other contingencies that might require the use of American military forces. Among the most serious, though one of the most unlikely, of these was a war with Great Britain alone (RED), which in the planners' estimate could conceivably arise from commercial rivalry between the two nations, or with Great Britain and Japan (RED-ORANGE). The latter contingency was conceded by all to present the gravest threat to American security, one that would require a full-scale mobilization and the greatest military effort.

In their study of these two contingencies, the military planners came to grips with strategic problems quite different from those presented by ORANGE. A war with Japan would be primarily a naval war fought in the Pacific. So far as anyone could foresee, there would be no requirement for large ground armies. There was a possibility, of course, that Japan would attack the Panama Canal, Hawaii, and even the West Coast of the United States, but no real danger that Japan could seize and occupy any of these places. In the unlikely event of a conflict between Great Britain and the United States, there was a real possibility of invasion of the United States, as well as attacks against the Canal and American interests in the Caribbean and Latin America. In such a war, the major threat clearly would lie in the Atlantic.

Plans developed to meet the remote danger of a RED war, in contrast to ORANGE, called for the immediate dispatch of the bulk of the U.S. Fleet to the Atlantic and large-scale ground operations to deprive the enemy of bases in the Western Hemisphere. As in ORANGE, it was assumed that neither side would have allies among the great powers of Europe and Asia, and no plans were made for an invasion of the enemy's homeland by an American expeditionary force. This was to be a limited war in which the United States would adopt a strategic defensive with the object of frustrating the enemy's assumed objective in opening hostilities.

The problems presented by a RED-ORANGE coalition, though highly theoretical, were more complicated. Here the American strategists had to face all the possibilities of an ORANGE and a RED war—seizure of American possessions in the western Pacific, violation of the Monroe Doctrine, attacks on the Panama Canal, Hawaii, and other places, and, finally, the invasion of the United States itself. Basically, the problem was to prepare for a war in both oceans against the two great naval powers, Great Britain and Japan.

As the planners viewed this problem, the strategic choices open to the United States were limited. Certainly the United States did not have the naval strength to conduct offensive operations simultaneously in both the Atlantic and Pacific Oceans; she must adopt a strategic defensive on both fronts or else assume the strategic offensive in one theater while standing on the defensive in the other. The recommended solution to this problem—and it was only a recommended solution, for no joint war plan was ever adopted—was "to concentrate on obtaining a favorable decision" in the Atlantic and to stand on the defensive in the Pacific with minimum forces. This solution was based on the assumption that since the Atlantic enemy was the stronger and since the vital areas of the United States were located in the northeast, the main effort of the hostile coalition would be made there. For this reason, the initial effort of the United States, the planners argued, should be in the Atlantic.

A strategic offensive-defensive in a two-front war, American strategists recognized, entailed serious disadvantages. It gave the hostile coalition freedom of action to attack at points of its own choosing, compelled the United States to be prepared to meet attacks practically everywhere, exposed all U.S. overseas possessions to capture, and imposed on the American people a restraint inconsistent with their traditions and spirit. Also it involved serious and humiliating defeats in the Pacific during the first phase of the war and the almost certain loss of outlying possessions in that region.

But the strategic offensive-defensive had definite advantages. It enabled the United States to conduct operations in close proximity to its home bases and to force the enemy to fight at great distance from his own home bases at the end of a long line of communications. Moreover, the forces raised in the process of producing a favorable decision in the Atlantic would give the United States such a superiority over Japan that the Japanese might well negotiate rather than fight the United States alone. "It is not unreasonable to hope," the planners observed, "that the situation at the end of the struggle with RED may be such as to induce ORANGE to yield rather than face a war carried to the western Pacific." [3]

This plan for a RED-ORANGE war was admittedly unrealistic in terms of the international situation during the 1920's and 1930's. The military planners knew this as well and better than most and often noted this fact in the draft plans they wrote.[4] But as a strategic exercise it was of great value, for it forced the military planners to consider seriously the problems presented by a war in which the United States would have to fight simultaneously in the Atlantic and Pacific Oceans. In an era when most war planning was focused on the Pacific and when Japan seemed the most likely enemy, this experience may have seemed irrelevant. But it was to prove immensely useful in the plans developed for World War II.

By late 1937 the assumptions that had given to ORANGE planning its prime importance during the past decade and a half had become of doubtful validity. International events had created a situation that made it increasingly unlikely that a war between the United States and Japan could be limited to these two nations. Germany, Italy, and Japan had joined hands in the Anti-Comintern Pact, and threats or direct acts of aggression were the order of the day in Europe and Asia. Great Britain and France, still suffering from the prolonged economic crisis of the early 1930's and weakened by domestic political upheavals, remained passive in the face of this threat, seeking to avert armed conflict by a policy of appeasement.

In the light of these developments, the Joint Board directed its planners to re-examine the ORANGE plan. In its view, the existing plan was now "unsound in general" and "wholly inapplicable to present conditions." The planners were to develop a new plan which should provide, the Board specified, for an initial *"position in readiness"* along the West Coast and the strategic triangle formed by Alaska, Hawaii, and Panama. In addition, the planners were to make "exploratory studies and estimates" of the various courses of action to be followed after the position of readiness had been assumed. Clearly implied in these instructions was the injunction to consider the possibility that the United States might become involved in a European conflict while engaged in offensive operations in the Pacific.[5]

In less than two weeks, the Joint Planning Committee reported its inability to reach an agreement. The Army members, viewing the uncertain situation in Europe, were reluctant to underwrite offensive operations in the Pacific beyond those essential to the security of the strategic triangle and the West Coast. With the European (Rome-Berlin) Axis in mind, they pointed out that political considerations might require limited action and purely defensive operations in the Pacific. To uncover vital areas in the Western Hemisphere for an offensive in the far Pacific seemed to the Army planners foolhardy indeed. Thus, their plan provided for purely defensive operations after the assumption by U.S. forces of a position of readiness.

To the Army planners, the primary problem was to determine the kind of war the United States should fight. Should the situation dictate operations designed only for the defense of the United States or of the Western Hemisphere, then the war in the Pacific might well take on a limited character. It was impossible to determine in advance just what the situation would be, whether the United States would be involved with one or more of the Axis Powers, or even what forces would be available. It might well be, declared the Army planners, that national policy and public opinion would neither require nor support a plan for offensive operations in the Pacific.

The Navy members of the Joint Planning Committee argued that American strategy could not be limited to a purely defensive position in readiness but must aim at the defeat of the enemy. Once war began, production could be quickly increased to provide the means required both for the security of the continental United States and for offensive operations in the Pacific. Should the European Axis give aid to the enemy, the naval planners assumed, with Great Britain clearly in mind, that the United States would have allies who would provide the assistance needed by the U.S. Fleet to maintain naval superiority over Japan. "The character, amount, and location of allied assistance," they hastened to add, "cannot be predicted." [6]

The separate reports submitted by the Army and Navy members of the Joint Planning Committee put the choice between the opposing strategies squarely up to the Joint Board. The Board avoided the choice by issuing new instructions to the planners on December 7, 1937. The new plan, it specified, should have as its basic objective the defeat of Japan and should provide for "an initial temporary position in readiness" for the Pacific coast and the strategic triangle. This last was to be the Army's job; the Navy's task would consist of "offensive operations against ORANGE armed forces and the interruption of ORANGE vital sea communications." [7]

Even under these revised instructions, the planners were unable to agree on the best way to meet an Axis threat. Faced with another split report, the Joint Board turned over the task of working out a compromise to the Deputy Chief of Staff and the Assistant Chief of Naval Operations. These two, after a month of discussion, finally came up with a new ORANGE plan on February 18, 1938. This plan maintained the traditional offensive strategy in the Pacific, but it also took into account the danger of a simultaneous conflict in the Atlantic—the first time this possibility was recognized in ORANGE planning. On the outbreak of a war with Japan, the United States would first assume a position in readiness and make preparations for the offensive against Japan. It would then be ready to meet any unexpected development that might arise, including an attack in the Atlantic. If none did, the Navy would then proceed to take the offensive against Japan with operations directed initially against the mandated islands and extending progressively westward across the Pacific. These operations combined with economic pressure (blockade) would, it was believed, result in the defeat of Japan and a settlement that would assure the peace and safeguard American interests in the Far East.[8]

The 1938 revision of ORANGE, with its emphasis on flexibility, represented an enormous advance in military planning. The Navy's single-minded insistence on an advance into the western Pacific was still present, but it was modified by an increased awareness of the uncertainties of a world threatened by the rising tide of Axis aggression. The Army, with its concern for the defense of the United States, was shifting away from the Pacific orientation that had dominated strategic planning since World War I and was turning anxious eyes toward Europe. A RED-ORANGE war was a theoretical probability no longer worth considering, and the Atlantic area occupied more and more the attention of the strategists. Moreover, all earlier plans had assumed the United States would fight alone; now that the world was becoming divided between two armed camps that assumption might have to be revised.

Though it was the Army planners who seemed most aware of the danger from Europe, it was the Navy that made the first move to strengthen America's Atlantic defenses. In December 1937, the director of the Navy War Plans Division, Captain Royal E. Ingersoll, was sent to London to discuss informally with the British Admiralty the new construction programs of the two navies and the conditions of U.S.-British naval cooperation in the event both nations were involved in a war against Japan. During the course of these discussions, the possibility of a German war inevitably arose. The British viewed this possibility with concern, for the Germans could be expected to attack British trade routes in the Atlantic. Should Italy join Germany, the prospects were even more alarming. The French, if they entered the war, would hold the western Mediterranean, but the British would still have to place the bulk of their forces in the Atlantic. They would have little, therefore, to send to the Far East. Here the United States could perform a valuable service in the common cause by taking up the slack in the Far East in return for the security the Royal Navy would provide in the Atlantic. Even if the United States became involved in the European conflict, Great Britain could still be relied upon to man the Atlantic barrier so long as the U.S. Fleet assumed responsibility for the Pacific. It is perhaps for this reason that the Navy members of the Joint Planning Committee seemed less concerned about the Atlantic and more interested in the Pacific than the Army planners.[9]

Events in Europe in 1938 fully justified the concern of American policy makers and planners, and the Munich crisis in September of that year provided the impetus to a comprehensive review of American strategy. Taking the lead from the public statements of President Roosevelt and Secretary of State Cordell Hull, the Joint Board directed its planning committee in November to make a study of the course the United States should follow if German and Italian aggression in Europe and simultaneous Japanese expansion in the Far East should threaten American security and interests in both the Atlantic and Pacific.[10]

Here, for the first time, was a specific directive to the planners to study (within the context of the current international situation) the problems presented by a two-ocean war in which the United States, acting in concert with allies, would be opposed by a coalition. These problems had been studied before in the ORANGE-RED plans, but under entirely different assumptions and in a completely unrealistic situation. They had been considered briefly and tangentially also in the latest revision of ORANGE with its provision for a position in readiness and cooperation with allies. The informal naval conversations in London in January 1938 were a clear recognition of the possibility of such a war and the first step toward the intimate military collaboration that marked the Anglo-American relationship during World War II.

For almost six months, the planners of the Joint Board considered the problem presented by simultaneous Axis aggression in the Atlantic and Pacific areas and finally, in April 1939, submitted their report. In it they reviewed the world situation, estimated the likelihood of war, calculated the probable objectives of the Axis in Europe and of Japan in the Far East, discussed the effects of concerted action by these powers on the United States, and analyzed the strategic problems involved in the various situations that might result from such action. So comprehensive was the report, such a model of strategic analysis, that it was characterized by the Joint Board as "a monument" to its planning committee and became the basis for much of the strategic planning before Pearl Harbor.[11]

In their effort to arrive at a sound military strategy for the United States, the joint planners examined the various contingencies that might arise as a result of Axis aggression. Based on this examination, their conclusions were that:

1. Germany and Italy would take overt action in the Western Hemisphere only if Great Britain and France remained neutral or were defeated.

2. Japan would continue to expand into China and southeast Asia at the expense of Great Britain and the United States, by peaceful means if possible but by force if necessary.

3. The three Axis Powers would act together whenever the international situation seemed favorable. If other countries, including the United States, reacted promptly and vigorously to such action, then a general war might well follow.

The reaction of the United States to these or any other situations that might arise, the planners pointed out, would depend in large measure on the forces available and the extent to which American interests were involved. In the event of a threat in both oceans simultaneously, the United States, they maintained, should assume the defensive in the Pacific, retaining adequate forces based on Hawaii to guard the strategic triangle. Arguing further in a manner reminiscent of RED-ORANGE planning, the strategists of the Joint Board declared that priority in a two-ocean war must go first to the defense of vital positions in the Western Hemisphere—the Panama Canal and the Caribbean area. From bases in that region, the U.S. Fleet could operate in either ocean as the situation demanded, but its primary obligation must always be to control the Atlantic approaches to the Western Hemisphere, especially to the south where the continent was most exposed. This task would not be difficult if Great Britain and France actively opposed Axis aggression; but if they did not, the security of the South Atlantic would become the major concern of

U.S. forces, and the active cooperation of the Latin American states the indispensable prerequisite for political and military action.

On the basis of their study, the joint planners recommended that a series of war plans be prepared, each of them to be applicable to a different situation. Priority in these plans, they held, must be given to the defense of the United States, and this would require safeguarding the security of the Western Hemisphere. To hold firm to these objectives would be no easy task, the planners recognized. Not only must strategy be linked to policy, but it must also take cognizance of such intangibles as tradition, the spirit of the nation, and "emotionalized public opinion."

The pioneering study by the joint planners in 1939 raised sharply and dramatically the question of American policy in the event of concerted aggression by Germany, Italy, and Japan. By focusing on the threat to the Caribbean and South America, the planners challenged strongly the long-standing orientation of American strategy toward the Pacific and gave weight to the Army's arguments against offensive operations in the western Pacific.

The planners raised another issue that needed to be resolved before the course of national policy could be charted. All the color plans had been based on the assumption the United States would act alone. Was this assumption valid in terms of the international situation and in the face of a threatening Axis coalition? Should the strategists, in drawing up their plans, therefore assume that the United States would have allies? And if so, who would they be and what would we be expected to do for them and they for us? Like the Atlantic-versus-Pacific issue, this question of allies involved political matters and would have to be resolved by the President himself.

It was perhaps as well that no firm answers were forthcoming in the spring of 1939, for the course of events was still far from clear. The planners recognized this when they proposed that alternative plans be prepared to meet different situations in which the United States would have to meet the combined threat of Germany, Italy, and Japan. The Joint Board, in approving the work of the planners, accepted this recommendation and in June 1939 laid down the guide lines for the development of these war plans, aptly designated RAINBOW to distinguish them from the color plans.[12]

There were to be five RAINBOW plans in all, each of them based on a different situation. The objective of all was the same—to defend the United States and the Western Hemisphere from Axis aggression and penetration, overt or concealed. In developing their plans, the planners were to assume that initially, at least, the United States would be alone and that the European as well as the Latin American democracies would remain neutral. But in each of the plans they were to "set forth the specific cooperation that should be sought from allied or neutral Democratic Powers, with respect to specific Theaters of Operations to render our efforts fully effective." Common to all of the plans was the assumption that the United States would face a coalition rather than a single power.

The five specific situations forming the basis of the five RAINBOW plans were defined by the Joint Board as follows:

RAINBOW 1 assumed the United States to be at war without major allies. United States forces would act jointly to prevent the violation of the Monroe Doctrine by protecting the territory of the Western Hemisphere north of 10° South Latitude, from which the vital interests of the United States might be threatened. The joint tasks of the Army and Navy included protection of the United States, its possessions, and its sea-borne trade. A strategic defensive was to be maintained in the Pacific, from behind the line Alaska-Hawaii-Panama, until developments in the Atlantic permitted concentration of the fleet in mid-Pacific for offensive action against Japan.

RAINBOW 2 assumed that the United States, Great Britain, and France would be acting in concert, with limited participation of U.S. forces in Continental Europe and in the Atlantic. The United States could, therefore, undertake immediate offensive operations across the Pacific to sustain the interests of democratic powers by the defeat of enemy forces.

RAINBOW 3 assumed the United States to be at war without major allies. Hemisphere defense was to be assured, as in RAINBOW 1, but with early projection of U.S. forces from Hawaii into the western Pacific.

RAINBOW 4 assumed the United States to be at war without major allies, employing its forces in defense of the whole of the Western Hemisphere, but also with provision for United States Army forces to be sent to the southern part of South America, and to be used in joint operations in eastern Atlantic areas. A strategic defensive, as in RAINBOW 1, was to be maintained in the Pacific until the situation in the Atlantic permitted transfer of major naval forces for an offensive against Japan.

RAINBOW 5 assumed the United States, Great Britain, and France to be acting in concert; hemisphere defense was to be assured as in RAINBOW 1, with early projection of U.S. forces to the eastern Atlantic, and to either or both the African and European Continents; offensive operations were to be conducted, in concert with British and allied forces, to effect the defeat of Germany and Italy. A strategic defensive was to be maintained in the Pacific until success against the European Axis Powers permitted transfer of major forces to the Pacific for an offensive against Japan.[13]

Of the five plans, RAINBOW 1 was basic, though most limited. Providing for the defense of the Western Hemisphere from the bulge of Brazil to Greenland and as far west as Midway in the Pacific, it established the necessary conditions that had to be met before any of the other plans could be executed. RAINBOW 2 and 3 called for offensive operation into the western Pacific, the former on the assumption that Great Britain and France would be allies, and the latter that they would not. In this respect, RAINBOW 3 established virtually the same conditions as the ORANGE plan. RAINBOW 4 also assumed that Great Britain and France would be neutral, presumably as a result of Axis military action, and therefore emphasized the defense of the Western Hemisphere against external aggression. Emphasis in this plan as in RAINBOW 1 was on limited action to fend off any Axis threat to the American republics. In neither case (RAINBOW 1 or 4) were major U.S. forces to be sent to Europe or to the far Pacific.

The situation envisaged in RAINBOW 5 came closer to the conditions of World War II than any of the others, though these were not foreseen at the time. Like RAINBOW 2, it assumed the active collaboration of Great Britain and France. But unlike that plan, which called for the United States to make the major effort in the Pacific, RAINBOW 5 envisaged the rapid projection of American forces across the Atlantic to Africa or Europe "in order to effect the decisive defeat of Germany, Italy, or both." Clearly implied in this statement was the concept that finally emerged as the basic strategy of World War II: that in a war with the European Axis and Japan, Germany was the major enemy and that the main effort therefore should be made in Europe to secure the decisive defeat of Germany at the earliest possible date.

In June 1939 the international situation seemed to point toward the concept outlined under RAINBOW 2, that is, the projection of U.S. forces into the western Pacific with Great Britain and France providing the defenses of the Atlantic. The Navy was particularly interested in this plan, for it would have to carry the major load in any drive across the Pacific. And since the plan assumed British and French allies, the Navy would be relieved of some of its responsibilities in the Atlantic to concentrate on the Pacific enemy. At the same time, the United States would have to protect the Far Eastern interests of its allies "as its major share in the concerted effort." Britain's plans for the defense of its Pacific and Asiatic possessions were, therefore, of the utmost importance to the American naval planners.

Captain Ingersoll's visit to London in December 1937 had opened the way for a helpful exchange of information and coordinated planning between the American and British staffs. By the summer of 1939 the time seemed ripe for further conversations, and in May an officer of the Admiralty Plans Division came to Washington to talk to U.S. naval planners.

The increasing closeness between American and British naval planning was a vital element in the emergence of an Atlantic-first strategy. From the American point of view, such a strategy and the naval collaboration that flowed from it had a sound basis in national self-interest. Admiral Mahan* had pointed this out at the turn of the century, and it had become a cardinal principle of American naval doctrine since. In the nineteenth century the Royal Navy alone had controlled the seas and thus made possible the development of the United States; in the twentieth century, declared Mahan, the cooperation of Great Britain and the United States would assure the safety of the Atlantic community. Together, the two navies could command all the important sea routes of the world.

Policy makers as well as naval officers understood very well the close dependence of American security on British sea power. President Roosevelt had been Assistant Secretary of the Navy from 1913 to 1920 and fully appreciated the importance of sea power to the United States. Control of the Atlantic, he knew, must be always in the hands of friendly powers. That was a fundamental tenet of American policy, and no effort would be too great to prevent any potential enemy from gaining command of the Atlantic approaches to the Western Hemisphere. Soon to become British Prime Minister, Churchill understood as well as Roosevelt the implications of naval power for the security of both countries.

The summer of 1939 was one of tense expectancy. Europe was on the verge of war and Japan showed no disposition to abandon aggression in Asia. During these months, a joint RAINBOW 1 plan, which had first priority, was completed and the two services hurriedly pushed forward completion of their own plans for hemisphere defense.[14]

There were important organizational changes, too, at this time. In an effort to keep in close touch with his military advisers, President Roosevelt, on July 5, 1939, placed the Joint Board under his immediate "supervision and direction." Up to that time, the Board, it will be recalled, had reported to the two service Secretaries, under whose authority it functioned. It now had a broader basis, but still

* Alfred Thayer Mahan (1840-1914), American naval historian, author of the widely studied *The Influence of Sea Power upon History* (1890).

sent its recommendations through the Secretaries, for the President had no desire to alter existing procedures.[15] This change coincided with a change in the high command. On August 1, Admiral Harold R. Stark was appointed Chief of Naval Operations to succeed Admiral William D. Leahy, and a month later General George C. Marshall formally succeeded Malin Craig as Chief of Staff of the Army after two months as Acting Chief of Staff.

The outbreak of war in Europe early in September 1939 gave a fresh urgency to RAINBOW planning. RAINBOW 2 seemed to fit the situation of the moment best, and while work went forward on the development of plans, the President took measures to strengthen the nation's defenses and to keep America out of war by keeping war away from America. Immediately on the outbreak of hostilities he proclaimed the neutrality of the United States, while ordering the Army and Navy to bring their strength up to the full authorized level. On his initiative, the foreign ministers of the American republics met at Panama at the end of September to proclaim their neutrality and to devise measures for their joint defense. An American security zone was proclaimed in the western Atlantic, and plans made to patrol the zone to keep war away from the Americas.

Throughout the winter of 1939-1940, the period of the "phony war," the joint planners sought to develop plans to meet the RAINBOW 2 contingency. The task proved a formidable one, indeed, for the range of possibilities was wide. Moreover, each proposed course of action in the Pacific had to be coordinated with the plans of the Allies. But without specific knowledge of these, the planners were faced with many uncertainties. In April 1940, therefore, they proposed that conversations should be held with the British, French, and Dutch "as soon as the diplomatic situation permits." By that time, the Army planners had prepared four drafts of a proposed RAINBOW 2 plan, on each of which the Navy had commented in detail.[16]

The planners were still trying to solve the problems posed by RAINBOW 2 when, in the spring of 1940, the nature of the war in Europe changed abruptly. Early in April German forces invaded Denmark and Norway and by the end of the month had occupied both countries. On May 10 the German campaign against France opened with the attack on the Netherlands and Belgium, and four days later German armor broke through the French defenses in the Ardennes. At the end of the month the British began the evacuation from Dunkirk, and on June 10 Italy declared war. A week later, the beaten and disorganized French Government sued for peace. With

France defeated and England open to attack and invasion, the threat from the Atlantic looked real indeed.

In this crisis, American strategy underwent a critical review. Clearly, RAINBOW 2 and 3 with their orientation toward the far Pacific were scarcely applicable to a situation in which the main threat seemed to lie in Europe. The defeat of France in June and the possibility that Great Britain might soon fall outweighed any danger that Japanese aggression could present to American security. Calling for an early decision from higher authority, the Army planners argued that since the United States could not fight everywhere—in the Far East, Europe, Africa, and South America—it should limit itself to a single course. Defense of the Western Hemisphere, they held, should constitute the main effort of American forces. In any case, the United States should not become involved with Japan and should concentrate on meeting the threat of Axis penetration into South America.[17]

The Army's concern about America's ability to meet a possible threat from an Axis-dominated Europe in which British and French Navies might be employed against the United States was shared by the Navy. As a result, the joint planners began work on RAINBOW 4, which only a month earlier had been accorded the lowest priority, and by the end of May had completed a plan. The situation envisaged now in RAINBOW 4 was a violation of the Monroe Doctrine by Germany and Italy, coupled with armed aggression in Asia after the elimination of British and French forces and the termination of the war in Europe. Under these conditions, the United States was to limit its actions to defense of the entire Western Hemisphere, with American forces occupying British and French bases in the western Atlantic.[18]

Acceptance by the Joint Board of the RAINBOW 4 plan was the beginning rather than the end of the comprehensive review of strategy precipitated by Germany's startling success in Europe. Still in doubt was the fate of Great Britain and the French Navy, and American policy depended to a very large degree on these two unknowns. Possession of the British and French Fleets would give the European Axis naval equality with the U.S. Fleet and make possible within six months hostile operations in the Western Hemisphere. Since six months was the time required to mobilize, equip, and train American forces, the planners asserted that "the date of the loss of the British or French Fleets automatically sets the date of our mobilization." [19]

During the dramatic weeks of May and June 1940, the President met with his military advisers almost daily and discussed with them every major development of the war. On June 13, shortly before the fall of France, he called in the intelligence chiefs of the Army and Navy and asked for an evaluation of the situation, posing a number of specific questions. This request precipitated an interim review of the various courses of action open to the United States in the light of the rapidly changing situation. As the planners saw it, there were three alternative courses open:

1. To maintain a strong position in the Pacific and to avoid commitment everywhere else.

2. To make every effort, including belligerent participation, to sustain Great Britain and France.

3. To take whatever measures were required to prevent Axis penetration into the Western Hemisphere.[20]

All three possibilities had already been considered in one or another of the RAINBOW plans, but, as the planners pointed out, the essence of the problem now was time. RAINBOW 4 was the best course to follow in this situation, in their view, and the end of British or French resistance, they held, should be the signal for American mobilization.

On the morning of June 17, the day after the planners had submitted their report, General Marshall discussed the problem with his immediate assistants. "Are we not forced," he asked, "into a question of reframing our national policy, that is, purely defensive action in the Pacific, with a main effort on the Atlantic side? We have to be prepared," Marshall told his staff, "to meet the worst situation that may develop, that is, if we do not have the Allied fleet in the Atlantic." The time had come, he thought, to mobilize the National Guard and to discontinue shipments to England of munitions that would be needed for American mobilization.[21]

On the basis of this discussion, the Chief of the War Plans Division, Brigadier General George V. Strong, recommended that same day that the Army Chief of Staff and the Chief of Naval Operations propose to the President as the basic policy of the United States: first, a purely defensive position in the Pacific; second, no further commitments for material aid to the Allies; and third, immediate mobilization for hemisphere defense. These recommendations reflected the pessimistic and strongly conservative outlook of the Army staff at the time, a view the Army planners made no effort to conceal. His proposal, Strong stated frankly, was "a recognition of the early defeat of the Allies, an admission of our inability to furnish means in quantities sufficient to affect the situation, and an acknowledgement that we recognize the probability that we are next on the list of Axis powers. . . ."[22]

General Marshall and Admiral Stark approved General Strong's recommendations in principle on June 18 and directed their planners to outline the measures required "to effect an immediate mobilization of national effort for hemisphere defense." The result was a comprehensive review of national policy during the latter part of June by the War and Navy Departments, the State Department, and the President. With the study of the questions proposed by Roosevelt on June 13, this review furnished an estimate of probable war developments and outlined the action required for full-scale mobilization and for aid to Britain and her allies. Though never approved by the President, the conclusions of the planners nevertheless reflected his views and constituted an important milestone in the development of U.S. strategy for World War II.[23]

The critical point at issue in the discussions was the fate of the French Fleet and the future of Great Britain. The military wished to base their plans on the worst of all possible contingencies—that England, if not the British Empire, would be forced out of the war and that the French Fleet would fall to the Axis. The President, on the other hand, believed that American action should be based on the assumption that Great Britain would remain an active belligerent and that the military situation in Europe would not alter appreciably in the next six months. He did not feel, either, that aid to Britain should be cut off entirely, and countered the planners' arguments with the observation that if a small amount of aid would see the British through without seriously retarding American preparations, then that aid should be furnished. Nor was the President willing to put the armed forces on a wartime basis or to support full mobilization of manpower and industry. He agreed on the necessity for defense of the Western Hemisphere and the protective occupation of European colonial possessions, as well as other strategic positions in the Caribbean area and in Central and South America, but only after consultation and negotiation with other nations concerned.

As a result of these discussions, the planners recommended that American policy be based on the following:

1. That the British Commonwealth and Empire would continue to exist in the fall and winter of 1940, though Great Britain itself might not remain an active combatant.

2. That France would be occupied by German forces, and even if the French in North Africa or elsewhere continued resistance, U.S. aid would not alter substantially the French position.

3. That U.S. participation in the war as an active belligerent could

not prevent the defeat of France or of Great Britain at this time.

This estimate of the situation at the end of June led the planners to recommend, as the "Basis for Immediate Decisions Concerning the National Defense," a defensive strategy in the Pacific, regardless of the fate of the French Fleet. But if that fleet did fall into German hands, the planners recognized they would have to consider the question of whether to move the major portion of the U.S. Fleet to the Atlantic. The planners thought, too, that the further release of war materials needed for American forces would seriously weaken the United States. But they did not rule out altogether aid to Britain and stipulated, in accordance with Roosevelt's wishes, that aid would be given "under certain circumstances." [24]

During the summer of 1940, American policy and strategy were shaped in large measure by President Roosevelt's conviction that Britain must be encouraged to resist and that the British Fleet must not be permitted to fall to Germany. In a real sense, therefore, American strategy was dependent upon British fortunes. Only "one force," said Henry Stimson, the Secretary of War, on the day after France's surrender, "remained between the Nazis and the Western Hemisphere—the British Fleet." If that fleet were lost, the United States would stand alone.[25]

Reassurances from the British that they had no intention of giving up the fight were gratifying to a President so closely committed to British support, but a more objective estimate of Great Britain's ability to resist invasion and detailed information on which to base plans were needed. To fill this need as well as to see for themselves how the British were fighting and what they needed most, the Army and Navy sent special observers to London in the summer of 1940 at Prime Minister Churchill's request. The Army observers were General Strong, Chief of the War Plans Division, and Major General Delos C. Emmons of the Air Corps. Both would remain for only a few weeks, but the Navy observer, Rear Admiral Robert L. Ghormley, was to remain in London on extended duty. Already, the British had appointed their own Admiralty Committee, headed by Admiral Sir Sidney Bailey, to consider "naval cooperation with the United States Navy" in the event of American entry into the war, and had made clear to the Americans in a general way how they intended to fight the war.[26]

With the arrival of the special observers in London in August 1940, the conversations which had been carried on informally by the Navy since December 1937 were broadened to include Army representatives and enlarged in scope to include basic questions of strategy, command arrangements, and matériel requirements. None of the observers doubted the determination of the British people to continue their resistance. In their month in England, Generals Emmons and Strong were greatly impressed by the coolness and confidence of the British under attack and by the organization, training, and techniques for defense against air attack.[27] The British faith in the efficacy of air bombardment and the independent position of the Royal Air Force also had an effect on the two Army observers. Implicit in their report was a reflection of the British belief that Germany could be so weakened ultimately by bombardment as to make ground operations on the Continent feasible.

The American observers also learned much about British strategy for the conduct of the war. In broad terms, the British chiefs outlined for the American observers their policy for the conduct of the war:

1. The security of the United Kingdom and Imperial possessions and interests.

2. Command of the home waters and the eastern Mediterranean, while seeking to regain command of the entire Mediterranean.

3. An intensified air offensive and economic pressures against both Germany and Italy.

4. Development of resources for major offensive ground operations when opportunity offered.[28]

As to the Far East, the British admitted frankly that their interests would be best served if the U.S. Fleet remained in the Pacific. Their original plan had been to send a naval force to the Far East in the event of a Japanese attack, but that was no longer possible. On the other hand, if Japan came into the war and if the United States sent a portion of the fleet into the Atlantic, British surface vessels from the Home Fleet and the force at Gibraltar could be sent to the Far East. "The support of the American battle fleet," observed the Chief of the Air Staff, "would obviously transform the whole strategical situation in the Far East."

On the question of American material aid, the British were equally frank. In response to a question from Admiral Ghormley as to whether the British were relying on economic support and eventual cooperation of the United States, they replied that in plans for the future "we were certainly relying on the continued economic and industrial cooperation of the United States in ever-increasing volume." These, they declared, "were fundamental to our whole strategy." But on the question of the "eventual active cooperation" of the United States, the British were somewhat evasive. "No account had been taken" of this possibility, they told the American observers, "since this was clearly a matter of high political policy."

For the British, Germany clearly was the main enemy and the "mainspring" of the Axis effort in Europe. Arguing from this basis, the British insisted that "whatever action may be necessary against any other country must, therefore, be related to our main object, which is the defeat of Germany"—a statement that came very close to the basic U.S. strategic decision of World War II. And when Admiral Ghormley asked the British how they expected to achieve this goal and whether the final issue would be decided on land, they replied that "in the long run it was inevitable that the Army should deliver the *coup de grâce.*" But they hoped that the Army's task could be made considerably easier by "a serious weakening in the morale and fighting efficiency of the German machine, if not a complete breakdown." How this would be accomplished the British did not specify, but their emphasis on bombardment indicated that air power would certainly play a leading role in the weakening of Germany.

Events in Europe after June 1940 gave hope for a brighter future than had seemed possible after the German offensives in April and May. The success of the British in beating off the attacks of the *Luftwaffe* and the reports of the special observers led to a more favorable program of support for the British war effort and to other measures of U.S. aid, such as the transfer of 50 old destroyers in return for a lease on air and naval base sites in British possessions in the western Atlantic. For the moment, the Axis threat in Europe seemed to be blunted and the way opened for cooperation with the British in the Far East.

But the summer calm gave way to the storms of September. On September 22, Japanese troops entered northern Indochina, and five days later the Japanese Government announced its adherence to the Rome-Berlin Axis. Just two days before the signing of the Tripartite Pact, the U.S. Army planners had completed a report on the ability of the United States to cope with the problems presented by the Axis threat. After reviewing the possibilities in Europe, the planners pointed out that the United States might soon face renewed advances in the Far East, possibly against the Netherlands Indies or the Philippines, but that it would not be possible to oppose such moves by a major effort in the Pacific in view of the greater danger in the

Atlantic. Operations in the Pacific, they maintained, should be held to the minimum.[29]

There was a general agreement in Washington with this view. The main problem was how to avoid a conflict with Japan and at the same time maintain American interests and defend American possessions in the Far East. The answer perhaps lay in Europe, for there was strong reason to believe that Japan would take no overt military action against the United States or Great Britain until German victory seemed assured. This line of reasoning served to strengthen the view that as long as Great Britain was in danger, the United States should remain on the defensive in the Pacific. It was also a powerful argument for continued aid to Britain and for opposition to any move that might risk serious hostilities with the Japanese.

Early in October the entire subject of American policy toward Japan was reviewed at the highest level in Washington. Inevitably the question of British cooperation arose. The military chiefs opposed strong action on the ground that the British would be unable to send any forces into the area and that the United States could not undertake to assume Allied obligations in the Far East. Despite the well-known views of the American staff, the British continued their efforts to persuade the Americans to join in the defense of their Far Eastern possessions by sending naval units to Singapore. In May 1940 Churchill had offered to let the Americans use Singapore "in any way convenient" in order, as he put it, to "keep the Japanese quiet in the Pacific." On October 4 he tried again. In a strong personal message to President Roosevelt discussing the Far Eastern situation, he asked, "Would it not be possible for you to send an American squadron, the bigger the better, to pay a friendly visit to Singapore? There they would be welcome in a perfectly normal and rightful way." [30]

Both Admiral Stark and General Marshall were opposed to the dispatch of an American naval force to Singapore and agreed that the greater danger was in the eastern Atlantic. Secretary Hull also opposed the move. As he told the British Ambassador: "It will not be wise, even from the British standpoint for two wars to be raging at the same time, one in the East and the other in the West. If this country should enter any war, this would immediately result in greatly cutting off military supplies to Great Britain." [31] The move would be politically inexpedient also, for this was an election year and Roosevelt was already in the midst of a campaign for election to a third term. A military gesture such as Churchill had proposed was likely to lose more votes than it would gain. Thus, on the ground of political expediency as well as strategy, the President turned down the Prime Minister's invitation.

Developments since the summer of 1940 had made the need for closer coordination of British and American plans increasingly evident. Almost every important problem faced by the military planners raised questions that could not be settled without a knowledge of British capabilities and plans. But the hectic months of a Presidential campaign and the uncertainty of the outcome discouraged any serious effort to lay the basis for such coordination. By early November, President Roosevelt's re-election seemed certain and on the eve of the election Admiral Stark made the first bid for a firm and clear statement of American policy that would provide the basis for coordinated U.S.-British plans.[32] It was the most comprehensive analysis thus far of the various courses of action open to the United States, the military effect of developments in Europe and Asia, and the close relationship between British fortunes and American policy. Known as the "Plan Dog" memorandum because the recommended course of action if the United States became a belligerent was contained in paragraph D ("dog" in military parlance), Admiral Stark's study constitutes perhaps the most important single document in the development of World War II strategy.

The central point of Admiral Stark's analysis was the recognition that American security depended to a very large extent on the fate of Great Britain. This note he sounded at the very outset with the assertion that "if Britain wins decisively against Germany we could win everywhere; but that if she loses the problem confronting us would be very great; and while we might not *lose everywhere,* we might, possibly, not *win* anywhere." Should the British Commonwealth and Empire collapse, it seemed probable to Stark that the victorious Axis Powers would seek to expand their control, economically at first and then politically and militarily, into the Western Hemisphere. The military consequences of a British defeat were so serious for the United States, Stark declared, that Britain ought to be assisted in every way possible. He did not believe, either, that Britain had the manpower or material to conquer Germany. Assistance by powerful allies would be necessary ultimately, and to be ready for this eventuality Britain "must not only continue to maintain the blockade, but she must also retain intact geographical positions from which successful land actions can later be launched."

In facing the consequences of close cooperation with the British, Admiral Stark boldly raised the possibility—thus far avoided—of active American participation in the war. Since Britain could not herself defeat Germany, the question was how American resources in men and supplies could be employed in combination with the British to achieve this end. Admiral Ghormley, it will be recalled, had raised this question with the British in London in August, asking whether large-scale ground operations would eventually be necessary. He had received an affirmative reply from the British then, and Stark now returned to this point. Blockade and bombardment, the chief means favored by the British, he did not think would do the job. The only certain way of defeating Germany was "by military success on shore," and for that, bases close to the European Continent would be required. "I believe," Stark declared, "that the United States, in addition to sending naval assistance, would also need to send large air and land forces to Europe or Africa, or both, and to participate strongly in this land offensive."

Considering the importance of the Atlantic to American security, Stark argued strongly against major commitments in the far Pacific that would involve the United States in an all-out effort against Japan such as was envisaged in ORANGE. Such a course would have the effect of drawing resources away from the Atlantic and cutting down aid to Britain. Even a limited war against Japan would require strong reinforcements in the southwest Pacific and southeast Asia to defend British and Dutch possessions. Also, it might prove very difficult indeed to prevent a limited war from becoming unlimited—as the Japanese later found out. Nor did Stark see how the defeat of Japan, even if this could be accomplished, would contribute materially to the more important objectives of the defense of the Western Hemisphere and the continued existence of the British Commonwealth Empire. To perform all the tasks required to achieve these objectives, the United States could "do little more in the Pacific than remain on a strict defensive."

The major alternative courses of action open to the United States, as Stark viewed the possibilities, were four, and he stated them as questions:

A. Shall our principal military effort be directed toward hemisphere defense and security in both oceans? [Similar to RAINBOW 1 and 4]

B. Shall we prepare for a full offensive against Japan, premised on assistance from the British and Dutch forces in the Far East, and remain on the strict defensive in the Atlantic? [Similar to RAINBOW 2, or RAINBOW 3 and ORANGE with allies]

C. Shall we plan for sending the strongest possible military assistance both to the British in Europe and to the British, Dutch, and Chinese in the Far East? [In effect, this would call for an equal effort on two fronts while defending the Western Hemisphere]

D. Shall we direct our efforts toward an eventual strong offensive in the Atlantic as an ally of the British, and a defensive in the Pacific? [Similar to RAINBOW 5]

There was no doubt in Admiral Stark's mind that the alternative outlined in paragraph "Dog" would best serve the national interests. It would enable the United States to exert all its efforts in a single direction, make possible the greatest assistance to Britain, and provide the strongest defense of the Western Hemisphere. The one great disadvantage of Plan Dog, of course, was that it would leave Japan free to pursue her program of expansion in Asia and the southwest Pacific. Therefore the United States, while making every effort to avoid war with Japan, should seek to keep that nation from occupying British and Dutch possessions in that area.

Plan Dog was the course to be followed in the event of war—and Stark seemed to have little doubt that the United States would soon be involved in the European conflict. But if war did not come, or, as he put it, "until such time as the United States should decide to engage its full forces in war," the best course to follow would be that outlined in paragraph A, that is, build up the defense of the Western Hemisphere and stand ready to fight off a threat in either ocean.

Should his proposals find favor with the President, Stark strongly urged measures to put them into effect. The first step would be to prepare a joint plan as a guide for Army and Navy planning, and at least the "skeleton" of alternative plans for other situations that might develop. Such plans, however, would be of limited value if there was not a "clear understanding between the nations involved as to the strength and extent of the participation which may be expected in any particular theater. . . ." For this reason, therefore, he recommended that secret staff talks be initiated with British military and naval authorities "to reach agreements and lay down plans for promoting unity of allied effort should the United States find it necessary to enter the war." The British had already suggested such conversations on various occasions, the most recent suggestions having been made in October by the British Ambassador to Secretary Hull in Washington, and by the First Sea Lord and Chief of the Naval Staff Admiral Sir Dudley Pound to Ghormley in London.

The reaction of General Marshall and the Army planners to Plan Dog was entirely favorable. As a matter of fact, the Army had argued substantially along these lines in June 1940, when the prospect of an Axis victory in Europe had seemed so great, and General Marshall had then asked whether it would not be advisable to reframe U.S. naval policy so as to place the main effort in the Atlantic with "purely defensive action in the Pacific." [33] Thus, except for minor comments, the Army planners endorsed the Stark proposals, which went forward to the President on November 13. On November 18 the Joint Board instructed its planning committee to study the questions raised by Admiral Stark and prepare recommendations for submission to the President and the Secretaries of War and Navy.[34]

The British, who presumably learned of Plan Dog from Admiral Ghormley, also agreed with Admiral Stark. Since the plan was based so largely on the need to maintain the British Commonwealth Empire, this is not surprising. Churchill thought the plan "strategically sound" and "highly adapted to our interests," as indeed it was, but only because of the identity of British and American interests. He was "much encouraged by the American naval view" and cautioned his staff "to strengthen the policy of Admiral Stark" and "not use arguments inconsistent with it." [35] Apparently the British chiefs took this advice seriously, for on November 23 Admiral Ghormley reported to Stark that in the view of the Admiralty, which he believed to be the view of the British Government, "the primary objective of the war is the defeat of Germany and Italy," and that in case Japan and the United States should enter the war, U.S.-British strategy in the Pacific should be to contain the Japanese and prevent extension of the operations to the south and to the Indian Ocean.[36] But the British clung to their faith in Singapore and still hoped the United States would send a naval force there to hold it against the Japanese.

While arrangements went forward for conversations with the British, the joint planners continued their efforts to produce a statement of national defense policy based on Admiral Stark's recommendation. If acceptable, this document was to be submitted for approval to the President by the Secretaries of State, War, and Navy and was to serve as the basis for instructions to the American representatives in the forthcoming staff conversations. On December 21 the joint planners completed their work. In all essential respects, their recommendations were similar to those of Admiral Stark. The major objective of U.S. defense policy, they said, was the security of the Western Hemisphere, and this was to be secured by full cooperation with the British Commonwealth and Empire. Until forced to enter the war, the United States should follow the course advocated in paragraph A of Stark's memorandum; if forced into war with Japan, the United States should at the same time enter the war in the Atlantic and limit operations in the mid-Pacific and Far East so as "to permit prompt movement to the Atlantic of forces fully adequate to conduct a major offensive in that ocean." [37] American policy and strategy, therefore, would be designed to defeat Germany and its allies in order to prevent the extension of Axis influence into the Western Hemisphere, while seeking to keep the Japanese from entering the war or from attacking British and Dutch territory in the Far East.

The Joint Board approved the work of its planners on December 21, and the Secretaries of War and Navy gave their approval soon after. The original intention was to have the Secretary of State join the two service Secretaries in submitting these recommendations to the President for his approval, as the basis for future action by all agencies of the government. But Secretary of State Hull refused. He was in general agreement with these policies, he declared, but was doubtful of the propriety of "joining in the submission to the President of a technical military statement of the present situation." [38]

Arrangements for staff conferences with the British were completed early in January 1941, and on January 15 the British delegation left for the United States. There had been preliminary exchanges of view by cable and a proposed set of instructions prepared for the American representatives. But the military authorities still did not have President Roosevelt's approval of the recommended national defense policy, which was to constitute the guidelines for the American delegates. Finally, on January 16, the President met with his principal advisers, the two Secretaries and the service Chiefs. Present at the meeting also was the Secretary of State. The group came to be known informally as the War Council.

The meeting opened with a consideration of the problems raised by the possibility of simultaneous action by Germany and Japan against the United States. The President thought there was only "one chance in five" of such an attack but he avoided any commitment on the basic question of whether to plan for a major effort in the Atlantic or Pacific. On one point, though, he left no doubt. There was to be no curtailment of aid to Britain, even in the event of a concerted attack in the Atlantic and Pacific. Clearly, the President's major concern was with Great Britain. In that sense, he was of the same mind as his chief military and civilian advisers. He thought the Navy should be prepared to convoy shipping in the Atlantic and continue to patrol the East Coast. But he was equally anxious that the Army should not be committed to any operations until it was fully prepared, and that American military policy should be "very conservative" until its strength had been greatly increased. In Latin America, the United States would have to be prepared, the President declared, to provide forces, properly trained, to assist the governments in their resistance to subversive Axis activity.

The President's view of American policy in the Pacific coincided closely with that of the military authorities. There the United States would stand on the defense with the fleet based on Hawaii. There was to be no naval reinforcement of the Philippines, and the commander of the Asiatic Fleet, based in the Philippines, was to have discretionary authority in the event of attack to withdraw when he thought it necessary. The choice was his and it would be up to him to decide whether to sail east toward Pearl Harbor or south to Singapore, as the British wished.[39]

By the middle of January 1941, the major lines of American strategy in World War II had emerged and the re-election of President Roosevelt assured a continuation of the policy established during the critical summer months of 1940. While hoping to achieve his aims by measures short of war, the President had publicly stressed during the preceding months America's unreadiness for war and the danger from Europe and the Far East. Army and Navy planners had defined the problem facing the United States in a series of studies and had made plans to meet various situations which might arise. The most likely contingency in early 1941 was that the United States, allied with Great Britain, might be involved in a two-ocean war against a combination of Germany, Italy, and Japan. In such a contingency, it was generally agreed, the United States would adopt a defensive role in the Pacific and make its main effort against the most powerful and dangerous enemy, Germany. But many matters still remained to be decided before firm plans could be made that would best serve the interests of the United States and the free nations of the world. First among these was the necessity for agreement between the United States and Great Britain on how best to secure these objectives.

During the first three weeks of January 1941 the planners of the Joint Board completed their arrangements for the American-British Staff Conference. On January 21 they submitted to the Board a proposed agenda for the meetings and a statement of the American position. The meetings were to be nonpolitical; no specific commitments were to be made (except for methods of cooperation) and agreements reached would be subject to approval by the two governments. Within this framework, the delegates were to determine the best methods by which the forces of both nations could defeat Germany and its allies should the United States be "compelled to resort to war" (a phrase introduced by the President), reach agreement on the methods and nature of military cooperation, and coordinate plans for the use of their forces.

As a guide for the delegates, American national objectives were defined in virtually the same terms that Admiral Stark used: (1) protection of the Western Hemisphere against military or political encroachment by any other power; (2) aid to the British Commonwealth and Empire; (3) opposition by diplomatic means to Japanese expansion. In the event of war, the "broad military objective" of the United States and Britain would be the defeat of Germany, which would be "most effectively attained" by placing the principal military effort in the Atlantic, or "navally in the Mediterranean"—another Presidential phrase. In the way of practical advice in negotiating with the British, the delegates were to keep the following in mind:

It is believed that we cannot afford, nor do we need, to entrust our national future to British direction. . . .

United States Army and Navy officials are in rather general agreement that Great Britain cannot encompass the defeat of Germany unless the United States provides that nation with direct military assistance. . . .

It is to be expected that proposals of the British representatives will have been drawn up with chief regard for the support of the British Commonwealth. Never absent from British minds are their postwar interests, commercial and military. We should likewise safeguard our own eventual interests.[40]

The Joint Board gave its approval to these instructions and procedures on January 22, submitting them in turn to the Secretaries of War and the Navy with the suggestion that the statement defining the military position and strategy governing the action of U.S. forces be approved by the President. As a result Navy Secretary Frank Knox personally submitted the report to the President on January 23, and three days later Roosevelt approved it with minor changes in wording.[41]

The American-British Staff conversations opened in Washington on January 29, 1941, and continued through fourteen sessions to March 29, when the delegates submitted a final report, commonly known as ABC-1.[42] At the outset, the British stated their position clearly:

1. The European theater is the vital theater where a decision must first be sought.

2. The general policy should therefore be to defeat Germany and Italy first, and then deal with Japan.

3. The security of the Far Eastern position, including Australia and New Zealand, is essential to the cohesion of the British Commonwealth and to the maintenance of its war effort. Singapore is the key to the defense of these interests and its retention must be assured. In line with this strategy, U.S. naval forces, after appropriate dispositions for defense of the Western Hemisphere, should be employed mainly in the Atlantic and Mediterranean, the British stated. But they also declared that the United States should maintain in the Pacific a fleet large enough to prevent the Japanese from prejudicing the main effort in the Atlantic.

There was no disagreement between the Americans and the British on the first two points. Both sides were agreed that Germany was the main enemy and their first objective. They agreed further that the Atlantic would be the decisive theater of the war and the principal effort of the two nations would be made there. The delegates also recognized the legitimate interests of each side, an indispensable basis for cooperation. On the American side, the security of the United States and the defense of the Western Hemisphere were considered of paramount interest, with first call on American forces. British interests were broader, encompassing the security of the Commonwealth and Empire. "A cardinal feature of British strategic policy," the delegates agreed, "is the retention of a position in the Far East such as will insure cohesion and security of the British Commonwealth and the maintenance of its war effort."

The third point of British strategy, the importance of Singapore, involved the whole question of Far Eastern strategy. On this, there was a fundamental disagreement between the British and the American delegates. This disagreement stemmed partly from different national interests. The British had to deal with problems of Commonwealth security, and in their view Singapore was essential to the defense of India, Australia, and New Zealand. American interests in the Far East, though substantial, were not as vital. The only American possession of importance in the area, the Philippines, had virtually been written off as indefensible in a war with Japan.

There was a basic difference in outlook also between the British and Americans. Reflecting their insular position and long tradition in wars against Continental powers, the British placed their main emphasis on sea and air power rather than large-scale ground forces. The reduction of Germany by these means would be a slow process, but the British were accustomed to long wars and had no doubt of ultimate victory. The final blow, they expected, would be delivered by ground armies, but to prepare for that eventuality they would first secure or regain the strategic positions required for the offensive— Singapore, the Mediterranean—and then concentrate on weakening the enemy's war machine. Victory with minimum losses and minimum risks, exploitation of superior naval power, and avoidance of large-scale Continental operations—that was the classic British strategy.

The Americans, conscious of their overwhelming material power and unwilling to face the prospects of a long war, wished to concentrate all their power at the earliest possible moment against the main enemy, Germany. To achieve this aim and end the war quickly with fewer casualties in the long run, they were willing to face the temporary loss to Japan of strategic positions like the Philippines and to risk substantial casualties initially rather than disperse their forces or adopt a purely defensive or delaying strategy.

These differences emerged sharply in the discussions over Singapore. What the British were asking the Americans to do was to underwrite the defense of the Commonwealth and incorporate as a central feature of Allied strategy the British concept of the importance of Singapore as the key to defense of the Far East, even at the expense of concentrating for a decisive blow against Germany at the earliest possible date. Though the Americans appreciated the political, economic, and symbolic significance of Singapore for the British Commonwealth, they doubted its strategic value and the wisdom of underwriting its defense. To accept the British proposal would not only have been contrary to their instructions but would constitute, the American delegates believed, "a strategic error of incalculable magnitude." [43] They therefore refused to budge from the position that the British must look after their own special interests, as the United States would look after its own in the Philippines, and that the two nations should act together where their interests coincided, that is, in the North Atlantic and the British Isles.

The report submitted by the American and British delegates laid down the basic guidelines of Allied cooperation in World War II. It defined clearly the policies, the "paramount interests" of both countries, and the general strategic concepts designed to support these policies. Among the major strategic objectives accepted by both sides were:

1. The early defeat of Germany, the predominant member of the Axis, the principal military effort of the United States being exerted in the Atlantic and European area, the decisive theater. Operations in other theaters were to be conducted in such a manner as to facilitate the main effort.

2. The maintenance of British and Allied positions in the Mediterranean area.

3. The strategic defensive in the Far East, with the U.S. Fleet employed offensively "in the manner best calculated to weaken Japanese economic power, and to support the defense of the Malay Barrier by directing Japanese strength away from Malaysia."

To secure these objectives, the delegates agreed on a number of specific measures, including economic pressure, a sustained air offensive against German military power, the early elimination of Italy from the war, raids and minor offensives at every opportunity, and the support of resistance movements in Axis-dominated countries. All these would be preparatory to the final offensive against Germany. For that it would be necessary to secure bases in the Mediterranean and on the west and northwest shores of Europe, and to gather "maximum land forces, composed largely of mobile armored divisions," to defeat and destroy the German Army.

The agreements reached between the American and British staffs and embodied in ABC-1 were never intended to be binding on the two nations, or to have any political or official character, but only to determine the way in which the United States and the British Commonwealth could defeat Germany "should the United States be compelled to resort to war." From the start it was understood that conclusions reached by the conferees would have to be confirmed by the Chiefs of Staff of both nations and were contingent upon political agreements by the two governments. In line with this understanding, General Marshall and Admiral Stark gave their tentative approval to the ABC-1 report and advised the British Chiefs that they would present it to the President for approval at an appropriate time.[44] At the same time, the Joint Board issued a new directive for the preparation of plans under RAINBOW 5, the situation most closely meeting the requirements laid down in ABC-1.

Work on RAINBOW 5 had been initiated originally in May 1940, after the German offensive in the West but before the fall of France.

In April of that year the Joint Board had established a new priority for the development of RAINBOW plans, placing 5 after 2 and 3.[45] The situation envisaged then in RAINBOW 5 was a war in which the United States, allied with Great Britain and France, would project its armed forces "to either or both of the African and European continents as rapidly as possible" to accomplish the decisive defeat of Germany. The planning done in May on this basis was rendered obsolete within a month by the fall of France. Moreover, it seemed doubtful at the time that Great Britain would survive, and the planners turned their efforts to other RAINBOW situations—first, RAINBOW 4 (hemisphere defense) and then RAINBOW 3 (United States alone in a major effort against Japan). By the end of 1940, when it appeared that Britain would survive and a revised RAINBOW 5 situation was the most likely contingency to plan for, arrangements were already under way for the American-British Staff conversations.

Once the Chief of Staff and Chief of Naval Operations had given their approval to ABC-1, work on RAINBOW 5 progressed rapidly. By April 30, 1941, the Army and Navy had agreed on a joint plan and on that date submitted their work to the Joint Board. For the purposes of this plan, the Allies—Associated Powers, they were called—were assumed to be the United States, the British Commonwealth (less Eire), the Netherlands Indies, Greece, Yugoslavia, China, the Governments-in-Exile, and the Free French; the Axis nations were assumed to be Germany, Italy, Rumania, Hungary, Bulgaria, and possibly Japan and Thailand. These last two, even if they were not in the war initially, were potential enemies, and the possibility of their intervention was therefore taken into account in the plan.[46]

RAINBOW 5 was virtually identical with ABC-1. As a matter of fact, one of the first assumptions of the plan was that the Allies would conduct the war "in accord with ABC-1" and the arrangements made with the Canadians. Thus, the strategic concepts, supporting measures, and missions enumerated in ABC-1 were repeated almost verbatim in RAINBOW 5. For the U.S. Army, "the primary immediate effort" would be to build up large land and air forces "for major offensive operations against the Axis powers," and other operations were to be restricted to those that would "not materially delay this effort." Just what these operations would consist of was not specified, although reference was made, as in ABC-1, to a large-scale attack by ground forces against Germany and to the capture of bases from which to launch such an offensive. As one of the Army planners explained at the time, "a plan must be formulated upon a situation and no prediction of the situation which will exist when such a plan can be implemented should be made." [47]

RAINBOW 5 was neither a blueprint for victory nor a plan of operations. It merely outlined the objectives and missions of American forces in case of war on the basis of assumptions that seemed sound at the time. Specific plans to achieve these objectives were still to be made. The first step was to secure authority to proceed.

Joint Board authority came on May 14 when the Board formally approved both RAINBOW 5 and ABC-1, which it had tentatively approved early in April. Approval of the Secretaries came on May 28 (Navy) and June 2 (Army), at which time both plans went to the President, with the explanation that the British Chiefs of Staff had approved ABC-1 provisionally and submitted it to their government for approval. The President apparently read the two documents carefully but withheld approval of ABC-1 on the ground that the British had not yet approved it. Nor would he approve RAINBOW 5, presumably because it was based on ABC-1, that is, on arrangements with the British which had not yet been accepted by their government. He did request, however, that "in case of war" the two plans be returned to him for his approval.[48]

The President's ambiguous response to the carefully worked out arrangements with the British, and to the American plans based on these arrangements, raised the question whether the Army and Navy were authorized to proceed with their own planning for war on a RAINBOW 5 contingency. This question was resolved on June 10 at a meeting in Secretary of War Stimson's office. General Marshall's view was that since the President had not disapproved the plan, the Army could proceed with its own arrangements. This seemed reasonable, and it was on that basis that the services proceeded to make detailed plans for the employment of their forces.[49]

Though the President had not given his approval, the decision on the course the United States would follow in the event it was "compelled to resort to war" had, in effect, been made. The United States would make the main effort in the Atlantic and European area where the major enemy, Germany, was located. Just how the final blow would be delivered was not yet known, but the Americans expected it would require a large-scale ground offensive. In the Pacific and Far East, United States strategy would be defensive, with greatest emphasis on the area encompassed by the strategic triangle, Alaska-Hawaii-Panama. Implicit in this concept was acceptance of the loss of the Philippines, Wake Island, and Guam. Thus, in a period of less than three years, the Pacific orientation of U.S. strategy, developed over a period of many years was completely reversed. By mid-1941, in response to the threat from Europe, the eyes of American strategists were focused on the Atlantic. It was there, they believed, that the war in which the United States was certain to be involved would be decided.

These expectations were more than fulfilled. Though the war, when it came, opened with an attack in the Pacific, the President and his military advisers made it clear at the outset in the first of the wartime conferences with the British held at Washington in December 1941-January 1942 (ARCADIA) that they would stand by their decision to defeat Germany first. Not once during the course of the war was this decision successfully challenged.

Earl F. Ziemke

The German Decision to Invade
Norway and Denmark
(1940)

The German invasion of Norway was a dramatically daring military operation. The decision to embark on the venture was made by Adolf Hitler as Chief of State and also (since December 1938) Commander in Chief of the Armed Forces of the German Reich. He arrived at the decision over a period of six months, during which the proposal was debated at length in the highest echelons of the German armed forces. Hitler's own attitude shifted during that time from luke-warmness verging on indifference to determination. Since the end of the war, the decision has been both praised and condemned; here it is presented as an example of decision-making in a developing situation.[1]

Even though the occupation of Norway and Denmark had no significant effect on the outcome of the war, it established a milestone in the history of warfare by demonstrating the effective reach of modern military forces. Although lacking the resources to capitalize on it, the Germans had made a move of potential value to them in the development of a global strategy. It confronted the United States as well as Great Britain with a strategic threat. It brought Germany, theoretically at least, into a position to strike outward from the mainland of Europe toward Iceland, Greenland, and possibly the North American Continent.

Immediately after the outbreak of war in September 1939, Norway, jointly with Sweden, Denmark, and Finland, announced its neutrality. In that action the Scandinavian states were following a policy they had adhered to consistently, if not always with complete success, since the middle of the nineteenth century. Germany, for its part, on September 2, 1939, presented a note in Oslo in which it declared its intention to respect the territorial integrity of Norway under all circumstances but warned that it expected the Norwegian Government to maintain an irreproachable neutrality and that it would not tolerate an infringement of that neutrality by a third power. A month later, on October 9, in a secret memorandum on the conduct of the war, Hitler stated that the neutrality of the "Nordic States" was to be assumed for the future and that a continuation of German trade with those countries appeared possible even in a war of long duration.[2]

With due allowance for Hitler's tendency to "play by ear," it can be said that the German interest in Norwegian neutrality at the beginning of the war was sincere. For Germany the advantages were substantial. Of the approximately six million tons of Swedish magnetite iron ore which Germany imported annually, about half passed through the Norwegian ice-free port of Narvik. From Narvik, as long as Norway remained neutral, ore ships could travel safely in the Leads, the passage inside the numberless islands fringing the Norwegian west coast. The Leads also made it much more costly and difficult for the Allies to blockade Germany, since blockade runners could steam up the long Norwegian coast and break out above the Arctic Circle in waters difficult to patrol. Consequently, in wartime the neutrality of Norway was a significant German asset, one which the British could be trusted not to overlook.

Passive exploitation of Norway's neutrality did not exhaust the German strategic interests in the Norwegian area. After World War I an opinion had developed in the German naval command which held that if the German Fleet had had bases in Norway and had not been bottled up in the North Sea, that war might have gone differently for the Navy. It was a return to this line of thought which brought forward a proposal for a shift to more aggressive action in Norway.

In the last week of September 1939, with the campaign against Poland drawing rapidly to a successful conclusion, Hitler and the Commander in Chief, Navy, Fleet Admiral Erich Raeder, began casting about for measures to be adopted in case the war against Great Britain and France had to be fought to the finish. One possibility was to proclaim a "siege of Britain," which would be put into effect by the Navy and the Air Force. In the days immediately following, even though Hitler, on September 27, announced his intention to open a land offensive in the West before the end of the year, the Armed Forces High Command and the service commands examined various

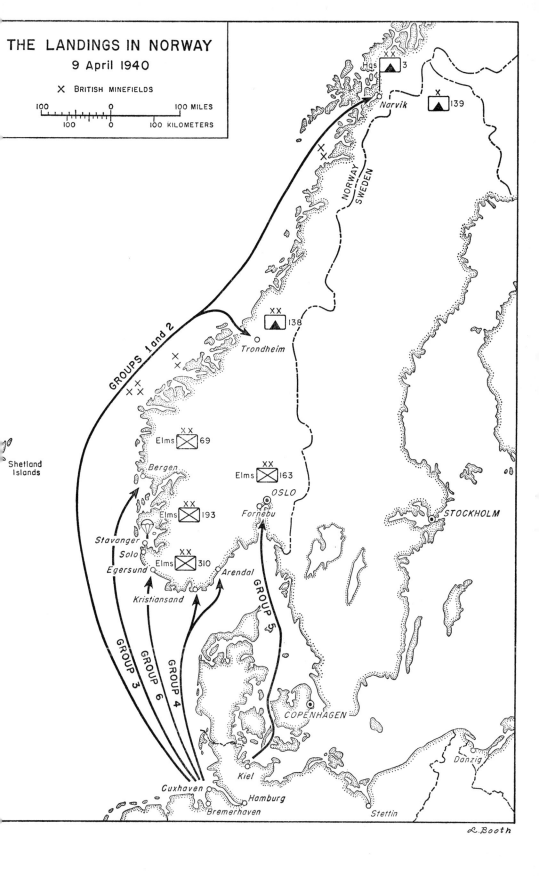

THE LANDINGS IN NORWAY
9 April 1940

X BRITISH MINEFIELDS

100 ————— 0 ————— 100 MILES

100 ————— 0 ————— 100 KILOMETERS

Hqs ▲ 3

X ▲ 139

Narvik

NORWAY

SWEDEN

GROUPS 1 and 2

▲ 138

Trondheim

Shetland
Islands

Elms ⊠ 69

Bergen

Elms ⊠ 163

OSLO

STOCKHOLM

Elms ⊠ 193

Fornebu

Stavanger

Solo

Egersund   Elms ⊠ 310

Arendal

Kristiansand

GROUP 5

GROUP 3

GROUP 6

GROUP 4

COPENHAGEN

Danzig

Cuxhaven

Kiel

Hamburg

Bremerhaven

Stettin

L. Booth

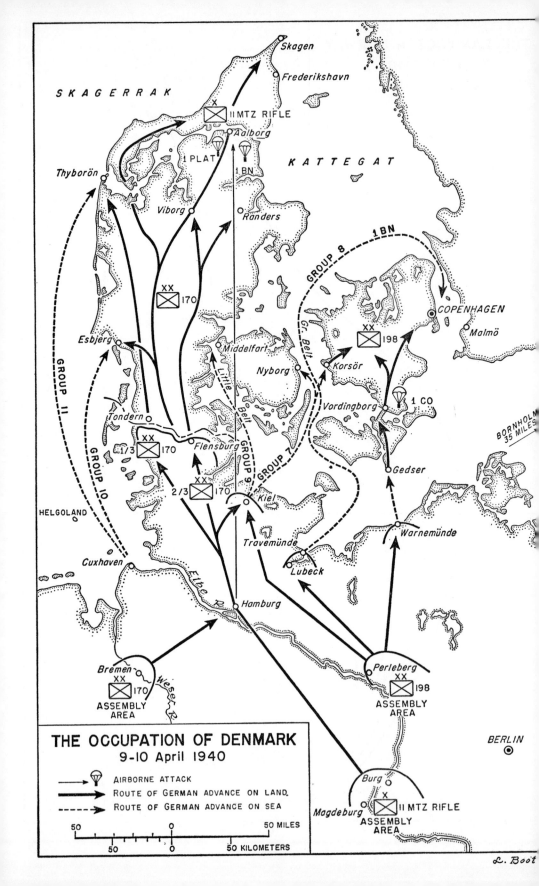

SKAGERRAK

Skagen

Frederikshavn

X
II MTZ RIFLE

Aalborg

1 PLAT

1 BN

KATTEGAT

Thyborön

Viborg

Randers

1 BN

GROUP 8

COPENHAGEN

Malmö

XX
170

Gr. Belt

XX
198

Esbjerg

Middelfart

Nyborg

Korsör

GROUP 11

GROUP 10

Tondern

Little Belt

GROUP 9

GROUP 7

Vordingborg

1 CO

BORNHOLM
35 MILES

XX
1/3   170

Flensburg

HELGOLAND

XX
2/3   170

Kiel

Gedser

Cuxhaven

Travemünde

Warnemünde

Elbe R.

Lübeck

Hamburg

Bremen

Weser R.

XX
170
ASSEMBLY
AREA

Perleberg

XX
198
ASSEMBLY
AREA

BERLIN

THE OCCUPATION OF DENMARK
9-10 April 1940

AIRBORNE ATTACK

ROUTE OF GERMAN ADVANCE ON LAND.

ROUTE OF GERMAN ADVANCE ON SEA

Burg

Magdeburg

X
II MTZ RIFLE
ASSEMBLY
AREA

50   0   50 MILES

50   50 KILOMETERS

0

L. Boot

possibilities for the future conduct of the war. On October 2 the Armed Forces High Command asked for the Navy's opinion on the following three: a land offensive in the West, the "siege of Britain," and delaying tactics. Raeder favored the siege of Britain and ordered the Naval Staff to draw up the supporting arguments.[3]

The siege of Britain offered the Navy a decisive role in the war—provided it could be carried out. The Submarine Command had only 29 Atlantic-type submarines; and the Navy had concluded in the "Battle Instructions" of May 1939 that in wartime the English Channel would be completely blocked and the British would spare no pains to close the northern route out of the North Sea, between the Shetland Islands and Norway.[4] Resolution of the first problem, that of the submarines, was a matter of time; the second, how to achieve freedom of action outside the North Sea, Raeder turned to on October 3. Informing the Naval Staff that he considered it necessary to acquaint Hitler as soon as possible with the considerations favorable to extending the Navy's operational bases to the north, he ordered an immediate investigation to determine what places in Norway would be most suitable as bases and how they could be acquired. He thought that the combined diplomatic pressure of Germany and the Soviet Union might be enough to secure the bases "peacefully." [5]

It was quickly agreed that Trondheim and Narvik offered the best sites, but on the questions of whether they could or should be acquired the estimates were almost entirely negative. When the Chief of Staff, Naval Staff, broached the question to the Chief of Staff, Army, he was told that difficult terrain, poor communications, and long supply lines placed almost insurmountable obstacles in the way of a military operation to secure the bases, and that, if it were attempted, the entire German war industry would have to be devoted to Army requirements. This would bring the submarine program to a halt, thereby making it impossible to exploit the bases.[6] The Army, having just had what it considered to be a narrow escape in Poland, was trying to talk Hitler out of opening an offensive against the Allies in France, and it was in no mood to contemplate additional adventures in Scandinavia. This timorousness, as Hitler saw it, caused him to lose confidence in the Army leadership and later to exclude the Army High Command almost entirely from the planning for the operation in Norway.

In its own considerations, set down on October 9, the Naval Staff was far from enthusiastic. A base on the coast of Norway, it conceded, would be of great value to the fleet which Germany planned to have after 1945, but until then it could be used profitably only by the submarines. While a base—at Trondheim, for instance—would undeniably be useful for submarine warfare, the length and vulnerability of its lines of communication to Germany would greatly reduce its value. Finally, to acquire such a base by a military operation would be difficult, and even if it could be acquired by political pressure, serious political disadvantages—among them, loss of the protection which Norwegian neutrality gave German shipping—would have to be taken into account.[7]

By this time Hitler's own thoughts on the future course of the war had crystallized, and on October 9 he put the finishing touches on a lengthy political and military analysis in which he reaffirmed his intention to launch an offensive in the West. On the same day, in Directive No. 6 for the Conduct of the War, he ordered the Army to prepare an offensive on the northern flank of the Western Front, with the objectives of smashing large elements of the French and Allied armies and taking as much territory as possible in the Netherlands, Belgium, and northern France to create favorable conditions for air and sea warfare against Great Britain and for the defense of the Ruhr. The next day Raeder explained to Hitler that the conquest of the Belgian coast (at the time even Hitler believed this would be the limit of the advance) would be of no advantage for submarine warfare, and then, mentioning Trondheim as a possibility, he pointed to the advantages of bases on the Norwegian coast. Hitler replied that bases close to Britain were essential for the Air Force but agreed to take the question of Norway under consideration.[8]

But in the succeeding weeks Hitler, preoccupied with his plans for an invasion of France and the Low Countries, left the Norwegian question in the background. Raeder himself did not return to it until November 25, when he told the Naval Staff that he saw a danger, in the event of a German attack on the Netherlands, that Britain might stage a surprise landing on the Norwegian coast and take possession of a base there. Two days later he emphasized the importance of attacks on sea traffic between Norway and the British Isles and stated that it was difficult to intercept ships leaving Norway because they could travel long distances in Norwegian territorial waters. In a conference with Hitler on December 8 he reverted to this problem and stated that it was important to occupy Norway.[9]

In December Raeder also came into contact with Vidkun Quisling, the leader of the Norwegian National Union party (*Nasjonal Samling*) modeled on the German Nazi party. The National Union party was small and had little influence in Norwegian politics; but Quisling, who had served as Norwegian Minister of War in the early 1930's, claimed to have well-placed contacts in the Norwegian Government and Army. He was also a protégé of Reichsleiter Alfred Rosenberg, head of the Foreign Political Office of the Nazi party. With Rosenberg's support he had attempted, without much success, in the summer of 1939 to drum up interest in a German occupation of Norway. In Raeder he found a receptive listener, and at their first meeting, on December 11, he told him that the danger of a British occupation of Norway was great, and he maintained that the Norwegian Government had already secretly agreed to permit such an occupation. The National Union party, he suggested, was in a position to forestall the British move by placing the necessary bases at the disposal of the German armed forces. In the coastal area men in important positions had already been bought for the purpose, but a change in Germany's attitude was absolutely necessary since months of negotiations with Rosenberg had not produced the desired results.

On the next day Raeder recounted these statements to Hitler and took the occasion to review the pros and cons of an operation in Norway. Quisling, he said, had made a trustworthy impression but had to be dealt with cautiously since he might only be attempting to further his own interests. A British occupation of Norway, in Raeder's opinion, would be intolerable because Sweden would then come entirely under British influence, the war would be carried into the Baltic, and German naval warfare would be completely disrupted in the Atlantic and the North Sea. On the other hand, a German occupation of bases in Norway would produce strong countermeasures by the British Navy for the purpose of interrupting the transport of ore from Narvik. The German Navy was not prepared to cope with this; nevertheless, Raeder believed the risks had to be taken and recommended that, if Quisling made a good impression on Hitler, permission be given for the Armed Forces High Command to collaborate with Quisling in preparing plans for an occupation, either by peaceful means—that is, by German forces being called in—or by force. On December 14, after talking with Quisling, Hitler ordered the Armed Forces High Command to "investigate how one can take possession of Norway." [10]

Hitler received Quisling again on December 18. Then, as at the previous meeting, Hitler expressed a personal desire to preserve the neutrality of Norway; but, he stated, if the enemy prepared to extend the war, he would be obliged to take countermeasures. He promised financial support for Quisling's party and indicated that the Armed Forces High Command would assign him missions and turn to him for information as the planning progressed. During the following months Quisling kept in close contact with Rosenberg, furnishing intelligence information and warnings of an impending Allied invasion. In Oslo, a representative of the Rosenberg office and the German Naval Attaché maintained close contact with the Quisling organization. But the idea of an operation dependent on support by Quisling and his followers was soon dropped because of the number of uncertain factors involved—not the least among them the suspicion that Quisling had vastly overstated his strength and capabilities—and the need to preserve secrecy. After December Quisling had no part in the planning.[11]

Although Hitler may have been impressed by Quisling's apparent offer of a cheap success in Norway, a more significant explanation for his sudden spurt of interest lies elsewhere. A new and serious element had been recently added to the Scandinavian situation by the Soviet attack on Finland, on November 30, 1939. The Soviet aggression had aroused immediate sympathy for Finland among the Allies and in the Scandinavian countries. Norway and Sweden feared an extension of Soviet influence into other Scandinavian countries. (Quisling, talking to Raeder, had said the Norwegian Government would turn to Great Britain for help against the Soviet advance.) Germany, bound by the Nazi-Soviet Pact in which Finland was declared to be outside the German sphere of interest, adopted a policy of strict neutrality which occasioned a strong wave of anti-German sentiment in Scandinavia. For Germany, the most serious consideration was that Allied intervention to aid Finland could be expected to entail an occupation of Norwegian ports.[12]

While the situation was by no means as dangerous as Raeder and Quisling painted it, German concern for Allied action in Scandinavia was not without substance. Since the beginning of the war, Allied expectations with respect to Norway had developed almost exactly along the lines predicted by Raeder; however, the devising of practical means for realizing these expectations had been quite another matter. In mid-September British Prime Minister Winston Churchill had presented his Plan CATHERINE, which involved sending naval forces through the straits leading from the North Sea into the Baltic Sea to gain control of those waters and to stop the Swedish ore traffic. Although CATHERINE was rejected as too dangerous and no other plan was devised, the Allies, influenced by the widely held thesis that

Germany did not have the resources to sustain a long war, continued to regard Norway, and Narvik in particular, as their most promising strategic objective. With the Soviet invasion of Finland, the moment of opportunity seemed to have come, especially when the early successes of the Finns made it appear that the Red Army was weak. The French Government, eager to draw the main action of the war away from the Franco-German frontier, went so far as to think of establishing a major theater of war in Scandinavia and of challenging both the Soviet Union and Germany there. The British, on the other hand, wanted to avoid offering excessive provocation to the Russians, with the result that while Allied hopes ran high it was not until the end of January 1940 that agreement came on the method of attaining them.

In the week following Hitler's first meeting with Quisling, Brigadier General Alfred Jodl, Chief of the Operations Staff, Armed Forces High Command, set in motion an investigation of the Norwegian problem. While the preliminary work was begun by the high commands of the three services, Jodl remained in doubt concerning the future handling of the matter. On December 18 he discussed it with the Chief of Staff of the Air Force, presumably on the assumption that the Air Force role would be predominant in any operation that might result. In the course of these preliminaries, preparations were made to assign targets in Norway to the Reconnaissance Squadron "Rowel," a special purpose unit which was supposed to be able to escape detection from the ground by flying at extremely high altitudes. As late as January 2, 1940, however, the "Rowel" Squadron had still not been committed, and the scope of the intelligence missions which had been assigned to the air attachés in Norway in December was still limited.[13]

At the end of December, reporting to Hitler, Raeder again declared it essential that Norway not fall into British hands. He feared that British volunteers "in disguise" would carry out a "cold" occupation and warned that it was necessary to be ready. That his feeling of urgency was not shared in other quarters was demonstrated on January 1, when General Franz Halder, Chief of Staff of the Army, and General Wilhelm Keitel, Chief of Staff of the Armed Forces High Command, agreed that it was in Germany's interest to keep Norway neutral and that a change in the German attitude would depend on whether or not Great Britain threatened Norway's neutrality.[14]

Shortly after the turn of the year Hitler's attention was drawn more sharply toward Norway by increasing Allied talk of intervention in the war between Russia and Finland, and, more particularly, by a British attempt on January 6 to secure Norwegian and Swedish acceptance of a proposal to allow British naval forces to operate inside Norwegian territorial waters. On January 10 he released to the service high commands the Armed Forces High Command memorandum *Studie Nord,* which had been completed ten days earlier and embodied the preliminary considerations of the services regarding an operation in Norway.

Studie Nord proceeded from the premise that Germany could not tolerate the establishment of British control in the Norwegian area and that only a German occupation could forestall such a development. As a result of the Russo-Finnish war, it was stated, anti-German opinion was on the increase in Scandinavia, and Norwegian resistance to a British occupation was hardly to be expected. It was also thought that the British might use a German attack in the West as an excuse to occupy Norway. Further work on the study was to be done under the direction of an Air Force general. The chief of staff was to be supplied by the Navy and the operations officer by the Army. From these assignments it appeared that the predominant roles were expected to fall to the Air Force and the Navy. The operation was estimated to require about one division of Army troops.[15]

During the review of *Studie Nord,* the Naval Staff once more argued strongly against an operation in Norway. It did not believe a British occupation of Norway was imminent, and it considered a German occupation, without any previous action having been taken by the British, as a strategically and economically dangerous venture that would result in loss of the security afforded by the territorial waters of a neutral Norway. At the end, Raeder agreed that the "best" solution was preservation of the *status quo.*[16]

Between January 14 and 19 the Naval Staff worked out an expansion of *Studie Nord.* Similar supplementary studies were prepared in the Army and Air Force High Commands, but both of those services were deeply involved in the planning for operations in the West and, therefore, gave the Norwegian question only cursory treatment. In its study the Naval Staff reached two important conclusions, namely, that surprise would be absolutely essential to the success of the operation and that part of the assault force could be transported by sea if fast warships of the fleet were used as transports. If surprise could be achieved, the Naval Staff contended, Norwegian resistance would be negligible and the only units of the British Navy that would need to be taken into account would be those which might be on patrol off the coast of Norway—possibly one or two cruisers. A decision to use warships as transports would overcome the limitations imposed by the short range of the air transports and would make it possible to consider the simultaneous occupation of a number of points along the Norwegian coast as far north as Narvik.[17]

During the first weeks of January Hitler's attention remained concentrated on the plan for invading France and the Low Countries, which he hoped to put into execution before the end of the month. However, after the middle of the month the weather predictions became increasingly less favorable, and on January 20 he announced that the operation could probably not begin before March. With that announcement it became possible to look at the Scandinavian situation in a new light. The delay in the German invasion of France could give the Allies time to intervene in the north, a contingency which Hitler, who had been impatient to resume the offensive since October 1939, may well have regarded as a welcome challenge. On January 23 he ordered *Studie Nord* recalled. The creation of a working staff in the Air Force High Command was to be dropped, and all further work was to be done in the Armed Forces High Command. Hitler thus, in fact, killed two birds with one stone, placing the planning for an operation in Norway on a somewhat firmer basis and at the same time finding an outlet for his rage over an incident that had occurred earlier in the month, which had resulted in plans for the invasion of France and the Low Countries falling into Allied hands when a German Air Force major made a forced landing on Belgian territory.[18] On January 27, in a letter to Commanders in Chief, Army, Navy, and Air Force, Keitel stated that henceforth work on *Studie Nord* would be carried out under Hitler's direct personal guidance, in closest conjunction with the over-all direction of the war. Keitel would take over supervision of the planning, and a working staff, which would provide a nucleus for the operations staff, would be formed in the Armed Forces High Command. Each of the services was to provide an officer suitable for operations work, who also, if possible, had training in organization and supply. The operation was assigned the code name WESERÜBUNG.[19]

In creating a planning staff for WESERÜBUNG, Hitler anticipated the next Allied step by less than a week. After the Commander in Chief of the Finnish Army, Field Marshal Carl Gustaf Mannerheim, appealed for help on January 29, the Allied Supreme War Council decided to send an expedition timed for mid-March. The French wanted to blockade Murmansk and attempt landings in the Pechenga region, and they talked of simultaneous operations in the Caucasus in addition to the occupation of parts of Norway and Sweden.[20] The British plan which was adopted was more modest. While ostensibly intended to bring Allied troops to the Finnish front, it laid its main emphasis on operations in northern Norway and Sweden. The main striking force was to land at Narvik and advance along the railroad to its eastern terminus at Luleå, occupying Kiruna and Gällivare along the way. By late April two Allied brigades were to be established along that line. Two additional brigades would then be sent to Finland.[21]

The staff for WESERÜBUNG assembled on February 5 and was installed as a special section of the Operations Staff, Armed Forces High Command. Its senior officer was Captain Theodor Krancke, commanding officer of the cruiser *Admiral Scheer*. On the first day Field Marshal Hermann Goering, obviously annoyed at having been relegated to a subsidiary role in what appeared to be developing as a primarily air operation, had not yet appointed an Air Force representative.

Although it was widely assumed after the failure of Allied counteroperations in Norway that the Germans had laid their plans well in advance, probably even before the outbreak of war, such was not the case. The Krancke staff began its work with very modest resources. German military experience offered no precedent for the type of operation contemplated, and the Armed Forces High Command and service memorandums prepared after December 1939 furnished little more guidance than tentative points of departure for operational planning. A certain amount of intelligence information on the Norwegian Army and military installations was available, which, while it was useful and later proved to be accurate, was not of decisive importance. For maps and general background information it was often necessary to rely on hydrographic charts, travel guides, tourist brochures, and other similar sources. The limitation on personnel imposed by the necessity for preserving secrecy was another handicap. Nevertheless, in the approximately three weeks of its existence the Krancke staff produced a workable operations plan.

The Krancke Plan for the first time focused clearly on the technical and tactical aspects of the projected operation. It envisioned simultaneous landings at Oslo, Kristiansand, Arendal, Stavanger, Bergen, Trondheim, and Narvik. Control of those fairly small areas, it was held, meant control of the entire country, since they were the principal centers of population, industry, and trade. Moreover, with the capture of those places and their garrisons, the Norwegians would lose eight of their sixteen regiments, nearly all of their artillery, and almost all of their airfields.* The operation was to be executed by a corps of approximately six divisions, the first assault wave of which was to be transported half by warship and half by plane. Primarily it would be an airborne operation. The 7th Air Division (Airborne Troop Command) was expected to supply eight transport groups and five battalions of parachute troops in the first wave, and thereafter to bring in the 22nd (Airborne) Infantry Division within three days.[22]

In mid-February the *Altmark* incident gave the first real sense of urgency to the preparations for WESERÜBUNG. On February 14 the German tanker *Altmark,* with 300 British seamen captured by the commerce raider *Graf Spee* aboard, entered Norwegian territorial waters on its return trip to Germany. Despite strong misgivings, the Norwegian Admiralty, though suspecting the nature of the "cargo," permitted the *Altmark* to proceed. On February 16, when six British destroyers put in an appearance, the *Altmark* took refuge in Jössing Fjord, near Egersund, escorted by two Norwegian torpedo boats. Disregarding protests from the Norwegian naval craft, the British destroyer *Cossack* entered the fjord and, sending a party aboard the *Altmark,* took off the prisoners after a brief skirmish.

The deliberate action of the *Cossack* convinced Hitler that the British no longer intended to respect Norway's neutrality, and on February 19 he ordered a speed-up in the planning for WESERÜBUNG. On Jodl's suggestion it was decided to turn the operation over to a corps commander and his staff. Lieutenant General Nikolaus von Falkenhorst, Commanding General, XXI Corps, was nominated for the task—largely because he had acquired some experience in overseas operations during the German intervention in Finland in 1918.[23]

At noon on February 21, von Falkenhorst reported to Hitler and was offered the mission of planning and—when and if the time came—commanding the operation against Norway. The planning was to be

* This method of operation took advantage of a major weakness of the Norwegian Army, namely, that it could not mobilize to fight as a unit. Because of the peculiar geography of the country, mobilization was by divisions, with single divisions—for the most part having no contact with each other—scattered throughout the major centers from Oslo to Harstad in the vicinity of Narvik. On paper, the Norwegian Army consisted of six divisions with a peacetime strength of 19,000 men and a war strength of 90,000. But up to April 1940 it had only 16,000 men under arms (including 1,800 for air defense, 950 in the Army Air Corps, and 300 security guards). The German intention, therefore, was not to meet and defeat each one of the divisions on its home ground but to capture the main centers before mobilization could begin.

carried out with two considerations in mind: (1) to forestall a British move by occupying the most important ports and localities, in particular, the ore port of Narvik; and (2) to take such firm control of the country that Norwegian resistance or collaboration with Great Britain would be impossible.[24] On the next day, after von Falkenhorst had reviewed and approved the Krancke Plan, his appointment was confirmed. Four days later, on February 26, a selected staff from Headquarters, XXI Corps, began work in Berlin.

The first major question to be decided concerned Denmark. As early as December 1939 the German Army had taken under consideration the question of occupying Denmark in conjunction with an operation against Norway. In a supplement to *Studie Nord,* the Naval Staff had recommended acquisition of bases in Denmark, particularly at the northern tip of Jutland, as a means of approaching the Shetlands-Norway passage and of facilitating naval and air control of the Skagerrak. The Krancke staff had assumed that the necessary bases in Denmark could be secured by diplomatic pressure, reinforced with the threat of a military occupation; but after the von Falkenhorst staff had been installed, it was decided not to rely on half measures of that sort. On February 28 von Falkenhorst outlined a plan to Keitel that included the occupation of Denmark. At the same time, the estimate of troop requirements was raised by two divisions.

On the same day an even more important new element was introduced, one which eventually made necessary a complete revision of the Krancke Plan. Jodl secured Hitler's approval for a proposal to prepare WESERÜBUNG in such a fashion that it could be executed independently of the forthcoming campaign in the West, both in terms of time and of forces employed. All of the planning up to that time had started from the assumption that WESERÜBUNG would have to come either before or after GELB (the invasion of France, the Netherlands, and Belgium) since the 7th Air Division, in particular, would be required for both operations. The Armed Forces High Command now proposed to reduce the commitment of parachute troops for WESERÜBUNG to four companies and to hold back one regiment of the 22nd Infantry Division. This change and that concerning Denmark were approved by Hitler on February 29.[25]

Two days later, on March 1, Hitler issued the "Directive for Case WESERÜBUNG," which set forth the general requirements for the operations and authorized the beginning of operational planning. The stated strategic objectives were to forestall British intervention in Scandinavia and the Baltic, provide security for the sources of Swedish iron ore, and give the German Navy and Air Force advanced bases for attacks on the British Isles. Daring and surprise were to be relied on, rather than strength in terms of numbers of troops. The idea of a "peaceful" occupation to provide armed protection for the neutrality of the Scandinavian countries was to be basic to the whole operation. Von Falkenhorst as Commanding General, Group XXI, was to be directly subordinate to Hitler.* Denmark and Norway were to be occupied simultaneously, with WESERÜBUNG SÜD involving the occupation of all of Denmark and WESERÜBUNG NORD the occupation of Norway by means of air and seaborne landings at the most important places along the coast.[26]

The appearance of the Führer directive brought an immediate wave of protests and objections from the Army and Air Force. With the campaign in the West impending, neither wanted to divert forces to a subsidiary theater of operations. The Army had not yet altered the negative attitude toward the projected campaign which Halder had expressed on October 5, 1939. Moreover, personal feelings were involved, since up to that time neither the Army nor the Air Force High Command had been brought directly into the planning for WESERÜBUNG. Halder noted in his diary that as of March 2 Hitler had not "exchanged a single word" with the Commander in Chief, Army, on the subject of Norway. The Army also objected to troop dispositions being made independently by the Armed Forces High Command. The Air Force protested that the demands on the 7th Air Division and other air units were too high.

On March 3, declaring that he expected Allied intervention in Finland in the near future, Hitler sharply ordered the services not to delay the preparations for WESERÜBUNG by further disputes. (On March 2 Great Britain and France had submitted notes to Norway and Sweden requesting the right of transit for troops which they intended to send to the aid of the Finns.) He demanded that the forces for WESERÜBUNG be assembled by March 10 and ready for the jump-off by March 13 so that a landing would be possible in northern Norway on approximately March 17.[27]

On March 5 WESERÜBUNG was discussed in a meeting with Hitler at which the three Commanders in Chief were present. Field Marshal Goering, angry and claiming he had been kept in the dark about the operation, condemned all planning so far as worthless. After Goering had given vent to his feelings, Hitler again stated that he

---

* In German military terminology "group" (*Gruppe*) was used to designate an intermediate unit, in this instance between a corps and an army.

expected Allied intervention in Scandinavia, under the guise of help
for Finland, in the near future and then demanded and secured
immediate agreement on the commitment of German forces. Two days
later Hitler signed a directive assigning the 3rd Mountain Division,
the 69th, 163rd, 196th, and 181st Infantry Divisions, and the 11th
Motorized Rifle Brigade for employment in Norway and the 170th,
198th, and 214th Infantry Divisions for Denmark. That disposition
of forces was declared to be final and no longer subject to change.
Simultaneously, WESERÜBUNG and GELB were completely divorced
from each other.[28] The 7th Air Division and 22nd Infantry Division
were released for GELB. It was no longer possible to contemplate airborne and parachute landings on the scale which had been envisioned
in the Krancke Plan.

Meanwhile, the staff of Group XXI had completed "Operations
Order No. 1 for the Occupation of Norway," which it issued on March
5. The order was concerned with the landings and consolidation of
the beachheads. Two possibilities were envisioned: (1) that the desired objectives of a peaceful occupation could be achieved, and (2)
that the landings and occupation would have to be carried out by
force. If the first possibility materialized, the Norwegian Government
was to be assured of extensive respect for its internal sovereignty and
the Norwegian troops were to be treated tactfully. If resistance was
encountered, the landings were to be forced by all possible means,
the beachheads secured, and nearby mobilization centers of the
Norwegian Army occupied. Complete destruction of the Norwegian
Army was not considered possible as an immediate objective because
of the size of the country and difficulty of the terrain, but it was
believed that the localities selected for landings comprised the
majority of the places needed to prevent an effective mobilization and
assembly of Norwegian forces and to control the country in general.
Attempted Allied landings were to be fought off, unnecessary losses
were to be avoided, and, if the enemy proved superior, the troops
were to withdraw inland until a counterattack could be launched.[29]

Landings in approximately regimental strength were to be made
at Narvik, Trondheim, Bergen, Kristiansand, and Oslo, and landing
parties of one company each sent ashore at Egersund and Arendal
to take possession of the cable stations. Stavanger was to be taken in
an airborne operation. The initial seaborne landing force of 8,850
men was to be carried in five groups of warships. No major reinforcement of the landing teams at the beachheads was contemplated until
contact had been established overland with Oslo, where the main

force was to debark—16,000 men (in addition to the 2,000 landed on W Day) to be brought in by three sea transport echelons during the first week, with another 40,000 to be transported in shuttle movements thereafter. An additional 8,000 troops were to be transported to Oslo by air within three days after W Day.[30]

"Operations Order No. 1 for the Occupation of Denmark" was also completed, although it was not issued until March 20. The principal military objective of WESERÜBUNG SÜD was Aalborg at the northern tip of Jutland. Its two airfields were to be taken two hours after the operation began by a parachute platoon and an airborne battalion. Full control of the airfields and the lines of communication from Germany would be secured by the 170th Infantry Division and the 11th Motorized Rifle Brigade in a rapid advance across Jutland from the German border. Five warship groups, consisting of light naval craft, merchant vessels, and the World War I battleship *Schleswig-Holstein,* were organized to stage landings on the west coast of Jutland and the Danish islands.[31] Command of operations in Denmark was given to XXXI Corps under Air Force General Leonard Kaupisch.

Since the first objective of WESERÜBUNG was to induce both Norway and Denmark to surrender without a fight, special provisions were made to open negotiations with both governments at the moment of the landings. The German Ministers in Oslo and Copenhagen, who were designated Plenipotentiaries of the German Reich, would present the German demands and thereafter, if the demands were accepted, would keep the Norwegian and Danish Governments under surveillance. The operations officer of Group XXI and the chief of staff of XXXI Corps were named Plenipotentiaries of the *Wehrmacht* (Armed Forces). Traveling in civilian clothes, they were to go to Oslo and Copenhagen two days before W Day. After making last-minute reconnaissances, they would instruct the Ministers (who were not to be informed of their missions until the night before the landings) and thereafter, using special codes, inform the headquarters and the landing teams of the outcome of the negotiations.

After March 5 the timing of WESERÜBUNG became the major concern at the highest German command level. Admiral Raeder, in conference with Hitler on March 9, declared that the execution of WESERÜBUNG was urgent. The British, he maintained, had the opportunity to occupy Norway and Sweden under the pretext of sending troops to help the Finns. Such an occupation would result in loss of the Swedish iron ore and could be decisive against Germany. WESERÜBUNG itself he characterized as contrary to all the principles of naval warfare, since Germany did not have naval supremacy but would have to carry out the operation in the face of a vastly superior British Fleet; nevertheless, he believed the operation would be successful if surprise were achieved.[32]

On March 12, with news of peace impending in the Soviet-Finnish war, which was expected to hasten Allied action, and with information that the Allies had again offered assistance to Finland, a speed-up in the German preparations was ordered.[33] The Navy had already canceled all other naval operations on March 4 and on that day had begun holding submarines in port for WESERÜBUNG. On March 11 long-range submarines were dispatched to the main ports on the Norwegian west coast, where they were to combat Allied invasion forces or, according to the circumstances, support WESERÜBUNG.[34]

The Allied effort, meanwhile, had moved slowly, and the Finnish Army, under the weight of massive Soviet offensives which had begun in February, was reaching the limits of its endurance. The British held back two divisions from France, intending to put them into the field in Norway, and planned to expand their force eventually to 100,000 men. The French intended to commit about 50,000 troops.[35] The British and French staffs agreed that the second half of March would be the best time for going into Norway; but, aside from the desire to exploit the situation created by the Russo-Finnish conflict, they saw no compelling reason to act quickly, since they were convinced that the important Trondheim-Narvik area was beyond the Germans' reach and could be taken at any time. Allied plans, furthermore, remained contingent on the Norwegian and Swedish Governments' granting rights of transit to Allied troops. They had turned down a request by Finland to that effect on February 27, and another by the British and French Governments on March 3. By that time Finland had decided to sue for peace. On March 9 the Allied governments told the Finnish Ministers in Paris and London that if a request were made the Allies would come to the aid of Finland with all possible speed. The French went so far as to urge that such a request be made. They promised delivery of a hundred bombers within two weeks but left the dispatch of troops still dependent on the attitude of Norway and Sweden. On the same day Field Marshal Mannerheim, who regarded the Allied proposal as too uncertain, gave his government categorical advice to conclude peace.[36]

At the last minute, on March 12, still hoping for an appeal from the Finns, the Allies decided, at the suggestion of the French, to attempt a semipeaceable invasion of Scandinavia. Assuming that the recent diplomatic responses of the Norwegian and Swedish Governments ran counter to public opinion in those countries, they proposed to "test on the Norwegian beaches the firmness of the opposition." A landing was to be made at Narvik; if it succeeded, it would be followed by one at Trondheim. Forces for Bergen and Stavanger were to be held ready. The objectives were to take Narvik, the railroad, and the Swedish ore fields; but the landing and the advance into Norway and Sweden were to take place only if they could be accomplished without serious fighting. The troops were not to fight their way through either Norway or Sweden and were to use force only "as an ultimate measure of self-defense." [37]

The signing of the peace treaty between Russia and Finland in Moscow on the night of March 12 put an end to the Allied plans. The Germans observed British submarines concentrated off the Skagerrak on March 13, and an intercepted radio message setting March 14 as the deadline for the preparation of transport groups indicated that the Allied operation was getting under way. But another message, intercepted on March 15, ordering the submarines to disperse, revealed that the peace had disrupted the Allied plan.[38]

General opinion in the German Armed Forces High Command and the Navy High Command was that, with the pretext for action gone, the Allies would not undertake an operation against Norway in the near future. Even Raeder for a time doubted whether a German operation in Norway was still necessary. The fact remained, however, that the Allies had intended to go into Scandinavia, and for Hitler that was enough. He was convinced, he stated, that the British would not abandon their strategic aim of cutting off the German ore imports and believed that the possibility of a future Allied occupation still existed; therefore, WESERÜBUNG would have to be executed.

Although Hitler was probably influenced in large part by his gambler's instinct and his disinclination to abandon an operation once it had been prepared and he thought it could be carried off successfully, he was more nearly right in his estimate of Allied intentions than he knew. On March 21 Paul Reynaud became the head of a French Government committed to a more aggressive prosecution of the war; and a week later, at a meeting of the Allied Supreme War Council, the Scandinavian question again came under consideration. The new Scandinavian undertaking was to consist of two separate but related operations, WILFRED and Plan R 4. WILFRED involved the laying of two mine fields in Norwegian waters, one in the approaches to the Vest Fjord, north of Bodö, and the other between Ålesund and

Bergen, with the pretense of laying of a third near Molde. WILFRED was to be justified by notes delivered to Norway and Sweden several days in advance protesting the inability of those nations to protect their neutrality. The supposition was that WILFRED would provoke German counteraction, and Plan R 4 was to become effective the moment the Germans landed in Norway "or showed they intended to do so." Narvik and the railroad to the Swedish frontier formed the principal objectives of Plan R 4. The port was to be occupied by one infantry brigade and an antiaircraft battery, with the total strength to be built up eventually to 18,000 men. One battalion, in a transport escorted by two cruisers, was to sail within a few hours after the mines had been laid. Five battalions were to be employed in occupying Trondheim and Bergen and in a raid on Stavanger to destroy Sola airfield, the largest in Norway and the closest to the British Isles. The plan depended heavily on the assumption that the Norwegians would not offer resistance, and, strangely, the possibility of a strong German reaction was left almost entirely out of account.[39]

On the German side, after the Finnish-Soviet peace was announced, Hitler hesitated briefly as he cast about for means of justifying the operation, but the time for decision had come. From the point of view of the Navy, an early execution was imperative because all other naval operations had been brought to a standstill by the preparations and because after April 15 the nights would become too short to afford proper cover for the naval forces. Reporting to Hitler on March 26, Raeder declared that the danger of an Allied landing in Norway was no longer acute, but since he believed WESERÜBUNG would have to be carried out sooner or later, he advised that it be done as soon as possible. Hitler agreed to set the day for sometime in the period of the next new moon, which would occur on April 7.[40]

On April 1, after a detailed review, Hitler approved the plans for WESERÜBUNG; on the following day, after having been assured by the Commanders in Chief, Navy and Air Force, that ice would not impede naval movements in the Baltic and that flying conditions would be satisfactory, he designated April 9 as W (WESER) Day and 5:15 A.M. as W Time. The first supply ships sailed on April 3 and the warships began putting out from German ports at midnight on April 6.[41]

It was not until after the first German ships were at sea that the Allies reached an agreement on their own operation. The execution of WILFRED and Plan R 4 was at first tied to Operation ROYAL MARINE, a British proposal for sowing fluvial mines in the Rhine to which the

French objected on the ground that it would provoke German bombing of French factories. WILFRED had been scheduled for April 5, but it was not until that date that the British Government agreed to carry out the Norwegian operations independently of ROYAL MARINE. In consequence, the WILFRED mines were not laid until the morning of April 8, by which time the German ships were advancing up the Norwegian coast. When it became known on the morning of April 8 that the German Fleet, which had been sighted by aircraft in the North Sea on the previous day, was at sea in the vicinity of Norway the mine-laying force was withdrawn and Plan R 4 was abandoned.

In the end the Allied venture accomplished nothing and gave Hitler the excuse he needed for WESERÜBUNG. The coincidence of Allied and German forces heading toward Norway at exactly the same time reinforced the myth of Hitler's "intuition" and gave rise to the *post hoc, ergo propter hoc* argument that WESERÜBUNG was forced on Germany by the aggressive intentions of the Allies. Actually there is no evidence that Hitler knew of WILFRED or Plan R 4, and it appears highly unlikely that he would have risked his Navy in Norwegian waters if he had known or suspected that the British Navy would be engaged in major operations in that area at the same time.

On W Day, despite the fact that Warship Groups 1 and 2 had been sighted by British reconnaissance planes in the North Sea on April 7 and that one of the ships of the 1st Sea Transport Echelon had been sunk off Norway on the same day and its survivors—some of them soldiers in uniform—had been taken ashore in Norway, surprise was achieved everywhere except at Oslo, where Germany's newest cruiser *Blücher* was sunk by the guns and torpedoes of coastal forts on the fjord outside the city. The Danish Government capitulated immediately, but the Government of Norway declared its intention to fight and, taking advantage of the delay in the German landing at Oslo, escaped into the interior. Within a week the Allies had committed forces at Narvik, Namsos, and Åndalsnes to aid the Norwegians. But the superiority of the German plan and preparations was quickly proved, and by the first week of May the Allies had been driven out of Namsos and Åndalsnes, leaving central and southern Norway firmly in German hands. British counteroperations at sea were not much more successful, and the German Air Force quickly demonstrated the ability of airpower—given the proper conditions—to neutralize superior sea power. At Narvik, nearly out of the striking range of the German Air Force, the situation was somewhat different. There the British Navy moved in quickly, and none of the ten German destroyers which had carried the landing force north managed to escape. By April 14, after Allied troops had begun landing, Hitler was on the verge of instructing the regiment at Narvik to withdraw into Sweden and be interned. It took the combined efforts of the Army and Armed Forces High Commands to dissuade him from performing that signal act of timidity, which would also have amounted to sacrificing the primary objective of WESERÜBUNG. Thereafter the Narvik regiment staged a skillful and stubborn defense until early June, when the Allies, under the pressure of catastrophic developments in France, decided to evacuate. On June 9, one day after the last Allied troops had sailed, the Norwegian Army surrendered.

In comparison with the expenditures of men and matériel which became commonplace later in the war, the cost of the Norwegian campaign was minor. German casualties were 1,317 killed, 1,604 wounded, and 2,375 lost at sea or otherwise missing. The British lost 1,869 men in ground fighting and upward of 2,500 more at sea. The Norwegian losses numbered 1,335 men, and those of the French and Poles, 530. Of the losses on both sides, the only ones of major significance were those sustained by the German Navy. At the end of June 1940, Germany had only one heavy cruiser, two light cruisers, and four destroyers fit for action. In the anxious days of the summer of 1940 that was a source of some comfort to the British. Winston Churchill has described it as a "fact of major importance potentially affecting the whole future of the war." [42] On the other hand, the Norwegian campaign constituted the high point in the German Navy's exploitation of its surface forces.

As an isolated military operation the German occupation of Norway was an outstanding success. Carried out in the teeth of vastly superior British sea power, it was, as Hitler said, "not only bold, but one of the sauciest undertakings in the history of modern warfare." [43] Well planned and skillfully executed, it showed the *Wehrmacht* at its best; nevertheless, some of the faults which were later to contribute greatly to the German defeat were already present, although not yet prominent enough to influence the outcome of the campaign. For success the operation depended heavily on daring and surprise combined with lack of preparedness and indecision on the part of the enemy. Those elements won campaigns but were not enough to win the war. Also in this campaign two serious defects of Hitler's personal leadership were revealed: his persistent meddling in the details of operations and his tendency to lose his nerve in a crisis.

To some extent, too, WESERÜBUNG gave evidence of Hitler's fatal weakness, his inability to keep his commitments within the bounds of his resources. Most German authorities still contend that Germany's strategic interests in Scandinavia and the existence of Allied intentions to open an offensive there created a compelling necessity for German action. However, two who qualify as experts of the first rank have concluded that WESERÜBUNG was not the sole solution for Germany, and probably not the best. Artillery General Walter Warlimont has pointed out that even if the Allies had been able to establish a foothold in Norway, they would have been forced to relinquish their hold there once Operation GELB (the invasion of the Netherlands, Belgium, and France) had started and that, if it were still necessary, the German occupation of Norway could have been accomplished more cheaply after GELB.[44] Professor Walther Hubatsch in his history of the Norwegian campaign reaches essentially the same conclusion and adds the observation that Germany "undoubtedly" had the strength at that time to force the Allies back out of Scandinavia. He observes also that in Scandinavia the Allies would have had to contend with strong opposition on the part of the Soviet Union as well as Germany.[45] These views find further support in the official British historian's statement that "given the political situation of 1939-40 British intervention in some form was inevitable; and given the paucity of the then resources in men and arms, a more or less calamitous issue from it was likewise inevitable." [46] Of course, the clock cannot be set back and the function of history is not to speculate on what might have been; yet the contentions of Warlimont and Hubatsch, although they may benefit to some extent from hindsight, do in fact reflect a strong body of opinion which existed in the German Command at the time and which, in essence, opposed the growing tendency to plunge in with a full-scale offensive at any point which was or might be threatened.

To return to the firmer ground of tangible gains, WESERÜBUNG brought Germany control of its supply line for Swedish iron ore (later also for Finnish nickel), a number of new naval and air bases, and some other economic advantages. The naval and air bases somewhat improved the German position with respect to the British Isles, increased the Navy's chances to break out into the Atlantic with raiders, and later made possible air and sea attacks on the Allied Murmansk convoys. However, a decisive improvement, particularly in the naval situation, was not achieved. Germany could still be shut off from the open sea, and for the Navy the advantages gained in the bases were offset by the losses in ships sustained during WESERÜBUNG.

In the further course of the war, Norway became the staging area for a German advance across Finland to Murmansk and the Murmansk Railroad. That attack bogged down in the summer of 1941 short of its objectives, and thereafter the fronts in Finland and Norway stagnated, tying down more than a half million men and tremendous amounts of matériel. Although Hitler insisted to the very last that Norway was the strategic key to Europe, the expected Allied invasion never came; and on May 8, 1945, the German Army in Norway surrendered without having fired a shot in the decisive battles of the war.

Louis Morton

Japan's Decision for War
(1941)

Few if any of the fateful decisions of history are as well documented as the one Japan made on December 1, 1941 to go to war with the United States and Great Britain. The sequence of events that led to this decision has been described in rich detail and at first hand by those who played the leading roles in this drama of national suicide, and, with somewhat more detachment, by the students of diplomacy and Far Eastern affairs. The rise and fall of cabinets in prewar Japan, the confidential deliberations of its highest political bodies, the tortuous path of its diplomacy, and the views of its most influential leaders have been analyzed and illuminated by jurists and scholars alike. For those who wish to retrace the road to Pearl Harbor, the signposts are indeed numerous and the way well lighted.

Not so well charted is the course taken by the Japanese Army and Navy to gain by force what the politicians and diplomats could not win by negotiation. The path is a faint one, but the journey along it rewards the traveler with an understanding of the strange mixture of reality and illusion which led Japan to attack the most powerful nations in the Pacific. It confirms and clarifies, too, the role of the military in Japan's political life and makes clear how the needs and capacities of the Army and Navy at once established and limited national objectives and ambitions. And along this path lies the explanation for Japan's dramatic blow against Pearl Harbor and its choice of time, place, and method of attack.[1]

The Army in Japan traditionally stood for a course of expansion which would make Japan the unchallenged leader of Asia. In 1936 the

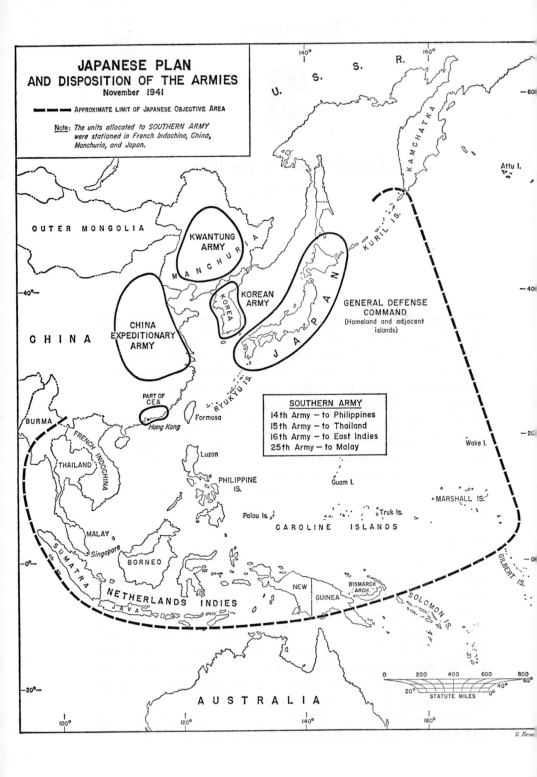

**JAPANESE PLAN
AND DISPOSITION OF THE ARMIES**
November 1941

▬ ▬ ▬ Approximate limit of Japanese Objective Area

Note: The units allocated to SOUTHERN ARMY
were stationed in French Indochina, China,
Manchuria, and Japan.

U. S. S. R.

KAMCHATKA

Attu I.

OUTER MONGOLIA

KWANTUNG
ARMY

MANCHURIA

KURIL IS.

KOREAN
ARMY

KOREA

GENERAL DEFENSE
COMMAND
(Homeland and adjacent
islands)

J A P A N

CHINA
EXPEDITIONARY
ARMY

C H I N A

PART OF
CEA

RYUKYU IS.

Formosa

Hong Kong

BURMA

FRENCH INDOCHINA

THAILAND

Luzon

SOUTHERN ARMY
14th Army — to Philippines
15th Army — to Thailand
16th Army — to East Indies
25th Army — to Malay

Wake I.

PHILIPPINE
IS.

Guam I.

MARSHALL IS.

Palau Is.

Truk Is.

MALAY

C A R O L I N E   I S L A N D S

Singapore

BORNEO

GILBERT IS.

N E T H E R L A N D S   I N D I E S

JAVA

SUMATRA

NEW
GUINEA

BISMARCK
ARCH.

SOLOMON IS.

0   200   400   600   800

STATUTE MILES

A U S T R A L I A

U. Brae

Army gained a predominant position in the political life of the nation and its program became the official policy of the government, and since then it had been preparing for war. The program adopted in that year called for, among other things, the establishment of a "firm position" on the Asiatic Continent—a euphemistic way of saying that China must be conquered; expansion into southeast Asia to secure the bases and raw materials needed to make Japan economically strong and self-sufficient; strengthening the military forces of the nation; development of critical war industries; and the improvement of air and sea transportation.[2]

Though this program was to be achieved gradually and peacefully, if possible, it clearly implied military action both in China and in southeast Asia. And to prepare for that contingency, the Japanese Government turned all its efforts into military channels. In 1936, appropriations for military expenditures rose sharply and continued to rise thereafter. The entire economy of the nation was placed under rigid controls and oriented toward war; heavy industries were expanded, the production of aircraft and munitions was increased, and every effort was made to stockpile weapons, equipment, and strategic raw materials.[3]

The shortage of oil was the key to Japan's military situation. It was the main problem for those preparing for war, and, at the same time, the reason why the nation was moving toward war. For the Navy the supply of oil was critical; for the Army it was always a limiting factor. And none of the measures taken to curtail civilian consumption or to manufacture substitutes ever gave Japan enough of this precious commodity to free it from the restraint exercised by the Dutch, the British, and the Americans, who controlled the sources of supply. Without oil, Japan's pretensions to empire were empty shadows.[4]

Japan's move into China in July 1937, eight months after it had signed the Anti-Comintern Pact with Germany, produced further difficulties. The vigor of the Chinese reaction soon led to full-scale war, an eventuality the Japanese military neither expected nor desired. Moreover, the United States, like other nations with interests in China, refused to acquiesce in this fresh assault on the *status quo* in Asia. In unmistakable terms, it made clear to Japan that it still stood by the open-door policy and the territorial integrity of China. Japan's action in China was in violation of all existing treaties, and, in the American view, the only solution to the "China incident" was the complete withdrawal of Japanese forces from China. This was a

price the military leaders of Japan would never pay for the good will
of the United States.

The war in China, from which Japan could extract neither honor
nor victory, proved a continuing drain on the resources of the nation,
requiring ever more stringent controls, higher appropriations, and
further expansion of war industries. By the end of 1941, Japan's industry and manpower had been so completely mobilized that the
transition to total war was scarcely noticed.

The growth of Japan's military forces matched its industrial
growth. Between 1936 and 1941 the size of the Army more than
doubled. The number of divisions rose from 20 to 50; air squadrons,
from 50 to 150. And China provided the testing ground for doctrine
and a reservoir of combat-trained veterans. Naval forces grew rapidly
also after 1936 when Japan withdrew from the international naval
conference of that year. By 1940 combat tonnage had jumped to
over one million tons, giving Japan a navy more powerful than the
combined American and British Fleets in the Pacific.[5]

Despite these preparations for war, neither the Army nor the Navy
developed during the decade of the thirties any specific plans for the
use of this formidable military machine against a coalition of Western
Powers. In the files of the High Command were general statements of
policy and annual operations plans, but, except for those that concerned China, they were defensive in concept and dealt only with
the United States and Soviet Russia. In no case, it was emphasized,
should Japan fight more than one enemy at a time. The plans were,
in the words of one Japanese officer, "outdated writings" and "utterly
nonsensical." [6]

The absence, during this period, of specific plans reflecting national
objectives and government policy is remarkable. The preparation of
such plans is the major function of a general staff and was routine in
the United States and other democratic countries where the military
was much more closely controlled than in Japan. The fact that the
Japanese General Staff—which had studied in the best schools in
Europe—had failed to prepare such plans as late as 1940 cannot be
attributed either to peaceful intentions or to a supreme confidence in
diplomacy. It was based solely on a realistic appreciation of Japan's
economic weakness and lack of the strategic resources required for
modern warfare.

Toward the end of 1940, after Germany had conquered most of
Western Europe, Japan set out to remedy its basic weaknesses by a
program of expansion in southeast Asia. There, in the crumbling

British, Dutch, and French empires, lay the oil, rubber, bauxite, and other vital resources Japan needed so badly. Only the United States and Soviet Russia stood in the way, and their interference, the Japanese believed, could be checkmated by political alliance. Thus, in the months that followed, Japan sought to immobilize the United States with the Tripartite Pact (between Germany, Italy, and Japan, signed on September 1940) and to gain the friendship of Russia with a five-year pact of nonaggression and neutrality.

Simultaneously with these diplomatic and political measures, the Japanese Army and Navy began to prepare more actively for a general war while laying the basis for military action in the south. Renewed efforts were made to stockpile vital resources, and in late October the Total War Research Institute was established. In December 1940 the Army ordered three divisions, then in South China, to begin training for operations in tropical areas. During the next few weeks special studies were made of the geography, terrain, and climate of Malaya, Indochina, the Netherlands Indies, Thailand, and Burma, and of the problems involved in military operations there. By January 1941 Japanese pilots were flying reconnaissance and taking aerial photographs over the Malayan coast and the Philippines, and the War Ministry and Foreign Office were printing military currency for use in the southern area. It was at this time, too, that Admiral Isoroku Yamamoto, commander of the Combined Fleet, conceived the idea of a carrier-based air attack on Pearl Harbor and ordered his staff to work out the problems posed by such an operation.[7] The Japanese Army and Navy were unmistakably moving away from the defensive concepts which had guided their planning during the preceding decade.

The summer of 1941 was the critical season for the diplomats as well as the soldiers of Japan. The war in China was still on, draining the meager oil reserves of the nation and creating an insoluble barrier to agreement with the United States. The Tripartite Pact had produced an effect opposite from that intended and erected another obstacle to an understanding between the two countries. And finally, the Dutch, backed by the Americans and British, had successfully resisted Japanese efforts to secure economic concessions in the Indies.

The German invasion of Russia in June 1941 forced the Japanese to review their program for the conquest of southeast Asia. For over a week they debated the question of the effect of Germany's action on Japan. Some thought it better to move north now rather than south, others that the time had come to make concessions and reach agreement with the United States, whose hand in the Pacific had been strengthened by the Russo-German war. President Roosevelt, who listened in on the debate through the medium of MAGIC—the code name applied to intercepted and decoded Japanese messages— characterized it as "a real drag-down and knock-out fight . . . to decide which way they were going to jump—attack Russia, attack the South Seas, [or] sit on the fence and be more friendly with us." [8] The Foreign Minister, Yosuke Matsuoka, favored the first course; the Army, the second; and the Premier, Prince Fumimaro Konoye, the third.

On July 2, 1941, at a conference in the Imperial Presence, the leaders of Japan made their decision. It was a clear-cut defeat for the pro-Axis Foreign Minister and those who believed with him that Japan should attack Russia. For the others it was a compromise of sorts. Negotiations with the United States, begun in February 1941, would be continued in an effort to settle the issues between the two countries. At the same time, the plans already made for the domination of Thailand and Indochina, the first objectives in the southern area, would be put into effect immediately. "We will not be deterred," the Imperial Conference decreed, "by the possibility of becoming in- volved in a war with England and America." [9] In short, Japan would attempt the difficult feat of sitting on the fence and advancing south at the same time.

The problems posed by Germany's attack on Russia were hardly settled and the decision made to abide by the Tripartite Pact and the drive southward when a new crisis arose. On June 21 U.S. Secretary of State Cordell Hull had handed the Japanese Ambassador, Admiral Kichisaburo Nomura, a note asking for some clear indica- tion of a genuine desire for peace and making allusions to the pro- German attitude of certain members of the Japanese Government. This communication was still unanswered; and now Matsuoka insisted on outright rejection of the note and the termination of the talks. The Premier, Prince Konoye, wished instead to reply with counter- proposals already prepared by the Army and Navy. Matsuoka would not budge from his position, and Konoye, given the nod by War Minister General Hideki Tojo and after consultation with the Em- peror, submitted the resignation of the entire Cabinet on July 16. Two days later he received the Imperial mandate to form a new Cabinet which, except for Matsuoka who was replaced by Admiral Soemu Toyoda, was the same as the old one. The Japanese could now go ahead with the program outlined at the Imperial Conference of July 2.[10]

The first move of the new government was the virtual occupation of French Indochina. Protesting that Indochina was being encircled, Japan issued what was in effect an ultimatum to the Vichy Government on July 19. On July 24 Roosevelt offered to guarantee to the Japanese equal access to the raw materials and food of Indochina in return for the neutralization of that country, but nothing came of the proposal. The following day Japanese troops moved into the southern portion of Indochina. Japan now possessed strategically located air and naval bases from which to launch attacks on Singapore, the Philippines, and the Netherlands Indies.

Although the French acquiesced in this raid on their empire, the United States was not so obliging. In the view of the State Department, this fresh Japanese aggression constituted a threat to American interests in the Far East and justified the imposition of additional economic restrictions, then being considered by the President, as a warning to Japan.[11] These restrictions were finally put into effect on July 26 when the President, against the advice of his Chief of Naval Operations, Admiral Harold R. Stark, issued an order freezing Japanese assets in the United States. Since Japan no longer had the dollars with which to purchase the urgently needed materials of war, the effect of this measure, which the British and Dutch supported, was to create an economic blockade of Japan. So seriously did Admiral Stark regard this move that he warned Admiral Thomas C. Hart, commander of the Asiatic Fleet, to take "appropriate precautionary measures against possible eventualities." [12]

The sharp American reaction to their move into Indochina came as a surprise to the Japanese and precipitated an intensive review of the nation's readiness to wage war. The picture was not encouraging. The powerful Planning Board which coordinated the vast, complex structure of Japan's war economy found the country's resources meager and only enough, in view of the recent action of the United States, for a quick, decisive war to gain the riches of the Indies. "If the present condition is left unchecked," asserted Teiichi Suzuki, President of the Board, "Japan will find herself totally exhausted and unable to rise in the future." The blockade, he believed, would bring about Japan's collapse within two years, and he urged that a final decision on war or peace be made "without hesitation." [13] The Navy's view was equally gloomy. There was only enough oil, Admiral Osami

Nagano told the Emperor, to maintain the fleet under war conditions for one and a half years and he was doubtful that Japan could win a "sweeping victory" in that time. His advice, therefore, was to drop the Tripartite Pact and reach agreement with the United States.

The Army and other powerful forces in the Japanese Government did not share these views. They thought there was enough oil on hand to wage war and that renunciation of the Tripartite Pact would not necessarily bring about a change in U.S.-Japanese relations. Marquis Koichi Kido, the Emperor's chief adviser, discussed the problem with Prince Konoye and agreed that before a decision on war or peace could be made, the Army and Navy would have to reach agreement.

By the middle of August the two services had agreed on a broad line of strategy. The impetus came from a series of studies presented by the Total War Research Institute, a subordinate body of the Planning Board. Forecasting the course of events during the next six months, the Institute called for the invasion of the Netherlands Indies in November, followed the next month by surprise attacks on British and American possessions in the Far East. Anticipating that the United States and Great Britain would utilize Soviet bases in a war against Japan, the Institute's studies dealt with the problems of economic mobilization; military planning, except in the most general sense, was left to the services.[14]

These studies, as well as others, were discussed heatedly during the tense days that followed the U.S. embargo. From these discussions emerged four alternative lines of strategy, all of them designed to accomplish the swift destruction of Allied forces in the Far East and the early seizure of the Netherlands Indies. The first was based on the Institute's studies and provided for the seizure of the Indies and then the Philippines and Malaya. The second called for a step-by-step advance from the Philippines to Borneo, Java, Sumatra, and Malaya. The reverse, from Malaya to the Philippines, constituted a third line of action and one which would have the advantage of delaying attack against American territory. The fourth plan proposed at this time consisted of simultaneous attacks against the Philippines and Malaya followed by a rapid advance along both axes to the Indies. Admiral Yamamoto's plan for an attack against Pearl Harbor, work on which had begun in January, did not enter into the calculations of the planners at this time.

Army and Navy planners agreed that the first plan was too risky for it would leave Japanese forces exposed to attack from the Philippines and Malaya. The Navy preferred the second plan; it was safe, provided for a step-by-step advance, and created no serious problems. The Army objected to it, however, on the ground that by the time the main objectives in the Netherlands Indies and Malaya were reached the Allies would have had time to strengthen their defenses. The third plan, with its early seizure of Malaya and bypassing of the Philippines, appealed greatly to the Army planners who hoped in this way to gain southeast Asia and delay American entry into the war. But this course, as the Navy pointed out, also placed American naval and air forces in the Philippines in a strategic position athwart Japan's line of communication and constituted a risk of the utmost magnitude. The fourth course, simultaneous attacks and advance along two axes, created serious problems of coordination and timing and a dangerous dispersion of forces. But because it was the only course which compromised the views of both groups, it was finally adopted. For the first time the Japanese had a strategic plan for offensive operations designed to achieve the goals of national policy against a coalition of enemies.[15] Operational plans for each objective were still to be made, forces organized, trained, and rehearsed.

Though the Army and Navy had agreed on strategy, the Japanese Government was still reluctant to take the final step. Contributing to this lack of resolution was the slowing down of Germany's advance in Russia and the Japanese Navy's concern over the shortage of oil reserves. From the end of July until his resignation in October, Premier Konoye sought to persuade his cabinet colleagues to adopt a less aggressive policy in an effort to reach agreement with the United States.

The first sign of this new policy was a proposal, delivered by Admiral Nomura in Washington on August 6, for a personal meeting—a "leaders' conference"—between the Japanese Premier and President Roosevelt. General Tojo had agreed to this proposal only on the understanding that Konoye would use the occasion to press the program for expansion to the south. The American reply on August 17 that a prerequisite to such a meeting was the settlement of the issues between the two countries confirmed Tojo and the Army leaders in their view that the United States would never yield to the Japanese demands and that war should begin as soon as the Army and Navy were ready.[16]

The difference between the two Japanese points of view was temporarily resolved early in September and formalized at an Imperial Conference held on September 6. The agreement, characteristically

Japanese, was expressed in language which both sides could accept and interpret in their own way. The negotiations with the United States, it was agreed, would be continued, as Konoye wished. But at the same time military preparations would be pushed to completion so that the nation would be ready for war by the end of October, that is, in six weeks. "If by the early part of October," the conferees decided, "there is no reasonable hope of having our demands agreed to in the diplomatic negotiations . . . we will immediately make up our minds to get ready for war. . . ." [17]

The Imperial Conference also fixed the minimum demands Japan would make and maximum concessions it would grant in the negotiations with the United States and Great Britain. The former were hardly likely to gain acceptance. First, both the Western Powers would have to promise to discontinue aid to China, close the Burma Road, and "neither meddle in nor interrupt" a settlement between Japan and China. Second, America and Britain would have to recognize Japan's special position in French Indochina and agree not to establish or reinforce their bases in the Far East or take any action which might threaten Japan. Finally, both nations would have to resume commercial relations with Japan, supply the materials "indispensable for her self-existence," and "gladly cooperate" in Japan's economic program in Thailand and Indochina. In return for these "minimum demands," the Japanese were willing to agree not to use Indochina as a base for further military advance, except in China, to withdraw from Indochina "after an impartial peace" had been established in the Far East, and, finally, to guarantee the neutrality of the Philippine Islands. [18]

While the negotiations with the U.S. went forward, the Army and Navy General Staffs continued their preparations for war and the troops earmarked for operations in the south intensified their training, usually under conditions approximating those of the areas in which they would fight. Since agreement had already been reached on the strategy for war, General Hajime Sugiyama, Army Chief of Staff, was able shortly after the September 6 Imperial Conference to direct that detailed operational plans for the seizure of Malaya, Java, Borneo, the Bismarck Archipelago, the Netherlands Indies, and the Philippines be prepared. [19] The Army planners immediately went to work and the next two months witnessed feverish activity in the General Staff.

By the end of August the Navy planners had worked out their plans for seizing bases in the western Pacific and had from Admiral

Yamamoto a separate plan for an attack on Pearl Harbor. "Table-top maneuvers" at Tokyo Naval War College between September 10 and 13 resulted in agreement on operations for the seizure of the Philippines, Malaya, the Netherlands Indies, Burma, and islands in the South Pacific, but there was still some doubt about Yamamoto's plan. The exercise had demonstrated that a Pearl Harbor strike was practicable, but many felt that it was too risky, that the U.S. Pacific Fleet might not be in port on the day of the attack, and that the danger of discovery during the long voyage to Hawaii was too great. But Admiral Yamamoto refused to give up his plan and finally, when he failed to convert his colleagues, offered to resign from the Navy. The combination of his strong argument that the success of the southward drive depended on the destruction of the American Fleet, his enormous prestige, and his threat to resign were too much for opponents of the plan. In mid-October, a month after the maneuvers, the Navy General Staff finally adopted his concept of a surprise carrier-based attack on Pearl Harbor and incorporated it into the larger plan for war.[20]

This larger plan, which was virtually complete by October 20 and was the one followed by the Japanese when war came, had as its immediate objective the capture of the rich Dutch and British possessions in southeast Asia. The greatest single threat to its success was the U.S. Pacific Fleet at Pearl Harbor, and this threat the Japanese now hoped to eliminate by the destruction or neutralization of the fleet at the start of the war. U.S. air and naval forces in the Philippines, which stood in position along the flank of their advance southward, the Japanese expected to destroy quickly also, seizing the islands later at their leisure. Finally, America's line of communications across the Pacific was to be cut by the capture of Wake Island and Guam. Once these threats had been removed and the coveted area to the south secured, Japanese military forces would occupy strategic positions in Asia and in the Pacific and fortify them immediately. These bases would form a powerful defensive perimeter around the newly acquired empire in the south, the home islands, and the vital shipping lanes connecting Japan with its new sources of supply. With these supplies the Japanese thought they could wage defensive war indefinitely.[21]

The area marked for conquest formed a vast triangle whose east arm stretched from the Kuril Islands in the north, through Wake Island, to the Marshall Islands. The base of the triangle was formed by a line connecting the Marshall Islands, the Bismarck Archipelago,

Java, and Sumatra. The western arm extended from Malaya and southern Burma, through Indochina, and thence along the China coast.

The acquisition of this area would give to Japan control of the resources of southeast Asia and would satisfy the national objectives in going to war. Perhaps later, if all went well, the area of conquest could be extended. But there is no evidence in the Japanese plans of an intention to invade the United States or to seek the total defeat of that nation. Japan planned to fight a war of limited objectives and, having gained what it wanted, expected to negotiate for a favorable settlement.

Japanese planners anticipated that certain events might require an alteration in their strategy and outlined alternative courses of action to be followed in each contingency. The first possibility was that the negotiations then in progress in Washington would prove successful. If this unexpected success was achieved, all operations were to be suspended even if the final orders to attack had been issued. The second possibility was that the United States might take hostile action before the attack on Pearl Harbor by sending elements of the Pacific Fleet to the Far East. In that event, the Japanese Combined Fleet would be deployed to intercept American naval forces while the attacks against the Philippines and Malaya proceeded according to schedule.

The possibility of a Soviet attack, or of a joint U.S.-Soviet invasion from the north, was a specter that haunted the Japanese. To meet such a contingency, Japanese ground forces in Manchuria were to be strengthened, while air units from the home islands and China were to be transferred to meet the new threat. Thereafter, the attack to the south would proceed on schedule.

The forces required to execute this vast plan for conquest were very carefully calculated by Imperial General Headquarters. A large force had to be left in Manchuria, and an even larger one in China. Garrisons for Korea, Formosa, the home islands, and other positions required additional forces. Thus, only a small fraction of the Japanese Army was available for operations in the south. Of the total strength of the Army's 51 divisions, 59 mixed brigades, and 1,500 first-line planes, Imperial General Headquarters could allocate only 11 divisions and 2 air groups (700 planes) to the operations in the south.

In the execution of this complicated and intricate plan, the Japanese planners realized, success would depend on careful timing and on the closest cooperation between ground, naval, and air forces. No provision was made for unified command of all services, then or later. Instead, separate agreements were made between Army and Fleet commanders for each operation. These agreements provided simply for cooperation at the time of landing and for the distribution of forces.

In addition to supporting the Army's operations in the south, the Combined Fleet had other important missions. Perhaps the most important, and certainly the most spectacular, was that assigned the Pearl Harbor Striking Force. Later, this force was to support operations of the 4th Fleet in the capture of Guam and the Bismarck Archipelago, and then assist in the southern operations. The 6th Fleet (submarines) was to operate in Hawaiian waters and along the West Coast of the United States to observe the movement of the U.S. Pacific Fleet and make surprise attacks on shipping. The 5th Fleet was to patrol the waters east of Japan, in readiness for enemy surprise attacks, and, above all, keep on the alert against Russia.

The Japanese plan for war was complete in all respects but one— the date when it would go into effect. That decision awaited the outcome of the negotiations then in progress and of the struggle in the Cabinet between those who advocated caution and those who pressed for immediate action. "Time had become the meter of strategy" and Japan "was crazed by the tick of the clock." [22]

The six-weeks' reprieve Konoye had won on September 6 to settle the outstanding issues by diplomacy went by quickly without producing a settlement. A new proposal, which Nomura delivered to Hull on September 27, was rejected by the Americans, who were unwavering in their position on China. Nomura renewed the request for a meeting between Roosevelt and Konoye but on October 10 was constrained to tell Foreign Minister Toyoda that there was not "the slightest chance on earth" of a "leaders' conference" so long as Japan refused to compromise. The negotiations, in the words of Toyoda, had "slowly but surely . . . reached the decisive stage." [23] There was apparently no way of reconciling the basic differences over China.

The domestic situation was no better. The demands of the Army and Navy for a decision on the question of war were becoming ever more insistent. Oil stocks were steadily diminishing, the most favorable season of the year for operations was approaching, and failure to act soon might force a delay of many months and expose the Japanese to a Soviet attack on Manchuria. Finally, on September 24, General Sugiyama and Admiral Nagano, the Army and Navy Chiefs of Staff, submitted a joint letter calling attention to the shortage of supplies, the effect of the weather on operations, and the problems of mobilizing, staging, and deploying their forces. "With all the force of their positions" they asked for a quick decision "by October 15 at the latest," so that they could start operations by mid-November.[24]

With no agreement in sight, Konoye sought to win an extension. On October 12 he invited War Minister Tojo, the Navy and Foreign Ministers, and the President of the Planning Board to his home for a final conference on the question of war and peace. At the meeting the Premier argued strongly for continuing the negotiations beyond the deadline, then set at October 15. The Navy Minister would not commit himself, but General Tojo, on the ground that success in the negotiations would require concessions in China, refused to go along with Konoye. The issue had now been narrowed to the withdrawal of Japanese troops from China, and on the morning of October 14 the Premier again sought Tojo's consent. "On this occasion," he urged the War Minister, "we ought to give in for a time . . . and save ourselves from the crisis of a Japanese-American war." Tojo again refused, and at a Cabinet meeting later in the day demanded that the negotiations be terminated. Finally, late that night, he sent Konoye a message stating that the Cabinet ought to resign, "declare insolvent everything that has happened up to now, and reconsider our plans once more." [25]

Without Tojo's support Konoye had no recourse but to resign. The Army, seeking possibly to avoid responsibility for the decision which must soon be made, suggested that his successor be a prince of the Imperial family. The suggestion was rejected as contrary to tradition and the Marquis Kido, together with the Council of Senior Statesmen (former premiers), recommended that Tojo himself be named Premier. The Emperor accepted this recommendation. On October 18 Tojo took office with an Imperial mandate to reconsider Japan's policy in relation to the world situation without regard for the September 6 decision. The fate of Japan was in the hands of its generals.

In Washington, where every Japanese move was carefully weighed and analyzed, the Japanese Cabinet crisis was cause for real concern and Ambassador Joseph C. Grew's cables from Tokyo did little to lessen it. On October 16, when Konoye resigned, Admiral Stark told Pacific and Asiatic Fleet commanders there was "a strong possibility" of war between Japan and Russia. Warning them that Japan might also attack the United States, Stark instructed the two commanders to take "due precautions." This message Admiral Hart and the commander of the Pacific Fleet at Pearl Harbor, Admiral Husband E. Kimmel, passed on to their Army colleagues, who, a few days later, received quite a different message from Washington informing them that they need not expect an "abrupt change in Japanese foreign policy." [26] Apparently the Army did not agree with the Navy's estimate of the international situation, and neither mentioned the possibility of an attack on Pearl Harbor.

The period from October 18 to November 5 was one of mounting tension and frantic preparations on both sides of the Pacific. In Tokyo the Tojo Cabinet and the High Command, meeting in an almost continuous series of "Liaison Conferences," considered every aspect of Japan's position and the possibilities of each line of action. Finally, on November 5, a decision was reached and confirmed by a conference in the Imperial Presence. This decision was substantially the same as that reached on September 6: to continue negotiations in an effort to reach an agreement with the United States, and, if no settlement was reached, to open hostilities. The deadline first set was November 25, later extended to November 29. The significance of this decision was revealed in a message the new Foreign Minister, Shigenori Togo, sent Admiral Nomura in Washington on November 4 telling him that relations between the two countries had "reached the edge." Next day he wrote that time was "exceedingly short" and the situation "very critical." "Absolutely no delays can be permitted. Please bear this in mind and do your best," Togo said. "I wish to stress this point over and over." [27]

The Imperial Conference agreed to make two more proposals to the United States. The first, Proposal A, was an amendment to the latest Japanese proposal and provided for a withdrawal from China and French Indochina, when and if a peace treaty was signed with Chiang Kai-shek. In certain areas in China, to be specified in the treaty, Japanese troops would remain for a "suitable period," vaguely and informally stated to be about twenty-five years. Further, the Japanese Government would interpret its obligations under the Tripartite Pact independently of the other Axis Powers. Lastly, Japan would agree not to discriminate in trade, provided all other nations did the same. In his instructions to Nomura, Foreign Minister Togo emphasized that while other matters could be compromised in his negotiations with the United States, Japan could not yield on the question of China.

In Proposal B, to be made if the first was rejected, no mention was made of the Tripartite Pact or the removal of Japanese troops from China. Japan would withdraw her troops from southern Indochina immediately and from the northern part of that country only after the negotiation of a peace treaty with Chiang Kai-shek, or after the conclusion of a "just peace" in the Pacific. In return, the United States was to agree not to interfere in the negotiations with China, and to cooperate with Japan in the acquisition and exploitation of natural resources in the Netherlands Indies. Finally, the United States was to resume commercial relations with Japan, and to provide that nation with oil.[28]

With the decision made and the deadline set, the Army and Navy drew up an agreement embodying the objectives of the war and an outline of operations. About the same time Admiral Nagano sent Yamamoto his final orders and told him to be ready to strike "by the first part of December." During the next few weeks the fleet was readied for action, and on November 26 the Pearl Harbor Striking Force left its lonely assembly area in the snowbound Kurils and sailed due east on its way to Hawaii.[29]

The Army acted with similar dispatch. On November 6 General Sugiyama issued instructions to the Southern Army, which had the task of taking the southern area, to prepare detailed plans for operations. Four days later the ranking Army and Navy officers of the Southern Army and the Combined Fleet met in Tokyo to work out final arrangements for joint operations. On November 20 the actual order for the attack was issued, but with the proviso that operations would not begin until the results of the diplomatic negotiations were known.[30]

In Washington, the privileged few followed each move of the Japanese in the mirror of MAGIC while observing in reports from all parts of the Far East increasing evidence of Japanese military preparations. Japanese ship movements toward Malaya and the concentration of shipping at Formosa, staging area for the attack on the Philippines, were quickly detected by American observers. Ambassador Grew, who had reported as early as January 27, 1941, that there was talk in Tokyo of a surprise attack on Pearl Harbor, warned on November 3 that recent troop movements placed Japan in a position to start operations "in either Siberia or the Southwest Pacific or in both" and that war might come with dramatic and dangerous suddenness." "Things seem to be moving steadily toward a crisis in the Pacific," wrote Admiral Stark to his Pacific Fleet commander, Admiral Kimmel, on

November 7. "A month may see, literally, most anything. . . . It doesn't look good." [31]

The first proposal agreed upon at the Imperial Conference of November 5 was handed to Secretary of State Hull by Ambassador Nomura two days later. On the 12th the Secretary told the Japanese Ambassador that the proposal was being studied and that he hoped to have a reply ready within three days. When it came, it proved to be rejection of Proposal A on the ground that the offer to withdraw troops from China and Indochina was indefinite and uncertain and that the United States could not agree to the Japanese definition of nondiscrimination in trade.

On November 20 Admiral Nomura, who now had the benefit of the advice of his colleague Saburo Kurusu, sent from Japan as a special envoy, presented Proposal B, virtually a restatement of the "minimum demands" and "maximum concessions" of the September 6 Imperial Conference. Intercepted Japanese messages had already revealed to Hull that this was to be Japan's last offer for a settlement.[32] To the Secretary of State, the new Japanese offer "put conditions that would have assured Japan's domination of the Pacific, placing us in serious danger for decades to come." The commitments which the United States would have had to make were, in his opinion, "virtually a surrender." [33]

The problem faced by American political and military leaders was a serious one. An outright rejection of Proposal B might well provide Japan with the pretext for war. Full acceptance was out of the question. The only way out of this dilemma was to find a "reasonable counterproposal" or a basis for temporary agreement. In support of this view, Admiral Stark and Brigadier General Leonard T. Gerow, who as chief of the Army War Plans Division acted for the Chief of Staff during his absence, pointed out to the Secretary of State that a *modus vivendi* would "attain one of our present major objectives—the avoidance of war with Japan." "Even a temporary peace in the Pacific," Gerow urged, "would permit us to complete defensive preparations in the Philippines and at the same time insure continuance of material assistance to the British—both of which are highly important." [34]

During the next four days, various drafts of a *modus vivendi* were prepared, and on November 25 the entire matter was reviewed at a meeting of the service Secretaries and the Secretary of State. The general view was that the *modus vivendi* should be adopted, but Hull was pessimistic and expressed the view that the Japanese might "break out any time with new acts of conquest by force" and that national security now "lies in the hands of the Army and Navy." [35] Nor could the American Government ignore the unfavorable reaction of the Allied Powers to the *modus vivendi*. The Chinese reaction was especially sharp, and from Chiang came a bitter protest, supported by a cable from Churchill.

The President was faced with a fateful decision. The Army and Navy wanted time to prepare for war and were willing to buy it with minor concessions. But the slight prospect of Japanese acceptance of the *modus vivendi* was, in the view of the Secretary of State, hardly worth the risk of lowering Chinese morale and resistance and opening the way for appeasement. President Roosevelt agreed. Thus the American reply to Proposal B, handed to the Japanese Ambassador on the afternoon of November 26, omitted the *modus vivendi*.[36]

In view of the seriousness of the situation, the Army and Navy chiefs felt that commanders in the Pacific should be warned immediately. The Navy had already sent out word on November 24—to be passed on to the Army commanders—that prospects for an agreement with Japan were slight and that Japanese troop movements indicated that "a surprise aggressive movement in any direction, including attack on Philippines or Guam" was a possibility.[37] Now, on November 27, War Secretary Stimson asked General Gerow whether the Army should not send a warning. Gerow showed him the Navy message of November 24, but this failed to satisfy Stimson, who observed that the President wanted a warning message sent to the Philippines. As a result, a fresh warning, considered a "final alert," was sent to Hawaii, the Philippines, Panama, and San Francisco. The commander of each of these garrisons was told of the status of the negotiations with Japan, the imminence of hostilities, and the desirability of having Japan commit the "first overt act." Each was instructed to "undertake such reconnaissance and other measures" as he thought necessary and to carry out the tasks assigned in the war plan if hostilities occurred. With the exception of MacArthur, each of the commanders was also warned not to alarm the civilian population or to "disclose intent." At the same time G-2 (intelligence) of the War Department sent an additional and briefer message to Hawaii and Panama, but not to the Philippines, warning against subversive activities.

The Navy warning of November 27, which was passed on to the Army commanders, was more strongly worded and definitely an alert for war. "This dispatch," it read, "is to be considered a war warning . . . and an aggressive move by Japan is expected within the next few days." Navy commanders were alerted to the likelihood of amphibious operations against either the Philippines, the Kra isthmus, or Borneo and instructed to "execute an appropriate defensive deployment preparatory to carrying out the tasks assigned in their war plans." The possibility of attack on Pearl Harbor was not mentioned in either message.[38]

Though the date November 26 marked the real end of negotiations, the Japanese were not yet ready to go to war. On November 27 a Liaison Conference summarily rejected the American note. But to gain a few days, the Japanese instructed Nomura and Kurusu November 28 to do their best to keep the conversation open. Now, on November 30, Tojo presented the Cabinet view for war, but even at this late date several of the senior statesmen expressed doubts about the wisdom of a war with the United States. Konoye asked why it was not possible to continue "with broken economic relations but without war," to which Tojo replied that the final consequence of such a course would be "gradual impoverishment."[39] Later that day the same group met with the Emperor and each man presented his views. Already the force scheduled to attack Pearl Harbor was on its way across the North Pacific and elements of the Southern Army were assembling for their various attacks.

Final details for the opening of hostilities were completed on November 30 at a meeting of the Liaison Conference. At that time the attack on Pearl Harbor was discussed and agreement reached on the form and substance of the note which would formally end the negotiations and sever the relations between the two countries. Hostilities would follow, but no declaration of war, it was decided, would be made in advance. The timing of the Japanese reply to Hull's note was discussed also and it was agreed that the Naval Staff would make the decision in order to gain the fullest advantage of surprise at Pearl Harbor and elsewhere.[40]

The decisions of the Liaison Conference were formalized and sanctioned by the council in the Imperial Presence on December 1. Tojo, who presided at the meeting, explained the purpose of the conference. Then the Ministers and the Chiefs of Staff discussed the question of war with the United States, Great Britain, and the Netherlands. The vote was unanimously for war. "Our negotiations with the United States regarding the execution of our national policy, adopted November 5, have finally failed," reads the record of the meeting. "Japan will open hostilities against the United States, Great Britain, and the Netherlands." The Emperor spoke not a single word during the meeting.[41]

All was in readiness; only the date for the start of war remained to be fixed and that was quickly decided. December 8 (Japanese Standard Time) was the date selected, and on December 2 the Army and Navy chiefs passed this information on to the forces moving into position for the attack. But on the slim chance that by a miracle the United States would agree to the Japanese terms, the Navy Chief of Staff added that should an amicable settlement be reached, "all forces of the Combined Fleet are to be ordered to reassemble and return to their bases." From Admiral Yamamoto's flagship at the Kure naval base went the message *Niitaka Yama Nobore* (Climb Mount Niitaka), the prearranged signal for the attack on Pearl Harbor.[42]

Various considerations underlay the choice of so early a date. Both the Army and Navy felt that delay would be disastrous. By March 1942 America's naval superiority as well as the reinforcements in the Philippines would make the plan extremely hazardous, if not impossible of execution. Moreover, by that time the Americans and British would have completed their preparations in the Philippines and Malaya. Weather, too, was a decisive consideration in the Japanese plan. The conquest of Malaya would require five months and would have to be completed by spring, the best time for military operations in Manchuria in the event that Russia should decide to attack. Finally, December and January were favorable months for amphibious operations in the Philippines and elsewhere, with the tide and moon favoring the attacker.

In arriving at their decision for war, the Japanese gave little or no thought to the interests and desires of their Axis partners. Carefully, they kept their plans secret from Mussolini and Hitler, although Hitler at least would have greatly preferred a Japanese attack on Soviet Russia or on the British base at Singapore. Only on December 4, three days after the decision for war was made, did the Japanese Ambassador in Berlin hint at the possibility of early hostilities when he cautiously inquired whether the German Government would declare war on the United States if Japan moved first, a contingency that was not covered in the Tripartite Pact. Even then Hitler suspected nothing, and so little did the Japanese regard his wishes that they did not make an official request for a declaration of war until the afternoon of December 8.[43]

The first week of December 1941 was one of strain and nervous tension in Tokyo and of suspense and somber watchfulness in Washington. The signs of an early break were too clear to be missed by those who could read the intercepted Japanese messages and intelligence reports, but there was no realization of the danger to Pearl Harbor. Nomura and Kurusu saw Hull several times, but both sides knew nothing could come of these meetings. On December 4, Thursday, Congress adjourned for a long weekend. Next day the Japanese Embassy began to leave Washington and Nomura reported to his home office the partial destruction of codes.

On December 6 President Roosevelt composed a last-minute plea for peace to the Emperor. On the same day a Liaison Conference in Tokyo approved the decision to have Nomura deliver Japan's final note at 1 P.M. (Washington time) the next day, thirty minutes before the scheduled launching of the attack on Pearl Harbor. This note, in fourteen parts, began to arrive in Washington late on December 6. Thirteen of the fourteen parts of the message were in American hands that night, together with reports of two large Japanese convoys off Indochina, headed south. Unidentified aircraft, presumably Japanese, had been observed over Luzon, where by this time a full air alert was in effect and where the troops had already moved into defensive positions along the beaches. In Manila, Admiral Sir Tom Phillips, alarmed over Japanese movements, was just leaving for his flagship, *Prince of Wales,* after concluding arrangements with Hart and MacArthur for concerted naval action in the event of an attack.

That same day, December 6, the Japanese forces were rapidly approaching their destinations. The Pearl Harbor Striking Force, after a voyage across the Pacific, was heading southeast for the final run and at 11 P.M. (Washington time) was about 600 miles north of Oahu. On Formosa airfields were the Japanese planes for the attack on Clark Field in Manila, and the troops scheduled to seize advance airfields in the Philippines had already left staging areas in Formosa and the Pescadores. The invasion force for Guam was in position fifty miles north of the island and the Wake Island force stood ready at Kwajalein. Advance units of the Japanese 25th Army had left Hainan in two convoys on December 4 on their way to Malaya and on December 6 were nearing southern Thailand and Kota Bahru.

On the morning of December 7, Sunday, the fourteenth and last part of the final Japanese note was in American hands. Though it did not indicate when or where war would start, its intent was clear. A short time later two additional messages were intercepted. Taken with the fourteen-part note breaking off the negotiations, they were starkly revealing. One instructed the Japanese Ambassador to destroy the code machines and secret documents; the other, to deliver the fourteen-part message at 1 P.M. (Washington time). At 10:30 that morning Stimson and Knox went to Hull's office, where they were closeted for well over an hour, and at 12:30 the President received the Chinese Ambassador, to whom he read his note of the day before to the Emperor. "This is," he told Hu Shih, "my last effort for peace. I am afraid it may fail." [44]

General Marshall spent Sunday morning on the bridle path and reached his office about 11 o'clock. The intercepted message giving the deadline (1 P.M. Washington time) for delivery of the fourteen-part note struck him as significant and he suggested to Admiral Stark that an additional warning be sent to the Pacific. He then composed a message to the commanders in Hawaii, the Philippines, Panama, and San Francisco telling them that the Japanese were destroying their coding machines and would present at 1 P.M. Washington time "what amounts to an ultimatum." "Just what significance the hour set may have," he added, "we do not know, but be on alert accordingly." Declining an offer from Admiral Stark for the use of the Navy's radio, Marshall turned the message over to an officer for transmission over the Army's network and was assured shortly before noon that it would be delivered in thirty minutes. By a series of ironical circumstances and unexpected delays, the message to Hawaii was in turn entrusted to commercial telegraph and radio and then to a bicycle messenger who, on his way from Honolulu to Fort Shafter, was caught in the attack with his still encoded message.[45]

President Roosevelt's personal note to the Emperor reached Tokyo at noon of December 7 (Tokyo time) but was not delivered to Ambassador Grew until 11 o'clock that night. Shortly after midnight (about 11 A.M., December 7, Washington time), he called on the Foreign Minister to request an audience with the Emperor, but Togo said he would deliver the message himself. Meanwhile in Washington Ambassador Nomura had made an appointment to see Mr. Hull at 1:45 P.M. He and Kurusu arrived at the State Department a half hour late and were admitted to Hull's office at 2:20, only a few minutes after the Secretary had received a telephone call from the President telling him of the attack on Pearl Harbor. The Japanese emissaries handed the Secretary the fourteen-part note, which he already had on his desk. Hull, after pretending to read the note, turned to the two envoys. "In all my fifty years of public service," he said with feeling,

"I have never seen a document that was more crowded with infamous falsehoods and distortions—infamous falsehoods and distortions on a scale so huge that I never imagined until today that any Government on this planet was capable of uttering them." [46] The Japanese left without making any comment.

At approximately 8 A.M. Tokyo time, Ambassador Grew received from Foreign Minister Togo the Japanese fourteen-part note breaking off the negotiations. Later that morning, after Japanese bombs had fallen on Hawaii, Guam, and Wake, after Japanese forces had attacked the Philippines, Hong Kong, and Shanghai, and Japanese troops had landed in Malaya, Grew received an announcement that a state of war existed between Japan and the United States. Around noon General Tojo read to "a stunned and silent nation" the Imperial Rescript declaring war. The broadcast closed on the martial strains of "Umi Yukaba":

> Across the sea, corpses in the water;
> Across the mountain, corpses in the field
> I shall die only for the Emperor,
> I shall never look back.

From the vantage point of hindsight, Japan's decision to go to war appears as a supreme act of folly. By this decision the Japanese leaders appear to have deliberately committed their country to a hopeless struggle against a combination of powers vastly superior in potential industrial and military strength. This view has perhaps been most effectively presented by Rear Admiral Samuel Morison (USNR ret.), who characterized the Pearl Harbor attack which brought the United States into the war as a politically disastrous and strategically idiotic move. "One can search military history in vain," concluded Morison, "for an operation more fatal to the aggressor." [47]

But to the Japanese, their decision, though it involved risks, was not a reckless and foolhardy one. It was based, for one thing, on the expectation that the United States would prefer to negotiate rather than fight. The Japanese leaders fully appreciated the industrial potential of the United States and that nation's ability to fight a major war on two fronts. But they had to accept this risk, as General Tojo said, "in order to tide over the present crisis for self-existence and self-defense." [48]

The Japanese, it must be emphasized, did not seek the total defeat of the United States and had no intention of invading this country. They planned to fight a war of limited objectives and, having once secured these objectives, to set up a defense in such depth that the United States would find a settlement favorable to Japan an attractive alternative to a long and costly war. To the Japanese leaders this seemed an entirely reasonable view. But there were fallacies in this concept which Admiral Yamamoto had pointed out when he wrote that it would not be enough "to take Guam and the Philippines, not even Hawaii and San Francisco." To gain victory, he warned his countrymen, they would have "to march into Washington and sign the treaty in the White House." [49] Here was a lesson about limited wars that went unheeded then and is still often neglected.

Perhaps the major Japanese error was the decision to attack the United States at all. The strategic objectives of the Japanese lay in southeast Asia and if they had limited their attacks to British and Dutch territory the United States might not have entered the war. Such a course would have involved risks but it would have forced the United States to act first. And there was, in 1941, strong opposition to a move that would have appeared to a large part of the American people as an effort to pull British and Dutch chestnuts out of the fire. As it was, the Japanese relieved the Roosevelt administration of the necessity of making a very difficult choice. The alternatives it faced on December 1941, when the Japanese were clearly moving southward, were either to seek from Congress a declaration of war if Japan attacked the British and the Dutch in southeast Asia or to stand by idly while the Japanese secured the rich resources of Malaya and the Indies which would enable them to prosecute the war in China vigorously to an early end. The Japanese attack on Pearl Harbor with one blow resolved all the problems and mobilized the American people as nothing else could have done.[50]

The Japanese based much of their hope for success on the situation in Europe. The war there favored their plans and they saw little possibility of an early peace. Germany, they believed, would defeat Russia, or at least gain military domination of the European Continent, but they doubted that the Germans would be able to launch a successful invasion of England. At any rate, it was clear that both the British and Russians would be too preoccupied in Europe for some time to come to devote their attention to the Far East. The United States had an important stake in Europe, too, and would be unwilling to concentrate its forces in the Pacific, the Japanese estimated, so long as the outcome in Europe remained in doubt.

The possibility of avoiding war with the United States was seriously considered and discussed at length in Tokyo, but the Japanese were apparently convinced that if they moved south the United States would go to war. Their only hope lay in knocking out the American Fleet and removing the Philippine threat, so that the United States would be unable to take offensive action for from eighteen months to two years. By that time, the Japanese estimated, they would have secured the southern area and established themselves firmly behind a strong outer line of defense. With the resources thus won—such as oil, rubber, bauxite—they would be in a position to wage defensive warfare almost indefinitely. The United States, they reasoned, would be unable to sustain the major effort required to break through this defensive screen in the face of the losses imposed by a determined and well-trained foe. As a result, the Japanese leaders felt justified in their hopes that the United States would be forced to compromise and allow Japan to retain a substantial portion of her gains, thus leaving the nation in a dominant position in Asia.

This plan was not entirely unrealistic in 1941, but it completely overlooked the American reaction to Pearl Harbor and the refusal of the United States to fight a limited war—or Japan's ability to so limit it. The risks were recognized, but the alternatives were not estimated correctly. Yet, even had the Japanese appreciated fully the extent of the risks, they would probably have made the same decision. To them, correctly or incorrectly, the only choice was submission or war, and they chose the latter in the hope that their initial advantages and the rapid conquest of southern Asia would offset the enormous industrial and military potential of the enemy.

In the final analysis, the Japanese decision for war was the result of the conviction, supported by the economic measures imposed by the United States and America's policy in China, that the United States was determined to reduce Japan to a position of secondary importance. The nation, Tojo and his supporters felt, was doomed if it did not meet the challenge. In their view, Japan had no alternative but to go to war while she still had the power to do so. She might lose, but defeat was better than humiliation and submission. "Japan entered the war," wrote a prince of the Imperial family, "with a tragic determination and in desperate self-abandonment." If she lost, "there will be nothing to regret because she is doomed to collapse even without war." [51]

Stetson Conn

The Decision to Evacuate the Japanese
from the Pacific Coast
(1942)

One of the U.S. Army's largest undertakings in the name of national defense during World War II was the mass evacuation of persons of Japanese ancestry from the Pacific coast states—from all of California and from the western halves of Oregon and Washington. The decision to evacuate the Japanese was one made at the highest level—by the President of the United States acting as Commander in Chief. What Army plans and recommendations lay behind this decision? With what alternatives was the President presented? To what extent was his decision based on military considerations? [1]

Initial plans for the evacuation of suspected persons from strategic areas along the Pacific coast concerned enemy aliens of all three Axis nations—Germany, Italy, and Japan—rather than persons of Japanese ancestry alone. Of the latter, the census of 1940 showed that, out of a total of 126,947 in the continental United States, 112,353 were living in the three Pacific states. California had 93,717 Japanese, or nearly three fourths of the national total. Of the West Coast Japanese 40,869 were aliens (called "issei") ineligible for citizenship through naturalization proceedings, and 71,484 were American-born (called "nisei") and therefore United States citizens. In early 1942 there were about 58,000 Italian and 22,000 German aliens in the Pacific states. A good many of the German aliens were recent refugees from Nazi Germany. Most of the Germans, and a large proportion of the Japanese and Italians, lived in or near the principal cities and adjacent strategic areas. For several decades the Japanese population had been the target of civilian hostility and restrictive action, a situa-

88

tion that unquestionably colored the measures taken against these people after Pearl Harbor.

An agreement of July 18, 1941, between the War and Justice Departments gave Justice responsibility for controlling enemy aliens in the continental United States in the event of war. Before Pearl Harbor both Justice (primarily, through its Federal Bureau of Investigation) and the armed services had closely scrutinized the records of prospective enemy aliens and compiled lists of those against whom there were grounds for suspicion of disloyalty. Presidential proclamations of December 7 and 8, 1941, dealing with the control of Japanese and of German and Italian aliens, respectively, provided the basis for immediate and subsequent action against any enemy aliens suspected of hostile intent or of action against the national security. On December 7 President Roosevelt authorized the Army to cooperate with the FBI in rounding up individual enemy aliens considered actually or potentially dangerous. By December 13 the Department of Justice had interned a total of 831 alien residents of the Pacific states, including 595 Japanese and 187 Germans; by February 16, 1942 the number of alien Japanese apprehended had increased to 1,266. By specifically authorizing the exclusion of enemy aliens "from any locality in which residence by an alien enemy shall be found to constitute a danger to the public peace and safety of the United States," the Presidential proclamation also provided a basis for evacuation on a larger scale.[2]

During the first few days after the Pearl Harbor attack, the West Coast was alarmed by a number of reports—all false—of enemy ships offshore. It was in the midst of this atmosphere that the first proposal for a mass evacuation of the Japanese developed. On December 10 a Treasury agent reported to Army authorities that "an estimated 20,000 Japanese in the San Francisco metropolitan area were ready for organized action." Without checking the authenticity of the report, the Ninth Corps Area staff worked until late that night on a plan for evacuation, which was then approved by the Corps Area Commander. The next morning the Army called the local FBI chief, who "scoffed at the whole affair as the wild imaginings of a discharged former F.B.I. man." This stopped any local action for the moment, but the Corps Area Commander duly reported the incident to Washington and expressed the hope that "it may have the effect of arousing the War Department to some action looking to the establishment of an area or areas for the detention of aliens."[3] His recommendation that "plans be made for large-scale internment" was forwarded by the Chief of Staff's office to G-2 (intelligence) and to the Provost Marshal General.[4]

On December 19, and apparently as one consequence of this initial flurry, the Western Defense Command sent the following recommendation to its Washington command post, at that time General Headquarters:

1. In view of the fact that the West Coast of the United States has now been designated and is functioning as an active Theater of Operations, it is recommended that action be initiated at the earliest practicable date to collect all alien subjects fourteen years of age and over, of enemy nations and remove them to the Zone of the Interior.

2. It is also recommended that these individuals be held under restraint after removal from the Theater of Operations in order to preclude their surreptitious return.

3. Records indicate that there are approximately 40,000 of such enemy aliens and it is believed that they constitute an immediate and potential menace to vital measures of defense.[5]

In making this recommendation the Army commander on the Pacific coast, Lieutenant General John L. DeWitt, was acting not only as commanding general of the Fourth Army and Western Defense Command but also as commander of the Western Theater of Operations, established on December 11 with the same territorial limits as those of the Defense Command. However General DeWitt may have felt during December about the treatment of enemy aliens, he was then firmly opposed to an evacuation of citizens. During a telephone conversation between Major General Allen W. Gullion, the War Department's Provost Marshal General, and General DeWitt on December 26, 1941, General Gullion remarked that he had just been visited by a representative of the Los Angeles Chamber of Commerce, who had asked for a roundup of all Japanese in the Los Angeles area. In response, General DeWitt said (and General Gullion expressed agreement with what he said):

I thought that thing out to my satisfaction. . . . If we go ahead and arrest the 93,000 Japanese, native born and foreign born, we are going to have an awful job on our hands and are very liable to alienate the loyal Japanese from disloyal. . . . I'm very doubtful that it would be common sense procedure to try and intern or to intern 117,000 Japanese in this theater. . . . I told the governors of all the states that those people should be watched better if they were watched by the police and people of the community in which they live and have been living for years . . . and then inform the F.B.I. or the military authorities of any suspicious action so we could take necessary steps to handle it . . . rather than try to intern all those people, men, women and children, and hold them under military control and under guard. I don't think it's a sensible thing to do. . . . I'd rather go along the way we are now . . . rather than attempt any such wholesale internment. . . . An American citizen, after all, is an American citizen. And while they all may not be loyal, I think we can weed the disloyal out of the loyal and lock them up if necessary.[6]

In any event, all planning for mass evacuation of either aliens or citizens of enemy ancestry from strategic areas was deferred pending new arrangements that were in the making with the Department of Justice for more effective control of enemy aliens.

While these arrangements were being worked out, the Provost Marshal General proposed that responsibility for the alien program be transferred from Justice to the War Department in all theaters of operations. After the decision to activate an Eastern Theater of Operations, he amended his proposal so that, in the continental United States, it would apply only in the Western Defense Command.[7] General DeWitt opposed the transfer, at least until it became evident that the Department of Justice through the FBI could not control the situation on the West Coast. He thought the FBI organization on the coast could handle matters effectively if Attorney General Francis Biddle would provide the FBI with adequate authority. General DeWitt also thought civil control of the alien program better than military control of it. General Gullion therefore decided to hold up his proposal until there was better evidence of its necessity.[8]

What General DeWitt wanted at this time was the issuance of clear instructions to FBI agents on the West Coast that would enable them to take more positive steps to prevent sabotage and espionage. At his urging Secretary of War Henry L. Stimson had conferred with Attorney General Biddle, who thereafter speeded up the implementation of the Presidential proclamations of December 7 and 8. In late December the Department of Justice announced regulations requiring enemy aliens in the Western Defense Command to surrender radio transmitters, short-wave radio receivers, and certain types of cameras by January 5, 1942. On December 30 General DeWitt was informed that the Attorney General had also authorized the issuance of warrants for search and arrest in any house where an enemy alien lived, upon representation by an FBI agent that there was reasonable cause to believe that there was contraband on the premises. In addition, the Department of Justice and the Provost Marshal General had arranged to send representatives to San Francisco to confer with General DeWitt in order to work out more specific arrangements for controlling enemy aliens. To centralize and expedite Army action in Washington,

Gullion also arranged for DeWitt to deal directly with the Provost Marshal General's office on West Coast alien problems, and for the latter to keep General Headquarters (GHQ) informed of developments. As a result of this arrangement, the responsible Army command headquarters in Washington had little to do during January and February 1942 with the plans and decision for Japanese evacuation.[9]

The San Francisco conference took place on January 4 and 5, 1942. Before the meetings the War Department's representative, Major Karl R. Bendetsen, chief of the Aliens Division, Provost Marshal General's office, recommended that General DeWitt insist on several measures beyond those already ordered by the Attorney General. In particular he urged the definition of strategic areas from which all enemy aliens were to be excluded and that authority to prescribe such areas be vested in the Army. He also insisted that there must be a new and complete registration of enemy aliens and a "pass and permit" system similar to the one prevalent in prewar Europe. The Justice representative, Assistant Attorney General James Rowe, Jr., also presented broader plans for action than any the Attorney General had hitherto approved. In opening the conferences, General DeWitt emphatically declared his serious concern over the alien situation and his distrust in particular of the Japanese population—both aliens and citizens. But, according to the later recollections of Rowe, General DeWitt during the meetings expressed strong opposition to a mass evacuation of the Japanese. What he wanted was a full implementation of the President's proclamations. He particularly wanted the FBI to have blanket authority to "search, enter, and arrest" at the homes and business premises of all suspected individuals. In a formal commentary on Rowe's proposals, General DeWitt expressed some apprehensions that they would prove inadequate, but further discussion on January 5 led to an exchange of identical memorandums on the following day representing a plan of action mutually agreeable to General DeWitt, to Rowe, and to N. J. L. Pieper, the chief FBI agent on the Pacific coast who had also attended these meetings. These memorandums provided for an alien registration with the least delay, for FBI searches of suspected premises under regulations that subsequently proved entirely satisfactory to General DeWitt, and for the designation of restricted areas from which enemy aliens would be barred by the Attorney General, who would "entertain" Army recommendations on this score if they were accompanied by an exact description of each area.[10]

The arrangements agreed upon at the San Francisco meetings took much longer to put into effect than either General DeWitt or the Justice Department representatives had anticipated. The registration of enemy aliens was finally undertaken between February 2 and 9, and the large-scale "spot" raids that General DeWitt was especially anxious to have launched did not get under way until the same week; thus both operations took place in the period when agitation against the Japanese was rapidly mounting. General DeWitt had anticipated that he could fix the boundaries of the restricted areas by January 9, but it was January 21 before he sent the first of his lists (for California only) to Washington for transmission to the Attorney General. One of his principal difficulties was to reconcile the recommendations of the Navy, which by agreement were to be made through General DeWitt, with the position of the Department of Justice. Navy commanders wanted to exclude not only enemy aliens but also all American-born Japanese who could not show "actual severance of all allegiance to the Japanese Government." [11]

General DeWitt's recommendation on January 21 dealing with California called for the exclusion of enemy aliens from 86 "Category A" restricted zones and their close control by a pass and permit system in 8 "Category B" zones. Many of the Category A areas, in the vicinity of strategic installations, were uninhabited or had no alien population, but the execution of the recommendation nevertheless would have required the evacuation of more than 7,000 persons. Only 40 per cent of these would have been Japanese aliens; the majority would have been Italians.[12]

The Secretary of War's letter (drafted in the Provost Marshal General's office), which forwarded this recommendation to the Attorney General, added the following comments:

In recent conferences with General DeWitt, he has expressed great apprehension because of the presence on the Pacific coast of many thousand alien enemies. As late as yesterday, 24 January, he stated over the telephone that shore-to-ship and ship-to-shore radio communications, undoubtedly coordinated by intelligent enemy control were continually operating. A few days ago it was reported by military observers on the Pacific coast that not a single ship had sailed from our Pacific ports without being subsequently attacked. General DeWitt's apprehensions have been confirmed by recent visits of military observers from the War Department to the Pacific coast.

The alarming and dangerous situation just described, in my opinion, calls for immediate and stringent action.[13]

Actually there had been no Japanese submarine or surface vessels anywhere near the West Coast during the preceding month, and careful investigation subsequently indicated that all claims of hostile shore-to-ship and ship-to-shore communications lacked any foundation whatsoever.[14] General DeWitt's recommendations for restricted areas in Arizona followed on January 24, and for Oregon and Washington on January 31; the recommendations were forwarded by the War Department to Justice on January 29 and February 3, respectively.[15] By the latter date the position of the Japanese population was under heavy attack, and in consequence the alien exclusion program was being eclipsed by a drive to evacuate all people of Japanese descent from the West Coast states.

Agitation for a mass evacuation of the Japanese did not reach significant dimensions until more than a month after the outbreak of war. Then, beginning in mid-January 1942, public and private demands for federal and state action increased rapidly in tempo and volume.[16]

Behind these demands lay a profound suspicion of the Japanese population, fanned, of course, by the nature and scope of Japan's early military successes in the Pacific. Army estimates of the situation reflected this suspicion. An intelligence bulletin of January 21 concluded that there was an "espionage net containing Japanese aliens, first and second generation Japanese, and other nationals . . . thoroughly organized and working underground." [17] In conversations with Brigadier General Mark W. Clark of GHQ on January 20 and 21, General DeWitt expressed his apprehension that any enemy raid on the West Coast would probably be accomplished by "a violent outburst of coordinated and controlled sabotage" among the Japanese population.[18] In talking with General Gullion on January 24, General DeWitt stated what was to become one of the principal arguments for evacuation. "The fact that nothing has happened so far is more or less . . . ominous," he said, "in that I feel that in view of the fact that we have had no sporadic attempts at sabotage there is control being exercised and when we have it it will be on a mass basis." But in this same conversation he also said that he was still opposed to any move to transfer authority from Justice to the War Department because he thought there was "every indication" that the arrangements made with the Department of Justice and its FBI were going to prove satisfactory.[19]

The publication, on January 25, of the report of the Roberts Commission, which had investigated the Pearl Harbor attack, had a large and immediate effect on both public opinion and government action. The report concluded that there had been widespread espionage in

Hawaii before Pearl Harbor, both by Japanese consular agents and by Japanese residents of Oahu who had "no open relations with the Japanese foreign service." [20] The latter charge, though proved false after the war was over, was especially inflammatory at the time it was made. On January 27 General DeWitt had a long talk with Governor Culbert L. Olson of California and afterward reported:

There's a tremendous volume of public opinion now developing against the Japanese of all classes, that is, aliens and non-aliens, to get them off the land, and in Southern California around Los Angeles—in that area too—they want and they are bringing pressure on the government to move all the Japanese out. As a matter of fact, it's not being instigated or developed by people who are not thinking but by the best people of California. Since the publication of the Roberts Report they feel that they are living in the midst of a lot of enemies. They don't trust the Japanese, none of them.[21]

Two days later DeWitt and Pieper, the FBI chief, met with the Attorney General of California, Earl Warren. General DeWitt reported that Warren was in thorough agreement with Governor Olson that the Japanese population should be removed from the state of California, and the general expressed his own unqualified concurrence in this proposal and also his willingness to accept responsibility for the enemy alien program if it were transferred to him.[22]

In Washington, as Major Bendetsen told General DeWitt on January 29, the California Congressional delegation was "beginning to get up in arms," and its representatives had scheduled an informal meeting for the following afternoon to formulate recommendations for action. Some Washington State congressmen also attended the meeting, to which representatives of the Justice and War Departments were invited. Major Bendetsen reported General DeWitt's views to the assembled congressmen and, though denying that he was authorized to speak for the War Department, nevertheless expressed the opinion that the Army would be entirely willing to take over from Justice, "provided they accorded the Army, and the Secretary of War, and the military commander under him, full authority to require the services of any other federal agency, and provided that federal agency was required to respond." [23] The congressmen unanimously approved a suggested program of action, which called for an evacuation of enemy aliens and "dual" citizens from critical areas, but which made no specific mention of the Japanese. In presenting the Congressional program to his chief, Major Bendetsen described it as actually "calling for the immediate evacuation of all Japanese from the Pacific coastal strip, including Japanese citizens of the age of 21 and under, and calling for an Executive Order of the President imposing full responsibility and authority (with power to requisition the services of other federal agencies) upon the War Department." [24] He also reported the Congressional recommendations, as adopted, to General DeWitt, who expressed general approval of them despite some technical objections. The next day, DeWitt recorded this opinion:

As a matter of fact, the steps now being taken by the Attorney General through the F.B.I. will do nothing more than exercise a controlling influence and preventative action against sabotage; it will not, in my opinion, be able to stop it. The only positive answer to this question is evacuation of all enemy aliens from the West Coast and resettlement or internment under positive control, military or otherwise.[25]

The Department of Justice in the meantime had agreed informally to accept General DeWitt's initial recommendation for restricted areas in California, and it was preparing to carry out this and other aspects of the alien control program. On January 28 it announced the appointment of Thomas C. Clark as Coordinator of the Alien Enemy Control program within the Western Defense Command, and Clark arrived on the scene of action on the following day. On January 29 the Justice Department made its first public announcement about the restricted Category A areas that were to be cleared of enemy aliens by February 24.[26]

As a result of the Congressional recommendations and other developments, Attorney General Biddle asked War Department representatives to attend a meeting in his office on Saturday afternoon, February 1. There he presented them with the draft of a press release to be issued jointly by the Justice and War Departments, indicating agreement on all alien control measures taken to date and including the following statement: "The Department of War and the Department of Justice are in agreement that the present military situation does not at this time require the removal of American citizens of the Japanese race." In opening the meeting Biddle stated that Justice would have nothing whatever to do with any interference with citizens or with a suspension of the writ of habeas corpus. The War Department representatives—Assistant Secretary of War John J. McCloy, General Gullion, and Major Bendetsen—agreed to the wording of the press release except for the sentence quoted. The meeting then adjourned, the War Department representatives withholding approval of any press release until General DeWitt's views could be obtained, and until they learned the outcome of a conference at Sacramento that had been arranged for February 2 between General DeWitt, Attorney General Clark, the Governor of California, and other federal and state officials. Major Bendetsen informed the Chief of Staff's office that the Justice Department's proposal had been held up also because General DeWitt in telephone conversations had been provisionally recommending the evacuation of the whole Japanese population from the Pacific coastal frontier. In the meantime the Provost Marshal General's office had been formulating plans for mass evacuation and had already located sufficient nontroop shelter to provide for substantially all of the West Coast Japanese. In a telephone conversation immediately after the meeting with Justice representatives, Major Bendetsen reported, General DeWitt agreed to submit a recommendation for mass evacuation in writing.[27]

Before General DeWitt could report the outcome of the Sacramento meeting, Secretary Stimson met, on February 3, with McCloy, General Gullion, and Major Bendetsen to confer about the proposed press release and the Japanese problem in general. They discussed a proposal under which military reservations would be established around the big aircraft factories and some port and harbor installations, and from which everyone could be excluded at the outset and until they were licensed to return. In practice, licenses would not be issued to Japanese residents or to other groups or individuals under suspicion. It appeared that under this plan citizens as well as aliens could be excluded legally without obvious discrimination.

During the February 3 discussion, Stimson was handed a record of a telephone conversation between General George C. Marshall, Chief of Staff, and General DeWitt, who had called just as the Secretary of War's meeting was getting under way. In it, General DeWitt said:

I had a conference yesterday with the Governor and several representatives from the Department of Justice and Department of Agriculture, with a view to removal of the Japanese from where they are now living to other portions of the state. And the Governor thinks it can be satisfactorily handled without having a resettlement somewhere in the central part of the United States and removing them entirely from the state of California. As you know the people out here are very much disturbed over these aliens, the Japanese being among them, and want to get them out of the several communities. And I've agreed that if they can solve the problem by getting them out of the areas limited as the combat zone, that it would be satisfactory. That would take them 100 to 150 miles from the coast, and they're working on it. The Department of Justice has a representative here and the Department of Agriculture, and they think the plan is an excellent one. I'm only concerned with getting them away from around these aircraft factories and other places.[28]

In other exchanges on this and succeeding days, General DeWitt explained that what the California authorities proposed to do was to move both citizen and alien Japanese (voluntarily if possible, and in collaboration with American-born Japanese leaders) from urban areas and from along the seacoast to agricultural areas within the state. They wanted to do this in particular, in order to avoid having to replace the Japanese with Mexican and Negro laborers who might otherwise have to be brought into California in considerable numbers. The California officials felt they needed about ten days to study the problem and come up with a workable plan. By February 4 it appeared to General DeWitt that they could produce a plan that would be satisfactory from the standpoint of defense.[29]

After meeting with Secretary Stimson on February 3, McCloy called DeWitt to tell him about the licensing plan and to caution him against taking any position in favor of mass Japanese evacuation. The next day General Gullion told General Clark that Stimson and McCloy were against mass evacuation of the Japanese. "They are pretty much against it," he said, "and they are also pretty much against interfering with citizens unless it can be done legally." While agreeing that the Stimson-McCloy point of view represented the War Department position for the moment, Gullion also said that personally he did not think the licensing action proposed was going to cure the situation.[30] On this same day, February 4, Colonel Bendetsen (just promoted to the rank of lieutenant colonel) in talking with General DeWitt remarked that he was sure that American citizens of Japanese extraction would have to be excluded from some areas at least. General DeWitt evaded a direct comment at this point in the conversation, but later he said:

You see, the situation is this: I have never on my own initiative recommended a mass evacuation, or the removal of any man, any Jap, other than an alien. In other words, I have made no distinction between an alien as to whether he is Jap, Italian, or German—that they must all get out of Area A, that is the Category A area. The agitation to move all the Japanese away from the Coast, and some suggestions, out of California entirely—is within the State, the population of the State, which has been espoused by the Governor. I have never been a body [sic] to that, but I have said, if you do that, and can solve that problem, it will be a positive step toward the protection of the coast. . . . But I have never said, "You've got to do it, in order to protect the coast." . . . I can take such measures as are necessary from a military standpoint to control the American Jap if he is going to cause trouble within those restricted areas.[31]

The projected joint press release of the War and Justice Departments, which had been submerged in this more fundamental issue, was finally issued in revised form on February 5 and in terms that differed from what either General DeWitt or the Provost Marshal General's office had wanted. With respect to citizens, it stated innocuously: "The Government is fully aware of the problem presented by dual nationalities, particularly among the Japanese. The appropriate Governmental agencies are now dealing with the problem." [32]

Three days earlier, on February 2, members of Congress from all three Pacific states had organized informally under the leadership of their senior senator, Hiram Johnson. He had appointed two subcommittees, one headed by Senator Rufus C. Holman of Oregon to consider plans for increased military strength along the Pacific coast and the other by Senator Mon C. Wallgren of Washington to deal with the questions of enemy aliens and the prevention of sabotage. On February 4, General Clark of GHQ and Admiral Harold R. Stark, Chief of Naval Operations, were asked to testify on the West Coast military outlook at a meeting of the first of these subcommittees. Before they spoke, Senator Holman summed up the situation by saying that the people on the West Coast were alarmed and horrified as to their persons, their employment, and their homes. General Clark said that he thought the Pacific states were unduly alarmed. While both he and Admiral Stark agreed that the West Coast defenses were not adequate to prevent the enemy from attacking, they also agreed that the chance of any sustained attack or of an invasion was—as General Clark put it—nil. They believed that sporadic air raids on key installations were a distinct possibility, but they also held that the West Coast military defenses were considerable and in fairly good shape; and as Admiral Stark said, from the military point of view the Pacific coast necessarily had a low priority as compared with Hawaii and the far Pacific. These authoritative Army and Navy views were passed on to the Wallgren subcommittee, but they do not seem to have made much impression.[33]

On this same day, February 4, the federal government's Office of Facts and Figures completed an analysis of a hasty survey of public opinion in California and concluded: "Even with such a small sample, . . . one can infer that the situation in California is serious; that it is loaded with potential dynamite; but that it is not as desperate as some people believe." [34] A contemporary Navy report described what was happening to the Japanese population in the Los Angeles area in these words: ". . . loss of employment and income due to anti-Japanese agitation by and among Caucasian Americans, continued personal attacks by Filipinos and other racial groups, denial of relief funds to desperately needy cases, cancellation of licenses for markets, produce houses, stores, etc., by California State authorities, discharge from jobs by the wholesale, unnecessarily harsh restrictions on travel including discriminatory regulations against all Nisei, preventing them from engaging in commercial fishing." While expressing opposition to any mass evacuation of the Japanese, the report concluded that if practices such as those described continued there would "most certainly be outbreaks of sabotage, riots, and other civil strife in the not too distant future." [35]

In fact, no proved instances of sabotage or of espionage after Pearl Harbor among the West Coast Japanese population were ever uncovered. The most damaging tangible evidence turned up against the Japanese was that produced by the intensive searches of their premises by the FBI from early February onward. By May it had seized 2,592 guns of various kinds, 199,000 rounds of ammunition, 1,652 sticks of dynamite, 1,458 radio receivers, 2,914 cameras, 37 motion picture cameras, and numerous other articles that the alien Japanese had been ordered to turn in at the beginning of January. A major portion of the guns and ammunition was picked up in a raid on a sporting goods shop. After assessing this evidence, Department of Justice officials concluded:

We have not, however, uncovered through these searches any dangerous persons that we could not otherwise know about. We have not found among all the sticks of dynamite and gun powder any evidence that any of it was to be used in bombs. We have not found a single machine gun nor have we found any gun in any circumstances indicating that it was to be used in a manner helpful to our enemies. We have not found a camera which we have reason to believe was for use in espionage. [36]

There were better if less tangible grounds for suspecting that some of the Japanese people—citizens as well as aliens—might become disloyal in the event of a Japanese invasion. The Navy report mentioned above indicated that a small but significant minority of the West Coast Japanese could be expected to be highly undependable in a crisis; and subsequently the War Relocation Authority concluded that for this reason "a selective evacuation of people of Japanese descent from the West Coast military area was justified and administratively feasible in the spring of 1942," although it concluded also that a mass evacuation such as was actually carried out was never justified.[37]

Within this setting Colonel Bendetsen on February 4 wrote a long memorandum to General Gullion that stated at the outset his conclusion that an enemy alien evacuation "would accomplish little as a measure of safety," since the alien Japanese were mostly elderly people who could do little harm if they would. Furthermore, their removal would inevitably antagonize large numbers of their relatives among the American-born Japanese. After considering the various alternatives that had been suggested for dealing with citizens, Colonel Bendetsen recommended the designation of military areas from which all persons who did not have permission to enter and remain would be excluded as a measure of military necessity. In his opinion, this plan was clearly legal and he recommended that it be executed by three steps: first, the issuance of an Executive Order by the President authorizing the Secretary of War to designate military areas; second, the designation of military areas upon the recommendation of General DeWitt; and, third, the immediate evacuation from areas so designated of all persons to whom it was not proposed to issue permits to re-enter or remain. Colonel Bendetsen assumed that, if military areas were established on the West Coast in place of all Category A restricted areas thus far recommended by General DeWitt, about 30,000 people would have to be evacuated.[38]

The Deputy Provost Marshal General, Colonel Archer L. Lerch, indorsed Colonel Bendetsen's proposals, and in doing so commented on what he called the "decided weakening of General DeWitt" on the question of Japanese evacuation, which he considered "most unfortunate." He also thought the plan for settlement within California being worked out between General DeWitt and the state authorities savored "too much of the spirit of Rotary" and overlooked "the necessary cold-bloodedness of war." [39] General Gullion presented a condensed version of Colonel Bendetsen's observations and recommendations in a memorandum to McCloy on the following day. In doing so, he also noted that General DeWitt had changed his position and now appeared to favor a more lenient treatment of the American-born Japanese to be worked out in cooperation with their leaders; in General Gullion's opinion, such cooperation was dangerous and the delay involved was "extremely dangerous." [40] A revision of this memorandum, with all reference to General DeWitt deleted, became the Provost Marshal General's recommendation of February 6 to McCloy that steps be taken immediately to eliminate what General Gullion de-

scribed as the great danger of Japanese-inspired sabotage on the West
Coast. He advised that these steps should include the internment, by
the Army, in areas east of the Sierra Nevada mountains of all alien
Japanese, together with as many citizen members of their families as
would voluntarily accompany them, and the exclusion of all citizen
Japanese from restricted zones and their resettlement with the assistance of various federal agencies.[41]

On the following day, February 7, Colonel Bendetsen read General
Gullion's memorandum to General DeWitt, who expressed some enthusiasm for its recommendations but did not want to indorse them
without further study.[42] By February 7, also, McCloy had decided to
send Colonel Bendetsen to the West Coast "to confer with General
DeWitt in connection with mass evacuation of all Japanese." [43]
When Colonel Bendetsen departed for San Francisco he carried new
instructions for the Army's West Coast commander. These instructions, together with President Roosevelt's decisions of February 11,
presently to be mentioned, were to produce new and detailed recommendations from General DeWitt.[44]

In the meantime, the War and Justice Departments had been approaching an impasse over the area evacuations contemplated under
the enemy alien control program. After agreeing informally to accept
General DeWitt's initial California recommendation, Justice officials
balked at accepting the very large size Category A areas he recommended for Washington and Oregon, since they included the entire
cities of Seattle, Tacoma, and Portland. The execution of this recommendation would have required the evacuation of about 10,700 additional enemy aliens and, as in the case of California, only about
40 per cent of these would have been Japanese. As a practical matter
the Department of Justice would have found it extremely difficult to
supply either the manpower or the internment facilities that a compulsory evacuation of 17 or 18 thousand enemy aliens would have
required, and by February 4 its Washington representatives were in-
timating that, if there were any further category A recommendations
or if the evacuation of any citizens were to be involved, Justice would
have to bow out and turn its evacuation responsibilities over to the
War Department. General DeWitt on February 4 was considering
putting the whole Los Angeles area into Category A because his air
commander had recommended Category A zones around 220 different installations that, when plotted on the map, almost blanketed the
area anyway. For the same reason, General DeWitt believed he might
have to put all of San Diego in Category A also.[45] He finally recom-

mended the blanket Category A coverage of the two cities in a letter of February 7, and five days later he recommended that almost all of the San Francisco Bay area be put in Category A. If all of General DeWitt's recommendations for Category A areas through February 12 had been accepted, it would have made necessary the evacuation of nearly 89,000 enemy aliens from areas along the Pacific coast—only 25,000 of whom would have been Japanese.[46]

It should be borne in mind that none of the enemy alien program recommendations submitted by General DeWitt through February 16 included American citizens of Japanese or other extraction. The concentration of the Japanese population near strategic points seemed in itself to be sinister in 1942. Actually, there was a greater proportionate concentration of German and Italian aliens near strategic points than there was of Japanese. General DeWitt's Category A recommendations would have affected nine-tenths of the West Coast German alien population and nearly three-fourths of the Italian aliens, but less than two-thirds of the Japanese aliens. Of course General DeWitt after February 3 was also counting upon the California State authorities to persuade the citizen Japanese to evacuate California's urban areas and other sensitive points along the coast.

In a letter to the Secretary of War on February 9, Attorney General Biddle formally agreed to announce the Category A areas initially recommended for Arizona, California, Oregon, and Washington as prohibited to enemy aliens by February 15 or 24—applying the latter date to those areas that had a considerable alien population. But Biddle questioned the necessity of forcibly excluding German and Italian aliens from all of these areas and wondered why whole cities had been included in Washington and Oregon and none in California. He added that if, as he had been informally advised, all of Los Angeles County was going to be recommended as a Category A area, the Department of Justice would have to step out of the picture because it did not have the physical means to carry out a mass evacuation of such scope. In conclusion, he stated that the Department of Justice was not authorized under any circumstances to evacuate American citizens; if the Army for reasons of military necessity wanted that done in particular areas, the Army itself would have to do it.[47]

The Attorney General's stand led naturally to the drafting of a War Department memorandum summarizing the "questions to be determined re Japanese exclusion" that needed to be presented to President Roosevelt for decision. These questions were:

1. Is the President willing to authorize us to move Japanese citizens as well as aliens from restricted areas?

2. Should we undertake withdrawal from the entire strip DeWitt originally recommended, which involves a number of over 100,000 people, if we included both aliens and Japanese citizens?

3. Should we undertake the intermediate step involving, say, 70,000, which includes large communities such as Los Angeles, San Diego, and Seattle?

4. Should we take any lesser step such as the establishment of restricted areas around airplane plants and critical installations, even though General DeWitt states that in several, at least, of the large communities this would be wasteful, involve difficult administrative problems, and might be a source of more continuous irritation and trouble than 100 per cent withdrawal from the area? [48] *

In the early afternoon on February 11 McCloy accompanied Stimson to the White House, where they obtained answers to the four questions. The President told the War Department secretaries to go ahead and do anything they thought necessary under the circumstances. "We have *carte blanche* to do what we want to as far as the President's concerned," McCloy informed Colonel Bendetsen immediately after the White House conference. The President specifically authorized the evacuation of citizens. In doing so he observed that there probably would be some repercussions to such action, but said that what was to be done had to be dictated by the military necessity of the situation. Mr. Roosevelt's only reported qualification was, "Be as reasonable as you can." McCloy also told Colonel Bendetsen that he thought the President was prepared to sign an Executive Order giving the War Department the authority to carry out whatever action it decided upon.[49]

The President's decisions gave an understandable impetus to the so-called final recommendation being prepared by General DeWitt, which with the assistance of Colonel Bendetsen he had begun to draft on the evening of February 10. Completed as a formal memorandum for the Secretary of War February 13, it was forwarded with a covering memorandum to GHQ via air mail.[50] General DeWitt's new recommendations differed from those he had already submitted under the enemy alien control program in only one important particular: he recommended the enforced evacuation by federal authority of the American-born Japanese from the Category A areas already recommended by him in previous letters to the Secretary of War.[51] His

---

* The figures given in (2) and (3) are about equal to the Japanese population that these steps would affect. It therefore appears that the memorandum did not contemplate a mass evacuation of German or Italian aliens.

memorandum reached GHQ at 5 P.M., February 18. On February 19 it was decided at a GHQ staff conference not to concur in General DeWitt's recommendations, and instead to recommend to General Clark that only enemy alien leaders be arrested and interned. General Clark, being aware of developments in the War Department, must have realized the futility of a GHQ nonconcurrence.[52] On February 20 GHQ sent General DeWitt's memorandums to the War Department through normal channels, with an indorsement that they were being "transmitted in view of the proposed action already decided upon by the War Department." [53] They finally reached the Provost Marshal General's office "for remark and recommendation" on February 24, the day after General DeWitt received new directives from the War Department that differed in many particulars from the recommendations he had submitted.[54]

In the meantime, on February 13, the Pacific coast Congressional subcommittee on aliens and sabotage had adopted the following recommendations:

We recommend the immediate evacuation of all persons of Japanese lineage and all others, aliens and citizens alike, whose presence shall be deemed dangerous or inimical to the defense of the United States from all strategic areas.

In defining said strategic areas we recommend that such areas include all military installations, war industries, water and power installations, oil fields, and refineries, transportation and other essential facilities, as well as adequate protective areas adjacent thereto.

We further recommend that such areas be enlarged as expeditiously as possible until they shall encompass the entire strategic area of the states of California, Oregon and Washington, and Territory of Alaska.

These recommendations were forwarded to President Roosevelt with a covering letter of the same date signed on behalf of the entire West Coast Congressional delegation.[55] On February 16 the President sent the letter and its enclosed recommendations to Secretary Stimson, with a memorandum that read: "Will you please be good enough to reply to Congressman Lea in regard to the enclosed letter." [56]

On the same day, February 16, Colonel Bendetsen boarded an airplane in San Francisco, reaching the War Department's offices in Washington about noon on February 17.[57] Before his arrival, the Provost Marshal General's office initiated a telegraphic survey among the Corps Area Commanders with the following message:

Probable that orders for very large evacuation of enemy aliens of all nationalities predominantly Japanese from Pacific Coast will issue within

48 hours. Internment facilities will be taxed to utmost. Report at once maximum you can care for, including housing, feeding, medical care, and supply. Your breakdown should include number of men, women, and children. Very important to keep this a closely guarded secret.[58]

A follow-up letter explained that 100,000 enemy aliens* would be involved, 60,000 of whom would be women and children, and that all were to be interned east of the Western Defense Command—"50 per cent in the Eighth Corps Area, 30 per cent in the Seventh, and 10 per cent each in the Fourth and Sixth." [59] There were three reasons for the intention (as of February 17) of removing the Pacific coast Japanese to areas east of the Western Defense Command. Since mid-December General DeWitt had insisted that internment of enemy aliens ought to be outside his theater of operations; some of the governments of the intermountain states had already indicated that they would not countenance any free settlement of the West Coast Japanese within their borders; and, lastly, an Army survey of existing facilities for internment in the five interior states of the Ninth Corps Area disclosed that they could not accommodate more than 2,500 people.

The final steps toward a decision on the evacuation of the West Coast Japanese began on February 17 with another conference between Secretary Stimson and President Roosevelt. Thereafter, Stimson met in the afternoon with McCloy, General Clark, General Gullion, and Colonel Bendetsen. General Clark protested that a mass evacuation would involve the use of too many troops. Stimson again expressed his dislike of mass evacuation. But finally the Secretary decided that General DeWitt should be instructed to commence an evacuation immediately and to the extent he deemed necessary for the protection of vital installations. At the conclusion of this meeting, General Clark consulted his GHQ chief, Lieutenant General Lesley J. McNair, who decided that General DeWitt should not be allotted any additional troops for evacuation purposes.[60]

On the evening of February 17, McCloy, Gullion, and Bendetsen met with Justice representatives at the home of Attorney General Biddle. After some preliminary discussion, General Gullion pulled from his pocket and proceeded to read the draft of a proposed Presidential Executive Order that would authorize the Secretary of War to remove both citizens and aliens from areas that he might designate. Biddle accepted the draft without further argument, because the

* The reference to all Japanese residents as "aliens" was rather frequent practice in Army exchanges on the subject during February 1942.

President had already indicated to him that this was a matter for military decision. After several more meetings between Justice and War Department officials during the next two days, the Executive Order was presented to the President and signed by him late on February 19.[61] Between February 18 and 20 McCloy, General Gullion, and Colonel Bendetsen drafted the instructions for General DeWitt to guide his execution of the evacuation plan and embodied them in two letter directives, both dated February 20. These directives and a copy of Executive Order 9066 reached General DeWitt on February 23.[62]

On February 21 the Secretary of War, in accordance with the President's request, answered the Congressional letter of February 13 by assuring the West Coast delegation that plans for the partial or complete evacuation of the Japanese from the Pacific coast were being formulated.[63] In consultation with the Department of Justice, War Department officials at this time also prepared a draft of legislation that would put teeth into the enforcement of the new evacuation program but did not submit it to Congress until March 9. This draft as a bill became Public Law 503 after brief debate; it was passed by a voice vote in both houses on March 19 and signed by the President on March 21. Three days later, the Western Defense Command issued its first compulsory exclusion order.[64]

As already noted, the plan for evacuation presented in the War Department's directives of February 20 differed materially from the plan recommended by General DeWitt in his memorandum of February 13.[65] The central objective of the DeWitt plan was to move all enemy aliens and American-born Japanese out of all Category A areas in California, Oregon, and Washington that the general had recommended through February 12. Although General DeWitt had repeatedly described the Japanese as the most dangerous element of the West Coast population, he also made it clear as late as February 17 that he was "opposed to any preferential treatment to any alien irrespective of race," and therefore that he wanted German and Italian aliens as well as all Japanese evacuated from Category A areas.[66] His plan assumed that all enemy aliens would be interned under guard outside the Western Defense Command, at least until arrangements could be made for their resettlement. Citizen evacuees would either accept internment voluntarily, or relocate themselves with such assistance as state and federal agencies might offer. Although this group would be permitted to resettle in Category B areas within the coastal zone, General DeWitt clearly preferred that they move inland. The central objective of the War Department plan was to move all Japanese out of the California Category A areas first, and they were not to be permitted to resettle within Category B areas or within a larger Military Area No. 1 to be established along the coast.[67] There was to be no evacuation of Italians without the express permission of the Secretary of War except on an individual basis. Although the War Department plan ostensibly provided that German aliens were to be treated in the same manner as the Japanese, it qualified this intention by providing for exemption of bona fide German refugees. This qualification automatically stayed the evacuation of German aliens until General DeWitt could discover who among them were genuine refugees. The War Department plan contemplated voluntary relocation of all types of evacuees to the maximum extent possible, with internment as necessary outside the Western Defense Command. Another major difference between the two plans was related to General DeWitt's recommendation of a licensing system for Category A areas; the President's Executive Order of February 19 did not require the application of the licensing plan, and licensing was not embodied in the War Department's directives of February 20.

There were other lesser differences between the two plans. General DeWitt had recommended that before any evacuation all preparations should be complete, including the "selection and establishment of internment facilities in the Sixth, Seventh, and Eighth Corps Areas." As already noted, the War Department at this time was also planning to put all internees east of the Ninth Corps Area, but its directives did not contemplate postponement of evacuation until internment facilities were ready. General DeWitt had also recommended the initial and separate internment of all enemy alien males over fourteen years of age until family units could be established in internment camps. The War Department plan had no such provision. As for the number of people to be involved, General DeWitt's memorandum contained an estimate that 133,000 people would have to be evacuated either voluntarily or by compulsion. A breakdown of the figure (based on his previous Category A recommendations) discloses that his plan would have involved about 69,000 Japanese (25,000 aliens and 44,000 American citizens), about 44,000 Italians, and about 20,000 Germans. The War Department planners apparently made no estimate of the numbers that their directives would involve, but eventually they did involve more than 110,000 Japanese residents—citizens and aliens—of the Pacific coast states.

Nearly three years later, in December 1944, the Supreme Court upheld the constitutionality of mass evacuation, in the test case of

Korematsu v. *United States.* Its decision, rendered in the midst of war, also had to be made without access to many pertinent records. The Court concluded:

Korematsu was not excluded from the Military Area because of hostility to him or his race. He *was* excluded because we are at war with the Japanese Empire, because the properly constituted military authorities feared an invasion of our West Coast and felt constrained to take proper security measures, because they decided that the military urgency of the situation demanded that all citizens of Japanese ancestry be segregated from the West Coast temporarily, and finally, because Congress, reposing its confidence in this time of war in our military leaders—as inevitably it must—determined that they should have the power to do just this. There was evidence of disloyalty on the part of some, the military authorities considered that the need for action was great, and time was short. We cannot—by availing ourselves of the calm perspective of hindsight—now say that these actions were unjustified.[68]

Would the Court's conclusion have been the same in the light of present knowledge? Considering the evidence now available, the reasonable deductions seem to be that General DeWitt's recommendation of February 13, 1942, was not used in drafting the War Department directives of February 20 for a mass evacuation of the Japanese people, and that the only responsible commander who backed the War Department's plan as a measure required by military necessity was the President himself, as Commander in Chief.

Louis Morton

The Decision to Withdraw
to Bataan
(1941)

On December 23, 1941, only two weeks after the Japanese attack on Pearl Harbor, General Douglas MacArthur—then commanding American forces in the Philippines—made one of the most difficult and important decisions of his long and famous military career. Under the threat of impending disaster, he determined on that day to withdraw his forces on the island of Luzon to the Bataan Peninsula, to declare the Philippine capital, Manila, an open city, and to transfer his headquarters to the tiny island of Corregidor in Manila Bay. The successful execution of this plan had far-reaching results: it saved the 75,000 troops on Luzon from immediate defeat, delayed the Japanese timetable for conquest by four months, and kept large Japanese combat forces tied up in the Philippines long after Malaya, Singapore, and the Indies had fallen. It is not the purpose of this essay to describe the masterly skill with which the elaborate maneuver—a double retrograde movement—was accomplished. Rather it is to examine the background and circumstances leading to the critical decision to withdraw to Bataan.

The war in the Philippines had begun on December 8 with a disastrous air attack against Clark Field, an attack which destroyed half the heavy bombers of MacArthur's Far East Air Force. In the tragic two weeks that followed, the Japanese continued to achieve astounding successes. During the first few days of the war, they made three preliminary landings on Luzon to secure airfields and to support the main landings to come. On December 22 they made their main assaults, putting the bulk of Lieutenant General Masaharu Homma's 14th

110

Army ashore at Lingayen Gulf, about 135 miles north of Manila. By December 23 the Japanese not only had landed a large number of troops north of the capital but had achieved aerial and naval supremacy in the Philippines and had isolated the archipelago from Australia to the south and from Hawaii and the United States to the east.[1] It was in these circumstances that MacArthur made his decision to withdraw to Bataan.

Plans for the defense of the Philippine Islands had been in existence for many years before General MacArthur took command in July 1941. The latest revision of these plans, completed in April 1941 and called WPO-3, was based on the joint Army-Navy ORANGE plan of 1938, one of the many "color" plans developed during the prewar years. Each color plan dealt with a different situation, ORANGE covering an emergency in which only the United States and Japan would be involved. In this sense, the plan was politically unrealistic and completely outdated by 1941. Tactically, however, the plan was an excellent one and its provisions for defense were applicable under any local situation.[2]

Under WPO-3, American troops were not to fight anywhere but in Central Luzon. The mission of the Philippine garrison was to hold the entrance to Manila Bay and deny its use to Japanese naval forces. U.S. Army forces, constituting an Initial Protective Force and consisting of regular U.S. Army troops, had the main task of preventing enemy landings. Failing in this, they were to defeat those Japanese forces which succeeded in landing. If, despite these attempts, the enemy proved successful, the Initial Protective Force was to engage in delaying action but not at the expense of the primary mission, the defense of Manila Bay. The Americans were to make every attempt to hold back the Japanese advance while withdrawing to the Bataan Peninsula. Bataan, recognized as the key to the control of Manila Bay, was to be defended to the "last extremity."

In addition to the regular U.S. Army troops, the defenders could rely on the military forces of the Commonwealth, the Philippine Army, which had been organized and trained by General MacArthur. If used as anticipated in WPO-3, the Philippine Army would be under the command of the Department Commander, a U.S. Army officer, and would be used to defend Manila Bay. The plan did not contemplate using Philippine Army troops for the defense of the entire archipelago.

WPO-3 divided Luzon, the principal theater of operations, into six sectors and provided a mobile reserve. Detailed plans for the defense

of each sector were made by the sector commanders. The commander of the Philippine Division, the only U.S. Army division in the Philippines, in addition to conducting operations in the sector or sectors assigned to him, was to organize the defenses of Bataan and to command operations there if necessary.

The supply plan in WPO-3 was a complicated one. Provision had to be made to supply the six sectors during the initial phase of operations, to withdraw supplies into Bataan, and to establish there a supply base capable of supporting defensive operations by a force of 31,000 men for a period of six months. The supplies required for this purpose were designated the defense reserves, and except for ammunition most of these had already reached the Philippines. Some were already on Bataan, but the greatest portion by far was stored in the Manila area, which was as yet without adequate protection from air attack. Since these supplies would have to be moved to Corregidor and Bataan in the event of war, WPO-3 stipulated that the Filipino-

American defenders would fight a delaying action to keep the roads open long enough to carry out this phase of the operation.

Nothing was said in WPO-3 about what was to happen after the defenses on Bataan crumbled. Presumably by that time, estimated at six months, the U.S. Pacific Fleet would have fought its way across the Pacific, won a victory over the Japanese Combined Fleet, and made secure the line of communications. The men and supplies collected on the West Coast in the United States during that time would then begin to reach the Philippines in a steady stream. The Philippine garrison, thus reinforced, could then counterattack and drive the enemy into the sea.

Actually, no one in a position of authority at that time (April 1941) believed that anything like this would happen. Informed naval opinion estimated that it would require at least two years for the Pacific Fleet to fight its way across the Pacific. There was no plan to concentrate on the West Coast and no schedule for the movement of men and supplies to the Philippines. Army planners in early 1941 believed that at the end of six months, if not sooner, supplies would be exhausted and the garrison would go down in defeat. WPO-3 did not say this; instead it said nothing at all. But everyone hoped that when the time came something could be done, some plan improvised to relieve or rescue the men stranded 7,000 miles across the Pacific.

General MacArthur had the answer for those who saw no way out of the difficulty in the Philippines: transform WPO-3, which he regarded as defeatist and defensive, into an aggressive plan whose object would be the defeat of any enemy that attempted the conquest of the Philippines. An optimist by nature, with implicit faith in the Philippine people, MacArthur was able to inspire the confidence and loyalty of his associates and staff. His optimism was contagious and infected the highest officials in the War Department and the government. By the fall of 1941 there was a firm conviction in Washington and in the Philippines that, given sufficient time, the defenders could successfully resist a Japanese attack.

In pressing for a more aggressive plan, enlarged in scope to include the entire archipelago, MacArthur could rely on having a far stronger force than any of his predecessors had had. His growing air force included by the end of November 1941 35 B-17's and almost a hundred fighters of the latest type. Many more were on their way. The performance of the heavy bombers in early 1941 justified the hope that the South China Sea would be successfully blockaded by air and that the islands could be made a "self-sustaining fortress." [3]

MacArthur could also count on the Philippine Army's one regular and ten reserve divisions, inducted into the service of the United States by Executive Order on the same day he was called back to active duty in July 1941. During his term as Military Adviser to the Philippine Commonwealth Government (1935-1937), he had worked out the general concept of his strategy as well as detailed plans for the use of this national army. As commander of U.S. Army Forces in the Far East (USAFFE) he could plan on the use of the regular U.S. Army garrison as well as the Philippine Army. He was in an excellent position, therefore, to persuade the War Department to approve his own concept for the defense of the Philippines.

Almost from the date that he was recalled to active duty in the Philippines, on July 26, 1941, MacArthur began to think about replacing WPO-3 with a new plan.[4] From the first, he apparently intended to defend the inland seas and the entrances to Manila and Subic Bays, and by September his plans had progressed so far that he informed Major General Jonathan M. Wainwright, commander of the Philippine Division, of his intention to reorganize the forces in the Philippines and to give that officer his choice of commands.[5]

The opportunity to request a change in plans for the defense of the Philippines came in October, after MacArthur received a copy of the new war plan, RAINBOW 5, prepared by the U.S. Army-Navy Joint Board some months earlier. This plan, which was world-wide in its provisions and conformed to arrangements with the British staff, called for a defensive strategy in the Pacific and Far East, and recognized Germany as the main enemy in the event of a war with the Axis. Based on the assumption that the United States would be at war with more than one nation and would be allied with Great Britain, RAINBOW accepted implicitly the loss of the Philippines, Wake, and Guam. Like ORANGE, it assigned Army and Navy forces in the Philippines the mission of defending the Philippine Coastal Frontier, defined as those land and sea areas which it would be necessary to hold in order to defend Manila and Subic Bays. Also, as in ORANGE, the defense was to be conducted entirely by Army and Navy forces already in the Philippines, augmented by such local forces as were available.[6] No reinforcements could be expected.

MacArthur immediately objected to those provisions of RAINBOW relating to the Philippines and called for the revision of the plan on the ground that it failed to recognize either the creation of a high command for the Far East or the mobilization of the Philippine Army. In a strong letter to the War Department on October 1, MacArthur pointed out that he would soon have a force of approximately 200,000 men organized into 11 divisions with corresponding air force, corps, and army troops. There could be no adequate defense of Manila Bay or of Luzon, he said, if an enemy were to be allowed to land and secure control of any of the southern islands, and with the "wide scope of possible enemy operations, especially aviation," he thought such landings possible. He urged, therefore, that the "citadel-type defense" of Manila Bay provided in the ORANGE and RAINBOW plans be changed to an active defense of all the islands in the Philippines. "The strength and composition of the defense forces projected here," General MacArthur asserted, "are believed to be sufficient to accomplish such a mission." [7]

The reply from Washington came promptly. On October 18 General George C. Marshall, Army Chief of Staff, prepared a memorandum for MacArthur informing him that a revision of the Army mission had been drafted in the War Department and was then awaiting action by the Joint Board, "with approval expected within the next ten days." The recommendation to redefine the Philippine Coastal Frontier to include all the islands in the archipelago would also be presented to the Joint Board for approval. The assignment of a broader mission than that contained in RAINBOW, Marshall explained, was made possible because of the increased importance of the Philippines "as a result of the alignment of Japan with the Axis, followed by the outbreak of war between Germany and Russia." [8]

With this notice that his plans would soon be approved by the Joint Board, MacArthur immediately organized his forces to execute the larger mission. On November 4 he formally established the North and South Luzon Forces and the Visayan-Mindanao Force, all of which had actually been in existence for several months already.[9] A month later, on December 3, he issued the orders defining the missions of these and his other principal tactical commands. The North Luzon Force, which had been under the command of Brigadier General Edward P. King, Jr., from November 3 to 28, now came under General Wainwright. This force had responsibility for the most critical sector in the Philippines, including part of the central plains area, Lingayen Gulf, the Zambales coast, and the Bataan Peninsula. General Wainwright was instructed to protect airfields and prevent hostile landings in his area, particularly at those points opening into the central plains and the road net leading to Manila. In case of a successful landing, the enemy was to be destroyed. In contrast to WPO-3, which provided for a withdrawal to Bataan, MacArthur's plan stated there was to be "no withdrawal from beach positions." The beaches were to "be held at all costs." [10]

The South Luzon Force under Brigadier General George H. Parker, Jr., was assigned the area generally south and east of Manila. Like the force to the north, it was to protect the airfields in its sector and prevent hostile landings. General Parker was also enjoined to hold the beaches at all costs. The South Luzon Force was much smaller than that in the north. It consisted initially of only two Philippine Army divisions, the 41st and 51st, and a battery of field artillery. Additional units were to be assigned at a later date when they became available.[11]

On Luzon, between the North and South Luzon Forces was the Reserve Area, including the city of Manila and the heavily congested area just to the north. This area was directly under the control of MacArthur's headquarters and contained the Philippine Division (less one battalion), the 71st and 91st Divisions (Philippine Army), the 86th Field Artillery (Philippine Scouts), the Far East Air Force, and the headquarters of the Philippine Department and the Philippine Army. The defense of the entrance to Manila and Subic Bays was left, as it always had been, to Major General George F. Moore's Harbor Defense augmented by the Philippine Coast Artillery Command.[12]

When the Japanese made their first landings on December 10 and 12 at the northern and southern extremities of Luzon, General Mac-Arthur made no disposition to contest them. He correctly surmised that these landings were designed to secure advance air bases and that the Japanese had no intention of driving on Manila from any of these beachheads. He did not regard the situation as serious enough to warrant a change in his plan to oppose the main attack, when it came, with an all-out defense at the beaches. The MacArthur Plan, then, remained in effect.[13]

Whether the Japanese landings represented the main attack or not, General MacArthur had to consider seriously the prospect of an eventual withdrawal to Bataan and the evacuation of Manila. To prepare the President of the Commonwealth, Manuel L. Quezon, for the worst, he sent word to him on the morning of December 12 to be ready to move to Corregidor on four-hours' notice. Shocked and wholly unprepared for this "startling message," Quezon arranged a conference with MacArthur that night at the Manila Hotel. At the meeting, MacArthur explained that there was no immediate cause for concern and that he was only "preparing for the worst in case the Japanese should land in great force at different places." In such event, it would be unwise, he told Quezon, to have his forces scattered. He intended to concentrate his army on Bataan and to move his headquarters, together with the High Commissioner and the Commonwealth Government, to Corregidor and declare Manila an open city. "Do you mean, General," asked Quezon, "that tomorrow you will declare Manila an open city and that some time during the day we shall have to go to Corregidor?" MacArthur's answer was an emphatic "No." He did not seem to be certain that the move would even be necessary and was evidently only preparing the President for such a possibility. The meeting closed with Quezon's promise to consider the matter further. Later he consented, with reluctance, to move to Corregidor if necessary.[14]

The possibility of a withdrawal seems to have been in the minds of other officers in MacArthur's headquarters before the main Japanese landings. During an inspection of the 21st Field Artillery (PA) position along Lingayen Gulf, Colonel Constant L. Irwin, MacArthur's G-3 (operations), showed little interest in the tactical placement of the guns. Instead, wrote Colonel Richard C. Mallonée, the regimental instructor, Colonel Irwin showed a great deal of interest in the location of the ammunition and supply routes, selected to conform with the mission of holding at the beaches. "He took a look at our ammunition disposition and the dangerous supply routes," declared Mallonée, "and very violently announced that it would be impossible to withdraw the ammunition in time to save it, and by God, he would crucify anyone who lost so much as one round." [15] This was the first time, remarked Mallonée that he heard the word "withdraw." He explained to Colonel Irwin that his orders were to hold at all costs, and he repeated Wainwright's order to the troops of the North Luzon Force that "we must die in our tracks, falling not backward but forward toward the enemy." The answer of the G-3 officer was "Don't believe everything you hear." [16]

The chief of staff of the 21st Division (PA), the senior instructor of the division, and Colonel Mallonée were all now thoroughly confused about the mission, and after a conference they decided to request clarification from General Wainwright's headquarters. They were told that the mission was still to hold at all costs, "but by the manner in which it was issued it was evident that there is considerable doubt in the minds of the North Luzon Force command as to whether the mission is actually as given." [17]

If any doubts existed they were quickly dispelled when the main force of General Homma's 14th Army came ashore at Lingayen Gulf on the morning of December 22. The two Philippine Army divisions guarding the 120-mile Lingayen coast line immediately took such action as they could to meet the invasion, while Wainwright quickly dispatched the 26th Cavalry of Philippine Scouts to hold the road leading from the beaches into the central Luzon plain. And from MacArthur's reserve came a tank battalion and 12 75-mm. guns on self-propelled mounts. Clearly, there was no question about the determination to resist the enemy at the beaches. But performance fell short of plans, and the Japanese succeeded that morning in landing three infantry regiments with supporting artillery and tanks. While these troops fanned out to the east and south, the rest of the 14th Army continued to come ashore. By the end of the day, the Japanese had secured most of their objectives and were in position to debouch onto the central plain.

Fighting on December 22 had been confused and indecisive. The stiffest resistance put up by the Scouts of the 26th Cavalry could not prevent the Japanese from moving south. The defiles leading east from the narrow beaches had fallen and the road to Baguio, the Philippine summer capital, lay open. With the mountains to their rear, and Japanese troops in front and north of them, the defenders had little choice but to retreat south. "My right [north] hand in a vise," the American commander told MacArthur before he left the Philippine summer capital to the Japanese, "my nose in an inverted funnel, constipated my bowels, open my south paw." [18]

The performance of the untrained and poorly equipped Philippine Army troops was the clearest sign of imminent disaster. At the first appearance of the enemy, they had broken and fled to the rear in a disorganized stream. When stopped, they always had the same story to tell—how they were subjected to heavy mortar and artillery fire, bombed and strafed by enemy planes, threatened by hostile tanks usually headed straight for them, deserted by their officers, and left all alone to meet the oncoming Japanese. Always they had stood their ground bravely, continued to fire their rifles, and only fallen back under the greatest necessity. Often they claimed to have been captured and then to have escaped. Now they were tired, hungry, and filled with a consuming desire to be transferred to the motor transport service where they could serve their country by driving a truck. [19]

The action of December 23 was critical. In the American line that morning was the 71st Division (PA) astride the critical Route 3 leading south. To its left was the 11th Division (PA), and along the southern coast of Lingayen Gulf was the 21st. The 26th Cavalry

(PS) was under orders to fall back to reorganize, and a combat team of the 91st Division (PA), attached to North Luzon Force from USAFFE reserve, was speeding north to reinforce the 71st Division.

The Japanese made their main effort along Route 3, where they soon made contact with the 71st Division. At this point the Japanese attack stalled, largely because of the action of the division artillery. Later, when Japanese planes and tanks entered the action, the Filipino infantry broke and fled, leaving the artillery uncovered. The line might have held if the 91st Combat Team had arrived in time, but at this critical moment it was far from the scene of combat.

The situation was serious. A meeting of the American commanders was hastily called and a revised plan adopted. The 71st Division was to establish a new line about five miles to the south, astride Route 3, where it would be reinforced by the 91st Combat Team when and if that unit arrived. The 26th Cavalry would set up an outpost line to the rear through which the troops could fall back if necessary.

It was now evident to General Wainwright that he could no longer hold back the Japanese flood. His only hope lay in retiring behind the Agno River, which curved in a huge arc from the southern shore of Lingayen Gulf to the mountains on the east and constituted the first formidable obstacle in the path of the advancing Japanese. Late on the afternoon of December 23, therefore, Wainwright telephoned General MacArthur's headquarters in Manila and requested permission to withdraw behind the Agno River. Any further defense of the Lingayen beaches, he declared, was entirely "impracticable," but if MacArthur would sanction this withdrawal and release to him the Regular Army Philippine Division from USAFFE reserve, Wainwright promised to mount a counterattack. MacArthur readily granted Wainwright permission to withdraw to the Agno River but would go no further. He wanted to know what plans Wainwright had made for a counterattack—he had none yet—and made it clear that his chances of getting the Philippine Division were very slight. It was on this note that the conversation ended.[20]

Wainwright's admission on the afternoon of December 23 that further defense of the beach was useless and his request for permission to withdraw behind the Agno could have come as no surprise to General MacArthur. The possibility of a withdrawal had been considered from the start, but it was the withdrawal to Bataan not the Agno River that was in his mind. A withdrawal to the Agno, he must have decided by this time, would only halt the Japanese temporarily. And he could have placed but slight faith in the chances of a successful counterattack. Only on this basis is it possible to explain his lukewarm reaction to Wainwright's proposal for a counterattack and his refusal to release the crack Philippine Division, the one division in the islands that consisted only of Americans and Philippine Scouts. Thus, Wainwright's telephone call must simply have confirmed his belief that the time had come to withdraw to Bataan.

Just when MacArthur made the decision to withdraw is not clear. We know that as early as December 12 he had alerted Quezon to this possibility. And, though he made no change in plans when the Japanese landed at Lingayen ten days later, his message to General Marshall on that date clearly indicated that he now believed he might have to withdraw quickly. He estimated that the Japanese force disembarking from 70 to 80 transports in Lingayen Gulf had a strength of 80,000 to 100,000 men, and he reported that he had on Luzon only about 40,000 men. He anticipated that this "enormous tactical discrepancy" between the two forces would eventually compel him "to operate in delaying action on successive lines through the central Luzon plain to final defensive positions on Bataan." When forced to do so, he told the Chief of Staff, he would declare Manila an open city and move his headquarters, together with the Commonwealth Government and the High Commissioner's office, to Corregidor, which, he said, "I intend to hold." General Marshall immediately replied that his proposed line of action was approved by the War Department and that he was doing his utmost to send aid. Implied also was approval by President Roosevelt, who, Marshall said, had seen all of MacArthur's messages.[21]

We now know that the actual strength of the Japanese force that came ashore in Lingayen Gulf was only 40,000, about half as large as MacArthur estimated it to be. On the other hand, the total strength of the troops on Luzon under General MacArthur's command at this time was considerably higher than the 40,000 figure he gave to the Chief of Staff. Even without the Air Force, the number of American troops alone could not have been less than 20,000. In addition, there were 12,000 Philippine Scouts. To the total of 32,000 must be added the strength of seven Philippine Army reserve divisions and one regular division, as well as the constabulary, inducted into the service of the United States by this time. Even at half-strength, and many of the units were undoubtedly at two-thirds strength at least, the total number of troops on Luzon at this time could not have been less than 65,000-70,000.[22] No evidence has come to hand that explains the discrepancy between the actual and reported strength of the forces on Luzon.

The events at Lingayen Gulf on December 22 and 23 could scarcely have given General MacArthur any reason to alter the bleak picture he had painted for the Chief of Staff. Wainwright's request on the afternoon of December 23 was simply the culmination of a series of events that narrowed down the choices open to him. Now he had only two: either to make a firm stand on the line of the Agno and give Wainwright his best unit, the Philippine Division, for a counterattack; or to withdraw all the way to Bataan in planned stages. He decided on the latter, thus abandoning his own plan for defense and reverting to the old ORANGE plan.

The reason for this decision is not difficult to discern, and it has nothing to do with the supposed numerical superiority of the Japanese landing force, as MacArthur had implied in his message to General Marshall. Rather it was the quality not the quantity of his troops that was responsible for the failure to halt the Japanese. Up to this time, General MacArthur seemed to have had the greatest confidence in the fighting qualities of the Philippine Army reservists, and in the ability of his forces to hold the central Luzon plain. The events of December 22 and 23 forced a revision of this view. "General MacArthur, viewing the broken, fleeing North Luzon Force," wrote Colonel James V. Collier, a G-3 officer on MacArthur's staff, "realized that his cherished plan of defeating an enemy attempt to advance toward Manila from the north was not now possible. . . ." [23] MacArthur never publicly acknowledged the poor performance of the Army he had done so much to organize and train, but it was noted by every American who served with the Philippine Army units and is the central fact that emerges from a study of the first days of the campaign. To this reason for the withdrawal must be added General MacArthur's desire to save the city of Manila from destruction.

Having made his decision to withdraw to Bataan, MacArthur notified all force commanders on the night of December 23 that "WPO-3 is in effect." [24] Nothing more was required. WPO-3 was well known to all U.S. Army officers who had been in the Philippines six months or more. Under it, the Philippine Department headquarters, after the experience of numerous maneuvers, had selected certain delaying positions along the central Luzon plain. These positions had been reconnoitered and were considered fairly strong defensive lines along the route of withdrawal to Bataan. It only remained to issue written orders to supplement the announcement that WPO-3 was in effect.

The next morning, December 24, at 11 o'clock, the USAFFE staff was called to a conference. Brigadier General Richard K. Sutherland, MacArthur's Chief of Staff, announced the decision and stated that the headquarters was to be moved to Corregidor that evening. By special order all officers in the headquarters, except those of high rank who had been promoted a few days earlier, were promoted one grade. To the War Department, General MacArthur sent news of his decision as well as the further information that the Japanese had landed at Atimonan and Mauban in southern Luzon that morning.[25] "Tonight," he told the Chief of Staff, "I plan to disengage my forces under cover of darkness. For the present, I am remaining in Manila, establishing an advanced headquarters on Corregidor." [26]

On the afternoon of December 24, President Quezon and High Commissioner Francis B. Sayre, with their personal and official families, sailed to Corregidor. MacArthur's headquarters began to move that night, Christmas Eve. Next morning Headquarters USAFFE opened at Topside on Corregidor and MacArthur reported his new position to Washington. A rear echelon, headed by the deputy chief of staff, Brigadier General Richard J. Marshall, remained behind in Manila to close out the headquarters and to supervise the shipment of supplies and the evacuation of the remaining troops.[27]

The decision to withdraw to Bataan altered completely the course of the campaign, and a new plan based on ORANGE was quickly devised. General Wainwright's new orders directed him to withdraw slowly, holding the Japanese until January 8 north of the key city of San Fernando where the main highway leading into the Bataan Peninsula began. That done, he would withdraw into Bataan. The two-week delay was designed to allow time for the movement of supplies, the preparation of defenses on Bataan, and the withdrawal of the South Luzon Force. During the withdrawal, Wainwright's troops were to occupy successive defensive positions, five in all. The intention was to delay the Japanese by forcing them to deploy for an organized attack against each position and to withdraw to the next line before a serious battle developed. Wainwright was also to cover the withdrawal of the troops located south of Manila, across the Pampanga River, over the Calumpit bridge to San Fernando, and thence to Bataan. All of the South Luzon Force was to clear the bridge before January 8. During the withdrawal, a Bataan Defense Force, organized on December 24, was to prepare defensive positions on Bataan. A total of almost three divisions was ordered into the peninsula immediately to establish a line behind which the withdrawing troops could fall for protection.[28]

This plan for the withdrawal to Bataan called for a difficult maneuver requiring accurate timing and the closest coordination. One slip, one road left unguarded, one bridge blown too soon or not soon enough might well imperil the entire plan. Should the forces in North and South Luzon fail to pull back to Bataan, or should the Japanese seize the road net leading into the peninsula, then the strategic objective of the withdrawal, the denial of Manila Bay to the enemy, would be jeopardized.

To support the movement to Bataan a new plan of supply was quickly drawn. Under War Plan ORANGE the movement of supplies to Bataan was to begin immediately on the outbreak of war and continue until the depots and warehouses there had been stocked with sufficient supplies to sustain a garrison of 43,000 men for six months. When MacArthur substituted for ORANGE his order to fight it out on the beaches, this supply plan was canceled. The supplies earmarked for Bataan under ORANGE therefore went to advance depots and railheads behind the beaches. When MacArthur ordered a return to ORANGE, many of the supplies needed on Bataan were scattered, and no measures had yet been taken to move them to Bataan. MacArthur's decision left only seven days, until January 1, when Manila was evacuated, in which to bring in the supplies, and instead of the 43,000 men provided for in ORANGE, the force withdrawing to Bataan would be closer to 80,000. This change in plans was destined to have a greater effect on the ability of the defenders to hold Bataan than any other phase of the operation.

The supply plan went into effect on the morning of December 24, when General R. J. Marshall called G-4 (supply) and the quartermaster into his office and told them of the decision to withdraw all troops on Luzon to Bataan and to evacuate Manila. Brigadier General Charles C. Drake, the quartermaster, was instructed to move his base of operations to Bataan immediately and to check on the reserves at Corregidor to be sure that there was enough to supply 10,000 men for six months. Small barges and boats required to move the supplies from Manila to Corregidor and Bataan were quickly gathered, and within twenty-four hours Corregidor was completely stocked with the supplies for a six-month campaign. At the same time, all supplies were immediately started on their way to Bataan by every available means—water, truck, and rail. Ammunition had already been stored in the peninsula, together with certain defense reserves including 300,000 gallons of gasoline, lubricating oil, and greases, and about 3,000 tons of canned meats and fish.[29]

In Manila, the rear echelon worked valiantly to get all the supplies out of the city before the Japanese moved in. Those small craft not transferred to Corregidor and Bataan were destroyed; demolitions were carried out with efficiency and dispatch. By the time R. J. Marshall and his men moved out on New Year's Eve, everything that might possibly be of value to the enemy had been destroyed or distributed to the civilian populace.[30]

In the rush of events on the evening of December 23, no one had remembered to inform the Navy of the change in plans. Admiral Thomas C. Hart, Commander in Chief of the Asiatic Fleet, had seen a copy of MacArthur's message to the Chief of Staff in Washington predicting such a move, however, and was not surprised to learn the next morning from his liaison officer that Manila was to be declared an open city and that all military forces were to be evacuated from the capital that day. He was now faced with the choice of moving to Corregidor, where Rear Admiral Francis W. Rockwell, commander of the 16th Naval District, was already established, or southward to the Netherlands Indies where most of the Asiatic Fleet had gone at the beginning of war in the Pacific, and where he had already decided to go ultimately.[31] Hart decided on the latter course, largely because it was evident that the submarines would soon have to go south, and announced his decision to his staff at a conference that day. Next morning he turned over to Rockwell full command of all naval activities in the Philippines and late that night left Manila aboard a submarine.[32]

With all fields capable of basing American bombers gone and with the prospect of the early loss of all fighter strips except those on Bataan, there seemed to be no justification for retaining the Far East Air Force in the Philippines. Already most of the B-17's which had survived the Clark Field attack had been sent to Darwin, Australia. On December 24 MacArthur called Major General Lewis H. Brereton, the Far East Air Force commander, to his office and told him that he was to go to Australia. His new mission would be to protect the line of communications southward and to support the defenses of the Philippines. Brereton offered to stay on, but MacArthur told him that he could perform a greater service in Australia. Brereton closed his headquarters in Manila at 4 o'clock on the afternoon of December 24 and left that evening in a PBY to join his bombers at Batchelor Field near Darwin. All that remained in the Philippines of the once formidable Far East Air Force was a handful of fighters. Since only a few men were required to fly and service these planes, most of the airmen who did not go south eventually became infantry soldiers on Bataan.[33]

On December 26 Manila was officially declared an open city and MacArthur's proclamation was published in the newspapers and broadcast over the radio. That night the blackout ended and the capital was ablaze with lights. The Japanese were not notified officially of the proclamation but learned of it through radio broadcasts. The next day, and thereafter, they bombed the port area, from which supplies were being shipped to Bataan and Corregidor.

With the evacuation of the Government and the Army a feeling of foreboding and terror spread through the city and the exodus, which had ceased after the first confusion of war, began again. "The roads back into the hills," noted a newspaper correspondent, "were black with people striving to reach their native villages. . . . The few trains still running into the provinces were literally jammed to the car tops." [34] The business district was deserted and there were few cars along Dewey Boulevard. "No girls in slacks and shorts were bicycling along the water front," wrote Major Carlos Romulo regretfully, "and there were no horseback riders on the bridle path. . . . The Yacht Club, the night clubs and hotels . . . all looked like funeral parlors." [35] Despite the lifting of the blackout, Manila seemed like a deserted city.

Meanwhile, in the early morning hours of December 24, two days after the landings at Lingayen Gulf, another Japanese force had landed at Lamon Bay, on the east coast of Luzon, below Manila. The Japanese now had troops north and south of Manila, in position to march on the capital. They had, moreover, forced General MacArthur to abandon his plans for the defense of Luzon and to order a withdrawal to Bataan and Corregidor. This decision had led the Asiatic Fleet and the Far East Air Force to fall back on the line from Soerabaja, in Java, to Darwin, 1,500 miles away, and left Manila, the "pearl of the Orient," open to the invaders. The Japanese could feel justly proud of their accomplishments.

But General Homma could draw small comfort from his success, for MacArthur's forces were still intact. In a period of two weeks, under the most difficult circumstances and under constant pressure from the enemy, the American and Philippine troops had completed a skillful and dangerous withdrawal and successfully escaped to

Bataan. So long as they could maintain their positions there, the Japanese would be unable to use Manila harbor.

If the decision to withdraw to Bataan had sealed the fate of Manila, it had also made possible the accomplishment of the mission assigned to War Plan ORANGE: to delay the Japanese and hold the entrance to Manila Bay. Thus, MacArthur's decision to withdraw his Luzon forces into Bataan forced upon the Japanese a difficult and costly four-month campaign to win a battle that must to them have seemed won on December 23.

It is interesting to contrast MacArthur's decision of December 23, 1941, with that reached by General Tomoyuki Yamashita, commanding the Japanese 14th Area Army in the Philippines three years later, when MacArthur's victorious Southwest Pacific Area forces were preparing to return to Luzon.[36] The situation MacArthur faced in December 1941 and that which confronted Yamashita in December 1944 were quite similar. Both commanders had to prepare their defenses against opponents with superior air and naval forces and with ground forces possessing mobility and fire power with which both were unable to cope. In both cases there was scant hope that the defending commanders could receive reinforcements or supplies once the battle was joined on Luzon. But there were important differences, for the commanders had different missions. While not explicitly stated, it was generally understood that MacArthur's mission under War Plan ORANGE was to hold Manila Bay for six months. Yamashita's mission, less specific, was to pin down on Luzon as many U.S. Army divisions as he could for as long as possible in the hope of slowing the Allied advance toward Japan.

When Yamashita assumed command in the Philippines on October 9, 1944, Imperial General Headquarters expected to fight the decisive battle for the archipelago on Luzon. But MacArthur's invasion of the central Philippines at Leyte that same month precipitated a quick switch. Imperial GHQ, despite Yamashita's remonstrances, decided to fight it out at Leyte. As a result, the Imperial Japanese Navy suffered a shattering defeat. Japan's airpower incurred grievous losses that it could ill afford; precious divisions from Luzon and China were ground up before the Allied onslaught; and irreplaceable Japanese cargo ships and transports were sunk. Leyte was indeed a graveyard of Japanese hopes and plans.

Yamashita was a realist. As early as the first week of November 1944 he concluded that Leyte was lost, and he requested higher authority to permit him to concentrate his efforts on preparing the defenses of Luzon. But Imperial GHQ denied him this until after MacArthur, on December 15, struck out boldly from Leyte to Mindoro, just south of Luzon. Then and then only did Imperial GHQ give Yamashita permission to cease the futile effort to hold Leyte and turn his attention to Luzon.

By late December Yamashita knew that Imperial GHQ must soon write Luzon off as a strategic loss. He could expect no help from the Japanese Navy nor any significant air reinforcements for the defense of Luzon. Whatever limited attempts higher headquarters might make to send him ground reinforcements would end, he knew, once MacArthur's troops reached Luzon. Realizing all this he had decided as early as the first half of November that his operations on Luzon would have to be primarily defensive. By late December he concluded that his defense would have to be a static one. To conduct this defense he had a variety of units, most of them underfed, understrength, and underequipped, totaling about 272,000 troops including air, ground, and naval services. The leadership, training, and organization of many units left much to be desired, and Yamashita did not obtain even nominal command of Army Air Forces and naval shore-based troops on Luzon until after the new year opened. Lacking adequate transportation and supplies of many types, his logistical situation approached the impossible.

Yamashita realized that within the framework of his mission to conduct a protracted delaying action on Luzon he had no hope of defending all the island. He did not have the troops, supplies, and equipment to do so, and the terrain over much of Luzon would not provide him with desired natural defensive positions. He could not hope to hold the vital central plains-Manila Bay region against the superiority in ground and air forces he knew MacArthur would bring to bear. To withdraw to Bataan, as MacArthur had, appeared an unwise move to Yamashita. Bataan he considered a cul-de-sac. On that small peninsula his 272,000 troops could not find food. Concentrated in such a limited area, they would be quickly cut to ribbons by the superior air, naval, and ground fire power available to MacArthur. In addition, he considered the city of Manila virtually indefensible and its defense of little significance unless tied to the defense of the entire bay region, which he could not, in any case, hope to hold for long. He concluded, therefore, that to attempt to deny Manila Bay to the Allies could lead only to the early annihilation of his forces, making it impossible for him to carry out plans to pin down major Allied forces on Luzon for a protracted period.

This was Yamashita's key decision. By making it, he fixed the strategy of MacArthur's campaign for the reconquest of Luzon.

Yamashita concentrated most of his strength in three mountainous strongholds. The strongest and most important of these defensive sectors covered all Luzon northeast and east of Lingayen Gulf and included within its area the island's roughest, most inhospitable mountains. In these mountains, with about 150,000 men, Yamashita intended to make his last stand. The second defensive groupment numbered approximately 30,000 troops, mainly of the Army Air Forces and the Navy. This force Yamashita located in mountain country west of the central plains and dominating the Clark Field air center. The third major concentration, 50,000 troops, he posted in mountains east and northeast of Manila, controlling the principal sources of the city's water supply.

As events turned out, a deviation from Yamashita's plans—a deviation that illustrates his command and control problems— served to deny the use of Manila Bay to the Allies for some time. Contrary to Yamashita's orders, a force of some 17,000 troops under naval command elected to defend Manila and held out until March 3, 1945. Salvage, repair, and construction problems in the bay area were of such magnitude that it was well into April before the Allies could profit by Manila's port facilities. Thus, directly or indirectly, the Japanese prevented the Allies from employing Manila Bay for roughly three months after MacArthur's initial landings on Luzon on January 9, 1945, as compared to the five months that MacArthur's and Wainwright's forces, by their stands on Bataan and on Corregidor, had denied the bay to the Japanese three years earlier. Yamashita's groupment west of Clark Field remained a threat for a little over a month after January 9. The Japanese in the mountains east and northeast of Manila retained their hold over Manila's water supply for nearly five months.

In 1942, American resistance on the Luzon mainland, except for minor, isolated forces, ended on April 9, almost four months to the day after the initial Japanese attacks against the Philippines. Corregidor lasted one more month. In 1945, Yamashita's main force did better. Holed up in the mountain fastnesses of northern Luzon, it was still resisting when Japan surrendered, seven and a half months after MacArthur's initial landings, and Yamashita estimated he could have continued the fight in those northern mountains for another month.

Who made the wiser decision—MacArthur or Yamashita?

Leo J. Meyer

The Decision to Invade
North Africa (TORCH)
(1942)

Before dawn on November 8, 1942, American soldiers waded through the surf of North African beaches in three widely separated areas to begin the largest amphibious operations that had ever been attempted in the history of warfare. These troops were the vanguard for a series of operations that eventually involved more than a million of their compatriots in action in the Mediterranean area. One campaign led to another. Before the German surrender in May 1945 put an end to hostilities in Europe, American units in the Mediterranean area had fought in North Africa, Sicily, Italy, Sardinia, Corsica, and southern France.[1]

The decision to take the initiative in the West with an Allied invasion of North Africa was made by Prime Minister Winston S. Churchill and President Franklin D. Roosevelt. It was one of the few strategic decisions of the war in which the President overrode the counsel of his military advisers.

The reasons for it were as much political as military. At first, TORCH, as the operation was called, had no specific military objective other than to effect a lodgment in French North Africa and to open the Mediterranean to Allied shipping. It stemmed mainly from a demand for early offensive action against the powers of the European Axis and ostensibly was designed to ease the pressure on the hard-pressed Soviet armies and to check the threatened advance of German power through Egypt into the Middle East.

A combined Anglo-American attack on North Africa might have come earlier had it not been for the pressing need to use the ex-

129

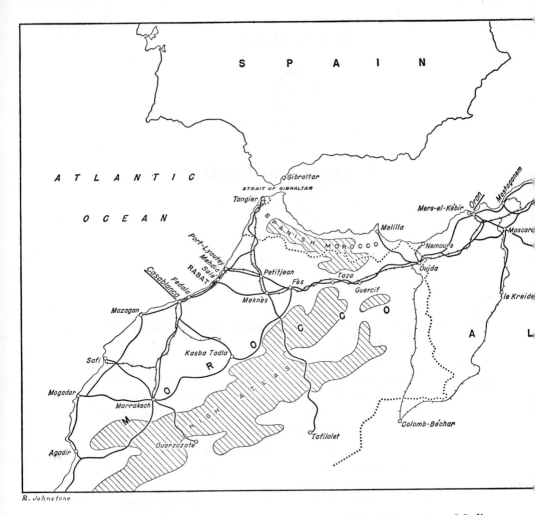

R. Johnstone

tremely limited resources of the Allies to defend the eastern Mediterranean and to stem the Japanese tidal wave that ultimately engulfed
Burma, Malaya, the East Indies, the Philippines, and large areas of the
southwest Pacific. In fact, the invasion of North Africa had been a
main topic of discussion between President Roosevelt, Prime Minister
Churchill, and their chief military advisers, known collectively as the
Combined Chiefs of Staff (CCS), at the first of the Allied wartime
conferences (ARCADIA) held in Washington during the week before
Christmas 1941.[2] The thought of a North African undertaking at that
time was inspired by hope of winning the initiative at relatively
small cost and "closing and tightening the ring" around Germany,
preparatory to a direct attack upon the core of its military power.[3]

American military leaders had long appreciated the fact that the
occupation of North Africa held the promise of producing valuable

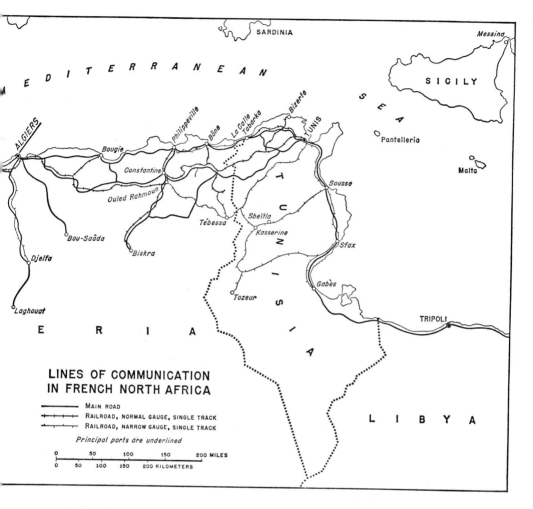

LINES OF COMMUNICATION
IN FRENCH NORTH AFRICA

——————— MAIN ROAD
—+—+—+—+— RAILROAD, NORMAL GAUGE, SINGLE TRACK
—·—·—·—·— RAILROAD, NARROW GAUGE, SINGLE TRACK

Principal ports are underlined

results for the Allied cause. It would prevent Axis penetration of the French dependencies in that region, help secure the British line of communication through the Mediterranean, and provide a potential base for future land operations in the Mediterranean and southern Europe.[4] Nevertheless, they were opposed on strategic grounds to the dissipation of Allied strength in secondary ventures.[5] Confident that America's great resources eventually would prove the decisive factor in the war, they favored a concentration of forces in the United Kingdom for a massive attack against Western Europe at the earliest possible time.*

The British accepted the American view that the main blow would eventually have to be delivered in Western Europe, but they hesitated

---

* The date for such an assault as estimated in early 1942 was to be sometime in the spring of 1943.

to commit themselves on when and where it should fall. Even at this early stage they showed a preference for peripheral campaigns to be followed by a direct attack on the enemy only after he had been seriously weakened by attrition. Such a "peripheral strategy" came naturally to British leaders. They had followed it so often in earlier wars against Continental powers that it had become deeply imbedded in England's military tradition. But another factor that led them to shy away from an immediate encounter with the enemy on his home grounds was the vivid memory of earlier disasters on the Continent. About these the British said little at this time, but that the fear of another debacle influenced their arguments can be taken for granted. Later it was to come more openly to the surface.

Churchill and General Sir Alan Brooke, Chief of the Imperial General Staff, from the outset stressed the advantages of a North African operation in 1942 or 1943. They made much of the tonnage that would be saved by opening the Mediterranean and the likelihood that the French in North Africa, despite the fact that they were torn by dissension, would cooperate with the Allies once they landed. Thus France would be brought back into the struggle against the Axis.

While the majority of American military leaders had their doubts about the value of a North African invasion and its chances of success, President Roosevelt was attracted to the idea largely because it afforded an early opportunity to carry the war to the Germans. In his opinion it was very important to give the people of the United States a stronger feeling that they were at war in the West as well as in the Pacific and to impress upon the Germans that they would have to face American power on their side of the Atlantic.[6] Because of the interest of the two political heads, who in many matters saw eye to eye, the Combined Chiefs of Staff, without committing themselves definitely to any operation, agreed at the ARCADIA conference to go ahead with a plan to invade North Africa.

The task of working out such a plan was given to General Headquarters (GHQ) in Washington. By combining the main features of GYMNAST and a British scheme to attack Tunisia, GHQ produced a plan in record time called SUPER-GYMNAST.* This plan was first submitted for review to Major General Joseph W. Stilwell, who had been working on plans to seize Dakar, and then to Major General Lloyd R. Fredendall, both attached to GHQ. On the basis of their

* The code name GYMNAST continued to be used loosely by many to apply to SUPER-GYMNAST as well as to the original plan.

comments a revised plan was drawn up and approved on February 19, 1942.[7]

Soon thereafter, unforeseen developments arose that prevented immediate implementation of the revised plan. Among these were the heavy losses the British Navy suffered in the Mediterranean and the Japanese advances in southeastern Asia, the Philippines, and the Netherlands Indies which made it imperative to give the Pacific area first call on American resources, particularly in ships. The shipment of men and supplies to the threatened areas put so great a strain on the Allied shipping pool, already seriously depleted by the spectacular success of German U-boats,[8] that little was available for an early venture into North Africa or anywhere else. Before the situation eased, preparations for meeting the German Army head on in Europe, known as BOLERO, had received the green light in priorities over SUPER-GYMNAST.

As in the case of SUPER-GYMNAST, BOLERO had its roots in strategic thinking that antedated Pearl Harbor. Months before December 7 basic Anglo-American strategy, in the event of America's entry into the war, called for the defeat of Germany, the strongest Axis power, first. This grand strategic concept was discussed as a hypothetical matter in pre-Pearl Harbor British-American staff conversations held in Washington between January 29 and March 27, 1941, and later set forth in the Allied agreement (ABC-1) and in the joint Army-Navy plan, RAINBOW 5, which were submitted to the President in June 1941.[9] While sympathetic toward the strategy in both ABC-1 and RAINBOW 5, Roosevelt refrained from approving either at the time, probably for political reasons. At the ARCADIA conference in December 1941, the basic strategic concept was confirmed and a decision was made to begin the establishment of an American force in the United Kingdom. This decision, however, "was not definitive" since it was essentially based on the need of protecting the British Isles and did not include their use as a base for future offensive operations against the Continent. The omission troubled many American leaders, including Secretary of War Henry L. Stimson, who in early March tried to persuade the President that "the proper and orthodox line of our help" was to send an overwhelming force to the British Isles which would threaten an attack on the Germans in France. In this he was supported by the Joint Chiefs of Staff who had accepted the detailed analysis of the military situation, worked out by the War Plans Division under Brigadier General Dwight D. Eisenhower in late

February. As a result, the President replied to the Prime Minister on March 8 that in general the British should assume responsibility for the Middle East, the United States for the Pacific, and that both should operate jointly in the Atlantic area. At the same time, the American planners were assigned the task of preparing plans for an invasion of northwest Europe in the spring of 1943.

The principal argument for selecting this area for the main British-American offensive was that it offered the shortest route to the heart of Germany and so was the most favorable place in the West where a vital blow could be struck. It was also the one area where the Allies could hope to gain the necessary air superiority, where the United States could "concentrate and maintain" the largest force, where the bulk of the British forces could be brought into action, and where the maximum support to the Soviet Union, whose continued participation in the war was considered essential to the defeat of Germany, could be given.[10] By April 1 an outline draft, which came to be known first as the Marshall Memorandum and later as BOLERO, was far enough advanced to be submitted to the President, who accepted it without reservation and immediately dispatched Harry Hopkins, his personal envoy to Russia and Britain, and General George C. Marshall, Army Chief of Staff, to London to obtain British approval.[11]

As originally conceived, BOLERO contemplated a build-up of military power in the United Kingdom simultaneously with continuous raids against the Continent, to be followed by a full-scale attack on Hitler's *"Festung Europa"* in the spring of 1943. Later the code name ROUNDUP was applied to the operational part of the plan. Under this plan, 48 divisions, 60 per cent of which would be American, were to be placed on the Continent of Europe by September of that year. Included in BOLERO was a contingent alternate plan known as SLEDGE-HAMMER, which provided for the establishment of a limited beach-head on the Continent in the fall of 1942 should Germany collapse or the situation on the Eastern Front become so desperate that quick action in the West would be needed to relieve German pressure on the Soviet Union.

In London Hopkins and Marshall outlined the American plan to the British. While stressing BOLERO as a means of maintaining the Soviet Army as a fighting force, they also emphasized the need of arriving at an early decision "in principle" on the location and timing of the main British-American effort so that production, allocation of resources, training, and troop movements could proceed without delay.[12]

Churchill seemed to be warmly sympathetic to the American proposal to strike the main blow in northwestern Europe and described it as a "momentous proposal" in accord with "the classic principle of war—namely, concentration against the main enemy." [13] But though the Prime Minister and his advisers agreed "in principle," Marshall was aware that most of them had "reservations regarding this and that" and stated that it would require "great firmness" to avoid further dispersions.[14] That he was right is borne out by the fact that Churchill later wrote that he regarded SLEDGEHAMMER as impractical and accepted it merely as an additional project to be considered along with invasion of North Africa and perhaps Norway as a possible operation for 1942.[15] At all events, BOLERO was approved by the British on April 14 with only one strongly implied reservation: it was not to interfere with Britain's determination to hold its vital positions in the Middle East and the Indian Ocean area.[16]

While BOLERO-SLEDGEHAMMER was acceptable to the British in mid-April, it remained so for less than two months.[17] By early May they were expressing strong doubts that the resources to launch an early cross-Channel operation could be found.[18] In part, the uncertainty was due to the state of the American landing-craft production program, which was not only lagging far behind schedule but was indefinite as to type and number. What the requirements in craft would be no one actually knew, for all estimates in regard to both number and type were impressionistic. In the original outline plan, the number needed had been placed at 7,000. This was soon raised to 8,100 by the Operations Division (OPD), still too conservative an estimate in the opinion of many. Lieutenant General Joseph T. McNarney, Deputy Chief of Staff, for example, considered 20,000 a more realistic figure.[19] As to type, the Army had placed orders with the Navy for some 2,300 craft, mostly small 36-foot vehicle and personnel carriers, for delivery in time for a limited operation in the fall. These, along with 50-foot WM boats (small tank lighters), were considered sufficiently seaworthy by the Navy to negotiate the waters of the English Channel. The rest of the 8,100 were expected to be ready for delivery in mid-April 1943, in time for ROUNDUP.[20]

This construction program, seemingly firm in early April, soon ran into difficulties. Toward the end of April the Navy, after re-examining its own requirements for amphibious operations in the Pacific and elsewhere, concluded it needed about 4,000 craft. If its estimates were allowed to stand, only about half of the Army's needs for SLEDGE-HAMMER could be met in the construction program. Some of the resulting deficit might possibly be made up by the British, but this seemed unlikely at the time, for their production was also behind schedule.

The second obstacle arose when the British questioned the ability of the landing craft on which construction had begun to weather the severe storms that prevailed in the Channel during the fall and winter months. They convinced the President that their objections to the type of craft under construction in the United States were sound, as indeed they were. The result was that a new program, which shifted the emphasis to the production of larger craft, was drawn up and placed under British guidance. Like the earlier program this one also underwent a series of upward revisions.[21]

As the requirements rose, the prospects of meeting them declined. In late May it was still possible to expect delivery in time for ROUNDUP in the spring of 1943, but the hope of obtaining enough craft for SLEDGEHAMMER had dwindled. If the latter operation was to be undertaken at all, it would have to be executed with what craft and shipping could be scraped together. This, of course, would increase the danger that SLEDGEHAMMER would become a sacrificial offering launched not in the hope of establishing a permanent lodgment but solely to ease the pressure on the Soviet armies. For this the British, who would be required to make the largest contribution in victims and equipment, naturally had no stomach.

In late May, when Vyacheslav M. Molotov, the Soviet Foreign Commissar, visited London to urge the early establishment of a second front in Western Europe, he found Churchill noncommittal. The Prime Minister informed him that the British would not hesitate to execute a cross-Channel attack before the year was up provided it was "sound and sensible," but, he emphasized, "wars are not won by unsuccessful operations." [22]

In Washington a few days later, Molotov found that a different view on SLEDGEHAMMER from the one he had encountered still prevailed. Roosevelt, much more optimistic than Churchill, told him that he "hoped" and "expected" the Allies to open a second front in 1942 and suggested that the Soviet Union might help its establishment by accepting a reduction in the shipment of Lend-Lease general supplies.[23] The conversations ended with a declaration drafted by Molotov and accepted by the President which stated that a "full understanding was reached with regard to the urgent tasks of creating a Second Front in Europe in 1942." [24] This statement, although not a definite assurance that a cross-Channel invasion would soon be launched, differed considerably from the noncommittal declarations of the Prime Minister. It clearly indicated that Washington and London were not in full accord on the strategy for 1942 and that further discussions between U.S. and British leaders were necessary to establish a firm agreement.

By the time of the second Washington conference in June 1942 (ARGONAUT), Churchill and his close military advisers, if they ever truly accepted the U.S. strategy proposed by Marshall, had definitely undergone a change of mind. They now contended that an emergency invasion in 1942 to aid Russia would preclude a second attempt for years to come and therefore no direct attack should be undertaken unless the German Army was "demoralized by failure against Russia." [25]

Aware of the fact that the British had grown cool to SLEDGE-HAMMER, if not to ROUNDUP, as the strategy for 1942 and 1943 and anxious to get American troops into action against the main enemy as quickly as possible, President Roosevelt in mid-June sounded out his military advisers on the resurrection of GYMNAST. The suggestion met with strong dissent from Secretary of War Stimson and General Marshall, both of whom now were convinced that the British were just as much opposed to ROUNDUP for 1943 as they were to SLEDGE-HAMMER in 1942.[26]

In deference to their views, Roosevelt refrained from openly supporting the British position during the June conference in Washington, with the result that the meetings ended with BOLERO and ROUNDUP-SLEDGEHAMMER ostensibly still intact as the basic Anglo-American strategy in the North Atlantic area. But Churchill's vigorous arguments against a 1942 cross-Channel invasion of the Continent and Roosevelt's lively and unconcealed interest in the Mediterranean basin as a possible alternative area of operations indicated that the opponents of diversionary projects were losing ground. The defeat of the British Eighth Army by General Erwin Rommel's Africa Corps in a spectacular tank battle at Knightsbridge in Libya on June 13 and the subsequent fall of Tobruk on June 21, followed by the rapid advance of Rommel's army toward Alexandria and the Suez Canal, further weakened the position of the U.S. military leaders, for as long as Commonwealth forces were fighting with their backs to the wall in Egypt no British Government could be expected to agree to a cross-Channel venture.

Churchill, who had hurriedly returned to England in the crisis created by Rommel's victories, soon made it unmistakably clear that he was adamant in his opposition to any plan to establish a bridge-head on the Continent in 1942.[27] A premature invasion, he reiterated in a cable to Roosevelt, would be disastrous. Instead, he recommended that the American military chiefs proceed with planning for GYMNAST while the British investigated the possibility of an attack on Norway (JUPITER), a pet project of his. To his representative in Washington, Field Marshal Sir John Dill, he sent a message making it clear that he wanted a North African operation. "GYMNAST," he stated, "affords the sole means by which the U.S. can strike at Hitler in 1942. . . . However if the President decided against GYMNAST the matter is settled" and both countries would have to remain "motionless in 1942." [28] But for the time being, the impetuous Prime Minister was in no position to press strongly for the early implementation of the project, eager though he was to assume the offensive. For weeks to come the military situation would demand that every ton of available shipping in the depleted Allied shipping pool be used to move men, tanks, and other materials around southern Africa to hold Egypt and bolster the Middle East against Rommel's army and to hold the even more potentially dangerous German forces in Russia that had conquered Crimea and were massing for an offensive that might carry them across the Caucasus into the vital oil-rich regions of Iraq and the Persian Gulf.[29]

Strong support for the Prime Minister's objections to a premature invasion of the Continent had come from the British Chiefs of Staff. After considering the advantages and disadvantages of SLEDGEHAM-MER, they stated in their report to the War Cabinet on July 2: "If we were free agents we could not recommend that the operation should be mounted." [30] In reaching this conclusion they were ostensibly persuaded by two reports, one from Lord Leathers, British Minister of War Transport, who had estimated that the operation would tie up about 250,000 tons of shipping at a time when shipping could ill be spared, and the other from Lord Louis Mountbatten, Chief of Combined Operations, which pointed out that, in the absence of sufficient landing craft in the United Kingdom, all amphibious training for other operations, including cross-Channel in 1943, would have to be suspended if SLEDGEHAMMER were undertaken. The War Cabinet immediately accepted the views of the British Chiefs of Staff and on July 8 notified the Joint Staff Mission in Washington of its decision against an operation on the Continent even if confined to a "tip and run" attack.[31]

In submitting its views on the strategy to be followed, the War

Cabinet carefully refrained from openly opposing ROUNDUP as an operation for 1943. But the effect was the same, since it was not possible to conduct both the African invasion and the cross-Channel attack with the means then at the disposal of the Allies.

Because of the lag in landing craft construction, the Joint Chiefs of Staff realized that SLEDGEHAMMER was rapidly becoming a forlorn hope. By the end of June, out of a total of 2,698 landing craft— LCP's, LCV's, and LCM's—estimated as likely to be available, only 238 were in the United Kingdom or on the way.[32] By mid-July General John E. Hull, Deputy Chief of OPD, informed Eisenhower, who had gone to London, "that all the craft available and en route could land less than 16,000 troops and 1,100 tanks and vehicles." [33] This was 5,000 troops and 2,200 tanks less than the estimates made in mid-May. Despite these discouraging figures, General Marshall and Admiral King (Ernest J. King, Chief of Naval Operations), stubbornly continued to object to dropping SLEDGEHAMMER from the books, not because they wanted it but because they clearly recognized that the fate of ROUNDUP was also at stake in the British Government's attitude toward the emergency operation. Whether in earnest or not, they now went so far as to advocate that the United States should turn its back on Europe and strike decisively against Japan unless the British adhered "unswervingly" to the "full BOLERO plan." [34] This attitude so impressed Field Marshal Dill that he seriously considered cabling his government that further pressure for GYMNAST at the expense of a cross-Channel operation would drive the Americans into saying, "We are finished off with the West and will go out in the Pacific." [35] What Dill did not know was that Roosevelt was opposed to any action that amounted to an "abandonment of the British." Nor did the President openly agree with his Joint Chiefs of Staff that the British would be as unwilling to accept a large-scale cross-Channel attack in 1943 as in 1942, whatever their present views.[36] He was still determined to commit the Western Allies to action against the Germans before the end of the year, somehow and somewhere. If an agreement with the British on a cross-Channel attack could not be reached, he was quite willing to settle for some other operation. Unlike his chief military advisers, he was far from hostile to a campaign in the Mediterranean, the Middle East, or elsewhere in the Atlantic area if circumstances ruled out SLEDGEHAMMER or ROUNDUP. In fact, Secretary Stimson believed he was weakening on BOLERO and considered him somewhat enamored of the idea of operations in the Mediterranean.[37] The President's willingness to accept a substitute for an early invasion of Europe appears in the instructions he gave Harry Hopkins, General Marshall, and Admiral King when he sent them to England on July 18 with large powers to make a final effort to secure agreement on a cross-Channel attack in 1942. Should they become convinced after exploring all its angles with the British that such an operation would not prevent "the annihilation of Russia" by drawing off enemy airpower, they were to consider other military possibilities.[38]

As might have been expected, the American delegates failed to convince Churchill or the British military chiefs that an early assault on the Continent was practical. The Prime Minister, after questioning both the urgency and feasibility of SLEDGEHAMMER, again emphasized the value of a North African operation and suggested that if the approaching battle for Egypt went well, it might be possible to carry the war to Sicily and Italy.[39]

A realistic estimate of the military situation at the time indicated that launching a successful operation against the mainland of Europe in 1942 was far from bright. Allied war production potential was still comparatively undeveloped and battle-tested divisions were unavailable. Landing craft, despite a high production priority ordered by the Navy in May, were still scarce, shipping was woefully short, and modern tanks, capable of meeting those of the enemy on equal terms, were just beginning to roll off the assembly lines. Even if the production of matériel could be speeded up, time was required to raise and organize a large force and train units in the difficult techniques of amphibious warfare. By according additional overriding priorities to BOLERO, the flow of men, equipment, and supplies to the United Kingdom could be increased, but this meant running the grave danger of crippling forces already engaged with the enemy elsewhere. Should this risk be accepted, there still remained the problem of erecting a logistical organization that could feed men, equipment, and supplies into the battle area without interruption. Considerable progress had been made in building such an organization in the United Kingdom, but it was still far from perfect. Taking all these matters into consideration, along with the likelihood that the Germans would have enough strength in France and the lowlands to contain an invasion without weakening their eastern front, the Combined Chiefs of Staff concluded that, at best, the only landing that could be made on the Continent in 1942 would be a minor one, aimed at securing a foothold at a port and holding and consolidating it during the winter. But the hard facts mutely argued against pitting any force against a veteran army on the chance that it could be sustained during the stormy winter weather.

The Americans saw this as clearly as the British. As realists, they knew that an operation in execution would take priority over one in contemplation, and that it would generate pressures that could upset the basic strategy agreed upon for Europe. The weakness of their stand was that nearly a year would probably elapse before more than a few Americans other than those in the Air Force would be in action against the Germans. Knowing this, Churchill and the British Chiefs of Staff reiterated time and again the advantages of a North African operation in conjunction with a counteroffensive in Libya. They stressed all the old arguments: it could lead to the liberation of Morocco, Algeria, and Tunisia, bring the French there back into the war against the Axis, open the Mediterranean to through traffic thus saving millions of tons of shipping, cause the withdrawal of German airpower from Russia, and force the Germans and Italians to extend themselves beyond their capacity in reinforcing their trans-Mediterranean and southern front. They would not admit that a North African operation in 1942 would rule out ROUNDUP and contended instead that early action in the Mediterranean would lead to a quick victory, which would still permit it to be launched in 1943.

The Americans, on the other hand, continued to hold out for SLEDGEHAMMER. They resisted the idea of dropping SLEDGEHAMMER, primarily in order to forestall a diversionary and indecisive operation which would siphon off resources and prevent a true second front from being established in 1943. Marshall and King, if not Hopkins, were certain that the fate of ROUNDUP was at stake and as firm as ever in the belief that a direct attack against the Continent was the only way to assist the hard-pressed Soviet armies and seriously threaten the military power of Germany. But because of the President's instructions to agree to some military operations somewhere in 1942, it was impossible for them to hold their ground indefinitely. Their position was not strengthened by the course of events in Russia, in the Middle East, and in the Atlantic, or by the opinion expressed by General Eisenhower—recently appointed Commanding General, European Theater of Operations, United States Army (ETOUSA)—that SLEDGEHAMMER had less than a fair chance of success.[40] Nor were they helped by the secret message from Roosevelt to Churchill, saying "that a Western front in 1942 was off" and that he was in favor of an invasion of North Africa and "was influencing his Chiefs in that direction." [41] Furthermore, since a cross-Channel operation to ease the pressure on the Soviet Union would have to be carried out primarily by British forces, because the shipping shortage precluded the flow of U.S. troops and aircraft to the United Kingdom in large proportions before the late fall of 1942, the American representatives could not insist on it. Marshall therefore refrained from pressing for the retention of SLEDGEHAMMER in the BOLERO plan after July 23 but continued to insist on ROUNDUP. This left the whole question of alternative action for 1942 undecided.

Informed by Marshall of the deadlock, Roosevelt sent additional instructions to his representatives in London, directing again that an agreement on an operation for 1942 be reached. This message specifically instructed the American delegation to settle with the British on one of five projects: (1) a combined British-American operation in North Africa (either Algeria or Morocco or both); (2) an entirely American operation against French Morocco (the original GYMNAST); (3) a combined operation against northern Norway (JUPITER); (4) the reinforcement of the British Eighth Army in Egypt; (5) the reinforcement of Iran.[42]

The American military chiefs, Marshall and King, now knew that SLEDGEHAMMER was dead, for no cross-Channel attack was possible in the face of British objections and without the President's strong support. Preferring the occupation of French North Africa with all its shortcomings to a campaign in the Middle East or Norway, they reluctantly accepted SUPER-GYMNAST.[43] On July 24 a carefully worded agreement, drawn up by Marshall and known as CCS 94, was accepted by the Combined Chiefs of Staff. It contained the important condition that the CCS would postpone until mid-September final decision on whether or not the North African operations should be undertaken. (The date September 15 was chosen because it was considered the earliest possible day on which the outcome in Russia could be forecast.) [44] If at that time the Russians clearly faced a collapse that would release so many German troops that a cross-Channel attack in the spring of 1943 would be impractical, the North African invasion would be launched sometime before December 1. Meanwhile, planning for ROUNDUP was to continue while a separate U.S. planning staff would work with the British on the North African project, now renamed TORCH.[45]

The door to later reconsideration of the agreement, deliberately left open in CCS 94 by General Marshall in order to save the ROUNDUP concept, did not remain open long. In a message to the President on July 25, Harry Hopkins urged an immediate decision on TORCH "to avoid procrastination and delays." [46] Without further consulting his military advisers, Roosevelt chose to assume that a North African campaign in 1942 had been definitely decided upon and at once cabled his emissaries that he was delighted with the "decision." At the same time he urged that a target date not later than October 30 be set for the invasion.[47] By ignoring the carefully framed conditions in CCS 94 and in suggesting a date for launching TORCH, the President actually made the decision. In so doing, he effectively jettisoned ROUNDUP for 1943, though he probably did not fully realize it at the time.

Although Marshall must have realized the fatal impact of Roosevelt's action on ROUNDUP, he was reluctant to view it as one that eliminated the conditions stipulated in CCS 94. At the first meeting of the Combined Chiefs of Staff held after his return to Washington he therefore refrained from accepting the "decision" as final and pointed out that the mounting of TORCH did not mean the abandonment of ROUNDUP.[48] At the same time, he recognized that a choice between the two operations would have to be made soon "because of the logistic consideration involved," particularly the conversion of vessels to combat loaders which, according to a "flash estimate" of the Navy, would require 96 days. Nor was Admiral King willing to admit that the President had fully decided to abandon ROUNDUP as well as SLEDGEHAMMER in favor of TORCH.[49]

If Marshall and King entertained any hope of getting the President to reopen the issue and make a definite choice between ROUNDUP and TORCH they were doomed to disappointment. Instead, on July 30, at a meeting at the White House with the Joint Chiefs of Staff, the President stated that "TORCH would be undertaken at the earliest possible date" but made no comment on its possible effect on ROUNDUP.[50] The next day his decision on TORCH was forwarded to the British Chiefs of Staff and to General Eisenhower.*

However loath the President's military advisers were to sidetrack plans for the direct invasion of the Continent and accept a secondary project in its place, an attack on French North Africa, alone among the operations considered, met strategic conditions for joint Anglo-American operations in 1942 on which both Churchill and Roosevelt could agree. Without the wholehearted support of the two top polit-

---

* Before leaving London, Marshall informed Eisenhower that he would be in command of the TORCH operation, if and when undertaken, in addition to being Commanding General, ETOUSA. This appointment was later confirmed by the CCS.

ical leaders in the United States and Great Britain, no combined operation could be mounted. In short, TORCH from the beginning had support on the highest political level in both countries, an advantage never enjoyed by either ROUNDUP or SLEDGEHAMMER.

The decision to invade North Africa restored Anglo-American cooperative planning, which had been showing signs of serious strain. It was now on a sound working basis that permitted the establishment of rights and priorities with relentless determination. What was still needed was a final agreement between Washington and London on the size, direction, and timing of the contemplated operation. Such an agreement was not easy to reach. The big question to be decided was where the main effort of the Allies should be made and when. On this issue Washington and London were at first far apart.

The strategic planners in Washington, mindful of the dangers in French opposition, hostile Spanish reaction, and a German counter-stroke against Gibraltar with or without the support of Spain, proposed making the main landings outside the Mediterranean on the Atlantic coast of French Morocco.[51] Troops would take Casablanca and adjacent minor ports, seize and hold the railroad and highways to the east as an auxiliary line of communications, secure all the approaches to Gibraltar, and consolidate Allied positions in French Morocco before moving into the Mediterranean. This, the planners estimated, would take about three months. The plan was a cautious one, dictated primarily by the fear that the Strait of Gibraltar might be closed by the Germans or the Spanish, acting singly or together.

The bold course, advocated by the strategic planners in London, including many Americans working with the British, was to strike deep into the Mediterranean with the main force at the outset and then, in coordination with the British Eighth Army moving west from Egypt, seize Tunisia before the Germans could reinforce the threatened area. They viewed with feelings approaching consternation the cautious Washington strategy that would waste precious months in taking ports and consolidating positions over a thousand miles distant from Tunisia, whose early occupation they believed to be vital to the success of TORCH. Should the Germans be permitted to establish themselves firmly in that province it was feared that they might, because of shorter lines of communications and land-based air-power, be able to hold out indefinitely, thus preventing the extension of Allied control to the strategic central Mediterranean.

The proponents of the inside approach also stressed the relative softness of the Algerian coastal area as compared with that around

Casablanca. In their view, Algeria with its favorable weather and tide conditions, more numerous and better ports, and proximity to Tunisia seemed to have every advantage over western Morocco as the main initial objective. They believed that even in the matter of securing communications it would be safer to move swiftly and boldly through the Strait of Gibraltar and seize ports along the Algerian coast as far east as Philippeville and Bône. Strong determined action there would cow the Spanish and make them hesitate to permit German entry into Spain for a joint attack on Gibraltar. On the other hand, they contended that an unsuccessful attack in the Casablanca area, where operations were extremely hazardous because of unfavorable surf conditions four days out of five, would almost certainly invite Spanish intervention.[52]

For weeks arguments for and against both strategic concepts were tossed back and forth across the Atlantic in what has aptly been called a "transatlantic essay contest." [53] Meanwhile, preparations for the attack languished. A logical solution to the problem was to reconcile the conflicting views by combining both into a single plan. This, General Eisenhower, who had been designated to command the operation before Marshall left London, attempted to do in his first outline plan of August 9 when he proposed approximately simultaneous landings inside and outside the Mediterranean, the first strong and the latter relatively weak.[54]

Almost immediately, the plan struck snags in the form of insufficient naval air support and assault shipping. Shortly after it was submitted, both the American and the British Navies suffered severe losses in naval units, particularly in aircraft carriers.* Since close land-based air support would be negligible, confined to a single airfield at Gibraltar under the domination of Spanish guns, carriers were necessary to protect assault and follow-up convoys for the operations. In view of the recent naval losses and needs elsewhere in the world, finding them would take time. The U.S. Navy quickly let it be known that it had no carriers immediately available to fill the void and was unwilling to commit itself on when they would be available. This meant that the burden of supplying sea-borne air protection would probably fall on the British.

Equally if not more important in determining the size and timing of the landings was the availability of assault shipping. Most of the

---

* The United States Navy lost a carrier and several cruisers in the Guadalcanal operation; the Royal Navy, one aircraft carrier sunk and one damaged in trying to reinforce Malta.

American APA's (assault troop transports) were tied up in the Pacific where they were vitally needed. To transport the 12 regimental combat teams, envisioned as the force needed to make the three landings, would require 36 APA's and 9 to 12 AKA's (attack cargo transports); and as yet the program for converting conventional transports to assault transports had hardly begun.* On August 2 the Navy estimated that sufficient assault shipping, trained crews, and rehearsed troops for an operation of the size originally contemplated would not be ready for landings before November 7. The British were against postponing the operation and, to gain time, were willing to skimp on the training and rehearsals of assault units and boat crews.[55] The President sided with them on an early attack and on August 12 directed Marshall to try for an October 7 landing date even if it meant the reduction of the assault by two-thirds. It now fell to Eisenhower and his planning staff to rearrange their plan in the light of available resources and under the pressure for quick action.

In his second outline plan of August 21, Eisenhower set October 15 as a tentative date for the invasion and proposed dropping the Casablanca operation entirely and concentrating on the capture of Oran in Algeria.[56] That having been accomplished, he would move in two directions, eastward into Tunisia and southwest across the mountains into Morocco. This plan seemed to ignore the danger to the Allies' line of communications from the direction of both Gibraltar and Spanish Morocco should Spain join the Axis Powers. It also failed to take sufficiently into account the shortage in naval escorts and the logistical problems involved in funneling all the men, equipment, and supplies needed to seize Algiers, French Morocco, and Tunisia into the port of Oran, whose facilities might not be found intact. The complicated convoy arrangements for the assault, follow-up, and build-up phases of the operation that would have to be made were enough by themselves to doom the plan in the eyes of the military chiefs in Washington as too risky.

In response to continuous pressure from the President and the Prime Minister for an early assault, Eisenhower advanced D Day from October 15 to October 7, when the moon would be in a phase that would facilitate surprise. This date he viewed as the earliest practicable time for the beginning of the invasion. But few informed leaders believed that this date could be met. Admiral King considered October 24 more likely, and even the British planners, who were consistently more optimistic about an early D Day than their American

* Conversion had begun on 10 small vessels taken off the BOLERO run.

colleagues, admitted that meeting the proposed date would require a "superhuman effort." [57]

The most serious problem confronting planners on both sides of the Atlantic continued to be the scarcity of assault shipping. The Navy's original estimate of 14 weeks as the time required to convert conventional ships to assault vessels, train crews, rehearse troops in embarkation and debarkation, load troops and cargo, and sail from ports of embarkation in the United States and the United Kingdom to the destination remained unchanged. This meant that November 7, the date given in the original estimate, would be the earliest possible day for the assault to begin. The Navy might also have pointed to the shortage of landing craft for transporting tanks and other assault vehicles as an argument against an early D Day. LST's were under construction at the time but none were expected to be available before October or November.*

Nevertheless, Roosevelt and Churchill, impatient of delay, continued to insist on an early invasion date. It was such pressure in the face of shipping, equipment, and training deficiencies that was responsible for Eisenhower's August 21 proposal to limit drastically the size of the assault and confine it entirely to the Mediterranean.

The plan found few supporters even among those who made it. Eisenhower himself regarded it as tentative and the date of execution probably too early, because as yet little progress had been made in planning the force to be organized in the United States and not enough was known about scheduling convoys, the availability of air and naval support, or the amount of resistance that could be expected.[58]

So widely varying were the reactions to the plan in Washington and London that a reconciliation of views appeared impossible. Fortunately for the success of the operation, a spirit of compromise developed. By August 24 the British military chiefs were willing to moderate their stand for an early invasion somewhat and even to accept the idea of a Casablanca landing, provided the scope of TORCH was enlarged to include an attack on Philippeville, a port close to Tunisia. Their willingness to make concessions, however, was contingent on a greater naval contribution by the United States.[59] The proposal was unacceptable to the American Joint Chiefs of Staff, who now used the August 21 plan to bolster their original argument that the main blow should be struck in the west, outside the Mediterra-

---

* No LST's actually became available in time for the initial landings but three "Maracaibos," forerunners of the LST's, were.

nean, at or near Casablanca. They would accept an assault on Oran
along with one on Casablanca but none against ports farther to the
east. They were also willing to adjust Eisenhower's directive as he
had requested, bringing his mission more in line with his resources,
but they stubbornly opposed any increase in the U.S. Navy's contribution which would weaken the fleet in critical areas elsewhere in the
world.

Such was the status of TORCH planning when Churchill returned
from Moscow, where he had been subjected to Stalin's taunts because
of the failure of the Western Allies to open up a second front on the
Continent.[60] Only by playing up the military advantages of TORCH
and giving assurances that the invasion would begin no later than
October 30 had he been able to win the Soviet leader's approval of
the operation. Thus committed, it is no wonder that Churchill was
alarmed at the turn matters had taken during his absence from London. With characteristic vigor he at once sprang into action to restore
the strategic concept of TORCH to the shape he believed essential to
success. In a series of messages to Roosevelt, he urged the establishment of a definite date for D Day,[61] and argued eloquently for an invasion along the broadest possible front in order to get to Tunisia
before the Germans. "The whole pith of the operation will be lost,"
he cabled, "if we do not take Algiers as well as Oran on the first
day." [62] At the same time, he urged Eisenhower to consider additional landings at Bône and Philippeville.[63] He was confident that a
foothold in both places could be attained with comparative ease and
expressed the opinion that a strong blow deep inside the Mediterranean would bring far more favorable political results vis-à-vis Spain
and the French in North Africa than would an assault on Casablanca.
He was not opposed to a feint on that port but he feared making it
the main objective of the initial landings. Because of the dangerous
surf conditions, he argued, "Casablanca might easily become an
isolated failure and let loose upon us . . . all the perils which have
anyway to be faced." [64] As to the time of the attack, he would launch
it by mid-October at the latest. To meet that target date, he believed
naval vessels and combat loaders could be found somewhere and out-
loading speeded up.

Roosevelt, equally unwilling to accept a delay, proposed in his reply two simultaneous landings of American troops, one near Casablanca, the other at Oran, to be followed by the seizure of the road
and rail communications between the two ports and the consolidation of a supply base in French Morocco that would be free from de-

pendence on the route through the Strait of Gibraltar. He appreciated the value of three landings but pointed out that there was not currently on hand or in sight enough combat shipping and naval and air cover for more than the two landings. He agreed, however, that both the Americans and the British should re-examine shipping resources "and strip everything to the bone to make the third landing possible." [65] In his reply Roosevelt also conveyed his views on the national composition of the forces to be used in the initial landings within the Mediterranean. Recent intelligence reports from Vichy and North Africa had convinced him that this was a matter of such great political import that the success or failure of TORCH might well depend on the decision made. These reports indicated that in the breasts of most Frenchmen in North Africa an anti-British sentiment still rankled in consequence of the evacuation at Dunkirk, the destruction visited on the French fleet at Mers-el-Kebir, British intervention in the French dependencies of Syria and Madagascar, and the abortive attack by British-sponsored de Gaulle forces on Dakar. Both the President and his advisers were convinced that the strength of this sentiment was such that the inclusion of British troops in the assault was extremely dangerous.[66] Roosevelt therefore insisted on confining the initial landings to American troops.

Churchill did not share the view that Americans "were so beloved by Vichy" or the British "so hated" that it would "make the difference between fighting and submission." [67] Nevertheless he was quite willing to go along with the President's contention that the British should come in after the political situation was favorable, provided the restriction did not compromise the size or employment of the assault forces. At the same time, he appropriately pointed out that the American view on the composition of the assault would affect shipping arrangements and possible subsequent operations. Since all the assault ships would be required to lift purely American units, British forces would have to be carried in conventional vessels that could enter and discharge at ports. This necessarily would delay follow-up for some considerable time should the landings be stubbornly opposed or even held up.[68]

As a result of the transatlantic messages between the two political leaders, a solution to the impasse of late August gradually but steadily began to emerge. On September 3 Roosevelt, who had promised to restudy the feasibility of more than two landings, came up with a new plan in which he proposed three simultaneous landings—at Casablanca, Oran, and Algiers. For Casablanca he proposed a force of

34,000 in the assault and 24,000 in the immediate follow-up (all United States); for Oran, 25,000 in the assault and 20,000 in the immediate follow-up (all United States); for Algiers, 10,000 in the initial beach landing (all United States) to be followed within an hour by British forces. All British forces in the follow-up, the size of which would be left to Eisenhower, would debark at the port of Algiers from noncombat-loaded vessels. All the American troops for the Casablanca landing were to come directly from the United States; all those for Oran and Algiers, from the American forces in the United Kingdom. As for shipping, the United States could furnish enough combat loaders, ready to sail on October 20, to lift 34,000 men and sufficient transports and cargo vessels to lift and support 52,000 additional troops. Total available shipping under U.S. control, he estimated, was enough to move the first three convoys of the proposed Casablanca force. This did not include either the American transports, sufficient to lift 15,000 men, or the nine cargo vessels in the United Kingdom that had previously been earmarked for the TORCH operation. Under the President's proposal, the British would have to furnish (1) all the shipping (including combat loaders) for the American units assigned to take Oran and Algiers except the aforementioned American vessels in the United Kingdom, (2) the additional British troops required for the Algiers assault and follow-up, and (3) the naval forces for the entire operation, less those that the United States could furnish for the Casablanca expedition.

Churchill replied to the American proposal at once, suggesting only one modification of importance, a shift of ten or twelve thousand troops from the Casablanca force to that at Oran in order to give more strength to the inside landings. Unless this was done, he pointed out, the shortage in combat loaders and landing craft would rule out an assault on Algiers.[69]

Roosevelt consented to a reduction of approximately 5,000 men in the Casablanca force and expressed the belief that this cut, along with a previous one made in the Oran force, would release enough combat loaders for use at Algiers. Whatever additional troops were needed for that landing the President believed could be found in the United Kingdom. To these proposals the Prime Minister agreed on September 5.

The scope and direction of the landings were now decided; the "transatlantic essay contest" was over. Only the date of the invasion remained to be settled. The planning staffs in both Washington and London, after six weeks of frustrating uncertainty, could now breathe a sigh of relief and proceed with definite operational and logistical preparation without the harassing fear that the work of one day would be upset by a new development in strategy the next.

The final decision represented a compromise on the conflicting strategic concepts of Washington and London. It sought to minimize the risks to the line of communications involved in putting the full strength of the Allied effort inside the Mediterranean with the ultimate hope of gaining Tunisia quickly. The plan to make initial landings east of Algiers at Philippeville and Bône, advocated by the British, was abandoned, but the assault on Algiers was retained at the expense of the forces operating against Casablanca and Oran. The political desirability of an all-American assault, though probably still valid, was compromised to the extent that British forces were to be used at Algiers in the immediate follow-up and for the eastward push into Tunisia after a lodgment had been attained.

No date was set for the attack. This decision the Combined Chiefs left to Eisenhower, who had a number of matters to consider in making it.[70] Because of broad political and strategic reasons and the normal deterioration in weather conditions in the area of impending operations during the late autumn, the earlier the landings, the better. The vital need for tactical surprise pointed to the desirability of a new-moon period. But in the final analysis, D Day would be determined by the time needed to assemble and prepare necessary shipping, acquire naval escorts, equip American units in the United Kingdom, and train assault troops and landing craft crews in amphibious operations. By mid-September Eisenhower was sufficiently convinced that his logistical and training problems could be solved by late October and so he set November 8 for the attack.[71]

His optimism that this date could be met was not shared by all his staff, particularly those acquainted with the tremendous logistical tasks that remained to be completed. More than the political leaders and strategic planners, they realized that no task forces of the size contemplated could be fully equipped and shipped in the short time remaining, no matter how strongly imbued with a sense of urgency everyone concerned might be.[72] If there was to be an invasion at all in November, they realized that the Allies would have to cut deeply into normal requirements and resort to considerable improvisation. Events were to prove that those who doubted the complete readiness to move on November 8 were correct.

Even in retrospect, it is debatable whether the decision to invade North Africa was the soundest strategic decision that could have been made at the time and under the existing circumstances. If there had to be an operation in the Atlantic area in 1942 that had a chance of success, few students of World War II will argue today with the view that TORCH was to be preferred over SLEDGEHAMMER. The shortage of landing craft and other resources necessary to attain a lodgment in northwest Europe and to sustain it afterward was sufficient reason for the rejection of SLEDGEHAMMER. There was little real doubt but that TORCH would siphon off the necessary men and equipment required for ROUNDUP in 1943. This the American military leaders saw clearly as did the British, although the latter never admitted it openly in conference. The real question therefore remains: Was it wise to embark on an operation in the northwest African area in 1942 at the expense of a possible direct attack against the Continent in 1943? The British as a group and some Americans, notably the President, believed it was; most of the American military leaders and strategic planners thought otherwise.

The preference of the British for TORCH undoubtedly stemmed fundamentally from their opposition to a premature frontal assault on *Festung Europa*. Their inclination for a peripheral strategy was based in part on tradition, in part on previous experience in the war, in part on the desirability of opening up the Mediterranean, and in part on the need of bolstering their bastions in the Middle East. More than the Americans, they knew what it meant to try to maintain a force in Western Europe in the face of an enemy who could move swiftly and powerfully along inner overland lines of communications. Having encountered the force of German arms on the Continent earlier in the war, they naturally shied away from the prospect of meeting it head on again until it had been thoroughly weakened by attrition.

The American military leaders, on the other hand, less bound by tradition and confident that productive capacity and organization would give the Allies overwhelming odds within a short time, believed the war could be brought to an end more quickly if a main thrust was early directed toward the heart of the enemy. In their opinion the enemy, softened by heavy and sustained preliminary bombardment from the air, would become a ready subject for such a thrust by the summer of 1943. They also believed that an early cross-Channel attack was the best way to help the Russians, whose continued participation in the war was a matter of paramount importance. They did not want SLEDGEHAMMER any more than the British, but fought against scrapping it before Russia's ability to hold out was certain. They opposed entry into North Africa because they did not consider it an area where a vital blow could be struck and because they wanted to save ROUNDUP. Churchill, Brooke, and others may assert, as they do, that no cross-Channel attack would have been feasible in 1942 or in 1943 because the Allies lacked the means and the experience in conducting amphibious warfare, and because the enemy was too strong in Western Europe. Marshall and his supporters can contend with equal vigor that had not TORCH and the preparations for subsequent operations in the Mediterranean drained off men and resources, depleted the reserves laboriously built up in the United Kingdom under the BOLERO program, wrecked the logistical organization in process of being established there, and given the enemy an added year to prepare his defenses, a cross-Channel operation could have been carried out successfully in 1943 and the costly war brought to an end earlier. Whose strategy was the sounder will never be known. The decision that was made was a momentous one in which political and military considerations were so intermingled that it is difficult to determine which carried the greater weight. For that reason if for no other, it will be the subject of controversy as long as men debate the strategy of World War II.

Robert W. Coakley

7

The Persian Corridor as a Route
for Aid to the U.S.S.R
(1942)

During World War II, the United States and Great Britain carried on a massive supply program for the U.S.S.R. based on the rationale that the Soviet Union's continuance in the war as an active and powerful ally was a fundamental condition for victory over Hitler's Germany. Until May 1945, common agreement on the necessity for defeating Germany, totally and finally, tended to obscure differences in political aims. American and British leaders—both military and political —agreed that without involvement of the major portion of the German Army on the Eastern Front, any invasion of Fortress Europe from the west would be rendered practically impossible. They therefore accorded to aid to the U.S.S.R. a claim of extremely high priority on Anglo-American material resources. But getting the promised supplies delivered and satisfying the demands of the Soviet Government, a most exacting ally, were onerous tasks. They involved some of the most difficult decisions that the Western Allies had to make. One of the most important of these, reached in August and September 1942, was to give the U.S. Army control of the movement of munitions and supplies to the U.S.S.R. through the so-called Persian Corridor, and to accord that project one of the highest priorities in the Allied scale. This decision was made at a critical juncture of the war against Germany, in a period before the tide had definitely turned in favor of the Allies, when any commitment, however small, of ships, supplies, and trained men had to be carefully weighed in the strategic balance.

Only President Roosevelt and Prime Minister Churchill could make the basic decision that the Americans should have responsibility. But before this basic decision could be given any practical effect, military agencies at several different levels had to formulate plans and estimate the impact of fulfilling them. And it was the United States-British Combined Chiefs of Staff (CCS) who gave the project the final stamp of approval after the military plan was drawn up. The whole process serves as a prime example of the complexity of the processes by which such politico-military decisions are arrived at in the conduct of coalition warfare.[1]

The supply program for the U.S.S.R. took the form of a series of "protocols"—definite diplomatic commitments negotiated at the highest governmental levels stipulating exact quantities of specific types of supplies to be made available to the U.S.S.R. by the United States and Great Britain over a given period of time. The First Protocol, signed at Moscow on October 1, 1941, while the United States was still at peace, covered the nine-month period from that date until June 30, 1942. The Second Protocol was negotiated to cover the period from July 1, 1942 to June 30, 1943 and the Third and Fourth for similar annual periods in 1943-44 and 1944-45.[2] These protocols were the bibles, so to speak, by which supply to the U.S.S.R. was governed. In this way they differed from any other of the Lend-Lease commitments of the United States Government before and during World War II.

To be sure, adjustments in protocol quantities could be made by negotiation with the Russians, and each protocol contained a safeguarding clause stipulating that the fortunes of war might make delivery impossible,* but neither adjustments nor safeguarding clauses provided any genuine avenue of escape from commitments except when the Russians were willing to agree. And pressure from the Russians was relentless, not only for fulfillment of existing commitments to the letter but also for additional quantities and for new weapons that the developing war on the Eastern Front led them to think desirable. The rationale behind the program gave these pressures almost irresistible force despite the sacrifices involved for the Anglo-American effort in the West.

These sacrifices were greatest during the years 1941 and 1942, when British and American resources were under heavy strain to meet even the minimum requirements of their own forces. Every

* For instance, in the Second Protocol the safeguarding clause read as follows: "It is understood that any program of this sort must be tentative in character and must be subject to unforeseen changes which the progress of the war may require from the standpoint of stores as well as from the standpoint of shipping." See footnote 2.

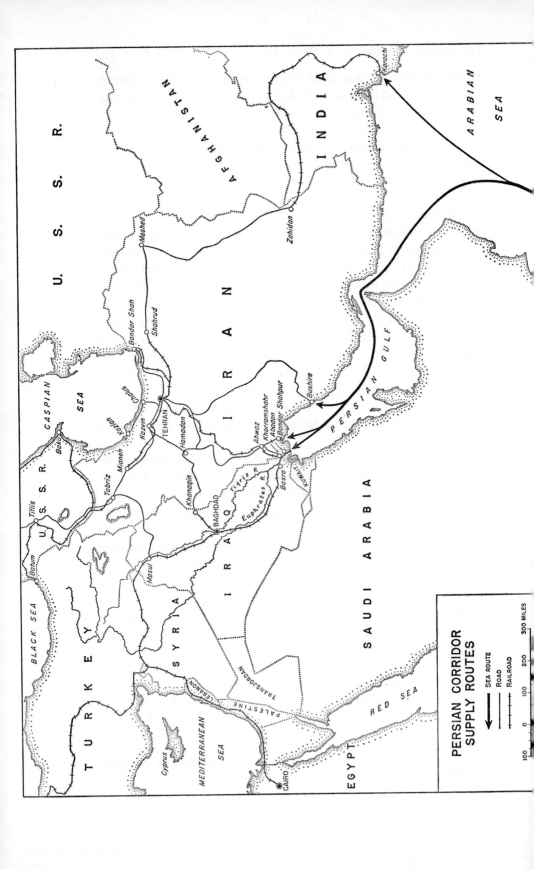

PERSIAN CORRIDOR
SUPPLY ROUTES

SEA ROUTE
ROAD
RAILROAD

0   100   200   300 MILES

military move required a close calculation of the availability of troops, of equipment, and of shipping to transport them. The supplies and equipment promised to the Soviet Union could be made available only at considerable sacrifice to a United States Army in training and a British Army fighting for its life in the Middle East. Shipping, the most crucial resource of all in the period following Pearl Harbor, could also be put on the supply run to the U.S.S.R. only by accepting limitations on the deployment of American and British forces to danger spots around the globe. Yet furnishing the supplies and the shipping in the end proved to be the less difficult part of the task of supplying the Russians; by mid-1942 the central problem had become that of opening or keeping open routes of delivery over which these ships and supplies, made available at such sacrifice, could move to the U.S.S.R.

These routes of delivery were long, roundabout, and difficult. With the Germans in control of most of Western Europe and of French North Africa, the Baltic and the Mediterranean were closed to Allied cargo vessels. This left three main alternative routes for the transport of supplies from the United States to the Soviet Union. The first ran across the Atlantic and around the coast of Norway to Soviet Arctic and White Sea ports, principally Murmansk and Archangel, the second across the Pacific to Vladivostok and over the Trans-Siberian Railway to European Russia, the third around the coast of Africa to the Persian Gulf and thence across Iran to the Soviet border. Each of these routes had its definite limitations. The northern route around Norway was the shortest, but it also was the most vulnerable to attack by German submarines and land-based aircraft. Moreover, winter cold and ice frequently blocked Soviet harbors and rendered sailing conditions for Allied merchantmen scarcely tolerable even without the German threat. The route to Vladivostok ran directly past the northernmost Japanese island of Hokkaido. Ships flying American or British flags could not proceed through waters controlled by the Japanese once Japan had gone to war against Britain and the United States. And even in Soviet-flag shipping, a very scarce commodity in 1941-42, the United States did not dare risk supplies and equipment definitely identifiable as being for military end use. Moreover, the rail line from Vladivostok to European Russia had initially a very limited capacity. The southern route via the Persian Gulf was the only one relatively free of the threat of enemy interference, but in 1941 it possessed an insignificant capacity. Iranian ports were undeveloped and the Trans-Iranian Railway running north to the U.S.S.R.

was rated in October 1941 as capable of transporting but 6,000 tons of Soviet aid supplies monthly, hardly the equivalent of a single ship-load.

In August 1941, by joint agreement with the U.S.S.R., the British moved into control of southern Iran while the Soviet Union took over the northern portion of the country. This joint occupation, regularized by treaty arrangements between the two powers and a new Iranian Government, secured the land area through which supplies trans-ported by sea over the southern route could be carried on to the U.S.S.R. Facilities in Iran to make any considerable flow of aid through this area possible were therefore a basic need from the mo-ment the Western Allies committed themselves to a large-scale Soviet aid program. For a year after the initial occupation, however, preoc-cupation with other tasks, in a period of scarcity of men and materials, combined with Soviet intransigence to delay any positive decision or practicable plan for providing such facilities. During that year the major effort was devoted to forwarding supplies to the Russians over the more vulnerable northern Atlantic route. Only after the Germans had demonstrated beyond any reasonable doubt that they could make this route prohibitively costly, did the United States and Britain de-cide on a concentrated effort to develop the Persian Corridor as an alternate route.

American and British transportation experts in September 1941 freely predicted that the southern route would eventually provide the best avenue for the flow of supplies to the U.S.S.R., but there was little immediate follow-up on this prediction. The Russians insisted on the use of the northern route, evidently both because it promised quicker delivery of supplies closer to their fighting fronts and because they feared the establishment, in Iran, of a strong British or American po-sition so close to the Soviet border. The British, faced with the ne-cessity of developing adequate supply lines for their own hard-pressed forces dispersed through the Middle East from Egypt to India, lacked resources to devote to developing facilities for Soviet aid. On the borders of Egypt and in Libya, the British Eighth Army was engaged in a seesaw battle with the Afrika Korps; in Syria and Iraq the British Tenth Army stood guard against a German drive southward through the Caucasus to the oil fields of Iraq and Iran whence the very lifeblood of the Commonwealth war effort flowed. Immediately after entry into southern Iran, the British prepared a plan for developing transport facilities through their zone to a point where they could carry, by the spring of 1942, 72,000 long tons of

Soviet aid supplies in addition to essential cargoes for British military forces and the Iranian civilian economy; but this plan proved to be more a hope than a promise. Soviet insistence on the use of the northern sea route left the British with no strong incentive to push developments in Iran when the limited manpower and materials available to them were sorely needed to develop supply lines more vital to their own military effort in the Middle East.

Initially, the American position in Iran was anomalous and it remained so even after Pearl Harbor. The United States was not a party to the agreement with the Iranian Government. The American Government, therefore, had to limit its actions in Iran to supporting the British. And before American entrance into the war against Germany, this support had to be rendered through Lend-Lease channels in such a way as not to compromise the neutrality of the United States. At the urgent request of the British, two missions were dispatched to the Middle East in the fall of 1941, one to Egypt under Brigadier General Russell L. Maxwell and the other to Iran under Brigadier General Raymond A. Wheeler, with the justification that they were necessary to make Lend-Lease aid "effective." These missions were instructed to aid the British in the development of their lines of communication, under conditions where British desires as to projects to be undertaken were to govern. Projects were to be financed with Lend-Lease funds and carried out by civilian contractors.

The British plan for development of Iranian facilities was conditioned on the expectation of assistance from Wheeler's mission as well as of large-scale shipments of American Lend-Lease supplies and equipment. Elaborate plans were drawn up, but Pearl Harbor completely disrupted them. Mission projects were shoved far down the scale of priorities while the United States carried out its initial deployments to the Pacific and the British Isles. Mission personnel and material waited at dockside for shipping that could not be allocated. And even when initial U.S. deployments were completed, these priorities were advanced very little. Under arrangements made by the Combined Chiefs of Staff shortly after Pearl Harbor, the whole Middle East was designated a British area of strategic responsibility, just as the Pacific was designated an American one. American strategic plans placed their emphasis on concentration of resources for an early invasion of Europe, and Army planners sought to keep their commitments in support of the British Middle East to a minimum. In the running argument between the British and American Chiefs of Staff over a peripheral strategy versus one of concentration, the Americans won at least a temporary victory in April 1942. In a conference in London at that time, it was agreed that preparations should be made for both an emergency entrance onto the Continent in 1942 to prevent Soviet collapse (SLEDGEHAMMER) and for full-scale invasion in 1943 (ROUNDUP). The build-up in the British Isles for both these purposes (BOLERO) was placed at the top of the American priority scale from April through July, and the Middle East missions continued to be treated as poor relations.

A War Department decision in February 1942 that the missions should be militarized served only to produce additional delays and confusion. Requisite numbers of service troops to perform the tasks planned for civilian contractors were simply not available under the priority the missions were granted. Against a request for more than 25,000 men submitted by General Wheeler as the requirement to carry out projects planned, the War Department decided it could allot but 6,950 troops, and only 654 of these could be moved to Iran before September 1, 1942. This decision, predicated on continuing use of contractor personnel, gradual rather than immediate militarization of contractor projects, and utmost use of indigenous labor, meant that the great bulk of Wheeler's projects had to be placed in a long-deferred second priority. Few even of the contractor personnel had arrived in the Persian Gulf by April 1942. During that month General Wheeler himself was transferred to India to become head of the Services of Supply there and was succeeded as head of the Iran mission by Colonel Don G. Shingler.

Without the extensive American assistance expected, the British were unable to devote enough resources to the development of Iranian facilities to increase significantly the transit capacity through their zone in Iran. Almost inevitably they concentrated their resources in the area on supply installations and facilities around the port of Basra in Iraq, designed to serve their own Tenth Army. The few American contractor personnel who did arrive were assigned the task of developing the port of Umm Qasr in Iraq, designed as a subsidiary port in the Basra complex. Thus the first opportunity to develop Persian Gulf facilities went largely by default.[3]

While the Persian Gulf languished, the Americans and British devoted their main energies toward forwarding supplies over the difficult northern sea route, basically in accordance with Russian desires. This effort mounted to its crescendo in April and May 1942, when the Americans, having completed initial deployments and finally found supplies and ships to transport them to the U.S.S.R., attempted to make up previous deficits in their commitments under the First Protocol. During April some 63 ships cleared American ports headed for north Russia, and plans were laid to send almost as many in May. For the long pull, the President proposed that some 50 American ships be placed in regular monthly service over the northern route from March through November each year, 25 from November through the following March. The Persian Gulf was given but a small role, and the Russians indicated they wanted only trucks and planes delivered thereby. In accordance with this preference, the goal for the southern route was set, in January 1942, at 2,000 trucks and 100 bombers monthly, these to be shipped knocked down, assembled in plants to be operated by contractor personnel under the American mission in Iran, and driven or flown to the Soviet Zone; only small additional quantities of general cargo were to be forwarded over the Trans-Iranian Railway and in the assembled trucks.[4]

This planning in early 1942 ignored latent German capabilities to interrupt shipments around the coast of Norway. Shipping over the northern route proceeded under convoy of the British Navy from Iceland onward, and during 1941 and the early part of 1942 the convoys were virtually unmolested by the Germans. As of the end of March 1942, only 1 ship had been lost out of the 110 that had sailed over the route. But in February Hitler began to shift the weight of his naval and air strength to Norway, and the March convoys, although they suffered small loss, were subject to heavy attack. As the daylight hours in the far north lengthened during April and May, attacks were stepped up, losses mounted, and each convoy became a serious fleet operation making a heavy drain on British naval resources. Churchill and the British Admiralty, fearing that if British naval strength was concentrated too heavily in protecting the Murmansk convoys the Germans would shift their naval strength to the mid-Atlantic, decided in late April that only 3 convoys of 25 to 35 ships each could be sent through every two months. Since planned loadings in the United States had been going forward on the supposition that 107 ships would move in these convoys during May alone, the proposed curtailment came as a heavy blow to Roosevelt's hopes that Allied commitments under the First Protocol could be fulfilled. But deplore the decision as he might, the American President was in no position to offer American naval convoy as a supplement to British, and on May 3, 1942, he acquiesced in Churchill's decision, expressing at the same time the hope that the convoys could at least be kept to the maximum of 35 ships. Even this hope was doomed to disappointment. In the 2 convoys started out from Iceland in May, only 57 ships sailed rather than 70, and of these, 9 were lost, despite heavy naval convoy. Many of the 63 ships sent out from the United States in April merely served to create a log jam of shipping at the Iceland convoy rendezvous, a log jam that was liquidated only by unloading many cargoes in British ports.[5]

Curtailment of the northern convoys made it impossible for the Allies to fulfill their promises under the First Protocol. Yet in the midst of these difficulties, a Second Protocol was negotiated covering the period July 1, 1942, through June 30, 1943, based on the premise, as stated by the President, that strategic considerations required that "aid to Russia should be continued and expanded to the maximum extent possible.[6] The British and American shipping authorities, basing their calculations on the British plan to send through 3 convoys every two months, estimated the capacity of the northern route at slightly more than 3 million short tons during the protocol year and optimistically added another million short tons to be carried via the Persian Gulf. The Pacific route was left entirely out of their calculations. Accepting these tenuous shipping figures as gospel, the President and his advisers offered the U.S.S.R. a total of 4.4 million short tons over the Second Protocol year, about three times as much as was actually delivered under the First Protocol. Though this Second Protocol was not officially signed until October 1942, it actually went into effect in July when the first expired, and from that date forward the Americans and British stood committed to the delivery of this massive tonnage to the U.S.S.R. And in contrast to the First Protocol, in which British and American obligations were approximately equal, the great majority of supplies under the second were to come from American sources.

This first crisis on the northern route inevitably threw the spotlight on the Persian Gulf as the only important alternative for forwarding war supplies to the U.S.S.R. The Russians, now taking a more realistic view of the situation, reversed their previous position and asked that not only planes and trucks but all sorts of military equipment in the largest quantities possible come via the southern route. In cutting back shipments scheduled to move over the northern route in May 1942, the shipping authorities decided to divert 12 ships to the Persian Gulf and to follow with 12 more in June. Harry Hopkins, the President's confidential adviser, wanted to increase this rate and send 8 more monthly if the Persian Gulf could handle them. The Second Protocol schedules, as noted above, proposed shipment of a million short tons via the southern route over the year beginning July 1, 1942.[7]

This decision in May 1942 to speed up shipments to the Persian Gulf was a premature one made in an atmosphere of crisis. It was soon obvious that the cargoes of even the 24 ships sent out in May and June could not be unloaded and sent on to the U.S.S.R. unless more drastic steps were taken to develop Iranian facilities. An effort began almost immediately to push this development, but it was unaccompanied by any realistic appraisal of what was needed, any fundamental upgrading of priorities, or more logical division of responsibilities. The major effort was simply devoted to accelerating unfulfilled plans already on the books. On the American side, the mission in Iran was given a clear directive stating that its primary responsibility would be to facilitate the flow of aid to Russia and not to aid the British, and that projects in Iran should be placed in first priority and those in Iraq and elsewhere in second. Colonel Shingler was told of the new million-ton goal for the Second Protocol year and designated the American representative for executing the program for "receipt, assembly, and forwarding" of the material to be shipped through Iran under these arrangements.[8] As a consequence, the handful of American construction personnel at Umm Qasr quickly transferred the center of their activities to the port of Khorramshahr in Iran. Nevertheless, the position of both the mission and the American Government remained anomalous. The British retained strategic responsibility for the area and direction of the effort to forward supplies to the U.S.S.R.; the American mission's task was still only that of aiding them to effect these deliveries. If the primacy of the task of forwarding supplies to the U.S.S.R. was recognized on the American side, the British were still in no position to place it above their own military needs.[9]

Nevertheless, when the American mission shifted its activities from Iraq to Iran in April 1942, the dimensions of the task to be performed in developing Iranian facilities had at least been generally defined. Reduced to bare essentials, this task involved development of port facilities and of egress roads, increase of the capacity of the Trans-Iranian Railway as far north as Tehran at least tenfold, improvement of existing roads and construction of new ones north from the Persian Gulf ports to the Soviet Zone, construction and operation of aircraft and truck assembly plants, and development of trucking facilities to supplement the carrying capacity of the railroad.

The best developed Iranian port was on the island of Abadan, the site of what was then one of the world's largest oil refineries, owned by the Anglo-Iranian Oil Company. But Abadan figured in British plans for supply to the U.S.S.R. only as a site for delivery of cased aircraft for assembly and of particularly heavy equipment that could not be unloaded elsewhere. The rest of the capacity of the port was reserved for oil shipments. Similarly, Basra in Iraq, the only other well-developed port in the area, was already overloaded with cargo for the British Army, although it also had to serve initially as the principal reliance for handling Soviet-aid cargoes. Any really significant augmentation of shipments to the U.S.S.R. would require development of the Iranian ports proper—Khorramshahr, Bandar Shahpur, Ahwaz, and Bushire—and of the lighterage basin at Tanuma (or Cheybassi) across the Shatt-al-Arab from Basra in Iraq. Khorramshahr and Bandar Shahpur were the key ports, and each initially possessed only one berth capable of handling large vessels. Ahwaz was a small barge port 100 miles up the Karun River from Khorramshahr, Bushire a small port on the east shore of the Persian Gulf whence the main highway in Iran ran north to Tehran.

From Bandar Shahpur the railway ran north via Ahwaz and Andimeshk to Tehran and thence through the Soviet Zone to Bandar Shah on the Caspian Sea, through some of the most difficult mountain terrain in the world. The railway was without adequate high-powered locomotives and rolling stock, the line was laid with light rail, and it lacked an automatic signal system to speed traffic. The British had placed the railway under military control and assigned a force of 4,000 soldiers to run it, but the locomotives and rolling stock promised from the United States were slow in arriving, and the increase in rail capacity came equally slow.

To supplement the railroad, the British had four trucking routes under development, all operated by a quasi-governmental corporation, the United Kingdom Commercial Corporation, using native drivers. Two routes ran wholly within Iran, from Bushire and Andimeshk, respectively, to Tabriz in the Soviet Zone in the northwest. A third ran northwest from Basra through Baghdad, crossed into Iran at Khanaqin on the Iraqi railway, and also terminated at Tabriz. The fourth involved a devious route running by rail out of Karachi, in what was then India, to Zahidan in southeastern Iran, and thence by truck to Meshed in the Soviet Zone in the northeast. This last route was used but infrequently and the Russians objected that deliveries over it provided supplies too far from the fighting fronts. All the routes were over the poorest sort of dirt roads, and United Kingdom Commercial Corporation operations were seriously handicapped by lack of trucks and efficient drivers.[10]

Once it had been concentrated in Iran, the American mission was assigned some of the most essential tasks—construction of additional docks at Khorramshahr, operation of truck assembly plants at Andimeshk and Khorramshahr and of an aircraft assembly plant at Abadan, construction of highways connecting Khorramshahr, Ahwaz, Andimeshk, Tanuma, and Tehran, and assistance to the British in the performance of a variety of other tasks. The British Army and the United Kingdom Commercial Corporation remained in control of all transport operations.[11]

When queried by Lieutenant General Brehon B. Somervell, chief of the Army Service Corps, in May 1942 about Hopkins' project for sending 20 ships per month via the Persian Gulf, Shingler replied that the ports would not be prepared to handle that many (120,000 tons of Soviet cargo) until the end of October 1942, when planned improvements were scheduled for completion, and that even then inland clearance would be limited to 78,000 tons monthly and there would be insufficient storage for the excess until clearance capacity had been improved. He offered little hope that the ports would be able to unload and clear in expeditious fashion the 87,000 long tons of Soviet aid dispatched from the United States during May and the 91,000 tons shipped in June when these cargoes arrived, in July and August. British shipping representatives in the area were even more pessimistic. Undeterred, the Washington authorities cut back these shipments only slightly in July and August, to 63,000 and 66,000 long tons, respectively.[12]

While forwarding these tonnages, Washington and London contributed more by way of pressure for accomplishment than they did by way of sending men and matériel to accelerate the pace of development. The British remained unable to spare either men or resources, and the Americans were reluctant to commit significant additional resources to the Middle East. The handful of Americans present in Iran in April had grown to only slightly more than 1,000 by July 1—817 civilians and 190 military personnel. Though shipments of necessary transportation, construction, and port equipment were expedited, all too frequently delays developed in shipping the most critical items such as port cranes, rail equipment, and heavy construction supplies. The effects of a lack of centralized responsibility and a coordinated plan with high priority were all too apparent.

As a result, in no particular did progress during the three months after the May decision justify optimism. The heavy shipments to the Gulf ports inevitably brought an increasing threat of port congestion. Development of the ports lagged behind Shingler's predictions, and inland clearance, ever the biggest bottleneck, lagged even further. The Trans-Iranian Railway, necessarily the primary reliance, was carrying, as late as August 1942, only 35,770 long tons of supplies for all purposes and of these only 12,400 were supplies for the U.S.S.R. The trucking operations of the United Kingdom Commercial Corporation, never characterized by a high degree of efficiency, were but a poor supplement. While the need for capacity for Soviet aid rose, the British found it necessary to add the burden of supply for the Polish Army they were evacuating through Iran to that of the British military and the Iranian civilian economy. While the two U.S. truck assembly plants at Andimeshk and Bandar Shahpur and the plane assembly plant at Abadan began operations in April, their capacity continued low and was further limited by the lack of adequate port and inland clearance facilities. Such was the situation in the Persian Corridor when the Allies found themselves facing a new and more serious crisis in their effort to maintain even a limited schedule of convoys over the northern route.[13]

On June 27, 1942, convoy PQ-17, the third of the three convoys the British had promised to push through during the two-month period of May-June, departed Reykjavík, Iceland, for the long run to the U.S.S.R. over the northern route. The convoy contained 33 merchantmen—22 American and 11 British—and had an unusually large naval escort. In a grim running battle with German air and sea raiders, 22 of the 33 merchant vessels were lost. Shocked by these heavy losses, the British Admiralty decided to suspend the northern convoys "at least till the northern ice packs melted and receded and until perpetual daylight passed." On July 17 Churchill informed Stalin of the decision, saying that continuation "would bring no benefit to you and would only involve dead loss to the common cause." Stalin's reply was a brutal rejection of the British reasons for halting the convoys and a bitter protest, in the strongest language, against the action taken.[14]

The decision to suspend the northern convoys came at a critical juncture in the affairs of the Anglo-American coalition, when their entire strategic concept for the year 1942 was undergoing drastic revision. In June the war in the Middle East took a dangerous turn. The German commander General Erwin Rommel launched a drive into Egypt opening up a new threat to the Suez Canal and the Middle East oil fields. At the same time, the German drive through the U.S.S.R. was plowing relentlessly forward through the Caucasus, threatening these same oil fields from another direction and raising the possibility of complete defeat of the Soviet Army. In this critical situation, the American staff was forced to reconsider its position and take immediate emergency steps to bolster the British position in the Middle East. Supply aid was stepped up and an American air force (the Ninth) established in Egypt. A new command was set up, United States Army Forces in the Middle East (USAFIME), under Major General Russell L. Maxwell, formerly head of the North Africa mission, and he was allotted the quota of service troops he had previously been denied.

The crisis in the Middle East gave the final death blow to any hopes that SLEDGEHAMMER, the plan to invade the Continent in 1942, could be carried out. The American staff continued to hope that commitments to the Middle East could be kept from interfering with the execution of ROUNDUP, the invasion plan in 1943. But this hope ran afoul of the President's determination that American troops must be put in action against the Germans in 1942. In instructions given to his staff for conferences with the British at London in mid-July, Roosevelt made it quite clear that unless SLEDGEHAMMER could be carried out either an American army must be committed to the Middle East or the invasion of North Africa undertaken. The decision taken at the conference (July 18-25, 1942) was on the invasion of North Africa in the fall (Operation TORCH).[15]

The TORCH decision vastly complicated relations with the Russians at precisely the same time that the northern convoys were suspended. In conversations in May with Soviet Foreign Commissar Vyacheslav M. Molotov, President Roosevelt had given more positive assurances of the opening of a second front in 1942 than the British or even his own staff thought justified. The TORCH decision, in the Russian view, did not conform to these assurances nor did it promise to take much of the pressure off the U.S.S.R. While both Roosevelt and Churchill continued to hope that it would not prevent invasion of the Continent in 1943, both the American and British military staffs were convinced that it would. Thus, the TORCH decision and the cancellation of the northern convoys created a doubly embarrassing situation for the President and the Prime Minister vis-à-vis Stalin. Even if the convoys were resumed in September, they would probably have to be suspended again for at least two months to provide the requisite naval support for TORCH in November. Thus, while the Russians battled for their very existence, the second front in Europe that they had been clamoring for was not to become a reality nor would they receive the supply aid promised under the Second Protocol unless some new means of delivery were found. It promised to be, as Churchill told Roosevelt in September, "a formidable moment in Anglo-American-Soviet relations.[16]

The July crisis evoked a diligent and almost frantic search for alternate means of delivery of supplies to the U.S.S.R. Churchill had long supported an operation (JUPITER) to secure the northern fringes of Norway and thus clear the route for the northern convoys, but neither his own nor the American staff ever looked with favor on this plan. It could, in any event, hardly be carried out except as a substitute for TORCH. The Pacific route to the U.S.S.R. also inevitably came in for increased consideration. Plans were developed for delivering the majority of all planes to the Russians via an air ferry from Alaska to Siberia, but the Russians were at first uncooperative and development of the ferry route was distressingly slow. For a brief moment, the Americans considered sending vessels on the long Arctic route through the Bering Sea and around the northern fringes of Siberia, and actually turned over seven vessels to the Russians for this purpose, but the Russians themselves evidently found the route impractical and placed the vessels instead on the run to Vladivostok. The transfer of more ships to the Soviet flag in the Pacific for use on this Vladivostok run was of course a possibility, but in July and August 1942 it had little to recommend it. The greatest Soviet needs seemed clearly to be for military equipment and supplies that could not be risked on the Pacific route; Vladivostok was a long way from the critical fighting front in the Caucasus; and the outright transfer of ships to the U.S.S.R. involved a complete loss of control over their future use, a very serious thing in view of the general shortage of cargo shipping in 1942.[17]

The finger thus pointed to the Persian Gulf as the only logical alternative to the northern route for the shipment of military supplies; indeed, it had already been pointing in that direction since the first difficulties with the northern convoys in April. But each turn of the strategic wheel had brought some new demand on British and American resources that prevented the assignment of sufficiently high priority, and the diffusion of responsibility between British and Americans had prevented the development of any coordinated plan. Paradoxically enough, the decision to commit additional American resources to the Middle East in June had the practical immediate effect of slowing shipments of men and material to the Persian Gulf, for the highest priority went to getting the Ninth Air Force to Egypt and supporting the British effort in the desert. There were no significant accretions of American personnel in Iran in July and August 1942. And under the new command arrangement, Colonel Shingler's Iran mission was made a service command in the USAFIME Services of Supply.

The crisis in July produced a situation in which either facilities in the Persian Gulf would have to be extensively developed or else the United States and Britain would have to renege completely on their promises under the Second Protocol. Whereas, under the shipping estimates that originally lay behind the Second Protocol, 1 million tons were to be forwarded through Iran during the protocol year, that goal had now to be more than doubled if the southern route was to compensate for the deficiencies of the northern. It was set, in fact, at 200,000 tons monthly, in a situation where the previous goal of 72,000 tons a month, proposed by the British in the fall of 1941, was still far short of attainment. The question for decision, by mid-July 1942, was less whether Iranian facilities should be developed than how, by whom, and to what extent. The welter of confused responsibilities that had characterized the earlier effort had to be resolved and a clear-cut decision rendered on the priority to be given the project. From the very beginning it had been clear that only the Americans had the resources to accomplish the task; but to turn it over to them would require delicate adjustments in relationships as long as the area remained one of British strategic responsibility and the military forces there under British command. In terms of priority, the basic question was the extent to which the BOLERO build-up for invasion of the Continent in 1943, already subordinated to TORCH, should be further subordinated to the effort to ensure continued deliveries of supplies to the U.S.S.R. These were questions that only the President, the Prime Minister, and the Combined Chiefs of Staff could decide. And both because it was primarily American commitments for delivery of supplies that were concerned and because only the Americans had the resources adequate to the task of developing the facilities in Iran to the desired extent, the responsibility for decision lay mainly with the President of the United States.

The President showed no inclination to view the obstacles that had arisen to the continued delivery of supplies to the U.S.S.R. as insuperable. In his instructions to his staff for the London negotiations in July, he answered categorically the question of whether a serious effort should be made to meet the Second Protocol:

> British and American matériel promises to Russia must be carried out in good faith. . . . This aid must continue as long as delivery is possible and Russia must be encouraged to continue resistance. Only complete collapse, which seems unthinkable, should alter this determination on our part.[18]

In taking this position, the President indicated clearly that he thought this aid must flow mainly via the Persian Gulf until the northern convoys could be resumed.

An intensive exploration of the question of how this could be accomplished followed. On July 13, 1942, evidently anticipating the British decision to suspend the northern convoys, Averell Harriman, the President's personal Lend-Lease representative in London, cabled Harry Hopkins calling attention to the need for speed in expanding transit facilities through Iran. His recommendation was that the U.S. Army should take over operation and control of the Trans-Iranian Railway in the British Zone. Admiral Ernest J. King, Chief of Naval Operations, General George C. Marshall, Army Chief of Staff, and General Somervell agreed generally that steps must be taken to increase Iranian transit facilities, but they stopped short of any positive recommendation that the Americans should take over the railroad, pending further study. The President, nonetheless, readily accepted Harriman's proposal. Replying on July 16 to Churchill's formal notification of the suspension of the northern convoys, he placed it before the Prime Minister. Churchill accepted the proposal immediately with some enthusiasm and informally communicated his views to Harry Hopkins, then in London, though he delayed a formal response to the President until the whole matter had been subjected to further study.[19]

In a sense, then, the basic decision that the Americans would take over the task of developing facilities in the Persian Gulf had been taken by the President and agreed to by the Prime Minister by mid-July. But it took two months to make that decision final enough to give it practical effect. Recognition on both sides that the matter needed further study reflected the immense complications of the problem and the fact that it seemed unlikely that merely turning the Iranian railway over to the Americans would provide an adequate solution. It was clear that a much more far-reaching decision was needed which would delineate clearly the dimensions of the task of supplying the U.S.S.R. through Iran, the cost of carrying out such a task, the division of responsibility and the best organization for it, and the priority to be accorded this effort in relation to other essential military and civilian activities in the area. The "further study" consequently took over a month. Many hands entered into it. Brigadier General Sidney P. Spalding, Assistant Executive of the Munitions Assignments Board, went out to the Middle East on a special mission in late July, as the personal representative of General Marshall and Harry Hopkins, to determine on the spot what steps should be taken to increase Persian Gulf capacity for Soviet aid. Churchill and Harriman, after a visit to Stalin in August, returned via Tehran and Cairo also to investigate the situation at first hand. At the hub of the fact-finding stood General Maxwell in Cairo, who, as commander of USAFIME, had a newly assigned responsibility for American operations in the Persian Gulf.

It was less on the highly placed dignitaries, nevertheless, than on the "pick-and-shovel" men, British and American, in the Persian Gulf, that the real job of fact-finding fell. The final estimates on which action was based were gathered together by Colonel Shingler, largely on information received from British transportation authorities in the area. Shingler's tables were postulated on the use of all the Iranian ports and partial use of Basra in Iraq and Karachi in India for cargoes to be cleared through Iran; against a current (August 1942) capacity of 189,000 long tons for all these ports, Shingler proposed a target of 399,500 tons for June 1943. Rail clearance currently running at little more than 35,000 long tons he thought could be increased to 180,000 in the same period under American operation. By providing trucking lines to haul 139,500 tons per month, he would bring total monthly inland clearance capacity to 319,500 tons. Deducting estimated essential requirements of the British military in Iran and the Iranian civilian economy, Shingler figured it would ultimately be possible to forward 241,000 long tons of supplies monthly to the U.S.S.R. This would provide enough capacity to meet the currently accepted goal of 200,000 long tons per month of Soviet aid supplies via the southern route, but it must be kept in mind that Shingler did not believe that target could be met until June 1943, much too late to meet the immediate need for an alternate to the northern route.

In mid-August most of the interested parties—Harriman, Churchill, Spalding, Maxwell, Shingler, and the British commanders in the

Middle East—gathered at Cairo in a conclave that lasted several days. Using Shingler's estimates as their point of departure, but modifying them in several ways, they arrived at a general estimate and plan for action. This plan and estimate Maxwell forwarded to the War Department in Washington on August 22. Excluding Shingler's figures for Basra and Karachi, it set the target for the Iranian ports at 261,000 long tons monthly. The monthly target for the railroad remained at 180,000 tons, but the trucking goal was expanded from 139,500 to 172,000 tons, making a total inland clearance target of 352,000 long tons monthly. To achieve these goals, Maxwell recommended that the U.S. Army take over the operation not only of the railway, but also of the ports—Khorramshahr, Bandar Shahpur, Bushire, and Tanuma—and operate a truck fleet to supplement that of the United Kingdom Commercial Corporation. Troop requirements to meet these objectives were calculated to be 3 port battalions, 2 railway operating battalions, 1 engineer battalion, and 2 truck regiments—a total of approximately 8,365 men, all of whom, Maxwell said, had been included in the troop pool for the Middle East on a deferred priority. Matériel requirements, in addition to organizational equipment for the service troops, were set at 75 additional steam locomotives, 2,200 20-ton freight cars or their equivalent, and 7,200 trucks averaging 7 tons in capacity.[20]

Maxwell's recommendations were contingent on receipt of "specific requests . . . from the British authorities." The specific request came from Winston Churchill to the President on the same day. Churchill said:

I have delayed my reply until I could study the Trans-Persian situation on the spot. This I have now done both at Tehran and here, and have conferred with Averell, General Maxwell, General Spalding and their railway experts. The traffic on the Trans-Persian Railway is expected to reach three thousand tons a day for all purposes by the end of the year. We are all convinced that it ought to be raised to six thousand tons. Only in this way can we ensure an expanding flow of supplies to Russia while building up the military forces which we must move into North Persia to meet a possible German advance.

To reach the higher figure, it will be necessary to increase largely the railway personnel and to provide additional quantities of rolling stock and technical equipment. Furthermore, the target will only be attained in reasonable time if enthusiasm and energy are devoted to the task and a high priority accorded its requirements.

I therefore welcome and accept your most helpful proposal contained in your telegram, that the railway should be taken over, developed and operated by the United States Army; with the railroad should be included the ports of Khorramshahr and Bandar Shahpur. Your people will thus undertake the great task of opening up the Persian Corridor, which will carry primarily your supplies to Russia. All our people here agree on the benefits which would follow your approval of this suggestion. We should be unable to find the resources without your help and our burden in the Middle East would be eased by the release for use elsewhere of the British units now operating the railway. The railway and ports would be managed entirely by your people, though the allocation of traffic would have to be retained in the hands of the British military authorities for whom the railway is an essential channel of communication for operational purposes. I see no obstacle in this to harmonious working.[21]

Harriman followed with a cable to the President the next day, strongly reinforcing the Prime Minister's arguments and Maxwell's recommendations. Maxwell, Spalding, and he all agreed, Harriman said,

(a) that with proper management and personnel and with additional equipment the capacity of the railroad to Teheran can be increased to six thousand long tons a day,

(b) that the British have not the resources or personnel to carry out this program even if we should supply the equipment,

(c) that unless the United States Army undertakes the task the flow of supplies to Russia will dry up as the requirements of the British forces in the theatre increase,

(d) that the importance of the development of the railroad to its maximum cannot be over-emphasized,

(e) that the condition in the Prime Minister's cable of the British retaining control of traffic to be moved is reasonable, offers no practicable difficulty and should be accepted.[22]

While placing his main emphasis on the railroad, Harriman also recommended the dispatch of the 3 port battalions and asked favorable action on the request for trucks and personnel to increase road transport, though he placed the last in a priority second to the railroad and the ports.

On August 25, the President turned both Churchill's and Harriman's cables over to General Marshall with a request that he have a plan drawn up to accomplish what was being proposed and to give his judgment as to whether the United States should accede to the request. Marshall assigned the task to General Somervell's Services of Supply (SOS). Within the SOS primary responsibility fell on Colonel D. O. Elliot, head of the Strategic Logistics Division, working under the general supervision of Brigadier General LeRoy Lutes, Assistant Chief of Staff for Operations. Somervell told his subordinates that he wanted to present the Army Chief of Staff with "a complete study in every respect . . . one that can be regarded as a model." [23]

The resultant SOS Plan, presented by Lutes to Somervell on September 4, 1942, met this high standard in almost every respect.[24] It brought all the earlier proposals on the railroad, ports, and trucking organization together in one single plan for a balanced and self-contained American service command in the Persian Gulf. This command was to be formed in the United States and shipped to Iran by increments to take over from Shingler's sparsely staffed mission, absorbing the latter in the process. Thus, while the SOS Plan was built on the recommendations drawn up at Cairo, it expanded the personnel and matériel recommendations contained in those recommendations considerably, producing a far more accurate estimate of what the project to develop the Persian Gulf would actually cost other efforts. In order to provide for a balanced service command, troop requirements were expanded from the 8,365 in the Maxwell cable to 23,876. While 4,515 of these, road maintenance personnel, were placed in a deferred category, they were to prove in the end as necessary as any of the others. Though the target figures and the estimated numbers of trucks, rail cars, and locomotives remained the same in the SOS Plan as in the Cairo recommendations, the additional organizational equipment for the service troops vastly expanded the total amount of matériel required.

Meeting these requirements, the planners found, would be difficult. The pool of service troops available was small, and a large proportion of those activated had either been earmarked for BOLERO or would be necessary for TORCH. The production of heavy equipment —locomotives, rail cars, and large trucks—was limited, and, outside domestic requirements, most of that under production had been earmarked for the British. As usual, shipping was the most critical commodity of all. The SOS Plan noted that "all troop and cargo ships have been assigned missions [and] any new operations must be at the expense of other projects." If the project was to succeed it must be given a priority second only to the operational requirements of TORCH, and above those of the build-up for the invasion of the Continent in 1943.

Presupposing this high priority, the SOS planners proposed that of the 19,361 troops considered essential for early shipment, 8,969 could be made available by diversion from BOLERO, 8,002 from other troop units already activated (mainly for second priority objectives in Iran and North Africa), and 1,501 from new activations. Of the road maintenance troops in a delayed category, 1,503 would also have to come from the BOLERO troop pool, the rest from miscellaneous sources. One port battalion of 889 men was to be diverted from General Wheeler's Service of Supplies in Karachi where it was reportedly not doing port work. Provision of the locomotives and rail cars would also require diversions from other sources in the Middle East and India, but the major portion would have to come from new production or from the domestic railroads. Trucks presented the most difficult problem of all. It was thought that 500 of 10-ton capacity could be repossessed from a number turned over to the British under Lend-Lease and 600 of capacity unknown withdrawn from a stock at Karachi intended for shipment into China, but for the rest it would be necessary to substitute 2 ½-ton cargo trucks in larger numbers for the trucks of 7-ton capacity requested.

Shipping requirements for men and materials added up, according to Transportation Corps estimates, to a total of 471,000 ship tons. The SOS Plan provided for movement of 11,000 men on the *West Point* and *Wakefield* in late October, the rest on British troopships to be released from deployment of U.S. Air Forces to the Middle East in January 1943. Both movements represented diversions from BOLERO. Cargo shipments should begin October 1 and continue through January at the rate of 110,000 tons, approximately 10 ships per month—again a diversion from BOLERO, but partially compensated for by the fact that the shipping pool would be increased by release of cargo ships originally scheduled to sail over the northern route.[25]

The most difficult question of all was timing. Shingler had estimated that the final targets for port capacity and inland clearance could not be met before June 1943. Both General Spalding and Averell Harriman insisted that this target date could be moved forward to February 1943, and Spalding presented estimates to Somervell on this basis on his return to Washington. The British, remembering their own experience, were extremely dubious that more than half the target could be achieved by February and felt that June would be far more realistic. The SOS planners refused to commit themselves definitely but postulated a "material advancement" of the June target date set by Shingler.[26] The SOS Plan for movement was geared to this "material advancement." Priorities were proposed as, first, rail operations; second, ports; and third, road operations. The 5,004 troops required for the railroads and the 5,016 for the ports (including miscellaneous service and headquarters elements necessary to complement them) could be taken care of in the first troop movement scheduled for October. The equipment for their operations could be made available and shipped in coordination with the troops. They should be in the theater and ready to take over operation of the ports and railroads by the end of the year. The 8,114 troops primarily for truck operations and in third priority would follow in January and should be in the theater at least by early March. The heavy trucks, whose availability was most in question, or smaller substitutes for them, could probably be made available by this time. The essence of the conclusion dictated by General Somervell was that, if high enough priority was given to the movement of troops and supplies, the whole operation was feasible. He ended with the recommendation "that this plan be accepted as the basis of future operation of supply routes in the Persian Corridor." [27]

Somervell submitted the plan to the Chief of Staff, General Marshall, with a draft cable for the President to send to the Prime Minister indicating his acceptance of the latter's proposal and his approval of a plan to put it into effect. But final approval of the plan was not to come through this channel. The Persian Gulf project involved both matters of combined strategy and division of military responsibility in the Middle East that required consideration by the Anglo-American Combined Chiefs of Staff. General Marshall therefore placed the plan before them, and it was they who rendered the final decision.

In consideration of the plan before the Combined Staff Planners (CPS), the British had their opportunity to present their views. The British planners in general accepted the SOS Plan, but they remained more pessimistic about the possible rate of development. They pointed to one glaring contradiction in the American calculations. Iranian ports would be unable, during the months following, to handle shipments of supplies on the scale contemplated for the new American command "without cutting the scheduled Russian shipments and the essential civil and military maintenance commitments." They therefore insisted on a reduction in the schedule of these cargo shipments from 10 to 5 ships per month at the outset, stipulating that it might be increased later at the discretion of the authorities on the spot. Beyond this, the only other revision in the plan proposed by the CPS was to add the barge port of Ahwaz to the list of facilities to be operated by the American command.[28]

Having made what they considered necessary revisions in the plan, the CPS turned to the question of its strategic implications and the problem of division of responsibility between British and Americans in Iran. Its strategic implications were clear. It would "increase the dispersion of . . . U.S. military resources" and "divert personnel, equipment, and ships that are at present set up for other theaters." The greatest effect would be on the build-up in the British Isles for invasion in 1943 and this effect would be felt most severely in the diversion of cargo shipping. The CPS noted:

Transportation required for this plan will reduce the number of sailings for BOLERO to the extent of about 2½ times the number of sailings for the project. On the assumption that 44 cargo ship sailings are required to complete the move, the cost to BOLERO would therefore be a total of 110 sailings during the period of the move. The longer turnaround to the Persian Gulf results in a proportionately larger quantity of shipping being removed from other military operations. The number of cargo sailings monthly may be increased in direct proportion to the reduction of ships allocated to the Persian Gulf for handling lend-lease to Russia. Personnel shipping in ships of 20 knots or better can be made available without interfering with present planned operations of higher priority.[29]

The planners could see no alternative to accepting this cost. "If our shipping losses continue at their present excessive rate along the northern Russian route," they noted, "it may become necessary to use the Persian Gulf route entirely." This statement had additional force in view of developments since July, when the planning for American operation of Persian Gulf facilities had begun. After the two months' suspension during July and August, the British resumed the northern convoys in September using a very heavy naval escort, only to lose some 13 cargo vessels out of 40. Neither this scale of escort nor this rate of loss could be sustained during the early stages of TORCH, and the President and Prime Minister were forced to the decision that the convoys must be canceled again during October and November. While the Combined Staff Planners were weighing the Persian Gulf plan, Churchill and Roosevelt were pondering the question how to break the bad news of the new suspension of convoys to Stalin. "My persisting anxiety is Russia," wrote the British Prime Minister, "and I do not see how we can reconcile it with our consciences or with our interests to have no more PQ's till 1943, no offer to make joint plans for JUPITER [the invasion of Norway], no signs of a spring, summer or even autumn offensive in Europe." [30] It is not therefore surprising that the CPS recommended to the Combined Chiefs "favorable consideration" of the proposition that "the U.S. Army accept responsibility for developing and operating the transportation and port facilities in the Persian Corridor" in accordance with the SOS Plan.[31]

In making this recommendation, the CPS had to resolve finally the old question of the relative responsibilities of British and Americans for movement control. The general principle of Churchill's cable that the United States should operate the transport facilities subject to British allocation of traffic required some definition, and the first version of the plan presented by the British raised definite fears on the American side that they wished to control shipments from the United States as well as internal traffic through the Corridor. American strategic planners in General Marshall's Operations Division, never very enthusiastic about this diversion of American resources from their primary objective of a cross-Channel invasion, thought the United States should not undertake the project with responsibility so divided in the theater. They wished to give first priority to supplies for the U.S.S.R. But British counterobjections to this produced a compromise, if not satisfactory to all, at least acceptable, in the tradition of nearly all Anglo-American wartime relations. The British were to continue to exercise strategic responsibility for the defense of the area against enemy attack and for security against internal disorders. In view of this responsibility, the British Commander-in-Chief of the Persia-Iraq Command would control "priority of traffic and allocation of freight" for movement from the Gulf ports northward. But, recognizing the primary objective of the United States as increasing and ensuring the uninterrupted flow of supplies to Russia, the CPS proposed this statement: "It is definitely understood that the British control of priorities and allocations must not be permitted to militate against attainment of such objective, subject always to the military requirements for preparing to meet a threat to the vital Persian Gulf oil areas." The U.S. Commanding General in the Persian Gulf was granted the right of appeal through the Joint Chiefs of Staff to the Combined Chiefs of Staff on any British decision which he thought would prejudice the flow of supplies to the U.S.S.R. General priority of movement was stated as follows: "Over and above the minimum requirements for British forces consistent with their combat mission, and essential civilian needs, Russian supplies must have highest priority." [32]

These provisions meant that the British control over allocation of freight would not be exercised except in case of imminent threat of a German attack or an Axis-inspired uprising. In normal circumstances, there would be fixed allocations for British military forces and for civilian needs which would be transported as first priority, and all additional capacity would go to the movement of Soviet aid supplies. This delicate matter decided, the Combined Chiefs approved the CPS recommendations on September 22, 1942, without any recorded discussion.

In rendering its decision, the CCS made no definite stipulation as to the priority to be given the Persian Gulf project, apparently on the theory that this must be left to the President. They had, nevertheless, in mid-August adjusted their shipping priorities to give Soviet aid cargoes going via the southern route priority equal to that of military shipments for TORCH and the Middle East and above those for the BOLERO build-up. A Presidential directive giving virtually the same priority to the project for developing Iranian facilities to handle these shipments was therefore almost a foregone conclusion. It was forthcoming on October 2, 1942, when the President instructed Secretary of War Henry L. Stimson that "the project for the operation and enlargement of the Persian Corridor be given sufficient priority and support in the form of men, equipment and ships to insure its early and effective accomplishment." [33] With this directive the SOS Plan as modified by the CCS decision was put into action.

Persian Gulf facilities under American operation eventually provided an adequate substitute for the northern sea route for delivery of supplies to the U.S.S.R., but this development came much later than the planners in August and September 1942 had hoped and much too late to permit fulfillment of American commitments under the Second Protocol. Shipments of both supplies and personnel for the Persian Gulf Command were delayed well beyond the schedule proposed in the SOS Plan. Mistakes were made both in the planning and in the early operations. A trucking fleet that would carry anything like the 172,000 tons proposed in the SOS Plan was never sent. The transition from British to American operation took longer than planned, and the Americans also took longer to make their operation effective. Under British operation, improvement was slow during the latter half of 1942. Approximately 40,000 long tons of Soviet aid were delivered through the Corridor in September 1942, only 51,000 in January 1943. Total tonnage on the Trans-Iranian Railway expanded only from 36,000 in August 1942 to 52,000 in January 1943. Between January and May 1943, the Americans assumed operation step by step and the turnover was generally complete by May 1. During this transition period, total tonnage delivered to the Russians expanded to 101,000 in April, with the railroad carrying 65,000 tons in March. Under complete American operation, the figure for tonnage delivered to the Russians was nearly doubled by September 1943, reaching 199,000, and the railroad achieved a capacity of 175,000 tons in

October. This achievement of the target loads came six months after the date predicted by Harriman and Spalding and three months after the more pessimistic goal proposed by Shingler in August 1942. After October 1943, the Persian Gulf was in a position to forward even more cargo than it proved necessary to send by that route. In the peak month of July 1944, some 282,097 long tons of supplies were delivered to the U.S.S.R. through the Corridor.[34]

The effects of the ultimate success achieved by the American command are clearly apparent in the figures on performance under the various Protocols. On the First and Second Protocols, deliveries were only about 75 per cent of the material promised, while on the third the United States exceeded its promises by 30 per cent and on the fourth had already met 95 per cent of its commitments when the war in Europe came to an end on May 8, 1945, and the schedules were revised. True, a shift in Soviet priorities, after Stalingrad, from military equipment to civilian-type supplies that made possible a far greater use of the Pacific route during this later period also influenced the result, but in large measure it was the opening of the Persian Gulf that made possible so high a scale of shipments, with the northern route intermittently closed throughout the war.[35]

Despite the delays in fulfillment of the goals, then, the decision must be evaluated as a sound one if the rationale of the program of aid to the U.S.S.R. is accepted. The cost involved to the build-up for invasion of the Continent was not a determining factor in postponing that operation until mid-1944. By the time the decision was finally rendered, there were so many other diversions and dispersions of American resources under way or in prospect that the Persian Corridor project was simply one of the minor factors contributing to the delay in concentration in the British Isles.

The principal criticism of the decision then must be that it was belated, unduly slow both in the making and in execution. It was reasonably apparent in October 1941 that the Persian Corridor would have to be extensively developed if supply commitments to the Soviet Union were to be met, and the crisis on the northern convoy route in April and May 1942 made it doubly certain. For a long period, there was a clear contradiction in American policy on aid to the U.S.S.R. Supplies and the ships to carry them were accorded almost the highest priority possible, while the means of developing the only secure route for delivery of the supplies were accorded one of the lowest. This situation had reached the point by July 1942, when the northern convoys had to be suspended, where only a decision at the highest level could resolve it. The President made that decision, ending the contradiction in policy. Yet the necessity for carrying out, almost *de novo,* a survey of requirements needed to perform the task and the means of meeting them delayed even the beginning of fulfillment of the decision for almost two months. It took another year for its complete effects to be felt. The lesson then appears to be that the plans for development of any line of communications must be prepared well in advance, and a decision taken as early as possible on the means to fulfill them. Otherwise, amid the competing claims of a global conflict, the relatively small requirements of such a project tend to get lost in the shuffle of major undertakings, despite the importance they may have for over-all strategy.

In 1942 the importance of the Persian Corridor project for over-all strategy was not inconsiderable. The need for speed must be evaluated in terms of developments on the Russian front in that year. While the Persian Gulf decision was in the making, the Germans were moving steadily forward to their rendezvous with destiny at Stalingrad. If the Persian Gulf facilities had been ready, the amount of British and American supplies reaching the Russians during this critical battle would have been much greater. As it was, the Russians won with what they had and what the British and Americans did in fact contribute. But had the battle gone the other way, as it nearly did, British and American leaders might well have had good cause to regret the fact that the decision to make a concentrated effort to develop the southern route had not been made earlier.

Richard M. Leighton

OVERLORD *versus the Mediterranean*
at the Cairo-Tehran Conferences
(1943)

The long debate between United States and British leaders over the strategy of the European war reached a climax and a turning point at the great mid-war conferences at Cairo and Tehran late in 1943.* Since the decision to invade North Africa, a year and a half earlier, the debate had focused on the war in the Mediterranean, the British generally advocating a bold, opportunistic strategy, the Americans a more cautious one. On the surface, they had disagreed on specifics rather than fundamentals. Few on the American side advocated complete withdrawal from the Mediterranean, and U.S. leaders were as quick as the British to respond to the opportunity offered by the disintegration of Italian resistance in early summer of 1943. They opposed the British primarily on the choice of objectives, especially east of Italy. For their part, the British never questioned the principle that the main attack against Germany in the West, and the decisive one, must eventually be made from the northwest (OVERLORD), not the south. In the meantime, they argued, aggressive operations in the Mediterranean were not merely profitable but even essential in order to waste the enemy's strength and to contain and divert enemy forces that might otherwise concentrate on other fronts. But the debate was embittered by American suspicions that the British intended somehow to sidetrack, weaken, or indefinitely postpone the invasion from the northwest, subordinating it to peripheral and indecisive ventures in the Mediterranean that would serve their own long-range political ends. Since the British consistently disclaimed such inten-

* Code-named SEXTANT and EUREKA, respectively.

182

tions, the issue of OVERLORD versus the Mediterranean could not be debated on that basis—and, indeed, cannot now be proved even to have existed outside the minds of the Americans. For them, nevertheless, it was the real issue, and the question actually debated at Cairo and Tehran—whether OVERLORD should be postponed a few weeks in order to permit small-scale operations in the eastern Mediterranean—was only the shadow.

From the American point of view, the great achievement of the conferences was not the compromise reached on the latter question —essentially a technical matter, worked out on the staff level—but the decision of the Big Three—Roosevelt, Stalin, and Churchill—to make OVERLORD and its southern France complement, ANVIL, the supreme effort of the Western Allies against Germany in 1944. After Cairo-Tehran, Mediterranean strategy continued to be a source of friction, but American leaders seemed to consider the cross-Channel invasion as assured and the issue of OVERLORD versus the Mediterranean as closed.[1]

In November 1943 Allied military fortunes were high. On the Eastern Front Soviet armies had crushed the Germans' summer offensive against Kursk before it had got well under way and had launched a series of powerful counteroffensives, which by late November had driven the enemy across the Dnieper, isolated the Crimea, and, farther north, pushed almost to the Polish border. British and Americans in the Mediterranean had swept through Sicily in July and August, forced the capitulation of Italy, and invaded the peninsula in September, bogging down finally in the mountains south of Rome. The strategic bombing offensive against the German homeland continued with mounting intensity, despite heavy losses, and in early autumn the hitherto lagging build-up of American invasion forces in the British Isles swelled to massive proportions. In the Pacific war, the New Guinea offensive had reached the Huon Peninsula with the capture of the important enemy base at Finschhafen, the South Pacific campaign had advanced to Bougainville in the northern Solomons, and the push across the Central Pacific had begun with fiercely contested landings on Tarawa and Makin in the Gilberts. In the Atlantic, the U-boats had been decisively defeated and shipping losses reduced to negligible proportions. On all fronts except Italy and Burma the Allies were advancing. Germany's defeat was now predicted for October 1944, and the American planning committees had been ordered to produce a scheme for ending the war against Japan within the following year. Optimism ran high.

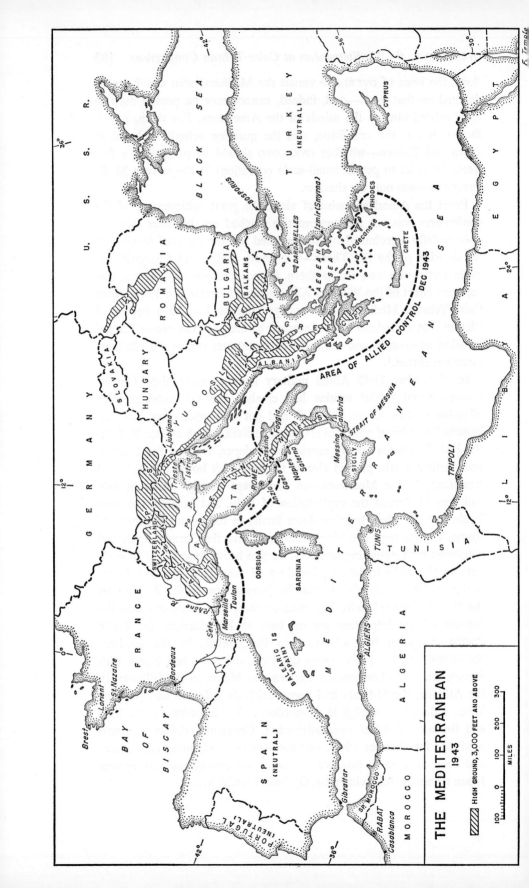

THE MEDITERRANEAN
1943

[///] HIGH GROUND, 3,000 FEET AND ABOVE

MILES
100   0   100   200   300

Behind this optimism lay the realization that men and materials would be available on the scale needed to sustain and quicken the momentum already gained. The immense weight of Soviet manpower and industry, after more than two years of mobilization, was now making itself felt; Soviet armies, backed by masses of reserves and munitions, now had a capacity for sustained offensive warfare that the enemy no longer possessed. In the West, Britain's war effort had passed its peak, with armed forces fully deployed and manpower and industrial capacity fully engaged. American armed forces, on the other hand, though approaching the limits of their planned expansion, were still mostly uncommitted; the bulk of the U.S. Army was at home, waiting to be deployed overseas, and only a handful of divisions had actually seen action in the West. American war industry by now had achieved a productivity that in many categories of munitions actually surpassed foreseeable needs. Military supply programs were already being cut back, and pressures were building up to expand production of civilian goods. The most spectacular achievement of American war production was in shipbuilding. American shipyards in this year poured out 19.2 million dead-weight tons of merchant shipping, which was more than two-and-one-third times as much as had been built in 1942. Early in August, the Joint Chiefs of Staff informed the chairman of the War Production Board that they no longer expected merchant shipping to be the bottleneck of the overseas war effort.[2]

Only one category of supply—landing craft—threatened seriously to limit Allied strategy in 1944. At Cairo and Tehran, indeed, the apparent necessity of choosing between a postponement of OVERLORD and an abandonment of planned or proposed amphibious operations elsewhere was dictated by the shortage of landing craft—more particularly, of one type of landing vessel, the LST (landing ship, tank). Less than 300 LST's were in existence in November 1943, almost all built in the United States. Of these, 139 were in the Mediterranean—67 of them allocated to the British under Lend-Lease—and, except for a small contingent, were all earmarked for transfer to the United Kingdom for OVERLORD as soon as the amphibious phases of the Italian campaign were completed. For OVERLORD, in addition, the United States had agreed the preceding spring to provide 62 more new LST's during the coming winter. The remaining new production of LST's was allocated to the war in the Pacific.[3] *

* A few LST's of special design were constructed in Britain early in the war. In origin, the LST was a British-designed vessel, like virtually all the landing

Production of LST's and other landing ships and craft in the United States had been late in getting under way, reaching large volume only in the winter of 1942-43 and then rapidly falling off. This first wave of production, aimed originally at the now discarded plan for a cross-Channel invasion in spring of 1943 (ROUNDUP), had proved generally adequate, together with the smaller output of British factories and yards, to meet the rather modest needs of Allied amphibious operations before mid-1943.* Even the invasion of Sicily, in some respects the most massive amphibious operation of the entire war (8 divisions were landed simultaneously), was adequately mounted without drawing upon a substantial reserve of U.S. assault shipping in the Atlantic or interfering with planned deployments of craft to the Pacific.[4]

From the Navy's point of view, the whole landing craft production program had been undertaken at the worst possible time—when the Navy was straining to rebuild sea power destroyed or immobilized at Pearl Harbor and in later engagements, in order to gain supremacy in the Pacific, while at the same time trying to break the stranglehold of enemy submarines upon the sea lanes in the Atlantic. The program competed with many other lines of war production for materials—above all, for the steel, engines, and facilities needed to build other types of combatant vessels. A Navy official commented bitterly in April 1943 that the high rate of landing craft construction achieved late in 1942 had been obtained "only by cutting across every single combatant shipbuilding program and giving the amphibious program overriding priority in every navy yard and every major shipbuilding company. The derangement . . . will not be corrected for about six months." [5] As landing craft schedules were terminated or cut back that winter and spring, the Navy pushed the building of escort vessels to meet the revived menace of the German U-boats in the Atlantic, which in March reaped a harvest of more than a million dead-weight tons of Allied shipping.[6] Navy officials candidly wanted no more emergency landing craft programs.

By August 1943, however, pressures were building up to increase the output of landing craft, at a time when, as a result of the abate-

---

ships and craft used in World War II. Under wartime agreements, the United States constructed most of the merchant and amphibious shipping used by both countries, thus enabling Britain, with limited building capacity, to concentrate on expanding its Navy.

* SLEDGEHAMMER, the tentatively planned emergency cross-Channel attack in fall of 1942, had been canceled, partly because of a shortage of assault lift, but for other reasons as well.

ment of the submarine menace, the Navy was cutting back its escort and antisubmarine vessel programs. While the landings on Sicily had been successful, with losses lower than anticipated, the greater part of the entire amphibious fleet in the Mediterranean was tied up for weeks after the initial landings, moving supplies over the beaches and performing other administrative tasks. Other amphibious undertakings were in prospect in the Mediterranean, in southeast Asia, and on the two main avenues of advance toward Japan across the Pacific. The biggest prospective deficit of amphibious shipping, however, loomed in the planned cross-Channel assault, then scheduled, as a result of decisions at the Washington Conference of May 1943, for the spring of 1944. For this undertaking, against what was expected to be the most heavily defended coastline in the world, the assault as then tentatively planned was to be on a scale of only about three and a half divisions with two more afloat, a limit imposed arbitrarily by the predicted availability of assault shipping. At the Quebec Conference* of August 1943 Prime Minister Churchill bluntly called for an immediate increase in American landing craft production, pledging at the same time a maximum effort in his own country, in order to strengthen the OVERLORD assault. The same demand was voiced on the American side in various quarters.

In September and again late in October the Navy, with JCS approval, ordered large increases in landing craft production. Navy officials framed the new program, however, with an eye to the war in the Pacific, not the war in Europe. Large segments of the program were devoted to new types of vessels mainly adapted to warfare in the Pacific—notably LVTA's (armored amphibious tractors—"amtracks") and the new LCT(7), actually a small landing ship—inevitably at the expense of the older types desperately needed in Europe. Nor would the increases become effective in time to help OVERLORD if the operation were carried out early in May 1944. Allocations of new production to OVERLORD were limited to about three months' output, at current low rates, at the end of 1943. To this Admiral Ernest J. King, Chief of Naval Operations, on November 5, promised to add something less than a month's production of LST's, LCI(L)'s, and LCT's, and not all of these seemed likely to arrive in the United Kingdom in time to be used in the invasion.[7]

A month before the Allied leaders assembled at Cairo, U.S. representatives at a conference of Foreign Ministers in Moscow pointed

* Code-named QUADRANT.

to the new landing craft program as indisputable proof that the long-postponed second front would be opened the following spring. In Washington, by contrast, the British were being warned privately that no more new landing craft would be forthcoming for OVERLORD.[8] It was the latter assumption that shaped the options laid before the conferences at Cairo and Tehran.

American military leaders and their staffs, on the eve of the Cairo-Tehran Conferences, were in a mood to force a showdown on the strategy of the European war.[9] As they viewed it, Allied strategy since the decision to invade North Africa had been drifting steadily away from the northwestern Europe orientation, agreed on in April 1942, and into a peripheral line of action that could only end in stalemate. Preparations for a cross-Channel invasion in spring of 1943 had been suspended, the British Isles almost denuded of American troops, and American resources had been diverted into the development of a new line of communications and a new invasion base in North Africa. The decision at Casablanca in January 1943 to attack Sicily had ensured that the Mediterranean would continue to be the main theater in Europe during 1943 and that no cross-Channel invasion could be attempted until 1944 at the earliest. Since then British persuasion and the ineluctable logic of momentum had drawn the Allies deeper into the Mediterranean—into Tunisia, Sicily, Italy, Sardinia, Corsica—and a long, uphill struggle still loomed ahead in Italy. Most alarming to the Americans was the persistent effort of the British to broaden the Mediterranean front eastward—by pressure on Turkey to enter the war, by proposals to seize ports on the Dalmatian coast of Yugoslavia and step up aid to the Balkan guerrillas, and, most recently, by an ill-advised incursion into the Dodecanese Islands which had cost the British several thousand troops killed and captured and untold loss of prestige. Persistent operations by the British in this region raised, in American minds, the dread specter of military operations and political involvement in the Balkan peninsula, a land of inhospitable terrain, primitive communications, and turbulent peoples.

In the light of developments in the Mediterranean, American military leaders discounted the repeated pledges of loyalty by the British to the cross-Channel invasion strategy. They tended to gloss over or ignore the immense investment Britain already had in the cross-Channel operation, the heavy contributions of British shipping to the build-up of American invasion forces and material in the United Kingdom (almost half the entire tonnage used), and the persistent pleas of British leaders for a strengthening of the OVERLORD assault. It was widely believed in American official circles that British leaders feared to come to grips with the German Army on equal terms, that they were haunted, as Secretary of War Stimson put it, by the "shadows of Passchendaele and Dunkirk." [10] Army staff officers, wrestling with the paradox, could only conclude that the great Anglo-American invasion army amassing in the United Kingdom was intended by the British to be "a gigantic deception plan and an occupying force" after the expected German collapse.[11]

In recent weeks American suspicions of British intentions had quickened. At the Quebec Conference in August, the OVERLORD plan prepared by the Anglo-American planning staff in London had been accepted by both sides with little discussion. But the British had rejected an American demand that OVERLORD be given an "overriding" priority over operations in the Mediterranean. Prime Minister Churchill, then and subsequently, had stressed, to a degree that aroused American misgivings, the stipulations written into the OVERLORD plan to the effect that additional forces would be needed if German strength in France exceeded certain levels. As yet, the Americans had not made an issue of this point, since the JCS had approved the stipulations along with the plan. Then, late in October, a crisis had suddenly developed in Italy when it appeared that the Germans were winning the build-up race south of Rome and might soon be in a position to launch a crushing counterattack. Churchill and the British Chiefs of Staff had reacted with what the Americans considered unjustified alarm. The British had proposed the temporary retention in the Mediterranean of all assault shipping earmarked for OVERLORD, and, more disturbing, had intimated that if the situation in Italy continued to deteriorate it might be necessary to postpone OVERLORD beyond its present target date of May 1, 1944. After some discussion, it had been agreed that 68 OVERLORD LST's should remain in the Mediterranean until mid-December, as the theater commander, General Dwight D. Eisenhower, had requested, to help mount an amphibious turning movement around the enemy's right flank south of Rome. But the JCS and their staffs were still worried, as the time for the Cairo meetings approached, over the implied British threat to OVERLORD. For the British Chiefs of Staff had bluntly warned that they intended, at the forthcoming conference, to bring up for reconsideration "the whole position of the campaign in the Mediterranean and its relation to OVERLORD." [12]

Finally, early in November, the Americans received a disturbing hint of the role the Soviet leaders might play at Tehran. At the Foreign Ministers' conference in Moscow late in October, Marshal Joseph Stalin had displayed a lively interest in the operations of his allies in the Mediterranean, and, to the astonishment of the Western representatives, had reacted with bland unconcern when British Foreign Secretary Anthony Eden had hinted that, owing to the worsening situation in Italy, it might be necessary to postpone OVERLORD. Following the conference, Major General John R. Deane, head of the U.S. military mission in Moscow, had been bombarded by complaints from the Soviet staff about Allied inaction in the Mediterranean. Deane had concluded from all this that the Soviets, as he informed Washington, "want to end the war quickly and feel they can do it," and therefore were less interested in OVERLORD, six months or more distant, than in immediate action to draw German strength from the Eastern Front. Deane warned his superiors to expect a Soviet demand at the forthcoming conference for a greater effort in the Mediterranean, including "some venture in the Balkans," even if that meant delaying OVERLORD.[13] Deane's warning caused a furor in Washington, where it was apparently taken at face value. Combined with the disturbing hints from London of an impending attack on OVERLORD, it conjured up nightmarish visions of a concerted Russo-British demand at Tehran for a major shift of effort to the Mediterranean—or worse, to the eastern Mediterranean—at the expense of OVERLORD.[14]

At Cairo in November 1943, the Americans found that the British, too, were ready for a showdown.* "It is certainly an odd way of helping the Russians," declared Churchill after a scathing review of recent setbacks in the Mediterranean, "to slow down the fight in the only theater where anything can be done for some months." [15] The British Chiefs of Staff seized the initiative with a blunt criticism of American insistence on the "sanctity of OVERLORD":

> We must not . . . regard OVERLORD on a fixed date as the pivot of our whole strategy on which all else turns. In actual fact, the German strength in France next spring may, at one end of the scale, be something which makes OVERLORD completely impossible, and, at the other end, something which makes RANKIN not only practical, but essential. . . .† This policy,

---

* The Cairo-Tehran meetings lasted from November 22 through December 7, 1943. At Cairo, Roosevelt, Churchill, and their military advisers met formally for the first time with the Chinese President, Chiang Kai-shek. The Tehran meetings (November 28-December 1) brought the two Western leaders together with Soviet Premier Stalin for the first time. A second series of meetings, attended by British and Americans only, was held at Cairo December 2-7.

† RANKIN was one of several alternative plans for crossing the English Channel in the event of a German collapse before the OVERLORD date.

if literally interpreted, will inevitably paralyze action in other theaters without guaranteeing action across the Channel. . . . It is, of course, valuable to have a target date to which all may work, but we are firmly opposed to allowing this date to become our master. . . .

They were prepared, they asserted, to carry out the cross-Channel invasion "as soon as the German strength in France and the general war situation gives us a good prospect of success," but they insisted that unless the Allies pursued an aggressive course of action in the Mediterranean during the coming winter and spring, such conditions were unlikely to develop.[16]

The ominous implications of this manifesto were hardly borne out, however, by the British Chiefs' concrete program for the Mediterranean. They wanted to advance beyond Rome only as far as the Pisa-Rimini line (the same limit the JCS had in mind); to extend more aid to the Balkan partisan forces in the form of weapons, supplies, technical assistance, and Commando raids; to try to bring Turkey into the war before the end of the year; and, with Turkish consent, to open the Dardanelles (shortest route to the U.S.S.R.) to Allied shipping. The opening move, provided Turkey's support were assured, would be an attack about February 1944 on the largest of the Dodecanese Islands, Rhodes, which commanded the approaches to the Aegean and the Dardanelles. Finally, control of the whole Mediterranean area would be unified under a British commander. (This last the Americans were already prepared to concede, in return for the appointment of a U.S. commander for OVERLORD.) In short, the British hoped by means of a major effort in Italy and what U.S. Ambassador Winant called "bush-league tactics" east of Italy to force the Germans back along the entire Mediterranean front. By the Prime Minister's reckoning, the eastern Mediterranean operations would involve not more than a tenth of the combined British and American resources in the whole theater. But, while all the troops and other means needed were available in the area, the landing ships and craft were scheduled for early transfer to the United Kingdom. To retain them for the required time might mean postponing OVERLORD as much as six weeks or two months—that is, until about July 1, 1944.[17]

As far as Italy and the Balkans were concerned, the U.S. Chiefs had no quarrel with these proposals. They even saw certain advantages in gaining Turkey as an active ally, provided the price paid for intervention was strictly limited. But they doubted the ability of the Turks to hold their own if attacked by the Germans and felt no enthusiasm for another try at Rhodes so soon after the recent disaster.

Moreover, the American staffs challenged the timetables and requirements of the British plan at many points. They doubted whether the
Rhodes operation could be fitted into the LST movement schedules,
even if OVERLORD were postponed to July 1.[18]

The British, however, had an alternative proposal: the necessary
assault shipping for the Rhodes operation might be taken from southeast Asia. In August a new Allied command had been set up in
southeast Asia under Vice Admiral Lord Louis Mountbatten, em-
bracing Burma, Ceylon, Siam, the Malay Peninsula, and Sumatra
(but neither China nor India). Since then the basic divergence of
British, American, and Chinese purposes in the area, not to mention
the differences within each camp, had been sharpened. British aspira-
tions looked primarily south and southeast, toward a restoration of
Britain's prewar possessions and influence in Malaya and the East
Indies. The Americans were more interested in increasing China's
effectiveness as an ally and in gaining bases in China for bombing
and, ultimately, invading Japan. For the British, therefore, Burma was
a stage on the road to Singapore and beyond—one that might, perhaps, be bypassed—while for the Americans it lay on the route over
the Himalayas into China. Although construction had begun early in
1943 on a road from Ledo, in India's Assam Province just over the
Burmese border, to connect with the old Burma Road where it
crossed into China, contact between China and her allies depended
for the present on the airlift. Throughout 1943 supplies delivered
over the "Hump" from India to China each month had not exceeded,
on the average, what could be carried by a single medium-sized
freighter. Competition for this trickle of cargo was fierce. Lieutenant
General Joseph W. Stilwell, Mountbatten's American deputy and
commander of the U.S. China-Burma-India theater (lying partly
within Mountbatten's command), wanted to use the supplies mainly
to equip Chinese forces in China in order to help in the reconquest of
northern Burma, scheduled to begin early in 1944 before the onset
of the spring monsoon. Major General Claire L. Chennault, commanding the U.S. air forces in China, believed the airlift should be
greatly expanded and devoted entirely to support of an air offensive
against Japanese communications in China and with the home islands.
Chennault's program, which promised quicker results at lower cost
than Stilwell's long-range plan of regenerating Chinese armies and
restoring land communications with China, appealed both to the
President and to Chiang Kai-shek, though the latter naturally demanded an airlift large enough to support both programs. Since the

preceding spring the bulk of supplies brought over the Hump had in fact gone to Chennault's air forces. However, Roosevelt's broader aims for China coincided with Stilwell's. His purpose in inviting Chiang to Cairo (over British objections) was, in part, to discuss further economic and military aid—which was imperative, Chiang said, if China were to continue fighting—and, in part, to enlist his cooperation in the forthcoming Burma offensive.

The general plan of this offensive was to launch converging drives into northern and central Burma—by British-Indian forces from the west, by Stilwell's American-trained Chinese from the northwest, and by Chiang's own armies from southern China. Subsidiary features of the plan included a British naval demonstration in the Bay of Bengal by fleet units released from the Mediterranean after the Italian surrender, and an amphibious operation—although where this would be carried out was still somewhat uncertain. A year earlier Stilwell's plan for the reconquest of Burma had included a major amphibious attack on Rangoon; at the Washington Conference of May 1943 this had been scrapped, for lack of assault shipping, in favor of smaller landings near Akyab and on Ramree Island, along the Burma coast just below the Indian border. To mount these operations, a contingent of 6 attack transports, 18 LST's, and a number of smaller craft had been sent to India, arriving there finally, after a protracted holdover in the Mediterranean, early in the fall. Churchill, meanwhile, had come out strongly for an "Asiatic-style TORCH" in the form of a surprise descent on the northern tip of Sumatra (CULVERIN), which the Americans opposed as eccentric to the main effort and his own advisers thought would require more resources than were available. Mountbatten, finally, had proposed a more modest substitute in the form of landings on the Andaman Islands, southwest of Rangoon, in March or April 1944. This operation (BUCCANEER) had been tentatively endorsed by both the British and U.S. Chiefs of Staff, though it, along with the remainder of the whole plan, still awaited formal approval. BUCCANEER was, then, the amphibious part of the general plan (CHAMPION) submitted to Chiang at Cairo.[19]

Immediately the plan ran into heavy weather. Hardly anyone, in fact, had much enthusiasm for BUCCANEER, except perhaps Chiang, who had not been informed of its objective but who independently suggested the Andamans as a suitable objective. Its most serious defect was that it seemed to have little connection with the mainland operations it was intended to support and hardly represented a threat serious enough to provoke a strong reaction. The U.S. Chiefs of Staff preferred it to CULVERIN but were not committed to any particular operation; Admiral King himself favored a landing on the mainland near Moulmein, with a view to cutting across the isthmus to Bangkok, but such an undertaking was not thought feasible with the assault shipping available. Evidently the most that could be said for BUCCA-NEER was that it would provide a base for future amphibious landings on the mainland and for bombing the new Bangkok-Moulmein railroad, which gave the Japanese in Burma direct overland connections with the Gulf of Siam.[20]

Churchill made no secret of his distaste for BUCCANEER and had earlier declared that if he could not have CULVERIN he would send the British assault shipping back to the Mediterranean. At Cairo he expanded on the idea: if the Americans would not accept CULVERIN, and if they refused to postpone OVERLORD the few weeks necessary to carry out the attack on Rhodes and move assault shipping back to the Mediterranean, then why not take the shipping needed for Rhodes from southeast Asia? BUCCANEER might be postponed rather than canceled. As Churchill remarked, "There really cannot be much hurry. The capture of the Andamans is a trivial prize compared with Rhodes, and also it can be undertaken at any time later in the year." [21]

That Churchill was willing to entertain the idea of doing BUCCA-NEER at all, despite his candidly expressed scorn for the operation, was the result of the position taken at Cairo by the Chinese Generalissimo. Chiang immediately branded the whole Burma plan (CHAM-PION) as inadequate. As a price for his participation in a more ambitious one, moreover, he demanded an immediate increase in the airlift far beyond the capacity of available transport aircraft and explicit guarantees from the British that the land operations would be supported simultaneously by major coordinated naval and amphibious attacks. The unreasonableness of the airlift demand, and the arrogance shown by Chiang's subordinates in discussing it with the Western military leaders, caused the latter to close ranks and drove even General Marshall, U.S. Army Chief of Staff, to exasperation.[22] A moderate increase in the airlift was ordered, but the Chinese were told unequivocally that they must choose between an offensive in Burma and expanded ferry operations, since both competed for transport aircraft. As for BUCCANEER, the U.S. Chiefs of Staff did not at first take a strong stand, agreeing to postpone action pending decisions yet to be taken on the broader strategy of the war against Japan and the British role in it. In the CCS, therefore, Chiang's demand for an amphibious operation was carefully and noncommittally "noted," with a promise merely of future "consideration." Churchill, however, sharply challenged Chiang's view of the interdependence of the naval and amphibious phases of CHAMPION and the land operations. He pointed out that, in the absence of accessible bases and because of the time needed to refit and redeploy British naval forces from the Mediterranean, direct naval support could not be provided in the forthcoming spring campaign, even though he could promise that by March strong naval forces would be operating in the Bay of Bengal. Finally, he told Chiang emphatically that no definite undertaking to carry out an amphibious operation in conjunction with the land campaign could be given.[23]

Chiang thus faced defeat on all his demands. Early in the afternoon of November 25 he agreed to the CHAMPION plan as drawn, with the sole stipulations that the British should gain naval superiority in the Bay of Bengal—which Churchill had already promised—and that the plan should include an amphibious operation—to which Churchill was willing to agree if the Americans met his own conditions in the Mediterranean. At the same time, however, Chiang was demanding that President Roosevelt give him something to show for having attended the conference.[24] The President obliged. On the same afternoon he told Stilwell and Marshall he had decided, as a further concession to Chiang, greatly to enlarge the program of equipping Chinese divisions, and, some time on the same day, he seems to have given Chiang a pledge that BUCCANEER would be carried out on the scale and at the time planned.[25]

The President's pledge, of which the British knew nothing, left his military chiefs very little room for maneuver. If the Soviet leaders at Tehran should insist, as the Joint Chiefs fully expected them to insist, on an immediate major effort by the Western Allies in the Mediterranean, with or without OVERLORD, approval of the British program seemed assured. The assault shipping allotted for BUCCANEER, now sacrosanct, could not be made available for Rhodes. If OVERLORD shipping currently in the Mediterranean were used instead, how could it be replaced in time to meet the OVERLORD target date? New American production after January was allotted to the Pacific, and Admiral King bristled at the suggestion of further inroads on this source. The only remaining possibility seemed to be to postpone OVERLORD a few weeks as the British had proposed, thus giving more time to redeploy assault shipping and, incidentally, making available another one or two months' production of landing craft. As Admiral William D. Leahy, remarked, the problem was brutally simple: the JCS had to decide whether or not they could accept a delay in OVERLORD; if they could not, "the problem appeared insoluble." [26]

The President, at least, had been thinking of delay. Back in Washington, former Justice James F. Byrnes, Director of the Office of War Mobilization, had received on November 23 a "very urgent" message from him inquiring whether the output of landing craft could be increased, by means of an overriding priority, during the *first five months of 1944*—an inquiry that made sense only under the assumption that OVERLORD might be postponed beyond May 1, 1944. Byrnes' reply, dispatched on November 25, indicated that substantial increases might be possible in April and later, but virtually none before then. Roosevelt probably knew, therefore, when he promised Chiang an amphibious operation, that if OVERLORD were postponed to July, it could be bolstered by the addition of some 22 new LST's, not to mention 10 more now allocated but unlikely to reach the United Kingdom in time for a May assault—and this without encroaching on Pacific allocations of February and later output.[27]

Final decision had to wait, then, until the Russians showed their hand. At the last Cairo meeting with the British (on November 26) before going to Tehran, the U.S. Chiefs of Staff stressed the sanctity of BUCCANEER, but said little about OVERLORD or the Mediterranean. General Sir Alan Brooke, British Chief of Staff, asked them whether they understood that "if the capture of Rhodes and Rome and Operation BUCCANEER were carried out, the date of OVERLORD must go back." Marshall assured him they did. Would it not be better, urged Brooke perplexedly, to postpone BUCCANEER rather than OVERLORD? What if the Russians should demand both a strong Mediterranean offensive and an early OVERLORD? The situation had become embarrassing. Finally, Admiral Leahy blurted out a broad hint: the U.S. Chiefs of Staff "were not in a position to agree to the abandonment of Operation BUCCANEER. This could only be decided by the President and the Prime Minister." There was little more to say. The Americans accepted the British program as a basis for discussion at Tehran, but on the contradictory assumption that it "would in no way interfere with the carrying-out of operation BUCCANEER." The British left with the distinct impression, as Lieutenant General Sir Hastings L. Ismay, Deputy Military Secretary to the Cabinet, reported to the Prime Minister, that the Americans, now rigid against any tampering with BUCCANEER, contemplated a postponement of OVERLORD "with equanimity." [28]

At the opening general meeting at Tehran, on November 28, the three principals, at Stalin's brusque suggestion, promptly got down to business. Roosevelt noted in his opening remarks the possibility that OVERLORD might have to be postponed "for one month or two or three," and he spoke of the various operations in the Mediterranean that were being considered to relieve enemy pressure on the Eastern Front—in the Aegean, at the head of the Adriatic, and in Italy. OVER-LORD, he pointed out, would draw away more German divisions than any of these, and he urged that, if possible, it not be delayed "beyond May or June." Churchill presented the British case, elaborating on the promising opportunities that could be exploited in the eastern Mediterranean without detriment either to the campaign in Italy or to OVERLORD. How would the Soviet Union, he asked, regard this prospect "even if it meant as much as about two months' delay in OVERLORD?" [29]

Up to this point the atmosphere had been cordial. To the pleased surprise of the Westerners, Stalin opened his remarks with an almost casual promise that the Soviet Union would intervene in the war against Japan as soon as Germany was defeated. This confirmed and strengthened the more tentative offers the Soviet Marshal had made on earlier occasions. But his next words brought the discussion abruptly to a tense climax. He declared bluntly that the whole Mediterranean program appeared to him to involve an excessive dispersion of forces. OVERLORD should be made the "basic" operation for 1944 and all other operations, however attractive, regarded as diversions. He saw only one useful possibility in the Mediterranean, an attack on southern France (which Churchill had mentioned in his opening remarks) followed by a drive northward toward an eventual junction with the main OVERLORD forces—the classic pincers formula, which the Russians had applied so often in their own theater. Why not, he suggested blandly, suspend the Italian campaign immediately in order to release forces for this operation, and then launch OVER-LORD two or three months later? [30]

General Marshall must have been reflecting sardonically, while Stalin was dropping his bombshell, on an innocent remark he himself had made in a meeting of the Joint Chiefs that morning, to the effect that the Soviet demands, whatever they might be, "would probably simplify the problem." [31] Whatever the reasons for the sudden evaporation of Stalin's recently displayed interest in Mediterranean operations, and for his return to the old familiar insistence on a second front—perhaps because, with Soviet armies now at a standstill in the Ukraine, a grand convergence on southeastern Europe no longer promised quick victory—his proposals immeasurably complicated what had been an essentially simple, if baffling, dilemma. The Mediterranean was a "going" theater of war in which the Western Allies had a heavy investment. To stop short on the present line in Italy would be almost as repugnant to the Americans as to the British, and Churchill promptly and emphatically asserted that from the British point of view the capture of Rome was both strategically and politically imperative. Stalin seemed, moreover, not to have grasped the limiting role of shipping and landing craft, or the central problem of timing and sequence that grew out of it. He had to be reminded that the troops in the Mediterranean, except for seven divisions already in transit to the United Kingdom, were irrevocably bound there for lack of shipping to deploy them elsewhere. He missed the point that the southern France operation and the landings in the Adriatic had been suggested as mutually exclusive alternatives and that the Rhodes operation was very modest in scope. When Churchill reminded him of this last fact, Stalin conceded that on those terms the capture of Rhodes might be worthwhile. But if both the Rome and Rhodes operations were to be carried out, or even only the latter, how could a landing in southern France two or three months before OVERLORD (for which Stalin had stipulated no date) be worked into the schedule—unless OVERLORD was postponed? [32]

At this juncture the President, who had been silent during the above exchange, suddenly interposed. Stalin's proposals, he said, had raised a serious problem of timing. A choice must be made: either undertake Churchill's Aegean operations, which would delay OVERLORD a month or two, or, as the Soviet Premier had suggested, "attack [southern] France one or two months *before the first of May* and then conduct OVERLORD *on the original date.*" His own preference, Roosevelt added, was for the latter alternative.[33]

Churchill was caught off balance. Nothing in the President's earlier remarks had suggested any intention to insist on adherence to the May 1 target date over OVERLORD. Roosevelt had, in fact, seemed to accept the idea of postponement, urging only that it be brief. His military advisers, by the end of the Cairo meetings, had seemed resigned to the inevitability of some delay. But by implying now that Stalin himself had demanded a May 1 date (which he had not, in fact, done), the President evidently hoped to enlist his support. If so, it was an adroit maneuver, for Stalin failed to challenge the President's implication. Its significance was not lost on Churchill, who immediately protested against the idea of condemning 20 or more divisions in the Mediterranean to inactivity "solely for the purpose of keeping the May date for OVERLORD," and chided the President for the "rigid timing" of the program he had proposed.[34]

The Russians had shown their hand. For the Americans the nightmare of an Anglo-Soviet demand for a shift to the Mediterranean had been dissipated in the comforting assurance that the Soviet leaders once more stood solidly for the primacy of OVERLORD and shared the American aversion for operations in the eastern Mediterranean. It quickly became clear, moreover, that the Russians also shared American suspicions as to British motives, for in the course of the next day, November 29, both Churchill and Brooke, under Soviet grilling, were repeatedly obliged to go through the ritual of affirming their loyalty to OVERLORD.[35] At a meeting of the military representatives on this same day, the Soviet leaders indicated no very specific notions as to what should be done in the Mediterranean or when. When General Brooke pointed out the risk that a landing in southern France so long in advance of OVERLORD might be crushed before OVERLORD could get under way, the Soviet representative, Marshal Klementy Voroshiloff, merely reiterated rather woodenly his master's statement that the operation would be a valuable complement to OVERLORD. Anyway, he added, Stalin did not insist on a southern France operation. All other undertakings in the Mediterranean, "such as Rome, Rhodes, and what not," were diversions that, if carried out at all, should be "planned to assist OVERLORD and certainly not to hinder it." Evidently the Soviet leader intended to let his allies squabble unhindered over Mediterranean strategy. According to Voroshiloff, however, Stalin did insist on OVERLORD—and "on the date already planned." [36]

Thus the issue was finally joined on the timing of OVERLORD. On this same day, November 29, Roosevelt, now committed to fight for a May OVERLORD and evidently confident that with Soviet support he could win, sent a message to Washington tardily instructing Byrnes to call off the proposed speed-up in landing craft production, since "the increase in critical types . . . does not become effective soon enough to justify change in present construction programs." [37]

At the plenary meeting that afternoon, Stalin set forth his position in the language of an ultimatum. He also pressed for an early appointment of a commander for the operation. Soviet forces, he promised, would match the invasion from the west by a simultaneous offensive from the east.[38] Churchill held the floor for most of the session with a spirited defense of the British Mediterranean program.

He vainly tried to draw out Stalin on his proposal for a southern
France operation, for which, as he pointed out, no plan had yet been
drafted, and he warned, as Brooke had already done, that if the
attack were too weak or launched too early, it would invite disaster.
If, on the other hand, a two-division amphibious lift could be left in
the Mediterranean, bright possibilities opened up—turning movements along the Italian coasts, then a swift capture of Rhodes, and
finally an invasion of southern France in conjunction with OVERLORD.
This might mean setting back OVERLORD by six or eight weeks, or—
and Churchill here introduced the alternative for the first time at
Tehran—the needed assault shipping could be brought back from
India. At all events, Churchill concluded, if the handful of vessels
needed for Rhodes could not somehow be found, it was unreasonable
to suppose that the larger number required for an invasion of southern
France or any other diversionary operation in support of OVERLORD
could be provided. He reminded the Soviet Premier that OVERLORD
could not be undertaken at all unless there was a reasonable expectation of success based on certain specified conditions of enemy strength.
This brought from Stalin his celebrated query: Would OVERLORD be
ruled out if there were 13 instead of 12 mobile German divisions in
France and the Low Countries on D Day? Churchill assured him it
would not.[39]

Stalin made no effort to answer Churchill's arguments. He ignored
the allusion to BUCCANEER, restated his demand for a May OVERLORD,
and indicated his preference for a southern France invasion two or
three months before OVERLORD; if this proved impossible, the operation might be launched simultaneously with OVERLORD or even a little
later. All other operations in the Mediterranean he regarded as diversions. Roosevelt finally interposed to suggest a date for OVERLORD
"certainly not later than 15 or 20 May, if possible." Stalin chimed
agreement. Churchill promptly and emphatically dissented, and the
atmosphere again became tense. Finally, the problem was referred
to the military representatives to work out before the next afternoon,
when final decisions would be reached.[40]

Despite the appearance of a deadlock, the germ of a compromise
had already emerged. Both Stalin and Roosevelt had refrained from
demanding a May 1 date. Before lunch the next day, November 30,
Churchill decided to agree to a date sometime in May, and the British
Chiefs of Staff came to the meeting with their American opposites
that morning with specific proposals worked out on this basis.[41] General Eisenhower would be allowed to keep the 68 OVERLORD LST's

in the Mediterranean until January 15, 1944, in order to ensure the early capture of Rome. This meant, by British calculations, that OVER-LORD could not be earlier than June—but the British Chiefs were willing, in order to satisfy Stalin, to define this as "in May." They were also prepared to support an operation against southern France and, most important, to agree that no assault shipping earmarked for OVER-LORD should be retained in the Mediterranean specifically for the Rhodes operation. The key to this last concession lay in their final proposition: as a result of Stalin's momentous pledge on November 28 to enter the war against Japan after Germany's defeat, they argued, the role of China in the coalition had been automatically reduced, and the whole case for an offensive in Burma in spring 1944, including BUCCANEER, had been weakened. The British now hoped, in short, to persuade the Americans to cancel BUCCANEER and send its assault shipping back to the Mediterranean, where it could be used to help mount the southern France operation—and, as a likely by-product, the attack on Rhodes as well. If the Americans refused to cancel BUCCANEER, the burden would be upon them to find the assault shipping for southern France elsewhere, leaving the same probability that it could also be used for Rhodes.[42]

Meanwhile, the U.S. Chiefs of Staff, feeling confident in the assurance of Soviet support, had worked out their own position. The assault shipping already in the Mediterranean could be safely kept there until mid-January, as General Eisenhower had asked, to support the Italian campaign, without endangering an early May OVERLORD. With what remained after the withdrawals, the Staff estimated, it would be possible to mount a two-division assault against southern France (now labeled ANVIL). This operation, for tactical and strategic reasons, should be launched no earlier than three or four weeks before OVERLORD rather than on the date suggested by Stalin. But the later date would not leave time, the Americans emphasized, to shift any of the landing craft over to the eastern Mediterranean for an attack on Rhodes and get them back to Corsica in time to refit for the ANVIL landings. *Ergo*—no Rhodes operation. The problem, as Admiral Leahy triumphantly summed up, "seemed to be a straightforward one of the date of OVERLORD." [43]

The argument that a southern France operation would be feasible but that a Rhodes operation would not hinged on logistical calculations of an extremely speculative character. While these calculations, involving forward projections of landing craft availability, could not be positively disproved at the time—although the British challenged them at every point—the case for the ANVIL landings seemed particularly flimsy. General Brooke could cite against it the verdict of General Eisenhower, a month earlier, that the assault shipping remaining in the Mediterranean would suffice for no more than a one-division lift, that the build-up following the assault would be very slow, and that no attack on such a scale would be likely to succeed.[44] The British did not believe the OVERLORD shipping could be moved back to the United Kingdom, after mid-January, in time for a May D Day, and they feared, incidentally, that the landing craft allotted for OVERLORD were inadequate.

Caught between contradictory logistical estimates, the discussion deadlocked. Nevertheless, the afternoon deadline was at hand, and the Russians had to be given an answer. The military leaders agreed, therefore (falling back on the subterfuge suggested by the British), that the Russians could be told "we will launch OVERLORD during May, in conjunction with a supporting operation against the south of France on the largest scale that is permitted by [available] landing craft," with a target date, for planning purposes, the same as that for OVERLORD. The advance in Italy would continue as far as the Pisa-Rimini line, and the 68 LST's requested by Eisenhower would be left in the Mediterranean until January 15. The fate of BUCCANEER and the Aegean operations was reserved for discussion at Cairo.[45] Thus, the difficult questions of timing and provision of means raised by Stalin's bombshell on November 28 were left unanswered, and no breath of discord ruffled the meeting of the principals on the afternoon of November 30, when the military decisions were ratified. It was inconceivable, Churchill declared, "that the two nations, with their great volume of production, could not make the necessary landing craft available." [46]

Whatever else they did, the Tehran decisions did not spell defeat for the British program in the Mediterranean. The heart of that program—capture of Rome and advance to a defensible line beyond—now seemed assured, even though it had been the first target of Stalin's attack. The modest proposals for the Balkans had been accepted. American opposition had centered on the Aegean operations, for which Admiral King had warned he would not under any circumstances turn over American landing craft.[47] Nevertheless, the prospects of mounting the attack on Rhodes had been immeasurably improved by the introduction of an assault lift requirement for ANVIL, and Stalin had supported the British view, which was written into the formal conclusions of the Tehran Conference, that Turkey should, if possible, be brought into the war before the end of the year. The attitude of the Turks themselves, on which the whole enterprise would depend, was soon to be tested anew in negotiations at Cairo. At all events, the British left no doubt in American minds that they intended to press forward with their Aegean plans, and that, in view of Stalin's firm pledge of participation in the war against Japan, they now regarded BUCCANEER as fair game.[48]

Back at Cairo, the Anglo-American CCS faced the task of finding enough assault lift to carry out (1) a late May or early June OVERLORD, (2) a simultaneous southern France operation, (3) the British attack on Rhodes, as soon as possible following the impending landings south of Rome, and (4) BUCCANEER, in southeast Asia, still scheduled for March. The British promptly renewed their attack on BUCCANEER. The operation was now even more vulnerable than before, according to Mountbatten's most recent plan which provided for a considerably stronger assault, with increased requirements for assault shipping and carrier-borne aviation. The ends in view seemed hardly commensurate with the cost, for more than 50,000 troops were to be concentrated against a garrison estimated at only about 5,000. The British insisted, moreover, on debating the larger issue of the whole campaign in Burma, which, in view of American plans for the Pacific and Stalin's firm promise to enter the lists against Japan, seemed to them to make little sense. The U.S. Joint Chiefs of Staff were mainly worried lest, in the absence of an Allied offensive in Burma, the Japanese might seize the initiative and overwhelm the precariously defended American air bases in China. But they found it difficult to defend BUCCANEER on its merits. General Marshall candidly admitted that if the operation could be dropped without wrecking the mainland campaign, "he personally would not be seriously disturbed." [49]

Whatever the defects of BUCCANEER, the JCS were, of course, no more inclined than before to release its assault shipping if the craft were to be used to mount an attack on Rhodes. But the British adroitly shifted ground. They now soft-pedaled their Aegean plans (which depended mainly on the outcome of negotiations with the Turks, anyway), and concentrated on the problem of mounting an adequate attack against southern France, to which the Americans were firmly committed. ANVIL, they argued, must not be tailored to the leavings of other undertakings (as implied in the Tehran formula) but should be made strong enough to form a genuine complement to OVERLORD. This meant an assault by at least two divisions, perhaps three. But when the staffs checked their hasty Tehran estimates against the more

ample data available at Cairo, they found that the residual assault lift
in the Mediterranean, after OVERLORD withdrawals, would not exceed
one and two-thirds divisions and might be even less. After a half-
hearted attempt to hew to the Tehran line, the JCS conceded the
need for at least a two-division assault, and on December 4 Admiral
King, in a surprise move, offered to meet the ANVIL assault shipping
deficit from new production previously allotted to the Pacific.[50]

King's offer opened no breach in the opposition of the JCS to the
Rhodes operation, since, as he made clear, the new ships and craft
could not reach the Mediterranean in time to be used for it. On the
other hand, although they almost covered the calculated deficit against
a two-division ANVIL assault, they did not guarantee this operation.[51]
They left no margin for unforeseen contingencies, and many on the
American as well as on the British side considered even a two-division
assault too weak. There was, moreover, growing uneasiness over
OVERLORD's own weakness, even after the allocations of November 5.
Time was growing short. OVERLORD and ANVIL were now designated
the supreme operations for 1944; the responsible commanders were
about to be named, and few doubted that when they reviewed the
existing plans they would demand a more ample provision of means.
At the plenary meeting on December 5 Harry Hopkins, President
Roosevelt's personal aide, elicited from the military leaders, after
some sharp cross-questioning, the remarkable admission that although
they had given the stamp of approval to a two-division ANVIL and a
three-and-a-half division OVERLORD, they believed nevertheless that
both operations should be strengthened.[52]

After two days of discussion at Cairo, the problem had thus taken
on new dimensions. It was no longer a question of mounting the
ANVIL assault at a fixed scale. Now it seemed necessary to provide a
pool of assault shipping large enough to mount both ANVIL and
OVERLORD on a scale as yet undetermined but adequate to give each
a reasonable margin of safety. Precisely how much shipping would
be needed could not be known until the plans themselves were revised and developed in detail. The very uncertainty on this score lent
force to the British argument that it would be folly to commit precious
assault shipping irrevocably to a venture in southeast Asia that even
the U.S. Chiefs of Staff conceded to be of secondary importance.

At the plenary meeting on December 5, Churchill bluntly pointed
out that only the President's unilateral pledge to Chiang stood
in the way of agreement. He suggested that Chiang might be offered
some lesser substitute for BUCCANEER, which itself would then be

postponed until after the monsoon. The remainder of the campaign could be carried out as planned. Hopkins supported this idea. The President, obviously unhappy, finally agreed to the suggestion that Mountbatten's representatives, then in Cairo, and Mountbatten himself should be queried as to what small-scale amphibious operations might be undertaken if he had to give up the bulk of his assault lift. At the same time, the CCS were ordered to re-examine forthwith the two main European operations "with a view to increasing the assaults in each case." Roosevelt's full capitulation swiftly followed. That same afternoon, after consulting with his advisers (only King, in the JCS, held out against postponing BUCCANEER), he sent Churchill a brief message: "BUCCANEER is off." [53]

The Joint Chiefs were not informed of the decision until the next day, but they must have realized, after their meeting with the President, that it could not long be delayed. What now had to be decided were the precise alternatives to be offered Chiang. On the night of December 5 the British and U.S. planners made a list of various amphibious operations that might be undertaken in Burma during the spring, assuming arbitrarily that the shipping to be withdrawn from the theater would comprise most of the LST's, combat loaders, and small aircraft carriers. It was not an impressive list. The Joint Chiefs, studying it the following morning, were inclined to conclude that it might be better to give up serious amphibious ventures in the Southeast Asia Command altogether during this season, and transfer all the BUCCANEER assault shipping back to European waters. The British agreed. The CCS accordingly recommended that major amphibious operations in the Bay of Bengal be delayed until after the monsoon, and that Chiang Kai-shek be offered two alternatives: the mainland offensive as planned, with British naval control of the Bay of Bengal assured, but without BUCCANEER, for which would be substituted carrier strikes, Commando raids, and bombardment of Bangkok and the railroads; or postponement of the mainland offensive, compensated for by increased airlift to China and more rapid development of the long-range bombardment program from bases in China. Later that day Mountbatten's reply came in, stating flatly that sea-borne operations smaller than BUCCANEER would not be worth the effort. He proposed that, in anticipation of Chiang's probable reaction, only limited land operations in northern and central Burma and along the Arakan coast be undertaken, and that the aim of opening the land route to China during this season be abandoned. [54]

By evening of December 6 all knew that the President, without

informing the JCS, had decided to abandon BUCCANEER and, moreover, had already cabled Chiang the bad news, presenting the same
alternatives arrived at by the Chiefs of Staff that morning.[55] Chiang's
reply had not yet been received, but the President was due to leave
Cairo the following morning and the conference decisions could not
wait. Accordingly, the two alternatives presented to Chiang were both
included in the final SEXTANT paper approved by the President and
Prime Minister at the plenary meeting on the night of December 6.

In the light of the Generalissimo's known attitude, there could
be little doubt that he would reject the first; there was considerable
doubt that he would accept even the second. Actually, by ruling out
any worthwhile substitute for BUCCANEER, and so informing the
Chinese leader forthwith, the President had thrown away an option
that might have been acceptable to Chiang, inasmuch as the latter
had never been told precisely what sort of operation was contemplated, but only that it would be a major one. At the time the
conference decisions were approved, however, the leaders had Mountbatten's word for it that nothing less than BUCCANEER would serve.
Later in the month Mountbatten changed his mind, but by then the
President's message had left Chiang in no mood for compromise. In
any case, Mountbatten's small residue of assault shipping was soon to
be swallowed up in the maw of swelling European requirements.
On December 7 the world-wide redeployment of assault shipping
dictated by the SEXTANT decisions began, as the CCS ordered
Mountbatten to send 15 LST's and 6 assault transports—the bulk of
his amphibious fleet—back to European waters.[56]

It has become almost a commonplace in American interpretations
of World War II to say that at Tehran the British were forced to
abandon their reservations concerning OVERLORD. Thus, it is asserted,
the primacy of OVERLORD vis-à-vis the Mediterranean, and, indeed,
its execution were finally assured.[57] Like the classic query, "When did
you stop beating your wife?" this interpretation accepts as fact what is
actually the nub of the issue, namely, the American allegation that
the British, and Churchill in particular, had never intended to go
through with OVERLORD and only resigned themselves to do so under
Soviet pressure at Tehran. In reality, both Churchill and Brooke,
forced repeatedly by the Russians to state their intentions concerning
OVERLORD, did not change their position. At the end of the conference
it was what it had been before: OVERLORD would be the main effort
of the Western Allies in Europe, and, as far as the British were concerned, it would be carried out, as Churchill told Stalin on November

30, "provided the enemy did not bring into France larger forces than the Americans and British could gather there." [58] In essence, this was the reservation already spelled out in the OVERLORD outline plan and accepted by the U.S. Chiefs of Staff themselves. Whether British leaders secretly harbored reservations of a more far-reaching nature is not known now (except by themselves) and probably will never be known. Certainly, the Americans had no basis at the time, other than hearsay, for suspecting that they did. The historian's position is likely to depend largely on where he decides to place the burden of proof—on the Americans to demonstrate that their suspicions were based on fact, or on the British to show that their professions were sincere.

As for Stalin's stand on OVERLORD, it was no more than a restatement of the familiar second front theme dinned into Western ears from the time of the German invasion of Russia down to the Moscow Conference of October 1943. It may be doubted whether Stalin was taken in by the transparently vague formula finally decided on to define the target date for the operation, but there is no indication that he attached any importance to it. His whole attitude at Tehran toward the timing of OVERLORD and supporting operations in the Mediterranean was one of lofty indifference. At all events, his pronouncements on OVERLORD added nothing to earlier Anglo-American agreements on the relation between the cross-Channel invasion and the Mediterranean. The most significant effect of Stalin's position was, not the essentially empty characterization of OVERLORD and ANVIL as "supreme" operations in 1944, but the CCS decision on December 5 to explore the possibility of strengthening the two assaults. This decision, which virtually invited the responsible commanders to demand the means they considered necessary, formally recognized—what the JCS since spring of 1943 had refused to concede—that the limit placed on the size of the OVERLORD assault at the May Washington Conference was arbitrary and unrealistic. In principle, it represented a real vindication of the stubborn efforts by the British since early 1942 to obtain more American landing craft for OVERLORD. How many would actually be forthcoming remained to be seen. For the present, over and above the allotments made at the Washington and Quebec (August 1943) Conferences, the planners could count on the vessels released from southeast Asia, most of about two months of American production of LST's, LCI(L)'s, and LCT's, pledged by Admiral King on November 5 and December 4, a handful of U.S. and British assault transports, and an indeterminate amount of new British LCT's. These additions, it was expected, "should provide a satisfactory lift both for OVERLORD and ANVIL." The expectation proved to be overoptimistic.[59]

With relation to the war in the Pacific, Stalin raised an issue that was welcome to the British and may have been embarrassing to the U.S. Chiefs of Staff. No debate on the question is recorded, but the CCS, in making OVERLORD and ANVIL the "supreme" operations for 1944, agreed that "nothing must be undertaken in any other part of the world" to jeopardize their success. Never before had the cross-Channel operation been underwritten in such sweeping terms; the statement wiped out provisos, insisted upon by the JCS at the Washington Conference in May, that in the face of reverses in the Pacific the United States would be obliged to expand her operations there, even at the expense of the effort in Europe. In principle, at least, the war in the Pacific was now subordinate to the war in Europe.[60]

Coming at the time they did, the decisions at Cairo and Tehran relating to the war in Europe have inevitably taken on a retroactive luster from the dramatic events of the following summer—the invasion of Normandy and southern France, the advance up the Italian peninsula, the sweep across France to the Rhine. The decisions foreshadowed the events; it is less certain that they shaped them as well. To contemporaries, indeed, it seemed as though the whole conference program was going awry almost before the ink was dry. As the Cairo meetings ended, the outlook for the attack on Rhodes was good. The British could reasonably count on using for it the ex-BUCCANEER assault shipping now on its way back to the Mediterranean, since the conference agreements stipulated only that any operations undertaken in the Aegean must be "without detriment" to OVERLORD and ANVIL.[61] Negotiations with the Turks were going well. Less than a week later, the Turks suddenly raised the ante on military aid demanded as the price of intervention, and by December 25 Churchill had abandoned his Aegean plans. Similarly, by the middle of the month the planned landings south of Rome, taken almost for granted at Cairo and Tehran, had been cancelled owing to the failure of the American Fifth Army to reach positions within supporting distance of the target area. Later in the month, they were revived on a larger scale and, after a frantic search for the necessary assault lift, finally carried out late in January at Anzio. ANVIL, too, came under fire almost immediately, as the OVERLORD commanders laid claim to its allotted assault lift, and after protracted debate the plan was canceled. When the Allies finally invaded southern France in mid-August, the operation (renamed DRAGOON) was no longer strategically related to OVERLORD and could not have been justified by the arguments used at Tehran.

As for OVERLORD itself, Stalin's unequivocal insistence upon the operation undoubtedly enhanced the likelihood that it would be carried out, even in the face of an unforeseen increase in German power. On the other hand, the massive preparations for the invasion had already generated a momentum difficult if not impossible to arrest. Any radical change of direction or of emphasis at this time—let alone later—would have caused an upheaval in plans and preparations more costly than many military defeats. As a practical matter, the war in Europe had progressed beyond the point of no return. Even the date was hardly any longer in the realm of strategic decision. After Tehran strategic planning was pointed toward a late May or early June OVERLORD (though the administrative staffs continued for some time to work toward an early May deadline), but in the end the actual date of the launching was shaped, as Churchill has remarked, "mainly by the moon and the weather." [62]

John Miller, Jr.

MacArthur
and the Admiralties
(1944)

On February 29, 1944, one thousand American soldiers landed on a small Japanese island in the Pacific. They were accompanied by a famous American general whose youthful appearance and physical vigor belied his sixty-four years. At the day's end they had killed a few Japanese, lost two killed and three wounded themselves, and captured an airfield. How many more Japanese opposed them was not clear, but in the afternoon the general told them to stay and defend their ground until reinforcements arrived.

The thousand soldiers came from the 1st U.S. Army Cavalry Division; the island was Los Negros in the Admiralties group of the Bismarck Archipelago; the general was Douglas MacArthur, Commander in Chief of all Allied forces in the Southwest Pacific Area. Behind his decision to go to the Admiralties with the thousand men, and to keep them there, lay a complex of decisions and operations. From these decisions blossomed a complex series of events which materially aided the Allied cause.[1]

Seizure of the Admiralties was an integral part of two major Allied offensives: the campaign against the great Japanese air and naval bases at Rabaul, New Britain, in the Bismarck Archipelago, which occupied the Allied forces of the South and Southwest Pacific Areas for nearly two years; and the Allied westward advance along the north coast of New Guinea and into the Philippines. When President Roosevelt, Prime Minister Churchill, and the U.S.-British Combined Chiefs of Staff met at Casablanca in January 1943 to determine

Allied courses of action for 1943, they approved, among other projects, a westward advance through the Central Pacific and a continuation of the campaigns against Rabaul which had begun in 1942 with the seizure of Guadalcanal in the Solomon Islands and the Japanese base at Buna on the Papuan peninsula of New Guinea. Plans of the U.S. Joint Chiefs of Staff and the theater commanders called for the Guadalcanal and Papuan operations to be followed by two coordinated advances involving Allied land, sea, and air forces. Admiral William F. Halsey's South Pacific forces would drive northward through the Solomons to Bougainville while MacArthur's Southwest Pacific forces advanced up the northeast New Guinea coast, crossed the Vitiaz and Dampier Straits, landed on New Britain, and seized the Admiralties to cut the Japanese line of communications to Rabaul. Once Rabaul was isolated by land, sea, and air action, both forces were to converge and capture the base. All operations against Rabaul by South and Southwest Pacific forces after the Guadalcanal campaign were under MacArthur's strategic direction, with Halsey in direct command of the Allied land, sea, and air forces in the South Pacific Area, with the exception of those assigned to the land defense of New Zealand. These were under the New Zealand Chiefs of Staff. Most of the Solomon Islands were in the Southwest Pacific Area.

Capture of Rabaul, as envisaged in early 1943, would advance the Allied cause in several respects. Initial operations in the great series of campaigns were defensive in purpose. They were designed to protect the Allied sea and air lines of communication from the United States to New Zealand and Australia which the Japanese had threatened by moving southward from Rabaul. Offensively, possession of Rabaul would give the Allies a great air and naval base to support MacArthur's projected, but not yet approved, advance along the north coast of New Guinea to the Philippines.[2]

The Joint Chiefs were hardly home from Casablanca when it became obvious that not enough planes and ships could be provided to complete the capture of Rabaul in 1943. In March, therefore, they postponed plans to seize it and its sister base, Kavieng, at the north end of New Ireland until 1944. Deciding on more limited objectives for 1943, they directed MacArthur to advance via the Lae-Salamaua-Finschhafen-Madang area of New Guinea and occupy western New Britain while Halsey moved up as far as southern Bougainville. MacArthur and Halsey executed these missions with efficiency, and by October 1943 New Georgia in the Solomons and Lae, Salamaua,

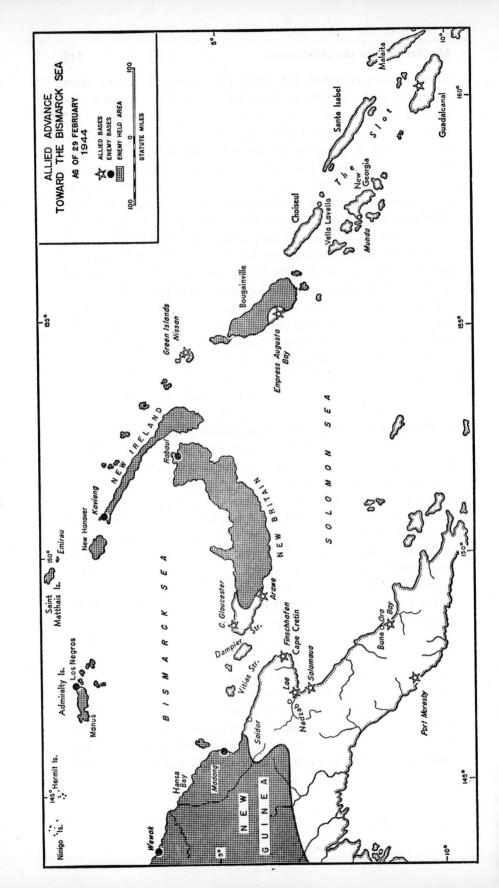

ALLIED ADVANCE
TOWARD THE BISMARCK SEA
AS OF 29 FEBRUARY
1944

ALLIED BASES
ENEMY BASES
ENEMY HELD AREA

STATUTE MILES
100   100

Finschhafen, and Nadzab in New Guinea were in Allied hands. The Allies controlled the air and the sea forward from their advanced bases, and bombers were attacking Rabaul.

But now the Joint Chiefs were considering another change in plans. Whereas in 1942 there had been general agreement that Rabaul should be captured, in June of 1943 members of various Washington planning committees who served the Joint Chiefs were more inclined to bypass Rabaul and neutralize it by air action. They argued that assaulting Rabaul directly was merely a reversal of Japanese strategy and would not gain, for the Allies, objectives worthy of the high price Rabaul's strong and well-equipped garrison would surely exact.[3]

At the same time the Joint Chiefs, preparing to mount amphibious offensives in the Central Pacific beginning with the Gilberts in November 1943, decided to transfer the 1st Marine Division from Mac-Arthur's area and the 2nd Marine Division from Halsey's to the Central Pacific. They also determined to use all of Halsey's assault transports and cargo ships, as well as most of his Third Fleet warships. On June 15 they informed MacArthur of these decisions, but not of their doubts concerning the capture of Rabaul, and asked him for specific information regarding target dates and organization of forces for future offensives so that they could effectively coordinate his moves with those of Admiral Chester W. Nimitz, Commander in Chief of all Allied forces in the Pacific Ocean Area and immediate commander of the Central Pacific subarea.[4] Thus faced with the possibility of a rival offensive that would use divisions and ships he had planned to employ against Rabaul, MacArthur hurled back a vigorous reply. Arguing against the Central Pacific offensive—calling it a "diversionary attack"—he expounded on one of his favorite themes, the virtues of advancing through New Guinea to the Philippines. Withdrawal of the two Marine divisions, he argued, would prevent the ultimate assault against Rabaul. Halsey joined MacArthur to protest removal of the 2nd Marine Division and most of his ships.[5]

The problem was resolved by compromise. Halsey kept part of his transports—enough to move one reinforced division—and some of his warships throughout November 1943. The 1st Marine Division stayed with MacArthur, and the 2nd Marine Division went to the Central Pacific to make its bloody, valorous assault on Tarawa in the Gilbert Islands in November 1943.[6]

By July 21, 1943, the arguments against assaulting Rabaul had so impressed General George C. Marshall, Army Chief of Staff, that he suggested to MacArthur that he seize Kavieng on New Ireland and

Manus in the Admiralties to isolate Rabaul and capture the Japanese
base at Wewak in New Guinea. MacArthur saw it otherwise. Marshall's plan, he asserted, involved too many hazards. Wewak was too
strong for direct assault and should be isolated by seizing a base
farther west. Rabaul would have to be captured rather than neutralized, he insisted, because its strategic location and excellent harbor
made it ideal to support a westward advance along New Guinea's
north coast.[7] His logic is not easy to follow here, as Rabaul was a
more powerful base than Wewak. On the other hand, it was an excellent naval base and Wewak was not.

MacArthur's argument failed to convince Marshall, and when the
Combined Chiefs met with President Roosevelt and Prime Minister
Churchill at Quebec in August they all agreed that Rabaul should
be neutralized and bypassed, that MacArthur and Halsey should
neutralize New Guinea as far west as Wewak and capture Manus and
Kavieng to use as naval bases, and that MacArthur should then ad-
vance along the New Guinea coast to the Vogelkop Peninsula in 1944.
Marshall indicated that Mindanao would be the next objective.[8]

Then followed, in October, November, and December 1943, and
January 1944, the continuous bombings of Rabaul and other Japa-
nese bases in the area, and the invasions of the Treasury Islands, the
Empress Augusta Bay region of Bougainville, Arawe and Cape
Gloucester in western New Britain, and Saidor on the Huon Peninsula
of New Guinea.

The Joint Chiefs and the Area Commanders now turned to preparing specific plans to carry out the general missions agreed on
at Quebec. Actually, operations in the Bismarck Archipelago, in addition to those at Arawe and Cape Gloucester, had been contemplated
for nearly two years as part of the campaign against Rabaul. The
Joint Chiefs' orders which launched the campaigns called for other
operations in the Archipelago, while MacArthur's early plans called
for the capture of Kavieng and of Manus in the Admiralties as well as
Rabaul. In late 1943, MacArthur's plans called for the invasion of
Hansa Bay, New Guinea, on February 1, 1944, to establish a light
naval and air base, and the capture of Manus as well as Kavieng (by
South Pacific forces) on March 1.[9]

The Admiralties, lying 260 miles west of Kavieng and 200 miles
northeast of Wewak, were admirably situated to assist in isolating
Rabaul. They also provided excellent facilities to support the approach
to the Philippines. Responsibility for base construction at Kavieng
and at Seeadler Harbor in the Admiralties was to be Halsey's. Kavieng

was to be a minor fleet base, a PT (patrol torpedo) boat base, and a major air base with six airfields. In the Admiralties, where the Japanese had already built two airfields, Manus would serve as an air base and Seeadler Harbor, 6 miles wide, 20 miles long, and 120 feet deep, was to be a major fleet base with complete repair facilities including drydocks. It would serve Admiral Nimitz' naval forces, as well as Halsey's and MacArthur's.[10]

Halsey, who conferred with MacArthur in Brisbane in late 1943 before departing on a trip to Hawaii and continental United States, opposed seizing Kavieng. He wanted to bypass Kavieng and occupy Emirau in the Saint Matthias group about 90 miles northwest of Kavieng, which had never been taken by the Japanese. Kavieng, on the other hand, was a major air and naval base and was reported to be strongly defended. In December MacArthur told members of Halsey's staff that an attack against Emirau or Kavieng would serve equally well in the isolation of Rabaul.[11]

Halsey spent four days with Nimitz at Pearl Harbor and then, in early January 1944, flew to San Francisco, where he and Nimitz conferred with Admiral Ernest J. King, Chief of Naval Operations. Here, and later in Washington, the South Pacific commander made known his views on Kavieng and Emirau.[12]

Halsey was not able to carry his point at this time. He did, however, discuss timing and naval support for Manus and Kavieng—important questions requiring close coordination now that the Central Pacific offensives were under way.[13] * Kavieng, almost 400 miles from the newly built Allied airfield at Empress Augusta Bay in Bougainville, lay beyond the range of land-based fighter planes from Halsey's most advanced air base. Thus aircraft carriers would have to provide cover for the Kavieng invasion forces, and Nimitz agreed to furnish them. General MacArthur, who had no carriers at this time, also wanted them for the invasion of Manus, in case bad weather kept his planes grounded in New Guinea and at Cape Gloucester. Nimitz warned that bad weather would limit carrier operations too.[14]

But now another problem involving ships had to be settled. Rear Admiral Robert B. Carney, Halsey's Chief of Staff, had visited Pearl Harbor in December and reported that the ships for Kavieng would not be available until May 1. This would certainly postpone the Admiralties operations.[15] Nimitz then suggested that by delaying his

* Nimitz' forces, having invaded the Gilberts in November 1943, were planning their initial move into the Marshalls (Kwajalein and Roi-Namur) in late January.

second Marshalls invasion (Eniwetok) until May 1 he could provide
support for Manus and Kavieng about April 1. MacArthur was ready
and willing to invade Manus and Kavieng in March before moving
to Hansa Bay in New Guinea, but the Joint Chiefs ordered Nimitz to
deliver a strong carrier strike, employing nearly every fast carrier
that was operational in the Pacific, against Truk in the Carolines during March to support and cover the Eniwetok invasion. Naval supporting forces would therefore not be available for Manus and Kavieng
until April at the earliest. Nimitz proposed that representatives of all
the Pacific commands meet in Pearl Harbor to coordinate details and
timing.[16]

The Joint Chiefs, reviewing plans for Pacific operations, ordered extension of operations in the Bismarck Archipelago, and directed
Nimitz to provide fleet support and cover for the Manus-Kavieng
operations but to keep his fleet units under his direct control. At the
same time, he was to attach some additional warships and assault
shipping to MacArthur and Halsey. The exact amounts were to be determined at the forthcoming Pearl Harbor conference, which would
make recommendations to Washington. MacArthur was to continue
his strategic control over Halsey's South Pacific forces.[17]

The conference at Pearl Harbor convened on January 27, 1944.
Halsey, flying out from Washington, had been grounded by bad
weather at Fort Worth and again at San Francisco, and so was not
present. Carney represented him as well as Lieutenant General Mil-
lard F. Harmon, who commanded all Army forces in the South
Pacific. Representing MacArthur were his chief of staff, Lieutenant
General Richard K. Sutherland, and his commanders of Allied air
and naval forces, Lieutenant General George C. Kenney and Vice
Admiral Thomas C. Kinkaid.

Sutherland made it clear that MacArthur wanted Halsey to take,
not Emirau, but Kavieng, for use as an air base. Besides discussing
operations in the Bismarck Archipelago, the conference covered a
wide range of other subjects—the value of the Marianas, B-29's, the
possibility of bypassing Truk, and the comparative merits of the
Central and Southwest Pacific routes to the Philippines. All agreed
that whether Truk was bypassed or taken, Seeadler Harbor was essential as a fleet base for the approach to the Philippines.

Nimitz proposed giving long-range support to the Manus-Kavieng
invasions, with a two-day strike against Truk starting about March
26. In addition, he agreed to send two divisions of fast carriers to

operate under Halsey's command during the invasions, while other carriers and fast battleships operated in covering positions.[18] Forces involved were large. Ironically, they were neither needed nor used, for the operations were not conducted in accordance with these plans.

The advancing Allies now had the initiative, but Japanese decisions and actions, which were forced on the enemy by the Allied offensives, must be understood to grasp the significance of the Allied decisions and actions. Continuous bombardments of Rabaul, and to a lesser degree of Kavieng, reduced Japanese strength so much that on February 19, 1943, there were no warships at Rabaul, and after that date no fighter planes rose to attack the Allied bombers. Such impotence was brought about largely by the South and Southwest Pacific air and naval campaigns, but it was also brought about by Nimitz' naval forces. The Central Pacific Forces invading Kwajalein and Roi-Namur on January 31 had encountered no resistance from the Japanese Combined Fleet, which had suffered crippling losses when it sent most of its planes to Rabaul in late 1943 and lost them. The Kwajalein and Roi-Namur operations came off so well that Allied reserve and garrison forces were not committed.

The Joint Chiefs of Staff told Nimitz they were willing to delay the Manus-Kavieng invasions in order to proceed directly to Eniwetok with the uncommitted troops. Nimitz decided to go there at once and invaded Eniwetok on February 17. In support of this move, he sent the main body of the Pacific Fleet to attack Truk on February 16 and 17, over one month ahead of schedule. The strike was an outstanding success. The Combined Fleet had already escaped toward safer waters, but the U.S. naval pilots destroyed 250–275 planes, as well as thousands of tons of shipping. The Commander in Chief of the Combined Fleet, almost bereft of planes, immediately ordered all naval aircraft out of the Southeast Area—the Japanese area which included eastern New Guinea, the Bismarck Archipelago, and the Solomon Islands. Army aircraft had already been sent to Wewak. Rabaul, though strong in ground troops (about 100,000 in early 1944), artillery, and machine guns, was "compelled to face the enemy with ground resources alone and completely isolated. . . ." [19]

When Halsey learned that Nimitz' plans would postpone invasion of Manus and Kavieng until April he decided to use what forces he could spare to seize a base within fighter range of Kavieng, a decision which culminated in the invasion of the Green Islands, 117 miles east of Rabaul and 220 miles southeast of Kavieng. This was accomplished by New Zealand troops between February 15 and 20, and by March 4 a fighter field was in operation, followed before the end of the month by a bomber field.

By the time Halsey invaded the Green Islands, Southwest Pacific plans for the invasions of the Admiralties and Hansa Bay were well developed. Target date for Manus and Kavieng was April 1. Assigned to the Admiralties were 45,110 men, with the 1st Cavalry Division providing the assaulting troops. All troops were to concentrate at Oro Bay and Cape Cretin, New Guinea. The 6th Infantry Division was designated as GHQ reserve. Hansa Bay, with April 26 as D Day, was to be taken by the 24th and 32nd Infantry Divisions.[20]

As was customary in MacArthur's area, GHQ prepared general plans which assigned forces, missions, and target dates. Operational plans were prepared by the ground, air, and naval commanders and their staffs. To Lieutenant General Walter Krueger, commanding the U.S. Sixth Army and ALAMO Force,* MacArthur gave responsibility for coordination of this planning. Krueger's responsibility gave him a pre-eminent position; he was *primus inter pares*.

During January and the first two weeks of February, General Kenney's planes bombed the Admiralties and Kavieng and also continued earlier attacks against the Wewak airfields. By February 6 the airfields at Momote on Los Negros and Lorengau on Manus in the Admiralties were unserviceable, and no Japanese planes were based at either field. Antiaircraft fire had stopped completely, but not because the guns were destroyed. Colonel Yoshio Ezaki, commanding in the Admiralties, had ordered his troops neither to fire nor to wander about in daylight in order to conceal his positions from the Allies.

At this time Kenney and Major General Ennis C. Whitehead, commanding the Fifth Air Force's Advanced Echelon, were eagerly seeking methods by which the whole advance could be speeded. Whitehead wanted to get the Admiralties out of the way soon so that he could concentrate on Wewak and Hollandia in the west. Kenney, having had experience in New Guinea with quick seizures of airfields by light forces, had another such operation in mind. Some time before February 23 he told Whitehead to hit Momote airfield hard but not to crater the runway. Hoping to force the Japanese to evacuate Los Negros and retire to Manus, he ordered frequent low-altitude photo reconnaissance missions.[21]

* ALAMO, actually the Sixth Army, was theoretically a task force directly under GHQ.

The Allies were not aware that Japanese air resistance in the Southeast Area was a thing of the past and that they had won the air battle. They knew, however, that the enemy was weakening. The runways at Rabaul were usually cratered. On February 21 Allied intelligence reasoned that Japanese aircraft were "absconding" from Rabaul, probably to Truk and other bases in the Carolines.[22]

On February 23—shortly after the great Truk raid and the withdrawal of Japanese aircraft from the Southeast Area, and after the Joint Chiefs and Nimitz had postponed Nimitz' fleet support for Manus and Kavieng by deciding on Eniwetok first—Whitehead forwarded to Kenney a reconnaissance report from three B-25's that had just spent ninety minutes at low altitudes over the Admiralties. They had not been fired on, saw no Japanese, no vehicles, and no laundry hung out to dry. The airfields were pitted and overgrown with grass. The whole area looked "completely washed out." Whitehead recommended that a ground reconnaissance party go in at once to check.[23]

During the year 1943 the Allies had won a resounding series of victories in the Southwest Pacific, and GHQ was now a headquarters wherein optimism prevailed. When Kenney, who even in GHQ was conspicuous for optimism, received Whitehead's message, he was at his office in Brisbane. Concluding that Whitehead was right and "Los Negros was ripe for the plucking," he hurried to MacArthur's office and proposed to MacArthur, Kinkaid, and part of MacArthur's staff that a few hundred troops go to Los Negros on APD's, seize it, and repair Momote airfield at once rather than capture Seeadler Harbor. They could be reinforced and resupplied by air. This should be a reconnaissance in force. If resistance proved too strong the invaders could withdraw. A quick seizure of the Admiralties, Kenney reasoned, would make possible the bypassing of Kavieng and Hansa Bay.[24]

MacArthur made his decision almost at once. Always a man of faith, self-confidence, and buoyant optimism, he saw opportunities where other men saw problems and difficulties. He agreed with Kenney's proposal. Next day he radioed orders to his subordinates to prepare for the reconnaissance at once. He directed that 800 men of the 1st Cavalry Division, a force he shortly increased to 1,000, board two APD's at Oro Bay and sail to Los Negros by February 29.[25]

This decision, obviously made in great haste without benefit of much staff study, but by a general of great experience, deserves examination. MacArthur was sending 1,000 men against an enemy island group approximately one month ahead of the time that his schedule had originally called for a whole division to make the invasion. Kenney's recommendation was based on aerial reconnaissance. Whitehead had said no Japanese troops were in sight, and on February 26 he estimated, but without indicating the basis for his conclusion, that no more than 300 Japanese were holding the Admiralties.[26]

MacArthur's own G-2 (intelligence) section had made a completely different estimate. Brigadier General Charles A. Willoughby, his G-2, kept close track of enemy strength and dispositions at all bases, and especially those slated for invasion. MacArthur and Kenney might be optimists, but a G-2 must be at least half skeptic. Willoughby had to base his conclusions on evidence and logic, not faith. On February 25 he estimated that there were 4,050 Japanese troops in the Admiralties.[27] The 1st Cavalry Division, which would have to pay the price of any faulty intelligence estimates, put enemy strength at 4,900, although its field order for the reconnaissance dutifully stated, "Recent air reconnaissance . . . results in no enemy action and no signs of enemy occupation." [28]

In actual fact, Colonel Ezaki's garrison consisted of the 51st Transport Regiment; the 2nd Battalion, 1st Independent Mixed Regiment; the 1st Battalion, 229th Infantry; and elements of the 14th Naval Base Force. Willoughby's estimate correctly identified these units as present. Although no exact figures for enemy strength can be given today, his figure of 4,050 seems about right. The airmen had not seen troops in the open because Ezaki had ordered them to lie low during daylight hours.[29]

Almost inevitable is the question whether General MacArthur actually accepted Whitehead's figure of 300 and rejected his own G-2's careful estimate. While no categorical answer can be given, the answer would seem to be in the negative. Willoughby's previous estimates of Japanese strength and dispositions in the area had been quite close to the mark. The fact that Willoughby served as MacArthur's G-2 from 1941 through 1951, leaving the post voluntarily and only when President Truman relieved MacArthur of his commands, indicates MacArthur's continued confidence in him. Further, MacArthur ordered the 1st Cavalry Division to prepare a support force—1,500 ground combat troops and 428 Seabees (Navy construction battalion)—to land on D plus 2 if the reconnaissance force stayed. He also alerted the rest of the division to get ready to follow if needed as soon as shipping became available. Sending such a force in to handle only 300 Japanese was surely overdoing the principle of concentration. In making his decision MacArthur apparently accepted the bold Kenney-Whitehead method without accepting their intelligence estimate.

MacArthur decided to accompany the thousand-man reconnaissance force himself to judge from his own observation whether to evacuate or hold. He invited Kinkaid to go along, whereupon the admiral added two cruisers and four destroyers to the four destroyers initially scheduled to escort the APD's. The additions were necessary because a destroyer had neither accommodations nor communications equipment suitable for a man of MacArthur's position. A single cruiser would have served, but it was poor practice to send but one ship of any type on a tactical mission. Kinkaid therefore sent two cruisers, and two cruisers required four additional destroyers as escorts.[30]

General Krueger had originally planned to send a preliminary scouting party to the western tip of Manus, but he now canceled this plan in favor of Los Negros. As plans called for the thousand-man reconnaissance force to slip in through Hyane Harbor, the back door to Los Negros, Krueger did not wish to risk betraying the point of landing by scouting Hyane Harbor and Momote. He therefore sent six scouts by PBY plane and rubber boat to a point one mile south of the harbor on the night of February 27. They found a large Japanese bivouac area on southeastern Los Negros and reported by radio that the area between the coast and Momote was "lousy with Japs." But when the report reached GHQ Kenney discounted it. He argued, and with some reason, that 25 of the enemy "in the woods at night" might give that impression.[31]

The reconnaissance force, supported by air and naval bombardment, landed successfully starting at 7:55 A.M. on February 29. By 9:50 Momote airfield was in American hands; little enemy resistance had been encountered except some shelling by coastal guns at the entrance to Hyane Harbor that gave the landing craft a hard time. By 12:50—H plus 4 hours, 55 minutes—the thousand men were ashore. Two soldiers had been killed, three wounded; sailors of the landing craft crews lost an identical number. Five Japanese were reported killed.

The force commander, Brigadier General William C. Chase, reported "enemy situation undetermined" at 9 A.M.[32] Few Japanese had been seen, but by afternoon it was clear that the island was occupied. Patrols found three kitchens and a warehouse full of rations, and a captured document indicated that some 200 antiaircraft artillerymen were camped nearby.

General MacArthur and Admiral Kinkaid came ashore at 4 P.M.

The General pinned a Distinguished Service Cross on the jacket of the first man ashore, 2nd Lieutenant Marvin J. Henshaw, toured the front, received reports, and quickly made his decision. He directed Chase to "remain here and hold the airstrip at any cost." [33] Having "ignored sniper fire . . . wet, cold, and dirty with mud up to the ears," he and Kinkaid returned to the cruiser *Phoenix,* whence MacArthur radioed orders to send more troops, supplies, and equipment to the Admiralties at the earliest possible moment.[34] The cruisers and six destroyers departed for New Guinea at 5:29 P.M. leaving behind two destroyers to support the cavalrymen.

In ordering the force to stay, MacArthur was obviously confident that it could hold out against the Japanese until supporting forces arrived. He did not say so, but it seems probable that he knew from previous experience that the Japanese would deliver piecemeal counterattacks. If so, he was right. Colonel Ezaki, who did not survive the campaign, received explicit orders from his superior at Rabaul to counterattack with his entire strength.[35] But instead, starting that very night, he launched a series of very resolute, but piecemeal, uncoordinated attacks that failed. The support forces arrived in time, cleared Los Negros hastily, then took Lorengau airfield and cleared the rest of Manus in more leisurely fashion.

Momote airfield, first used by Allied aircraft in March, was ready for heavy bombers by May 18. Lorengau airfield proved unusable, but Army aviation engineers and Seabees finished another one on April 21. Seabees installed two runways for carrier aircraft on the outlying islands and developed Seeadler Harbor into one of the largest naval bases in the Pacific.[36] As planned, the naval base serviced the Third, Fifth, and Seventh Fleets in later operations, and the airfields supported the drives along the New Guinea coast and through the Central Pacific.

MacArthur's bold decisions had repercussions that made themselves manifest far beyond the confines of Hyane Harbor. He and his staff for some time had been convinced that the invasion of Hansa Bay in New Guinea was not a worthwhile move. On March 3, just after the reconnaissance force had landed in the Admiralties, his staff agreed that since Rabaul and Kavieng were now so much weaker it might be possible to bypass Hansa Bay and advance beyond Wewak in a long leap forward beyond the range of land-based fighter planes if carrier aviation could be provided.[37] MacArthur took up the question with the Joint Chiefs of Staff by radio two days later. Explaining that complete occupation of the Admiralties would soon follow, he urged that the success of the reconnaissance provided an excellent opportunity to speed up the war and advance west along the north coast of New Guinea. He suggested that his forces seize Kavieng at once, bypass Hansa Bay, and advance beyond Wewak all the way to Hollandia in Netherlands New Guinea if Admiral Nimitz' carriers could provide fighter cover. This would bypass the main strength of the Japanese 18th Army, then at Madang and Wewak, and speed the advance to the Vogelkop by several months.[38]

The Joint Chiefs, undoubtedly influenced by Halsey's arguments against Kavieng, as well as by MacArthur's proposals, told MacArthur on March 12 that his cherished dream of returning to the Philippines would come true. They ordered that the Kavieng plan be canceled, that Emirau be seized instead, that Kavieng and Rabaul be isolated with minimum forces, and authorized bypassing Hansa Bay in favor of the invasion of Hollandia which Nimitz' aircraft carriers would support. The latter would be the first direct move in MacArthur's long-hoped-for advance to the Philippines.[39]

As a result, MacArthur's forces invaded Hollandia on April 22, just a little later than the time the Manus-Kavieng operations might have been executed had he not made the decisions in February to go to the Admiralties to reconnoiter—and to stay there. These decisions, as they turned out, had the very great virtue of hastening victory while reducing the number of dead and wounded. Along with the decisions of Admirals Nimitz and Halsey, they shortened the war by at least one month, rendered several scheduled invasions unnecessary, and thus saved precious lives.

Ralph S. Mavrogordato

10

Hitler's Decision on the
Defense of Italy
(1943-1944)

Hitler's decision on the defense of Italy falls into the category of decisions made by a chief of state acting as commander in chief of the state's armed forces. In his decision on a counteroffensive through the Ardennes, he overruled his military advisers; in his decisions on the defense of Italy, he chose between the conflicting recommendations of the two commanders best qualified to advise him.

The decision not to yield southern Italy after the Anglo-American invasion of the mainland in September 1943 led to some of the bloodiest battles of the war. The Rapido River, Monte Cassino, and Anzio left an indelible imprint on the history of World War II. These battles became necessary when Hitler reversed an earlier decision to withdraw his forces to the northern Apennines. He had decided not to defend southern and central Italy while the Allies were fighting on Sicily (invaded in July) and when he already had reason to expect that the Italian Government, no longer directed by his Axis partner, Mussolini, would switch its allegiance from Germany to the Allies; he reversed himself only after Marshal Pietro Badoglio's government had defected from the Axis and the Allies had established their lodgment in southern Italy.[1]

Not until almost a month after the Allies invaded the Italian mainland did Hitler make a final decision on the defense of Italy. His indecision reflected a conflict between two alternative courses of action, each proposed by a field marshal—on the one hand, Field Marshal Erwin Rommel, who was convinced that the Gemans could and should hold only northern Italy; on the other, Field Marshal Albert Kessel-

224

ring, who was persuaded that a defense south of Rome was not only possible but also advisable.

In a situation already complex because of the necessity for anticipating possible Italian defection as well as estimating Allied offensive intentions, the presence of both field marshals in Italy—Rommel in the north and Kesselring in the south—complicated the problem of command. Hitler's choice of strategy in the final analysis determined his choice of commander.

The armistice between Italy and the Allies, announced September 8, 1943, on the eve of the Salerno landings, was no surprise to Hitler and the *Oberkommando der Wehrmacht* (OKW), the German High Command. German distrust of Italian intentions long before the Italian surrender—as early as May of that year—had caused plans to be made for that expected event. Benito Mussolini's deposition from power in July and the assumption of power by the Badoglio government convinced Hitler, despite Badoglio's protestations to the contrary, that Italy had no intention of continuing the war. Yet Hitler was loath to take the first step in an open break between the two Axis governments or to give the Italians the slightest excuse for defection. As long as Italy remained a formal ally, there was still chance of cooperation, particularly since the Allies' insistence on unconditional surrender was well known.

By 1943 Hitler needed all the help he could get. Germany was on the defensive in the East as well as in the Mediterranean, and no strategic goal determined the German over-all effort—unless it was Hitler's resolve to hold on to every foot of occupied territory.

The basic prerequisite of a strategic defensive plan is a substantial strategic reserve, but after the German losses at Stalingrad during the winter of 1942-43 and in Tunisia in the spring of 1943 no such reserve existed. A reserve could have been made available only if even limited offensive plans in the East had been abandoned and a relatively short front established. But this required retrograde movements on a grand scale, and Hitler refused to consider them. The result was that one theater could be reinforced only at the expense of another.

During a conference between Hitler and Mussolini at Feltre on July 19, 1943, Marshal Vittorio Ambrosio, Chief of the Italian High Command, asked Field Marshal Wilhelm Keitel, Chief of Staff of the OKW, what was happening on the Russian Front. Keitel could say no more than that the Germans were wearing the Russians down. "This," replied Ambrosio, "is not an active program but the renunciation of

GERMANY

AUSTRIA

HUNGARY

SWITZERLAND

BRENNER PASS

A   L   P   S

Trent ○   ○ *Feltre*   ○ *Ljubljana*

LAKE GARDA   *TRIESTE*

MILAN ○   ○ *Verona*

FRANCE

TURIN ○   Po R.

YUGOSLAVIA

GENOA

A   P   E   N   N

Rimini

FLORENCE   *Ancona*

Pisa ○   Arno R.

Arezzo   A   D   R   I   A   T   I   C

CORSICA   I   N   E   S   Tiber R.   S   E   A

(FR.)   ROME ○

Capistrello   *Ortona*

Ferentino   Rapido   BERNHARD LINE

Priverno   R.

Anzio ○   *Monte Cassino*   *Foggia* ○

Terracina ○   *Gaeta*   Garigliano R.   A   P   U   L   I   A

NAPLES ○   ○ *Salerno*   *Taranto*

TYRRHENIAN

SEA   C   A   L   A   B   R   I   A

SARDINIA

M

E

D   PALERMO

I   T   E   Strait of Messina

R

ITALY   R

1943-1944   A   SICILY

N

E

50 ⊢ 0 ⊣ 50 MILES   A

50 ⊢ 0 ⊣ 50 KILOMETERS   N   S   E   A

the initiative in operations. In substance the Axis is besieged, it is in a closed ring; it is necessary to get out. What prospects have you for doing this?" There were no prospects and Keitel eluded the question.[2] Nor did Hitler have a positive plan for victory. His belief in the *Endsieg* (final victory) was founded more and more on irrational hopes for which there was no positive foundation. First he wanted to wear down Russia by continuously reducing its strength in offensive operation;[3] later he merely hoped that a split between the Eastern and Western Allies would bring about a change in the fortunes of war.

By May 1943 North Africa was lost and with it over 100,000 Germans. One of the most serious consequences of the Allied conquest of Tunisia was its effect on Italian morale and determination to resist. Italy had never been prepared for the requirements of global warfare; now it had lost its best divisions in Greece, Russia, and North Africa. Criticism against Mussolini's conduct of the war mounted, particularly in Army and monarchist circles. Hitler recognized the unstable internal situation in Italy and in May 1943 the OKW began drafting plans to take over the defense of all of Italy and the Balkans in the event that Italian resistance should collapse or that the Italian Government should enter into a "treacherous" agreement with the Allies.[4] The Germans believed that further Allied offensive operations in the Mediterranean were imminent and, at the same time, that the Italians could no longer be relied on to contribute their share in the defense of their homeland or of the Balkans should either one be attacked—not a pleasant contemplation since only a few thousand German troops were on Italian soil in May 1943, troops that constituted the backlog of soldiers originally scheduled for transport to North Africa. By contrast, less than one year ago, in the early summer of 1942, Hitler had had visions of his armored columns advancing through North Africa and the Caucasus and meeting somewhere in the Near East in a gigantic pincer movement.

Faced with the prospect of losing his strongest ally, Hitler contemplated several strategic alternatives. Germany could assume the defense of Italy and Greece (with the latter occupied primarily by Italian troops). Germany could surrender all of Italy to the Allies, thereby avoiding the commitment of additional troops in what could only be a secondary theater of operations. Or Germany could defend in Italy along a geographic line that would prevent loss of the Po Valley and its rich agricultural and industrial resources.

Hitler never seriously considered evacuating all of Italy. In addition to giving up the resources of the Po Valley, withdrawal from Italy would have meant placing Allied armies on the southern border of Germany. Though the Alps provided an obstacle to invasion, the Allies would be able to establish air bases within easy striking distance of south and central Germany, and northern Italy would give the Allies an ideal staging area for amphibious operations against southern France or southeastern Europe. Withdrawal to the Alps might also suggest to Hungary and other Balkan satellites that they too could disengage from the none-too-popular war; finally, withdrawal from Italy might easily have adverse effects on Turkey's neutrality. Similar and stronger arguments existed against evacuating Greece.

The plan to occupy and defend all of Italy and the Balkans was the first plan adopted by Hitler. He charged Field Marshal Rommel with the activation of a skeleton army group headquarters in Munich to work out plans to occupy and defend Italy.[5] For Rommel's use, 6 good Panzer (armored) or Panzer grenadier divisions were to come from the East; 2 Panzer grenadier and 6 infantry divisions (reconstituted units that had been virtually destroyed at Stalingrad) were to come from France. Furthermore, 2 parachute divisions were to be made available by the *Luftwaffe*. The secrecy surrounding these plans was such that not even the senior German general in Italy, Field Marshal Kesselring, was informed of the early discussions.

In June 1943, his fears concerning Italy temporarily eased, Hitler decided to carry out a limited offensive in Russia with the result that Rommel could no longer rely on the Panzer divisions from the east for the execution of his task. Rommel thereupon informed Hitler that he could no longer undertake the defense of all of Italy with the troops expected to be available to him.[6] Hitler seemingly accepted Rommel's judgment, for subsequent plans envisaged the defense of Italy only in the Apennines, north of Rome, and in July he stated unequivocally that "without the Italian Army we cannot hold the entire peninsula." [7]

While Hitler, Rommel, and the OKW made plans in anticipation of Italy's defection, Kesselring was planning for the further conduct of the war in cooperation with Mussolini and the Italian High Command, the Comando Supremo. In agreement with the Comando Supremo, German forces in Italy had been built up independently of Rommel's plans in preparation for Allied attacks. By the time the Allies invaded Sicily in July, Kesselring had placed two German divisions on Sicily, 1 Panzer and 1 Panzer grenadier, both organized out of the troops that had been scheduled for North Africa before the Axis defeat. One Panzer grenadier division, still in process of organization, was on Sardinia, and 2 Panzer grenadier divisions and 1 Panzer division recently transferred from France were in central and southern Italy. Though these units were officially under command of the Comando Supremo, German strength and Italian weakness, as well as the fact that German troops bore the main burden of the battle for Sicily, made their subordination to Italian commands quite perfunctory. Kesselring was in fact the responsible commander.[8]

A natural optimist and political idealist whose Italophile views prevented him from a realistic appraisal of the Italian scene, Kesselring had, partly for this reason, not been taken into Hitler's confidence on plans to deal with Italy's possible defection. Kesselring was convinced that Italy would continue the war and that the Italian Army, though weak, would fight side by side with German troops. Hitler's distrust of the Italians was repugnant to Kesselring, and plans for the evacuation of southern Italy seemed to him less than necessary. Not only did he object strongly to Rommel's ideas concerning Italy and the Italians, but he resented the fact that while his own influence with Hitler had declined, Rommel's had increased. Kesselring's view was that all of Italy could and should be defended, even if Sicily had to be given up.[9]

When Mussolini fell on July 25, 1943, King Victor Emmanuel's appointment of Pietro Badoglio, Marshal of Italy, to be his successor shocked Kesselring; yet he believed Badoglio's solemn declarations that the war would continue. Hitler, Rommel, and the OKW worked under different assumptions. With the fall of Mussolini and Badoglio's assumption of control over the Italian Government, German plans covering an Italian collapse, rather vague and still in embryonic stages, suddenly acquired great importance and urgency. In his first excitement, Hitler—greatly disturbed over the fate of his fellow dictator —wanted to take immediate action by staging a *coup d'état* with German troops, arresting Badoglio and the King, liberating Mussolini, and re-establishing the fascist regime under German protection. Elements of the 2nd Parachute Division were at once flown to Rome to bolster German strength. But caution, ignorance of Mussolini's whereabouts, and the apparent willingness of the Italians to maintain the alliance with Germany restrained Hitler. However, the idea was not dropped, and General Kurt Student was charged with preparing the overthrow of Badoglio's government with the XI Air Corps, a parachute unit, now dispatched to Italy. At the same time Otto Skorzeny, a daredevil-type SS officer, received the mission of locating and liberating Mussolini.[10] Instead of a sudden and dramatic move, Hitler decided to occupy Italy unobtrusively and gradually by increasing the number of German divisions in the country—if possible, in agreement with the Comando Supremo.[11]

Even before this time German strength in Italy had been increased because of the fighting on Sicily and the danger of further Allied moves.

On August 1, 1943, the OKW issued a new and revised version of the plan to take over the country. Assigned the code name ACHSE, the plan recognized the danger to German troops in Italy that would come about from Italian defection and Allied landings on the Italian mainland. There were as yet no strong German forces in northern Italy and Rommel's headquarters was still in Munich. German forces in southern and central Italy and on Sicily had been increased to 8 divisions. Of these, 3 divisions and part of another were fighting on Sicily, 1 division was located on Sardinia, and 1 SS brigade occupied Corsica. At this time it was believed that Italian "treachery" could isolate all the German forces in southern and central Italy as well as those fighting on Sicily. Hitler, Rommel, and the OKW feared that Allied forces might attempt an amphibious operation against northern Italy, while strong Italian forces there might attempt to block the Alpine and Apennine passes. Even more likely seemed a landing near Rome where 5 Italian divisions could assist Allied operations, thereby cutting off all German troops south of the capital. Allied operations against Calabria and Apulia in the south were equally possible; so was an invasion of Sardinia as a prelude to further operations against northern Italy or southern France, for which the airfields on the island would make fighter cover possible. An invasion of Calabria with or without Italian cooperation would cut off German forces fighting on Sicily, while the air bases at Foggia in Apulia would simplify Allied operations against the Balkans. A landing in the Naples-Salerno area was not seriously considered during the first days of August because other areas seemed to offer greater tactical and strategic advantages to the Allies.[12] Moreover, a large-scale invasion of the Italian mainland was not thought likely, except by prior Allied agreement with Italy to use opportunities which that country's defection might bring about. The strategic goal of the Allies was thought to be the Balkans and not primarily Italy.

In this, all responsible German generals and military advisers of Hitler, including Kesselring, Rommel, and Admiral Karl Doenitz, Commander-in-Chief Navy, agreed. On July 17 Hitler had informed

Admiral Doenitz, that "at present it appears that the next enemy landing will be attempted there [in the Balkans]. It is as important to reinforce the Balkans as it is to hold Italy." [13] The reasoning behind the opinion that the Balkans were more immediately threatened than the Italian mainland included political, economic, and military factors. Placing himself in the position of the Allies, a spokesman for the OKW argued that a campaign in Italy would meet with the immediate and strong reaction of German-Italian forces which could use the extensive and functioning network of communications to counter any Allied move. In Greece, on the other hand, all Axis reinforcements and supplies would have to be shipped over the one existing railroad line of limited capacity, 1,300 kilometers long, and vulnerable to attack both from the air and by partisans. Political repercussions on Germany's southeastern allies, Hungary and Rumania, would be likely, while Allied pressure might persuade Turkey to give up her neutral status. Proximity of the Balkans to the vital Rumanian oil fields and Germany's economic dependence on the bauxite, copper, and other economic resources of the southeast were further reasons for fearing an invasion of that region.[14]

In addition to the difficulties of supplying German forces in Greece, other military factors seemed to favor the Balkans as an Allied goal. In Italy the Alps formed an insurmountable barrier to an invasion of Germany proper; the Ljubljana Gap, on the other hand, had provided the classic invasion route into Central Europe throughout history. Finally, an invasion of the Balkans would enable the Western Allies and Russia to join hands and coordinate their military strategy, while the presence of Western troops would constitute a check against Russian ambitions in the southeast, a point thought to be of particular concern to Great Britain. Thus Plan ACHSE was divided into two major parts, one for the Balkans and the other for Italy and southern France. The number of German divisions in the Balkans had been increased from 5 in January to more than 13 in July.[15]

Hitler, as yet, did not entertain the idea of defending Italy anywhere south of Rome in case of Italian defection. According to Plan ACHSE, effective on order from the OKW, Rommel was to occupy all the important passes, roads, and railroads leading out of Italy, disarm Italian Army units, and secure the Apennine passes. Kesselring was to withdraw his forces toward northern Italy, disarming the Italian Army and crushing any resistance. The island of Sardinia was to be evacuated by transferring the troops to Corsica and from there to the mainland. Rommel was to assume command over all German forces in Italy as soon as "the movements in northern Italy should become operationally connected with those in southern Italy." [16]

Under the impact of the Italian change of government and the increased danger of concerted action by Italy and the Allies, Hitler approved the plan to withdraw to the northern Apennines. Although he was always reluctant to give up ground without fighting "to the end," it is possible that his recent experiences at Stalingrad and in Tunisia had momentarily inclined him to be less rigid. Both times he had listened to the advice of optimists. For Italy, he listened to Rommel, who had learned to be more cautious.

During this time Kesselring remained convinced that all was well in Italy; he saw no danger to his troops or to his lines of communications. He continued to clamor for reinforcements in the south for the defense of Calabria and Apulia. On August 5 he sent a memorandum to Hitler and the OKW in which he stated: "At the moment it is certain that the Italian leadership and armed forces want to co-operate with us. . . . I repeat my previously expressed opinion that Calabria and Apulia are not sufficiently secure. Also, in view of the strategic importance of these regions as a springboard to the Balkans, I ask again for reinforcements of German troops in southern Italy." On August 19 he still thought that Italian "commands and troops will do everything possible to frustrate [Allied] attacks." [17] Actually a few days earlier, on August 15 and 16, Brigadier General Giuseppi Castellano, with full powers from Badoglio, had secretly entered into contact with the British Ambassadors at Madrid and Lisbon, to negotiate an armistice with the Allies and to offer active military assistance to any Allied venture on the mainland.[18]

Hitler refused to accede to Kesselring's wishes and to commit additional troops in the south. According to General Alfred Jodl, Chief of the Armed Forces Operations Staff of OKW, additional forces in the south would only increase the difficulties of supply. The security of the forces in southern Italy could be strengthened, Jodl argued, only by evacuating Sicily and thereby augmenting the defensive potential of Kesselring's forces. Jodl never doubted the necessity of withdrawing north in case of Italy's defection.[19] Hitler's disregard of Kesselring's views and the latter's knowledge that Rommel was eventually to succeed him in command prompted Kesselring to submit his resignation on August 14. Hitler refused to accept it.[20]

On August 1, 1943, Rommel's divisions began their infiltration into northern Italy. Some crossed the border with the consent of the

Comando Supremo, others despite Italian opposition. As a result of these movements, tension between the OKW and the Comando Supremo increased considerably, but as yet neither wanted to assume responsibility for an open break. Italy felt too insecure as long as no agreement with the Allies had been reached, while Germany wanted to commit as many troops in Italy as possible before open hostility made such movements more difficult. Besides, there was still a possibility that Italy might remain in the war, although Hitler was convinced that he had positive proof of Italy's armistice negotiations. During August the OKW dispatched 5 infantry and 2 Panzer divisions to northern Italy and on August 16 Rommel's headquarters moved to Lake Garda in northern Italy and assumed open command as Army Group B. The Comando Supremo and the Italian Government were in no doubt that Army Group B constituted in effect an occupation force, but they felt too weak to protest and pretended to accept the German version that Army Group B was to be a strategic reserve for the Balkans, southern France, or Italy in case of Allied landings at any of these points.[21] The Comando Supremo urged the OKW to use the German divisions in the north to strengthen the defenses in southern Italy where, on the assumption that Italy would remain loyal to the Axis, an Allied attack was much more likely, while the OKW applied pressure on the Comando Supremo to withdraw its divisions from the north for the same reason.[22] Neither trusted the other and neither wanted to take the first step. After the German divisions were firmly established in northern Italy, the OKW no longer feared an Allied invasion north of the Apennines.

During the second half of August the German position in southern Italy had also become more secure. By August 17 all the German troops in Sicily, exceeding 60,000 men, had been evacuated with their equipment. On August 22 the newly activated Tenth Army assumed command over German units in the Gaeta-Naples-Salerno region (the XIV Panzer Corps with 3 divisions) and in Calabria and Apulia (LXXVI Panzer Corps with 2 divisions and elements of a third). Two divisions and part of a third were grouped near Rome under the direct command of Kesselring.[23] * Yet, despite the more favorable

---

* General von Vietinghoff, who commanded the Tenth Army, considered it a costly mistake on the part of the Allies not to have attempted an invasion of Calabria before the close of the Sicilian campaign. Overcoming the resistance of the one and a half German divisions in Calabria, was, he believed, well within Allied capabilities. Such a landing would have cut off German troops on Sicily from their sources of supply, thereby shortening the length of time they could have resisted, and, most important, evacuation of German troops from

German position in Italy, Hitler did not change his plans. He personally informed General von Vietinghoff, Commanding General, Tenth Army, that Italian defection was only a matter of time and that the most important task was a safe withdrawal of the army to the north. Despite the weakness of the Italian Army, Hitler still feared that its cooperation with the Allies could place German troops in the south in a very precarious position.[24] The German army was to withdraw first to the Rome area and from there to the northern Apennines.

Even before General Castellano's offer of an armistice, the Allies had definitely decided on an invasion of the Italian mainland to secure the important port of Naples as a base for further operations in Italy. The Allies too had been aware that Italy was about to collapse, and the invasion of the mainland had originally been intended to deliver the knockout blow. Shortly after General Castellano started negotiating with the Allies, German reinforcements and the successful evacuation of German troops from Sicily had changed the picture substantially. Italy was no longer master in its own house and needed Allied help even to effect its surrender. At the same time, the Allies needed the assurance that Italy would offer no resistance to a landing operation.[25]

Allied concentration of troops and shipping in the western Mediterranean indicated to the Germans preparations for amphibious operations in the near future. Since northern Italy was no longer considered a likely target, the OKW now regarded the region of Naples-Salerno and the island of Sardinia most threatened, while the Rome area was thought of as particularly endangered in case of Allied landings and simultaneous defection of Italy. Kesselring recognized the possibility of a landing near Naples-Salerno, but showed greater concern for Apulia with its air bases at Foggia and suitability as a staging area against the Balkans. Hitler admitted the possibility of an invasion at Apulia, but he refused to permit Kesselring to dissipate his forces in order to reinforce that area and also brushed aside new demands by Kesselring to commit more troops in the south.[26] Hitler reaffirmed his views, which the OKW passed on to Kesselring in the form of an order dated August 18, 1943. Overriding his objections, the order instructed Kesselring—in his deployment and movement of the Tenth Army— to take into account the fact that Italy would capitulate sooner or later. The army was to put itself in a position to assure its withdrawal

---

Sicily would have been impossible. Without these forces, Vietinghoff maintains with considerable logic, the Germans could not have attempted resistance in southern and central Italy.

to central Italy even in case of Allied landings and active or passive resistance of the Italians. The order further directed the Tenth Army to defend the most threatened coastal area of Naples and Salerno with at least 3 mobile divisions and to hold it against Allied landings. Only mobile forces were to remain in southern Calabria and they would execute a fighting withdrawal to the north. In case political developments made a continuation of the fight in southern Italy impossible, the Tenth Army would fall back to the Rome area, Sardinia would be evacuated, and further action would be taken in accordance with ACHSE.[27]

Events now rapidly approached a climax. On August 30, the OKW issued a final revised version of ACHSE which adhered to the original concept but provided instructions more detailed and in closer accord with existing German troop dispositions. The directive still envisaged Kesselring directing a withdrawal to the Rome area, which was to be held until all troops had escaped from the south and from Sardinia. The Germans were to disarm the Italian Army in the process and to treat evacuated territory as hostile country. Rommel was to secure and occupy all the Alpine and Apennine passes as well as the major northern ports. The Italian Army was to be disarmed and the region of northern Italy pacified with the help of fascist organizations. Other sections contained instructions to the Commander-in-Chief Southeast for taking over the defense of the Balkans and disarming Italian troops in that region.[28]

Hitler's strategy in Italy on the eve of the Allied invasion can be summarized as follows. As long as Italy at least outwardly maintained the alliance, German troops in southern Italy were to execute a fighting withdrawal from the tip of Calabria; they were to hold the Naples-Salerno area to secure vital routes of communications to the north; only weak German units were to assist the Italians in Apulia. Deployment of all troops in southern Italy was to be such that lines of communications to the north were secured. As soon as Italy surrendered, the overriding consideration would become the safety of German troops in southern Italy, and their best chance of survival was seen in a well-organized withdrawal to central Italy where all troops under Kesselring would be assembled in preparation for a final withdrawal to the northern Apennines.

Allied intentions were somewhat clarified on September 3 when the British Eighth Army crossed the Strait of Messina into Calabria. In accordance with the instructions from the OKW, Kesselring ordered the Tenth Army to delay the Eighth Army while withdrawing its troops from Calabria to the north.[29] Five days later, the armistice was announced and ACHSE went into effect. The next morning the 16th Panzer Division fought troops of the U.S. Fifth Army on the beaches of Salerno.

Unknown to the Germans, Italy had signed an unconditional surrender on September 3 and reached agreement with the Allies that the armistice would not be announced until just before the planned invasion.

The moment which Hitler, Rommel, and the OKW had feared and anticipated had come: Italy had surrendered while two Allied armies were establishing themselves on the mainland. Kesselring was faced with the dual task of opposing the Allied armies and rendering the Italian armed forces ineffective. In this mission he was aided by the lack of Italian fighting spirit and poor planning on the part of the Comando Supremo. In the Tenth Army sector, Italian troops all but disappeared overnight; near Rome Kesselring needed only two days to convince the 5 Italian divisions located there to go home; in the north Rommel methodically disarmed and dissolved all Italian Army units. Italy had ceased to be an ally, but she also ceased to be a threat. Unhampered by the previously necessary regard for the sensitivity of the Comando Supremo and the Italian Government, the Germans proceeded to conduct the defense of Italy with no considerations except self-interest.[30]

Kesselring's and Hitler's great fear—an Allied landing near Rome and active resistance of Italian forces near the capital—proved groundless. Neither Kesselring nor Hitler knew that such a course had been definitely abandoned by Italy and the Allies. The 82nd Airborne Division was to have landed on the airports of Rome to occupy the city and prevent the Germans from assuming control. The operation was canceled at the last minute because Italy failed to guarantee the security of the airfields for the time the operation was scheduled.[31]

The simultaneous announcement of the armistice and the landing at Salerno might have resulted in a very grave situation for all German troops in the south. By a quirk of fate it probably had much to do with making necessary the long and costly campaign of the Allies in Italy. Only the day before, on September 7, Hitler had finally decided to cut the knot of Germany's entangled relations with Italy by sending an ultimatum to the Italian Government to accede to German demands. The demands themselves were not new, but up to that time the Italian Government and the Comando Supremo had been evasive without refusing outright to make the demands the basis of discussion. Hitler instructed the OKW to have the draft ready for his signature by September 9. The more important points of the ultimatum, as drafted by the OKW, included demands for (a) complete freedom of movement for German troop units—this was particularly directed against Italian reluctance to allow German troops near major ports; (b) withdrawal of all Italian troops from the German-Italian border area and subordination of Italian divisions in the Po Valley to Army Group B; (c) creation of a strong Italian front in southern Italy *behind* which Tenth Army could gain sufficient freedom of movement to counterattack against an invading enemy; (d) joint leadership (meaning in effect German leadership) of all armed forces. In case of Italian refusal, the draft ultimatum stated that Germany would have to take all steps it considered necessary to assure the safety of its troops.[32]

There seems no doubt that these steps would have included withdrawal of the Tenth Army at least to the Rome area. Because of the announced armistice on September 8 the ultimatum was not sent. Curiously, the Italians too were caught by surprise by the announcement of the armistice; they did not expect it until September 12 and had failed to give precise instructions to their officers, including army commanders. By September 12 Germany would probably have delivered the ultimatum and Italy—having already signed the armistice— could only have refused or stalled for time. There is at least the possibility that the Tenth Army would have been in the process of withdrawing if the invasion had been delayed for a few days.[33] Thus the German defense of Italy south of Rome at the time of the Salerno landings was due, first, to Hitler's reluctance to give the Italians an excuse for defection by withdrawing his troops to the north before an Allied invasion and as long as there remained the slightest possibility that Italy might remain in the war, and, later, to the timing of the invasion and the announcement of the armistice, which prevented Germany from delivering its ultimatum to the Italian Government.

Kesselring's resourcefulness and unexpected success in coping with the Italians and the two Allied armies during the first days after Salerno gained him at least temporary control over the conduct of operations. On September 12 Hitler informed Kesselring and Rommel —in response to Kesselring's request for clarification of the command situation in Italy—that Rommel was not yet authorized to issue directives to Kesselring; this authorization was to be issued by Hitler personally only after the forces of Commander-in-Chief South came within close proximity to the territory of Army Group B.[34] The dividing line between the two army groups was the line Pisa-Arezzo-Ancona. Kesselring's advocacy of a defense of Italy as far south of Rome as possible had gained considerable force after the Italian Army ceased to be dangerous and after the Allies had failed to land in the area of Rome. But Hitler did not yet see his way clear to accepting Kesselring's strategic concept. Kesselring complied with the letter of the OKW's instruction by ordering the Tenth Army on September 14 "to fall back upon the Rome area" after completion of the operations at Salerno, regardless of whether the Fifth Army had been forced back into the sea or not. "The objective," the order continued, "is to gain time for the evacuation of important materials as well as for the destruction of lines of communications and war industries." [35]

Still anticipating withdrawal, Hitler saw as yet no need to reinforce Kesselring and thus enable him to make a permanent stand in the south. Kesselring asked for no reinforcements from Rommel and received none. After it had become obvious that the Germans could not dislodge the Fifth Army from Salerno and were threatened with envelopment by the Eighth Army, he directed the Tenth Army to withdraw to a succession of defensive lines, one of which was the "B" line, later called the Bernhard, or Winter, Line. This line crossed the narrowest sector of the Italian peninsula, roughly between Gaeta and Ortona. Kesselring's written and oral directives and orders indicated that the Bernhard Line was but one of a series of defensive lines to be occupied by Tenth Army in the retrograde movement toward Rome. In a postwar account Kesselring maintained that he had never had any intention of complying with the "absurd" idea of withdrawing to the north. He accused the OKW and Rommel of writing off his forces. With two more Panzer divisions, which Rommel could well have spared, Kesselring in retrospect claimed he would have been assured of success at Salerno.[36] He also accused Hitler, in the same postwar account, of being inconsistent. If Hitler refused to send reinforcements to southern Italy, he should have withdrawn the Tenth Army before the Italian armistice.[37] In this argument Kesselring forgot that he, more than anyone else, had assured Hitler that there was no danger from the Italians as long as Germany was willing to assist in the defense of Italy. A German withdrawal from southern Italy before the armistice would have given the Italians every reason to break the alliance, since they were in no position to defend southern Italy without German help. In order to defend a line south of Rome—still a self-imposed mission—Kesselring instructed Tenth Army to fight to gain time for building up the Bernhard Line.[38]

It is a matter of conjecture when Hitler first entertained the idea that a more permanent defense of the Bernhard Line would serve Germany's greater strategic interests in the Balkans and in France. The belief that the Balkans remained the strategic goal of the Allies was still held throughout September and October. On September 15 Kesselring informed the OKW that he expected the next Allied attack to be launched, not against central or northern Italy, but against the Balkans after the air bases at Foggia had been taken.[39] Similar ideas were expressed by the Armed Forces Operations Staff of the OKW, by Admiral Doenitz, by Rommel, and by Hitler himself. Kesselring and Doenitz believed that a prolonged defense of southern Italy would delay an Allied attack against the Balkans, while the Armed Forces Operations Staff was of the opinion that withdrawal to the Apennines north of Rome would save 3 to 4 divisions which would be needed to reinforce the Balkans against the increased danger of an invasion.[40] Kesselring thought it of utmost importance to deny the Allies the undisputed possession of a staging area against the Balkans. Also a defensive line in the south would keep Allied bombers farther from southern Germany and the Po Valley, thus making strategic bombing more difficult. The Bernhard Line could be held with 11 divisions, including 2 mobile divisions in reserve on both flanks to prevent amphibious flanking operations, while estimates for holding the Apennine line in the north ranged from 13 to 20 divisions.[41] Defending the Bernhard Line would enable German forces to execute a delaying action including, if necessary, a withdrawal to the northern Apennines. Immediate withdrawal, on the other hand, would endanger the vital Po Valley, for once the Allies breached the Apennine line, no terrain suitable for defense was available short of the Alps. An additional advantage, in the eyes of Kesselring, lay in the possession of Rome. To prevent the Allies from occupying this city, he urged, would deny them the opportunity to exploit this fact for propaganda purposes. Finally, holding the Bernhard Line would make it possible for the German Army to execute a counteroffensive against Apulia, in case Allied preparations for an attack against the Balkans resulted in a withdrawal of Allied forces from the Italian front. The latter argument probably had considerable impact on Hitler, for later in Oc-

tober he summoned both Kesselring and Rommel to his headquarters
to hear them express their views on the feasibility of a counteroffensive.[42]

The arguments presented to Hitler in favor of a northern stand
were less dramatic, but probably equally valid. Rommel, maybe
overestimating the amphibious capabilities of the Allies, felt that a
line too far south represented a great danger for which he would not
want to assume the responsibility, even though he admitted that the
Bernhard Line could be held with half the divisions necessary in the
northern Apennines.[43] Rommel probably shared the opinion of some
members of the Armed Forces Operations Staff that withdrawal from
southern Italy meant simultaneous withdrawal from Greece, in order
to avoid dispersal of German forces over a large area vulnerable to
attack.[44] Hitler refused to consider withdrawal from Greece and gradually turned toward Kesselring's view. On September 17 Hitler informed Kesselring that he approved his plan for a slow withdrawal
northward and indicated that it was important to hold the Bernhard
Line "for a longer period of time." [45]

Kesselring had not succeeded in forcing the Fifth Army from its
beachhead, but German troops had exacted a heavy toll in men and
equipment. They kept the port of Naples in their hands throughout
September, and the Allies seemed checked. Thus, while Kesselring
successfully delayed the Allied advance north, Hitler gained time to
consider and reconsider arguments for and against a permanent defense of the Bernhard Line. Kesselring's optimism, a source of irritation to Hitler before the Italian surrender, now turned in his favor.
Rommel, in contrast, appeared too pessimistic, as Hitler indicated
later. Probably somewhat bitter over the outcome of his North African
campaign, Rommel did not relish the danger of exposing another
army to annihilation by flanking attacks from the sea. On the other
hand, Hitler apparently had never forgiven Rommel his "unauthor-
ized" retreat at El Alamein.[46]

Such considerations may well have passed through Hitler's mind
on September 24, 1943, when Admiral Doenitz presented his estimate
of the situation. Southern Italy, Doenitz argued, was especially important to the enemy as a bridgehead to the Balkans. "Therefore,"
Doenitz continued, "it is necessary for us to do all in our power to
block this route as long as possible. . . . Sicily . . . was worth
every sacrifice from this point of view. Now another opportunity for
determined resistance presents itself in Apulia. To prepare, follow
through, and secure a beachhead for a possible assault on the Balkans,

the enemy needs the airports near Foggia. This was the pattern followed in Sicily and at Salerno. If these airfields remain in our hands the attack on the Balkans will be effectively delayed." Hitler agreed with these observations and informed Doenitz that he would "issue directives for the conduct of the war accordingly." [47]

Hitler was coming closer to Kesselring's point of view. A few days later the force of Doenitz' argument was considerably lessened when the airfields at Foggia fell into British hands. Yet his argument remained valid if the airfields could be recaptured in a counteroffensive timed to coincide with an Allied build-up against the Balkans. Kesselring and Rommel, on September 30, expressed their opinions on the chances for a counteroffensive, and, though their views were not recorded, it seems more than likely that Kesselring expressed himself positively in accordance with his earlier statements, while Rommel, at the very least, expressed doubt.[48]

As a result of the conference with Kesselring and Rommel, Hitler definitely decided to reverse his earlier plans in favor of the defense of the Bernhard Line.[49] Though a formal order to this effect was signed by Hitler and issued on October 4, the two commands in Italy—Kesselring's and Rommel's—remained active, both continuing to function directly under the OKW. Hitler did not yet completely accept Kesselring's optimistic prediction of being able to hold the Allies away from the northern Apennines from six to nine months, for the same order that instructed Kesselring to build up and hold the Bernhard Line charged Rommel with the construction of a defensive line in the northern Apennines. For planning purposes, Rommel could still count on all his forces as well as those of Kesselring. However, for the first time since the invasion, Rommel's army group was ordered to send reinforcements to Kesselring consisting of 2 infantry divisions and some artillery units.[50] Rommel was not yet out of the picture, but Kesselring had won a major victory in the battle of concepts. Kesselring would hold on to Rome and tie down Allied divisions in a battle of attrition, thereby keeping them, he thought, from attacking the Balkans.

The political role assigned Italy after the Italian armistice and the dissolution of the Italian Army may have strengthened Hitler's decision of October 4, 1943, to hold on to Rome and to defend the Bernhard Line. On September 12 Otto Skorzeny realized Hitler's wish to liberate Mussolini.[51] With Mussolini liberated and the Italian Army disbanded, the road was open for the establishment of a fascist puppet regime and for the activation of some Italian Army units to be composed of loyal fascist volunteers. The chief of the new army was to be Marshal Rodolfo Graziani, who was invited to a conference with Hitler on October 9 to discuss means by which Italy could again share in the conduct of the war. During the course of the conference, Hitler and Graziani agreed that German-occupied Italy was to be treated as a "friendly" country in which the fascist government was to be given some measure of independence, excepting large areas designated as "zones of operation," and that the loss of Rome would seriously impair any chance of establishing Mussolini's puppet regime. Therefore, Hitler concluded, "the intended defense of the [Bernhard] Line is of decisive importance to the continuance of a joint struggle." [52]

While it is doubtful that Hitler took any strategic risks for the sake of his former ally, it is true that he felt considerable loyalty toward Mussolini. Moreover, the cooperation even of a puppet government would simplify coercive measures for obtaining labor and economic products for Germany. The decision to defend the Bernhard Line was probably strengthened by these considerations. In turn, it not only expedited the establishment of a fascist government but also made possible the later propagandistic exploitation of its existence.

Between October 4 and November 6 Hitler vacillated in his decision as to whom to give supreme command in Italy. He seemed to swing from Kesselring to Rommel and back to Kesselring. Both commanders were again summoned to present their views. Asked whether he thought he could defend the Bernhard Line and hold on to Rome and central Italy, Rommel, according to a postwar source, expressed himself negatively.[53] By November 6 Hitler had the draft of two orders in front of him, one appointing Rommel, the other appointing Kesselring. On that date, he signed the latter, with its detailed instructions regarding the defense of Italy which affirmed that "the Bernhard Line will mark the end of withdrawals." [54] Hitler had made the final decision regarding the strategy to be followed in the defense of Italy. Rommel was transferred out of the theater on November 21 and Army Group B discontinued as an active command, while Kesselring's command, now comprising the entire Italian theater, was redesignated Commander-in-Chief Southwest and Army Group C.[55]

Hitler's decision to hold and defend the Bernhard Line set the stage for the bloody battles of the Rapido River, Monte Cassino, and Anzio. Without Hitler's decision to reappraise the strategic defense of Italy, these places probably would have fallen to the Allies after light skirmishes or perhaps even unopposed. Kesselring's capable leadership made the decision pay off at least in time gained. The Allies did not take Rome until June 4, 1944.

Hitler's decision was a gamble. He could not be sure that the Allies would not commit stronger forces in the Mediterranean in an attempt to cut off and annihilate the German forces in the south, as they did later in their abortive attempt to cut the lines of communications at Anzio. Ironically enough, Hitler decided to hold the Bernhard Line primarily to prevent the Allies from going into the Balkans. The Allies had no intention of going there, although rapid conquest of southern and central Italy might have tempted them into such a venture.

The validity of Hitler's decision is difficult to test. Kesselring's best claim for success can only be that he lost a campaign more slowly. The time Kesselring may have gained for Hitler could not be put to use to change the fortune of war. Possibly Rommel felt at the time that the chances for winning the war were negligible and that, there-fore, needless sacrifice of blood for the sake of gaining time was pointless. Yet from a military point of view, defense of the Bernhard Line was perhaps the better choice, even though some of the basic assumptions, such as the counterattack against Apulia, could not be tested. Psychologically, the slow progress enforced on Allied armies advancing on Rome was not without detrimental effects on the Allied soldier and possibly even on the neutral nations, especially Turkey, and on Germany's southeastern allies.

Martin Blumenson

11

General Lucas at Anzio
(1944)

A commander can make a decision simply by ruling out what appears to him to be impractical or unfeasible. This was how Major General John P. Lucas, commander of the VI Corps in Italy, viewed and resolved his command problem immediately after the Anzio landing in January 1944. He rejected a course of action that to him appeared unwise or imprudent.

Yet two alternatives were in fact valid and open to him, though neither satisfied him completely. One seemed to him to verge on recklessness, the other could perhaps be criticized as overcautious. With orders from the next higher echelon of command deliberately left vague, General Lucas was free to choose. Thus he alone would shape the pattern of events that was to develop at Anzio.

The responsibility was great. If he made his choice on the side of safety or security, he would lessen the risks of an inherently hazardous operation. By gambling, he might lose the entire force under his command. On the other hand, if he refused to gamble, he might throw away the opportunity to secure a strategic objective at little cost and in one master stroke bring to an end an arduous phase of the Italian campaign.

The issues of this, the most significant command decision at Anzio, were rooted in the Allied motives for waging war on the Italian mainland. According to the formal directive of the U.S.-British Combined Chiefs of Staff, the object of invading the peninsula was to knock Italy out of the war and tie down as many German forces as possible. The Allies had achieved the first purpose even as they prepared to invade the Italian mainland at the toe and at Salerno: Italy had surrendered in September 1943. The Allies, therefore, in fighting up the boot of Italy, were serving the cause of the second, engaging German forces that otherwise might be employed in battle on the Russian Front or in preparations to repel the Allied invasion of north-west Europe (OVERLORD) scheduled for the spring of 1944.[1]

While containing the maximum number of German forces in Italy by means of offensive operations, the Allies had their minds fixed on Rome. Though the Combined Chiefs had not mentioned Rome as a goal of the Italian campaign, Prime Minister Winston Churchill "passionately" desired to capture the Eternal City, and this fact was well known among the Allied echelons of command.[2] President Franklin D. Roosevelt also had his eye on Rome. "Keep on giving it all you have," he wrote to the commander of the Fifth Army in December 1943, "and Rome will be ours and more beyond." [3]

Liberating Rome would be a dramatic act. The first Axis capital to fall to the Allies, it would demonstrate irrefutably the progress of Allied arms on the European Continent, perhaps stimulate revolt or increased guerrilla activity in German-occupied Europe, and without doubt strike a serious blow against German morale.

In support of the Allied predilection for Rome, military reasons could be marshaled. Nearby airfields were valuable. More important, Rome was the center of the Italian communications system. Through Rome passed the troops and supplies nourishing the implacable resistance that was preventing the Allies from marching up the Italian boot. South of Rome the terrain was eminently suitable for the tenacious defense holding the Allies in check, but north of Rome the first terrain on which the Germans could anchor a defense seemed no closer than the Pisa-Rimini line—which would represent a sizable Allied step toward Germany and provide more than adequate depth and security for the important Allied air and ground installations in south Italy.

The desire for Rome, balked by successful German opposition in the intervening mountainous ground in southern Italy, led directly to the amphibious landing at Anzio. Even before the invasion of Italy, Allied leaders had recognized the difficulties of making swift overland advance in the difficult terrain south of Rome. Lacking numerically superior forces, constricted by the width of the Italian peninsula to a relatively short front, and limited by the mountains to well-defined corridors of advance, the Allied ground forces were restricted to frontal attack. Maneuver was possible only by means of sea-borne

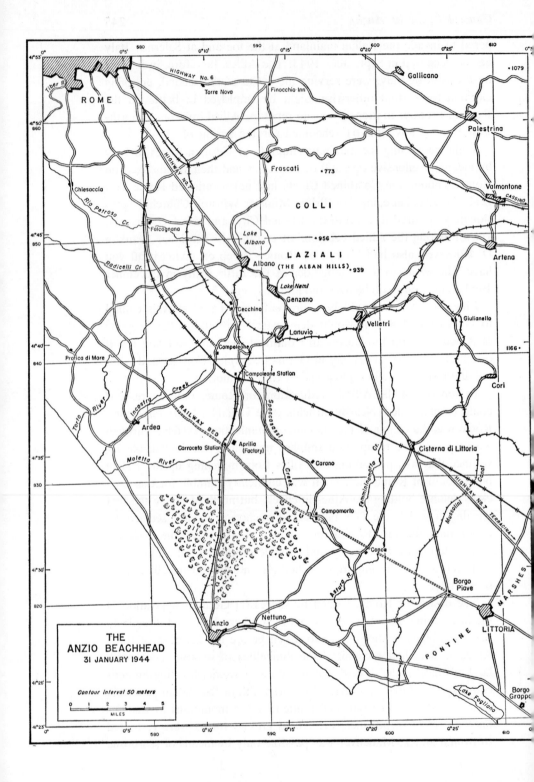

THE
ANZIO BEACHHEAD
31 JANUARY 1944

Contour interval 50 meters

0 1 2 3 4 5
MILES

hooks—the Allies could envelop the enemy positions only by amphibious end runs.[4]

Though there had been talk in the area of launching such operations on the Italian west coast, the necessity to do so became increasingly clear as the autumn of 1943 turned to winter. Not only did the Germans continue resourcefully to deny the Allies quick access to Rome, but the bitterly fought campaign in southern Italy seemed to be approaching a stalemate. In these circumstances, a surprise amphibious landing behind the enemy lines appeared the only way of transforming the static warfare of the Italian campaign into a swift war of movement where the superior mechanized equipment of the Allies could be employed to advantage.

Within this frame of reference, two place names became prominent: Anzio and the Alban Hills. The beaches near Anzio, 33 miles due south of Rome, were suitable for amphibious landings, and the open terrain of the low, relatively level coastal plain around Anzio was favorable for maneuver. Good roads led from there to the Alban Hills, some 20 miles inland. The Alban high ground, 15 miles southwest of the center of Rome, rises between the two main west coast highways leading to the capital. Dominating the southern approaches to the city, the hill complex was the last barrier the Germans could use to bar an Allied entry into Rome.

Early in October 1943, a month after the Salerno invasion, Lieutenant General Mark W. Clark, Commander of the U.S. Fifth Army, was sufficiently interested in sea-borne end runs to form a special amphibious planning staff and make it part of his G-3 (operations) Section.[5] The function of the special group was to investigate in detail all possible amphibious opportunities on the west coast of Italy, a task complicated by the lack of available troops and landing craft, the difficulty of finding suitable beaches within supporting distance of the main Fifth Army forces, and the generally unfavorable tactical situation.

During late October and early November, General Dwight D. Eisenhower, the Supreme Allied Commander in the Mediterranean theater, discussed with his senior subordinate commanders the possibility of making amphibious landings on the west coast as a means of maintaining the momentum of the lagging offensive in Italy. The major problem was to secure enough landing vessels to make such an effort feasible. More than two-thirds of the 90 LST's (landing ships, tanks) then in the Mediterranean had to be released by December 15 for employment elsewhere in future operations already planned; until that date the ships were needed to transport ground troops and supplies, as well as Strategic Air Force units, from North Africa and Sicily into Italy to accelerate the build-up of Allied forces.

The senior commanders in the theater were in agreement that if enough landing ships and craft could be retained beyond mid-December, an amphibious operation ought to be mounted to support the main offensive oriented on Rome. General Sir Harold R. L. G. Alexander, Commander in Chief of the Allied Armies in Italy (15th Army Group), felt that if the Allies could penetrate the main German defenses in south Italy, Allied troops landed on the enemy flank below Rome might so threaten German communications as to compel the enemy to retreat.

As the first step in clarifying the requirements of such an operation, Alexander, on November 8, 1943, instructed the Fifth Army to draw a plan. To guide the army staff, Alexander's 15th Army Group headquarters set forth his general concept. As part of a drive on Rome, an amphibious operation south of Rome was to be directed on the Alban Hills; combined with a frontal assault on the main enemy line, the landing threatening the enemy rear was to dispossess the Germans of the last defensive position on the southern approaches to Rome.[6]

The Fifth Army drew an outline plan, and on November 25 General Clark approved what was code-named Operation SHINGLE. An amphibious landing at Anzio was to take place after the Fifth Army reached the Capistrello-Ferentino-Priverno line near Frosinone (about 40 miles southeast of Rome) and was ready to institute an all-out drive toward the Alban Hills. The Anzio force was to be small and its effort subsidiary. Its function was to assist the major Fifth Army forces in their main effort to capture the Alban Hills mass. Link-up between the main and the Anzio fronts, it was assumed, would take place no later than seven days after the landing.

Though complying with Alexander's general desire, Clark's army plan reversed the roles of the participating forces. According to Alexander, the Anzio force was to capture the Alban Hills. According to Clark, the main Fifth Army forces were to seize the hill mass.

Reconciliation of the two concepts did not seem important for the moment, for it began to appear that SHINGLE was doomed to indefinite postponement. Though the theater received permission to retain sufficient landing ships and craft to make an amphibious operation feasible, enemy resistance, mountainous terrain, and bad weather so bogged down the Fifth Army advance to the north that the army could not get within supporting distance of the projected landing site.

SHINGLE gained a new lease on life on December 10 when General Clark suggested, despite little prospect of reaching in the near future positions from which to support a landing at Anzio, that the amphibious landing be mounted nevertheless. A strengthened Anzio force, if assured continuous resupply by water, could, he believed, consolidate a beachhead and remain separated from the main Fifth Army forces for more than seven days. Its mere presence deep in the German rear would constitute a considerable threat to German security and thereby facilitate the Fifth Army advance up the peninsula toward Rome.

The idea of making an amphibious envelopment at Anzio took concrete form on Christmas Day of 1943 at a conference in Tunis attended by Prime Minister Churchill and Generals Eisenhower and Alexander. British General Sir Henry Maitland Wilson was also present, for he had been designated the successor to Eisenhower, who was leaving the theater in a few days to assume command of the OVERLORD forces in England. With Eisenhower reluctant to influence the discussion because of his impending departure, and with Wilson virtually an observer, Churchill and Alexander decided in favor of SHINGLE. But instead of a landing to assist a main Fifth Army effort when the army was near Frosinone, SHINGLE was to be a larger operation launched regardless of where the Fifth Army stood in south Italy. Despite the opinion of the theater G-2 (intelligence), who opposed the operation on the basis that the Germans were too strong—the "seamier side of the question," as Churchill characterized the issue—Churchill and Alexander were convinced that an amphibious landing of not less than two assault divisions was "essential for a decision in Italy." [7]

Such an operation required further retention in the Mediterranean of landing ships and craft. Churchill and Alexander met at Marrakech, Morocco, on January 8, 1944, to discuss this problem. Shortly thereafter, the Combined Chiefs of Staff allowed the theater to hold through the month of February sufficient vessels to execute SHINGLE. [8]

According to General Clark, the Anzio landing was to "exercise a decisive influence in the operation to capture Rome." [9] The purpose of the amphibious venture was to outflank the enemy positions then established along the Garigliano and Rapido Rivers, some 60 miles south of Anzio. Whether the 60 miles between Anzio and the Garigliano was too great a distance for action on one front to influence the other was discussed, but it was accepted as an unavoidable risk.

An amphibious landing in the Terracina area, closer to the main front, would permit better integration of amphibious and main front activities, but it would be too close to warrant hope of securing a strategic effect—a direct threat against Rome.

It was, of course, impossible to predict the exact German reaction to a landing, but the most probable reactions seemed desirable from the Allied standpoint. By cutting the enemy main line of communications immediately south of Rome, the Anzio force might provoke the Germans at the Garigliano and Rapido to withdraw. The threat alone of a large force in the German rear might compel German withdrawal. Or the Germans might find it necessary to weaken the Garigliano-Rapido front in order to meet the threat at Anzio, and in so doing open the gate to an Allied surge up the Liri Valley toward Rome.

To implement the strategic intent of the operation, the force scheduled to land far behind the enemy front had to be of sufficient strength not only to provoke a desired reaction but also to sustain itself independently until the main Allied forces followed up the expected German withdrawal and made contact with the enveloping force. Yet the size and composition of the force was limited by the reservoir of Allied units available in the theater. The make-up of the force was also largely determined by the number of naval vessels on hand to carry out the amphibious landing. Furthermore, the operation had to be executed within a certain period of time so that landing ships and craft, as well as other naval vessels, could be released from the Mediterranean for the impending OVERLORD cross-Channel invasion of northwest Europe.

These factors determined the size of the Anzio force and the date of the amphibious operation. General Lucas' VI Corps—originally with 2 divisions, 3 Ranger battalions, 2 Commando battalions, a parachute regiment, and an additional parachute battalion, plus supporting units—later augmented by an armored division (less a combat command) and an infantry regimental combat team—was to make an amphibious assault on the Anzio beaches on January 22, 1944.

According to General Alexander's final instructions, the Fifth Army was "to carry out an assault landing on the beaches in the vicinity of Rome with the object of cutting the enemy lines of communication and threatening the rear of the German 14th Corps [defending the Italian west coast along the lower Garigliano River]." In support of the landing, the Fifth Army was to make a strong thrust on the main front toward Cassino and Frosinone "shortly prior to the assault landing to draw in enemy reserves which might be employed against the landing forces and then to create a breach in his front through which every opportunity will be taken to link up rapidly with the seaborne operation." [10]

Unlike the theater G-2, intelligence officers of the 15th Army Group were rather optimistic. They judged that the enemy had the equivalent of two divisions in reserve near Rome, which was correct. They also felt that various troop movements and reliefs already in progress in January could increase the reserves able to oppose a landing at Anzio. But they counted on the effect of weather and on harassment by the Allied air forces to interfere not only with troop movements but with the German defensive dispositions. It seemed probable, therefore, that the Germans in the Rome area would lack balance and organization in their dispositions. Thus, there was good reason to hope for success at Anzio, where two divisions in the initial landing were to be reinforced by a strong and fully mobile striking force of armor and infantry. The object of the Anzio operation, Alexander repeated, was "to cut the enemy's main communications in the Colli Laziali [Alban Hills] area southeast of Rome, and to threaten the rear of the 14th German Corps." These results, in Alexander's view, were expected:

> The enemy will be compelled to react to the threat of his communications and rear, and advantage must be taken of this to break through his main defenses [along the Garigliano and Rapido Rivers], and to insure that the two forces operating under Comd [sic] Fifth Army join hands at the earliest possible moment. Once this junction has been effected Comd Fifth Army will continue the advance North of Rome with the utmost possible speed. . . .[11]

General Clark translated General Alexander's desires as follows: "Mission. Fifth Army will launch attacks in the Anzio area. . . . (a) To seize and secure a beachhead in the vicinity of Anzio. (b) Advance on Colli Laziali." [12] What seemed on the surface to be perfectly clear—a mission to be executed in two logically consecutive parts—was in reality deliberately vague on the second portion. The VI Corps was to establish a beachhead, but then was it to advance *toward* the Alban Hills or *to* the Alban Hills?

The reason for the deliberate vagueness stemmed from the desire to keep the VI Corps flexible rather than to commit it to a single unalterable line of action. This in turn arose from the difficulty of judging the German reaction at Anzio.

The Fifth Army intelligence estimates, differing from those of the army group, were less optimistic, primarily because of belief that the seriousness of the threat carried by the landing would force the Germans into a violent reaction:

An attack on the coast line in the vicinity of Anzio by a force the size of a Corps will become an emergency to be met by all the resources and strength available to the German High Command in Italy. It will threaten the safety of the Tenth Army [controlling the defense of south Italy]. It will also threaten to seize Rome and the airfields in the vicinity thereof which are of such great importance.[13]

As soon as the Germans appreciated the magnitude of the Anzio landing and realized no other attacks would occur at other points along the coast, they would, the Fifth Army believed, have to concentrate forces to defeat the landing. If they were unable to do so because of Allied air action, other interruptions, or lack of available forces, they would have to isolate the landing force and try to prevent further build-up and advance. If the Germans could not prevent the movement of Allied forces to the Alban Hills, the safety of the Tenth Army would be seriously threatened to the extent of making withdrawal necessary and bringing to an end the successful defense in south Italy.

To defend against the landing, the enemy was judged to have immediately available near Rome a corps headquarters and two divisions, plus paratroop and armored elements. By the third day of the operation, the Germans could perhaps draw a division from the Adriatic front facing General Sir Bernard L. Montgomery's British Eighth Army. Two additional divisions could probably be near Anzio no sooner than D plus 16.[14]

Despite the relatively few German units immediately available to defend at Anzio, the Fifth Army assumed that the VI Corps would meet strong initial resistance on the beaches; it expected the Corps to receive heavy counterattacks as soon as the Germans became aware of the extent and the purport of the operation. Perhaps the lesson of having underestimated German strength at the time of the Salerno invasion had been too well learned. The Fifth Army—and with it the VI Corps—expected the same pattern of opposition to develop at Anzio as had come close to inflicting defeat on the Allies at Salerno. The emphasis consequently turned toward defense. The VI Corps at Anzio was to maintain a strong reserve. Troops were to dig in on initial objectives at once, to hold the beachhead against armored counterattacks.

With additional landing craft becoming available, the Fifth Army decided to augment the Anzio force. In addition to the original units —the 3rd U.S. and 1st British Divisions, the 504th U.S. Parachute Infantry Regiment, the 509th U.S. Parachute Infantry Battalion, a British Special Service Brigade of 2 Commando battalions, and the U.S. Ranger Force of 3 battalions—the army made available the 1st U.S. Armored Division (less Combat Command B), a regimental combat team of the 45th U.S. Division, and 3 more battalions of light and medium artillery than had originally been assigned. Should even more strength be necessary at Anzio, the remainder of the 1st Armored and 45th Divisions could be moved to the beachhead.

The result was a SHINGLE force that had grown from a tentative original figure of 24,000 men to an expected eventual strength of more than 110,000. From a subsidiary operation on the left flank of a nearby Fifth Army, the Anzio landing had developed into a major operation deep in the enemy rear. Assisting the landing was to be a major Fifth Army attack on the main front and a demonstration on the part of General Montgomery's British Eighth Army (deployed beside the Fifth), both designed to pin down the enemy troops in south Italy.

The Fifth Army effort along the Garigliano and Rapido Rivers was in direct support of the Anzio landing. Its primary purpose was to prevent the Germans from immediately reinforcing the defenders at Anzio. If Clark could at the same time break through the Garigliano-Rapido line, he might precipitate a German withdrawal which the Anzio invasion might well turn into a rout.

Toward these ends, Clark planned a three-corps assault across the Garigliano and Rapido. The attack was to begin on January 12 and to culminate on January 20 in a thrust by the II Corps across the Rapido in the shadow of the enemy-held height of Monte Cassino. The climax of these efforts was to come two days later far in the enemy rear as General Lucas' VI Corps landed at Anzio.

The Fifth Army expected the VI Corps to be ready to do one of two things upon landing. If the enemy reacted in strength, the Corps was to take the defensive and assemble reserves to meet German counterattacks. If, on the other hand, the Corps could take the offensive, it was to advance "on" the Alban Hills by one of two routes: directly up the Albano road to cut Highway 7; or by way of Cisterna and Velletri to cut not only Highway 7 but also Highway 6 near Val-

montone. Whether the VI Corps assumed a defensive or offensive attitude after landing would depend on how General Lucas saw the
situation and on how he decided to act.

What were General Lucas' qualifications for this difficult assignment? Well thought of by General George C. Marshall, U.S. Army
Chief of Staff, Lucas had commanded the 3rd Infantry Division in
training in the United States. He had been with the Seventh Army
during the Sicily operation as General Eisenhower's deputy and
"Personal Representative with the Combat Troops." At the end of
the Sicily campaign, he had replaced Major General Omar N. Bradley as the II Corps commander. On September 20, eleven days after
the Salerno invasion, he had been appointed commander of the VI
Corps.[15] Since then he had competently directed the Corps in the
Italian campaign.

The mountain warfare in Italy had fatigued General Lucas, so that
by the end of 1943 he sometimes appeared dispirited and perhaps
even discouraged. In mid-January 1944, eight days before the Anzio
landing, he became fifty-four years old. "I am afraid I feel every year
of it," he wrote in his diary.[16] "I must keep from thinking of the
fact," he wrote on the following day, "that my order will send these
men into a desperate attack. . . ."[17] Though some feeling of this
sort must almost always be present in the mind of a commander, the
extent of General Lucas' feeling appears to have been more than
normal. Indeed, before the Anzio operation he seemed more impressed by its difficulties than by its opportunities.

General Lucas first learned of SHINGLE in late December 1943,
when General Clark informed him that the VI Corps would be relieved of responsibility for its front so that the Corps staff and the
units assigned could plan and train for the operation. Lucas' immediate reaction was to urge that his Corps headquarters be relieved at
once in order to ensure enough time for planning and training.[18]

The relief occurred on January 3, 1944, and General Lucas grap-
pled with the problem of shipping. "Unless we can get what we want
[in the way of vessels]," he confided to his diary, "the operation becomes such a desperate undertaking that it should not, in my opinion,
be attempted." Otherwise, "a crack on the chin is certain." Lucas
would do what he was ordered to do, "but these 'Battles of the Little
Big Horn' aren't much fun and a failure now would ruin Clark, probably kill me, and certainly prolong the war."[19]

A high-powered conference, with General Alexander presiding,
took place on January 9, with staff members of the 15th Army Group,

the Fifth Army, and the VI Corps in attendance. General Lucas' impressions revealed his own state of mind:

Apparently SHINGLE has become the most important operation in the present scheme of things. Sir Harold started the conference by stating that the operation would take place on January 22 with the troops as scheduled and that there would be no more discussion of these points. He quoted Mr. Churchill as saying, "It will astonish the world," and added, "it will certainly frighten Kesselring [the German commander in Italy]." I feel like a lamb being led to the slaughter but thought I was entitled to one bleat so I registered a protest against the target date as it gave me too little time for rehearsal. This is vital to the success of anything as terribly complicated as this. I was ruled down, as I knew I would be, many reasons being advanced as to the necessity for this speed. The real reasons cannot be military.

I have the bare minimum of ships and craft. The ones that are sunk cannot be replaced. The force that can be gotten ashore in a hurry is weak and I haven't sufficient artillery to hold me over but, on the other hand, I will have more air support than any similar operation ever had before. A week of fine weather at the proper time and I will make it.

After the conference Alexander told him, "We have every confidence in you. That is why you were picked." Lucas was hardly reassured. To him, "the whole affair has a strong odor of Gallipoli and apparently the same amateur was still on the coach's bench."

What most troubled General Lucas during the preparatory period was the contrast between his own concern to ensure proper planning and training and what he considered nonchalance in the higher echelons of command toward these matters. His urgent demands for more training time were met with the statement that both divisions scheduled to make the initial assault were experienced in amphibious operations. Lucas was not so sure. The 1st British Division, he remarked in his diary, had landed on Pantelleria more than six months earlier against no opposition and had not been in action since. The 3rd U.S. Division, which had landed in Sicily in July 1943 against opposition, had hardly been out of action since then, with the result that the turnover of infantry lieutenants totaled 115 per cent of authorized strength—"The men that knew the answers were gone."

The potential of the troops in the two initial assault divisions impressed Lucas. Time was "so pitifully short," however, that all aspects of training required to realize this potential could hardly, he felt, be covered adequately. "The Higher Levels just can't see that."

A final landing rehearsal conducted on January 19, three days before the Anzio operation, bore out General Lucas' pessimism. Everything went wrong. The British were bad, but the 3rd Division was worse—in fact "terrible"—for it lost some forty DUKW's (2½ ton amphibious trucks) and 10 105-mm. howitzers in the sea.[20] Yet Admiral Sir Andrew B. Cunningham, the Allied naval commander in the Mediterranean, assured Lucas that "the chances are seventy to thirty that, by the time you reach Anzio, the Germans will be north of Rome." Lucas commented in his diary, "Apparently everyone was in on the secret of the German intentions except me."

Lucas often wondered whether higher commanders had intelligence information not available to him. There must have been indications, he told himself desperately, that the enemy intended to pull out and move north of Rome. If so, he felt, all the more reason for making a strong end run with well-equipped forces that could intercept and destroy the withdrawing enemy units. But he believed his forces lacked the strength to do so, and he found only exaggeration, no ground for confidence, in Alexander's statement that Anzio would make OVER-LORD (the cross-Channel invasion) unnecessary.

When Lucas learned that Clark was planning to establish an advance Fifth Army command post near him at Anzio, he was upset. "I wish to hell he wouldn't. I don't need any help." Yet he was far from confident. "Army has gone nuts again," he wrote:

> The general idea seems to be that the Germans are licked and are fleeing in disorder and nothing remains but to mop up. The only reason for such a belief is that we have recently been able to advance a few miles against them with comparative ease. The Hun has pulled back a bit but I haven't seen the desperate fighting I have during the last four months without learning something. We are not (repeat not) in Rome yet.
>
> They will end up by putting me ashore with inadequate forces and get me in a serious jam. Then, who will take the blame.

On January 20, in an uncertain frame of mind, General Lucas boarded the USS *Biscayne* for the voyage to Anzio. "I have many misgivings," he wrote, "but am also optimistic." The weather was good, and if it continued that way for four or five days, Lucas felt, "I should be all right." The enemy did not seem to have discovered the SHINGLE intention. "I think we have a good chance to make a killing." Yet he was apprehensive because he believed that his assault troops still lacked training. "I wish the higher levels were not so over-optimistic. The Fifth Army is attacking violently towards the Cassino line and has sucked many German troops to the south and the high command seems to think they will stay there. I don't see why. They can still slow us up there and move against me at the same time."

General Lucas' uncertainty on the eve of the Anzio landing could be attributed not only to his own physical and mental fatigue but also to the inclination of a sensitive man to worry now that things were unalterably fixed—the preparations, for better or worse, were finished, and no deficiencies, imagined or real, could be remedied. There was nothing further to do but execute the mission. Under other circumstances, General Lucas might, on these very grounds, have dismissed worrisome thoughts. But part of his uncertainty arose from two events that had occurred shortly before the embarkation of his Corps.

The first was the visit of the Fifth Army G-3 (operations) chief, Brigadier General Donald W. Brann, to Lucas' headquarters on January 12. Brann carried with him and delivered personally the newly issued Fifth Army order on SHINGLE in order to discuss with Lucas, his chief of staff, and his G-3 the vague wording of the projected advance "on" the Alban Hills. Brann made it clear that Lucas' primary mission was to seize and secure a beachhead. This was all Fifth Army expected. Brann explained that much thought had gone into the wording of the order so as not to force Lucas to push on to the Alban Hill mass at the risk of sacrificing his Corps. Should conditions warrant a move to the heights, however, Lucas was free to take advantage of them. Such a possibility appeared slim to the Fifth Army staff, which questioned Lucas' ability to reach the hill mass and at the same time hold the beachhead to protect the port and the landing beaches. It was perfectly obvious what the loss of the supply base would mean. If the enemy came to Anzio in strength and destroyed this base, the isolated Allied force would be in an exceedingly tough spot.[21]

The second event bolstered this line of reasoning. According to an early conception of SHINGLE, the 504th Parachute Infantry Regiment was to have been dropped at H hour minus 1 on the Anzio-Albano road about 10 miles north of Anzio.[22] Such an operation was in accord with an offensive orientation, a reflection of the intent to reach and take the Alban Hills. Unfortunately, the British objected to the presence of paratroopers behind enemy lines. The British feared they might mistake the Americans for Germans and perhaps take them under fire. At the same time, Navy representatives pointed out that the paratroopers would be within range of naval guns supporting the landing. The relatively flat terrain of the Anzio coastal plain would offer little cover against naval shellfire. The result was cancellation of the parachute drop; the paratroopers were to come into Anzio across the beaches immediately after the infantry assault divisions.

The removal of a powerful incentive for pushing the VI Corps out from the landing beaches in order to make contact with the paratroopers thus coincided with the doubts expressed on the army level that Lucas could do more than seize and secure a beachhead. Since Lucas himself had reservations on the strength and the training of the troops under him, a successful landing and a subsequent securing of the beachhead despite hardy opposition would to him represent a successful operation.

What everyone had overlooked, even while bending every effort toward that end, was the possibility of achieving complete surprise. No one had taken seriously the thought that the Allies might actually gain total surprise in the landing. Yet this is what happened. "We achieved what is certainly one of the most complete surprises in history," General Lucas wrote, ". . . practically no opposition to the landing. . . . The *Biscayne* was anchored 3½ miles off shore, and I could not believe my eyes when I stood on the bridge and saw no machine gun or other fire on the beach." The fact was that the VI Corps had embarked at Naples for a water movement of 120 miles with an assault force of almost 50,000 men and 5,200 vehicles—a total of 27 infantry battalions comprising about the same strength as the force landed at Salerno—and arrived at Anzio without having been detected by the Germans.

American and British planes of the Mediterranean Air Forces flew more than 1,200 sorties on D Day in direct support of the Anzio landing; they were hardly necessary. The only resistance offered the landing came from a few small coast artillery and antiaircraft detachments. Two batteries fired wildly for a few minutes before daylight until they were quickly silenced by naval guns. A few other 88-mm. guns and miscellaneous artillery pieces of French, Italian, and Yugoslav manufacture near the beaches had no chance to fire.

Small scattered mine fields, mostly in the port of Anzio, proved the greatest hazard to the troops coming ashore. The only opposition to the push immediately inland came from elements of two depleted coast-watching battalions which, along with two other battalions, had been recently relieved from the Garigliano front for rest and rehabilitation.

How had it happened? The Germans had always regarded the long sea flanks in Italy as being very much exposed to Allied amphibious attacks, and in December 1943 the German High Command—OKW —issued a directive on how to cope with possible landings on the Italian coast. In the event of an Allied invasion near Rome, the OKW planned to reinforce Field Marshal Albert Kesselring, the commander in Italy, with 2 infantry divisions sent from France, 2 infantry divisions moved from the Balkans, and about the equivalent of a division dispatched from Germany.[23]

Kesselring and his Army Group C headquarters also made prior arrangements as to how to meet Allied landings, among them a possible descent on the coast near Rome. To deal immediately with such a landing, Kesselring counted on having in army group reserve a parachute division in the process of organization and one or two mobile divisions, plus a corps headquarters. To reinforce these elements, he expected to call upon the Tenth Army for a division to be pulled out of the active front in south Italy; he hoped to have the Fourteenth Army in north Italy move elements in process of activation, reconstitution, training, or rehabilitation—the equivalent of about one or two divisions.

Why, then, had the VI Corps found no German units of any importance in immediate opposition at Anzio? Despite Kesselring's intention to retain reserve units around Rome, he had sent them—only a few days before the Anzio landing—to reinforce the Tenth Army front. Fearing that the Fifth Army was about to make a breakthrough along the lower Garigliano River, feeling that the fate of the Tenth Army right flank "hung by a slender thread," Kesselring between January 18 and 20 yielded to urgent requests for additional troops and dispatched from the Rome area the I Parachute Corps headquarters and the 29th and 90th Panzer Grenadier Divisions. These troops assumed responsibility for a portion of the XIV Panzer Corps front.[24] They had barely been committed along the Garigliano when the VI Corps came ashore at Anzio. As a result, there were no forces near Rome to counter the Anzio landings, there was no staff available to organize even an emergency defense. According to the first German estimate, the landing had a good chance of bringing the main front "to a state of collapse" because of the absence of immediate German reserves.[25] The troops in the coastal areas around Rome were so few that they could be counted on merely for coastal observation.

With German defense virtually nil, Allied troops quickly moved ashore. The 3rd Division reached its initial objectives and made ready to repel a counterattack that did not come. All organic division light artillery and the combat elements of the attached tank and antiaircraft battalions were brought to land by DUKW's and LCT's before daylight. Patrols seized and destroyed four bridges across the Mussolini Canal along the division right flank. By midmorning the 3rd Division commander radioed Lucas he was established and ready for further orders.

At the same time, the Ranger Force seized the port of Anzio. The 509th Parachute Infantry Battalion occupied Nettuno. British troops, delayed somewhat by mines and shallow water, were two miles inland shortly after midday. Commandos established a roadblock across the Albano road just north of Anzio.

Meanwhile, Field Marshal Kesselring, as soon as he learned of the invasion at Anzio, assumed that the disembarking troops would probably try to seize the Alban Hills. At 5 A.M., January 22, three hours after the initial landing, he ordered the 4th Parachute Division, in the process of activation near Rome, and certain nearby replacement units of the Hermann Goering Panzer Division to block the roads leading to the Alban Hills and to Rome. An hour later, he reported the landing to the OKW and requested troops. The OKW responded that day by ordering the 715th Motorized Infantry Division to move from southern France to Italy, the 114th Light (Jaeger) Division from the Balkans, miscellaneous units in about division strength from Germany, and, furthermore, the 92nd Infantry Division to be activated in Italy.

Since units outside the theater could not arrive near Anzio before a few days at the earliest, Kesselring, at 7:10 A.M., January 22, ordered the Fourteenth Army to make forces available. The army ordered the 65th Division (less one regiment) at Genoa, the 362nd Infantry Division (less one regiment) at Rimini, and the newly formed 16th SS Panzer Grenadier Division (with two regiments) to proceed immediately to the beachhead. Movement started that evening and continued through the following day.

At 8:30, Kesselring ordered the Tenth Army to transfer to Anzio a corps headquarters and all the combat troops that could be spared. The army pulled the I Parachute Corps out of the line and sent combat troops then in reserve—the 3rd Panzer Grenadier Division (less one regiment), the 71st Infantry Division, and parts of the Hermann Goering Panzer Division, all of which began to move toward Anzio that day. From the Adriatic portion of the Tenth Army front were soon to come the 26th Panzer Division and elements of the 1st Parachute Division.

At 5 P.M., January 22, the I Parachute Corps headquarters took command in the Anzio sector and, with arriving troops—miscellaneous battalions—as they became available, established a defensive line around the beachhead.

Having acted with coolness and dispatch, the Germans were considerably reassured by Allied behavior at the scene of the landing.

The Allies on the beachhead on the first day of the landing did not conform to the German High Command's expectations. Instead of moving northward with the first wave to seize the Alban Mountains . . . as the target, the landing forces limited their objective. Their initial action was to occupy a small beachhead. . . . As the Allied forces made no preparations for a large-scale attack on the first day of the landings, the German Command estimated that the Allies would improve their positions, and bring up more troops. . . . During this time, sufficient German troops would arrive to prevent an Allied breakthrough.[26]

By the evening of January 22, Kesselring decided that the lack of VI Corps aggressiveness would permit him to fashion a successful defense. Despite recommendations by the Tenth Army and XIV Panzer Corps commanders, who advocated immediate withdrawal and shortening of the Garigliano-Rapido front in order to get two seasoned divisions to Anzio, Kesselring instructed them to stand fast.[27] This was a courageous decision and in the nature of a gamble, for the first strong defense contingents at Anzio would come from the Tenth Army, and the earliest they could be expected was January 24. If the Allies launched an attack on January 23 or 24, German forces, Kesselring estimated, would not be strong enough to hold.[28]

There was no major action at the beachhead on January 23, and that evening Kesselring told the Tenth Army commander that he "believed that the danger of a large-scale expansion at the beachhead was no longer imminent." [29]

Operations on January 24 were also uneventful. As the Germans hoped, "the Allied landing forces limited themselves to reconnaissance and patrol . . . as well as adjusting their artillery fire on German positions. By this time, the German defenses had been strongly reinforced, and the German Command considered the danger of an Allied breakthrough to be removed." [30] By restricting its forces to consolidation of the beachhead, the Allied VI Corps restricted its efforts to local attacks, and with these, the Germans felt, they could cope.

On the Allied side, Generals Alexander and Clark had visited Anzio on D Day and both seemed satisfied. Alexander was very optimistic, Clark somewhat subdued. General Lucas thought Clark depressed by the offensive on his main Garigliano-Rapido front. The troops there had failed to breach the German line at Cassino, the entrance to the Liri Valley. Though the British 10th Corps had secured a bridgehead across the lower Garigliano, though the French Expeditionary Corps had made unexpectedly good progress fighting in the mountains near Cassino, the U.S. II Corps had been unable to get across and remain across the Rapido River in strength, the 36th Division in the attempt sustaining very heavy casualties in assault crossings on January 20 and 21. "The last thing Clark said to me on D Day before he embarked for [the return trip to] Naples," General Lucas later remembered, "was 'Don't stick your neck out, Johnny. I did at Salerno and got into trouble.' " [31]

General Lucas was not about to "stick his neck out." Having gained surprise in the landing, he proceeded to disregard the advantage it gave him. Two days after coming ashore, on January 24, he was thinking of pushing out from the beachhead. "I must keep in motion if my first success is to be of any value." But his push outward was in no sense an all-out drive toward the Alban Hills; it was no more than preliminary or preparatory movement.

The fact was that General Lucas showed more interest in building up his beachhead. Capturing the Anzio harbor intact and putting it into operation immediately to handle incoming troops and supplies were to him the most important achievements of the landing. He saw the port as his "salvation," the most significant part of the supply line stretching between Naples and Anzio, an umbilical cord tying the Anzio force to the Fifth Army. To keep the line intact, General Lucas personally supervised setting up an antiaircraft warning system, building an airfield, clearing the clutter of supplies and equipment that jammed the beachhead behind the first row of dunes.

His concern with the logistical aspects of the landing came not only from prudence but also from apprehension that had been haunting him from the outset. He believed that the Germans, using land communications, could increase their build-up faster than he could with his reliance on water transport. And he feared that the Germans would stop his VI Corps before it could cut their lines of communication. His intelligence officers informed him that the Germans were taking troops from the Fifth Army main front to oppose him. This might permit the Fifth Army to advance to the north of Rome, but the Fifth Army, Lucas was certain, would still have to fight powerful rear guards. He expected no spectacular rapidity of movement on the part of the Fifth Army, and thus, harking back to an earlier conception in which the VI Corps landing was to assist the advance of the Fifth Army main front, he saw his force at Anzio consigned to at least temporary isolation. Consequently, he sought to build up his strength and his supplies to enable his force to remain intact even though isolated. "The strain of a thing like this is a terrible burden," he confessed. "Who the hell wants to be a general."

"My days are filled with excitement and anxiety," General Lucas wrote on January 25, the fourth day of the landing operation, "although I feel now that the beachhead is safe and I can plan for the future with some assurance." A regimental combat team of the 45th Division was coming ashore that day, and Lucas expected the 1st Armored Division to arrive soon, to be followed by the remainder of the 45th. "That is about all I can supply but I think it will be enough." Meanwhile, the 1st British and 3rd U.S. Divisions were advancing "to extend the beachhead a little."

General Clark visited Lucas that day and revealed that he was disturbed over developments on the main army front, "where the bloodiest fight of the war is in progress. . . . That situation," Lucas felt, "will not be resolved, I am afraid, until I can get my feet under me and make some further progress. I am doing my best but it seems terribly slow. . . . I must keep my feet on the ground and my forces in hand and do nothing foolish. This is the most important thing I have ever tried to do and I will not be stampeded."

General Alexander also paid Lucas a visit and complimented him. "What a splendid piece of work," he said. Lucas reminded him that the task was not yet finished, even though the beachhead was now nearly 10 miles deep—not bad, Lucas thought, for D Day plus 3. "I must hold it," he wrote, "and think I can."

While General Lucas was building up his beachhead, Field Marshal Kesselring came to the conclusion that the Allies were preparing a full-scale attack. The best defense, he felt, was an attack of his own. To prepare such an effort, he ordered the Fourteenth Army headquarters to move from north Italy and take command at the beachhead. At 6 P.M., January 25, the Fourteenth Army did so and began to plan an attack designed to throw the VI Corps back into the sea.

Rain, hail, and sleet came on January 26 to disrupt General Lucas' logistical efforts. "This waiting is terrible," Lucas wrote. "I want an all-out Corps effort but the time hasn't come yet and the weather will not help matters. Bad for tanks. . . . I hope to get moving soon.

Must move before the enemy build-up gets too great." He thought he could attack in a few days, but he felt he needed to have the entire 45th Division on hand or on the way before he did.

Two heavy air raids occurred that night, doing considerable damage—trucks destroyed, ammunition exploding, people killed, fires everywhere, craters in the roads—but the port was still operating, the ships were unloading, "thank God."

Division commanders met with Lucas on January 27 to talk over future plans, and Lucas felt better about prospects. He expected 30 LST's to be unloaded at Anzio that day as compared with 7 the day before, and he looked forward to getting more than 30 unloaded on the following day.

Unknown to Lucas, General Alexander that day, January 27, was expressing dissatisfaction to General Clark. Alexander thought the VI Corps was not pushing rapidly enough. This statement prodded Clark, who had vaguely felt also that progress was lagging. So he went to Anzio the next day and there received the impression that the outcome of the struggle depended on who could increase his forces more quickly. Though the situation was still not clear to Clark, he urged Lucas to take bold offensive action. As he remembered later, what he wanted Lucas to do was to secure Cisterna as a strongpoint in a defensive line.[32]

But either Clark did not remember correctly or Lucas misinterpreted his remarks. For as the result of Clark's comments, Lucas that evening felt obliged to explain his whole course of action:

Apparently some of the higher levels think I have not advanced with maximum speed. I think more has been accomplished than anyone had a right to expect. This venture was always a desperate one and I could never see much chance for it to succeed, if success means driving the German north of Rome. The one factor that has allowed us to get established ashore has been the port of Anzio. Without it our situation by this time would have been desperate with little chance of a build-up to adequate strength. As it is, we are doing well and, in addition to troops, unloaded over 4,000 tons of supplies yesterday.

Had I been able to rush to the high ground around Albano and Velletri immediately upon landing, nothing would have been accomplished except to weaken my force by that amount because the troops sent, being completely beyond supporting distance, would have been immediately destroyed. The only thing to do was what I did. Get a proper beachhead and prepare to hold it. Keep the enemy off balance by a constant advance against him by small units, not committing anything as large as a division until the Corps was ashore and everything was set. Then make a coordinated attack to defeat the enemy and seize the objective. Follow this by exploitation.

This is what I have been doing but I had to have troops in to do it with.

By this time, on the seventh day of the operation, with more troops arriving on schedule—and to the point where Lucas could envisage holding some in corps reserve—he was ready to make his offensive bid. The effort was to start the night of January 29 with the 3rd Division and Ranger Force attacking toward Cisterna, northeast from Anzio, to cut Highway 7 and be ready to advance toward Cori— in the direction of Valmontone and eventual control of Highway 6. The British were to attack to the north to seize the area near the juncture of the Anzio-Albano road and the Cisterna-Rome railway, which would represent not only a breakthrough of the German defenses around the beachhead but a foothold on the foothills of the Alban mass. Units of the 1st Armored Division were then to deploy to the northern slope of the hill complex. Since the attacks were divergent, Lucas kept tight control, for he feared that if his forces became overextended, the Germans would try to come between them and cut the beachhead in two.

Soon after the VI Corps jumped off, it was "engaged in a hell of a struggle. . . . There is never a big breakthrough except in story books. . . . The situation, from where I sit, is crowded with doubt and uncertainty. I expect to be counterattacked in some force, maybe considerable force, tomorrow morning."

General Clark came to Anzio on January 29 with the intention perhaps of remaining for several days. General Lucas was not entirely happy with the prospect:

His gloomy attitude is certainly bad for me. He thinks I should have been more aggressive on D-Day and should have gotten tanks and things out to the front. I think he realizes the serious nature of the whole operation. His forces are divided in the face of a superior enemy on interior lines and now neither of the parts is capable of inflicting a real defeat on those facing it. There has been no chance, with available shipping, to build "Shingle" up to a decisive strength and anyone with any knowledge of logistics could have seen that from the start. I have done what I was ordered to do, desperate though it was. I can win if I am let alone but I don't know whether I can stand the strain of having so many people looking over my shoulder. We must continue to push the Germans.

Clark was still at Anzio on the last day of the month. "I don't blame him for being terribly disappointed," Lucas wrote. "He and those above him thought this landing would shake the Cassino line loose at once but they had no right to think that, because the German is strong in Italy and will give no ground if he can help it."

It was clear by then that Lucas' attack had failed to accomplish much. Furthermore, a disastrous engagement comparable to the 36th Division experience at the Rapido had occurred: the Ranger Force had lost two battalions—about 800 men—near Cisterna, having met unanticipated opposition at an unexpectedly strong and well-organized defensive position. It seemed clear also that the Germans had built up their forces around Anzio to the point where prospects of cutting the enemy lines of communication immediately south of Rome were fading rapidly.

What the Allies did not know was how close they came to breaking out of the beachhead. The Germans repulsed the large-scale attack of the VI Corps, but only with the greatest exertion. Not only did they have to postpone their own offensive preparations but they had to go over entirely to defense. They maintained their defensive line by a desperate juggling of forces and the commitment of all reserves, even those being held for the all-out counterattack (principally the 26th Panzer Division). The 715th Division arrived from France in time to enter the battle piecemeal near Cisterna.

What to Allied intelligence officers seemed like overwhelming German strength was in reality what Kesselring characterized as "a higgledy-piggledy jumble—units of numerous divisions fighting confusedly side by side." [33] Identifying many different divisional units, Allied intelligence officers had to assume, by the very nature of their profession, that each of those divisions was present in entirety. Total numbers then, like total units, they guessed, outnumbered the VI Corps. Yet actually, opposing the approximately 100,000 men of the VI Corps, of which about 25,000 were service troops, were less than 90,000 troops of the Fourteenth Army, of which probably 30,000 were noncombatant.

Though numbers were almost equal, the VI Corps enjoyed a distinct advantage. Whereas by comparison the VI Corps amphibious operation had been thoroughly planned and prepared, the German countermeasures were taken on the spur of the moment in time of stress and emergency. The German defenders at Anzio had been hastily assembled, the defenses hastily established. For the most part, fragments, remnants, and splinters of divisions, depleted units, recently organized units, provisional commands, barely trained troops manned the line. Because the great majority of the German troops at

Anzio were unseasoned, the fact that they held was rather miraculous from the German point of view.[34]

General Alexander arrived at Anzio on February 1, and General Lucas found him

. . . kind enough but I am afraid he is not pleased. My head will probably fall in the basket but I have done my best. There were just too many Germans here for me to lick and they could build up faster than I could. As I told Clark yesterday, I was sent on a desperate mission, one where the odds were greatly against success, and I went without saying anything because I was given an order and my opinion was not asked. The condition in which I find myself is much better than I ever antici- pated or had any right to expect.

When Clark and Alexander both departed Anzio, Lucas felt some- what reassured. He had suspected they had come to see whether he should be relieved of command. He was pleased they had been at Anzio, for at least, he felt, his superiors had seen the desperate nature of the fighting and could appreciate the rapidity of the German build-up opposite the VI Corps. Also, he was proud to show that the port and the beaches were working at capacity. Supplies amassed at the beachhead were fully ten days ahead of schedule.

The supply situation was so favorable that Lucas thought that he could support two more divisions in the beachhead. When he broached the matter to Alexander, he received only an enigmatic smile in reply.[35]

He did not know that Alexander and Clark had already decided on February 1 that the enemy build-up on the Anzio front dictated a switch to defensive tactics. Security of the beachhead became the overriding priority. In an order dated February 2, Alexander in- structed Lucas to hold his front with a minimum number of troops and prepare reserve positions to stop large-scale penetrations by the enemy. He was to protect the main approaches to the beachhead by establishing strongpoints reinforced by mines and wire in depth. The VI Corps was to turn its attention to active patrolling, to forming small but highly mobile reserve forces, and to rehearsing defensive arrangements.[36]

Lucas received the same order from Fifth Army early on February 3. He was to cease offensive action and consolidate his positions. "I hate to stop attacking," Lucas wrote. "We must keep him [the enemy] off balance all we can." [37]

By that time, keeping the enemy "off balance" was a forlorn hope. The initiative had passed to the Germans, and the VI Corps was about to start fighting for its life, seeking to preserve the precious ground it held. "Things get worse and worse," Lucas wrote on February 10, and five days later, "I am afraid the top side is not completely satisfied with my work. . . . They are naturally disappointed that I failed to chase the Hun out of Italy but there was no military reason why I should have been able to do so. In fact, there is no military reason for 'Shingle.' "

Lieutenant General Jacob L. Devers, deputy theater commander to General Wilson, who replaced Eisenhower in January, visited Lucas on February 16. He seemed to think that as soon as Lucas was ashore he should have gone on as fast as possible to disrupt enemy communications. He intimated that higher levels thought so and still did. "Had I done so," Lucas wrote, "I would have lost my Corps and nothing would have been accomplished except to raise the prestige and morale of the enemy. Besides," he added, "my orders didn't read that way."

The Germans launched their all-out effort on February 16 to drive the VI Corps back into the sea, and on the following day the commander of the 3rd Division was appointed Lucas' deputy. "I think this means my relief and that he gets the Corps," Lucas wrote. Still, "I hope I am not to be relieved from command. I knew when I came in here that I was jeopardizing my career because I knew the Germans would not fold up because of two divisions landing on their flank. . . . I do not feel that I should have sacrificed my command [by driving on to the Alban Hills]."

General Lucas was in fact relieved from command of the VI Corps on February 22, one month after the landing—not because he had failed to take the Alban Hills, but because Alexander thought him exhausted and defeated, Devers thought him tired, and Clark believed he was worn out. Explaining that he, Clark, "could no longer resist the pressure . . . from both Alexander and Devers," Clark relieved Lucas without prejudice. He had not lost confidence in Lucas, for he felt that Lucas had done all he could have at Anzio. Lucas, though shocked by the actual occurrence, was not entirely surprised by his relief. What bothered him most: "I thought I was winning something of a victory." [38]

General Clark, as a matter of fact, thought so too. He felt that Lucas could have taken the Alban Hills but could not have held them. Had Lucas moved immediately to the hill mass objective, he would have so extended his force that the Germans would have cut it to pieces. This was why he had seen to it that his order to Lucas had been carefully phrased—so that the VI Corps would not be assigned a "foolhardy mission." Clark had not thought it wise to tell Lucas before the operation, "you are to take the Alban Hills." For Lucas would then have been obliged to push to the objective before he secured his initial beachhead line.

Clark completely approved Lucas' course of action during the first few days of the operation; he was not disappointed. Alexander, Clark felt, was disappointed, and Clark thought that the cause of his disappointment was "British G-2 intelligence sources which were always over optimistic about the German resistance in Italy." The Germans built up their defenses at Anzio much faster than the British had believed possible, though Clark himself had always felt that Anzio had had little chance of success because it was not mounted in sufficient strength.[39]

Quite some time after the event, General Clark, thinking about the blood spilled along the Garigliano and at Anzio, came to the conclusion that it might better have been spilled entirely at the main front rather than on a "dangerous and unorganized beachhead" where a powerful counterattack could well have wrecked the entire Italian campaign. It was true that by the end of January Clark was disappointed by Lucas' lack of aggressiveness. Where Lucas was at fault, Clark believed, was in having failed to make a reconnaissance in force at once to capture Cisterna and Campoleone—an effort, Clark thought, not incommensurate with the strength of his forces.[40]

Others felt much the same way about the strength available to Lucas. General Marshall was of the opinion that Lucas could have managed to get to the Alban Hills, but he thought Lucas acted wisely —"for every mile of advance there were seven or more miles [to be] added to the perimeter." Lucas, Marshall believed, did not have enough men to get to the hills, to hold them, and also to hold the beachhead and the Anzio port.[41]

Such was the opinion of the theater G-2 who had opposed the operation at the Christmas Day conference at Tunis. The Anzio force could have advanced to the Alban Hills the first day or two, he was sure, but the force would then have been in a bad way without a concurrent Allied breakthrough on the main front. The Allies were unable to keep the Germans from shifting forces to Anzio from south as well as from north Italy and from southern France and the Balkans.[42]

Brigadier General Lyman L. Lemnitzer, General Alexander's American deputy, also felt the Allies did not have the strength to hold the Alban Hills. General Alexander had hoped, as Lemnitzer understood the idea, that the threat posed by the operation, coupled with the attack on the main (Garigliano-Rapido) front, might force the Germans to withdraw. The Fifth Army order for Lucas to advance "on" the hills was exactly what Alexander thought possible. And when Alexander visited the beachhead on D Day, he was in full agreement with Lucas' decision not to push out far from Anzio. He thoroughly approved Lucas' caution.

What inclined Alexander toward relieving Lucas, Lemnitzer thought, was his feeling that Lucas was unequal to the physical strain of the critical Anzio situation, not any feeling that Lucas had done anything wrong. Alexander, according to Lemnitzer, sensed that Lucas, "harried looking and under tremendous strain, would not be able to stand up physically to the hard, long struggle which by that time it was clear the Anzio operation would involve." [43]

It would seem then that Lucas' course of action during the first few days of the Anzio landing was justified. The Germans facing the main Fifth Army front along the Garigliano and Rapido showed no signs of withdrawing, and consequently the Allies saw no immediate prospect of forcing a general retreat and quickly linking the main front with the beachhead. It became far more likely that the Germans would move in strength against the VI Corps at Anzio. If the VI Corps went too far inland, it might be so extended as to risk annihilation. So Lucas had consolidated his positions, awaited reinforcements, and probed along the two main axes of advance toward the intermediate objectives of Cisterna and Campoleone to secure pivots for the advance on the Alban Hills. When he was ready to make his major effort, the Germans by then—after a week—had assembled sufficient forces to repel his attack.

Sufficient forces, but not overwhelming strength, as pictured by Allied intelligence during the battle and by Allied participants later. That the Germans were skillful at Anzio, no less in their build-up than in their actual defense, would be an understatement. Yet it would seem that Allied hesitation on the Anzio shore came from an appreciation of German invincibility that was little more than an apparition bred of doubt and uncertainty both before and during the operation, a myth to explain, afterward, a course of events that seemed inevitable because it happened that way. The opportunity for doing something else had come and gone, and after the first few days it was too late to do otherwise. And this was how General Lucas saw it:

The only thing that ever really disturbed me at Anzio, except, of course, my inability to make speedier headway against the weight opposing me, was the necessity to safeguard the port. At any cost this must be preserved as, without it, the swift destruction of the Corps was inevitable. . . . My orders were, to me, very clear and did not include any rash, piecemeal effort. These orders were never changed although the Army and the Army Group Commanders were constantly on the ground and could have changed them had they seen fit to do so.[44]

Despite his feeling that he could not have done otherwise, the alternative course of action open to General Lucas immediately after the landing remained a disturbing possibility to him. He could see many things that could have been done differently. A mass of armor and motorized infantry, he admitted, might perhaps have been able to make a sudden raid inland on D Day and reach the Alban Hills. But in his final analysis, Lucas was sure he could not have maintained the force there. The Germans had moved so swiftly that any force that far from home would have been in the greatest jeopardy. Lucas did not see how such a force could have escaped annihilation. "As it turned out," Lucas wrote, "the proper decision was made and we were able to reach and establish ourselves in positions from which the enemy was unable to drive us, in spite of his great advantage in strength." [45]

The whole idea of the Anzio operation, General Lucas continued to believe, was a mistake. If anyone expected him to push to the Alban Hills, he was bound to be disappointed. Lucas had never expected to push to the hill mass with the troops he had. He had seen his main mission as taking the port and securing the area around it. Perhaps part of his preoccupation with the port came from the Navy. "Make it clear to the Commanding General," Admiral Cunningham had advised the Anzio task force commander, "that no reliance can be placed on maintenance over beaches, owing to the probability of unfavorable weather. . . ." [46] As for the idea of taking Rome, General Clark had told him, "you can forget this goddam Rome business." [47]

If security rather than an offensive intention had become the most important aspect of the operation, the Alban Hills still figured prominently. The capture of the Anzio port was an obvious objective. But because of the commanding position of the Alban Hills, early occupation of this terrain feature was vital, to secure a limited force landed in a beachhead.[48] The VI Corps forces that remained isolated in the Anzio beachhead for four long months of agony were to appreciate the importance of the dominating terrain. German observers enjoyed an excellent view over the entire beachhead, a view obscured occasionally by atmospheric haze, more frequently by a heroic Allied expenditure of smoke, and German artillerymen found all parts of the beachhead within range of their guns.[49]

Was, then, General Lucas completely justified in building up the beachhead for seven days before starting his offensive? Or could he have got away with the gamble of an immediate drive to the Alban Hills? Certainly the complete surprise achieved at Anzio could have been exploited. And according to Tenth Army estimates, only a quick cutting of the lines of communication would have led to major Allied success, a success more than likely encompassing the capture of Rome.[50] According to Kesselring's Chief of Staff, "The road to Rome was open, and an audacious flying column could have penetrated to the city. . . . The enemy remained astonishingly passive." [51]

What if General Lucas had taken advantage of the surprise gained? Suppose he had not waited but had instead made an immediate aggressive move to the heights dominating the southern approaches to Rome. Could the Germans have massed enough forces to withstand a dynamic front as they did against the static front at Anzio? In view of the greater mechanization and mobility of Allied forces, would the Germans have dared to hold on to both the Anzio and Garigliano fronts if threatened by the much greater menace that an Allied force ensconced on the Alban Hills would have posed?

The answers may be found within the realm of speculation only. But the wisp of a nagging doubt remains. According to General Alexander, an aggressive commander at Anzio would have given the Fifth Army order to advance "on" the Alban Hills an interpretation different from that of General Lucas. Seizing upon the surprise attained, he would have—and could have—pushed patrols and light forces, in perhaps regimental strength, to the Alban Hills. The shock of finding Allied troops directly threatening Rome and the vital lines of communication might have so demoralized the Germans as to make possible Allied retention both of the hill mass and of a corridor between Anzio and the hills. A bluff—if prosecuted with imagination and daring, if carried through with vigor, if executed with the intention of raising havoc in the German rear—might have worked. Suppose, for example, General Patton had commanded the corps that came ashore at Anzio. . . .[52]

Sidney T. Mathews

12

*General Clark's Decision
to Drive on Rome
(1944)*

By the last week of May 1944, the Allied front in Italy had exploded
into action.* To the men on the Allied side who were doing the fighting, it seemed high time, for the forces in Italy had seen few real successes since the fall of 1943 when they had come ashore in Salerno
Bay and pushed northward beyond Naples to the so-called Winter
Line. Every attempt to engineer a far-reaching success had met with
bitter frustration.

But now the U.S. Fifth Army along the west coast had penetrated
the enemy's most imposing line of prepared defenses short of Rome.
The adjacent British Eighth Army also had made notable gains up
the valley of the Liri River, the route affording the most favorable
terrain for an advance on Rome. At the same time, the U.S. VI
Corps, which for nearly four months had been contained by a
strong enemy cordon in a shallow beachhead at Anzio, 33 miles
south of Rome, had broken its confinement. The VI Corps and the
rest of the Fifth Army at last had established contact.[1]

The commander of Allied forces in Italy, General Sir Harold
R. L. G. Alexander, already had indicated how the Fifth and Eighth
Armies were to capitalize on the early successes of the offensive.
While the Eighth Army and the bulk of the Fifth were to continue to
push northwestward in the general direction of Rome, the VI Corps
from the Anzio beachhead was to strike northeastward to seize the
town of Valmontone, astride Highway 6, the line of communications
to the German Tenth Army, which was opposing the main Allied at-

* See map on p. 246.

tack farther south.[2] Thus the VI Corps was to block the Tenth Army's logical route of withdrawal, possibly trapping the main body of the enemy, but certainly embarrassing further enemy operations on the southern front. This strike to Valmontone, General Alexander believed, was the most rewarding possibility open to the VI Corps for making a sizable contribution to the big offensive.

The commander of the U.S. Fifth Army, Lieutenant General Mark W. Clark, whose command included the VI Corps, was not so sure. General Clark's doubts about the Valmontone maneuver dated back to the period of planning before the start of the offensive when the Allied commander first had indicated his broad concept of the operation.[3] Unlike Alexander, Clark had believed that the decisive role would fall, not to the Eighth Army attacking frontally against the main enemy defenses in the Liri Valley, but to the Fifth Army, attacking through mountainous terrain west of the Liri and thereby outflanking German strength in the valley. Clark also disagreed with Alexander's estimate of what the VI Corps, with limited forces, could accomplish by a strike into the enemy's rear and flank. In keeping with his doubts, Clark early had instructed the VI Corps commander, Major General Lucian K. Truscott, to draw up alternate plans.[4] Now, on the morning of May 25, as forces from Anzio and from the south made contact and as the VI Corps reached positions from which the strike to Valmontone might be launched, the time for a final decision on the form and direction of the VI Corps exploitation was at hand.

The decision facing General Clark was no ordinary command decision. Indeed, since the views of the Army Group commander, General Alexander, had been spelled out so specifically, some army commanders would have considered that there was no room for decision at an army level at all. Yet Clark was determined that the action of the VI Corps should not be compromised by some predetermined concept but that the Corps should be used in what he considered the most advantageous manner in keeping with the situation at the time.

Throughout the planning before the offensive, General Clark had expressed uncertainty as to the most suitable direction for exploitation and had sought to defer a decision until the nature of the enemy's reaction to the offensive on the southern front became apparent. Indeed, he had even delayed a decision on the direction of the initial axis of attack to break out of the beachhead until the enemy reaction was clear. Though aware early that Alexander held an almost single-minded devotion to a drive from the beachhead through the German stronghold of Cisterna to Valmontone, Clark still did not consider himself bound to accept this as the only course of action. All through the planning period, Clark's freedom to consider alternate plans had been facilitated by the failure of Alexander to issue a direct written order, even though he had expounded the general concept of the Valmontone maneuver at several conferences. Clark himself had expressed no opinion at these conferences about Alexander's concept.[5]

Insisting on the necessity of flexibility, Clark, in directing the VI Corps to draw up alternate schemes of maneuver, had suggested four different axes of advance and had specified that the Corps be ready, on forty-eight-hours' notice, to carry out whichever seemed appropriate.[6] When, on May 5, Alexander issued a formal field order prescribing the Valmontone axis and during a visit to the beachhead personally directed the Corps commander, General Truscott, to concentrate his preparations on the Valmontone maneuver, Clark still did not swerve from his conviction that Truscott should be prepared for other eventualities.[7] To Alexander, Clark did not protest the substance of either Alexander's formal orders or his informal instructions to Truscott, but he did object to Alexander's bypassing the army command channel to deal directly with Truscott. With Truscott himself, Clark in effect contravened his superior's order by directing the Corps commander to make full preparations for carrying out either of the two main alternative schemes: the Cisterna-Valmontone attack, which Alexander favored, or a thrust northwestward along the west side of the Alban Hills through Albano on the most direct route to Rome.[8]

On May 17, after progress of the big offensive on the southern front had made clear that favorable conditions for an attack from argued that it might not be the decisive operation which Alexander the question of the direction of the VI Corps attack. Stressing the difficulties of the Valmontone maneuver, the Fifth Army commander argued that it might not be the decisive operation which Alexander contemplated and that, in any case, the selection of the axis of attack should be deferred until the enemy's situation became clearer. Unmoved, General Alexander indicated that he favored the Valmontone maneuver regardless of the enemy situation. For the first time, apparently, Alexander spelled out how the maneuver would be carried out beyond Valmontone—by light, mobile patrols striking to cut other roads available to the Germans north of Highway 6.[9]

His skepticism heightened by this additional information on the proposed maneuver, Clark nevertheless decided that in the face of

Alexander's continued stand he must at least order the VI Corps to attack initially in the direction of Valmontone, with the mission of breaking the German defenses at Cisterna.[10]

This he did, but he still did not feel rigidly bound to pursue the attack all the way to Valmontone to the exclusion of other operations that circumstances might indicate. He reserved his freedom to decide what course to pursue after Cisterna, even though he had no expectation that Alexander would alter the scope or form of the Valmontone maneuver. In short, Clark recognized that if the situation developed favorably for an attack directly toward Rome, he would have to make his decision independently.[11]

Without notifying Alexander, Clark instructed Truscott to be ready after taking Cisterna to shift the main axis of attack to the northwest toward Rome. He had not decided to adopt this course, but he wanted the VI Corps to be ready to carry it out if favorable conditions developed. The conditions which Clark had in mind included an Allied breakthrough of the last of the enemy's prepared defenses on the southern front and enemy withdrawal to the Caesar Line, another prepared position based on the southern slopes of the Alban Hills south and southeast of Rome.

By the early afternoon of May 25, it seemed to Clark that the desired developments had occurred. In addition, the VI Corps at Cisterna had scored a smashing success. The time for a decision had come.[12]

In the circumstances, General Clark could contemplate three feasible courses of action. He could throw the entire weight of the VI Corps (which rested on the striking power of five good U.S. divisions) toward Valmontone to cut Highway 6, threaten the rear of the German Tenth Army, and cut the enemy's main line of communication to the southern front. Or, he could turn the entire Corps northwest from the Cisterna area in an attack against the Alban Hills along the most direct route toward Rome. Or, finally, he could ride both horses, striking simultaneously in both directions.

Despite substantial losses in nearly three days of intensive action, Clark felt that the combat troops of the VI Corps were still in good fighting shape. Only the 1st Armored and 3rd Infantry Divisions had been involved in the heavy fighting around Cisterna. The 36th Infantry Division had been in reserve, while the 34th and 45th Infantry Divisions and a specially trained mobile group, the First Special Service Force, had played only supporting roles.[13]

The enemy, on the other hand, Clark believed, was in a state of rapid deterioration, incapable of halting a VI Corps offensive, either against the Alban Hills or toward Valmontone. The two divisions of the German Fourteenth Army which had unsuccessfully opposed the VI Corps' main effort on either side of Cisterna obviously had incurred heavy losses. Clark could discern no significant local reserves. The enemy had, Clark believed, only one possible source of major reinforcement, the Herman Goering Panzer Division, which he had good reason to believe was en route to the battlefield from reserve positions far north of Rome. The other three general reserve divisions available to the German theater commander, Field Marshal Albert Kesselring, had already been committed on the southern front.

Clark's evaluation of the enemy reserve situation was basically correct, but he underestimated the strength of the Caesar position at the base of the Alban Hills and the defensive capabilities of three good German divisions of the I Parachute Corps, which comprised the right (west) wing of the Fourteenth Army. Although the bulk of the reserves of these divisions had been ordered during the night of May 24 to buttress the sagging left flank of the Fourteenth Army, no part of them had reached the threatened sector by the next morning. These units, therefore, still remained for the most part in their main battle positions. They were thus available, along with the other units of the divisions, in position opposite the western half of the Anzio beachhead, for defense of the Caesar position in the Alban Hills or for delaying action in front of it.[14]

Should the full weight of the VI Corps be employed in the Valmontone maneuver, General Clark still doubted that the effort would accomplish the decisive results contemplated by Alexander. Though Clark recognized that a concentrated thrust by the VI Corps could cut Highway 6 at Valmontone, he felt it was optimistic to expect that this alone might trap large enemy forces in the south. The Tenth Army still might use other routes of withdrawal which led north from the Liri Valley through the mountains to Highway 5, a main lateral road running from the Adriatic coast through Tivoli to Rome. General Clark believed further that such a thrust was unnecessary to facilitate the advance of the Eighth Army, for the British had driven through the last prepared positions on the southern front. Finally, a thrust to Valmontone might lead the VI Corps away from, not toward, Rome.[15]

Clark was reluctant to encourage British competition for the capture of Rome.[16] He considered Rome a gem belonging rightly in the crown of his Fifth Army. The brunt of the early Italian campaign,

Clark knew, had fallen more heavily on the American elements of the Fifth Army than on either the British troops under his command or the Eighth Army. Clark and the Fifth Army in general believed that the Fifth Army's attack had been decisive in the breakout on the southern front. Clark repeatedly observed with pride that he had expanded the role originally assigned the Fifth Army and thereby found the key to the success of the operation. Not only had the Fifth Army made the first effective penetration of the enemy's prepared defenses: keeping the enemy off balance by successive envelopments in the Liri Valley, the Fifth Army, Clark believed, had been the primary factor in the Eighth Army's advance up the Liri Valley along what Alexander always had regarded as the "only way to Rome."[17] The Eighth Army, in Clark's opinion, had, in turn, been slow in capitalizing on this assistance, particularly in failing to launch strong frontal attacks to support the envelopments. In view of this experience, he doubted if the Eighth Army would provide the kind of strong frontal effort that he thought necessary to justify throwing the main weight of the VI Corps toward Valmontone. In short, the Fifth Army commander was reluctant to carry out further operations to envelop the enemy in front of the British unless the British also assisted the Fifth Army's advance to Rome.[18]

That General Clark did not see the Valmontone attack itself as an excellent opportunity for quick advance to Rome is puzzling. Terrain, the nature of the enemy's defenses, and the enemy's lack of substantial forces to halt a drive on Rome via Valmontone, all favored the adoption of this course. By continuing past Cisterna up the rolling swells of the Velletri-Artena Gap, between the Alban Hills and the Lepini Mountains, and along the northwest shoulder of the Lepini, the VI Corps might reach and cut Highway 6 northwest of Valmontone. The Corps then could wheel northwest across fairly open country to breach the Caesar Line northeast of the Alban Hills, and push rapidly to Rome. German defenses in the Caesar Line between the Alban Hills and Valmontone were weaker than elsewhere and had no strong natural features to buttress man-made barriers. Neither army nor corps intelligence estimates indicated substantial enemy forces in this area, though the VI Corps strongly suspected that the enemy might divert forces there either from the Adriatic coast or from the I Parachute Corps.[19] But Clark was perturbed by this prospect not at all and believed the only German reinforcement likely to appear in the area was the Hermann Goering Panzer Division.[20] He could hardly have considered it likely that this division alone could halt the full weight of the VI Corps.[21] The only reasonable explanation of why Clark failed to appreciate the opportunity presented by the Valmontone attack for a rapid drive to Rome lies in his belief that the German situation had so deteriorated that the VI Corps with less than maximum force could reach Rome more rapidly by a more direct route.[22]

The second alternative which General Clark could adopt—throwing the whole weight of the VI Corps into a drive west of the Alban Hills—had strong appeal because it was on the most direct route to Rome. By attacking northwest from Cisterna, he thought he could exploit the initial success of the beachhead attack and what appeared to be the enemy's rampant disorganization, by driving through the last prepared German position in front of Rome between Campoleone and Lanuvio at the southwest base of the Alban Hills before the Germans had time to settle down into it.[23] Using the entire corps would ensure quick success. The maneuver offered the incidental advantage of destroying the rest of the Fourteenth Army by frontal assault, after which local turning movements could pin the bulk of the I Parachute Corps against the coast or cut the rear of any forces attempting to defend along the base of the Alban Hills. Concentrating maximum force in this direction would have little effect on the southern front but would, Clark believed, destroy far more German forces than the Valmontone maneuver.[24]

The great magnet of this alternative was, of course, Rome. Clark, like many other Allied commanders and the British Prime Minister himself, regarded the city as the "great prize" of the entire spring offensive—indeed, of the whole Italian campaign.[25] He had told Truscott that it was the "only worthwhile objective" for the VI Corps.[26] Clark had only an incidental interest in the military value of the Italian capital—its airfields and its role as a communications hub ("All roads lead to Rome"). He wanted Rome because of the prestige associated with capturing it and the success such a feat would symbolize. In recompense for all the frustrations of the winter stalemate in the south of Italy and for the fact that, in Clark's opinion, the Fifth Army had borne the brunt of the fighting, Clark felt that his men deserved the honor. Allied strategy, which had exaggerated the value of Rome out of proportion to its military importance, must be taken into account in explaining the emphasis Clark put on taking the city. Capturing Rome would represent to the people in the United States tangible evidence of American success in Italy, a dramatic event which could be more easily grasped by the American public than the destruction of large numbers of the enemy. Clark also wanted Rome in the shortest possible time because he suspected that Alexander wished the Eighth Army to share in the triumph. Alexander, for example, had constantly referred to the Liri Valley, up which the British Eighth Army was driving, as the "only route" to Rome. Clark did not intend to divide the prize with the British and believed that he had in his grasp an opportunity to make this unnecessary.[27]

Finally, General Clark wanted Rome as quickly as possible because, as he was aware, the Allied cross-Channel invasion of France was imminent. This invasion, the main effort against Germany, would, Clark knew, draw the spotlight from Italy.[28]

The third alternative open to General Clark was a compromise between the other two. By dividing his forces and attacking in both directions, northwest toward the Alban Hills and northeast toward Valmontone, he could exploit the opportunity to drive on Rome rapidly and at the same time comply with Alexander's order for cutting the enemy's main line of communications to the southern front. In the face of the estimated enemy disorganization and the commitment on the southern front of all major German reserves except the Hermann Goering Panzer Division, Clark felt that he could carry out Alexander's maneuver to cut Highway 6 at Valmontone with one reinforced American division, while shifting the main weight of the VI Corps attack toward the Italian capital.[29] This course of action had the advantage of complying with the letter, if not the spirit, of the order from Clark's superior.

General Clark made his decision in favor of the third alternative. Though he expected that the enemy would commit the Hermann Goering Panzer Division at Valmontone, he believed that a reinforced American division could handle the opposition. Even if this proved to be a considerable gamble, it was a gamble in the direction which Clark personally thought most economical. The bigger bet he placed on the drive on Rome.[30]

The final plan for the VI Corps designated four divisions for the main effort northwest against the Alban Hills. The 34th and 45th Infantry Divisions were to lead the assault on either side of the Rome-Naples railroad northwest from Cisterna, while the 36th Infantry Division and the 1st Armored Division maintained a strong supporting attack on the right flank toward Velletri. The 3rd Infantry Division, supported by an armored task force and the First Special Service

Force to cover the flanks, was to make the secondary thrust, to seize Artena and cut Highway 6 at Valmontone.[31]

After completing the plan, Clark flew to his command post on the southern front to explain the operation to his chief of staff, Major General Alfred M. Gruenther, and to discuss operations on the southern front. He left his G-3 (operations) officer, Brigadier General Donald W. Brann, to explain the plan to the VI Corps commander, General Truscott. It appears on the basis of contemporary evidence, that Truscott supported Clark's decision, reacting favorably to the shift of main effort to the northwest and expressing confidence that the weaker force could reach Valmontone and cut Highway 6. His only objection appears to have been against a strong frontal attack on Velletri along Highway 7, northwest of Cisterna, apparently because of heavy resistance which a combat command of the 1st Armored Division had met for two days in that area. At 3:55 P.M. on May 25, General Brann radioed General Clark that Truscott was "entirely in accord" with the Army commander's plan.[32] At 5:55 Truscott telephoned Brann, saying, "I feel very strongly we should do this thing [the attack to the northwest]. We should do it tomorrow."[33]

In the evening of May 25, Clark returned to the Anzio beachhead where, in conference with Truscott, details of the attack plan were worked out. As the two leaders met, latest intelligence reports confirmed earlier views of the seriousness of the enemy's setback.[34] The final Corps plan was precisely that decided on originally by Clark except that it removed the feature of a strong frontal assault on Velletri, which Truscott had found objectionable. "I am launching this new attack," Clark radioed his chief of staff, "with all speed possible in order to take advantage of the impetus of our advance and in order to overwhelm the enemy in what may be a demoralized condition at the present time. You can assure General Alexander this is an all-out attack. We are shooting the works!"[35] General Truscott, when he met his division commanders later in the evening, was equally confident. In the area which included the zone of the VI Corps main effort, he said, "the Boche is badly disorganized, has a hodge-podge of units and if we can drive as hard tomorrow as we have done the last three days, a great victory is in our grasp." [36]

By the decision to head directly for Rome, General Clark had, in effect, altered drastically Alexander's basic scheme of maneuver against the Tenth Army's rear. By diluting the force oriented toward

Valmontone he had made that effort distinctly secondary, and by its very nature primarily defensive should the enemy move in sufficient force in time. Yet the Army commander had given no inkling of his intentions to Alexander, the Army Group commander. He had decided to act first and explain later.[37]

During the afternoon of May 25 General Clark had prepared the way for breaking the news to Alexander. When visiting the Fifth Army command post on the southern front, he briefed General Gruenther, his chief of staff, with the idea that Gruenther could explain the plan to Alexander the next day, after the unilateral decision had become irrevocable. Once this had happened, Clark was anxious for Alexander to know that it was an "all-out attack" and that a strong force would be used against Valmontone.[38] At 11:15 A.M. on May 26, nearly twenty-four hours after Clark made his decision and fifteen minutes after the newly oriented attack jumped off, General Alexander arrived at the Fifth Army command post and received the news from General Gruenther.

In the presentation of his case, Clark could have had no abler advocate than his chief of staff or one whom Alexander liked as much. Alexander appeared "well pleased with the entire situation and was most complimentary in his reference to the Fifth Army" and to Clark. Far from objecting to the shift of the main axis, Alexander stated: "I am for any line which the army commander believes will offer a chance to continue his present success." A little later, he asked Gruenther, "I am sure the army commander will continue to push toward Valmontone, won't he? I know that he appreciates the importance of gaining the high ground just south of Artena. As soon as he captures that he will be absolutely safe!" Gruenther was equal to the occasion. "I assured him," he reported later to Clark, "that you had that situation thoroughly in mind and that he could depend on you to execute a vigorous plan with all the push in the world!" Gruenther was convinced that Alexander "left with no mental reservations as to the wisdom" of Clark's decision. In fact, he commented that "if the Anzio Force could capture the high ground north of Velletri, it would put the enemy at a serious disadvantage and would practically assure the success of the bridgehead attack."[39]

Either Alexander was accepting with grace a virtual *fait accompli* or the Valmontone maneuver had lost its principal champion. Whichever the case, Alexander's acquiescence was strongly conditioned, if not determined, by the success which the Fifth Army already had achieved in the spring offensive and by his conception of the role of an Allied Army Group commander, especially in relation to an American Army commander like Clark. In the wake of the smashing success which the VI Corps had achieved at Cisterna and the reported disorganization of the Fourteenth Army, Alexander could have no readily defensible grounds for questioning Clark's judgment of the best course of action in Clark's own zone of responsibility.[40]

As events developed, Clark's decision neither unlocked the door to Rome nor cut the enemy's rear at Valmontone. Though the two German divisions which had opposed the VI Corps attack from the beachhead had been almost destroyed, the Fourteenth Army was able to employ against the new thrust the three good divisions of the I Parachute Corps. Also, the Fourteenth Army shifted to the threatened sector additional units from a division which had been manning coast defenses nearby. Kesselring, for his part, diverted some contingents of the Tenth Army. With these forces the Germans delayed the VI Corps main effort in front of the Caesar Line at the base of the Alban Hills for two days and then halted repeated, bloody, and fruitless efforts by three American divisions at Lanuvio and along the Anzio-Albano-Rome road. The German defensive success was attributable to the time required for the VI Corps to shift its direction of attack, to the two days' delaying action which afforded time for the main German forces to reorganize, to the strength of the Caesar position in this sector, and to the undiminished fighting qualities of the three good divisions of the I Parachute Corps. In the optimistic glow of the sweeping victory against the Fourteenth Army's center and left wing on both sides of Cisterna, Clark, Truscott, and their intelligence officers had badly underestimated the defensive capabilities of the I Parachute Corps.

German commanders actually did not recognize for several days the shift in the VI Corps main axis of attack. They were still too worried about the weak point in the Caesar Line between the Alban Hills and Valmontone. But the U.S. 3rd Division, tired from three days' heavy fighting, did not cut Highway 6. Moving into the gap, the American division, in the face of resistance from scattered German units and first arrivals of the Hermann Goering Division, assumed a primarily defensive role. Under strength in tanks to start with, the Hermann Goering Division actually had been severely damaged by Allied air attacks en route to the south and had been slowed by a gasoline shortage. Only its reconnaissance battalion had been released to the Fourteenth Army by the morning of May 26, and its other units were committed piecemeal in the days following in small counterattacks. For at least three days German strength in front of Valmontone and westward to the Alban Hills was not sufficient to have stopped a strong attack by even a secondary effort; even in subsequent days German strength was not sufficient to have halted the main effort of the VI Corps had it been made in that direction. For more than a week before the capture of Rome, the rear and the right (west) flank of the German Tenth Army, withdrawing slowly toward the Caesar Line, were exposed and threatened with a trap which the German commanders feared would be closed, but which was not.

The greatest irony was that if the VI Corps' main effort had continued on the Valmontone axis on May 26 and the days following, Clark could undoubtedly have reached Rome more quickly than he was able to do by the route northwest from Cisterna. The VI Corps also could have cut Highway 6 and put far greater pressure on the Tenth Army than it did.

Ironically, too, when the Fifth Army finally broke through the last of the Fourteenth Army's defenses, it accomplished this by a surprise night infiltration along the eastern side of the Alban Hills between the hills and Valmontone. When this breach had been widened, Clark again wheeled his forces northwest toward Rome and away from the withdrawing Tenth Army. Though the British Eighth Army in the advance up the Liri Valley failed to keep heavy pressure against the main body of the Tenth Army, the Fifth Army still might have closed the trap had Clark struck toward Tivoli and then eastward along the lateral highway toward the Adriatic coast.[41]

Yet the fact remains, General Clark and the Fifth Army got to Rome. They captured the city on June 4, only two days before Allied landing craft touched down in France.

Maurice Matloff

The ANVIL Decision:
Crossroads of Strategy
(1944)

On August 15, 1944, Allied forces invaded southern France east of
the Rhone—the last of a long series of triphibious operations in the
Mediterranean. Within a month they swept up the valley of the
Rhone and linked up with General George S. Patton's U.S. Third
Army. The landing took place nine weeks after the launching of the
Normandy invasion and after some six months of indecision. To
President Roosevelt, General George C. Marshall (U.S. Army Chief
of Staff), and most U.S. strategic planners, the operation was a logical
part of the grand design fashioned at the Cairo-Tehran Conferences
to defeat Germany decisively. To Prime Minister Churchill and most
of the British staff, it was an operation at the wrong time and in the
wrong place—an undertaking that prevented the completion of the
Italian campaign and an advance through the Ljubljana Gap toward
Vienna.

Behind the landings on the coast of southern France lay one of the
most controversial decisions of World War II. No wartime debate
between the Americans and the British showed a sharper divergence
of opinion; none reflected a greater contrast in national approaches
to war strategy. As the rift between the Soviet Union and the West
has widened in the postwar period, the controversy that began in the
secret Anglo-American war councils of 1944 has flared into the
open. A growing chorus of opinion on both sides of the Atlantic has
charged that the peace was lost as a result of political and strategic
mistakes of World War II. No decision has drawn more fire from
participants and "Monday morning quarterbacks" alike than that to

invade southern France. It becomes all the more important, therefore, at this stage of the "cold war," to take stock of this key decision
—particularly to consider whether it really was as great a mistake as
its critics have alleged it to be.[1]

First, it is important to remember that, though the decision to
undertake the southern France venture—the ANVIL (renamed DRA-
GOON) operation—was made by the Americans and the British, it
was definitely influenced by their Soviet ally. It grew out of discussions of the "Big Three" at the Cairo-Tehran Conferences in November-December 1943. That conference was a showdown meeting
among the Allies on European strategy, a climax to two years of debate between the Americans and British and of growing Soviet impa-
tience for action in the West. A word must be said therefore about
the three principal partners in the European war and their divergent approaches to that conflict.

Great Britain, the island empire, dependent on sea lanes for its
very existence and situated precariously on the edge of Hitler's European fortress, had for centuries put its faith in the "balance of power."
It could be expected to seek to revive and rally the smaller nations
and to continue to throw its weight against any strong power that
threatened to upset the balance on the Continent. It would also be
expected to intervene actively in the Mediterranean and the Middle
East, through which ran the lifeline to its empire in the Orient. Experienced in war, diplomacy, and empire, Great Britain had a long
history of alliances with European powers, and its military leaders
were accustomed to working closely with its politicians and diplomats.

Across the Atlantic stood the other Western partner in the alliance,
the United States—young, impatient, rich in resources, highly in-
dustrialized, the country with the technical know-how. This was the
country whose whole tradition in war had been first to declare, then
to prepare. Traditionally opposed to becoming involved in European
quarrels, it nevertheless had strong bonds with Western Europe—
especially England. The American approach to European war, based
on U.S. experience in World War I, seemed to be to hold off as long
as possible, enter only long enough to give the bully who started it a
sound thrashing, get the boys home, and then try to remain as unin-
volved as before. Furthermore, throughout World War II, the President and his military staff could never forget the war against Japan,
which to many Americans appeared to be a more natural enemy
than Germany.

The third member in the alliance against Germany, the Soviet

Union, was a land power with completely internal lines of communication. The Soviet Union represented an enigmatic, restless, and dynamic force, devoted to the political and economic ideology of Communism, totally different from that of the Western partners. As we get more perspective on the role of the U.S.S.R. in World War II, it becomes evident that the period of its defensive struggle against Germany was merely a pause in twin drives for security and expansion. But for almost two years after the German attack, the Soviet Union was engaged in a desperate fight for its very existence, and while political and territorial ambitions were by no means absent, military considerations were more immediately paramount. Still fearful of capitalist encirclement, suspicious of friend and foe alike, it occupied an uneasy position in the partnership which Major General John R. Deane, chief of the U.S. military mission in Moscow from 1943 to 1945, has so fittingly called "the Strange Alliance."[2]

The divergent approaches of the Allies toward the European war were at first most clearly reflected in the conflict between British and American strategy—between the peripheral theory, espoused by Churchill and the British staff, and the theory of mass and concentration advocated by General Marshall and his staff. The British wanted to hit the German Army at the edges of the Continent and launch a large-scale landing on the Continent only as the last blow against an enemy already in process of collapse; the Americans wanted to concentrate forces early at a selected time and place to meet the main body of the enemy head on and defeat it decisively. Both justified their theories and plans in terms of relieving the pressure on the Russians. Neither side could readily win the other to its concept of strategy, and the long debate that ensued led to a delicate relationship with the Soviet Union. From the beginning the Russians, locked in a death struggle on the Eastern Front, had no doubts about the proper Western strategy. They wanted a second front, they wanted it soon, and they wanted it in the West. Each Anglo-American postponement of this second front added fuel to the fire.[3]

By November 1943—on the eve of Cairo-Tehran Conferences—a critical point had been reached in Allied war planning. Almost two years had gone by since Pearl Harbor. Firm agreement among the three Allies on how, when, and where to beat even the primary foe—Germany—was still lacking. One Mediterranean operation had followed another. North Africa had led to Sicily; Sicily, to the invasion of Italy. Always the skillful and resourceful arguments of the Prime Minister had urged the need to sustain the momentum and acquire the immediate advantages, the "great prizes" to be picked up in the Mediterranean, while the Allies were waiting for the right opportunity to cross the Channel in force. True, the Western partners had in August 1943 agreed on a major cross-Channel attack to be launched in the spring of 1944—Operation OVERLORD. But disturbing reports had been reaching Washington from London and Moscow. The Russians were hinting that they might accept increased pressure on the Germans in the Mediterranean even at the price of a delay in OVERLORD and might even accept aggressive action in Italy as a substitute for the second front.[4] These hints of a reversal in the Soviet position, coming on the heels of reported British cooling on OVERLORD, gave the U.S. staff much concern.[5]

What appeared to the Americans to be at stake was far more than the date or even the ultimate fate of OVERLORD. The whole strategy of the global war, the "beat Germany first" concept, the roles of the respective Allies in the coalition effort—all were in the balance. If in the war against Germany the British were still wedded to the theory of attritional opportunism, the Americans had staked heavily on the principle of concentration; from early in the war their global strategy, manpower and production balance, and strategic deployment had all been planned with that primary end in view. OVERLORD represented the hope—perhaps the last hope—of realizing their basic strategic faith, and they were determined to accept no further delay in the long-promised and much postponed invasion across the Channel. While the U.S. staff was apprehensive over the British and Soviet attitudes, both Roosevelt and Churchill were anxious to demonstrate their good faith to Soviet Premier Stalin.

The meeting at Tehran was the decisive conference in European strategy.[6] Preliminary exchanges between the Americans and British at Cairo were inconclusive. At Tehran, for the first time in the war, the President, the Prime Minister, and their staffs met with Marshal Stalin and his staff. The Prime Minister made eloquent appeals for operations in Italy, the Aegean, and the eastern Mediterranean, even at the expense of a delay in OVERLORD. Stalin at this point unequivocally put his weight behind the American concept of strategy. Confident of Russia's capabilities, he asserted his full power as an equal member of the coalition and came out strongly in favor of OVERLORD. Further operations in the Mediterranean, he insisted, should be limited to the invasion of southern France in support of OVERLORD. Soviet experience over the past two years, he declared, had shown that a large offensive from one direction was not wise;

that pincer operations of the type represented by simultaneous operations against northern and southern France were most fruitful. These operations would best help the Soviet Union. In turn, the Russians promised to launch a simultaneous all-out offensive on the Eastern Front.

Stalin's stand put the capstone on Anglo-American strategy. In a sense, therefore, he fixed Western strategy. Churchill lost out, and the Americans gained the decision they had so long desired. The final blueprint for Allied victory in Europe had taken shape.

It was typical of the President at Tehran to act as arbitrator, if not judge, between the other two leaders, as different in their methods as in the views they represented. The President did not appear completely indifferent to Churchill's eloquence and persuasiveness and to the possibilities of eastern Mediterranean ventures, particularly in the Adriatic. At the same time, he was under strong pressure from his military advisers to see that nothing delay OVERLORD, and in the end he held fast.[7] The President's task in this respect was undoubtedly made easier, as was that of the U.S. staff, by Stalin's firm stand. Years later, Churchill, still convinced that the failure at Tehran to adopt his eastern Mediterranean policy was a fateful error, wrote: "I could have gained Stalin, but the President was oppressed by the prejudices of his military advisers, and drifted to and fro in the argument, with the result that the whole of these subsidiary but gleaming opportunities were cast aside unused." [8]

On the morning of November 30, the Combined Chiefs of Staff (CCS) agreed to recommend that OVERLORD be launched during May 1944, in conjunction with a supporting operation against southern France, code-named ANVIL. The operation against southern France was to be mounted on as big a scale as the available landing craft permitted. For planning purposes, D Day for ANVIL was to be the same as D Day for OVERLORD.[9] The plan for an operation against southern France to which the Combined Chiefs made reference was, to say the least, vague. It was actually an old plan, newly dusted off. Stalin's expressed interest at the opening session of the conference in an invasion of southern France linked to OVERLORD had caught the U.S. and British delegations somewhat by surprise. It is true that for a long time the Americans and British had been thinking about some kind of southern France operation to be carried out eventually. As far back as April 1943, there had been talk of such an operation, and at the Quebec Conference in August 1943 the CCS had put on the planning books a proposal for a diversionary operation against south-

ern France to be launched in connection with OVERLORD. Considerable
staff planning had already been done on such an operation. But the
bulk of the Anglo-American planning staff had been left at Cairo, and
the only available study at hand was a copy of a joint outline plan
drawn up on August 9, 1943—a plan already much out of date.
Working feverishly with this plan as a basis, the few U.S. planners at
Tehran had ready on November 29 a study for the U.S. chiefs and the
President. It called for a two-division assault launched on France
from Corsica and Sardinia, building up to ten divisions, and, optimistically, if vaguely, it assumed that the landing craft and the other
resources would probably be available.[10] It was on the basis of this
study that the Americans and the British, urged on by the Russians,
committed themselves at Tehran to a southern France operation.

The Tehran decisions represented far more than the fashioning, at
long last, of a grand design and a pattern for victory. They marked a
still subtle but significant change in the balance of military power
within the coalition. Britain was growing relatively weaker, the
United States and the U.S.S.R. stronger. Capitalizing on Lend-
Lease, its production behind the Urals, the sacrifice of its armies and
people, and the effects of a war of attrition on the German invaders,
the Soviet Union had been able to make its weight felt in the strategic
scales at a critical point in Allied councils. The Russian bear was
coming into its own.

The United States, too, had grown stronger. By the close of 1943,
when Britain had practically completed its mobilization and strains
and stresses had begun to show up in its economy, America's industrial and military machine was in high gear. In mid-war, the
Americans drew up to and threatened to pass the British in deployed
strength in the European theater. The growing flow of U.S. military
strength and supplies to the theater assured the triumph of the U.S.
staff concept of a concentrated, decisive war, an objective reinforced by the addition, from the Casablanca Conference (January
1943) onward, of the unconditional surrender formula. Via the military doctrine of concentration, the strategists of the Kremlin and of
the Pentagon had found common ground. Tehran, which fixed the
European strategy, marked the beginning of a wartime realignment
in the European power balance.

The upshot of the concluding Anglo-American discussions in Cairo
was to confirm that OVERLORD and ANVIL were to be the "supreme
operations for 1944" and that nothing was to be done in any part of
the world to jeopardize their success.[11] But in the months that followed

Tehran, the southern France operation came perilously close to being abandoned in favor of further exploitation in Italy and possibly in the Balkans. A drawn-out debate ensued—marked by long discussions in the theater and numerous exchanges between Washington and London. Plans and preparations seesawed—now the operation was on, now it was off—not once, but several times.

The controversy over ANVIL in the months that followed Tehran falls into two main phases, roughly divided by June 1944 when the Allies captured Rome and went ashore in Normandy. The first phase is a story of confusion, uncertainty, and the temporary abandonment of the operation; the second, of gradual recovery and triumph.

The details of the Anglo-American debate in the early months of 1944 need not concern us here.[12] A variety of interlocking pressures built up against the operation. The widespread demands to strengthen the forthcoming OVERLORD assault, the slow progress of the Italian campaign and the move to speed it up, the lukewarmness of the British, the lack of landing craft, and shortage of other key re-sources—all contributed to ANVIL's decline. The debate developed first as between OVERLORD and ANVIL and then as between ANVIL and the Italian campaign. The resultant keen competition for that ever-precious commodity—landing craft—demonstrated the existing gap in planning between the strategists and the logisticians and gave further proof of that old axiom in strategy that, to be effective, plans and means must match. As priorities for an expanded OVERLORD assault and the Italian campaign rose, ANVIL received the short end of the stick.

By the beginning of February 1944, the British attitude hardened in opposition to the operation. The British were as much con-cerned by the additional needs of the Italian campaign as they were by those of the OVERLORD assault. The end run at Anzio, spurred by Churchill, had failed so far to break the stalemate in south Italy and pave the way for a subsequent drive on Rome. The British were convinced that the badly stalled Italian campaign must be started up again in earnest. The familiar specter of the draining powers of secondary operations rose to haunt the Washington Army staff. But Churchill, who firmly believed that a vigorous campaign in Italy would offer the greatest assistance to OVERLORD, felt that some flexi-bility in disposing Allied strength and resources in the Mediterranean was fully justified.

General Marshall and his planning assistants were not opposed to the prosecution of the Italian campaign as far as Rome, or slightly north thereof, but they also believed that planning and preparations for ANVIL had to be continued at least until April if it was to have any chance of being launched in the spring. To the Washington staff ANVIL and OVERLORD were essential parts of the same undertaking.[13]

Between the War Department struggling to keep ANVIL alive and Churchill intent on prosecuting the Italian campaign, the Supreme Allied Commander in Western Europe, General Dwight D. Eisenhower, found himself in a difficult position. He agreed with the War Department's estimate of the significance of ANVIL, but he was charged with the success of OVERLORD, and from his driver's seat the planning hazards began to make ANVIL appear less feasible. To help settle the issue, the American Joint Chiefs, at Marshall's suggestion, delegated their authority to Eisenhower.[14]

On February 24 General Eisenhower and the British Chiefs reached a compromise. The campaign in Italy was to have overriding priority over all other operations in the Mediterranean, at least until March 20, at which time the situation would be reviewed. In the interval, planning for ANVIL was to continue.[15] That the President and the Prime Minister accepted the compromise did not really settle the question. General Eisenhower became more and more uneasy over the shortage of landing craft for OVERLORD. Despite vigorous and costly Allied attacks, the situation in Italy did not improve. The stalemate continued. When the time set for reviewing the situation came around, General "Jumbo" Wilson (General Sir Henry Maitland Wilson), the Allied commander in the Mediterranean, and the British Chiefs insisted that an ANVIL simultaneous with OVERLORD be abandoned. On March 21 Eisenhower also concluded that ANVIL as a simultaneous attack must be canceled. Their recommendations were adopted.[16]

The decision in late March to forego a simultaneous ANVIL did not end the debate over ANVIL versus the Italian campaign. Old differences between the staffs were reargued. They now boiled down to a matter of options—the British wished to retain the option to continue the Italian campaign; the Americans, to launch ANVIL. The British argued that when an all-out offensive was launched in Italy it should continue until June, and then a final decision could be made on ANVIL, depending on the situation on the Italian and Normandy fronts. The U.S. Chiefs insisted that once the two Italian fronts were joined, nothing should interfere with ANVIL.

Back of the continued U.S. pressure for keeping ANVIL alive lay the familiar staff concern with ending the war against Germany quickly and decisively and with the least political embroilments. As Brigadier General Frank N. Roberts, the chief Army planner, summed it up:

> If we cancel ANVIL completely, the following will be true:
> *a.* We get into political difficulties with the French.
> *b.* Overlord will lose at least ten fighting divisions.
> *c.* Our service forces continue to support the western Mediterranean.
> *d.* Our divisions and the French divisions will be committed to a costly, unremunerative, inching advance in Italy. The people of both the United States and France may or may not take this indefinitely.
> *e.* Once committed to Italy, we have our forces pointed towards Southeastern Europe and will have the greatest difficulty in preventing their use for occupation forces in Austria, Hungary and southern Germany.[17]

As a way out of the impasse, the British Chiefs proposed a new compromise, and to get on with operations in the Mediterranean, the U.S. Chiefs agreed on April 18 to go along with it.[18] Allied resources in the Mediterranean were to be thrown into an all-out offensive in Italy, which was to have first priority. ANVIL was deferred indefinitely. OVERLORD would have to make its own way.

The end of the first phase of the debate over ANVIL permitted both the Normandy and Italian campaigns to go forward. On May 12 the Allied command in Italy launched the full-scale offensive. The Anzio bridgehead and the main battle line in the Liri Valley were soon linked up and the deadlock in Italy was broken. On June 4, two days before the Normandy invasion, the Allies finally captured Rome.

As the Allied armies swept into Rome and Normandy, the debate between the British and Americans reopened. Would the prize be the occupation of all Italy, the capture of Istria and Trieste, and an advance through the Ljubljana Gap, with political and strategic consequences for the Balkans? Or the direct strengthening of OVERLORD and of the subsequent Continental drive? The Allies must either continue the Mediterranean drive and commit themselves to a strong and active offense in the south, or throw their might into the assault on Germany from the west and content themselves with a holding role in Italy.

In June 1944, shortly after D Day, the U.S. Chiefs flew to London for an informal conference with the British. The Americans held firmly to an operation in the western Mediterranean but were willing to consider other plans of action. In the end, the CCS decided to explore several possibilities. General Wilson was asked to furnish plans and estimates for operations at Sète, 90 miles west of the Rhone, and Istria in the northern Adriatic as well as for ANVIL; and Eisenhower for an operation on the Bay of Biscay. Each operation was to be planned on the basis of a three-division lift and to be mounted about July 25.[19]

In the days that followed, the divergent views came into clearer focus. General Wilson came out strongly for a push in Italy toward the Ljubljana Gap and southern Hungary. He thus advanced the British thesis that OVERLORD could be aided elsewhere than in southern France. General Eisenhower countered with a recommendation that ANVIL be launched by August 15. Concerned because his operations in Normandy were behind schedule, he argued that ANVIL would give him an additional port, open a route to the Ruhr, and help the French Maquis. He firmly believed that the Allies could support but one major theater in the European war—the OVERLORD battle area. Both General Marshall and General Eisenhower stressed the need for a major port through which to pour some forty to fifty divisions waiting in the United States for battle in France. Since the SHAEF (Supreme Headquarters, Allied Expeditionary Force) staff frowned on Bay of Biscay operations and viewed the Sète movement as impractical because of timing, the Americans swung back to the original ANVIL to stay. The U.S. Chiefs of Staff now lined up solidly in back of General Eisenhower, the British behind General Wilson. The Prime Minister directed his attack on the President and Eisenhower, while the British Chiefs sought to sway their American opposites. In the face of these new onslaughts, the American lines held surprisingly firm.[20]

Churchill was willing to help General Eisenhower but not, he stated, at the expense of the complete ruin "of our great affairs in the Mediterranean." [21] He argued that, to hasten the end of the European war, "political considerations, such as the revolt of populations against the enemy or the submission and coming over of his satellites, are a valid and important factor." [22]

The President would not yield. To him the courses of action decided upon at Tehran still were the best means of bringing about the unconditional surrender of Germany. He agreed that the political factors mentioned by Churchill were significant, but the most important task at hand was to advance into Germany. Any operations into Istria and the Balkans would be diversionary and secondary. He could not agree to the employment of U.S. forces in that area. Nor did he think the French would support the use of their troops in the

Balkans. Plans laid at Tehran had gone well so far. Any change in ANVIL would have to be cleared with Stalin. The President concluded by reminding Churchill: "Finally, for purely political considerations over here, I should never survive even a slight setback in 'Overlord' if it were known that fairly large forces had been diverted to the Balkans." [23]

Years later a still annoyed Churchill was to write, "It was his [the President's] objections to a descent on the Istria Peninsula and a thrust against Vienna through the Ljubljana Gap that revealed both the rigidity of the American military plans and his own suspicion of what he called a campaign 'in the Balkans.' " [24] Churchill vigorously denied that anyone involved in these discussions had "ever thought of moving armies *into the Balkans.*" [25]

Whatever would have been the ultimate political or military effects of Churchill's Balkan policy—and this is still a moot point—he was not to win out. The President, in complete agreement with his staff, held firm. On July 2 he asked the Prime Minister to direct General Wilson to set the wheels in motion for an early ANVIL. He declared, "I am compelled by the logic of not dispersing our main efforts to a new theatre to agree with my Chiefs of Staff. . . . I always think of my early geometry—'a straight line is the shortest distance between two points.' " [26] General Marshall and his staff could ask for nothing more.

The President's personal pleas broke through the Prime Minister's adamant position, and he consented to the issuance of the directive to Wilson. On July 2 the CCS issued the directive: ANVIL would be launched with a target date of August 15 on a three-division assault basis and an airborne lift to be decided later. The build-up would be to ten divisions.[27] After months of uncertainty, ANVIL had apparently become a firm commitment—only six weeks before it was to be launched.

Nevertheless, in spite of their consent there were indications that the British did not consider the matter closed. When the Allied breakthrough at Saint-Lô proved successful during the last week in July, the British made their final effort to cancel ANVIL—now renamed DRAGOON. With the possibility of using the ports in Brittany to reinforce OVERLORD, Churchill and the British Chiefs tried again. Eisenhower was subjected to intense pressure from the Prime Minister to alter his stand. To Harry Hopkins, Roosevelt's special assistant, Churchill also sent a last-minute appeal to intercede and influence Marshall.[28]

Any worries that the Army planners may have had proved ground-less, for Eisenhower clung firmly to DRAGOON as OVERLORD's best con-comitant. To Churchill, Eisenhower suggested that he was willing to change his plan of campaign only if the Prime Minister and the President ruled that political considerations were to be paramount; on military grounds alone he would not yield in favor of a Balkan cam-paign. With the U.S. Chiefs, Hopkins, and the President in turn standing behind the decision, the British finally conceded defeat. On August 10 the British Chiefs notified General Wilson he was to pro-ceed with DRAGOON as planned, a directive that the CCS confirmed on the following day—just four days before the landing. The British would have to salvage the Italian campaign as best they could.[29]

After more than two years of discussion, frequently warm and spirited, the great debate over the Mediterranean and the cross-Chan-nel attack was finally laid to rest. The debate over the southern France operation in the summer of 1944 may be viewed as the last gasp of the peripheral strategy advocated by Churchill and his staff from the beginning of the European struggle. But the war had al-ready entered a new era. And in his arguments for canceling the southern France operation, Churchill was, in effect, giving peripheral strategy a new twist and a more openly political form, applying it now to the Soviet Union as well as to Germany. Despite the valiant efforts of the British to win another reprieve for the Mediterranean, the United States insistence on supplying extra power to OVERLORD had carried the day and sounded the knell for any ambitious plans in southeast Europe.

So much for the wartime debate, decisions, and revisions. It is clear that the differences of opinion between the Americans and British over ANVIL were but one expression of the underlying dis-agreement over the type of war to be fought and the objectives to be sought by the Anglo-American coalition. What of the postwar charge that the decision to undertake the southern France operation was a great mistake—a prime example of American political and strategic naïveté, one of the worst blunders of the war, a blunder that helped throw the victory to the Russians? This charge has taken two chief forms. One, that the operation—designed as it was to buttress the "big blow" strategy of the Americans—must share the general round of criticism that has been directed against that strategy. This repre-sents a postwar version of the case for peripheral strategy over that of mass and concentration. The other form of attack is more specific —that strategically and politically the Western partners would have gained far more by an operation against the Balkans. Both have in common the notion that American strategists concentrated too heavily on winning the military victory over Germany and not enough on political considerations.

Much of postwar writing on the grand strategy of World War II has been dominated by British writers—led by the incomparable Churchill—and the arguments advanced have become generally familiar. One can hardly pick up a book on World War II without coming across them, or find articles on World War II in our popular magazines that do not mention examples of American strategic and political naïveté.[30]*

From all the latest reports, the southern France decision is still holding its high rating on the "big blunder hit parade." What must be noted is that the eloquence of the British writers, the plausibility of their case, and the frustrations of the postwar years as tensions with the U.S.S.R. have increased—all have given their case great prominence. The resultant criticism of the United States strategy runs the gamut from the nostalgic "I told you so" of the Prime Minister and the reasoned historical analysis of a Liddell Hart in favor of a counterstrategy to a vindictive search for scapegoats by certain sections of the American press. What has been lost in all this barrage is the American case, its compulsions, its strong points, its logic. Obscured, too, are the positive results derived from the southern France operation, although General Eisenhower has stated in retrospect: "There was no development of that period which added more decisively to our advantages or aided us more in accomplishing the final and complete defeat of the German forces than did this secondary attack coming up the Rhone Valley." [31]

There is not space here to examine in detail the general charges against American strategy around which most of the postwar criticisms on the conduct of the war have centered. Churchill has lashed out at what he terms the American "logical, large-scale, mass-production style of thought." [32] General J. F. C. Fuller, the British student of strategy, has expressed the same thought in referring to this type of strategy as "ironmongering." [33] Chester Wilmot, the late Australian writer and B.B.C. war correspondent, concluded that the Americans were "militarily unsophisticated." [34] In this representation of their strategy, the Americans pursued relentlessly and rig-

---

* Incidentally, the list of so-called blunders of World War II is apparently growing. Hanson Baldwin's original modest six were recently tripled by Captain W. D. Puleston, USN ret. See footnote 30.

idly a kind of "big business" strategy built around the notion of concentrating tons of hardware in the British Isles and hurling it across
the Channel on a definite time schedule in such great quantities that
the hapless Germans would be all but submerged. This criticism begs
the question whether the Churchillian approach—the peripheral approach—however suitable to British manpower, economy, and traditions, was suited to U.S. capacities and traditions. Gordon Harrison,
author of *Cross-Channel Attack,* has remarked: "To accuse the
Americans of mass-production thinking is only to accuse them of having a mass-production economy and recognizing the military advantage of such an economy. The Americans were power-minded." From
the beginning they thought in terms of taking on the main German
armies and beating them. What they wanted was a "power drive,"
not a "mop-up." [35]

Back of the U.S. Chiefs' fear of a policy of attritional and peripheral warfare against Germany in mid-war lay their continued anxiety over its ultimate costs in men, money, and time. This anxiety
was intensified by their concern over getting on with the war against
Japan. Basic in their thought was a growing realization of the ultimate
limits of U.S. manpower available for war purposes. To the military,
the discernible ceilings in military manpower, and anxiety about the
effects of a long-continued period of maximum mobilization, confirmed their doctrine of concentration. But it is a mistake to believe
that the Americans remained opposed to all Mediterranean operations. As the debate over the southern France operation shows, a
good part of their labors in 1943 and 1944 was actually spent in
reconciling Mediterranean operations with the cross-Channel operation. It should also be carefully noted that the weakening of Great
Britain and its close dependence on the United States were well advanced before the end of 1943—when the peripheral strategy to
which the Prime Minister was so dedicated was still in vogue.

The controversy that has arisen over the question of a Balkan
operation demands special attention. Would it not have been wiser
to have invaded the Continent through the Balkans and thereby fore-
stalled Soviet domination of Central Europe? The fact must be emphasized that this is a postwar debate. The Balkan invasion was
never proposed by any responsible leader in Allied strategy councils
as an alternative to OVERLORD, and no Allied debate or planning took
place in those terms. The evidence is clear on this point. The Balkan
versus southern France argument is another kettle of fish. Churchill
has steadfastly denied that he wanted a Balkan invasion, and the

evidence, though not entirely clear, seems to bear him out.[36] But there are ambiguities in his position that remain to be explained. Undoubtedly, he was in favor of raids, assistance for native populations, throwing in a few armored divisions, and like measures, but nowhere in his wartime and postwar writing has he faced up to the question that so frightened the U.S. staff—the ultimate costs and requirements of an operation in the Balkans, an area of poor terrain and poor communications. This question is all the more valid in the light of World War II experience with Mediterranean operations in Italy—a striking demonstration of how great the costs of war of attrition can be. What is also clear is that both the President and the U.S. staff were determined to stay out of the thorny politics of the Balkan area. Suffice it to say, the Balkan question was never argued out in full and frank military or political terms during World War II.

Before we accept the case for the Balkan alternative to the southern France operation, there are other points to be pondered. With all due respect to the greatest phrasemaker of them all, there probably was no worse misnomer than the so-called "soft underbelly" of Europe. There is nothing "soft" about the European underbelly. As any good contour map will show, the Balkan area has a hard-shelled back —certainly not one ideally suited for armored warfare. Aside from terrain, logistical factors must be considered. Suppose an operation in the Balkans had bogged down or developed into a big campaign? In that case, additional bases would have had to be built in the Middle East to support it. Then there was the question of turnaround time. To have reoriented the Allied effort to the Balkans would have required a great diversion from the OVERLORD build-up and might have slowed plans for redeployment to the Pacific. To have reoriented that effort to the Balkans would itself have required considerable time. That the Allies were not diverted from the northern campaign may even have been England's salvation. For otherwise, Hitler might eventually have pulverized Britain with V-2 projectiles from launching platforms in the Low Countries.

Then there is the important factor of public opinion. Would the American people in the summer of 1944 have tolerated a shift from the much-publicized second front to an effort in the Balkans? The judgment of the President, the responsible American policy maker, was "no." Here it is important to consider the divergent approaches of the Prime Minister and the President to the European war. To Churchill, anxiously watching the rapid Soviet advance into Poland and the Balkans, the war had become more than ever a contest for

great political stakes, and he wished Western Allied strength diverted
to fill the vacuum left by the retreating Germans and thereby forestall
the Soviet surge. Had the President joined with the Prime Minister as
he often had in the past, the U.S. military staff's concentration on
bringing the war against Germany to a swift military conclusion might
still have been tempered and the war steered into more direct political
channels. But the President would not, and the Prime Minister by
himself could not. Many reasons may account for the President's
position—state of his health, anxiety to conclude the Japanese conflict, desire to get on with the tasks of peace. In any event, by the
last year of the war the American Commander in Chief was caught
on the horns of a political dilemma. There is reason to believe that
he was not unconcerned about the unilateral efforts of the Soviet
Union to put its impress on the shape of postwar Europe. But domestic political considerations required him to fight a quick and decisive war—one that would justify America's entry and the dispatch
of American troops abroad. He had done the job of educating the
American people to the need for active participation in the European
conflict, but whether he could have led them to a prolonged war or
to a prolonged stay of U.S. troops in occupation duties—such as
might have resulted from the more active U.S. role in southeastern
Europe desired by the Prime Minister—was more doubtful. Besides,
President Roosevelt's policy for peace, like President Woodrow Wilson's, seemed to rest on national self-determination and an international organization to maintain peace—not on the balance of power.
To achieve this aim he had to take the calculated risk of being able
to handle Stalin and of winning and keeping the friendship of the
Soviet Union. To use U.S. military strength to play the game of European power politics might have defeated both aims.

While the Prime Minister appeared willing to go a long way in
the same direction, he hedged more toward the traditional balance of
power theory. Churchill's inability in the last year of the war to reverse the trend bore eloquent testimony to the changed relationships
between United States and British military weight and to the shifting
bases of the Grand Alliance. The United States had the power but did
not choose to use it; the Prime Minister had the purpose but not
the power. After the middle of 1944 British war production became
increasingly unbalanced, and the British fought the remainder of the
war under a contracting economy. Clearly, the last year of the war
saw the foundations of the Alliance in further transition—British in-

fluence waning and the United States and the Soviet Union emerging as the two strongest powers in the world.

It is in the light of this shift in the power balance that we must consider the Prime Minister's alternatives. The strong presumption in the postwar debate is that had the Allies entered the Balkans the Russians would somehow have been held in check. The counterarguments must also be weighed. Aside from questions of military feasibility, there is no certainty that such a move would have produced the desired peace. Had the Western partners become involved in the Balkans, the Russians might have gone all the way to the Channel, perhaps picking up the strategic Ruhr along the way. Had the Western Allies entered the Balkans in force in the face of the advancing Russians, there is also no assurance that new embroilments might not have been begun then and there as the Americans feared. With the traditional balance of power upset, Great Britain growing weaker, the Russians intent on pushing their strategic frontiers westward, and the United States determined to leave Europe soon, more drastic measures than the temporary diversion of some Western military power—largely United States power at that—would seem to have been required to check the Russians and assure the peace in Europe.

It appears clear that back of Churchill's Balkan policy lay the traditional British balance of power theory. But there is a serious question here too for students of strategy to consider. At the risk of oversimplification, it may be said that traditionally the British practice rested on its wealth, its Navy, and some ground forces—all placed where they could do the most good. By the summer of 1944, Britain had neither the wealth nor the uncommitted ground forces to give, and its Navy could serve little against a land power such as the Soviet Union. Clearly it would have required Allied help—especially American—to make the theory work. With United States public opinion unprepared for a sudden shift in objective—from Germany to the Soviet Union—and with American tradition opposed to involving U.S. forces in European power politics, how realistic was the Churchillian policy? Furthermore, Communism has been called "an ideology in arms"—an ideology with its own body of doctrine, tactics, and ethics that operates on a global scale and assumes many forms of power—political, economic, psychological, as well as military; a colossus that can apparently wait generations to attain its ends. That the balance of power theory was a useful concept in Britain's history vis-à-vis Continental Europe is undoubtedly true. Whether the British experience with the traditional balance of power theory in Europe is the answer to the Communist threat now, any more than it could have been in the summer of 1944, is questionable. Willy-nilly, the power balance in the world has changed, and power itself has assumed new forms.

Martin Blumenson

14

*General Bradley's Decision
at Argentan
(1944)*

In August 1944, a few weeks after the Allied breakout in Normandy, Lieutenant General Omar N. Bradley, commanding the U.S. 12th Army Group, abruptly halted the advance of the XV Corps of Lieutenant General George S. Patton's Third Army. He thus prevented its movement northward through Argentan toward a juncture with Canadian forces coming south from Caen toward Falaise; as a consequence, the Allies failed to close the Argentan-Falaise pocket. The virtually surrounded German forces in Normandy, escaping through the Argentan-Falaise gap, avoided complete encirclement and almost certain destruction.

Why General Bradley made his decision and whether he was correct are questions that have stirred discussion ever since World War II.

The story starts during the breakout in Normandy in July 1944, when the U.S. First Army under General Bradley broke out of the confinement imposed by the Germans in the hedgerow country of the Cotentin Peninsula and streamed in triumph toward Avranches.[1] There, on the first day of August, as General Patton's Third Army became operational, General Bradley relinquished command of the First Army to Lieutenant General Courtney H. Hodges and assumed command of the 12th Army Group. Allied ground forces in Western Europe then comprised two U.S. armies under Bradley, and a British and a Canadian army, both under General Sir Bernard L. Montgomery's 21st Army Group. Until General Dwight D. Eisenhower, the Supreme Allied Commander, assumed personal direction of the

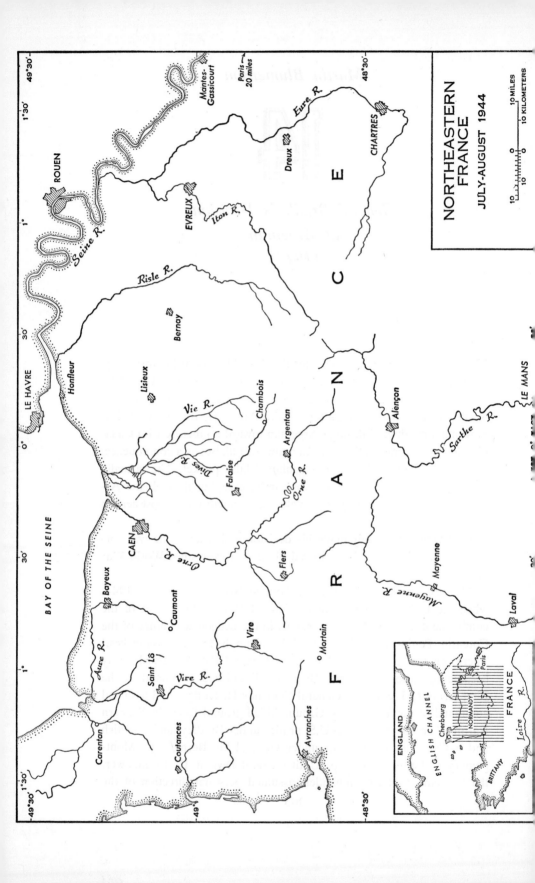

NORTHEASTERN FRANCE
JULY-AUGUST 1944

ground campaign—a task he undertook on the first day of September —Montgomery functioned as the commander of the land forces executing Operation OVERLORD.

The objective of OVERLORD, the cross-Channel attack, was lodgment of the Allied forces in roughly that portion of northwestern France which lies between the Seine and the Loire Rivers. According to preinvasion plans, the Allies hoped to gain the lodgment through the following maneuver: Patton's Third Army was to go westward from Avranches to take Brittany and its vital ports; Hodges' First Army was to protect the commitment of Patton's forces into Brittany, wheel on the right of the British and Canadian armies to the southeast and east, and then move eastward with those armies to the Seine River.[2]

The Allies started this operation with Patton's drive into Brittany as the main effort of the 12th Army Group. But the obvious scarcity of enemy forces in Brittany, the disorganization of the German left-flank forces near Avranches, and the fact that in driving to Avranches the Americans had outflanked the German defensive line in Normandy quickly led to an alteration of plans. On August 3 the Allies decided to clear Brittany with "a minimum of forces" (one corps), while the remainder wheeled eastward with their eventual sights on the Seine.[3] The new Allied intention was to swing the right flank toward the Seine in order to push the Germans back against the lower part of the river, where all the bridges had been destroyed by air bombardment. Pressed against the river and unable to cross with sufficient speed to escape, the Germans west of the Seine—the bulk of the forces in Western Europe—would in effect be encircled and face destruction.[4] Coincidentally, the Allies would come into possession of the lodgment area.

The XV Corps, commanded by Major General Wade H. Haislip and under Third Army control, had by this time been committed to action near Avranches—between the VIII Corps of the Third Army (clearing Brittany) and the VII Corps of the First Army (expecting orders to drive eastward from Avranches). Because the XV Corps was already around the German left and oriented generally southeastward, Haislip drew the assignment of initiating the sweep of the Allied right flank toward the successive objectives of Laval and Le Mans, the first objectives of what presumably was the encircling maneuver eastward to the Seine.[5]

According to General Montgomery's analysis of the situation produced by the breakout, "the only hope" the Germans had of saving

their armies was a "staged withdrawal to the Seine." By swinging
the Allied right flank "round towards Paris," Montgomery hoped to
hasten and disrupt that withdrawal. If the Germans withdrew to the
Seine, their immediate move, Montgomery believed, would be to
positions east of the Orne River, generally along a line between Caen
and Flers. If Montgomery could act quickly enough and drive south
from Caen to Falaise, he would cut behind this first stage of the German withdrawal he anticipated and place the Germans "in a very
awkward situation." Thus, although the broad Allied intent was to
pin the Germans back against the Seine, the immediate opportunity
was present to "cut off the enemy . . . and render their withdrawing
east difficult—if not impossible." This would be but the beginning of
a "wide encirclement of success," presumably meaning a wide swing
around the German armies west of the Seine by the U.S. XV Corps.
Meanwhile, the main instrument with which to harass the first part
of the German withdrawal had become the Canadian First Army,
which was to attack toward Falaise *as early as possible* and in any
case not later than August 8." [6]

General Montgomery reviewed his estimate of the situation and
also his own intentions two days later. To him, the Germans faced
terrifying alternatives in making their withdrawal to the Seine, which
seemed to Montgomery to be the only course of action open to them.
Not only on the basis of the troops available but also in the absence
of established alternate lines in the rear, the Germans could neither
hold any long front in strength nor let go both ends of their defensive
line. If they persisted in holding near Caen on the right, they offered
the Allies the opportunity of swinging completely around their left
and cutting off their escape. If they endeavored to buttress their encircled left flank near Vire and thereby weakened the pivot point near
Caen, they gave the Allies access to the shortest route to the Seine.
In either case, they invited destruction of their forces west of the Seine
River.

Judging that the Germans would try to escape the breakout consequences by accepting the lesser evil and pivoting on the Caen area
as they fell back, Montgomery planned to unhinge the German withdrawal by robbing the troops of their pivot point near Caen. Lieutenant General Henry D. G. Crerar's Canadian First Army was to
accomplish this by driving southward to Falaise from positions near
Caen (then later swinging northeast from Falaise to the Seine near
Rouen). As a complementary maneuver, Lieutenant General Miles
C. Dempsey's British Second Army, which had been attacking south-

east from near Caumont since July 30, was to continue to push out in an arc and drive eastward through Argentan on its way to the Seine. On the Allied right, Bradley's 12th Army Group was to make its main effort on the right flank by thrusting rapidly east and northeast toward the Seine near Paris.[7]

In brief, Montgomery's intentions were postulated on the belief that the Germans had no alternative but to withdraw to and across the Seine. On this premise, he sought to disorganize, harass, and pursue them, transform their retreat into a rout, and destroy their forces while they were still west of the Seine—within the confines of the OVERLORD lodgment area. On this basis, Crerar prepared to jump off toward Falaise, Dempsey made ready to push southeast toward Argentan, Hodges displaced part of his forces for a drive generally eastward from Avranches toward Alençon, and Patton sent the XV Corps southeastward from Avranches toward Le Mans. That was the Allied frame of reference on the day before the Germans disregarded Montgomery's logic and launched what became known as the Mortain counterattack.

From ground east of Mortain, the Germans attacked westward on August 7 to recover Avranches. They wished to establish Avranches as the left (west) flank anchor of a new continuous defensive line. They hoped thereby to halt the mobile warfare developing from the breakout and re-create the static conditions that had made possible their successful containment of the Allies during June and much of July.

In the course of their attack, the Germans overran Mortain and made a serious pentration on the VII Corps front, but they were halted on the first day of their attack by tenacious American resistance on the ground and effective Allied operations in the air. As General Bradley assembled and concentrated American strength near Mortain to guarantee Allied retention of Avranches, he conceived the idea of countering the attack by trapping the Germans.

Allied commanders first discussed the idea of ensnaring the Germans on August 8, the day after the German attack, when Bradley, in the presence of General Eisenhower (who was visiting Bradley's headquarters), telephoned General Montgomery and secured approval for a change in plan. His proposal was based on the fact that while the Allied armies in Normandy had fought hard during the first week in August against bitter opposition conducted from good defensive positions, General Haislip's XV Corps had rounded the left flank of those defensive positions and was attacking through lightly defended territory in a slashing advance. The XV Corps had already taken Laval and was well on its way to Le Mans. By capturing Le Mans, the XV Corps would, in less than a week, have moved an enveloping Allied arm around the German left flank to a point 85 air miles southeast of Avranches. By turning the XV Corps north from Le Mans toward Alençon, the Americans would threaten the German counterattacking forces from the south. This action seemed doubly attractive because the Canadian First Army on that day, August 8, had launched its attack south from positions near Caen toward Falaise and was thereby threatening the Germans from the north.[8]

The timing of the Canadian attack, as related to the Mortain counterattack, was of course accidental, but it could hardly have been more fortunate. Coming twenty-four hours after the unexpected German attack, the Canadian effort, in preparation for almost a week, had been launched in an entirely different context. With a massive application of air support, the Canadians had a good chance of reaching and taking Falaise.[9]

It suddenly became apparent to the Allied commanders that the Germans in Normandy, by attacking westward toward Avranches, had pushed their heads into a noose. The bulk of their forces—two field armies amounting to more than 100,000 men—were west of a north-south line through Caen, Falaise, Argentan, Alençon, and Le Mans. If the Canadians attacking from the north took Falaise and if the XV Corps attacking from the south took Alençon, 35 miles would separate the two Allied flanks and the Germans would be virtually surrounded. Allied possession of Falaise and Alençon, besides threatening the Germans with complete encirclement, would deprive them of two of the three main east-west roads they still controlled. If the Canadians attacking from the north and the XV Corps attacking from the south pressed on beyond Falaise and Alençon, respectively, and met at Argentan, or as General Montgomery put it, "if we can close the gap completely . . . we shall have put the enemy in the most awkward predicament." [10]

The prospect of doing just that caused the Allies to suspend the drive to the Seine in favor of encirclement in the Falaise-Alençon area. Instead of continuing eastward toward the Seine, the XV Corps was to turn north toward Alençon after reaching Le Mans.[11]

On August 9 the Canadian attack bogged down in the Caen-Falaise corridor 8 miles north of Falaise. But on the same day the XV Corps took Le Mans, and the following day it jumped off to the north.

General Montgomery made a new analysis of the situation on

August 11 and attempted to anticipate the probable consequences of the implicit juncture of Canadian and American troops. As the gap between Canadians and Americans narrowed, he estimated, the Germans could bring up additional divisions from the east, or, more probably, could move their armored and mobile forces eastward out of the pocket toward ammunition and gasoline supplies. If the Germans chose the latter course of action, they would probably operate in the Argentan-Alençon area "to have the benefit of the difficult 'bocage' country" there. Their purpose would be to hold off the Americans while they used the more advantageous terrain in that region to cover their withdrawal. Expecting, then, the Germans to mass stronger forces in defense of Alençon than of Falaise, Montgomery concluded that it would be easier for the Canadians to make rapid progress. The Canadians could probably reach Argentan from the north before the XV Corps could attain Argentan from the south.

General Montgomery therefore ordered the Canadians to continue their efforts to capture Falaise and proceed from there to Argentan. Meanwhile, the XV Corps was to advance through Alençon to the Army Group boundary just south of Argentan, a line drawn by Montgomery to separate the zones of operation of the American (12th Army Group) and the British-Canadian forces (21st Army Group). He projected a meeting of Canadian and American forces just south of Argentan, which would form a literal encirclement of the Germans. The British Second Army and the U.S. First Army, pressing from the west, were to herd the Germans into the Canadian-American line and assist in the total destruction of the surrounded enemy forces. Should the Germans somehow evade encirclement at Argentan, Montgomery was ready with an alternate plan: the Allies were to reinstate the drive earlier projected to the Seine.[12]

While the Canadians endeavored to resume their attack toward Falaise, the XV Corps drove north from Le Mans on August 10 and secured Alençon two days later. General Patton had set the Corps objective at the Army Group boundary—north of Alençon and just south of Argentan—so Haislip's forces continued their attack. Since Patton's order had also directed preparation for a "further advance" beyond the Army Group boundary, and since the Army Group boundary seemed within reach, Haislip—on the basis of the "further advance" inferentially authorized—established Argentan as the new Corps objective. With 2 armored divisions and 2 infantry divisions comprising his forces, Haislip judged that he could hold a solid shoulder between Alençon and Argentan, and with the Canadians, who were to reach Argentan from the north, thus encircle the German forces to the west.[13]

As the XV Corps attacked toward Argentan, General Haislip pointedly notified General Patton that he was about to capture the last objective furnished by the army commander. By implication, Haislip requested authority to proceed north of Argentan if the Canadians were not yet there. He suggested that additional troops be placed under his command so that he could block all the east-west roads under his control north of Alençon.[14]

Since the Canadians had made no further progress toward Falaise while the XV Corps had moved rapidly, Patton sent word for Haislip to go beyond Argentan. Haislip was to "push on slowly in the direction of Falaise." After reaching Falaise, Haislip was to "continue to push on slowly until . . . contact [is made with] our Allies," the Canadians.[15]

Attacking toward Argentan on the morning of August 13, the XV Corps struck surprising resistance. The advance halted temporarily. But as the Corps was preparing to make a renewed effort to get to and through Argentan, a surprising message came from the Third Army. General Bradley had forbidden further movement northward. General Patton had to order General Haislip to stop. Instead of continuing to the north to an eventual meeting with the Canadians, the XV Corps was to hold in place.[16]

This is the controversial command decision. Less than 25 miles separated Canadians and Americans—the Argentan-Falaise gap, through which the Germans tried to escape. Why Bradley did not allow Patton to let the XV Corps continue north and seal the Argentan-Falaise pocket is the main question of debate.

Montgomery believed—with good logic and a sound estimate of the probable course of German action—that the Canadians could cover the shorter distance to Argentan from the north more quickly than the XV Corps could from the south. His belief turned out to be overoptimistic. Despite his injunction for speed in getting to Falaise and beyond, the Canadians, halted 8 miles short of Falaise by August 9, were unable to mount a renewed attack until August 14. They did not secure Falaise until the last hours of August 16. According to Chester Wilmot, "the evidence suggests that the [Canadian] thrust from the north was not pressed with sufficient speed and strength." [17]

When the Canadians reached Falaise, U.S. troops were still just south of Argentan, where they had been halted by Bradley's order three days before. The gap between the two Allied forces had been narrowed, but 15 miles still separated them. Through this gap German forces withdrew to the east. "Due to the extraordinary measures taken by the enemy north of Falaise," General Eisenhower wrote to General Marshall, U.S. Army Chief of Staff, "it is possible that our total bag of prisoners [from the Argentan-Falaise pocket] will not be so great as I first anticipated." [18]

The failure of the Canadians to reach Falaise more quickly made General Bradley's decision to halt the XV Corps appear in retrospect to many commanders, both Allied and German, to have been a tactical error, a failure to take full advantage of German vulnerability. [19] It seemed particularly true because General Bradley himself had suggested and General Montgomery had accepted the idea of literal encirclement. So, too, had General Patton. If, as Patton said, the "purpose of the operation is to surround and destroy the German west of the Seine," as he understood it to be, the Germans had first to be surrounded so that their destruction would be inevitable. He envisioned pincers—the Canadians and the XV Corps on opposite sides —cutting through the German rear on relatively narrow fronts and actually encircling the enemy as a preliminary to destruction. Thus, he gave the XV Corps the task of making contact with the Canadians on the opposite Allied flank. [20]

Yet it would seem that General Bradley was less interested in encirclement than in destruction. Judging, like the others, that the Germans by attacking had "incurred the risk of encirclement from the south and north," he immediately visualized destruction occurring as the result of the closing of two Allied jaws. The upper jaw was to consist of the Canadian army, the British army, and part of the U.S. First Army on the north; the lower jaw was to be formed by part of the U.S. First Army (the VII Corps) and part of the U.S. Third Army (the XV Corps) on the south. In this concept, the Canadian army and the XV Corps were merely the front teeth of the upper and lower jaws, respectively; the remainder of the Allied forces were also to have a part in crushing the enemy forces caught between them. Artillery and tank fire, as well as air attack, had important roles to play. Holding the XV Corps at Argentan conformed with General Bradley's idea of destroying the enemy by the mashing effect of two jaws in process of closing. [21]

In actuality, the XV Corps at Argentan was already in an exposed position and vulnerable on both flanks. Though few enemy troops were on the XV Corps' east (right) flank, the west flank was open to the German forces partially bottled up in the pocket. As the Allies increased the pressure, they had to expect the Germans to make a break for safety. There was no better place for such an effort by the German forces concentrated for the Mortain counterattack than against the relatively weak left flank of the XV Corps. On August 13, when Bradley stopped further northward effort by the XV Corps, the contingents of the U.S. First Army on the XV Corps left were just starting to come up from Mayenne. In the extremely fluid situation of that day, a gap somewhere between 25 and 50 miles between U.S. forces near Mayenne and Argentan existed; it could not have been reassuring to General Bradley. And though he has not mentioned this as a factor in his decision, it was reasonable for him to be more concerned at that time with security than with encirclement.

Though the Allied commanders did not seem to be anxious about the Mayenne-Argentan gap, the Germans were preparing to launch a massive attack against the deep left flank of the XV Corps. Had the Germans been successful in getting off their attack, they would have struck exactly in the area between Mayenne and Argentan.[22] This alone would seem to justify Bradley's decision to halt the XV Corps and turn it from offensive orientation to defensive preparation. The continuous existence of the Argentan-Falaise gap led the Germans naturally into this escape corridor, where they were vulnerable to destruction from Allied artillery and air.

Long after the event, General Bradley explained that a head-on juncture of Canadians and Americans would have been a "dangerous and uncontrollable maneuver." According to General Eisenhower, it might have caused a "calamitous battle between friends." [23] Yet Bradley himself later offered two solutions to coordinate the artillery fires of the forces coming together: a distinctive terrain feature or conspicuous landmark could have been selected as the place of juncture; or the Canadian or American axis of advance could have been shifted several miles east or west to provide a double and stronger cordon of encirclement and avoid the danger of a head-on meeting.[24]

Bringing Canadians and Americans closer together had a more immediate disadvantage—the hampering of artillery and air activity, particularly the latter. Close support missions would have become increasingly restricted and the danger of bombing errors greater. As it was, the extremely fluid front necessitated considerable shifting of bomb safety lines and made the work of Allied pilots a delicate matter. Yet for all the hazards of error, Allied aircraft operated in the Argentan-Falaise area with excellent results until August 17, when the bomb line in that sector was removed and air activity, at least theoretically or officially, ceased.[25] Had an actual meeting of Canadians and Americans occurred near Falaise or Argentan, air activity would have come to an end much sooner, and artillery fire would have had to be curtailed.

Another reason contributing to General Bradley's reluctance to send American troops beyond Argentan was that he preferred, as he later said, "a solid shoulder at Argentan to a broken neck at Falaise." Although he afterward stated that he had not doubted the ability of the XV Corps to close the gap—and this despite increasing resistance encountered by the Corps on the morning of August 13—he had questioned the ability of the Corps to keep the gap closed. The increasing resistance met that morning and the fact that Haislip had called for additional troops to ensure retention of the Alençon-Argentan area—again, even though General Bradley did not mention these factors in his later account—argue in support of his decision. Furthermore, Bradley incorrectly believed that the bulk of the German forces west of the Alençon-Caen line were already stampeding across the Argentan plain and through the gap. Nineteen divisions, he feared, would trample the thin line of American troops if the latter went beyond Argentan.[26] Though the Germans were not stampeding, the belief that they were helps to explain the decision to stop the XV Corps. Perhaps the Canadians, too, were aware of the possible overextension of forces on their side of the gap.

Two arguments advanced to explain General Bradley's decision must be considered even though they appear to have little validity. First, rumor soon after the event ascribed the halt of the XV Corps to warnings by the Allied air forces that time bombs had been dropped along the highways in the Argentan-Falaise area to harass German movements. Further northward advance by the XV Corps, therefore, would have exposed American ground troops to these bombs. Whether this had a part in shaping General Bradley's decision or not, the fact was that fighter-bomber pilots had sown delayed-action explosives over a wide area between August 10 and 13. However, the bombs were fused for a maximum of twelve hours' delay, and they therefore could not have endangered the American ground troops.[27]

Second, it has been suggested that bringing the Canadians and Americans together head-on would have disarranged plans to "get the U.S. and British forces lined up and started together going east."[28] This explanation is patently weak. Arguing from hindsight, it invents a cause that seems to fit the results.

Perhaps the most controversial aspect of the whole question is

General Bradley's statement that he could not have let the XV Corps go beyond Argentan in any event because he lacked the authority to do so. The Corps was already at the Army Group boundary and indeed slightly across it and into the 21st Army Group zone. Since General Montgomery commanded the ground forces in France, and since Bradley had already violated the demarcation delineating his own sphere of operations, Bradley needed Montgomery's permission to go farther to the north. Though it is true that Montgomery did not sanction an American advance beyond Argentan, neither did Bradley propose it.[29] Perhaps the main reason why they both accepted the situation was the impending Canadian attack toward Falaise, the second attack, scheduled for the following day, August 14. Canadian success in attaining not only Falaise but Argentan would have made unnecessary any further intrusion into the 21st Army Group zone by the U.S. XV Corps.

General Bradley himself later considered the failure to close the gap a mistake, and he placed the responsibility on Montgomery. He recalled that he and Patton had doubted "Monty's ability to close the gap at Argentan" from the north, and they had "waited impatiently" for word from Montgomery to authorize continuation of the XV Corps advance. While waiting, according to Bradley, he and Patton had seen the Germans reinforce the shoulders of the Argentan-Falaise gap and watched the enemy pour troops and matériel eastward to escape the unsealed pocket. It seemed to him and Patton, Bradley remembered, that Dempsey's British Second Army, driving from the northwest, accelerated German movement eastward and facilitated German escape by pushing the Germans out of the open end of the pocket like squeezing a tube of toothpaste. "If Monty's tactics mystified me," Bradley wrote later, "they dismayed Eisenhower even more. And . . . a shocked Third Army looked on helplessly as its quarry fled [while] Patton raged at Montgomery's blunder."[30]

It is true that the Germans were building up the shoulders of the gap by August 13, but they were not fleeing eastward to escape encirclement by that date. The Germans had started on August 11 to withdraw to some extent their salient at Mortain, but Hitler was still insisting that another attack toward Avranches was necessary; to maintain the conditions that would make it possible, he ordered an attack against the deep left flank of the XV Corps. Not until August 13, several hours before Bradley halted the XV Corps, did a high-ranking commander state officially for the first time what in retrospect all German commanders later claimed to have thought—that it was time to begin to escape the threatening Allied encirclement.[31] Not until the following day, August 14, did Hitler admit that further retraction of the Mortain salient was necessary and that a renewed attack toward Avranches was, at least for the moment, impossible. Not until the afternoon of August 16 did the Germans begin to organize a withdrawal through the Argentan-Falaise gap.[32]

That Bradley claimed to have seen this as early as August 13 is due either to bad memory or to overanxious expectation of what, in his opinion, the Germans would have to do. If American intelligence was at fault, it was in anticipating the difficulty of securing and transmitting—in time to be of use—information on a situation so fluid that reports were out of date as they were being made. Thus, Allied predictions were ahead of the facts.

If Patton, in a subordinate role, could only rage at Montgomery's tactics, and if Bradley thought he might offend a sensitive Montgomery by requesting permission to cross the Army Group boundary, Eisenhower, who was in France and following the combat developments, might have resolved the situation had he thought it necessary. Yet General Eisenhower did not intervene. Interfering with a tactical decision made by a commander in closer contact with the situation was not Eisenhower's method of exercising command. Long afterward, General Eisenhower stated that he thought Montgomery should have closed the gap and that closing the gap "might have won us a complete battle of annihilation." [33] Montgomery's chief of staff, Major General Sir Francis de Guingand, also believed that the Argentan-Falaise gap might have been closed if Montgomery had not restricted the Americans by means of the existing Army Group boundary, a restriction, Guingand thought, American commanders felt strongly.[34]

Despite the foregoing observations made after the event, there is no doubt that the basis for General Bradley's decision at Argentan included four justifiable tactical considerations: (1) on the evidence of the increasing resistance to the XV Corps on the morning of August 13, there was no certainty that American troops could move through or around Argentan and beyond; (2) since the XV Corps left flank was already exposed, there was no point in closing the Argentan-Falaise gap at the expense of enlarging the Mayenne-Argentan gap on its deep left; (3) the Canadians were about to launch their second attack toward Falaise, an effort that, it was hoped, would get them beyond Falaise to Argentan and make unnecessary a further

American advance into the 21st Army Group zone; (4) bringing
American and Canadian lines together would have inhibited the full
use of the superior strength of Allied air and artillery.

What were the consequences of the decision? General Patton was
unhappy with the halt imposed on the XV Corps and impatient to
keep moving. Bradley estimated that, "due to the delay in closing the
gap between Argentan and Falaise, many of the German divisions
which were in the pocket have now escaped." Thus it was unnecessary
to retain a large force at Argentan. Montgomery had earlier authorized, in the event the Germans escaped encirclement at Argentan,
the drive to the Seine. The virtual absence of enemy forces in the
region east of Argentan to the Seine and the greater mobility of American forces as compared to the Germans thought to be fleeing the
pocket made it reasonable to turn Patton toward the eastern boundary
of the OVERLORD lodgment area, which now appeared within reach.
It was true that the Mayenne gap on the XV Corps left appeared
well on its way to elimination because of the excellent advance of the
VII Corps on August 13, and thus the XV Corps could have attacked
northward through Argentan with greater security on August 14. But
since Montgomery had had twenty-four hours to invite the XV Corps
across the Army Group boundary and had not done so, Bradley,
without consulting Montgomery, decided to retain part of the XV
Corps at Argentan and send the rest eastward toward the Seine
River.[35] General Patton seems to have had a hand in the decision,
for he secured approval by telephone to institute this course of action,
and on August 14 he instructed General Haislip to attack eastward.[36]

This of course changed the pattern of the battle. The reduced
forces of the XV Corps reached the Seine River and crossed it at
Mantes-Gassicourt on the night of August 19, thereby trapping the
German forces in Normandy. Simultaneously, the Corps dispatched
an armored division downstream from Mantes-Gassicourt on the left
bank of the Seine to drive the Germans toward the mouth where
escape crossings were more difficult. Eventually, a corps of the First
Army (the XIX Corps) joined this effort to deny the Germans easy
crossings over the Seine.

Meanwhile, at Argentan the Germans were implementing their decision of August 16 to escape through the Argentan-Falaise gap.
The withdrawal they started that evening increased pressure on the
remaining XV Corps forces still in place. It became evident, contrary
to earlier Allied intelligence estimates, that a large proportion of the

German forces in Normandy still remained within the Argentan-Falaise pocket. What the Americans had earlier judged to be escape efforts had in reality been troop movements to positions east of Argentan-Falaise, defensive movements designed to blunt the threats to Argentan and Falaise.[37]

Closing the gap by joining Canadians and Americans was thus as desirable as it had seemed on August 13, when Bradley had halted the XV Corps, but closing the gap three days later was bound to be more difficult, not only because of the German withdrawal of the Mortain salient and the concentration of enemy troops at the shoulders of the gap, but also because Bradley had allowed Patton to reduce the forces at Argentan in favor of the drive to the Seine.[38]* On the same day, August 16, Montgomery phoned Bradley and suggested that Canadians and Americans endeavor to meet—not somewhere between Argentan and Falaise, but 7 miles northeast of Argentan, near Chambois.[39]

No corps headquarters was on hand to direct the American part of the projected meeting, and the attack did not get under way until August 18. The actual meeting of Canadian and American forces occurred near Chambois on August 19, but not until the following day was the pocket securely closed. By that time, American troops were crossing the Seine. The Germans were roped into a relatively small area bounded by the Seine and the sea. With Allied control of the air (over the Seine) and the coastal waters, the Germans were encircled at the Seine.

By not closing the Argentan-Falaise pocket, as it happened, the Allies were able to reach the Seine more quickly and encircle the Germans there at much less cost in terms of Allied casualties. The Germans within the Argentan-Falaise pocket were not so disorganized or so vulnerable as is sometimes thought. Considering the disadvantages under which they were operating—Allied air supremacy, the limited road network, the close proximity of Allied artillery, the relative absence of cover on the Argentan plain—the Germans made a well-organized and well-executed withdrawal out of the pocket. Overextending the XV Corps by sending it beyond Argentan could have proved disastrous to it. Leaving the gap open provided a safety valve for German escape. The psychological effect of finding more Allied troops at the Seine after having escaped through the Argentan-

---

* From 4 divisions and 22 artillery battalions in the area between Alençon and Argentan on August 14, the American forces were reduced to 3 divisions and 7 artillery battalions.

Falaise gap must have been doubly discouraging and depressing to the Germans.

Was the shallow encirclement at Argentan ever possible? It would appear so, but whether it could have been maintained for long remains questionable. General Haislip had recognized that the Forêt d'Ecouves, a large wooded area just south of Argentan, provided the Germans with excellent terrain from which to deny Argentan to the XV Corps. Haislip had therefore instructed the French 2nd Armored Division to bypass the forest on the left (west) and the U.S. 5th Armored Division to drive around the eastern edge. Disregarding the order, the French division commander split his command into three columns and sent one each around the western edge, through the forest, and around the eastern limit. The column on the right consequently usurped a road reserved for the American armored division and blocked its advance for six hours during the afternoon of August 12. During those hours, the German commander, Lieutenant General Heinrich Eberbach, hastily assembled Panzer elements into a coherent defense that blocked the subsequent American effort. By the following morning, August 13, defensive preparations had progressed even further, to the point where German guns well sited and skillfully concealed on dominating terrain wrought a surprising amount of damage on the XV Corps attack formations. Yet as gratifying as this was to the Germans, it was also obvious to them that they were spent. They had stopped the American attack, but they did not expect to maintain for long the slender defensive line hastily established to oppose the XV Corps. The halt of the XV Corps attack early that afternoon came as a welcome surprise.[40]

Despite the increased resistance met at Argentan, with continued effort the XV Corps would more than likely have been able at the least to take physical possession of Argentan and thereby control the vital road net centering on that town. Obviously, this would have provoked violent German counteraction by the concentrated forces within the pocket. How far beyond Argentan the XV Corps might have gone, and how long it could have maintained positions in or beyond Argentan, are of course questions impossible to answer with certainty.

What critics of Bradley's decision sometimes overlook is the fact that by escaping through the Argentan-Falaise gap, the Germans ran a gantlet of fire that stretched virtually from Mortain to the Seine. Artillery and air attacks took a fearful toll of the withdrawing enemy troops. No one knows how many Germans escaped Argentan-Falaise and later Chambois. Estimates vary between 20,000 and 40,000 men.

Not many more than 50 medium and heavy artillery pieces and perhaps that many tanks reached eventual safety. Radios, vehicles, trains, supplies were lost; "even the number of rescued machineguns was insignificant."[41] All that remained were fragments of two field armies, the Fifth Panzer and the Seventh, which had effectively bottled up the Allies in Normandy during June and July, before the American breakout. The Allies took 50,000 prisoners in the Argentan-Falaise area; 10,000 dead were found on the field.[42] Those who escaped had still to reckon with the Allied forces at the Seine. An indication of the additional losses suffered by the Germans there may be found in the fact that 7 armored divisions managed to get the infinitesimal total of 1,300 men, 24 tanks, and 60 artillery pieces of varying caliber across the Seine.[43] The German remnants east of the Seine, lacking armament, equipment, even demolitions to destroy bridges behind them, could do nothing more than retreat toward Germany.

In the holocaust of the German defeat in Normandy, General Bradley's decision at Argentan was perhaps the major factor. Assuming the most advantageous conditions, how much better could the Allies have destroyed the Germans by closing the Argentan-Falaise gap? If any part of Bradley's decision might be considered a mistake, it is only that he halted the XV Corps before it took and secured Argentan, and this in retrospect seems far less momentous than it may have seemed at the time.

In other respects, General Bradley's decision seems justified, particularly by the turn of events. First and foremost, he remained within the operational framework established by his superior in command, General Montgomery—both in terms of boundaries and objectives. Whether he planned the rest that way or not, the results were fortunate. He achieved security at Argentan by sacrificing offensive maneuver and thereby prevented what could have been a disastrous overextension of the XV Corps; he ensured the destruction of two German armies at little cost; relinquishing the slim possibility of making and maintaining effective contact with the Canadians, he sent Patton to the Seine and secured not only a successful encirclement in double-quick time but also the goal of the cross-Channel attack, the lodgment area of the Allied armies on the Continent.

By the end of August, the Allies were at the Seine. The Germans were also at the Seine, but their shattered and disorganized elements could do little to oppose the Allied pursuit that was to take the Allied armies swiftly to the frontier of the enemy homeland.

Roland G. Ruppenthal

15

*Logistics and
the Broad-Front Strategy
(1944)*

Of all decisions made at the level of the Supreme Allied Commander in Western Europe during World War II, perhaps none has excited more polemics than that which raised the "one-thrust–broad-front" controversy. This has revolved about the decision that General Dwight D. Eisenhower made in September 1944 to build up his forces along the Rhine through the whole length of the Western Front, from the North Sea to Switzerland, before launching a final drive into the heart of Germany. It embodied what has come to be known as the "broad-front strategy."

There are those who endorse the view held by the top British commander in the theater, Field Marshal Sir Bernard L. Montgomery, that had General Eisenhower decided—preferably several weeks earlier, say, in mid-August—to concentrate all available resources in the north and halt all other offensive operations, the Allies with one bold, powerful thrust deep into Germany might have ended the war in late summer or early fall. Others maintain that the same end might have been accomplished had General Eisenhower banked all on a single thrust by the U.S. 12th Army Group, or even by the Third Army alone.

The factor that adherents to both these theories have neglected or underestimated is logistics. Seldom a subject for news headlines, logistic considerations nevertheless exert a strong influence not only on strategic planning but also on the conduct of operations once the battle has begun. What is not always recognized is that General Eisenhower's decision in mid-September 1944 was a decision based in large measure on logistic factors.[1]

By mid-September 1944 the Allied armies, having driven the Germans from Normandy and then pursued them across northern France and Belgium, stood at the German border in the north and at the Moselle River in the south. The enemy was building up a capacity for increased resistance in the frontier defenses of the West Wall (Siegfried Line) and along the Moselle. But even before this had made itself felt, the Allies' triumphant pursuit was slowed down and, in some sectors, brought to a temporary halt by supply shortages. These were the more exasperating because they occurred in the midst of spectacular successes and because they contributed so strongly to frustrating a short-lived hope that the war might be brought quickly to an end.

The supply situation which set the stage for General Eisenhower's decision was indeed all but desperate, but the reasons for it should not have been difficult to see. It is hardly surprising that combat commanders, in their exasperation over the denial to them of the means to continue the pursuit or to launch one bold thrust into Germany, should, on the American front, have immediately vented their annoyance on the Communications Zone, the organization responsible for their support. But their annoyance reflected both an unawareness of the impact of pursuit on supply capabilities and conveniently short memories concerning the invasion plan and the expected course of operations.

On its operational side, OVERLORD, the plan for the invasion of the European Continent, had been predicated on an estimate that the enemy would make successive stands on the major water barriers across France and Belgium. In accordance with this assumption, it was expected that he would make a stand at the Seine, a line that would not be reached until D Day plus 90. Furthermore, plans had contemplated a fairly steady rate of advance and not the pursuit of a disorganized enemy. While such a forecast of progress admittedly was conjectural, it formed, necessarily, the basis of logistic preparations. In the belief, for example, that the Seine ports would not become available quickly, great emphasis was placed on the development of the Brittany area, including the port of Brest. In addition, at least a month's pause at the Seine was expected to be necessary to develop an administrative base capable of supporting further offensives. Even on these assumptions, the margin of safety of the OVERLORD logistic plan was believed to be nonexistent.[2]

Since the OVERLORD operation developed quite differently from what had been expected, the assumptions on which the schedules had been based were largely voided. For the first seven weeks the advance was much slower than anticipated, and the Allied forces were confined to a shallow Normandy beachhead. From the viewpoint of logistical support, the lag in operations was not immediately serious, for it resulted in short lines of communications and gave the service forces added time to develop the port of Cherbourg whose capture had been delayed.

Whatever temporary advantage accrued from this situation quickly disappeared after the breakout at the end of July. By D Day plus 79 (August 24), Allied forces had closed to the Seine, 11 days ahead of schedule despite a lag of approximately 30 days at the beginning of the breakout. Tactically, the spectacular drive of early August brought definite advantages, for it resulted in the almost complete destruction of the German Seventh Army, and it greatly accelerated the advance to the enemy's border. From the point of view of logistic support, however, the rapid advance to the Seine foreshadowed serious complications. The fact that the OVERLORD objective for D plus 90 was reached on D plus 79 was, in theory, not too serious, for the supply structure was sufficiently flexible to accommodate itself to a variation of 11 days. But the actual departures from the scheduled advance involved a variation of 40, not 11 days: Because of the initial lag in operations, American forces were still at the D plus 20 line at D plus 49, and then between D plus 49 and D plus 79, a period of 30 days, they had actually advanced a distance which, by plan, was to have taken 70 days (i.e., logistically, from D plus 20 to D plus 90). The lines of communications could not be developed at the speed with which tanks and other combat vehicles were able to race forward. The result was that the armies already had used up their operational reserves by the time they reached the Seine.

Since rail and pipelines could not be pushed forward quickly enough, motor transport facilities were strained to the breaking point to meet even the minimum needs of the armies. The Communications Zone, consequently, found it impossible to establish stocks in advance depots. Furthermore, none of the Brittany ports had as yet been captured, and only one major port in Normandy—Cherbourg—was operational.

The arrival at the Seine marked only the beginning of supply difficulties. Despite the logistic complications which the rapid advance had already foreshadowed, decisions now were made to establish a bridgehead across the Seine, then to encircle Paris, and, finally, to continue the pursuit without pause all along the front. On purely tactical grounds these decisions were logically indicated, for the Allies now enjoyed a definite superiority, and the disintegration of enemy resistance offered opportunities that it would have been folly to ignore. From the point of view of logistics, however, these decisions carried with them a supply task out of all proportion to planned capabilities. With the supply structure already severely strained, these decisions entailed the risk of a complete breakdown.[3]

The continued advance, late in August and at the beginning of September, consequently brought hectic days and sleepless nights to supply officers. All the difficulties which had already begun to appear during the approach to the Seine now were further aggravated. The main problem, as before, was the deficiency in transport. Despite great efforts, rail reconstruction was unable to keep pace with the advance. Air supply repeatedly failed to match its predicted capacity. Motor transport therefore continued to bear the principal burden of the forward movement of supplies, and it was unable to deliver even daily needs, to say nothing of stocking advance supply depots.

The unbearable supply task which the continued advance created can best be appreciated by comparing planned with actual developments. At D plus 90 it had been assumed that no more than 12 United States divisions would have to be supported at the Seine. Not until D plus 120 was it thought feasible to support these divisions in their first offensive action beyond that barrier. In actuality, at D plus 90 (September 4) 16 divisions already were being supported at a distance of 150 miles *beyond* the Seine, and, within another week, U.S. First Army forces were operating at the German border in the vicinity of Aachen, well over 200 miles beyond Paris. By D plus 98 (September 12), the armies had advanced to a line which forecasts had indicated would not be reached until D plus 350. Between August 25 and September 12 they had advanced from the D plus 90 to the D plus 350 phase line, thus covering 260 phase-line days in 19 days. The record actually was more phenomenal than these figures indicate, because, in the earlier dash to the Seine, the armies had overcome an initial lag of 30 days. The city of Paris also had become an additional supply liability because of its liberation 55 days ahead of schedule.

Contrary to plan, therefore, and as a direct consequence of the August decisions, considerably greater forces were being maintained at much greater distances than contemplated. This was accomplished

despite an insufficiency of motor transport (which had been predicted even before D Day), despite the failure to open the Brittany
ports, and despite the premature assumption of responsibilities in
connection with the civil relief of Paris.

The probability that logistic limitations might strait-jacket tactical
operations had been realized as early as August 24, when General
Eisenhower expressed anxiety over the Allies' inability to undertake,
simultaneously, the various operations which appeared desirable.[4]
Flushed with success, however, the Allies had begun to develop ambitions which they had not dared consider a month earlier. The uninterrupted advance in the next two weeks continued to nourish the
hope that strong offensives, both north and south of the Ardennes,
might be sustained. In the first week of September, General Eisenhower decided that such simultaneous drives to both the Ruhr and
the Saar were still within Allied capabilities, and on September 10
he accordingly authorized an advance across the West Wall by both
United States armies—the First and the Third.[5] He admitted that the
supply organization already was stretched to the breaking point, but
he believed the operation was a gamble worth taking in order to
profit fully by the disorganized state of the German forces.

The maintenance of the armies was a touch-and-go matter at this
time, however, and it was necessary to keep a constant finger on the
logistic pulse. Supply capabilities clearly were unequal to the support
of sustained operations by both armies against determined opposition,
for deliveries were being made at the rate of only 3,300 tons a day to
the First Army and 2,500 tons to the Third—about one-half of what
they required. The dual offensive was supportable only if it could
achieve quick success. Lieutenant General George S. Patton, Jr.,
Third Army commander, was informed, therefore, that unless he was
able to force a crossing of the Moselle with the mass of his forces
within the next few days, he was to discontinue the attacks and assume
the defensive.[6]

Within the next ten days increasing resistance in both the First and
Third Army sectors forced General Eisenhower to make the decision
which he had hoped to avoid. A survey of supply capabilities at this
time showed that United States port discharge was averaging less than
35,000 tons a day, several thousand tons below requirements. Even
this was more than could be cleared from the ports, for the number
of truck companies had been greatly reduced as a result of the demands for line-of-communications hauling. The net effect of these
basic deficiencies was inescapable: a restriction on the number of

divisions that could be supported in active operations and, consequently, a limitation in the scale of combat operations. As early as the middle of August it had become impossible to maintain in combat all the divisions which were available. By early September three had been immobilized and their motor transportation used to form provisional truck companies. Two more divisions arrived in the middle of the month, and it was thought that their motor vehicles might have to be utilized in the same way. Logistic planners estimated that there would be 29 divisions in the 12th Army Group by October 1 but thought it unlikely, on the basis of the current logistic outlook, that more than 20 could be maintained in combat as far forward as the Rhine at that date.[7]

This gloomy forecast served to underscore two conclusions which already had been accepted at Supreme Headquarters: that, even should it prove possible to capture both the Saar and Ruhr objectives, these areas were at the absolute maximum distance at which Allied forces could be supported for the time being; and that it would be absolutely imperative to develop additional logistic capacity before attempting a power thrust deep into Germany.[8]

The situation in mid-September clearly indicated an urgent need both to shorten the lines of communications and to secure additional port capacity. The maximum force which could be supported through Cherbourg and the beaches was being reached rapidly. In fact, the capacity of the beaches was certain to decrease with the advent of bad weather, and new capacity also was required to compensate for that lost in Brittany. The obvious solution to this dual requirement lay in the development of the Seine ports and Antwerp.[9]

In the light of these circumstances, General Eisenhower, in mid-September, considered two possible courses of action: the concentration of all resources behind a single blow on a narrow front directed toward the center of Germany (the proposal favored by Field Marshal Montgomery); or an advance along the entire front with the aim of seizing suitable positions on the German frontier where the Allied forces could regroup, establish maintenance facilities, and mount a broad drive into Germany.[10] The first course, often referred to as a "knife-like thrust" to Berlin, was rejected on both tactical and administrative grounds. Logistic resources likewise were lacking for the full implementation of the second course. The Supreme Commander, nevertheless, decided in favor of the second plan, which provided that the Allies push forward to the Rhine, secure bridgeheads over the river, seize the Ruhr, and concentrate on preparations for the final nonstop drive into Germany. Because of the limited logistic capabilities, however, the timing of the Allies' efforts toward the attainment of immediate objectives now became of utmost importance. The implementation of this plan, consequently, required a succession of attacks, first by the 21st Army Group, then by the U.S. First Army, and, finally, by the U.S. Third Army, with supply priorities shifting as necessary.

Future logistic needs also were a major factor in the assignment of missions, for General Eisenhower specified that additional ports must be secured simultaneously with the attacks eastward. Accordingly, Field Marshal Montgomery's 21st Army Group was given the mission of securing the approaches to Antwerp or Rotterdam and capturing additional Channel ports; Lieutenant General Omar N. Bradley's 12th Army Group was to reduce Brest as quickly as possible and make physical junction with the Allied forces from the south of France (Operation DRAGOON), so that the supply lines leading from Marseille might assist in the support of his 12th Army Group.[11]

On September 17 Montgomery had launched a combined United States-British airborne operation in Holland to secure a bridgehead over the Rhine and to turn the enemy's flank in the north. General Eisenhower had conceived of this operation as having only a limited objective, however, and he emphasized this point to his top commanders and staff officers, stating that he wanted general acceptance of the fact that the possession of an additional major deepwater port on the north flank was an indispensable prerequisite for the final drive into Germany. He considered even the present operation in the north to be a bold bid for a big prize in view of the current maintenance situation. He considered the operation amply worth the risk. But he stressed repeatedly the conviction that a large-scale drive into the "enemy's heart" was unthinkable without building up additional administrative capacity, and this meant the opening of Antwerp.[12] He was, in effect, reiterating his decision, based in large measure on the logistical situation, to make no "one-thrust" push into Germany, but to advance on a broad front once adequate logistic support was insured.

The dilemma in which the Allies found themselves at this time was, as previously noted, a direct outcome of the earlier decisions by which logistic considerations had been subordinated repeatedly to the enticing prospects which beckoned eastward. General Eisenhower himself admitted that he had been willing to defer the capture of ports in favor of the bolder actions which had taken the Allied armies to the German border. The first such deferment had been made on August 3, when the bulk of the U.S. Third Army was turned eastward rather than into Brittany as originally planned. Two weeks later the Supreme Commander had again subordinated logistic considerations when he decided to cross the Seine and continue to drive eastward. Such deferments were no longer permissible.[13]

Though the British had captured Antwerp early in September, estimates made later in the month indicated that the port, whose approaches were still in German hands, might not begin operating before November 1. As a result, there was every prospect that United States forces would have to depend on lines of communications reaching all the way back to Normandy. Because of this, the total tonnages which the Communications Zone could guarantee to deliver were sufficient to support an attack by one American army and only if all the other United States forces reverted to the defensive. Even such a commitment would require the postponement of many essential administrative measures, such as building advance airfields, winterizing troops and equipment, and replacing worn-out material. Since the Ruhr rather than the Saar was the most important objective, it was inevitable that the burden of the sacrifice should be borne by those 12th Army Group forces operating south of the Ardennes in the direction of the Saar—General Patton's Third Army.[14]

The developments of the next few weeks produced little cause for altering the conclusions reached in mid-September. At the very end of the month the Communications Zone presented figures on its delivery capabilities which revealed even more clearly the impossibility of supporting large-scale operations east of the Rhine. The 12th Army Group had indicated, on the basis of daily maintenance needs of 650 tons a division, that its requirements would total 19,000 tons a day during the first half of October, assuming the employment of 22 divisions, and 23,000 tons a day by November 1, when the strength of the army group would reach 28 divisions. In addition, however, the army group requested that the Communications Zone deliver 100,000 tons of supplies over and above these daily requirements in order to meet deficiencies in equipment and establish minimum reserves. The Communications Zone's reply was discouraging indeed. It announced that it would be approximately 60 days before any substantial tonnages could be built up in the forward area. September deliveries had averaged only 8,000 to 10,000 tons a day to the forward areas, and for the entire month of October deliveries would not

even meet daily maintenance needs. Not until mid-November did the
Communications Zone expect its port and transportation situation to
improve sufficiently to permit the build-up of reserves, over and
above daily needs, in all the army areas. The outlook for the next six
to eight weeks was, therefore, a depressing one, for there appeared
no escaping the prospect that the forces which the 12th Army Group
could maintain actively operational would either have to be reduced
in size or continue on the starvation scale that had characterized their
support for the past several weeks.[15]

It also was clear that the maintenance of large-scale operations
would remain unsatisfactory until the port of Antwerp and adequate
rail lines of communications were made available. The operations of
the 21st and 12th Army Groups, consequently, were to be dominated throughout the fall of 1944 by the necessity of developing a
new administrative base in closer proximity to the front lines.

Tactical operations, to paraphrase an old maxim, had definitely
become the art of the logistically feasible.

Charles B. MacDonald

16

The Decision to Launch
Operation MARKET-GARDEN
(1944)

Was the decision to launch the largest airborne attack of World War II right or wrong?

It was the decision of a theater commander to commit what was, in effect, his strategic reserve. It was a decision to reinforce one success among a number of successes that had been achieved. Unfortunately, it was a failure.

The commander was General Dwight D. Eisenhower, Supreme Allied Commander in the invasion of Europe during World War II. The operation was an airborne attack (code-named MARKET) deep in the enemy's rear areas to be launched in mid-September 1944 in conjunction with a ground attack by the British Second Army (code-named GARDEN). The two attacks were known collectively as Operation MARKET-GARDEN.[1]

The airborne attack was designed to lay a carpet of airborne troops along a narrow corridor extending approximately 80 miles into Holland from Eindhoven northward to Arnhem. The airborne troops were to secure bridges across a number of canals as well as across three major water barriers—the Maas, the Waal (the main downstream branch of the Rhine), and the Neder Rijn (Lower Rhine) Rivers. Through this corridor were to pass British ground troops in a push beyond Arnhem to the IJsselmeer (Zuider Zee). The principal objective of the operation was to get Allied troops across the Rhine. Three main advantages were expected to accrue: cutting the land exit of those Germans remaining in western Holland; outflanking the enemy's frontier defenses, the West Wall, or Siegfried Line; and position-

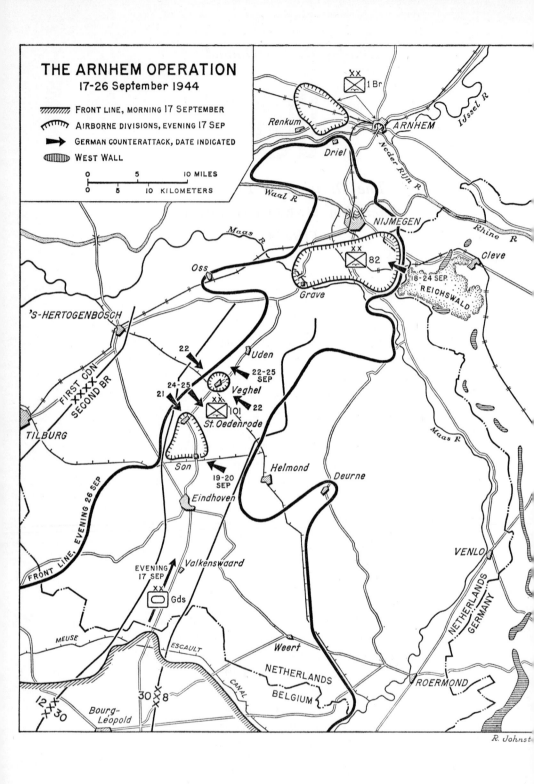

THE ARNHEM OPERATION
17-26 September 1944

FRONT LINE, MORNING 17 SEPTEMBER

AIRBORNE DIVISIONS, EVENING 17 SEP

GERMAN COUNTERATTACK, DATE INDICATED

WEST WALL

0   5   10 MILES
0   5   10 KILOMETERS

1 Br

ARNHEM

Renkum

Driel

IJssel R

Neder Rijn R

NIJMEGEN

Rhine R

Waal R

Maas R

82

Cleve

Oss

Grave

18-24 SEP

REICHSWALD

'S-HERTOGENBOSCH

Uden

22

22-25
SEP

Veghel

22

FIRST CDN
XXXX
SECOND BR

24-25

21

101

St. Oedenrode

Maas R

TILBURG

Son

19-20
SEP

Helmond

Deurne

FRONT LINE, EVENING 26 SEP

Eindhoven

VENLO

FRONT LINE, EVENING 17 SEP

Valkenswaard

EVENING
17 SEP

Gds

NETHERLANDS
GERMANY

MEUSE

ESCAULT

Weert

ROERMOND

CANAL

NETHERLANDS

BELGIUM

12 X 30

30 X 8

Bourg-
Léopold

R. Johnst

ing British ground forces for a subsequent drive into Germany along the North German plain.

In retrospect, General Eisenhower's decision can be analyzed by means of three questions:

1. Was an airborne attack of any kind to exploit success advisable at the time?

2. Was General Eisenhower justified in delaying the opening of the port of Antwerp while the airborne attack took place?

3. If an airborne assault was advisable, why Operation MARKET instead of some other airborne attack?

Consideration of the first question involves recalling the aura of optimism which pervaded Allied ranks in September 1944. These were the glorious days, the halcyon days of pursuit. The heartbreak of near stalemate among the hedgerows of Normandy, which had followed close on the Allied cross-Channel invasion of France in June, was past—an event belonging, it seemed, to yesteryear when the war still had to be won. In the place of heartbreak had come heady optimism. Having crossed the Seine, Allied commanders had raised their sights, not to the next obstacle, the West Wall, but beyond the West Wall to the Rhine itself.[2] No less an authority than the G-2 (intelligence officer) at Supreme Headquarters, Allied Expeditionary Force (SHAEF), had put the matter this way: "The August battles have done it and the enemy in the West has had it. Two and a half months of bitter fighting have brought the end of the war in Europe within sight, almost within reach." [3]

More specifically, the 21st Army Group, composed of British and Canadian troops, had dashed more than 250 miles since the breakout in Normandy. The lowlands of Flanders and the V-bomb launching sites in the Pas-de-Calais were behind. Brussels had fallen. A rapid armored thrust had taken Antwerp. As the day of the decision to launch Operation MARKET approached, the British reached the Dutch-Belgian frontier.

The U.S. First Army had raced across Belgium and Luxembourg to the very gates of Germany. The U.S. Third Army had reached and crossed the Moselle River in northeastern France. The newly created U.S. Ninth Army was operational in Brittany and engaged in besieging the port of Brest. The 6th Army Group, arriving from southern France (Operation DRAGOON), was at the point of uniting with the Third Army to create a unified Western Front that would stretch from Antwerp to Switzerland.

There was one cloud in this bright blue sky. Those who looked carefully at the scene of intertwined Allied success and German chaos could see that the Allies had their own private chaos in the field of logistics.[4] For logistical purposes, the invasion of Europe had been geared to a methodical advance. Yet Allied moves from the beaches to the Seine had been erratic, culminating in an explosive dash that secured the line of the Seine 11 days ahead of schedule and neared the German border on D Day plus 96, as against a predicted date of about D plus 300. The supply services could not keep up with this advance. The difficulty at first was not a lack of sufficient supplies on the Continent, for the build-up of supplies in Normandy had exceeded expectations. The difficulty was transport. With depots far behind the front and the Continental railway system crippled by Allied bombing and German destruction, the logisticians did not have the means of getting the supplies to the armies, which in some instances were 500 miles away. The situation spawned many supply problems, the most dramatic being a gasoline drought which immobilized the Third Army for five days at the Meuse River and a corps of the First Army for four days at the Belgian frontier.[5] A corps of the British Second Army was held for about two weeks west of the Seine so that its vehicles could augment the transport of the remainder of the Army.[6]

It was obvious that a solution of the transportation problem could not be found until ports nearer the fighting front were secured. As consumption of supplies mounted and as prospects of approaching winter and bad weather threatened the unprotected Normandy beaches, where the bulk of supplies was still arriving, the question of ports assumed increasing importance. As General Eisenhower put it on September 13: "Our port position today is such that any stretch of a week or ten days of bad Channel weather—a condition that grows increasingly probable with the receding summer—would paralyze our activities and make the maintenance of our forces even in defensive roles exceedingly difficult." [7]

In early September the Allies were using only Cherbourg, though they hoped soon to open a badly damaged Le Havre. Antwerp, captured virtually intact, could not be used until the Germans were cleared from the banks of the Schelde estuary, a 60-mile-long waterway connecting Antwerp with the North Sea.

General Eisenhower and his tactical commanders were not unaware of the logistical problems. But the tactical opportunities that lay before them were irresistible. If the Supreme Commander thought in terms of immediate objectives—like destroying enemy reserves in the Pas-de-Calais—his subordinates accepted no such mental discipline. As early as the latter part of August, the army groups and the armies were issuing operational orders couched in terms of the cities along the Rhine River—Mannheim, Darmstadt, Frankfurt, Koblenz. "It is contemplated," noted the 12th Army Group on August 27, "that the Armies will go as far as practicable and then wait until the supply system in rear will permit further advance." Yet the operational orders made clear that the 12th Army Group hoped that "as far as practicable" meant the Rhine.[8]

The Americans by September 10 were no more than 40 miles from the Rhine, the British no more than 60. Yet the Allied war machine was showing signs of creaking to a halt because of logistical weakness. Should the Allies stop for repairs, or should they try to get across the last big ditch—the Rhine River—that separated them from quick and apparently certain victory?

Paved with opportunity, the road taken by the Allies in late August and early September had not been without rough spots that assumed the form of controversy. Basically, these were the conflicts of opinion over the much discussed theories of what have come to be called the broad-front strategy and the one-thrust concept.[9] The aptness of General Eisenhower's decision—in effect a compromise between the two —is of concern here only insofar as it affected the alignment of the Allied forces at the time of Operation MARKET.

During the preinvasion planning, four routes leading from northern France through Belgium toward the objective of the Ruhr industrial area had been considered: (1) through the flatlands of Flanders, criss-crossed by waterways; (2) northeast via Liége and Aachen along the northern edge of the Ardennes; (3) across the Ardennes, a mountainous woodland with a restricted road net; and (4) south of the Ardennes via Metz, the Saar, and Frankfurt. Terrain considerations having largely eliminated two of the routes, General Eisenhower had determined to advance Field Marshal Sir Bernard L. Montgomery's 21st Army Group (British and Canadian armies) along the route north of the Ardennes, Lieutenant General Omar N. Bradley's 12th Army Group (American armies) south of the Ardennes. The main effort was to be vested in the former. To strengthen the main effort, Eisenhower allotted Montgomery the various Allied airborne forces available in the theater.[10]

As the pursuit toward the German border during late August and early September gathered momentum, Montgomery called for additional assistance. He wanted an entire American army to move along his right flank north of the Ardennes. Though Bradley thought a corps would be sufficient and though Eisenhower believed Montgomery was being overcautious, the Supreme Commander was inclined to favor Montgomery's request. Eisenhower was particularly anxious to attain the objectives that lay to the north. Montgomery might trap the remaining German reserves in the Pas-de-Calais; he would secure the Channel ports as far as Antwerp; and he would eliminate the V-bomb launching sites in the Pas-de-Calais. Acceding to Montgomery's request, Eisenhower directed the U.S. First Army to advance alongside the British north of the Ardennes. At the same time, Eisenhower emphasized his desire to gain the objectives in the north by reaffirming his earlier decision to put the airborne forces in the theater at Montgomery's disposal.[11]

Shifting the First Army to the right of the northern force placed that army along what had been considered the best route into Germany, the route via Liége and Aachen. The British and the Canadians, the latter scheduled to invest the Channel ports, were to push directly through Flanders, a region earlier ruled out for major advance by the planners because of its many water barriers. This divergence from plan affected Operation MARKET-GARDEN, for, as it turned out, the main Allied effort did not go through the Aachen Gap but through the canal-creased lowlands of Holland.

The airborne forces General Eisenhower allotted to the 21st Army Group were organized under the newly created headquarters of the First Allied Airborne Army. Commanded by Lieutenant General Lewis H. Brereton, the headquarters controlled two British and three American airborne divisions, a Polish parachute brigade, the American troop carrier command, and two British troop carrier groups.[12]

One of the principal reasons underlying the creation of the First Allied Airborne Army was the insistence by the U.S. War Department on greater strategic use of airborne troops. From February 1944 Generals George C. Marshall, U.S. Chief of Staff, and Henry H. Arnold, commander of the Army Air Forces, had let General Eisenhower know unmistakably that they attached great importance to the employment of airborne units in actual operations deep in enemy territory.[13]

As had been contemplated, creation of the airborne army facilitated planning for airborne operations. The first plan was tentatively scheduled for execution on August 20 but was canceled, presumably because of concern over supply to the ground forces; supplies were being delivered by aircraft that would have to transport the airborne troops, and the ground troops would soon overrun the target area of the airborne forces. Even as the first plan withered, alternative plans were under consideration. By early September when American patrols approached the German border, 18 separate airborne plans had been considered. Five had reached the stage of detailed planning; three had progressed almost to the point of launching; but none had matured. In most cases, the cancellations had been prompted by recognition that the fast-moving ground troops would overrun the objectives before an airborne force could land.[14]

The fact was that the paratroopers and glidermen resting and training in England had in effect become coins burning holes in SHAEF's pocket. This is not to say that SHAEF intended to spend the airborne troops in a wild or extravagant fashion. Rather, SHAEF had decided to buy an airborne product and was shopping around. The impetus to buy did not come from General Eisenhower alone. As late as August, General Arnold had again voiced his desire for an airborne operation that would have strategic implications. The War Department obviously wanted to see what airborne troops could do in actual combat; pursuit warfare, many believed, provided an excellent opportunity for their use.

Not everyone advocated this approach at this particular time. General Arnold wanted the airborne army used because he felt that missions of troop carrier planes were not "comparing at all favorably with combat plane missions (other than supply and training) . . ."[15] But some commanders, notably General Bradley, believed that this was as it should be. Impressed by the success his ground troops were achieving, Bradley wanted continued use of the aircraft to supply his ground columns.[16]

The most notable example of General Bradley's antipathy to an airborne operation occurred at Tournai. Though this city lay outside his 12th Army Group sector and inside the British zone, Bradley ensured its capture before an airdrop could be staged, by ordering the First Army to rush ahead and take it. The ground troops arrived in good time to make an airborne operation there unnecessary. But Bradley had nevertheless lost a measure of air supply because the troop carrier planes had been withdrawn from supply missions to prepare for the drop. "Although we had made good on our boast and Ike's air drop was washed out," General Bradley later wrote, "even our smugness could not compensate for the critical loss we had suffered in tonnage. . . . During the six-day stoppage that had resulted from SHAEF's planned drop at Tournai, we lost an average of 823 tons per day. In gasoline, this loss would have equaled one and a half million gallons. . . ." [17]

Whether General Bradley's armies could have gone considerably farther than they did had air supply not again been halted by Operation MARKET is a matter of conjecture. It should be noted that the halt of both the First and the Third Armies in mid-September cannot be attributed specifically to the lack of everyday supplies that airlift might have provided. The halts were due more to a combination of many causes, among them the rugged terrain along the German frontier, the presence of the West Wall, the exhaustion of American combat units, the worn-out condition of their equipment, the rebirth of German strength, and, it has been argued, the thinly spread formation in which American troops approached the German frontier.

In any plan for an airborne operation, the matter of weather is important. For Operation MARKET, the planners before the attack were fairly optimistic on this point. One of the field orders noted that the weather in the region was "very unreliable and subject to rapid change" but that conditions were supposed to be at their best during summer and early autumn. However, the First Allied Airborne Army, after the event, admitted that though the weather had been poor during the operation, it had been no worse than could have been expected.[18]

Along with the question whether an airborne attack of any kind was called for should be considered the matter of Allied intelligence. Accurate or not, the intelligence estimates current when General Eisenhower decided to approve Operation MARKET were the only basis available to the Supreme Commander for evaluating the enemy. These were the times when the First Army G-2 was predicting the possibility of German political upheaval within thirty to sixty days.[19] Some intelligence officers, notably the Third Army G-2, expressed more caution.[20] But SHAEF's estimate of the situation a week before the airborne attack was fairly typical of the optimistic Allied point of view.[21]

According to this estimate, the SHAEF intelligence chief believed that the enemy force available to defend the entire West Wall was no greater than 11 infantry and 4 armored divisions at full strength. As for reinforcements, an estimate believed to be unduly generous noted that a "speculative dozen" divisions might "struggle up" in the course of the month. It was considered "most unlikely that more than the true equivalent of 4 Panzer grenadier divisions with 600 tanks" would be found. The G-2 section declared flatly: "The West

Wall cannot be held with this amount. . . ." [22] Four days before the attack, the headquarters of the British Airborne Corps noted that the enemy's total armored strength in the Netherlands and vicinity amounted to not more than 50 to 100 tanks. [23] The only warning against such optimism sounded before the operation was that two SS Panzer divisions might be refitting near Arnhem. [24] This turned out to be true, but the warning had come too late to affect Eisenhower's decision.

Thus, in considering the question whether an airborne attack of any kind was justified at the time of Operation MARKET, points for and against emerge. Most significantly, the tactical picture, from the Allied outlook and from intelligence estimates, was receptive to an exploitation maneuver. Also, as we have seen, demands for an airborne operation were great; the troops were at hand and military leaders, on the high echelons of command as well as in the field, wanted to see them used. On the other side, antipathy to an airborne operation did exist on the part of at least one army group commander who did not want the troop carrier aircraft diverted from supply missions to ground forces. Also, since the airborne troops would support the 21st Army Group, they would not be employed to reinforce the attack along the axis that the Allied planners had deemed most advantageous for entrance into Germany.

The second question—was General Eisenhower justified in delaying the opening of the port of Antwerp in favor of the airborne attack?—is pertinent because British ground troops would be tied up in Operation MARKET's companion piece, Operation GARDEN. Thus, to authorize the airborne attack was to give tacit approval to delay at Antwerp. [25]

The principal factor in this decision was the preoccupation of Allied commanders with the Rhine River. Field Marshal Montgomery's main objective was "to 'bounce' a crossing over the Rhine with the utmost speed." Some of the Allied preoccupation was based on a natural desire to gain and cross this formidable historic water barrier before the Germans could regroup behind it. Also, the Rhine was virtually synonymous with what the Supreme Commander considered his primary objective—the Ruhr industrial area. Anything short of the Ruhr—and thus, by inference, the Rhine—was in effect an intermediate objective, even secondary. "The envelopment of the Ruhr from the north by 21st Army Group, supported by First Army," General Eisenhower said, even after the success of Operation MARKET was in doubt, "is the main effort of the present phase of operations." [26]

It would, however, be quoting out of context if it were not mentioned that almost every time General Eisenhower made this stipulation about the Ruhr, which he did on several occasions, he added that "on the way" the Allies wanted Antwerp "as a matter of urgency." [27] Nevertheless, in the Supreme Commander's words, written after the war, "The attractive possibility of quickly turning the German north flank [that is, of getting across the Rhine] led me to approve the temporary delay in freeing the vital port of Antwerp. . . ." [28]

It should also be noted that General Eisenhower's concern about the port situation during the pursuit appears to date only from September 10, the day he agreed to delay on Antwerp. The Supreme Commander had made little written comment about the port situation up to that time, but the failure to secure hoped-for usable ports was only then becoming marked. Little more than a week before September 10, the possibility still existed of using the Brittany ports, in particular Brest and Quiberon Bay. Because the entire 12th Army Group was scheduled at that time to advance south of the Ardennes, these ports would still have been valuable. The Channel ports, except for Antwerp, were likely to be open to shipping in the near future. And in any event, the invasion beaches and Cherbourg were operating efficiently. A minor delay in opening Antwerp, it seemed, could well be countenanced.

This is not to try in any way to minimize the importance of Antwerp to the eventual Allied victory. Even before the invasion, Allied planners had noted that "until after the development of Antwerp, the availability of port capacity will . . . limit the forces which can be maintained." [29] Getting Antwerp was one of the main reasons why Eisenhower had strengthened Montgomery's northern thrust. With the possible exception of Rotterdam, which seemed out of reach at the moment, there was no substitute for Antwerp. Eisenhower appreciated this. Yet he knew also how formidable the Rhine was.

Though Antwerp would have to wait, the airborne attack, if successful, might facilitate the task of opening the port. From the bridgehead that airborne troops were to establish across the Lower Rhine in Operation MARKET, British ground troops in Operation GARDEN were to push on to the IJsselmeer. Thus Holland would be split in two and all Germans in western Holland isolated, including those denying both Antwerp and Rotterdam to the Allies. Though the Germans were great ones for wringing the most from bypassed, so-called "fortress defenses," it is axiomatic that an enemy who is isolated is more easily subdued. Even if Operation MARKET-GARDEN failed to achieve more than a bridgehead beyond the Lower Rhine, the territory gained might serve as a buffer for subsequent moves to open Antwerp. From the Lower Rhine to the IJsselmeer the Germans would retain only a narrow corridor little more than 25 miles wide, and through that they would have to funnel the supplies for all their forces in western Holland, a distinct disadvantage.

The fact remained that if Operation MARKET was launched, an all-out campaign to open Antwerp would be delayed. The MARKET-GARDEN maneuver would in any case have to be staged on a thin logistical margin. As it turned out, three newly arrived American divisions had to be immobilized in Normandy so that their vehicles might be used to rush five hundred tons of supplies per day to the British. Obviously, little or no supplies would be left over for Antwerp. In manpower, MARKET-GARDEN would tie up the entire British Second Army; only the Canadian First Army, already busy with investiture of other Channel ports, would be available to open Antwerp.[30]

Among responsible Allied commanders were some who believed in early September that Antwerp was a dead issue. They remembered World War I, when the pursuit phase had marked the beginning of the end—the start of swift German collapse. If events ran true to the earlier experience, neither Antwerp nor any other port would be needed except to support the occupation of Germany. Whether General Eisenhower entertained similar thoughts is pure conjecture; but there is no doubt that some of his subordinates did. The U.S. First Army G-2 estimate of possible political upheaval is a clear example.

To recapitulate, the Ruhr—and thus, by inference, getting across the Rhine—was the main objective of operations at the time of Eisenhower's decision in regard to MARKET. Antwerp, for all its value, was a secondary objective—perhaps more correctly, an intermediate objective. The port situation had not become critical by September 10, despite serious and even alarming indications. Without Antwerp, the logistical situation was imminently risky. Even though MARKET-GARDEN might eventually lighten the task of opening Antwerp, the airborne operation would delay the start of that task.

The third question—why MARKET? why not some other airborne attack?—may be introduced by a prior question: what were the alternatives to Operation MARKET? Eighteen suggested airborne plans preceded MARKET but in most cases were canceled because of the rapid ground advance. One plan, Operation COMET, was virtually identical with MARKET, except that the latter employed more troops.

There were in addition eight other proposed operations that could have been considered current or worthwhile at the time of the MARKET decision. One plan to seize airfields at Berlin and the German naval base at Kiel was suitable only if the Germans were at the point of surrender or collapse. Another, to secure Walcheren Island at the mouth of the Schelde estuary for the purpose of assisting the opening of the port of Antwerp, was canceled because the island could easily be flooded by the Germans. The remaining six, planned variously to get the U.S. First or Third Army through the West Wall or across the Rhine, were all to take place in General Bradley's sector and thus required his approval. Whether Bradley's reluctance to have troop carrier planes diverted from ground supply missions had anything to do with the fact that none of these plans was chosen over MARKET is a matter for conjecture.

One other alternative was suggested. General Sir Miles C. Dempsey, the commander of the British Second Army, advocated, on the day of the MARKET decision, September 10, an airborne attack to get the British across the Rhine, not, as in MARKET, at Arnhem but upstream at Wesel, in Germany.[31] In many respects, this made sense. In earlier directives, Montgomery had oriented the 21st Army Group toward Wesel, close to the left flank of the U.S. First Army.[32] An airborne drop at Wesel would have conformed with announced direction and also would have prevented a gap from opening between the British and Americans. The gap, which caused serious concern, developed later as the British turned northward to Arnhem and the First Army moved eastward toward Aachen. A drop at Wesel also would have avoided what had begun to look like increasing German strength along the Dutch-Belgian border. But despite the advantages offered by a drop at Wesel, Field Marshal Montgomery overruled Dempsey's suggestion on the recommendation of air force commanders, for Wesel, on the fringe of the Ruhr, was in one of the most concentrated flak belts in Europe.[33]

Alternatives aside, Operation MARKET had certain advantages of its own. In the official history of General Eisenhower's headquarters, Forrest C. Pogue has listed these in a manner that bears repeating. Operation MARKET, he has written,

. . . seemed to fit the pattern of current Allied strategy. It conformed to General Arnold's recommendation for an operation some distance east of the enemy's forward positions and beyond the area where enemy reserves were normally located; it afforded an opportunity for using the long-idle airborne resources; it was in accord with Field Marshal Montgomery's desire for a thrust north of the Rhine while the enemy was disorganized; it would help reorient the Allied drive in the direction 21 Army Group thought it should go; and it appeared to General Eisenhower to be the boldest and best move the Allies could make at the moment. The Supreme Commander realized that the momentum of the drive into Germany was being lost and thought that by this action it might be possible to get a bridgehead across the Rhine before the Allies were stopped. The airborne divisions, he knew, were in good condition and could be supported without throwing a crushing burden on the already overstrained supply lines. At worst, General Eisenhower thought the operation would strengthen the 21 Army Group in its later fight to clear the Schelde estuary. Field Marshal Montgomery examined the objections that the proposed route of advance "involved the additional obstacle of the Lower Rhine . . . as compared with more easterly approaches, and would carry us to an area relatively remote from the Ruhr." He considered that these were overridden by certain major advantages: (1) the operation would outflank the Siegfried Line defenses; (2) it would be on the line which the enemy would consider the least likely for the Allies to use; and (3) the area was the one with the easiest range for the Allied airborne forces.[34]

Contrary to appearances, the military climate at the time of the MARKET decision was unsettled. Erratic winds were blowing in several directions. There was also the likelihood of a calm, a period of recuperation after the whirlwind of the pursuit. In this turbulent period emerged the decision to launch Operation MARKET-GARDEN.

The operation was a daring strategic maneuver that failed. That the decision to launch it has not prompted the kind of controversy surrounding other command decisions is somewhat singular. Here was no southern France, where one ally wanted it, the other opposed. Here was no Argentan-Falaise, where either ally could accuse the other of being at fault in failing to close the pocket. Even General Bradley, surely one of Field Marshal Montgomery's severest critics, has reserved his more pungent criticisms for other decisions.

Perhaps the reason for the lack of acrimony can be found in the narrow margin by which MARKET-GARDEN failed, or, perhaps more to the point, in the license afforded commanders under conditions of success such as existed in September 1944. As British Field Marshal Sir Douglas Haig put it on August 22, 1918, "Risks which a month ago would have been criminal to incur ought now to be incurred as a duty."

Charles V. P. von Luttichau

17

The German Counteroffensive
in the Ardennes
(1944)

The German counteroffensive through the Ardennes in the winter of 1944—the Battle of the Bulge—will long be recalled in American military annals of World War II as having inflicted on the U.S. 12th Army Group the first and only serious reverse it suffered in its sweep from Normandy to the Rhine. The heady optimism of the breakout from Normandy and the pursuit across France into Belgium and Luxembourg in August and September had been dashed by the failure of logistics to keep up with the speed of pursuit and the unexpectedly stubborn resistance of the Germans as they fell back on their West Wall. But in November, General Eisenhower, Supreme Allied Commander, believing that he now had available the strength to disregard unfavorable weather and the approach of winter, directed Lieutenant General Omar N. Bradley to launch the U.S. 12th Army Group on an offensive north and south of the Ardennes with the Rhine as its objective. In December, the U.S. First Army was attacking east of Aachen toward the Roer and Lieutenant General George S. Patton's Third Army, south of the Ardennes, was punching its way toward the Saar. Counting on the defensive strength of the terrain, General Bradley was holding his line in the Ardennes with minimum forces.

On December 16 the Germans crashed through these forces with a massive counteroffensive. It came as a complete surprise, created widespread if momentary consternation, halted the Allied offensive, and cost the Americans and British over 70,000 casualties before they could contain it.[1]

The German decision to launch an offensive in the Ardennes was

342

Hitler's. It was a decision in which the Chief of State, acting as Commander in Chief of the *Wehrmacht,* overrode the judgment of his military advisers. Hitler was the originator of the idea. He was the driving force behind the astounding feat of assembling the necessary forces. He came to the west in person to supervise the preparations and direct the operation. He personally prescribed the ambitious objectives and attached the extravagant hopes to a victorious outcome that converted an otherwise strictly tactical operation into a fateful strategic decision.[2]

The late hour of the war and the fact that Hitler was committing Germany's last reserves in men and resources gave the venture a character of finality and grave political significance. In Hitler's own words, the outcome of the battle would spell either life or death for the German nation. Over the years the Führer had come to identify his person with the German people and their destiny. Seen in this light, the Ardennes was a battle for Hitler's survival and that of the Nazi regime. If the events to be recounted seem to defy military logic, it was, in part, because the founder of a Reich that was to "last a thousand years" was a fanatic whose intuition had long since triumphed over sound reasoning.

In the middle of September 1944, Hitler startled his closest advisers with the announcement that he would launch a large-scale offensive through the Ardennes in November. The decision was not a sudden inspiration. Indeed, the origins of the idea for a counteroffensive can be traced as far back as the end of July, when Hitler was more immediately concerned with the aftermath of the July 20 conspiracy that had culminated in the well-known attempt on his life at his East Prussian headquarters and with plans to counteract the Allied breakthrough at Avranches. A succession of abortive attempts to turn the tide of invasion and stop the Allied advance across France by counterattacking at Mortain and later in Alsace appeared to have merely confirmed Hitler in his determination to inflict upon the Western Allies a crushing defeat that would influence in his favor the final outcome of the war.[3]

The plan for the big counteroffensive took shape during a period of internal insecurity and catastrophic Axis defeats on the fronts in the East and West.

In the East, the Soviet summer offensive in 1944 had driven in one sweep from the Dnieper to the gates of Warsaw and the banks of the Vistula, had isolated—temporarily—an army group in the Baltic States, and had brought the Russians within reach of the German

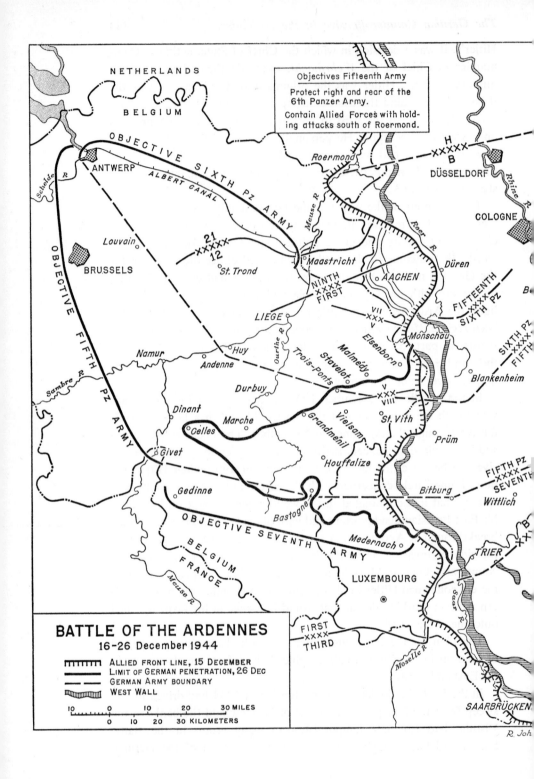

NETHERLANDS

BELGIUM

OBJECTIVE SIXTH PZ ARMY

Roermond

H
B
XXXX

DÜSSELDORF

Schelde R.

ANTWERP

ALBERT CANAL

Meuse R.

COLOGNE

Rhine R.

Roer R.

OBJECTIVE FIFTH PZ ARMY

Louvain

21
XXXXX
12

St. Trond

Maastricht

AACHEN

Düren

BRUSSELS

NINTH
XXXX
FIRST

FIFTEENTH
XXXX
SIXTH PZ

B

Sambre R.

LIEGE

VII
XXXX
V

Elsenborn

Monschau

SIXTH PZ
XXXX
FIFTH

Namur

Huy

Ourthe R.

Trois-Ponts

Malmédy

Stavelot

Blankenheim

Andenne

Durbuy

V
XXX
VIII

Dinant

Marche

Grandménil

Vielsam

St. Vith

Prüm

Celles

Givet

Houffalize

FIFTH PZ
XXXX
SEVENTH

Gedinne

Bastogne

Bitburg

Wittlich

OBJECTIVE SEVENTH ARMY

BELGIUM

FRANCE

Medernach

TRIER

B
XX

Meuse R.

LUXEMBOURG

Saar R.

BATTLE OF THE ARDENNES
16–26 December 1944

	ALLIED FRONT LINE, 15 DECEMBER
	LIMIT OF GERMAN PENETRATION, 26 DEC
	GERMAN ARMY BOUNDARY
	WEST WALL

10   0   10   20   30 MILES

0   10   20   30 KILOMETERS

R. Joh

homeland. Here their spectacular advance, having outrun its supplies, ground to a halt. In the Balkans, the Russians had occupied Rumania, then Bulgaria, and continued an almost unopposed advance toward Hungary. This movement threatened to cut off the German forces in Greece, Albania, and Yugoslavia, and force Hitler to order the evacuation of the first two of these occupied countries.

In Italy the Germans had fallen back to the Gothic Line, last transpeninsular defense position short of the Po Valley. In the far north the capitulation of Finland to the Russians had rendered untenable the advanced German positions in the Scandinavian theater of operations.

The catastrophes in the East were matched, if not surpassed, by the dangers in the West. By mid-September the Allies had liberated most of France, Belgium, and Luxembourg and were threatening the all-important Ruhr area, the industrial heart of Germany. They had also captured the vital harbor of Antwerp, a strategic objective of whose importance for the conduct of future operations both Eisenhower and Hitler were equally convinced. To meet the mounting crisis in the West, Hitler had recalled from temporary retirement Field Marshal Gerd von Rundstedt, charging him with the defense of the western approaches to the Reich. Rundstedt achieved what seemed impossible: with their backs to the imaginary safety of the Siegfried Line, the armies in the West once more formed a coherent defense line, taut and precariously thin but strong enough to frustrate the daring Allied bid (Operation MARKET-GARDEN) to jump the formidable obstacles of the lower Maas and Rhine.

Within three months, the *Wehrmacht* had lost in battle 50 divisions in the East and another 28 in the West, an appalling total of 78 divisions, or one and a half million men, and an area several times as big as Germany.[4]

Air Marshal Hermann Goering's once powerful *Luftwaffe* (air force) had ceased to be a factor that could influence decisively the outcome of the struggle. At this stage of the war, the *Luftwaffe* had to all purposes shot its bolt. Outclassed by Allied airpower, short of trained personnel and fuel, incapable of replacing mounting losses, the German Air Force had fallen into disgrace in Hitler's eyes. Recalling Goering's boastful prewar remarks that his fighters would sweep enemy intruders out of the skies, the people sarcastically referred to Allied bomber formations penetrating the heart of the Reich almost without challenge as *"Parteitag Flüge"* (prewar demonstration flights staged by the *Luftwaffe* for the Nazi Party at Nuremberg).

So paralyzed was this once imposing sword of the German blitz campaigns that it could not even prevent the ever-increasing bombardments of vital synthetic fuel plants.[5]

Yet the offensive spirit of the German fighter arm, under its able commander General Adolf Galland, had not been broken. Indeed, during the worst setbacks Galland was busy assembling a last reserve of pilots and planes to strike a potentially decisive blow at Allied airpower. Suicidal as the plan for this large-scale operation against Allied daylight bombers may have been, it might well have brought startling results had Hitler accepted it; but he did not. And thus one of the most daring operations planned in World War II never came to a full-blown test.[6]

Analogously, the German Navy had lost its former important position. As the *Luftwaffe* was reduced to abstemious use of its fighter arm, so was the Navy regarding its U-boats. After the Allies had captured or sealed off all submarine bases in France, the remaining ones nearer the Reich had become more vulnerable. The rapid advance of the Soviet armies along the shores of the Baltic Sea threatened to deprive the Navy of the training waters that Grand Admiral Karl Doenitz considered essential for breaking in the revolutionary new U-boats now under construction in German shipyards. Only with these faster, snorkel-equipped submarines could he hope to resume the U-boat offensive that had once threatened to destroy the tenuous communication lines of Allied global warfare. So vital appeared the retention of control of the Baltic Sea coast to Doenitz that he persuaded Hitler, against the sound advice of the Army's Chief of Staff, to hold on to this northern sector of the Eastern Front at the extreme risk of strategic breakthrough in the weakened center to the heart of Germany.[7]

The burden of defending Hitler's *Festung Europa* thus had to be shouldered by the Army. As Napoleon I said, an army marches on its stomach, but in modern warfare the "stomach" had grown to include the resources and productive capacity of the entire nation. Vast areas that so far had supplied the German war machine with essential raw materials had now been recaptured by the Allies. It was obvious, even to Hitler, that Germany could not continue the struggle indefinitely. Under the direction of the War Production Minister, Albert Speer, German production experienced a tremendous growth despite stepped-up Allied bombings. In September 1944 the economy still profited from the peak production level reached during the summer. Yet accumulated stocks, effective dispersion of industries, and a radical curtailment of civilian needs could assure continued adequate supply of the armed forces for only about six more months. Estimates for a longer lease on life were unrealistic. In September the breakdown of transportation, which later was to deprive the German High Command of the advantage of interior lines, was still a dreaded specter. Not until the end of the year did the paralysis of railroad communications hit an already collapsing economy. While the transportation crisis was still a matter of the future, the fuel oil drought was a present reality. It had contributed decisively to the grounding of the *Luftwaffe*. Now it threatened to immobilize the Army. To supply Hitler's final offensive in the West with fuel, the meager allotments to all other theaters of operations had to be cut below the minimum subsistence levels. With this decision Hitler incurred the grave risk of depriving already inadequate armored reserves, especially on the Eastern Front, of their ability to maneuver in the event of large-scale attack.[8]

The abortive July 20 uprising by a small group of German military leaders affected the Ardennes decision in two ways:

1. The failure of the attempt confirmed Hitler in his obsession that he was the leader chosen by "Providence" for his mission and gave him the opportunity to smash all opposition within Germany and establish complete control over the nation via the Gestapo and the Nazi Party.

2. He reacted to it by immediately putting into effect a series of drastic "total war" measures, designed to supply him with additional forces for a final counteroffensive. By lowering the draft age to 16 years and extending it to include the 50-year-olds and by combing out the home front and armed forces, he put an additional three quarters of a million men under arms. He thus built up a new strategic reserve consisting of 25 *Volksgrenadier* divisions and at least 6 Panzer divisions. These were raised and trained under the newly appointed commander of the Replacement Army, Gestapo Chief Heinrich Himmler. In addition, a great number of artillery, *Werfer* (rocket projectors), and armored units were being formed, thus theoretically creating a very flexible instrument in the hands of a capable supreme commander.[9]

In October the Germans once more achieved stabilization of the fronts in the main theaters of operation. Even in the Balkans and Hungary, where the Russians continued their advance, German resistance was stiffening. By scraping the bottom of the barrel, the German economy and war machine appeared capable of mounting one final large-scale offensive. It was now up to Hitler to decide where to launch it.

After the defeats of the summer of 1944, the remaining German war potential was so seriously reduced that Hitler might have concluded that he no longer could win the war and should seek an armistice. Germany's allies—Japan, Italy, and Finland—had undertaken, late in 1942, to induce Hitler to seek an agreement with the Soviet Union. The Japanese continued such efforts to the day when Hitler appears to have made the decision to attack in the Ardennes. Late in 1943, Hitler himself is reported to have sounded out the Western Allies for a definition of the "unconditional surrender" formula. But Allied insistence upon these terms before and after the July 20, 1944, plot all but ruled out the possibility of ending the war by negotiation.[10]

Unconditional surrender would have been difficult even for a German democratic government after a successful overthrow of Hitler's dictatorship. Certainly the "greatest captain of all times," as the Führer liked to be referred to, was the last person to admit that Germany's situation was hopeless. Even after the Ardennes offensive had failed, Hitler, on December 28, addressing the generals who were to lead a subsidiary attack in Alsace, pointed out that the war was an ideological conflict that could end only in Germany's victory or extinction. "By no means," he said, "am I entertaining the thought that the war could be lost. I have never in my life known the term 'capitulation.' . . ."[11]

If capitulation was wholly unacceptable to him, Hitler could only pursue the alternative of continuing the war, in the vague hope that the unfavorable course of events could be eventually reversed by determination, perseverance, and time. Arguing that a period of grave military defeats was inopportune for political decisions, he resolved to "continue this struggle until, as Frederick the Great said, one of our 'damned enemies give up.' Only then shall we get a peace that will guarantee the future existence of the German nation."[12]

After the period of victorious blitz campaigns had ended in the disastrous defeats in Stalingrad and Tunisia in 1943, Hitler's exuberant optimism changed to the almost mesmeric belief that he could be the winner of a long-drawn-out struggle in which one of his enemies would weary and give up. Only the fittest would win in this struggle for survival, and unless the German people could qualify they deserved extinction. Toward the end of the war this nihilistic attitude completely overshadowed all his plans and decisions.[13]

Forced into the defense on all fronts, Hitler still refused to sub-scribe to a purely defensive strategy and continued to think in terms of an offensive. Like Clausewitz, he maintained that offense is the best defense. But at the same time he violated the principle that suc-cessful defense requires preservation of strength, which in turn is possible only if space can be traded for time. In 1944 Hitler was fast running out of both. This consideration, perhaps, precipitated the decision to attack in the Ardennes, for to persist in the "rot of barren defense" (to use Hitler's words) would merely aggravate Germany's position, a statement General Alfred Jodl amplified: "We could not hope to escape the evil fate hanging over us. By fighting, rather than waiting, we might save something." [14]

Once Hitler had made the decision to go over to the offensive at any cost, he had to decide next whether to wait until he could throw into an all-out effort the whole remaining war potential of the nation and its armed forces. This course of action, proposed in separate plans to Hitler by military and civilian advisers, amounted to a radical revision of strategy. The offensive would have carried the punch of the combined forces of total mobilization of Germany's economy and armed might with a grand effort of the *Luftwaffe*'s fighter arm concentrated around a core of the dreaded jet planes now ready in limited numbers and steadily multiplying. The new offensive strategy would have confronted the Allies with a danger that they feared.

This alternative to an immediate throw of the dice was the essence of a plan advanced by the Chief of the Armed Forces Operations Staff, General Jodl, and his deputy, General Horst von Buttlar-Bran-denfels. They proposed to: (1) shift the main effort of the war to the West; (2) redeploy a considerable number of divisions from Scan-dinavia and Italy, authorizing large-scale withdrawals on these fronts; (3) transfer the bulk of Navy and *Luftwaffe* personnel to the Army; (4) convert the entire Replacement Army (about two million men), including all training units, into combat divisions; (5) totally mo-bilize all German resources far beyond the measures adopted in the July crisis; and (6) turn Germany into a fortress under martial law.[15]

To supplement such a course of action Hitler might have accepted the separate proposal submitted by Albert Speer and General Galland: to strike a devastating blow at Allied daylight bombers with the massed strength of 2,500 fighters (including the jets) trained and assembled expressly for that purpose. Their estimate was that 400 to 500 Allied bombers could thus be destroyed for the loss of an equal number of German fighters and that an air victory of such proportions would break the stranglehold of the air blockade.[16]

While there can be no doubt that adoption of these proposals in combination and their application in a great ground and air offensive could not have prevented the final collapse of Germany, their effect on Allied strategy would have been grave. But Hitler was perhaps too apprehensive, certainly too impatient, to adopt this radical solution. He had never fully grasped the significance of airpower, even during the early phase of the war when Goering's *Luftwaffe* was victorious in the East and West. Now, as the conflict entered the sixth year, the decline of the *Luftwaffe* had been painfully demonstrated. Hitler was disillusioned and distrustful of his air force's capacity to deliver the stroke Speer and Galland proposed and frustrated the plan even before it could be tested. Nor did the Jodl–Buttlar-Brandenfels proposal appeal to Hitler at this time. Six months later, after the Russian armies had penetrated the heart of the Reich, he was finally ready to apply extreme measures, but in the fall of 1944 Hitler was evidently unwilling to admit that the seriousness of the situation called for such a radical course. There is evidence that Hitler considered withdrawing troops from the northern and southern theaters of war, even to the extent of pulling back behind the Alps and giving up Italy altogether, in order to redeploy these divisions in the West. But this was at the end of July, at the height of the crisis in Normandy, and the thought then tentatively weighed was subsequently allowed to die.[17]

In rejecting the radical proposals for an all-out offensive, Hitler thus settled for a strategic compromise.

The question now arose as to where to launch the offensive on which he had decided. Initially, Hitler's military advisers explored all theaters of operations for possibilities. But the criterion that the offensive must gain a decisive success automatically reduced the choice to the theaters in the East and West.[18]

Panzer General Guderian, responsible for operations on the Eastern Front, continually urged that the strategic reserve be sent to his theater to thwart any Soviet attempt to invade the German homeland. In October, Guderian's fears were vividly confirmed by Soviet drives that cut off an army group in the Courland peninsula and penetrated the East Prussia defenses. During the same period, the Russians had captured Belgrade and crossed the natural barrier of the Danube on a wide front. By Christmas they encircled Budapest and threatened

Vienna. But Hitler refused to listen to the counsel of the Army's Chief of Staff and ridiculed intelligence estimates of Soviet strength and capabilities.[19]

In the beginning of August, Hitler and his staff actually considered a carefully prepared operation in the East, while planning to fight a defensive battle with their backs to the Siegfried Line. These plans were based upon the assumption that the withdrawal from France could be effected gradually with successive stands to be made along prepared defense positions well ahead of the West Wall. After a victory over the Russians, the forces could then be shifted to the West with a view to repeating the exploit against the Western Allies. This hope faded rapidly as the Allied armies swept relentlessly across France driving the remnants of the German armies in the West before them. Concurrently, the high-level planners realized that the Soviet Union's apparently inexhaustible manpower reserves and its advantage of unlimited terrain would frustrate German efforts to gain a strategic decision in the East.[20]

Explaining his position after the war, General Jodl stated that the attack had to be launched "in the West because the Russians had so many troops that even if we had succeeded in destroying 30 divisions it would have made no difference. On the other hand, if we destroyed 30 divisions in the West, it would amount to more than one third of the whole invasion army." [21] Actually, this would have been almost one-half of the Allied Expeditionary Force.

This consideration tipped the scales in favor of the West and coincided with Hitler's firm conviction that Germany's fate would be decided there. The geographical limits of the area—as compared to the endlessness of the U.S.S.R.—and the far smaller number of Allied units would give him the chance he was seeking. A major factor in this connection was Hitler's view that the leadership of the West would waver under the impact of a massive crisis and that public opinion, especially in the United States, would demand a withdrawal from Europe.[22]

Once the theater had been determined, the Armed Forces Operations Staff planners investigated feasible courses of action, bearing in mind Hitler's strategic objective, available German forces (amounting to 30 divisions), and Allied strength and capabilities. An important factor was the realization that Allied control of the air could not be broken by the *Luftwaffe* and had to be countered by other means.

Hitler specified the prerequisites that would ensure success: (1)

holding the positions in the West against all Allied breakthrough attempts without committing the forces being assembled for the big offensive; (2) achieving complete tactical surprise; (3) a period of bad weather extending for at least ten days to keep Allied air forces grounded during the initial phase of the operation; (4) speedy exploitation of the breakthrough; (5) a relatively quiet period on other fronts, especially in the East.[23]

German intelligence methodically evaluated Allied strength and capabilities. In September the Germans estimated that General Eisenhower's forces in France numbered 60 divisions with 5 more to be shipped to the Continent in October. It was a slight consolation to the German planners that their intelligence had failed to turn up any strategic reserves available to the Supreme Allied Commander at this time. Allied main-effort sectors were recognized in the Aachen area, where the Allies were expected to aim at closing to the Rhine on a broad front north of Cologne, and at Metz, where the objective was evidently the Saar Basin. Despite a relative shortage of ammunition, the Germans credited the Allied armies with the capability of launching and sustaining large-scale offensives. The numerical strength ratio between Allied and German forces was estimated at two to one. While Navy intelligence was still fearful of an amphibious landing in the area of the Ems estuary, Army intelligence discounted this possibility as well as that of a repetition of an airborne landing similar to the one launched at Arnhem.[24]

On the basis of these considerations the Germans weighed five possible courses of action to realize Hitler's intention: (1) Operation HOLLAND, consisting of a single-thrust attack to be launched from the bridgehead of Venlo with the objective Antwerp; (2) Operation LIÉGE-AACHEN, a double envelopment with the main effort originating in the area of northern Luxembourg, driving through the Ardennes in a northwesterly direction, then turning north to meet a secondary attack launched simultaneously from the area northwest of Aachen with the objective of destroying the Allied forces in that salient; (3) Operation LUXEMBOURG, a two-pronged attack from central Luxembourg and the area of Metz with the objective Longwy; (4) Operation LORRAINE and (5) Operation ALSACE, envelopment operations aimed at gaining Nancy and Vesoul, respectively.

The range of choice was soon reduced to the first two solutions because they offered the best prospect of a decisive success. From a strategic point of view Operation HOLLAND was very tempting, but was recognized to contain an element of grave risk. The second course, LIÉGE-AACHEN, which was later to become known as the "small solution," appeared more likely to succeed.[25]

Faced with these two alternatives, Hitler reached the momentous decision of combining them in what von Rundstedt, student of von Schlieffen, sarcastically characterized as an operational idea that could "almost" be called a stroke of genius. With this "big solution," however, Hitler gave the offensive two objectives to be attained with a force adequate only for one.

Some of the reasons behind this decision were tactical, others were psychological and find their explanation only in Hitler's personality. The tactical considerations that he regarded as favorable were: (1) the opportunity to slice through the Allied front along its national seam, thus adding to expected military crisis the cumulative effect of anticipated political disunion; (2) the strategic and psychological importance of Antwerp, seemingly within reach of a bold thrust, if speedily executed; (3) the weakness of the Allied dispositions in the Ardennes sector inviting repetition of the classic breakthrough victories in 1914 and 1940; and (4) the suitability of the wooded Eifel region for concealing a large-scale build-up and achieving surprise. Hitler had persuaded himself that he could assemble an adequate force to execute the offensive. He was determined to carry out the operation in the face of powerful Allied attacks astride Metz and the imminent thrust toward the Ruhr district. Distasteful as it was to him to give up valuable terrain and laboriously built defense positions, Hitler was willing to sacrifice both if he could thus hold intact the attack forces he was concentrating. A dangerously grave element in the structure of Hitler's consideration was the gross underestimation of Allied strength and determination and, conversely, an exaggerated overrating of the power and effectiveness of his own forces, especially the elite SS Panzer divisions.[26] The overriding psychological incitement, however, for undertaking the venture of a great counteroffensive was Hitler's recurring delusion that his military genius would permit him to regain the initiative and decisively alter the course of the war.[27]

Proponents of the "small solution" (LIÉGE-AACHEN), mainly Field Marshals von Rundstedt and Walter Model, based their objections to Hitler's concept on the following considerations: (1) the paucity of forces available for an objective so ambitious; (2) the serious lack of reserves to hold the shoulders and feed the offensive; (3) the uncertainty that the forces Hitler had promised could be held in reserve until the start of the offensive, in view of the impending resumption of Allied attacks; and (4) the conviction that the offensive, as planned by Hitler, would result only in a bulge in the German lines and not in the destruction of sizable Allied forces.[28]

Hitler categorically rejected all pleas in favor of the "small solution," and in his operation directive of November 10 marked the distant objective of Antwerp and even the disposition of the attack forces as "unalterable." To get what he wanted, he freely disregarded the counsel of his advisers and commanders, staking everything on what General Jodl later called "an act of desperation." [29]

The mission of the operation, decreed by Hitler, was "to destroy the enemy forces north of the line Antwerp-Brussels-Luxembourg, thus to achieve a decisive turn of the campaign in the West, and possibly of the entire war." The Commander in Chief West (von Rundstedt) was ordered to break through the weakly held front of the U.S. First Army between Monschau and Wasserbillig with Army Group B (Model), cross the Meuse between Liége and Dinant, seize Antwerp and the western bank of the Schelde estuary, and destroy the Allied forces thus cut off from their lines of supply, and, in conjunction with this main attack, launch strong elements of the adjoining Army Group H in a supporting attack from the north.

In the main attack with Field Marshal Model's Army Group B, the Sixth Panzer Army (with 4 armored and 4 infantry divisions) was to break through the Allied front north of the Schnee Eifel, seize undestroyed Meuse crossings astride Liége in cooperation with the 150th Panzer Brigade (SS Colonel Otto Skorzeny, famed for his exploit of having freed Mussolini), and subsequently close to the Albert Canal between Maastricht and Antwerp (inclusive). To cover its right (northern) flank, the Panzer army would seize and hold defense positions along the Vesdre River with the bulk of its infantry divisions and artillery.

Army Group B's center force, the Fifth Panzer Army (with 4 armored and 4 infantry divisions), was to use as its main axis of advance the road Bastogne-Namur, break through the Allied front in northern Luxembourg, and cross the Meuse between Amay and Namur. Advanced elements were to rush into the area around Brussels and that west of Antwerp to protect the Sixth Panzer Army's open western flank on the line Antwerp-Brussels-Dinant. To fulfill this task, the Fifth Panzer Army would stay abreast of its right neighbor—the Sixth Panzer Army—and disregard its own extended left flank.

The Seventh Army (with 1 armored and 5 infantry divisions) was given the task of protecting the southern and southwestern flank of the operation and gaining defense positions starting astride Luxembourg city and ending south of Dinant along the Semois River. This army's forceful advance was to gain the time and terrain essential to build up strong defense positions farther to the rear.

In a supporting attack from the north, the Fifteenth Army—reassigned for the offensive from Army Group H to Army Group B— had a dual mission. With 3 armored and 6 infantry divisions it was to launch holding attacks between Roermond and Eupen to tie down Allied forces in that sector and ultimately destroy them in a secondary attack. In addition, the Fifteenth Army had the task of assuming control over those units of the Sixth Panzer Army committed in the defensive position along the Vesdre River, after the mobile elements of the Sixth Panzer Army had crossed the Meuse.

The reserve was reckoned at 3 armored and 4 infantry divisions.

Hitler directed von Rundstedt to complete the concentration by the end of November—a date dictated by weather forecasts. The necessary fuel (four million gallons) and ammunition (50 trainloads from the sacrosanct Führer reserve), above and beyond the current needs of the theater, were promised. The *Luftwaffe,* Hitler assured his commanders, would support the attack of the ground forces with 1,500 fighters, including 100 jets.[30]

This was Hitler's original concept put into a directive. Except for the number and effective strength of units, it remained virtually unchanged until the offensive began on the morning of December 16, 1944.

On the eve of his offensive, Hitler could point with satisfaction to the fulfillment of the basic prerequisites he had specified when he had ordered the attack. The Western Front had withstood Allied breakthrough attempts at Aachen and in Lorraine, although 9 Panzer and an equal number of infantry divisions had been drawn into battle and suffered in varying degrees. Secrecy had been preserved, the weather was favorable, and the front in the East except for the sector in Hungary had remained relatively quiet. A tremendous effort had gone into the planning and preparations for Germany's last offensive. As the grenadiers and Panzers moved into their jump-off positions, expectation was high, and success appeared within close reach.

Almost immediately the operation fell short of the high hopes that had been attached to it. On the third day Hitler canceled the subsidiary attack of the Fifteenth Army and thus altered the tactical concept of the operation. The double envelopment was thus reduced to a far less effective single thrust. On the fourth day it was evident that the powerful Sixth Panzer Army would be unable to break through the Allied lines and that the distant objective of Antwerp could not be reached. After one week had passed, even the prospect of closing to the Meuse had faded. When General Patton's Third Army armor broke through to Bastogne on December 26, the battle was reduced to a fight for that city, and it was clear that the offensive had failed altogether.[31]

For the Germans, the Ardennes did not officially end until January 28, when Field Marshal Model's armies had been forced back to their original jump-off positions. They could claim to have drawn into the battle 29 U.S. and 4 British divisions and to have inflicted on them about 75,000 casualties.[32] The offensive had achieved a temporary respite though Hitler now referred to it as "a tremendous easing of the situation." [33] The Allies had been forced to abandon their attacks on the Roer dams and the Saar and to delay their final offensive toward the Rhine for two months. But even Hitler had to admit that it had not gained "the decisive success that might have been expected." [34] For this modest achievement compared to the ambitious aim, Hitler had paid an exorbitant price. Exact figures are not available, but reliable estimates indicate that German casualties were in the neighborhood of 100,000 men (about one-third of the attacking force); at least 800 tanks (out of over 2,000 employed); and about 1,000 planes (about half of the total fighter force assembled, including almost 300 lost in the "Big Strike" against Allied ground installations delivered on January 2, 1945).[35]

These losses were irreplaceable. They left the Western theater of operations with no appreciable fuel reserves. Ammunition stockpiles were down to one-third of estimated needs. Replacements for the casualties suffered could no longer be expected. The Ardennes had hurt the Allies, but, in the words of von Rundstedt's historian, it had literally "broken the backbone of the (German) western front." [36]

Long before the official end of the offensive in the West, the full impact of the strategic consequences of the Ardennes was felt in the East. The weakness of the 1,500-mile Eastern Front is best illustrated by the fact that almost half of the German divisions were either isolated in the north (on the Courland peninsula in Latvia) or tied down in the south (in Hungary) without a chance to influence the outcome of the impending battle in the center. When the Russians struck on January 12, 1945, it was too late for remedial measures. The reinforcements and supplies that for the past four months had consistently gone to the West and into the Ardennes had been spent in the short-lived Battle of the Bulge, while the Russians gained an awesome bulge of far greater permanence. They swept across Poland, captured almost all of East Prussia, drove deep into Silesia, and, finally, came to a halt less than 50 miles short of Berlin. Hitler's desperate gamble in the West had invited disaster in the East and hastened the final and inevitable defeat of Germany.

Robert Ross Smith

18

Luzon versus Formosa
(1944)

One of the thorniest problems of strategic planning for the war against Japan in 1944 was to decide whether the principal objective of drives that had brought the Allies into the western Pacific should be Luzon in the northern Philippines or Formosa. The decision was made by the U.S. Joint Chiefs of Staff, since the Pacific was an American area of strategic responsibility. They made it after long debate and careful study of the views of the commanders in the Central and Southwest Pacific theaters. Among the considerations that determined their choice when they finally made it, logistical factors played the major role, but here, as in other connections, they had to take into account the commitments and progress of the Allies in other theaters, and particularly in Europe. It was in this sense a decision in global strategy.

In January 1945, after more than three years of war, United States forces returned to Luzon, where in 1942 American troops had suffered a historic defeat.[1] The loss of the Philippines in May of that year, after the disaster that befell the U.S. Pacific Fleet at Pearl Harbor, had rendered obsolete the American prewar plans for action in the Pacific in the event of war with Japan.[2] By the late spring of 1943 the U.S. Joint Chiefs of Staff (who, by agreement of the U.S.-British Combined Chiefs of Staff, were responsible for the conduct of the war in the Pacific) had developed a new strategic plan for the defeat of Japan. The plan was neither sacrosanct nor immutable—it was not intended to be—but its underlying concepts governed the planning and execution of operations in the Pacific during a year and a half of debate over the relative priority of Luzon and Formosa as primary objectives of an Allied drive into the western Pacific.[3]

The plan was premised upon the concept that the Allies might very well find it necessary to invade Japan in order to end the war in the Pacific. The Joint Chiefs of Staff foresaw that intensive aerial bombardment of the Japanese home islands would be prerequisite to invasion, and that such bombardment would have to be coordinated with combined air, surface, and submarine operations aimed at cutting Japan's overwater lines of communication to the rich territories she had seized in the Netherlands Indies and southeastern Asia. The Joint Chiefs believed that the Allies could best undertake the necessary bombardment of Japan from airfields in eastern China. They decided that to secure and develop adequate air bases in China, Allied forces would have to seize at least one major port on the South China coast. The Allies would require such a port to replace the poor overland and air routes from India and Burma as the principal means of moving men and matériel into China.

To secure a port on the China coast, and simultaneously to cut Japan's line of communication to the south, the Allies would have to gain control of the South China Sea. Gaining this control, the Joint Chiefs realized, would in turn involve the seizure and development of large air, naval, and logistical bases in the strategic triangle formed by the South China coast, Formosa, and Luzon. But before they could safely move into this triangle, the Joint Chiefs decided, the Allies would have to secure air bases in the southern or central Philippines from which to neutralize Japanese airpower on Luzon. The Allies might also need staging bases in the southern and central Philippines from which to mount amphibious attacks against Luzon, Formosa, and the China coast.

In accordance with these 1943 plans, Allied forces in the Pacific had struck westward toward the strategic triangle along two axes of advance. Air, ground, and naval forces of the Southwest Pacific Area, under General Douglas MacArthur, had driven up the north coast of New Guinea to Morotai Island, lying between the northwestern tip of New Guinea and Mindanao, southernmost large island of the Philippine archipelago. Simultaneously, Admiral Chester W. Nimitz, commander of the Pacific Ocean Areas, had directed the forces of the Central Pacific Area in a drive through the Gilberts, Marshalls, and Marianas to the Palau Islands, some 500 miles east of Mindanao.*

---

* Nimitz' Pacific Ocean Areas included the North, Central, and South Pacific Areas.

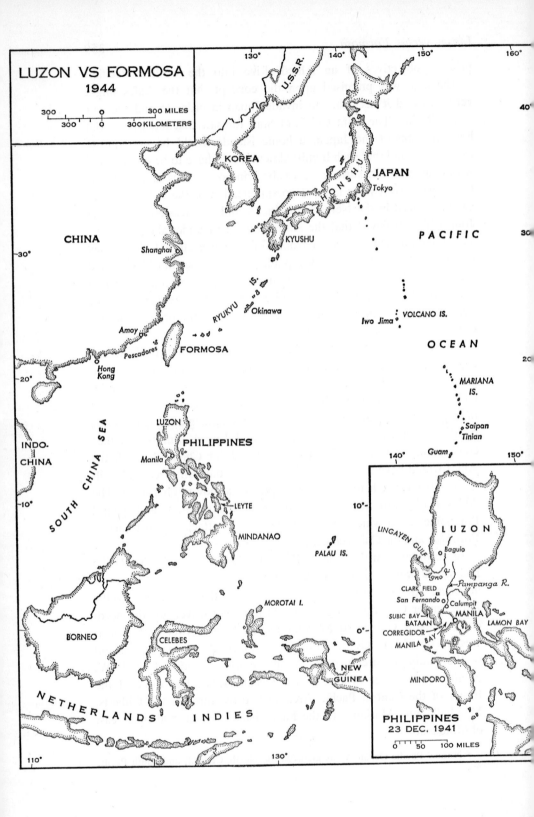

LUZON VS FORMOSA
1944

300 ——— 0 ——— 300 MILES
300 ——— 0 ——— 300 KILOMETERS

U.S.S.R.

KOREA

JAPAN

HONSHU

Tokyo

CHINA

KYUSHU

PACIFIC

Shanghai

RYUKYU IS.

Okinawa

Iwo Jima   VOLCANO IS.

Amoy

Pescadores   FORMOSA

OCEAN

Hong
Kong

MARIANA
IS.

INDO-
CHINA

LUZON

Saipan
Tinian

PHILIPPINES

Manila

Guam

SOUTH CHINA SEA

LEYTE

MINDANAO

PALAU IS.

MOROTAI I.

BORNEO

CELEBES

NEW
GUINEA

NETHERLANDS   INDIES

PHILIPPINES
23 DEC. 1941

0 —— 50 —— 100 MILES

LUZON

LINGAYEN GULF

Baguio

Agno

Pampanga R.

CLARK FIELD

San Fernando   Calumpit

SUBIC BAY   MANILA
BATAAN
CORREGIDOR
MANILA BAY   LAMON BAY

MINDORO

Studying various plans for Allied entry into the strategic triangle, the Joint Chiefs and their subordinate advisory committees concluded that Formosa constituted the most important single objective in the target area.[4] The island possessed so many obvious advantages and was located in such a strategically important position that most planners in Washington believed the Allies would have to seize it no matter what other operations they conducted in the western Pacific. Until they seized Formosa, the Allies would be unable to establish and secure an overwater supply route to China. Formosa, therefore, seemed a necessary steppingstone to the China coast. Moreover, Allied air and naval forces could sever the Japanese lines of communication to the south much more effectively from Formosa than from either Luzon or the South China coast alone. Furthermore, from fields in northern Formosa, the Army Air Forces' new B-29's could carry heavier bomb loads against Japan than from more distant Luzon.*

Many planners considered Formosa such a valuable strategic prize that they devoted considerable attention to the possibility of bypassing all the Philippines in favor of a direct descent upon Formosa. Discussion of this proposal waxed and waned in Washington during much of 1943 and 1944 despite the fact that the strategic outline plan for the defeat of Japan called for the seizure of bases in the southern or central Philippines before going on into the Luzon-Formosa-China coast triangle. Such discussions found the War and Navy Departments internally divided. Admiral Ernest J. King, Chief of Naval Operations and Navy member of the Joint Chiefs of Staff, was a leading advocate of plans to bypass the Philippines entirely. On the other hand, Admiral Nimitz and other ranking naval commanders in the Pacific favored at least reoccupying the southern or central Philippines before striking on toward Formosa. These officers believed it would be impossible to secure the Allied line of communications to Formosa until Allied land-based aircraft from southern Philippine bases had neutralized Japanese airpower on Luzon.[5]

General George C. Marshall, Chief of Staff and Army member of the Joint Chiefs, played a relatively inactive part in the debate until late 1944, but at one time at least seemed inclined toward bypassing both the Philippines *and* Formosa in favor of a direct invasion of Kyushu in southern Japan. Some officers high in Army counsels, including Lieutenant General Joseph T. McNarney, Deputy Chief of

---

* Northern Formosa, affording some good airfield sites, lies 300-odd nautical miles closer to Tokyo than the best airfield areas of northern Luzon.

Staff, strongly advocated bypassing the Philippines on the way to Formosa. General Henry H. Arnold, Army Air Forces member of the Joint Chiefs, also appears to have maintained through much of 1943 and 1944 that it might prove desirable to bypass the Philippines.[6] Other Army planners, including those of the chief logistician, Lieutenant General Brehon B. Somervell, commander of the Army Service Forces, favored taking the entire Philippine archipelago before making any move toward Formosa or the China coast. In the field, General MacArthur stood adamant against bypassing any part of the Philippines, a stand in which he had the support of most other ranking Army officers in the Pacific.[7]

In March 1944 the Joint Chiefs had directed MacArthur to be ready to move into the southern Philippines before the end of the year and to make plans to invade Luzon during February 1945. Simultaneously, they had ordered Nimitz to prepare plans for an assault against Formosa in February 1945.[8] These directives, which left in abeyance the relative priority of Luzon and Formosa, ostensibly settled the question of re-entry into the Philippines, but in mid-June the Joint Chiefs of Staff reopened the question of bypassing the archipelago.

Developments in the Pacific, Asia, and Europe between mid-March and mid-June 1944 tended to support those planners who wanted to bypass the Philippines. The U.S. Army had acquired new intelligence indicating that the Japanese were rapidly reinforcing their bastions throughout the western Pacific, including Formosa. Thus, the longer the Allies delayed an attack on Formosa, the more the operation would ultimately cost. Army planners suggested that the Allies might be able to reach Formosa during November 1944 if the Joint Chiefs immediately decided to bypass the Philippines. Moreover, the Joint Chiefs were beginning to fear an imminent collapse of Chinese resistance—some planners felt that the only way to avert such an eventuality would be the early seizure of Formosa and a port on the China coast without undertaking intermediary operations in the Philippines.[9] The Joint Chiefs were probably also stimulated by the success of the invasion of Normandy in early June and by the impending invasion of the Marianas in the Central Pacific, set for June 15. At any rate, on June 13, seeking ways and means to accelerate the pace of operations in the Pacific and feeling that the time might be ripe for acceleration, the Joint Chiefs asked Admiral Nimitz and General MacArthur to consider the possibilities of bypassing, in favor of a direct invasion of Japan, all objectives already selected in the western Pacific, including both the Philippines and Formosa.[10]

Neither Nimitz nor MacArthur gave the Joint Chiefs any encouragement. Both declared that the next major step in the Pacific after the advance to the Palaus-Morotai line would have to be the seizure of air bases in the southern or central Philippines. The Joint Chiefs' subordinate committees, examining the theater commanders' replies and undertaking new studies of their own, reaffirmed the concept that the Allies would have to move into the central or southern Philippines before advancing to either Luzon or Formosa. Like MacArthur and Nimitz, the advisory bodies saw no possibility of a direct jump to Japan. The Joint Chiefs of Staff, apparently with some reluctance, agreed.[11]

Meeting with President Franklin D. Roosevelt in a conference at Pearl Harbor in late July 1944, both MacArthur and Nimitz again emphasized that MacArthur's forces would have to be firmly established in the southern or central Philippines before any advance to either Formosa or Luzon could take place—on this point almost everyone was agreed. MacArthur then argued persuasively that it was both necessary and proper to take Luzon before going on to Formosa, while Nimitz expounded a plan for striking straight across the western Pacific to Formosa, bypassing Luzon. Apparently, no decisions on strategy were reached at the Pearl Harbor conferences.[12] The Formosa versus Luzon debate continued without let-up at the highest planning levels for over two months, and even the question of bypassing the Philippines entirely in favor of a direct move on Formosa again came up for serious discussion.[13] The net result of debate through July 1944 was reaffirmation of the decision to strike into the southern or central Philippines before advancing to either Formosa or Luzon. The Joint Chiefs still had to decide whether to seize Luzon or Formosa, or both, before executing any other major attacks against Japan.

General MacArthur was a most vigorous adherent of the view that the Allies would have to secure Luzon before moving any farther toward Japan. Contrary to the views held by the Joint Chiefs of Staff, MacArthur believed that Luzon was a more valuable strategic prize than Formosa. He declared that the Allies would need to reoccupy the entire Philippine archipelago before they could completely sever Japan's lines of communication to the south. MacArthur also believed that an invasion of Formosa would prove unduly hazardous unless he provided air and logistical support from Luzon. Finally, he suggested, if the Allies took Luzon first they could then bypass Formosa and strike for targets farther north, thus hastening the end of the war. The Luzon-first course of action, he averred, would be the cheaper in terms of time, men, and money.[14]

In addition, MacArthur considered that bypassing part of the Philippines would have the "sinister implication" of imposing a food blockade upon unoccupied portions of the archipelago. (His meaning here is not clear, inasmuch as his own plans called for seizing a foothold in southeastern Mindanao, jumping thence to Leyte in the east-central Philippines, and then going on to Luzon, initially bypassing the bulk of Mindanao, the Sulu Archipelago, and most of the Visayan Islands.)[15] MacArthur had a more cogent argument, and one that was bound to have some influence upon planning in Washington. The reoccupation of the entire Philippine archipelago as quickly and early as possible, was, MacArthur said, a national obligation and political necessity. To bypass any or all the islands, he declared, would destroy American honor and prestige throughout the Far East, if not in the rest of the world as well.

Just as General MacArthur was the most vigorous proponent of Luzon, so Admiral King was the most persistent advocate of the Formosa-first strategy. King believed that the seizure of Luzon before Formosa could only delay the execution of more decisive operations to the north. He also argued that the capture of Formosa first would greatly facilitate the subsequent occupation of Luzon. Moreover, King pointed out, the Allies could not secure and maintain a foothold on the China coast until they had seized Formosa. Finally, he suggested, if the Allies should bypass Formosa, then the principal objective in the western Pacific should be Japan itself, not Luzon.[16]

MacArthur believed that the plans to bypass Luzon were purely Navy-inspired.[17] Actually, the War and Navy Departments were as internally split during the Luzon-versus-Formosa debate as they had been earlier over the question of bypassing all the Philippines. For example, at least until mid-September 1944 General Marshall favored the Formosa-first strategy and like Admiral King had expressed the opinion that Japan itself, rather than Luzon, should be considered the substitute, if any, for Formosa. Most Army members of the Joint Chiefs' subordinate committees held similar views, and until September consistently pressed for an early decision in favor of Formosa. Army Air Forces planners, during the summer of 1944, expressed their interest in Formosa as a site for B-29 bases.[18]

Admiral Nimitz, the ranking naval officer in the Pacific, went on record until late September as favoring Formosa first. However, there are indications that his views were not enthusiastically shared by his staff, and there are grounds to believe that Nimitz grew steadily more lukewarm toward the idea of seizing Formosa. Nimitz had been at variance with Admiral King on the question of bypassing the entire Philippine archipelago, and it is possible that his support of the Formosa-first strategy stemmed at least in part from deference to King's judgment. A hint of Nimitz' attitude is apparent in the fact that his staff was preparing plans to seize Okinawa in the Ryukyu Islands, as a substitute for Formosa, well before such an operation gained serious consideration among high-level planners in Washington.[19]

The next ranking naval officer in the Pacific, Admiral William F. Halsey, commander of the Third Fleet (and until June 15, 1944, commander of the South Pacific Area as well), steadfastly opposed the Formosa-first plan. He wanted to go to Luzon and bypass Formosa in favor of seizing Okinawa. In this connection, Halsey relates a classic story concerning a discussion between his chief of staff, Vice Admiral Robert B. Carney, and Admiral King. King, propounding his Formosa plan to Carney, who was arguing in favor of Luzon, asked, "Do you want to make a London out of Manila?" Carney's reply was: "No sir, I want to make an England out of Luzon." [20]

Most of the other senior Army and Navy officers on duty in the Pacific also favored the Luzon-first strategy and advocated bypassing Formosa. Lieutenant General Robert C. Richardson, commanding U.S. Army Forces, Pacific Ocean Areas, strongly advised against Formosa. So, too, did MacArthur's air commander, Lieutenant General George C. Kenney, and the Southwest Pacific Area's naval commander, Vice Admiral Thomas C. Kinkaid. But among the Joint Chiefs of Staff during the summer and early fall of 1944 only Admiral William D. Leahy, the President's Chief of Staff, favored going to Luzon instead of Formosa, and this stand represented a reversal of Leahy's earlier thinking on the subject.[21]

It is noteworthy that, with the possible exception of Nimitz, the ranking Army and Navy commanders in the Pacific—the men responsible for executing or supporting the operation—were opposed to the seizure of Formosa. In general, they favored a program calling for the capture of Luzon and a subsequent jump to Okinawa or Japan. In the face of this opinion of the commanders on the spot, the consensus of most high-ranking Army and Navy planners in Washington—with Leahy and General Somervell as outstanding exceptions—was that the Formosa-first course of action was strategically the sounder and, therefore, the most desirable course for the Allies to follow in the western Pacific.

The Washington planners, however, had to give careful consideration to many factors other than ideal strategy. Study of these factors brought the Luzon versus Formosa debate to a climax in late September 1944.

Perhaps the most influential event helping to precipitate the climax was a drastic change in the target date for the initial invasion of the Philippines. Until mid-September 1944, General MacArthur's plans had called for the first entry into the Philippines to take place in southeastern Mindanao on November 15, while the major assault into the archipelago would occur at Leyte on December 20. On September 15, with the approval of the Joint Chiefs of Staff, MacArthur canceled preliminary Mindanao operations in favor of a direct jump from the Palaus-Morotai line to Leyte on October 20.[22]

Soon after this change of schedule, MacArthur informed the Joint Chiefs that he could push on from Leyte to Luzon on December 20, two months earlier than the date currently under consideration for an attack on either Luzon or Formosa. This new plan, MacArthur suggested, would permit the Allies to execute the Formosa operation on the date already selected, but, he went on, the prior seizure of Luzon would render unnecessary the occupation of Formosa.[23]

MacArthur's new schedule contained much to recommend it to the Joint Chiefs of Staff. His proposed sequence of operations—Leyte on October 20, Luzon on December 20, and Formosa, possibly, on February 20, 1945—would permit the Allies to maintain steady pressure against the Japanese. Should the Allies drop Luzon out of the sequence, the Japanese would have ample time to realign their defenses during the interval between the Leyte and Formosa operations. Moreover, dropping out Luzon could in no way accelerate the advance to Formosa—logistical problems would make it impossible for the Allies to mount an invasion of Formosa under any circumstances before late February 1945.

While MacArthur's proposals were gaining some favor in Washington, especially among Army planners, Nimitz' proposals for advancing to Formosa and the South China coast were losing ground.[24] Plans developed in Washington had long called for the seizure of all Formosa, after which amphibious forces would strike on westward to secure a port on the mainland. But Nimitz' latest plans provided for simultaneous assaults on southern Formosa and in the Amoy area of the China coast. Nimitz proposed to occupy the bulk of Formosa only if such a step proved necessary and feasible after he had established a firm bridgehead at Amoy.

Army planners quickly decided that Nimitz' new plans possessed major drawbacks. The Japanese would hardly allow Allied forces to sit unmolested in southern Formosa. Instead, the Japanese would mount strong counterattacks from northern Formosa with troops already on the island and with reinforcements staged in from China. Occupying and defending one beachhead on southern Formosa and another at Amoy would involve problems far different from those the Allies had encountered previously in the Pacific. So far during the war, the Japanese had usually been hard put to move air and ground reinforcements against the island perimeters Allied amphibious task forces had seized. In the southern Formosa-Amoy area, on the other hand, the Allies would not have the protection of distance from major Japanese bases they had enjoyed in earlier campaigns. The Allies did not have sufficient aircraft in the Pacific to keep neutralized all existing Japanese airfields within range of southern Formosa and Amoy. In addition, experience in the Pacific had demonstrated that Allied air and naval forces could not be expected to forestall all Japanese efforts to move strong reinforcements across the narrow strait between China and Formosa.

Having considered these factors, Army planners swung to the opinion that a southern Formosa-Amoy operation would be impractical. They believed that it would inevitably lead to protracted, costly campaigns to secure all Formosa and large areas of the adjacent China mainland as well. Major ground campaigns of such scope could delay progress toward Japan and would prove an unacceptable drain upon Allied manpower resources.

Further study of the manpower needed for the southern Formosa-Amoy operation revealed additional difficulties. Army intelligence estimates of Japanese strength in that region, for example, were far higher than those Nimitz' staff had produced. Army planners therefore believed that the southern Formosa-Amoy campaign would require many more combat units than Nimitz was planning to employ. Furthermore, according to various estimates made during September, Nimitz would lack from 77,000 to 200,000 of the service troops needed for the campaign he proposed.

Planners studied a number of suggestions for securing the necessary service forces. One thought, originating with the Navy, which was seeking ways to accelerate the Formosa target date, proposed taking service units from the Southwest Pacific Area. But MacArthur's command was already short of service troops. To remove any from his area might jeopardize the success of the Leyte operation and would certainly immobilize his forces in the central Philippines until long after Nimitz had secured the southern Formosa-Amoy region. Although the southern Formosa-Amoy and Luzon operations would each require about the same number of U.S. combat troops in the assault phase, MacArthur could count upon hundreds of thousands of loyal Filipinos to augment both his service and his combat strength. No similar source of friendly manpower would be available on Formosa.

By mid-September 1944 so few service units were available in the United States that the only way Army planners could see to solve the service troop shortage for Nimitz' proposed operation was to await redeployment from Europe. Army planners and the Joint Logistic Committee both estimated that Nimitz could launch the southern Formosa-Amoy campaign even as early as March 1, 1945, only if the war in Europe ended by November 1, 1944, thereby permitting timely redeployment of service units to the Pacific. And even if the Allies could effect such redeployment from Europe, logistical planners still felt that Nimitz would be unable to move against Formosa by March 1, 1945, unless the Joint Chiefs of Staff immediately decided to cancel the Luzon operation, thus providing for an early and unbroken build-up of the resources required to execute Nimitz' campaign. On the other hand, the logistical experts were convinced that MacArthur could move to Luzon before the end of 1944 regardless of developments in Europe. Army planners, not as optimistic as they had been a few months earlier about an early end to the war in Europe, pointed out that it would be unsound to schedule the southern Formosa-Amoy operation on the presumption of a German collapse by November 1, 1944. Events were to prove this argument sound.

Army planners saw other combined logistical-tactical disadvantages in Nimitz' plan. They believed, for instance, that the campaign would tie down so many troops, ships, landing craft, and planes that an invasion of Luzon, assuming Formosa came first, could not take place until November 1945. By the same token, any other major step toward Japan, such as the seizure of Okinawa, would be equally delayed. A hiatus of this length would be unacceptable for tactical reasons alone. In addition, the Luzon-first course, it appeared, would be far safer logistically than the southern Formosa-Amoy undertaking. As Army Service Forces planners pointed out, the Allied lines of communication to Luzon would be shorter and easier to protect than those to Formosa. The logisticians predicted that the Allies would find it especially difficult to safeguard the lines of communication to Formosa if Luzon remained in Japanese hands.

Other aspects of the logistical problems attained disturbing overtones. Admiral Leahy, for example, believed that although the Formosa-first course of action might ultimately hasten the end of the war in the Pacific, capturing Luzon and bypassing Formosa would prove far cheaper in terms of lives and other resources. By mid-September he, as well as most Army planners, was favoring what promised to be the longer course at the lesser cost. General MacArthur, meanwhile, expressed the opinion that the Formosa-first strategy would cost not only more lives but also more time. He was prepared to guarantee to the Joint Chiefs that he could secure the most strategically important areas of Luzon—the Central Plains-Manila Bay region—within four to six weeks after initial landings on the island.

General Marshall also began to show misgivings about the cost of the southern Formosa-Amoy operation vis-à-vis Luzon, although he remained convinced that the Formosa-first course was strategically the more desirable. Admiral Nimitz expressed no strong opinion on the relative cost of the two campaigns, but, "backing" into the problem, stated that the occupation of Luzon after Formosa need not delay the pace of the war in the Pacific. If Formosa came first, Nimitz pointed out, MacArthur's task on Luzon would be considerably eased and, presumably, less costly. Admiral King, however, declared himself convinced that the Formosa-first course would save time and, therefore, reduce casualties over the long run. By late September 1944, King alone among the upper-level planners seems to have retained a strong conviction along these lines.

While the discussions over tactical and logistical problems continued in Washington, the Allied position in China had been steadily deteriorating. In mid-September General Joseph W. Stilwell, commanding U.S. Army Forces in China, Burma, and India, and Allied Chief of Staff to Generalissimo Chiang Kai-shek, reported to the Joint Chiefs that Japanese offensives in eastern and southeastern China were overrunning the last air bases from which the China-based U.S. Fourteenth Air Force could effectively support invasions of either Luzon or Formosa. Chiang's armies were unable to either hold or recapture these air bases.[25]

This news had an obvious impact upon the thinking of both the ground and the air planners in Washington. The Army Air Forces had intended to expand airfields in eastern China as staging bases for B-29's flying against targets in Japan, Korea, Manchuria, and Formosa, and to base on these fields much of the tactical bombardment preceding the actual invasion of Japan. The East China fields now appeared irretrievably lost, and the Allies could not afford to expend the manpower necessary to retake and hold them. The need for seizure and development of a port on the China coast was therefore deprived of much of its urgency, since the Allies had needed such a port primarily to open a good supply route into China for the development of air bases. By the same token, one of the principal reasons for seizing Formosa—to secure a stepping stone to the China coast—became much less compelling.

This line of thinking forced naval planners to reconsider the southern Formosa-Amoy plan. To most Navy planners, a move to Formosa without the concomitant seizure of a mainland port would prove unsound, because Formosa lacked the anchorages and ports required for the large fleet and logistical bases the Allies needed in the western Pacific. Inevitably the question arose: If it was no longer feasible or desirable to seize and develop a port on the South China coast, was it feasible or desirable to occupy any part of Formosa? Since early September 1944 Army planners had been answering that question with an emphatic "no." [26]

The loss of existing and potential air base sites in eastern China, together with the limitations inherent in Nimitz' plans to occupy only southern Formosa, weighed heavily with Army Air Forces planners. There was no question but that B-29's could operate more effectively against Japan from northern Formosa than they could from northern Luzon, the Mariana Islands, or western China, but the big bombers could accomplish little more from southern Formosa than they could from the other base areas. Indeed, Saipan and Tinian in the Marianas lay closer to Tokyo than Nimitz' proposed base area in southern Formosa, and the two islands of the Marianas were secure from Japanese air attack. Even northern Luzon, some 200 miles farther from Tokyo than southern Formosa, had some advantages over southern Formosa—it had more room for B-29 fields and was safer from air attack. Finally, assuming that Nimitz could meet the most optimistic target date for the invasion of southern Formosa—March 1, 1945—B-29's could not begin operations from that island until the late spring or early summer. The Army Air Forces were already planning to initiate B-29 operations from the Marianas before the end of 1944. In brief, by mid-September, the Army Air Forces had lost interest in Formosa and had begun to see eye to eye with other Army elements on the disadvantages and drawbacks of the southern Formosa-Amoy scheme.

An obvious political consideration may have had a bearing on the ultimate decision in the Luzon versus Formosa debate. General Mac-Arthur's argument that it would be disastrous to United States prestige to bypass any part of the Philippines could not be dismissed. Perhaps more important, Admiral Leahy took the same point of view. By virtue of his intimate contact with President Roosevelt, it must be presumed that his colleagues of the Joint Chiefs of Staff gave Leahy's opinion careful consideration.

Whatever the political implication involved, the Formosa versus Luzon question was decided primarily upon its military merits. By the end of September 1944 almost all the military considerations—especially the closely interrelated logistical problems concerning troops and timing—had weighted the scales heavily in favor of seizing Luzon, bypassing Formosa, forgetting about a port on the China coast, and jumping on to Okinawa. Admiral King was the only member of the Joint Chiefs of Staff, if not the only prominent military figure as well, who still maintained a strong stand in favor of bypassing Luzon and executing the southern Formosa-Amoy operation.

Realizing that the military and political factors had undermined his position, King took a new, negative tack in the debate by raising objections to the Luzon operation per se. He argued that the Luzon campaign as MacArthur had planned it would tie up all the Pacific Fleet's fast carrier task forces for at least six weeks for the purposes of protecting the Luzon beachhead and Luzon-bound convoys and neutralizing Japanese airpower on both Luzon and Formosa. To pin down the carriers for so long would be unsound, King averred, and he therefore declared MacArthur's plan unacceptable to the U.S. Navy.[27]

Alerted by his deputy chief of staff (Major General Richard J. Marshall, then in Washington on official business), General MacArthur was able to provide Army planners with ammunition to counter King's last-ditch arguments.[28] MacArthur informed the Joint Chiefs that his only requirement for carriers after the initial assault on Luzon would be for a small group of escort carriers to remain off the island for a few days to provide support for ground operations until his engineers could ready a field for land-based planes at the invasion beaches. MacArthur continued by pointing out that only the first assault convoys would be routed through dangerous waters north of Luzon and consequently require protection from the fast carrier task forces. Resupply and reinforcement convoys would come through the central Philippines under an umbrella of land-based aircraft from Mindoro Island, south of Luzon, and would require no carrier-based air cover. Thus, MacArthur declared he would have no long-term requirement for the fast carrier task forces, which he could quickly release so that Nimitz could employ them elsewhere. Mac-Arthur concluded with the counterargument that the fast carriers would be tied down to a specific area much longer during the proposed southern Formosa-Amoy operation, especially if Luzon remained in Japanese hands, than would be the case for the Luzon invasion.[29]

This exchange took much of the wind out of King's sails. Next, Admiral Nimitz withdrew whatever support he was still giving the Formosa plan. He had concluded that sufficient troops could not be made available for him to execute the southern Formosa-Amoy campaign within the foreseeable future. Accordingly, at the end of September, he threw the weight of his opinion behind the Luzon operation, proposing that plans to seize Formosa be at least temporarily dropped. Simultaneously, Nimitz presented for Admiral King's consideration a planned series of operations designed to maintain steady pressure against the Japanese and carry Allied forces speedily on toward Japan: MacArthur's forces would initiate the Luzon campaign on December 20, 1944; Central Pacific forces would move against Iwo Jima, in the Volcano Islands some 650 miles south of Tokyo, late in January 1945; and the Central Pacific would next attack Okinawa, 850 miles southwest of Tokyo, and other targets in the Ryukyu Islands, beginning on March 1, 1945.[30]

King accepted Nimitz' recommendations, with one last reservation. King felt that the hazards involved in routing the Luzon assault convoys into the waters between Luzon and Formosa were so great that approval for such action should come directly from the Joint Chiefs of Staff. He raised similar objections to plans for having the Pacific Fleet's fast carrier task forces operate in the same restricted waters. The other three members of the Joint Chiefs of Staff, however, agreed to leave the decision on these problems up to Nimitz and MacArthur, a settlement that King finally accepted.[31]

After King's eleventh-hour change of position, the Joint Chiefs were able to attain the unanimity that their major strategic decisions required. On October 3, 1944, they directed General MacArthur to launch the invasion of Luzon on or about December 20 and instructed Admiral Nimitz to execute the Iwo Jima and Okinawa operations on the dates he had proposed. Nimitz would provide naval cover and support, including fast and escort carriers, for the invasion of Luzon; MacArthur would provide Nimitz with as much air support as he could from Luzon for the attack on Okinawa. The two commanders would coordinate their plans with those of B-29 units in the Pacific and India and with the plans of General Stilwell and the Fourteenth Air Force in China.[32]

The Joint Chiefs of Staff did not formally cancel the Formosa operation. Instead, they left in abeyance a final decision on the seizure of that island, but thereafter the occupation of Formosa as an operation of World War II never came up for serious consideration at the higher levels of Washington planning councils.

The Joint Chiefs had not reached their decision to take Luzon, bypass Formosa, and, in effect, substitute Okinawa for Formosa, either lightly or easily. From the beginning of the Luzon versus Formosa debate they had believed the seizure of Formosa and a port on the South China coast—bypassing Luzon—to be the best strategy the Allies could follow in the western Pacific. In the end, however, the Joint Chiefs had had to face the fact that the Allies could not assemble the resources required to execute that strategy, at least until after the end of the war in Europe. They could not seriously consider delaying the progress of the war in the Pacific until Germany collapsed. In the last analysis, then, logistical considerations alone would have forced the Joint Chiefs to the decision they reached in favor of Luzon, although other military realities, and possibly political factors as well, had some influence upon the outcome of strategic planning for operations in the western Pacific.

For the Allied forces of the Pacific theaters, the Joint Chiefs' directive of October 3, 1944, ended months of uncertainty. The die was cast. Luzon would be taken; Formosa would be bypassed. United States forces would recapture the entire Philippine archipelago in a consecutive series of advances, just as General MacArthur had been planning ever since he had left Corregidor in March 1942.

Forrest C. Pogue

19

The Decision to Halt
at the Elbe
(1945)

On April 12, 1945, the day of President Roosevelt's death and eighteen days before the Russians took Berlin, U.S. Ninth Army units
crossed the Elbe River near Magdeburg, some 50 miles from the
German capital. They established a second bridgehead farther south
on the following day. German counterattacks forced them to withdraw from the northern position on April 14, but the Americans held
the southern bridgehead. These elements were ordered to hold in
place while other units arriving at the Elbe were turned toward objectives south and north along the west bank of the river. On May 5,
a week before the Russians liberated Prague, the U.S. Third Army
pushed spearheads inside the Czechoslovak frontier and, on the day
the war ended, was in a position to advance in force to the Czechoslovak capital. Despite the pleas of Czechoslovak leaders and the appeals of British Prime Minister Churchill, these units were not sent
forward. Many observers have concluded that only a political decision, perhaps made weeks before, could have held General
Dwight D. Eisenhower's forces at the Elbe. Careful examination of
the Supreme Allied Commander's action indicates that he halted his
troops short of Berlin and Prague for military reasons only.[1]

It is important to remember that before April 1, 1945—the time
at which General Eisenhower decided to halt his forces when they
reached the Elbe—the zones of occupation for Germany and the
sectors of occupation for Berlin had been agreed upon by the United
States, Great Britain, and the Soviet Union. France had been invited
to participate in the arrangements. The zones had been outlined,

along general lines suggested by the British, by the European Advisory Commission (EAC) as early as January 1944. The United States and Great Britain had agreed on the main proposals at the Quebec Conference in September 1944 and had settled everything except the control of the Bremen-Bremerhaven enclave when their representatives met at Malta in January on their way to the Yalta Conference. The Soviet Union accepted the EAC recommendations at Yalta in early February 1945, and the fact that zones of occupation had been established was announced at the close of the meeting. As a result, many people assumed that the zones were worked out at this time and some bargain made in regard to Berlin and Prague. Prime Minister Churchill, in writing of this question, has made the situation clear in his statement: "The Soviet armies were at this very moment swarming over the prewar frontiers, and we wished them all success. . . . It was well understood by everyone that the agreed occupational zones must not hamper the operational movements of the armies. Berlin, Prague, and Vienna could be taken by whoever got there first. . . ." [2]

At the time of the Yalta Conference, when final plans for the defeat and occupation of Germany were being discussed, it was reasonable to assume that Berlin, Prague, and even cities west of the Elbe might fall to the Red forces.[3] The Allied forces, which were just recovering from the effects of the Ardennes counteroffensive, not only were still west of the Rhine, but still faced heavy fighting along the flooded Roer. There were disquieting reports, later proved inaccurate, that the Germans were preparing a mountain redoubt in southern Germany and Austria from which they could harry the Allies and prolong the war for months to come. This was a particularly unpleasant prospect for the United States, which wanted to end the war quickly in Europe in order to shift men and supplies to General MacArthur in the Pacific. Moreover, it is doubtful if American public opinion—far more favorable to a return to normal than to political arrangements for the future, especially arrangements considered to be more in the interest of Britain and France than of the United States—would have backed any action which required new commitments in Europe, particularly east of the Elbe.

So far as military commanders were concerned, their desire was to end the war in Europe as quickly as possible and to avoid political complications. This view seems to have been shared to some extent by members of the State Department.[4] General Eisenhower, schooled in a military tradition which held that commanders should keep their

GERMANY
APRIL 1945

MILES
50   50
50   50
KILOMETERS

eyes on the military road to victory and leave political decisions to civil authorities, was operating under a directive which called only for military action against Germany. This initial directive, which was not changed during the war, stated that his task was to "enter the continent of Europe, and, in conjunction with the other United Nations, undertake operations aimed at the heart of Germany and the destruction of her armed forces." In the absence of any requirement from the U.S.-British Combined Chiefs of Staff (CCS) to take measures which would strengthen the position of the Western Allies against future Soviet aggression, he emphasized a military rather than a political approach in planning the final offensive. Nothing in the contemporary record indicates that he deviated from the position which he stated after the war when writing about the effect on his plans of the division of Germany into occupation zones. This division, he wrote, "did not influence our military plans for the final conquest of the country. Military plans, I believed, should be devised with the single aim of speeding victory; by later adjustment, troops of the several nations could be concentrated in their own national sectors." [5]

Berlin was listed as the military goal of the Western Powers by the Supreme Headquarters, Allied Expeditionary Force (SHAEF) in a pre-D-Day plan of May 1944.[6] However, by mid-September 1944, when Soviet forces had reached the gates of Warsaw and had forced the collapse of Rumania, the Supreme Commander declared that while Berlin was still "the main prize," Allied strategy would have to be coordinated with that of the Russians. He thought that, should the Red forces "beat us to Berlin," the British forces under Field Marshal Sir Bernard L. Montgomery, ought to be pushed northward to take the Hanover area and the ports around Hamburg and that Lieutenant General Omar N. Bradley's U.S. forces should seize part or all of the Leipzig-Dresden area "depending upon the progress of the Russian advance." [7]

In the fall of 1944, Montgomery pressed repeatedly for a single Allied thrust toward Berlin, northeastward from the Rhine, preferably by his 21st Army Group aided by an American army under his command. In discussions over the "broad front" versus "narrow front" strategy, General Eisenhower made clear that for the moment he was more interested in the Ruhr than in Berlin. Germany, he believed, had two hearts: one industrial (the Ruhr), and the other political (Berlin). He wished to concentrate on the Ruhr on the theory that if the industrial heart stopped, the political heart would also die.[8]

After the Ardennes battle, the British commander revived his proposals for a single thrust to Berlin. Any chance which he had for leading the main offensive in his sector was ended in March when Bradley's forces seized the Remagen bridge and developed a major bridgehead across the Rhine. With the United States forces, which now far outnumbered the British troops on the Continent,[9] in a strong position to attack through central Germany to the Leipzig-Dresden area, it is not surprising that General Bradley's advice stressed the difficulties of the advance on Berlin and the value of striking toward Dresden. The U.S. commander has summarized the situation as he then saw it in *A Soldier's Story*. Nearly 200 miles separated Montgomery's Rhine bridgehead from the Elbe, while Soviet Marshal Georgi K. Zhukov had nearly a million men on the Oder with some elements within 30 or 40 miles of the German capital. Even if the Allies reached the Elbe before Zhukov crossed the Oder, the British and U.S. forces would still have to cross 50 miles of lowlands marked by lakes, streams, and canals to get to Berlin. When asked by General Eisenhower for an opinion, General Bradley estimated that a breakthrough from the Elbe would cost 100,000 casualties. "A pretty stiff price to pay for a prestige objective," he told the Supreme Commander. And, remembering that the Allies had already agreed that the Russian occupation zone would run within 100 miles of the Rhine, he added, "Especially when we've got to fall back and let the other fellow take over." He says candidly of his thinking of this period:

> I could see no political advantage accruing from the capture of Berlin that would offset the need for quick destruction of the German army on our front. As soldiers we looked naïvely on this British inclination [the desire to go on to Berlin] to complicate the war with political foresight and nonmilitary objectives.[10]

With these arguments in mind and fearing that the enemy might successfully establish his redoubt in the south, General Eisenhower concluded near the end of March that he should push his main force from the Kassel-Frankfurt area to the Elbe, split the German forces, cut off Berlin from the so-called "National Redoubt" area, and then turn his forces directly to the north and to the southwest of the Elbe. These maneuvers would enable him to seize ports on the North Sea and the Baltic and also clean up the area to the south before the enemy could assemble a force there. This meant that the main offensive would be under Bradley's command.[11] On March 28 he asked the Allied military missions in Moscow to inform Marshal Stalin of his intentions.

The British Chiefs objected strongly, saying that the Supreme Commander had gone outside proper channels in notifying Stalin of his plan to stop at the Elbe. They held that Eisenhower's proposals were contrary to his previous assurances that the main battle would be fought in the north; that they relegated the British forces to a secondary position; and that they failed to include capture of Berlin—an important political prize. It was apparent that the minimizing of the British position in the final offensive was of great importance at this stage of the debate. Prime Minister Churchill made this clear in a private memorandum to the British Chiefs of Staff on March 31 when he said:

> It seems to me that the chief criticism of the new Eisenhower plan is that it shifts the axis of the main advance upon Berlin to the direction through Leipzig to Dresden, and thus raises the question of whether the Twenty-one Army Group will not be so stretched as to lose its offensive power, especially after it has been deprived of the Ninth United States Army. Thus we might be condemned to an almost static role in the north and virtually prevented from crossing the Elbe until an altogether later stage in the operations has been reached. All prospect also of the British entering Berlin with the Americans is ruled out.[12]

Churchill had warned the British Chiefs of Staff that Eisenhower's credit with the U.S. Joint Chiefs of Staff stood very high as a result of recent victories and that they might "riposte heavily." "The Americans will feel that, as the victorious Supreme Commander, he has a right, and indeed a vital need, to try to elicit from the Russians their views as to the best point for making contact by the armies of the West and of the East." In a sharp exchange, in which the American Chiefs of Staff seemed to criticize British strategy and operations in the Rhineland, they held that in the existing fluid state of fighting, Eisenhower was the only person in a position to judge what measures were best for destroying the armies and their will to resist.[13]

The Prime Minister, in communications to President Roosevelt, moved quickly to deal with and dispose of "these misunderstandings between the truest friends and comrades that ever fought side by side as allies." He denied any attempt to disparage or lower the prestige of the Supreme Commander. While indicating that he felt that the U.S. Joint Chiefs had done less than justice to British efforts by their remarks, he made clear that his great concern was that the shift in the direction of the attack would leave the British forces in a static condition along the Elbe when and if they reached it. He then proceeded to shift the argument from the military to the political level by noting that the Russians were already in a position to overrun Austria and take Vienna. He asked: "If they also take Berlin, will not their impression that they have been the overwhelming contributor to the common victory be unduly imprinted in their minds, and may this not lead them into a mood which will raise grave and formidable difficulties in the future? I therefore consider that from a political standpoint we should march as far east into Germany as possible, and that should Berlin be in our grasp we should certainly take it. This also appears sound on military grounds." [14]

The President, in a reply which clearly reflected the U.S. Army's views, held the debate to military considerations. He explained that the U.S. Chiefs' insistence on upholding the Supreme Commander was an enunciation of a well-known military principle rather than an anti-British reaction. Any impression that they were reflecting on the performances of the 21st Army Group arose, he thought, from a failure to stress factors such as military obstacles and the strength and quality of opposing forces which had contributed to the difficulties facing Field Marshal Montgomery's units. The President could not see that Eisenhower's plans involved any far-reaching changes from the strategy approved at Malta. He regretted that at the moment of a great victory the Allies should "become involved in such unfortunate reactions." [15]

General Eisenhower, on his part, assured the British Prime Minister that he had no intention of relegating the British forces to a restricted sphere. He thought it likely that once Allied forces reached the Elbe, U.S. forces would be shifted to Field Marshal Montgomery, who would then be sent across the river in the north and to a line reaching at least to Lübeck on the Baltic coast. As for the drive to Berlin, he made no promises. If it could be brought into the Allied orbit, he declared, honors would be equally shared between the British and U.S. forces.[16] Churchill informed the President that the changes in strategy were fewer than he had initially believed and assured Roosevelt that relations with Eisenhower were still of the most friendly nature.[17] *

---

* Churchill's message ended with the Latin quotation: *"Amantium irae amoris integratio est"* which the War Department translated as "Lovers' quarrels are a part of love" and sent to General Eisenhower.

Churchill's words ended the discussion over the British role in future campaigns, but they did not dispose of the question of Berlin as a political matter. Made suspicious by the alacrity with which Marshal Stalin agreed to General Eisenhower's decision to drive for Leipzig instead of Berlin and by Soviet agreement that Berlin was no longer of strategic importance, the British Chiefs urged that this point be reconsidered. The U.S. Chiefs replied that "only Eisenhower is in a position to know how to fight his battle, and to exploit to the full the changing situation." As for Berlin, they felt that such "psychological and political advantages as would result from the possible capture of Berlin ahead of the Russians should not override the imperative military consideration, which in our opinion is the destruction and dismemberment of the German armed forces." [18]

On April 7, General Eisenhower presented his views to the Combined Chiefs of Staff. He said he was reluctant to make Berlin a major objective since it had lost much of its military importance; it was in ruins and many of the government offices had left the city. His chief interest at the moment was in dividing the enemy armed forces by a thrust to the Elbe near Leipzig and by establishing the Allied left flank on the Baltic near Lübeck. His only political reaction was shown in his statement that the push to the Baltic coast would prevent the Red Army from occupying any part of the Danish peninsula. If, after accomplishing these aims, his forces could take Berlin, well and good. He made it quite clear that while he was working on a basis of military objectives, he was willing to consider political factors in his decisions. He then added:

> But I regard it as militarily unsound at this stage of the proceedings to make Berlin a major objective, particularly in view of the fact that it is only 35 miles from the Russian lines. I am the first to admit that a war is waged in pursuance of political aims, and if the Combined Chiefs of Staff should decide that the Allied effort to take Berlin outweighs purely military considerations in this theater, I would cheerfully readjust my plans and my thinking so as to carry out such an operation.[19]

Admiral William D. Leahy, Chief of Staff to President Roosevelt, has written that there is no evidence in his notes that the Combined Chiefs of Staff ever took up the question of Berlin. The decision was thus left to the Supreme Commander, who was free to make it on purely military bases. Eisenhower's attitude was made clear on April 8 when, in answer to Montgomery's request for 10 U.S. divisions for a main thrust toward Lübeck and Berlin, he said:

As regards Berlin I am quite ready to admit that it has political and psychological significance, but of far greater importance will be the location of the remaining German forces in relation to Berlin. It is on them that I am going to concentrate my attention. Naturally, if I can get a chance to take Berlin cheaply, I shall take it.[20]

That General Eisenhower's decision was not based on a desire to favor American forces over the British was made clear less than a week later when the U.S. Ninth Army reached the Elbe and its commander, Lieutenant General William H. Simpson, asked permission to go to the German capital. The Supreme Commander reiterated his order to hold on the Elbe and to turn units northward in the direction of Lübeck and southward toward the National Redoubt. His action recalled the strategy which he had suggested as early as September 1944. In informing the War Department of his action, General Eisenhower said that not only were the Baltic and Bavarian objectives more important than Berlin, but that to plan for an immediate effort against the German capital "would be foolish in view of the relative situation of the Russians and ourselves. . . . While it is true we have seized a small bridgehead over the Elbe, it must be remembered that only our spearheads are up to that river; our center of gravity is well back of there." [21]

By the third week in April, Churchill seems to have accepted the Supreme Commander's views on Berlin. He cabled Foreign Minister Anthony Eden, then in the United States, on April 19:

. . . It would seem that the Western Allies are not immediately in a position to force their way into Berlin. The Russians have two and a half million troops on the section of the front opposite that city. The Americans have only their spearheads, say twenty-five divisions, which are covering an immense front and are at many points engaged with the Germans. . . .

In views which paralleled earlier suggestions of General Eisenhower's, he emphasized that it was most important for Montgomery to take Lübeck, since his arrival there "before our Russian friends from Stettin would save a lot of argument later on." He also believed it important to push on to Linz in Austria to meet the Red forces there and to gain the region south of Stuttgart where the main German installations connected with atomic research were located. Eden agreed completely, adding: "I am sure that you still have Prague in mind. It might do the Russians much good if the Americans were to occupy the Czech capital. . . ." [22]

It is not clear whether the British Foreign Minister discussed

Churchill's views with the new U.S. President, Harry S. Truman. The President, who had taken office upon Roosevelt's death on April 12, made his views evident on April 21 when, in answer to Churchill's cable regarding arrangements relative to zones of occupation, he replied that "the tactical deployment of American troops is a military one" and suggested that a certain latitude and discretion be permitted the Supreme Commander in these matters. Admiral Leahy, in commenting on the President's message, sums up the Berlin situation admirably for our purposes:

. . . He [Eisenhower] made a military decision in the field to rest on the Elbe, to which he knew he would have to withdraw anyway as soon as the German resistance collapsed. My notes do not show that the matter ever came before the Combined Chiefs of Staff. The Russians, after overcoming savage street-by-street resistance, announced the complete capture of Berlin on May 2, 1945.[23]

Thus far the discussion has dealt with military objectives which General Eisenhower hoped to seize by stopping west of the Elbe. It is now necessary to consider a second factor—one which affected Prague as well as Berlin—namely, the effort to establish an easily recognized line of demarcation where the advancing armies could stop. Efforts had been made since late 1943 to establish bomb-lines and, since the June 1944 landings, to provide closer liaison between Soviet and Western land forces. Near the end of March 1945, the War Department recalled that in 1939 armed clashes occurred between German and Soviet troops in Poland until both accepted the Vistula River as a line of demarcation. Perhaps prompted by this recollection, General Marshall wrote the Supreme Commander on March 26:

One of the problems which arises . . . is that of meeting the Russians. What are your ideas on control and coordination to prevent unfortunate incidents and to sort out the two advancing forces? One possibility is an agreed line of demarcation. The arrangements we now have with the Russians appear quite inadequate for the situation you may face and it seems that steps ought to be initiated without delay to provide for the communication and liaison you will need with them during the period when your forces may be mopping up in close proximity or in contact with the Russian forces.[24]

General Eisenhower and his advisers initially preferred that no set line be established and that his forces be allowed to go forward until contact was made with the Russians, using recognition signals to avoid incidents. After considering the matter, the Combined Chiefs of Staff authorized General Eisenhower to tell the Russians that Allied troops would advance until contact was imminent. Army group commanders were then to agree on zones of responsibility. This soon led to complications, as the Soviet leaders suspected that the Allies were trying to change the zones of occupation and would not be satisfied until General Eisenhower personally assured them that there was no such intent.[25]

On April 21 the Supreme Commander notified the Russians that since the logistical position of the Western Allies was stretched in the center as a result of the rapid drive to the Elbe, they would make no move at that point for some weeks at least. He added that he expected to cross the Elbe in the north to open the northern German ports and to drive the Germans north of the Kiel Canal. Other Allied forces were to go southward into the Danube valley. On the following day he suggested that, since a meeting of the converging armies appeared likely in the Wittenberg-Dresden area, he would choose the line of the Elbe-Mulde on the central front as an easily identified line.* If the Russians wanted to stop on the Elbe and desired the Western Allies to advance to Dresden, he was willing to do so. He suggested a firm junction on a recognizable line before final mutual adjustments based on local tactical situations were made.[26]

The Russians accepted the line of the Elbe and the Mulde on April 24. General Alexei Antonov, Red Army Chief of Staff, added that the Soviet Command contemplated occupying Berlin and clearing the Germans from the east bank of the Elbe north and south of Berlin and from the Moldau River valley in Czechoslovakia.[27] This last provision meant that Prague would be taken by the Russians.

Near the end of April the British Chiefs of Staff pointed out that the Western Allies could derive remarkable political advantages from liberating Prague and as much of the rest of Czechoslovakia as possible. General Marshall passed this on to General Eisenhower, adding: "Personally, and aside from all logistic, tactical, or strategical implications, I would be loath to hazard American lives for purely political purposes." [28]

General Eisenhower insisted that the northern thrust toward Lü-

* While, for convenience sake, the Allied halt is usually spoken of as "the halt on the Elbe," it is not a strictly accurate statement. North of Wittenberge (northwest of Berlin, to be distinguished from Wittenberg southwest of Berlin), the Allied forces crossed the Elbe; from Wittenberge to a point near the Czechoslovak border they used the Elbe-Mulde line; south of that, in Czechoslovakia itself, they followed the Karlsbad-Pilsen line. In the Dresden area, the Elbe was east of the area where Eisenhower planned to stop.

beck and Kiel and the southern drive in the direction of Linz and the National Redoubt be given priority. Provided additional means were at hand, he planned to attack the enemy also in Czechoslovakia, Denmark, and Norway. He thought that the Western Allies would be able to deal with Denmark and Norway, but concluded that the Red Army was in a perfect position to clean out Czechoslovakia and would certainly reach Prague before the U.S. forces. He assured General Marshall: "I shall not attempt any move I deem militarily unwise merely to gain a political advantage unless I receive specific orders from the Combined Chiefs of Staff." There is nothing to indicate that they gave him any such orders.[29]

The Supreme Commander informed the Russians on April 30 that while the operational position was being adjusted along the Elbe and the Mulde, he would cross the lower Elbe to establish a firm flank near Wismar. From the headwaters of the Mulde southward, he intended to hold the line approximately along the 1937 frontiers of Czechoslovakia. Later, Allied forces could advance to Karlsbad, Pilsen, and Budejovice. On the southern flank, he proposed to advance in the general area of Linz. If at any time the situation required the Allies to advance farther, he was willing to take such action.[30]

When, on May 4, General Eisenhower indicated his willingness to move from the Pilsen-Karlsbad area to the line of the Elbe and Moldau and to clear their western banks, the Russians strongly dissented. To avoid possible incidents, General Antonov asked General Eisenhower not to move his forces in Czechoslovakia east of the line Budejovice-Pilsen-Karlsbad. He pointedly reminded the Supreme Commander that the Red Army had stopped east of Wismar on the Baltic at his request, and hoped by the same token that the Allies would stop their advance in Czechoslovakia. General Eisenhower agreed not to move farther. Thus he left Prague to be liberated by the Russians.[31]

SHAEF was notified on May 5 that Czech partisans, in an independent action, had liberated Prague. Before the day's end, German armored forces converged on the city from the outskirts, and on the following morning Czechoslovak representatives asked for aid. They also requested that Czechoslovak forces, then with General Bradley's 12th Army Group, be sent into Prague. Czechoslovak appeals were also made directly to Lieutenant General George S. Patton, Jr., whose Third Army forces were near Pilsen. This word reached Colonel Anthony J. Drexel Biddle, Jr., of the European Allied Contact Section at SHAEF, on the morning of May 7 after the Germans had surrendered at Reims. He naturally said that Prague was included in the terms of surrender and that hostilities had ended.[32]

Unfortunately, seizure of the radio station in Prague by Czechoslovak partisans had led to confusion on the part of German troops in Czechoslovakia, who were inclined to discredit the report and continue fighting. Therefore, although the war was ended, Prague was still in danger from the German forces near that city. Churchill wired Eisenhower on May 7 that he hoped the latter's statements as to his intentions would not prevent an advance to Prague if forces were available and they did not meet the Russians first.[33]

More urgent appeals came from the Czechoslovaks on May 7 and 8, some being made directly to the Prime Minister. When the Czechs talked later to SHAEF officials, they were told that the proper procedure had been followed, since if Churchill felt that something could be done he had the facilities for taking up the matter directly with the U.S. Government.[34]

General Eisenhower continued to honor General Antonov's request of May 5 that the U.S. forces remain west of the Pilsen-Karlsbad line, while keeping the Russians informed of Czechoslovak pleas for aid. Thus, when on May 8 the Czechs asked for bombers to be sent to Prague, SHAEF forwarded the message to Moscow with the comment that no action was being taken. On the same day, a report was passed on to the effect that Czech partisans were under attack by the Germans. The Czechs were notified that Allied forces had stopped at the Soviet's request and that all appeals for help should go to the Russians.[35]

In order to stop the enemy attacks, a U.S. patrol was sent with a German representative of Admiral Karl Doenitz' headquarters* to Field Marshal Ferdinand Schoerner, who commanded the forces in Czechoslovakia, and warned him of the serious consequences which would follow if he did not speedily bring hostilities to an end. General Eisenhower warned all German soldiers by radio that any continuation of hostilities would be severely punished by the Allies.[36]

The Russian forces ultimately entered Prague on May 12. Some eighteen days passed before they gave permission for Czechoslovaks in General Bradley's army group to come to the city.

The decision in 1945 to halt Allied troops short of Berlin and Prague has since been severely criticized both in Europe and the

* Doenitz assumed supreme command of the German forces on April 30.

United States on political grounds. It is urged that Churchill was right in suggesting that we proceed as far as possible into Germany in order to strengthen our hands for later negotiation with the Russians.[37] Others say that we should have recognized the Russian menace earlier and have prepared our strategy to block the Soviet advance into Central Europe. This obviously takes us beyond the scope of this study into the making of foreign policy. We should also have to answer such questions as: (1) what would the Russians have done if we had embarked on a policy of racing them to various European capitals in the spring of 1945? And (2) what would have been the effect of the action on the war in the Pacific?

It is evident that the political leaders in the United States had framed no policy for dealing with an aggressive Soviet Union in Central Europe. It is equally clear that no political directive was ever issued to General Eisenhower by his American superiors or by the U.S.-British Combined Chiefs of Staff. His initial directive called for the defeat of Germany's armed forces, and it was obvious from messages that he received from Washington that military solutions were preferred. In this situation, the Supreme Commander reached his decisions relative to Berlin and Prague on military rather than political grounds. It is difficult to believe that critics of his decision would argue that he should have taken political action on his own initiative. When considered from the purely military viewpoint of the quickest way to end the war in Germany with the fewest number of casualties to our troops, leaving the maximum number available for rapid redeployment to the Pacific, his decision was certainly the proper one.

Louis Morton

20

The Decision to
Use the Atomic Bomb
(1945)

On August 6, 1945, the United States exploded an atomic bomb over Hiroshima and revealed to the world in one blinding flash the start of the atomic age. As the meaning of this explosion and the nature of the force unleashed became apparent, a chorus of voices rose in protest against the decision that had opened the Pandora's box of atomic warfare.

The final decision to use the atomic bomb was made by President Truman. There was never any doubt of that, and despite the rising tide of criticism he took full responsibility for his action. Only recently succeeded to the Presidency after the death of Roosevelt in April and beset by a multitude of problems of enormous significance for the postwar world, Truman leaned heavily on the counsel of his senior and most trusted advisers on the question of the bomb. But the final decision was his and his alone.[1]

The justification for using the atomic bomb was that it ended the war, or at least ended it sooner and thereby saved countless American and Japanese lives. But had it? Had not Japan been defeated and was she not already on the verge of surrender? What circumstances, it was asked, justified the fateful decision that "blasted the web of history and, like the discovery of fire, severed past from present"?[2]

The first authoritative explanation of how and why it was decided to use the bomb came in February 1947 from Henry L. Stimson, wartime Secretary of War and the man who more than any other was responsible for advising the President in this matter.[3] This explanation did not answer all the questions or still the critics. During the years that have followed others have revealed their part in the decision and in the events shaping it. These explanations have not ended the controversy, but they have brought to light additional facts bearing on the decision to use the bomb.

The epic story of the development of the atomic bomb is well known.[4] It began in 1939 when a small group of eminent scientists in this country called to the attention of the United States Government the vast potentialities of atomic energy for military purposes and warned that the Germans were already carrying on experiments in this field. The program initiated in October of that year with a very modest appropriation and later expanded into the two-billion-dollar Manhattan Project had only one purpose—to harness the energy of the atom in a chain reaction to produce a bomb that could be carried by aircraft if possible, and to produce it before the Germans could.[5] That such a bomb, if produced, would be used, no responsible official even questioned. "At no time from 1941 to 1945," declared Stimson, "did I ever hear it suggested by the President, or by another responsible member of the Government, that atomic energy should not be used in the war." And Dr. J. Robert Oppenheimer, who directed the Los Alamos laboratory where the bomb was developed, recalled in 1954 that "we always assumed if they [atomic bombs] were needed, they would be used." [6]

So long as the success of the project remained in doubt there seems to have been little or no discussion of the effects of an atomic weapon or the circumstances under which it would be used. "During the early days of the project," one scientist recalled, "we spent little time thinking about the possible effects of the bomb we were trying to make." [7] It was a "neck-and-neck race with the Germans," the outcome of which might well determine who would be the victor in World War II. But as Germany approached defeat and as the Allied effort to produce an atomic bomb offered increasing promise of success, those few men who knew what was being done and who appreciated the enormous implications of atomic energy became more and more concerned. Most of this concern came from the scientists in the Metallurgical Laboratory at Chicago, where by early 1945 small groups began to question the advisability of using the weapon they were trying so hard to build.[8] It was almost as if they hoped the bomb would not work after it was completed.

On the military side, realization that a bomb would probably be ready for testing in the summer of 1945 led to concrete planning by the few who knew about it for the use of the new weapon, on the assumption that the bomb when completed would work. By the end of 1944 a list of possible targets in Japan had been selected, and a B-29 squadron was trained for the specific job of delivering the bomb.[9] It was also necessary to inform certain commanders in the Pacific about the project, and on December 30, 1944, Major General Leslie R. Groves, head of the Manhattan District, recommended that this be done.[10]

Even at this stage of development, no one could estimate accurately when the bomb would be ready or guarantee that, when ready, it would work. It is perhaps for this reason—and because of the complete secrecy surrounding the project—that the possibility of an atomic weapon never entered into the deliberations of the strategic planners. It was, said Admiral William D. Leahy, "the best kept secret of the entire war" and only a handful of the top civilian and military officials in Washington knew about the bomb.[11] As a matter of fact, one bright brigadier general who innocently suggested that the Army might do well to look into the possibilities of atomic energy suddenly found himself the object of the most intensive investigation.[12] So secret was the project, says John J. McCloy, former Assistant Secretary of War, that when he raised the subject at a White House meeting of the Joint Chiefs of Staff in June 1945 it "caused a sense of shock even among that select group." [13] It was not until March 1945 that it became possible to predict with certainty that the bomb would be completed in time for testing in July. On March 15, Secretary of War Stimson discussed the project for the last time with President Roosevelt, but their conversation dealt mainly with the effects of the use of the bomb, not with the question of whether it ought to be used.[14] Even at this late date, there does not seem to have been any doubt at the highest levels that the bomb would be used against Japan if it would help bring the war to an early end. But on lower levels, and especially among the scientists at the Chicago laboratory, there was considerable reservation about the advisability of using the bomb.[15]

After President Roosevelt's death (April 12), it fell to Stimson to brief the new President about the atomic weapon. At a White House meeting on April 25, he outlined the history and status of the program and predicted that "within four months we shall in all probability have completed the most terrible weapon ever known in human history." [16] This meeting, like Stimson's last meeting with Roosevelt, dealt largely with the political and diplomatic consequences of the use of such a weapon rather than with the timing and manner of employment, the circumstances under which it would be used, or whether it would be used at all. The answers to these questions depended on factors not yet known. But Stimson recommended, and the President approved, the appointment of a special committee to consider them.[17]

This special committee, known as the Interim Committee, played a vital role in the decision to use the bomb. Secretary Stimson was chairman, and George L. Harrison, President of the New York Life Insurance Company and special consultant in the Secretary's office, took the chair when he was absent. James F. Byrnes, who held no official position at the time, was President Truman's personal representative. Other members were Ralph A. Bard, Under Secretary of the Navy, William L. Clayton, Assistant Secretary of State, and the eminent scientists Drs. Vannevar Bush, Karl T. Compton, and James B. Conant. General George C. Marshall, Army Chief of Staff, and General Groves attended at least one and possibly more of the meetings of the committee.[18]

The work of the Interim Committee, in Stimson's words, "ranged over the whole field of atomic energy, in its political, military, and scientific aspects." [19] During the first meeting, the scientific members reviewed for their colleagues the development of the Manhattan Project and described vividly the destructive power of the atomic bomb. They made it clear also that there was no known defense against this kind of attack. Another day was spent with the engineers and industrialists who had designed and built the huge atomic plants at Oak Ridge, Tennessee, and Hanford, Washington. Of particular concern to the committee was the question of how long it would take another country, particularly the Soviet Union, to produce an atomic bomb. "Much of the discussion," recalled Dr. Oppenheimer, who attended the June 1 meeting as a member of a scientific panel, "revolved around the question raised by Secretary Stimson as to whether there was any hope at all of using this development to get less barbarous relations with the Russians." [20]

The work of the Interim Committee was completed June 1, 1945,[21] when it submitted its report to the President, recommending unanimously that:

1. The bomb should be used against Japan as soon as possible.

2. It should be used against a military target surrounded by other buildings.

3. It should be used without prior warning of the nature of the

weapon. (One member, Ralph A. Bard, Under Secretary of the Navy, later dissented from this portion of the Committee's recommendation.)

"The conclusions of the Committee," wrote Stimson, "were similar to my own, although I reached mine independently. I felt that to extract a genuine surrender from the Emperor and his miltairy advisers, they must be administered a tremendous shock which would carry convincing proof of our power to destroy the empire. Such an effective shock would save many times the number of lives, both American and Japanese, that it would cost." [22]

Among the scientists working on the Manhattan Project were many who did not agree. To them, the "wave of horror and repulsion" that might follow the sudden use of an atomic bomb would more than outweigh its military advantages. "It may be very difficult," they declared, "to persuade the world that a nation which was capable of secretly preparing and suddenly releasing a new weapon, as indiscriminate as the rocket bomb and a thousand times more destructive, is to be trusted in its proclaimed desire of having such weapons abolished by international agreement." [23] The procedure these scientists recommended was, first, to demonstrate the new weapon "before the eyes of representatives of all the United Nations on the desert or a barren island," and then to issue "a preliminary ultimatum" to Japan. If this ultimatum was rejected, and "if sanction of the United Nations (and of public opinion at home) were obtained," then and only then, said the scientists, should the United States consider using the bomb. "This may sound fantastic," they said, "but in nuclear weapons we have something entirely new in order of magnitude of destructive power, and if we want to capitalize fully on the advantage their possession gives us, we must use new and imaginative methods." [24]

These views, which were forwarded to the Secretary of War on June 11, 1945, were strongly supported by sixty-four of the scientists in the Chicago Metallurgical Laboratory in a petition sent directly to the President. At about the same time, at the request of Dr. Arthur H. Compton, a poll was taken of the views of more than a hundred and fifty scientists at the Chicago laboratory. Five alternatives ranging from all-out use of the bomb to "keeping the existence of the bomb a secret" were presented. Of those polled, about two-thirds voted for a preliminary demonstration, either on a military objective or an uninhabited locality; the rest were split on all-out use and no use at all.[25]

These views, and presumably others, were referred by Secretary Stimson to a distinguished Scientific Panel consisting of Drs. Arthur Compton, Enrico Fermi, E. O. Lawrence, and Oppenheimer, all nuclear physicists of the first rank. "We didn't know beans about the military situation," Oppenheimer later said. "We didn't know whether they [the Japanese] could be caused to surrender by other means or whether the invasion [of Japan] was really inevitable. . . . We thought the two overriding considerations were the saving of lives in the war and the effect of our actions on the stability of the postwar world." [26] On June 16 the panel reported that it had studied carefully the proposals made by the scientists but could see no practical way of ending the war by a technical demonstration. Almost regretfully, it seemed, the four members of the panel concluded that there was "no acceptable alternative to direct military use." [27] "Nothing would have been more damaging to our effort," wrote Stimson, "than a warning or demonstration followed by a dud—and this was a real possibility." With this went the fear expressed by Byrnes, that if the Japanese were warned that an atomic bomb would be exploded over a military target in Japan as a demonstration, "they might bring our boys who were prisoners of war to that area." [28] Furthermore, only two bombs would be available by August, the number General Groves estimated would be needed to end the war; these two would have to obtain the desired effect quickly. And no one yet knew, nor would the scheduled ground test in New Mexico prove, whether a bomb dropped from an airplane would explode. [29]

Nor, for that matter, were all those concerned certain that the bomb would work at all, on the ground or in the air. Of these doubters, the greatest was Admiral Leahy, who until the end remained unconvinced. "This is the biggest fool thing we have ever done," he told Truman after Vannevar Bush had explained to the President how the bomb worked. "The bomb will never go off, and I speak as an expert in explosives." [30]

Thus, by mid-June 1945, there was virtual unanimity among the President's civilian advisers on the use of the bomb. The arguments of the opponents had been considered and rejected. So far as is known, the President did not solicit the views of the military or naval staffs, nor were they offered.

The military situation on June 1, 1945, when the Interim Committee submitted its recommendations on the use of the atomic bomb, was distinctly favorable to the Allied cause. Germany had surrendered in May and troops from Europe would soon be available for redeployment in the Pacific. Manila had fallen in February; Iwo Jima was in American hands; and the success of the Okinawa invasion was assured. Air and submarine attacks had all but cut off Japan from the resources of the Indies, and B-29's from the Marianas were pulverizing Japan's cities and factories. The Pacific Fleet had virtually driven the Imperial Navy from the ocean, and planes of the fast carrier forces were striking Japanese naval bases in the Inland Sea. Clearly, Japan was a defeated nation.

Though defeated in a military sense, Japan showed no disposition to surrender unconditionally. And Japanese troops had demonstrated time and again that they could fight and inflict heavy casualties even when the outlook was hopeless. Allied plans in the spring of 1945 took these facts into account and proceeded on the assumption that an invasion of the home islands would be required to achieve at the earliest possible date the unconditional surrender of Japan— the announced objective of the war and the first requirement of all strategic planning.[31]

Other means of achieving this objective had been considered and, in early June, had not yet been entirely discarded. One of these called for the occupation of a string of bases around Japan to increase the intensity of air bombardment. Combined with a tight naval block-ade, such a course would, many believed, produce the same results as an invasion and at far less cost in lives.[32] "I was unable to see any justification," Admiral Leahy later wrote, "for an invasion of an already thoroughly defeated Japan. I feared the cost would be enor-mous in both lives and treasure." Admiral Ernest J. King, Chief of Naval Operations, and other senior naval officers agreed. To them it had always seemed, in King's words, "that the defeat of Japan could be accomplished by sea and air power alone, without the neces-sity of actual invasion of the Japanese home islands by ground troops." [33]

The main arguments for an invasion of Japan—the plans called for an assault against Kyushu (code-named OLYMPIC) on November 1, 1945, and against Honshu (CORONET) five months later—are per-haps best summarized by General Douglas MacArthur, Commander, U.S. Army Forces, Pacific. Writing to the Chief of Staff on April 20, 1945, he declared that this course was the only one that would permit application of the full power of our combined resources— ground, naval, and air—on the decisive objective. Japan, he be-lieved, would probably be more difficult to invade the following year. An invasion of Kyushu at an early date would, moreover, place

United States forces in the most favorable position for the decisive assault against Honshu in 1946, and would "continue the offensive methods which have proved so successful in Pacific campaigns." [34] Reliance upon bombing alone, MacArthur asserted, was still an unproved formula for success, as was evidenced by the bomber offensive against Germany. The seizure of a ring of bases around Japan would disperse Allied forces even more than they already were, MacArthur pointed out, and (if an attempt was made to seize positions on the China coast) might very well lead to long-drawn-out operations on the Asiatic mainland.

Though the Joint Chiefs had accepted the invasion concept as the basis for preparations, and had issued a directive for the Kyushu assault on May 25, it was well understood that the final decision was yet to be made. By mid-June the time had come for such a decision and during that period the Joint Chiefs reviewed the whole problem of Japanese strategy. Finally, on June 18, at a meeting in the White House, they presented the alternatives to President Truman. Also present (according to the minutes) were Secretary of War Stimson, Secretary of the Navy James V. Forrestal, and Assistant Secretary of War McCloy.[35]

General Marshall presented the case for invasion and carried his colleagues with him, although both Admirals Leahy and King later declared they did not favor the plan. After considerable discussion of casualties and of the difficulties ahead, President Truman made his decision. Kyushu would be invaded in November as planned and preparations for the landing were to be pushed through to completion. Preparations for the Honshu assault would continue, but no final decision would be made until preparations had reached the point "beyond which there would not be opportunity for a free choice." [36] The program thus approved by Truman called for:

1. Air bombardment and blockade of Japan from bases in Okinawa, Iwo Jima, the Marianas, and the Philippines.

2. Assault of Kyushu on November 1, 1945, and intensification of blockade and air bombardment.

3. Invasion of the industrial heart of Japan through the Tokyo Plain in central Honshu, tentative target date March 1, 1946.[37]

During the White House meeting of June 18, there was discussion of the possibility of ending the war by political means. The President displayed a deep interest in the subject and both Stimson and McCloy emphasized the importance of the "large submerged class in Japan who do not favor the present war and whose full opinion and influence had never yet been felt." [38] There was discussion also of the atomic bomb, since everyone present knew about the bomb and the recommendations of the Interim Committee. The suggestion was made that before the bomb was dropped, the Japanese should be warned that the United States had such a weapon. "Not one of the Chiefs nor the Secretary," recalled McCloy, "thought well of a bomb warning, an effective argument being that no one could be certain, in spite of the assurances of the scientists, that the 'thing would go off.' " [39]

Though the defeat of the enemy's armed forces in the Japanese homeland was considered a prerequisite to Japan's surrender, it did not follow that Japanese forces elsewhere, especially those on the Asiatic mainland, would surrender also. It was to provide for just this contingency, as well as to pin down those forces during the invasion of the home islands, that the Joint Chiefs had recommended Soviet entry into the war against Japan.

Soviet participation was a goal long pursued by the Americans.[40] Both political and military authorities seem to have been convinced from the start that Soviet assistance, conceived in various ways, would shorten the war and lessen the cost. In October 1943, Marshal Stalin had told Secretary of State Cordell Hull then in Moscow for a conference, that the Soviet Union would eventually declare war on Japan. At the Tehran Conference in November-December of that year, Stalin had given the Allies formal notice of this intention and reaffirmed it in October 1944. In February 1945, at the Yalta Conference, Roosevelt and Stalin had agreed on the terms of Soviet participation in the Far Eastern war. Thus, by June 1945, the Americans could look forward to Soviet intervention at a date estimated as three months after the defeat of Germany.

But by the summer of 1945 the Americans had undergone a change of heart. Though the official position of the War Department still held that "Russian entry will have a profound military effect in that almost certainly it will materially shorten the war and thus save American lives," [41] few responsible American officials were eager for Soviet intervention or as willing to make concessions as they had been at an earlier period.[42] What had once appeared extremely desirable appeared less so now that the war in Europe was over and Japan virtually defeated. President Truman, one official recalled, stated during a meeting devoted to the question of Soviet policy that agreements with Stalin had up to that time been "a one-way street" and that "he intended thereafter to be firm in his dealings with the Russians." [43] And at the June 18 meeting of the Joint Chiefs of Staff with the President, Admiral King had declared that "regardless of the desirability of the Russians entering the war, they were not indispensable and he did not think we should go as far as to beg them to come in." [44] Though the cost would be greater, he had no doubt "we could handle it alone."

The failure of the Soviets to abide by certain agreements made at Yalta had also done much to discourage the American desire for further cooperation with them. But after urging Stalin for three years to declare war on Japan, the United States Government could hardly ask him now to remain neutral. Moreover, there was no way of keeping the Russians out even if there had been a will to do so. In Harriman's view, "Russia would come into the war regardless of what we might do." [45]

A further difficulty was that Allied intelligence still indicated that Soviet intervention would be desirable, if not necessary, for the success of the invasion strategy. In Allied intelligence, Japan was portrayed as a defeated nation whose military leaders were blind to defeat. Though her industries had been seriously crippled by air bombardment and naval blockade and her armed forces were critically deficient in many of the resources of war, Japan was still far from surrender. She had ample reserves of weapons and ammunition and an army of 5,000,000 troops, 2,000,000 of them in the home islands. The latter could be expected to put up a strong resistance to invasion. In the opinion of the intelligence experts, neither blockade nor bombing alone would produce unconditional surrender before the date set for invasion. And the invasion itself, they believed, would be costly and possibly prolonged.[46]

According to these intelligence reports, the Japanese leaders were fully aware of their desperate situation but would continue to fight in the hope of avoiding complete defeat by securing a better bargaining position. Allied war-weariness and disunity, or some miracle, they hoped, would offer them a way out. "The Japanese believe," declared an intelligence estimate of June 30, "that unconditional surrender would be the equivalent of national extinction, and there are as yet no indications that they are ready to accept such terms." [47] It appeared also to the intelligence experts that Japan might surrender at any time "depending upon the conditions of surrender" the Allies might offer. Clearly these conditions, to have any chance of acceptance, would have to include retention of the imperial system.[48]

How accurate were these estimates? Judging from postwar accounts of Japan, they were very close to the truth. Since the defeat at Saipan in July 1944, when Prime Minister Tojo had been forced to resign, the strength of the peace party had been increasing. In September 1944, the Swedish Minister in Tokyo had been approached unofficially, presumably in the name of Prince Konoye, to sound out the Allies on terms of peace. This overture came to naught, as did another the following March. But the Swedish Minister did learn that those who advocated peace in Japan regarded the Allied demand for unconditional surrender as their greatest obstacle.[49]

The Suzuki Cabinet that came into power in April 1945 had an unspoken mandate from the Emperor to end the war as quickly as possible. But it was faced immediately with an additional problem when the Soviet Government announced it would not renew the neutrality pact after April 1946. The German surrender in May produced another crisis in the Japanese Government and led, after considerable discussion, to a decision to seek Soviet mediation. But the first approach, made on June 3 to Jacob Malik, the Soviet Ambassador, produced no results. Malik was noncommittal and merely said the problem needed further study.[50]

At the end of June, the Japanese finally approached the Soviet Government directly through Ambassador Sato in Moscow, asking that it mediate with the Allies to bring the Far Eastern war to an end. In a series of messages between Tokyo and Moscow, which the Americans intercepted and decoded, the Japanese Foreign Office outlined the position of the government and instructed Ambassador Sato to make arrangements for a special envoy from the Emperor who would be empowered to make terms for Soviet mediation. Unconditional surrender, he was told, was completely unacceptable, and time was of the essence. But the Russians, on one pretext and another, delayed their answer until mid-July when Stalin and Molotov left for Potsdam. Thus, the Japanese Government had by then accepted defeat and was seeking desperately for a way out; but it was not willing even at this late date to surrender unconditionally and would accept no terms that did not include the preservation of the imperial system.

Allied intelligence had estimated the situation in Japan correctly. Allied invasion strategy had been re-examined and confirmed in mid-June and the date for the invasion fixed. The desirability of Soviet assistance had been confirmed also and plans for Russian entry into the war during August could now be made. No decision had been reached on the use of the atomic bomb, but the President's advisers had recommended it. The decision was the President's and he faced it squarely. But before he could make it he would want to know whether the measures already agreed upon would produce unconditional surrender at the earliest moment and at the lowest cost. If they would not, then he would have to decide whether circumstances warranted employment of a bomb that Stimson had already labeled as "the most terrible weapon ever known in human history."

Though responsibility for the decision to use the atomic bomb was the President's, he exercised it only after careful study of the recommendations of his senior advisers. Chief among these was the Secretary of War, under whose broad supervision the Manhattan Project had been placed. Already deeply concerned over the cost of the projected invasion, the political effects of Soviet intervention, and the potential consequences of the use of the atomic bomb, Stimson sought a course that would avoid all these evils. The difficulty, as he saw it, lay in the requirement for unconditional surrender. It was a phrase that might make the Japanese desperate and lead to a long and unnecessary campaign of attrition that would be extremely costly to both sides.[51] But there was no way of getting around the term; it was firmly rooted in Allied war aims and its renunciation was certain to lead to charges of appeasement.

But if this difficulty could be overcome, would the Japanese respond if terms were offered? The intelligence experts thought so, and the radio intercepts from Tokyo to Moscow bore them out.[52] So far as the Army was concerned there was much to be gained by such a course. Not only might it reduce the enormous cost of the war, but it would also make possible a settlement in the western Pacific "before too many of our allies are committed there and have made substantial contributions toward the defeat of Japan."[53] In the view of the War Department, these aims justified "any concessions which might be attractive to the Japanese, so long as our realistic aims for peace in the Pacific are not adversely affected."[54]

The problem was to formulate terms that would meet these conditions. There was considerable discussion of this problem in Washington in the spring of 1945 by officials in the Department of State and in the War and Navy Departments. Joseph C. Grew, Acting Secretary of State, proposed to the President late in May that he issue a proclamation urging the Japanese to surrender and assuring them that they could keep the Emperor. Though Truman did not act on the suggestion, he thought it "a sound idea" and told Grew to discuss it with his Cabinet colleagues and the Joint Chiefs. On June 18, Grew was back with the report that these groups favored the idea, but that there were differences on the timing.[55]

Grew's ideas, as well as those of others concerned, were summarized by Stimson in a long and carefully considered memorandum to the President on July 2.[56] Representing the most informed military and political estimate of the situation at this time, this memorandum constitutes a state paper of the first importance. If any one document can be said to provide the basis for the President's warning to Japan and his final decision to use the atomic bomb, this is it.

The gist of Stimson's argument was that the most promising alternative to the long and costly struggle certain to follow invasion was to warn the Japanese "of what is to come" and to give them an opportunity to surrender. There was, he thought, enough of a chance that such a course would work to make the effort worthwhile. Japan no longer had any allies, her navy was virtually destroyed, and she was increasingly vulnerable to air attack and naval blockade. Against her were arrayed the increasingly powerful forces of the Allies, with their "inexhaustible and untouched industrial resources." In these circumstances, Stimson believed the Japanese people would be susceptible to reason if properly approached. "Japan," he pointed out, "is not a nation composed of mad fanatics of an entirely different mentality from ours. On the contrary, she has within the past century shown herself to possess extremely intelligent people. . . ." But any attempt, Stimson added, "to exterminate her armies and her population by gunfire or other means will tend to produce a fusion of race solidity and antipathy. . . ."

A warning to Japan, Stimson contended, should be carefully timed. It should come before the actual invasion, before destruction had reduced the Japanese "to fanatical despair," and, if the Soviet Union had already entered the war, before the Russian attack had progressed too far.[57] It should also emphasize, Stimson believed, the inevitability and completeness of the destruction ahead and the determination of the Allies to strip Japan of her conquests and to destroy the influence of the military clique. It should be a strong warning and should leave no doubt in Japanese minds that they would have to surrender unconditionally and submit to Allied occupation.

The warning, as Stimson envisaged it, had a double character. While promising destruction and devastation, it was also to hold out hope to the Japanese if they heeded its message. In his memorandum, therefore, Stimson stressed the positive features of the warning and recommended that it include a disavowal of any intention to destroy the Japanese nation or to occupy the country permanently. Once Japan's military clique had been removed from power and her capacity to wage war destroyed, it was Stimson's belief that the Allies should withdraw and resume normal trade relations with the new and peaceful Japanese Government. "I personally think," he declared, "that if in saying this we should add that we do not exclude a constitutional monarchy under the present dynasty, it would substantially add to the chance of acceptance."

Not once in the course of this lengthy memorandum was mention made of the atomic bomb. There was no need to do so. Everyone concerned understood clearly that if the warning was unheeded the bomb was the instrument that, by its powers of destruction, would impress on the Japanese Government the hopelessness of any course but surrender. As Stimson expressed it, the atomic bomb was "the best possible sanction," the single weapon that would convince the Japanese "of our power to destroy the Empire." [58]

Though Stimson considered a warning combined with an offer of terms, which, if refused, was to be backed up by the sanction of the atomic bomb, as the most promising means of inducing surrender at any early date, there were other courses that some thought might produce the same result. One was continuation and intensification of air bombardment coupled with surface and underwater blockade. This course had already been considered and rejected as insufficient to produce surrender, though its advocates were by no means convinced that this decision was a wise one. And Stimson himself later justified the use of the bomb on the ground that by November 1 conventional bombardment would have caused greater destruction than the bomb. This apparent contradiction is explained by the fact that the atomic bomb was considered to be capable of a psychological effect entirely apart from the damage wrought.[59]

Nor did Stimson, in his memorandum, consider the effect of the Soviet Union's entry into the war. By itself, this action could not be counted on to force Japan to capitulate, but combined with bombardment and blockade it might do so. At least that was the view of Brigadier General George A. Lincoln, one of the Army's top planners, who wrote in June that "probably it will take Russian entry into the war, coupled with a landing, or imminent threat of landing, on Japan proper by us, to convince them [the Japanese] of the hopelessness of their position." [60] Why, therefore, was it not possible to issue the warning before a Soviet declaration of war against Japan and rely on that event, together with an intensified air bombardment, to produce the desired result? If together they could not secure Japan's surrender, would there not still be time to use the bomb before the scheduled invasion of Kyushu in November? [61]

No final answer to this question is possible with the evidence at hand. But one cannot ignore the fact that some responsible officials feared the political consequences of Soviet intervention and hoped that ultimately it would prove unnecessary. This feeling may unconsciously have made the atom bomb solution more acceptable than it might otherwise have been.[62] Some officials may have believed, too, that the bomb could be used as a powerful deterrent to Soviet expansion in Europe, where the Red tide had successively engulfed Rumania, Bulgaria, Yugoslavia, Czechoslovakia, and Hungary. In an interview with three of the top scientists in the Manhattan Project early in June, Byrnes did not, according to Leo Szilard, a physicist at the Chicago laboratory, argue that the bomb was needed to defeat Japan, but rather that it should be dropped to "make Russia more manageable in Europe." [63]

It has been asserted also that the desire to justify the expenditure of the two billion dollars spent on the Manhattan Project may have disposed some favorably toward the use of the bomb. Already questions had been asked in Congress,[64] and the end of the war would almost certainly bring on a full-scale investigation. What more striking justification of the Manhattan Project than a new weapon that had ended the war in one sudden blow and saved countless American lives? "It was my reaction," wrote Admiral Leahy, "that the scientists and others wanted to make this test because of the vast sums that had been spent on the project. Truman knew that, and so did other people involved." [65]

This explanation hardly does credit to those involved in the Manhattan Project, and not even the British physicist P. M. S. Blackett, one of the severest critics of the decision to use the bomb, accepted it. "The wit of man," he declared, "could hardly devise a theory of the dropping of the bomb, both more insulting to the American people, or more likely to lead to an energetically pursued Soviet defense policy." [66]

But even if the need to justify these huge expenditures is discounted —and certainly by itself it could not have produced the decision— the question still remains whether those who held in their hands a weapon thought capable of ending the war in one stroke could justify withholding that weapon. Would they not be open to criticism for failing to use every means at their disposal to defeat the enemy as quickly as possible, thereby saving many American lives?

And even at that time there were some who believed that the new weapon would ultimately prove the most effective deterrent to war yet produced. How better to outlaw war forever than to demonstrate the tremendous destructive power of this weapon by using it against an actual target?

By early July 1945 the stage had been set for the final decision, Stimson's memorandum had been approved in principle and on July 4 the British had given their consent to the use of the bomb against Japan.[67] It remained only to decide on the terms and timing of the warning. This was the situation when the Potsdam Conference opened on July 17, one day after the bomb had been successfully exploded in a spectacular demonstration at Alamogordo, New Mexico. The atomic bomb was a reality and when the news reached Potsdam it aroused great excitement among those who were let in on the secret. Instead of the prospect of long and bitter months of fighting the Japanese, there was now a vision, "fair and bright indeed it seemed" to Churchill, "of the end of the whole war in one or two violent shocks." [68]

President Truman's first action was to call together his chief advisers—Byrnes, Stimson, Leahy, Marshall, King, and Arnold (Air Force General Henry H. Arnold). "I asked for their opinion whether the bomb should be used," he later wrote. The consensus was that it should.[69] Here at last was the miracle to end the war and solve all the perplexing problems posed by the necessity for invasion. But because no one could tell what effect the bomb might have "physically or psychologically," it was decided to proceed with the military plans for the invasion.

No one at this time, or later in the conference, raised the question of whether the Japanese should be informed of the existence of the bomb. That question, it will be recalled, had been discussed by the Scientific Panel on June 16 and at the White House meeting with the Joint Chiefs of Staff, the War and Navy Secretaries, and McCloy on June 18. For a variety of reasons, including uncertainty as to whether the bomb would work, it had been decided that the Japanese should not be warned of the existence of the new weapon. The successful explosion of the first bomb on July 17 did not apparently outweigh the reasons advanced earlier for keeping the bomb a secret; and evidently none of the men involved thought the question needed to be reviewed. The Japanese would learn of the atomic bomb only when it was dropped on them.

The secrecy that had shrouded the development of the atomic bomb was torn aside briefly at Potsdam, but with no visible effect. On July 24, at the suggestion of his chief advisers, Truman informed Marshal Stalin "casually" that the Americans had "a new weapon of unusual destructive force." "The Russian Premier," he recalled, "showed no special interest. All he said was that he was glad to hear it and hoped we would make 'good use of it against the Japanese.' " [70] One cannot but wonder whether the Marshal was preoccupied at the moment or simulating a lack of interest.

On the military side, the Potsdam Conference developed nothing new. The plans already made were noted and approved. Even at this late stage the question of the bomb was divorced entirely from military plans and the final report of the conference accepted as the main effort the invasion of the Japanese home islands. November 15, 1946, was accepted as the planning date for the end of the war against Japan. [71]

During the conference, Stalin told Truman about the Japanese overtures—information that the Americans already had. The Marshal spoke of the matter also to Churchill, who discussed it with Truman, suggesting cautiously that some offer be made to Japan. "Mr. Stimson, General Marshall, and the President," he later wrote, "were evidently searching their hearts, and we had no need to press them. We knew of course that the Japanese were ready to give up all conquests made in the war." That same night, after dining with Stalin and Truman, the Prime Minister wrote that the Russians intended to attack Japan soon after August 8—perhaps within two weeks of that date. [72] Truman presumably received the same information, confirming his special assistant's, Harry Hopkins', report of his conversation with Stalin in Moscow in May. [73]

All that remained now was to warn Japan and give her an opportunity to surrender before using the bomb. In this matter Stimson's and Grew's views, as outlined in the memorandum of July 2, were accepted, but apparently on the advice of the former Secretary of State Cordell Hull it was decided to omit any reference to the Emperor. [74] Hull's view, solicited by Byrnes, newly appointed Secretary of State, before his departure for Potsdam, was that the proposal smacked of appeasement and "seemed to guarantee continuance not only of the Emperor but also of the feudal privileges of a ruling caste." And, should the Japanese reject the warning, the proposal to retain the imperial system might well encourage resistance and have "terrible political repercussions" in the United States. For these reasons he recommended that no statement about the Emperor be made until "the climax of Allied bombing and Russia's entry into the war." [75] Thus, the final terms offered to the Japanese in the Potsdam Declaration on July 26 made no mention of the Emperor or of the imperial system. Neither did the declaration contain any reference to the atom bomb but simply warned the Japanese of the consequences of continued resistance.[76] Only those already familiar with the weapon could have read the references to inevitable and complete destruction as a warning of atomic warfare.[77]

The receipt of the Potsdam Declaration in Japan led to frantic meetings to decide what should be done. It was finally decided not to reject the note but to await the results of the Soviet overture. At this point, the military insisted that the government make some statement to the people, and on July 28 Premier Suzuki declared to the press that Japan would ignore the declaration, a statement that was interpreted by the Allies as a rejection.[78]

To the Americans, the rejection of the Potsdam Declaration confirmed the view that the military clique was still in control of Japan and that only a decisive act of violence could remove it. The instrument for such action lay at hand in the atomic bomb; events now seemed to justify its use. But in the hope that the Japanese might still change their minds, Truman held off orders on the use of the bomb for a few days. Only silence came from Tokyo, for the Japanese were waiting for a reply from the Soviet Government, which would not come until the return of Stalin and Molotov from Potsdam on August 6. Prophetically, Foreign Minister Togo wrote Ambassador Sato on August 2, the day the Potsdam Conference ended, that he could not afford to lose a single day in his efforts to conclude arrangements with the Russians "if we were to end the war before the assault on our mainland." [79] By that time, President Truman had already decided on the use of the bomb.

Preparations for dropping the two atomic bombs produced thus far had been under way for some time. The components of the bombs had been sent by cruiser to Tinian in May and the fissionable material was flown out in mid-July. The B-29's and crews were ready and trained, standing by for orders, which would come through the Commanding General, U.S. Army Strategic Air Forces in the Pacific, Lieutenant General Carl A. Spaatz. Detailed arrangements and schedules were completed and all that was necessary was to issue orders.[80]

At General Arnold's insistence, the responsibility for selecting the particular target and fixing the exact date and hour of the attack was assigned to the field commander, General Spaatz. In orders issued on July 25 and approved by Stimson and Marshall, Spaatz was ordered to drop the "first special bomb as soon as weather will permit visual bombing after about 3 August 1945 on one of the targets: Hiroshima, Kokura, Niigata, and Nagasaki." He was instructed also to deliver a copy of this order personally to MacArthur and Admiral Chester Nimitz, naval commander in the Pacific. Weather was the critical factor because the bomb had to be dropped by visual means, and Spaatz delegated to his chief of staff, Major General Curtis E. LeMay, the job of deciding when the weather was right for this most important mission.

From the dating of the order to General Spaatz, it has been argued that President Truman was certain the warning would be rejected and had fixed the date for the bombing of Hiroshima even before the issuance of the Potsdam Declaration.[81] But such an argument ignored the military necessities. For operational reasons, the orders had to be issued in sufficient time "to set the military wheels in motion." In a sense, therefore, the decision was made on July 25. It would stand unless the President changed his mind. "I had made the decision," wrote Truman in 1955. "I also instructed Stimson that the order would stand unless I notified him that the Japanese reply to our ultimatum was acceptable." [82] The rejection by the Japanese of the Potsdam Declaration confirmed the orders Spaatz had already received.

On Tinian and Guam in the Marianas, preparations for dropping the bomb had been completed by August 3. The original plan was to carry out the operation on August 4, but General LeMay deferred the attack because of bad weather over the target. On August 5 the forecasts were favorable, and he gave the word to proceed with the mission the following day. At 2:45 A.M. on August 6, the bomb-carrying plane was airborne. Six and a half hours later the bomb was released over Hiroshima, Japan's eighth largest city, to explode fifty seconds later at a height of about 2,000 feet. The age of atomic warfare had opened.*

---

* Two other dates can be said to have opened the atomic age: December 2, 1942, when Enrico Fermi, in the Chicago laboratory, succeeded in establish-

Aboard the cruiser *Augusta* on his way back to the United States from the Potsdam Conference, President Truman received the news by radio. That same day, a previously prepared release from Washington announced to the world that an atomic bomb had been dropped on Hiroshima and warned the Japanese that if they did not surrender they could expect "a rain of ruin from the air, the like of which has never been seen on this earth." [83]

On August 7, Ambassador Sato in Moscow received word at last that Molotov would see him the next afternoon. At the appointed hour he arrived at the Kremlin, full of hope that he would receive a favorable reply to the Japanese proposal for Soviet mediation with the Allies to end the war. Instead he was handed the Soviet declaration of war, effective on August 9.[84] Thus, three months to the day after Germany's surrender, Marshal Stalin had lived up to his promise to the Allies.

Meanwhile, President Truman had authorized the use of the second bomb—the last then available. The objective was Kokura, the date August 9. But the plane carrying the bomb failed to make its run over the primary target and hit the secondary target, Nagasaki, instead.[85] The next day Japan sued for peace.

The close sequence of events between August 6 and 10, combined with the fact that the bomb was dropped almost three months before the scheduled invasion of Kyushu and while the Japanese were trying desperately to get out of the war, has suggested to some that the bombing of Hiroshima had a deeper purpose than the desire to end the war quickly. This purpose, it is claimed, was nothing less than a desire to forestall Soviet intervention in the Far Eastern war. Else why this necessity for speed? Certainly nothing in the military situation seemed to call for such hasty action. But if the purpose was to forestall Soviet intervention, then there was every reason for speed. And even if the Russians could not be kept out of the war, at least they would be prevented from making more than a token contribution to victory over Japan. In this sense, it may be argued that the bomb proved a success, for the war ended with the United States in full control of Japan.[86]

This theory leaves several matters unexplained. In the first place, the Americans did not know the exact date on which the Soviet Union would declare war but believed it would be within a week or two of August 8. If they had wished to forestall a Soviet declaration of

ing a chain reaction; and July 16, 1945, when the test bomb was exploded in New Mexico.

war, then they could reasonably have been expected to act sooner than they did. Such close timing left little if any margin for error. Secondly, had the United States desired above everything else to keep the Russians out, it could have responded to one of the several unofficial Japanese overtures, or made the Potsdam Declaration more attractive to Japan. Certainly the failure to put a time limit on the Declaration suggests that speed was not of the essence in American calculations. Finally, the date and time of the bombing were left to Generals Spaatz and LeMay, who certainly had no way of knowing Soviet intentions. Bad weather or any other untoward incident could have delayed the attack a week or more.

There is reason to believe that the Russians at the last moved more quickly than they had intended. In his conversations with Harry Hopkins in Moscow in May 1945 and at Potsdam, Marshal Stalin had linked Soviet entry with negotiations then in progress with Chinese representatives in Moscow.[87] When these were completed, he had said, he would act. On August 8 these negotiations were still in progress.

Did the atomic bomb accomplish its purpose? Was it, in fact, as Stimson said, "the best possible sanction" after Japan rejected the Potsdam Declaration? The sequence of events argues strongly that it was, for bombs were dropped on August 6 and 9, and on August 10 Japan surrendered. But in the excitement over the announcement of the first use of an atomic bomb and then of Japan's surrender, many overlooked the significance of the Soviet Union's entry into the war on August 9. The first bomb had produced consternation and confusion among the leaders of Japan, but no disposition to surrender. The Soviet declaration of war, though not entirely unexpected, was a devastating blow and, by removing all hope of Soviet mediation, gave the advocates of peace their first opportunity to come boldly out into the open. When Premier Suzuki arrived at the Palace on the morning of the 9th, he was told that the Emperor believed Japan's only course now was to accept the Potsdam Declaration. The militarists could and did minimize the effects of the bomb, but they could not evade the obvious consequences of Soviet intervention, which ended all hope of dividing their enemies and securing softer peace terms.[88]

In this atmosphere, the leaders of Japan held a series of meetings on August 9 but were unable to come to an agreement. In the morning came word of the fate of Nagasaki. This additional disaster failed to resolve the issues between the military and those who advocated surrender. Finally the Emperor took the unprecedented step of calling an Imperial Conference, which lasted until 3 o'clock the next morning. When it, too, failed to produce agreement, the Emperor told his minister that he wished the war brought to an end. The constitutional significance of this action is difficult for Westerners to comprehend, but it resolved the crisis and produced in the Cabinet a formal decision to accept the Potsdam Declaration, provided it did not prejudice the position of the Emperor.

What finally forced the Japanese to surrender? Was it air bombardment, naval power, the atomic bomb, or Soviet entry? The United States Strategic Bombing Survey concluded that Japan would have surrendered by the end of the year, without invasion and without the atomic bomb.[89] Other equally informed opinion maintained that it was the atomic bomb that forced Japan to surrender. "Without its use," Dr. Compton asserted, "the war would have continued for many months." [90] Admiral Nimitz believed firmly that the decisive factor was "the complete impunity with which the Pacific Fleet pounded Japan," and General Arnold claimed it was air bombardment that had brought Japan to the verge of collapse.[91] But Major General Claire L. Chennault, wartime air commander in China, maintained that Soviet entry into the Far Eastern war brought about the surrender of Japan and would have done so "even if no atomic bombs had been dropped." [92]

It would be a fruitless task to weigh accurately the relative importance of all the factors leading to the Japanese surrender. There is no doubt that Japan had been defeated by the summer of 1945, if not earlier. But defeat did not mean that the military clique had given up; the Army intended to fight on and had made elaborate preparations for the defense of the homeland. Whether air bombardment and naval blockade or the threat of invasion would have produced an early surrender and averted the heavy losses almost certain to accompany the actual landings in Japan is a moot question. Certainly they had a profound effect on the Japanese position. It is equally difficult to assert categorically that the atomic bomb alone or Soviet intervention alone was the decisive factor in bringing the war to an end. All that can be said on the available evidence is that Japan was defeated in the military sense by August 1945 and that the bombing of Hiroshima, followed by the Soviet Union's declaration of war and the bombing of Nagasaki and the threat of still further bombing, acted as catalytic agents to produce the Japanese decision to surrender. Together they created so extreme a crisis that the Emperor himself, in an unprecedented move, took matters into his own hands and ordered his ministers to surrender. Whether any other set of circumstances would have resolved the crisis and produced the final decision to surrender is a question history cannot yet answer.

Biographies

MARTIN BLUMENSON, Historian with OCMH since 1952. M.A., Bucknell University; M.A., Harvard University. Instructor: U.S. Merchant Marine Academy; Hofstra College. Historical Officer, European Theater, World War II; Commanding Officer, 3rd Historical Detachment, Korean War; Historian, Joint Task Force SEVEN. Bronze Star Medal, Commendation Ribbon. Captain, USAR. Author: *Breakout and Pursuit* and *Salerno to Cassino* (in preparation), in *United States Army in World War II; Special Problems of the Korean Conflict* (Washington, 1952); *Operation* REDWING: *The Atomic Weapons Tests in the Pacific, 1956* (Washington, 1957); and numerous articles in military and historical journals.

ROBERT W. COAKLEY, Historian with OCMH since 1948. William and Mary College, University of Virginia, Ph.D. Taught: University of Virginia, Tulane University, University of Arkansas, Fairmont State College. Historian, Headquarters, European Theater of Operations, U.S. Army, and U.S. Forces, European Theater, 1945-46. Coauthor: *Global Logistics and Strategy, 1940-1943* (Washington, 1955) and *Global Logistics and Strategy, 1943-1945* (in preparation), in *United States Army in World War II.*

STETSON CONN, Historian with OCMH since 1946. Ph.D. in history, Yale University. Taught: Yale University, Amherst College, and The George Washington University. Author: *Gibraltar in British Diplomacy in the Eighteenth Century* (New Haven, 1942). Coauthor: *The Framework of Hemisphere Defense* and *Guarding the United States and Its Outposts,* to be published in *United States Army in World War II.*

RICHARD M. LEIGHTON, Historian with OCMH since 1948. Harvard University, University of Cincinnati, Cornell University, Ph.D. Taught: Brooklyn College, University of Cincinnati, The George Washington University. Historical Officer, Headquarters, Army Service Forces, 1943-46. Coauthor: *Global Logistics and Strategy, 1940-1943* (Washington, 1955) and *Global Logistics and Strategy, 1943-1945* (in preparation), in *United States Army in World War II.*

CHARLES V. P. VON LUTTICHAU, Historian with OCMH since 1951. Graduate student, Universities of Berlin and Munich; M.A., American University. Lecturer: Army War College. German Air Force, World War II.

411

Author: Narratives in support of volumes in *United States Army in World War II;* various articles in military journals.

CHARLES B. MacDONALD, Historian with OCMH since 1948. B.A., Presbyterian College; Secretary of the Army Fellowship, 1957-58. Rifle company commander, European theater, World War II. Silver Star, Bronze Star, Purple Heart. Author: *Company Commander* (Washington, 1947); *The Siegfried Line Campaign* (in preparation); and (coauthor) *Three Battles* (Washington, 1952), in *United States Army in World War II.*

SIDNEY T. MATHEWS, Staff Member, Johns Hopkins Operations Research Office. Ph.D. in history, The Johns Hopkins University. Taught: University of Richmond. Lecturer: Army War College, Senior Marine Corps School. Combat Historian, Fifth U.S. Army in Italy, World War II. Captain, USAR. Historian, OCMH, 1947-52. Author: "Santa Maria Infante," *Small Unit Actions* in *American Forces in Action* (Washington, 1946); "Altuzzo," *Three Battles* (Washington, 1952) and *The Drive on Rome* (in preparation), in *United States Army in World War II.*

MAURICE MATLOFF, Historian with OCMH since 1947. Graduate fellow, Ph.D. in history, Harvard University. Taught: Brooklyn College, University of Maryland. Lecturer: Naval War College, Army War College. Member of the American Historical Association's Committee on the Historian and the Federal Government. U.S. Air Forces, World War II. Coauthor: *Strategic Planning for Coalition Warfare, 1941-1942* (Washington, 1953), and author: *Strategic Planning for Coalition Warfare, 1943-1944* (in preparation), in *United States Army in World War II;* and numerous articles and reviews in military and historical journals.

RALPH S. MAVROGORDATO, Staff Member, Special Operations Research Office, American University. B.A., Bucknell University; graduate study in political science and history, Duke University; staff member, Bureau of Applied Social Research, Columbia University. U.S. Army Medical Corps, World War II; Intelligence Analyst, G-2, Headquarters, U.S. Forces in Austria, 1948-51. Historian, OCMH, 1955-58. Author: Narratives in support of volumes in *United States Army in World War II.*

LEO J. MEYER, Historian with OCMH since 1948. B.A., M.A., Wesleyan University; Ph.D., Clark University. Taught: Clark University, Worcester Polytechnical Institute, New York University. Deputy Chief Historian, OCMH. Troop Movement Officer, New York Port of Embarkation; Chief of Movements, G-4 European theater; Commanding Officer, 14th Major Port, Southampton, England; Secretariat, Transportation Board. Legion of Merit, Bronze Star, O.B.E. Colonel, TC (Ret.). Author: *Relations Between the United States and Cuba, 1898-1917* (Worcester, 1928); articles in *Encyclopedia Americana, Encyclopaedia Britannica, Dictionary of American Biography, Dictionary of American History,* and various professional journals. Coauthor: *The Strategic and Logistical History of the Mediterranean Theater of Operations,* to be published in *United States Army in World War II.*

JOHN MILLER, Jr., Historian with OCMH since 1945. Ph.D., University of Iowa. Taught: University of Omaha; University of Iowa; Graduate School, U.S. Department of Agriculture; American University. U.S. Marine Corps, Pacific Theater, in World War II. Author: *Guadalcanal: The First Offensive* (Washington, 1949) and *Cartwheel: The Reduction of Rabaul* (in press), in *United States Army in World War II*. Coauthor: *Korea 1951-1953* (Washington, 1956); *Combat in Korea,* Volume II, to be published in *United States Army in the Conflict with the Communist Powers.*

LOUIS MORTON, Historian with OCMH since 1945. Ph.D., Duke University. Lieutenant Colonel, USAR. Author: *Robert Carter of Nomini Hall* (Princeton, 1941); *The Fall of the Philippines* (Washington, 1953), *Strategy and Command: Turning the Tide, 1941-1943* (in preparation), (coauthor) *Strategy and Command: The Road to Victory, 1943-1945* (in preparation), in *United States Army in World War II;* numerous articles in military and historical journals; and lectures at National War College, Army War College, and various Service schools and universities.

FORREST C. POGUE, Director, George C. Marshall Research Center. Ph.D. in history, Clark University; American Exchange Fellow, Paris, 1937-38. Taught: Murray State Teachers College. Combat historian with the First U.S. Army, World War II. Croix de Guerre. Historian, OCMH, 1947-52. Author: *The Supreme Command* (Washington, 1954), in *United States Army in World War II.*

ROLAND G. RUPPENTHAL, Staff Member, Johns Hopkins Operations Research Office. Ph.D. in history, University of Wisconsin. Taught: Akron University, Albert Lea, Jr., College. Historical Officer and assistant theater historian, European Theater, World War II. Lieutenant Colonel, USAR. Historian, OCMH, 1947-53. Author: *Utah Beach to Cherbourg* (Washington, 1948), in *American Forces in Action; Logistical Support of the Armies,* Vol. I (Washington, 1953), and *Logistical Support of the Armies,* Vol. II (in preparation), in *United States Army in World War II.*

ROBERT ROSS SMITH, Historian with OCMH since 1947. B.A. and M.A. in history, Duke University. Historical Officer, General Headquarters, Southwest Pacific Area and U.S. Army Forces, Pacific, World War II. Major, Infantry, USAR. Author: *The Approach to the Philippines* (Washington, 1953), *Triumph in the Philippines* (in preparation), and *Southern France and Alsace* (in preparation), in *United States Army in World War II.*

EARL F. ZIEMKE, Historian with OCMH since 1955. B.A., M.A., and Ph.D. in history, University of Wisconsin; staff member, Bureau of Applied Social Research, Columbia University. U.S. Marine Corps, World War II. Author: *The German Northern Theater of War, 1940-1945* (in preparation), Foreign Studies series, OCMH.

Footnotes

CHAPTER 1

[1] In preparing this essay the author has relied principally on the official records found in the Army's files and has cited these wherever applicable. But he owes a large debt also to his colleagues in the Office, Chief of Military History, who have studied these events in their own works, and to many others who have dealt with this complex subject in whole or in part. Among the volumes in the *United States Army in World War II* that should be consulted in connection with the present study are: Stetson Conn and Byron Fairchild, *The Framework of Hemisphere Defense* (in press); Richard M. Leighton and Robert W. Coakley, *Global Logistics and Strategy, 1940-1943* (Washington, 1956); Maurice Matloff and Edwin M. Snell, *Strategic Planning for Coalition Warfare, 1941-1942* (Washington, 1953); Louis Morton, *The Pacific War: Strategy and Command,* Vol. I (in preparation); Mark Skinner Watson, *Chief of Staff: Prewar Plans and Preparations* (1950). The official British volume by J. R. M. Butler, *Grand Strategy,* Vol. II: *September 1939-June 1941,* is also useful, as are the semiofficial volumes of Samuel Eliot Morison's *History of United States Naval Operations in World War II,* Vol. III: *The Rising Sun in the Pacific, 1931-April 1942* (Boston: Little, Brown, 1948), and Vol. I: *The Battle of the Atlantic, September 1939-May 1943* (Boston: Little, Brown, 1947). The two volumes of William L. Langer and S. Everett Gleason, *The Challenge to Isolation* (New York: Harper, 1952) and *The Undeclared War* (New York: Harper, 1953), though not official, are based on a thorough study of the State Department records and are an indispensable source for a study of American policy in this period. The reader may also wish to consult a work written from the revisionist point of view, the best statement of which can be found in Charles A. Beard, *President Roosevelt and the Coming of the War, 1941* (New Haven: Yale University Press, 1948). Among the most important sources for the present study is the memoir and biographical literature of the period, valuable as a supplement to the official records. Most useful are Winston Churchill, *Their Finest Hour* (Boston: Houghton Mifflin, 1949) and *The Grand Alliance* (Boston: Houghton Mifflin, 1950); Cordell Hull, *The Memoirs of Cordell Hull,* 2 vols. (New York: Macmillan, 1948); Robert E. Sherwood, *Roosevelt and Hopkins: An Intimate History* (New York: Harper, 1948); and Henry L. Stimson and McGeorge Bundy, *On Active Service in Peace and War* (New York: Harper, 1948). These works represent only a small portion of those that may be used with profit, but they should serve as the basis for further investigation into this complex subject.

[2] Joint Army-Navy Basic War Plan ORANGE, 1924, Joint Board (JB) 325, Ser. 228. After numerous drafts, the plan was completed and approved by the Joint Board and the Secretary of the Navy in August 1924 and by the Secretary of War the following month. The Preliminary Estimates of the Situation, Joint War Plan ORANGE, and other relevant studies are filed in War Plans Division (WPD) 368; JB 325, Ser. 207; JB 305, Sers. 208 and 209; General Board 425, Ser. 1136.

[3] Proposed Joint Estimate and Plan—RED-ORANGE, prepared in WPD (Army) and approved by Chief of Staff, 3 June 1930 as basis for joint plan, G-3 Obsolete Plans, Reg. Doc. 245-C. Additional material on RED-ORANGE may be found in same file 245-A through F and in WPD 3202. No joint plan was ever approved.

[4] In 1923, the Army draft of RED-ORANGE started with the statement, "Under existing conditions a coalition of RED and ORANGE is unlikely," and twelve years later the Director of Naval Intelligence, commenting on another draft plan, stated that a RED-ORANGE combination was "highly improbable" in the next decade, if at all. Army Draft RED-ORANGE, 1923, Reg. Doc. 245-F; Ltr, Director ONI to Director WPD, 27 Jun 35, sub: Joint Estimate of Situation, RED-ORANGE, copy in WPD 3202. By 1935, planning for such a war had virtually ended.

[5] Memos, JB for JPC, 10 Nov 37, sub: Joint Basic War Plan ORANGE, JB 325, Ser. 617, and Col S. D. Embick for WPD, 3 Nov 37, same sub, AG 225.

[6] Ltrs, Army and Navy Members JPC to JB, 28 and 30 Nov 37, sub: Joint Basic War Plan ORANGE, JB 325, Ser. 617; the Army plan is in Appendix A, the Navy's in Appendix B. See also Draft Memo, Col W. J. Krueger, 22 Nov 37, sub: Some Thoughts on Joint War Plans, AG 225.

[7] Directive, JB to JPC, 7 Dec 37, sub: Joint Basic War Plan ORANGE, JB 325, Ser. 618.

[8] Joint Basic War Plan ORANGE, 21 Feb 38, JB 325, Ser. 618. The plan was approved by the Secretary of the Navy on February 26 and by the Secretary of War two days later.

[9] For an account of the Staff Conversations in London early in 1938, see Pearl Harbor Report, Part 9, pages 4,272-78, and Capt. Tracy B. Kittredge, U.S.-British Naval Cooperation, 1939-1945, Section I, Part C. pp. 37-38.

[10] Min, JB Mtg, 9 Nov 38.

[11] Min, JB Mtg, 6 May 39; Ltr, JPC Rpt, Exploratory Studies, 21 Apr 39, JB 325, Ser. 634. The discussion of the report is based on the Exploratory Studies and related papers in the same file.

[12] The first directive of the Joint Board was dated May 11, 1939, but on further study was revised and amended instructions issued on June 30. Min, JB Mtgs, 6 May and 30 Jun 39, JB 325, Ser. 634; Ltrs, JB to JPC, 11 May 39, sub: Joint Army and Navy Basic War Plans, RAINBOWS 1, 2, 3, and 4; JPC to JB, 23 Jun 39 same sub; and JB to JPC, 30 Jun 39, same sub, all in JB 325, Ser. 642 and 642-1.

[13] Kittredge, U.S.-British Naval Cooperation, Sec. I, Part D, Notes, pp. 42-46; Memo, JPC to JB, 23 Jun 39; Min, JB Mtg, 30 Jun 39, JB 325, Ser. 642.

[14] Joint War Plan RAINBOW 1, JB 325, Ser. 642-1. Approved by the Joint Board on August 9, 1939, by the Secretary of War and Secretary of Navy on August 14, and by the President orally two months later.

[15] Military Order, 5 Jul 39; Memo of Secy JB, 20 Jul 39. JB 346, Ser. 646.

[16] The various drafts of RAINBOW 2 can be found in the Army files of the JPC, JB 325, Ser. 642-2.

[17] Memos, WPD for CofS, 22 May 40, sub: National Strategic Decisions, and

CofS for WPD, 23 May 40, no sub: *Aide-Mémoire,* Maj M. B. Ridgway, 23 May 40, all in WPD 4175-10.

[18] Ltr, JPC to JB, 31 May 40, sub: Joint Army and Navy Basic War Plan— RAINBOW 4. The Joint Board approved the plan early in June and the Secretaries soon after. It was not approved by the President until August 14. Relevant papers are in JB 325, Ser. 642-4.

[19] Joint RAINBOW 4, JB 325, Ser. 642-4.

[20] Memo, Senior Army and Navy Members JPC to Directors WPD, 16 Jun 1940, WPD 4250-3.

[21] Notes on Conference in OCS, 17 Jun 40, Misc Conf, Binder 3.

[22] Memo, WPD for CofS, 17 Jun 40, sub: National Defense Policy WPD 4250-3.

[23] The relevant papers are filed in WPD 4250-3.

[24] Memo, CofS and CNO for President, 27 Jun 40, sub: Basis for Immediate Decisions. . . . See also preliminary studies by the planners, with the President's comments, in WPD 4250-3.

[25] Stimson and Bundy, *On Active Service,* pp. 318-19.

[26] For a complete account of these developments and naval conversations, see Kittredge, U.S.-British Naval Cooperation, Section III, Parts A and B.

[27] Memo, Emmons and Strong for CofS, 22 Sep 40, sub: Observations in England, WPD 4368.

[28] Minutes of the Meetings with the British are in WPD 4402-1.

[29] Memo, WPD for CofS, 25 Sep 40, sub: Problem of Production . . . , WPD 4321-9.

[30] The message is quoted in Churchill, *Their Finest Hour,* pp. 497-98; see also p. 25.

[31] Hull, *Memoirs,* Vol. I, p. 906.

[32] Memo, Stark for Secy of Navy, 12 Nov 40, no sub. This is a revision of the original November 4 memo, no copies of which are in the Army file, revised to include the Army WPD comments and sent to the President. All papers relevant to this memo are filed in WPD 4175-15.

[33] Notes of Conference in OCS, 17 Jun 40, sub: Defense Problems, OCS Misc Conf.

[34] Ltr, CofS to JB, 18 Nov 40, sub: National Defense Policy for the United States, JB 325, Ser. 670; Memos, WPD for CofS, 13 Nov 40, sub: National Policy of the U.S.; Secy Gen Staff for WPD, same date, no sub; and CofS for Secy of War, same date, no sub, all in WPD 4175-15.

[35] Churchill, *Their Finest Hour,* pp. 690-91. The quotes are from his message of November 22, 1940, to the First Sea Lord.

[36] Ghormley to Stark, 23 Nov 40, quoted in Kittredge, U.S.-British Naval Relations, Sec. II, Part D, p. 313, and notes, App. B, Record of Admiralty Meeting, 22 Nov 40.

[37] Ltr, JPC to JB, 21 Dec 40, sub: National Defense Policy for the U.S., JB 325, Ser. 670. Earlier drafts and directives are in the same file. See also relevant papers in WPD 4175-15 and JB 325, Ser. 674.

[38] Memo, Brig Gen L. T. Gerow for CofS, 3 Jan 41, sub: Conf with Secy of State, WPD 4175-15.

[39] Memo, CofS for WPD, 17 Jan 41, sub: White House Conf of 16 Jan 41, WPD 4175-18.

[40] JPC to JB, 21 Jan 41, sub: Jt Instruction for Army and Navy Representatives . . . , JB 325, Ser. 674.

[41] Memo, FDR for Secy of Navy, 26 Jan 41, JB 325, Ser 674; Min, JB Mtg, 22 Jan 41.

42 Papers relating to the meeting are located in OPD Executive Office Files, Item 11, Executive 4, and WPD 4402-1, *passim.* The report itself is found in several files but is available in printed form in the *Pearl Harbor Attack Hearings,* Exhibit 49, Part 15, pages 1485-1542.

43 Memo, Army Delegates for CofS, 12 Feb 41, sub: Dispatch of U.S. Forces to Singapore, WPD 4402-3.

44 Ltr, CofS and CNO to Special Army and Navy Observers in London, 4 Apr 41, sub: Tentative Approval of ABC-1, WPD 4402-18. See notation on Copy 98, *Pearl Harbor Attack Hearings,* Part 15, 1485.

45 Ltr, JPC to JB, 9 Apr 40, sub: Joint Plans—RAINBOW, Approved 10 Apr, JB 325, Ser. 642-1.

46 Ltr, JPC to JB, 30 Apr 41, sub: Joint Basic War Plan—RAINBOW 5, Encl A, JB 325, Ser. 642-5.

47 Memo, WPD for CofS [May 1941], sub: Analysis of Plans for Overseas Expeditions, cited in Matloff and Snell, *Strategic Planning for Coalition Warfare, 1941-42,* pp. 45-46.

48 Min, JB Mtg, 14 May. The correspondence relating to the approval by the Secretaries and the statement recording the President's reaction are filed in JB 325, Ser. 642-5.

49 Min, Conference OSW, 10 Jun 41, WDCSA, Secy of War Conf, I.

CHAPTER 2

1 A more extensive discussion of the German planning and operations appears in Earl F. Ziemke, *The German Northern Theater of War, 1940-1945,* Department of the Army Pamphlet 20-271 (Washington, 1959). The British and Allied side of the Norwegian operation is presented in T. K. Derry, *The Campaign in Norway* (London: H.M. Stationery Office, 1952) and in J. R. M. Butler, *Grand Strategy,* Vol. II (London: H.M. Stationery Office, 1957), Chs. V and VI.

2 *Nazi Conspiracy and Aggression* (Washington, 1946), Vol. VII, Doc. 052-L.

3 *War Diary of the German Naval Staff, Operations Division, Part A* (hereafter cited as *Naval War Diary*) (ONI: Washington, 1948), Vol. 1, p. 113, and Vol. 2, p. 8.

4 Battle Instructions for the Navy (edition of May 1939), in *Führer Directives and Other Top-Level Directives of the German Armed Forces, 1939-1941* (ONI: Washington, 1948), p. 25.

5 *Trials of the Major War Criminals Before the International Military Tribunal* (hereafter cited as *International Military Tribunal*) (Nuremberg, 1947), Doc. 122-C.

6 *Naval War Diary,* Vol. 2, p. 39.

7 *OKM, SKL, Überlegungen zur Frage der Stützpunktgewinnung für die Nordsee-Kriegführung, 9.10.39.* Copies of the captured German Navy records are in the custody of the Director of Naval History, U.S. Navy Department.

8 *Denkschrift und Richtlinien über die Führung des Krieges im Westen, 9.10.1939* and *Der Oberste Befehlshaber der Wehrmacht, OKW Nr. 172/39, WFA/L, Weisung Nr. 6 für die Kampfführung, 9.10.39,* in *OKM, Weisungen OKW (Führer).* Office of the Chief of Military History (OCMH): *Führer Conferences on Matters Dealing with the German Navy* (hereafter cited as *Führer Conferences*) (ONI: Washington, 1947), 1939, p. 14.

9 *Naval War Diary,* Vol. 3, pp. 155, 168; *Führer Conferences,* 1939, p. 45.

10 *Führer Conferences,* 1939, pp. 54-57. *Tagebuch General Jodl* (WFA), 13

Oct 39-30 Jan 40, *International Military Tribunal*, Doc. 1811-PS (hereafter cited as *Jodl Diary*), 13 Dec 39.

[11] *International Military Tribunal*, Doc. 004-PS.

[12] *Führer Conferences*, 1939, p. 56; *Naval War Diary*, Vol. 4, p. 56.

[13] *Jodl Diary*, 18, 19, 20 Dec 39, and 2 Jan 40.

[14] *Kriegstagebuch des Generalobersten Franz Halder, International Military Tribunal*, Doc. NOKW-3140 (hereafter referred to as *Halder Diary*), III, 13.

[15] *International Military Tribunal*, Doc. 021-C; *Halder Diary*, III, 3, 18.

[16] *International Military Tribunal*, Doc. 021-C.

[17] *OKM, SKL, I Op. 73/40, Überlegungen Studie Nord, 19.1.40.*

[18] *Halder Diary*, III, 19, 29.

[19] *Jodl Diary*, 23 Jan 40; *International Military Tribunal*, Doc. 063-C.

[20] *International Military Tribunal*, Doc. 82-Raeder.

[21] Derry, *The Campaign in Norway*, p. 13.

[22] *OKW, WFA, Abt. III, Weisung an Oberbefehlshaber "Weserübung," 26.2.40.*

[23] *Jodl Diary*, 19 Feb 40; *Halder Diary*, III, 62, 64.

[24] *Gruppe XXI, Ia, Kriegstagebuch Nr. 1, 20.2.40-8.4.40,* 21 Feb 40; AOK 20 E 180/5. Copies of the captured German Army records are on file at the National Archives in Washington.

[25] *Gruppe XXI, Ia, Kriegstagebuch Nr. 1,* 26-29 Feb 40; *Jodl Diary*, 28 Feb 40.

[26] *International Military Tribunal*, Doc. 174-C.

[27] Karl Jesko von Puttkamer, *Die Unheimliche See* (Vienna: Verlag Karl Kuhne, 1952), p. 31; *Halder Diary*, III, 64; *Jodl Diary*, 1, 2, and 3 Mar 40.

[28] *Jodl Diary*, 5 and 7 Mar 40; *Gruppe XXI, Ia, Kriegstagebuch Nr. 1,* 5 Mar 40; *OKW, WFA, Abt. L, Nr. 22082/40, in Anlagenband 1 zum K.T.B. 1, Anlagen 1-52;* AOK 20 E 180/7.

[29] *Gruppe XXI, Ia, Nr. 20/40, Operationsbefehl für die Besetzung Norwegens, Nr. 1, in Anlagenband zum K.T.B. 1, Anlagen 1-52;* AOK 20 E 180/7.

[30] *Verbindungsstab Marine, B. Nr. 130, Seetransportübersicht nach dem Stande vom 22.3.40, in Gruppe XXI, Anlagenband 5 zum K.T.B. Nr. 1.* AOK 20 E 180/10; Kurt Assmann, *The German Campaign in Norway, Origin of the Plan, Execution of the Operation, and Measures Against Allied Counterattack* (London, 1948), p. 13.

[31] *Gruppe XXI, Ia, 126/40, Operationsbefehl für die Besetzung von Dänemark, Nr. 1, in Anlagenband zum K.T.B. 1, Anlagen 1-52;* AOK 20 E 180/7.

[32] *Führer Conferences*, 1940, I, 20.

[33] *Gruppe XXI, Ia, Kriegstagebuch Nr. 1, 12 Mar 40.*

[34] *Naval War Diary*, Vol. 7, p. 63.

[35] Derry, *The Campaign in Norway*, p. 13.

[36] Carl Gustaf Mannerheim, *The Memoirs of Marshal Mannerheim* (New York: Dutton, 1954), pp. 380-87.

[37] Butler, *Grand Strategy*, Vol. II, p. 113.

[38] *Führer Conferences*, 1940, I, 22; *Naval War Diary*, Vol. 7, p. 100.

[39] Derry, *The Campaign in Norway*, pp. 15ff.

[40] *Führer Conferences*, 1940, I, 22.

[41] *Gruppe XXI, Kriegstagebuch Nr. 1,* 1 and 2 Apr 40.

[42] Winston S. Churchill, *The Gathering Storm* (Boston: Houghton Mifflin, 1948), p. 657.

[43] *Gruppe XXI, Notiz für das Kriegstagebuch, 1.4.40, in Anlagenband 1 zum K.T.B. Nr. 1, Anlagen 1-52;* AOK 20 E 180/7.

[44] Walter Warlimont, *Gutachten zu der Kriegstagebuch-Ausarbeitung OKW/WFSt "Der nördliche Kriegsschauplatz,"* p. 19, MS # C-099 1, OCMH.

45 Walther Hubatsch, *Die deutsche Besetzung von Dänemark und Norwegen 1940* (Göttingen, 1952), pp. 266ff.

46 Derry, *The Campaign in Norway,* p. 246.

CHAPTER 3

1 The substance of the present essay is contained in the author's article entitled "The Japanese Decision For War," published in *U.S. Naval Institute Proceedings,* LXXX (December, 1954), 1325-34. Other published accounts in English of the events leading to Japan's decision may be found in Herbert Feis, *The Road to Pearl Harbor* (Princeton: Princeton University Press, 1950); Samuel Eliot Morison, *History of United States Naval Operations in World War II,* Vol. III: *The Rising Sun in the Pacific, 1931-April 1942* (Boston: Little, Brown, 1948); the two volumes of William L. Langer and S. Everett Gleason, *Challenge to Isolation* (New York: Harper, 1952), and *The Undeclared War, 1940-1941* (New York: Harper, 1953); U.S. Department of State, *Foreign Relations of the United States, Japan: 1931-1941* (Washington, 1943). A number of other works dealing in part with this subject will be found in the present author's critical essay on the bibliography of the Pearl Harbor attack, published in *U.S. Naval Institute Proceedings,* Vol. 81, No. 4 (April, 1955), 462-69.

2 International Military Tribunal of the Far East (IMTFE), Exhibit 216; Political Strategy Prior to the Outbreak of War, Part I, App. I, Japanese Studies in World War II, No. 147. These Japanese studies were written by Japanese Army and Navy officers at the direction of G-2, Far East Command. Mimeographed translations are on file at OCMH.

3 Jerome B. Cohen, *Japan's Economy in War and Reconstruction* (Minneapolis: University of Minnesota Press, 1949), Chap. I; United States Strategic Bombing Survey (USSBS), *The Effect of Strategic Bombing on Japan's War Economy* (Washington, 1946), p. 12; IMTFE, Judgment, Part B, pp. 114ff, 353; History of the Army Section, Imperial General Headquarters, 1941-1945, Japanese Studies in World War II, No. 72, p. 5.

4 USSBS, *Oil in Japan's War* (Washington, 1946), p. 1; IMTFE, Judgment, p. 902.

5 Hist Army Sec, Imperial GHQ, pp. 2-3; USSBS, *Japanese Air Power* (Washington, 1946), pp. 4-5; USSBS, *Japanese Naval Shipbuilding* (Washington, 1946), App. A.

6 Political Strategy Prior to Outbreak of War, Part IV, Japanese Studies in World War II, No. 150, pp. 1-2; IMTFE, Deposition of Shinichi Tanaka, Exhibit 3027.

7 IMTFE, Tanaka Deposition; Imperial GHQ Army Dept Directive No. 791, 6 Dec 40, No. 810, 16 Jan 41, No. 812, 18 Jan 41, all in Imperial GHQ Army Directives, Vol. I; IMTFE, Judgment, pp. 878-81; Robert E. Ward, "The Inside Story of the Pearl Harbor Plan," *U.S. Naval Institute Proceedings,* LXXVII (December, 1951), pp. 1272-75.

8 Ltr, Roosevelt to Ickes, 1 Jul 41, cited in Langer and Gleason, *The Undeclared War, 1940-1941,* p. 646. The July 2 decision is included among the IMTFE Exhibits as No. 588; Ltr, Grew to author, 19 Jun 41, OCMH.

9 IMTFE, Exhibit 585. The events leading to the decision are covered in Political Strategy Prior to Outbreak of War, Part IV, and Feis, *Road to Pearl Harbor,* pp. 209-19.

10 IMTFE, Judgment, pp. 928-30; Feis, *Road to Pearl Harbor,* pp. 223-26.

The American position, which remained virtually unchanged throughout the negotiations, was outlined by Cordell Hull in four points:

1. Respect for the territorial integrity and the sovereignty of each and all nations;

2. Support of the principle of noninterference in the internal affairs of other countries;

3. Support of the principle of equality, including equality of commercial opportunity;

4. Nondisturbance of the *status quo* in the Pacific except as the *status quo* may be altered by peaceful means.

Report of the Joint Committee on the Investigation of the Pearl Harbor Attack, 79th Cong., 2nd Sess., Doc. 244 (Washington, 1946), p. 294.

[11] *Foreign Relations of the United States, Japan,* Vol. II, p. 342.

[12] Rad, CNO to CINCAF, 25 Jul 41, in *Pearl Harbor Attack, Hearings Before the Joint Committee on the Investigation of the Pearl Harbor Attack* (Washington, 1946), Part 14, pp. 1400-01.

[13] Political Strategy Prior to Outbreak of War, Part IV, pp. 9, 73-77.

[14] IMTFE, Exhibits 870, 870-A, and 871.

[15] Political Strategy Prior to Outbreak of War, Part IV, pp. 9-10.

[16] Konoye Memoirs, *Pearl Harbor Attack Hearings,* Part 20, pp. 3998-4000, 4009-10; *Pearl Harbor Attack Report,* pp. 298, 302-07, 310; *Foreign Relations of the United States, Japan,* Vol. II, pp. 549-55.

[17] Konoye Memoirs, *Pearl Harbor Attack Hearings,* Part 20, pp. 4022-23. The wording of this important statement varies in different documents. IMTFE Defense Document 1579 gives a slightly different wording as does Judgment, Chapter VII, page 939. The Japanese phrase "Kaiseno Ketsui su" may be translated literally "decide to open hostilities." Konoye apparently did not interpret the phrase as meaning that it was a decision for war; Tojo did.

[18] Konoye Memoirs, *Pearl Harbor Attack Hearings,* Part 20, pp. 4022-23; IMTFE, Doc. 1652, Exhibit 588.

[19] IMTFE, Tanaka Deposition, Exhibit 2244.

[20] For a full account of the evolution of the Pearl Harbor plan, see Ward, "The Inside Story of the Pearl Harbor Plan," *U.S. Naval Institute Proceedings,* LXXVII, 1272-81.

[21] Japanese Army-Navy Central Agreement, Nov 41, copy in USSBS, *The Campaigns of the Pacific War,* pp. 43-46; *Combined Fleet,* Top Secret Order No. 1, copy in *Pearl Harbor Attack Hearings,* Part 13, pp. 431-84; Political Strategy Prior to Outbreak of War, Part IV, pp. 47-123; Hist Army Sec, Imperial GHQ, rev. ed., pp. 29-39; History of the *Southern Area Army,* 1941-1945, Japanese Studies in World War II, No. 24, pp. 4-8; Army and Navy Directives, Imperial GHQ Directive, Vol. I.

[22] Feis, *Road to Pearl Harbor,* p. 270.

[23] *Pearl Harbor Attack Report,* p. 322.

[24] Political Strategy Prior to Outbreak of War, Part IV, pp. 13-15.

[25] Konoye Memoirs, *Pearl Harbor Attack Hearings,* Part 20, p. 4010.

[26] Memo, Gerow for CofS, 18 Oct 41, sub: Resignation of Japanese Cabinet; Rad, CNO to CINCPAC and CINCAF, 16 Oct 41, both in *Pearl Harbor Attack Hearings,* Part 14, pp. 1389, 1402. See also Ltr, Grew to author, 19 Jun 49, OCMH.

[27] Dispatch, Togo to Nomura, 4 and 5 Nov 41, in *Pearl Harbor Attack Hearings,* Part 12, Exhibit 1, p. 92.

[28] The text of the two proposals is reproduced in IMTFE, Exhibit 770.

[29] USSBS, *The Campaigns of the Pacific War,* App. 12, pp. 43-46; App. 14,

p. 49. The Combined Fleet Top Secret Order Number 1 is printed in *Pearl Harbor Attack Hearings,* Part 13, pp. 431-84.

30 Hist of *Southern Army,* 1941-45, pp. 4-8; Hist Army Sec, Imperial GHQ, pp. 29-39.

31 Telgs, Grew to Hull, 27 Jan and 3 Nov 41, in *Pearl Harbor Attack Hearings,* Part 14, Exhibit 15, pp. 1042, 1045-60; Ltr, CNO to Kimmel, 7 Nov 41.

32 Rad, Tokyo to Washington, No. 812, 22 Nov 41, IMTFE, Doc. 2593, Item 17.

33 Cordell Hull, *The Memoirs of Cordell Hull,* 2 vols. (New York: Macmillan, 1948), Vol. II, p. 1069.

34 Memos, Stark and Gerow for Secretary of State, 21 Nov 41, in *Pearl Harbor Attack Hearings,* Part 14, pp. 1104-07. General Marshall was attending the maneuvers in North Carolina.

35 Hull, Memoirs, Vol. II, p. 1180.

36 *Foreign Relations of the United States, Japan,* Vol. II, pp. 766-70; Hull, *Memoirs,* Vol. II, pp. 1077-82; *Pearl Harbor Attack Report,* pp. 35-43.

37 Rad, Op NAV to Comdrs Pacific and Asiatic Fleets, 242005 Nov 41, *Pearl Harbor Attack Hearings,* Part 14, p. 1405.

38 Memo, Gerow for Marshall, 27 Nov 41, sub: Far Eastern Situation; Rads, Marshall to CG USAFFE, Hawaiian Dept, Carib Def Comd, Nos. 624, 472, 451, 27 Nov 41, OCS 18136-118 and WPD 4544-16; Miles to G-2 Hawaiian Dept, No. 472, 27 Nov 41. Most of these are published in *Pearl Harbor Attack Hearings,* Part 3, p. 1021, Part 14, pp. 1328-30. Stimson's account of these events is in Part 39, p. 84. The Navy message is in Part 14, p. 1406. See also *Pearl Harbor Attack Report,* pp. 199-201.

39 Konoye Memoirs, *Pearl Harbor Attack Hearings,* Part 20, p. 4012.

40 IMTFE, Exhibits 2954 and 2955, Depositions of Tojo and Togo.

41 IMTFE, Exhibit 588, Doc. 1652, Records of Imperial Conferences.

42 These messages are reproduced in USSBS, *The Campaigns of the Pacific War,* p. 51, and elsewhere.

43 Feis, *Road to Pearl Harbor,* p. 331; Langer and Gleason, *The Undeclared War,* pp. 910-11; *The Ciano Diaries, 1939-1943,* ed. by Hugh Gibson (Garden City, N.Y.: Doubleday, 1946), entries for 3 and 4 December 1941. On November 30, Foreign Minister Togo had told his Ambassador in Berlin that "war may suddenly break out between the Anglo-Saxon nations and Japan . . . quicker than anyone dreams." Quoted in Feis, *Road to Pearl Harbor,* p. 336.

44 Feis, *Road to Pearl Harbor,* p. 340.

45 *Pearl Harbor Attack Report,* pp. 219-28.

46 *Pearl Harbor Attack Report,* p. 41.

47 Morison, *The Rising Sun in the Pacific, 1931-April 1942,* p. 132.

48 Political Strategy Prior to Outbreak of War, Part V, p. 37.

49 Masuo Kato, *The Lost War* (New York: Knopf, 1946), p. 89.

50 Henry L. Stimson and McGeorge Bundy, *On Active Service in Peace and War* (New York: Harper, 1948), p. 390. Evidence on public opinion is not conclusive. A Gallup poll reported in the New York *Times* for February 23, 1941, found that although 56 per cent of those polled were in favor of an effort "to keep Japan from seizing the Dutch East Indies and Singapore," only 39 per cent supported risking war in such an attempt. Again, in August 1941, a *Fortune* poll showed that 33.7 per cent of those polled were in favor of defending the Philippines, East Indies, and Australia, and only 22.3 per cent favored the defense of an unspecified portion of this area. The conclusion of John W. Masland, writing in 1941, was that "powerful com-

mercial interests and articulate isolationist pressure groups" opposed American opposition to Japan; see John W. Masland, "American Attitudes Toward Japan," *Annals of the American Academy of Political and Social Science* (May, 1941), p. 165. See also *Public Opinion, 1935-1946,* prepared by Mildred Strunk under the editorial direction of Hadley Cantril (Princeton: Princeton University Press, 1951), p. 1077.

51 Statement of Prince Naruhiko Higashikuni, 9 Jun 49, ATIS, G-12 FEC, copy in OCMH.

CHAPTER 4

1 This study is part of a chapter, "The Army and Japanese Evacuation," written for inclusion in a volume entitled *Guarding the United States and Its Outposts,* which is being prepared for publication in *United States Army in World War II.* That chapter covers the proposal for the mass evacuation of Japanese residents from Hawaii as well as the West Coast decision. The principal published works on various facets of the subject include: United States War Department, *Final Report: Japanese Evacuation from the West Coast, 1942* (Washington, 1943) (hereafter cited as *Final Report*); Morton Grodzins, *Americans Betrayed: Politics and the Japanese Evacuation* (Chicago: University of Chicago Press, 1949) (hereafter cited as *Japanese Evacuation*); Dorothy S. Thomas and Richard S. Nishimoto, *The Spoilage* (Berkeley: University of California Press, 1946) and *The Salvage* (Berkeley: University of California Press, 1952); Jacobus tenBroek, Edward N. Barnhart, and Floyd W. Watson, *Prejudice, War, and the Constitution* (Berkeley: University of California Press, 1954); and the United States Department of the Interior, War Relocation Authority, *WRA: A Story of Human Conservation* (Washington, 1946) (hereafter cited as *WRA*).

2 Ltr, TAG to CGs, 29 Jul 41, inclosing copy of the SW-Atty Gen agreement of 18 Jul 41, in Adjutant General Central File (AG) 014.311 (1-13-41), Sec. 1; Proclamations of 7 and 8 Dec 41, copies in Provost Marshal General (PMG) File 014.311 WDC and PMG 383.01 Hawaii; Tel Conv, SGS with Lt Gen John L. DeWitt, 7 Dec 41, Western Defense Command (WDC) File 381 RAINBOW 4; Memo, Special Asst to SW for PMG, 13 Dec 41, PMG 014.311 WDC; J. Edgar Hoover, "Alien Enemy Control," *Iowa Law Review,* XXIX (March, 1944), 396-408.

3 Memo, G-2 Fourth Army for CofS Fourth Army, 11 Dec 41, Western Defense Command–Civil Affairs Division (WDC-CAD) File 014.31 Enemy Aliens.

4 Office, Chief of Staff (OCS) File Index, 11 Dec 41, Tally Card info re OCS 21227-38 and 39.

5 Ltr, CG WDC to CG GHQ, 19 Dec 41, WDC-CAD 014.31.

6 Tel Conv, DeWitt with Gullion, 26 Dec 41, WDC-CAD 311.3 Tel Convs (DeWitt, 42-43).

7 Memo, PMG for SW, 22 Dec 41, and Memo, PMG for G-2, 30 Dec 41, both in PMG 014.311 Gen P/W.

8 Tel Convs, DeWitt with Gullion, 26 and 27 Dec 41, and Tel Conv, DeWitt with Col Archer L. Lerch, Deputy PMG, 1 Jan 42, all in WDC-CAD 311.3 Tel Convs (DeWitt, 42-43); Memo for File, Lerch, 1 Jan 42, General Headquarters (GHQ) G-1 file, Subversive Activities, WDC.

9 Memo, Lerch for TAG, 30 Dec 41, PMG 014.311 WDC; Memo, PMG for ACofS G-1, GHQ, 1 Jan 42, and inclosed copy of Ltr, PMG to DeWitt, 1 Jan 42, GHQ G-1 file, Subversive Activities, WDC.

[10] Memo, Maj Bendetsen for DeWitt, 3 Jan 42, and Notes on Conf in Office of DeWitt, 4 Jan 42, both in WDC-CAD 014.31 Aliens; Memo, CG WDC for Rowe, 5 Jan 42, the attached Tab A, entitled Summary of Communication (*i.e.,* Rowe to DeWitt), 4 Jan 42, and memos of 6 Jan 42, all reproduced in *Final Report,* pp. 4-6, 19-24; Tel Conv, DeWitt with Col Raymond R. Tourtillott, 5 Jan 42, WDC-CAD 311.3 Tel Convs (DeWitt, 42-43); tenBroek *et al., Prejudice, War, and the Constitution,* pp. 104-05.

[11] The Twelfth and Thirteenth Naval District commanders made recommendations in identical language on this score. Memo, Adm John W. Greenslade, Commandant Twelfth Naval District, for CG Northern California Sector, 8 Jan 42, and Ltr, CG IX Army Corps to CG WDC, 8 Jan 42, both in WDC-CAD 014.31 Aliens.

[12] Ltr and Incls, CG WDC to Atty Gen (through PMG), 21 Jan 42, PMG 384.4 (California) General.

[13] Ltr, SW to Atty Gen, 25 Jan 42, PMG 384.4 (California) General. The transcript of General DeWitt's telephone remarks referred to reads, "We know there are radios along the coast; and we know they are communicating at sea. They may be communicating with each other. . . ." Tel Conv, DeWitt with Gullion, 24 Jan 42, WDC-CAD 311.3 Tel Convs (DeWitt 42-43).

[14] Ltr, James L. Fly, Chairman Federal Communications Commission, to Atty Gen Biddle, 4 Apr 44, quoted in WRA monograph by Ruth E. McKee, *Wartime Exile: The Exclusion of Japanese-Americans from the West Coast* (Washington, 1946), pp. 154-58.

[15] General DeWitt's final recommendation in this series, with respect to Utah, dated February 16, 1942 (copy in PMG 384.4 WDC), lists and describes the seven preceding ones.

[16] Grodzins, *Japanese Evacuation,* contains the most detailed analysis of the pressures that developed during January and February for Japanese evacuation.

[17] GHQ G-2 Info Bull 6, 21 Jan 42, copy in Assistant Secretary of War (ASW) McCloy File 014.311 WDC Gen.

[18] Memo, Clark for Judge Advocate GHQ, 24 Jan 42, GHQ file, WDC: Enemy Aliens.

[19] Tel Conv, DeWitt with Gullion, 24 Jan 42, WDC-CAD 311.3 Tel Convs (DeWitt, 42-43).

[20] The Roberts Report is published in *Pearl Harbor Attack: Hearings Before the Joint Committee on the Investigation of the Pearl Harbor Attack* (39 parts) (Washington, 1946), Part 39, pp. 1-21.

[21] Tel Conv, DeWitt with Bendetsen, 28 Jan 42, WDC-CAD 311.3 Tel Convs (DeWitt, 42-43).

[22] Tel Conv, DeWitt with Bendetsen, 29 Jan 42, as recorded both in WDC-CAD 311.3 Tel Convs (DeWitt, 42-43) and in PMG 384.4 WDC; PMG Daily Record of Operations, 29 Jan 42, PMG 384.4 WDC.

[23] Tel Conv, DeWitt with Bendetsen, 30 Jan 42, PMG 384.4 WDC.

[24] Memo, Bendetsen for PMG, 31 Jan 42, PMG 384.4 WDC.

[25] Memo for Record, 31 Jan 42, dictated but not signed by DeWitt, WDC-CAD 014.31.

[26] Department of Justice press releases, printed as Appendix, pp. 302-14, to *H. Doc. 2124, 77th Cong., 2d Sess.*

[27] Tel Conv, DeWitt with Bendetsen, 1 Feb 42, and Tel Conv, Gullion with Clark, 4 Feb 42, both in PMG 384.4 WDC; Tel Conv, DeWitt with Gullion,

1 Feb 42, GHQ G-1 file, Subversive Activities, WDC: Enemy Aliens; Memo, Bendetsen for SGS, 2 Feb 42, AG 014.311 (1-13-41), Sec. 10.

28 Tel Conv, Marshall with DeWitt and accompanying notes of Col Deane, 3 Feb 42, in OCS Tel Convs Binder 2.

29 Memo, DeWitt for ASW McCloy, 3 Feb 42, PMG 384.4 WDC; Tel Convs, DeWitt with Joyce, 3 Feb 42, DeWitt with Bendetsen, 4 Feb 42, and DeWitt with Gullion, 5 Feb 42, WDC-CAD 311.3 Tel Convs (DeWitt, 42-43).

30 Tel Conv, DeWitt with McCloy, 3 Feb 42, GHQ file, WDC: Enemy Aliens; Tel Conv, Gullion with Clark, 4 Feb 42, PMG 384.4 WDC.

31 Tel Conv, Gen DeWitt with Col Bendetsen, 4 Feb 42, WDC-CAD 311.3 Tel Convs (DeWitt, 42-43).

32 Press release of Feb 5, 1942, quoted in Grodzins, *Japanese Evacuation,* p. 258.

33 Memo for Record, Chief WD Liaison Br, 6 Feb 42, GHQ file, WDC: Protection of Vital Installations; Grodzins, *Japanese Evacuation,* pp. 71-73; *H. Doc. 1911, 77th Cong., 2d Sess.,* pp. 2-3.

34 Memo, Bur of Intelligence for Dir OFF, 4 Feb 42, copy in ASW 014.33 Enemy Aliens on the West Coast (hereafter cited as ASW 014.311 EAWC).

35 Report, Lieutenant Commander K. D. Ringle, Eleventh Naval District, through Commandant to CNO, no date, copy in ASW 014.311 EAWC.

36 Draft of Memo, early May 42, Atty Gen for Roosevelt, as quoted in Grodzins, *Japanese Evacuation,* pp. 134-36.

37 *WRA,* p. 182.

38 Memo, Bendetsen for PMG, 4 Feb 42, PMG 014.311 Gen P/W.

39 Memo, Deputy PMG for PMG, 4 Feb 42, PMG 384.4 WDC.

40 Memo, PMG for ASW, 5 Feb 42, ASW 014.311 EAWC.

41 Memo, PMG for ASW, 6 Feb 42, ASW 014.311 EAWC.

42 Two Tel Convs, DeWitt with Bendetsen, 7 Feb 42, WDC-CAD 311.3 Tel Convs (DeWitt, 42-43).

43 Talley Card 31 in re OCS 21227-88.

44 On 11 February General DeWitt referred to his new recommendations collectively as "the plan that Mr. McCloy wanted me to submit." Tel Conv, DeWitt and Bendetsen with Gullion, 11 Feb 42, WDC-CAD 311.3 Tel Convs (DeWitt, 42-43).

45 Tel Conv, DeWitt with Bendetsen, 4 Feb 42, and DeWitt with Gullion and Bendetsen, 4 Feb 42, both in GHQ G-1 file, Subversive Activities, WDC; Memo, CG WDC for PMG, 5 Feb 42, PMG 384.4 WDC.

46 The statistics in this paragraph have been compiled from General DeWitt's several recommendations and supplementary communications that he wrote in justification of them, which are located in various Provost Marshal General files.

47 Tel Conv, Col Bryan with Bendetsen, 11 Feb 42, WDC-CAD 311.3 Tel Convs (Bendetsen, Feb/Mar 42).

48 Memo for Record (unsigned), 11 Feb 42, ASW 014.311 EAWC.

49 Tel Convs, McCloy with Bendetsen, 11 Feb 42, at 10:00 A.M. and 11:15 A.M. Pacific time (the White House conference occurring between the two calls), WDC-CAD 311.3 Tel Convs (Bendetsen, Feb/Mar 42); Tel Conv, DeWitt and Bendetsen with Gullion, 11 Feb 42, WDC-CAD 311.3 Tel Convs (DeWitt, 42-43).

50 Memo, CG WDC for SW (through CG FF), 13 Feb 42, and covering Memo, CG WDC for CG FF GHQ, 14 Feb 42, originals in PMG 014.311 WDC. The basic memorandum is published in *Final Report,* pp. 33-38,

where it is erroneously dated February 14. As of February 11, General DeWitt was planning to have Colonel Bendetsen carry his recommendations back to Washington, but on February 12, because of the general's doubt that GHQ and General Marshall had been "thoroughly informed" of developments, he decided to submit them through the normal channels of communication. Tel Conv, DeWitt with Clark, 12 Feb 42, and Gullion with Bendetsen, 14 Feb 42, both in WDC-CAD 311.3 Tel Convs (DeWitt, 42-43).

51 The recommendations of the 13 February memorandum are described below at greater length in connection with the discussion of the War Department's directives of 20 February.

52 Both the original and the carbon of General DeWitt's recommendations in AG 014.311 (1-13-41), Sec. 10, are stamped to indicate receipt in GHQ on the date and at the hour indicated. As Colonel Bendetsen said on February 19, the DeWitt recommendations "must have hit the wrong air line." Tel Conv, Bendetsen with Donald A. Stroh, 19 Feb 42, PMG 384.4 WDC. The GHQ action is recorded in GHQ 337 Staff Confs Binder 2, entry of 19 Feb 42; and in Memo, G-5 Sec GHQ for Clark, 19 Feb 42, GHQ file, WDC: Enemy Aliens.

53 1st Ind, GHQ for TAG, 20 Feb 42, on Memo, CG WDC for CG FF, 14 Feb 42, GHQ file, WDC: Enemy Aliens.

54 2d Ind, TAG for PMG, 22 Feb 42, on Memo, CG WDC for CG FF, 14 Feb 42, PMG 014.311 WDC; (stamped "RECEIVED IN PMG, 11:00 A.M. 24 Feb 42.").

55 Recommendations inclosed in Ltr, Senator Holman, Senator Wallgren, Representative Lea, *et al.*, to President Roosevelt, 13 Feb 42, AG 014.311 (2-16-42).

56 Memo, President Roosevelt for SW, 16 Feb 42, AG 014.311 (2-16-42), received in Secretary's office at 9:11 A.M., 17 Feb 42.

57 Tel Conv, DeWitt with Gullion, 17 Feb 42, ASW 014.311 EAWC.

58 Memo, PMG for TAG, 17 Feb 42, PMG 384.4 WDC. This copy bears the notation: "Gen. Gullion took this up in person with Mr. McCloy who approves."

59 Ltr, TAG to CGs Corps Areas, 17 Feb 42, PMG 384.4 WDC.

60 Memo for Record, Gen Clark, 17 Feb 42, GHQ file, WDC: Enemy Aliens. General Clark also told General Marshall about the meeting and the decision about troops, but the author has been unable to find any evidence in Army records that the advice of the Chief of Staff was sought in the formulation of the War Department plan for Japanese evacuation.

61 Memo, PMG for CofS, 20 Feb 42, OCS 21227-113; Ltr, Mr. Biddle to the author, 31 Aug 56. See also, Grodzins, *Japanese Evacuation,* pp. 266-67, and tenBroek *et al., Prejudice, War, and the Constitution,* pp. 111-12.

62 Ltrs, SW to CG WDC, 20 Feb 42, PMG 384.4 WDC; Notes on Conf in ODCofS, 20 Feb 42, OCS Conf Binder 32. The longer of the letters became the Outline Memorandum published in part in *Final Report,* pp. 28-29, and attached to a letter from the Assistant Secretary of War to General DeWitt, 20 February 1942, p. 27 of the report. Executive Order 9066, 19 February 1942, and the shorter Secretary of War letter of 20 February 1942 are also published in *Final Report,* pp. 25-27. The letters were apparently handcarried by Colonel Bendetsen to San Francisco when he flew there on February 22.

63 Ltr, SW to Representative Lea, 21 Feb 42, AG 014.311 (2-16-42).

64 Grodzins, *Japanese Evacuation,* pp. 331-39; *Final Report,* pp. 29-31, 49.

On the legal aspects and consequences of the Presidential and Congressional decisions, see Clinton Rossiter, *The Supreme Court and the Commander in Chief* (Ithaca: Cornell University Press, 1951), pp. 42-54.

[65] The analysis that follows, unless otherwise noted, is based on the original of the DeWitt memorandum in PMG 014.311 WDC, and the copies of the WD directives in AG 014.311 (1-13-41), Sec. 1.

[66] Tel Conv, DeWitt with Gullion, 17 Feb 42, ASW 014.311 EAWC.

[67] The central objective of the War Department plan is clearly outlined in paragraphs 1-6 of the Outline Memorandum of February 20, paragraphs omitted in the publication of the memorandum in *Final Report,* pp. 28-29.

[68] *323 United States Reports,* pp. 223-24.

CHAPTER 5

[1] For a full account of the campaign, see Louis Morton, *The Fall of the Philippines,* in *United States Army in World War II* (Washington, 1953). The account that follows is based upon this volume and includes material taken from it.

[2] Unless otherwise noted, this description is based on the Philippine Department Plan ORANGE, 1940 Revision (short title: HPD WPO-3), AGO No. 326. The author has also had the benefit of conversations with the former Philippine Department Commander, Maj. Gen. George Grunert, MacArthur's chief of staff, Lt. Gen. R. K. Sutherland, his deputy chief of staff, Maj. Gen. R. J. Marshall, and various division commanders and staff officers who participated in the planning and execution of the plan.

[3] Henry L. Stimson and McGeorge Bundy, *On Active Service in Peace and War* (New York: Harper, 1948), p. 388.

[4] Interv with Col Legrande A. Diller, formerly aide to General MacArthur, 20 May 49. Gen. Wainwright mentions also that as Philippine Division commander he worked during May, June, and July 1941 to secure revisions of WPO-3. See General Jonathan M. Wainwright, *General Wainwright's Story, the Account of Four Years of Humiliating Defeat, Surrender, and Captivity* (Garden City, N.Y.: Doubleday, 1946), p. 10.

[5] Wainwright, *General Wainwright's Story,* p. 21.

[6] Joint Army and Navy Basic Plan RAINBOW 5, Joint Board No. 325, Serial 642-5, OPD Reg Docs.

[7] Ltr, MacArthur to TAG, 1 Oct 41, sub: Operations Plan R-5, WPD 4178-18. MacArthur repeated the same request, in virtually the same language, in a personal letter to Marshall on October 28, 1941. WPD 4477-2.

[8] Memo, Marshall for MacArthur, 18 Oct 41, sub: U.S. Army Forces in the Far East, WPD 4175-18.

[9] USAFFE-USFIP Rpt of Opns, p. 15, copy in OCMH.

[10] Ltr Order, CG USAFFE to CG North Luzon Force, 3 Dec 41, sub: Defense of the Philippines, AG 381 (12-3-41), Phil Records.

[11] Ltr Order, CG USAFFE to CG South Luzon Force, 3 Dec 41, sub: Defense of the Philippines, AG 381 (12-3-41), Phil Records.

[12] USAFFE-USFIP Rpt of Opns, pp. 17-18; Ltr Orders, CG USAFFE to CG Philippine Division, 6 Dec 41, sub: Movement Plans.

[13] For an account of these early landings, see Morton, *Fall of the Philippines,* pp. 98-115.

[14] Manuel L. Quezon, *The Good Fight* (New York: Appleton-Century, 1946), pp. 194-98. Present at the meeting also were Col. Manuel Nieto, the president's aide, and Lt. Col. Sidney L. Huff, MacArthur's aide.

[15] Col Richard C. Mallonée, Bataan Diary, I, p. 56, copy in OCMH.

[16] *Ibid.* The conversation between Irwin and Mallonée took place in the presence of the senior American instructor and chief of staff of the 21st Division (PA), and several other officers. Ltr, Col R. N. O'Day to author, 16 Nov 49, OCMH.

[17] *Ibid.,* p. 57.

[18] Rad, Lt Col John P. Horan to MacArthur, 24 Dec 41, AG 370.2 (19 Dec 41), Phil Records.

[19] Mallonée, Bataan Diary, I, pp. 62-63. See also Col James V. Collier, Notebooks, II, pp. 35-38, copy in OCMH.

[20] Wainwright, *General Wainwright's Story,* pp. 35-36.

[21] Rads, MacArthur to Marshall, No. 3, 22 Dec 41, and Marshall to MacArthur, same date, both in AG 381 (11-27-41 Gen), Far East.

[22] For a breakdown of the forces in the Philippines on the eve of war, see Morton, *Fall of the Philippines,* pp. 48-50.

[23] Collier Notebooks, II, p. 38.

[24] Wainwright, *General Wainwright's Story,* p. 36.

[25] Rad, CG USAFFE to AGWAR, 24 Dec 41, AG 381 (11-27-41 Gen), Far East. MacArthur mistakenly reported that the Japanese were standing off Nasugbu. No landing was ever made there.

[26] Rad, MacArthur to Marshall, 24 Dec 41, AG 381 (11-28-41 Gen), Far East.

[27] USAFFE Rpt of Opns, pp. 33, 40; Interv with General Marshall, 7 Apr 48, copy in OCMH.

[28] USAFFE Rpt of Opns, pp. 33-35; Collier Notebooks, II, p. 47; Sutherland to CG 51st Div, 24 Dec 41, sub: Operations Orders, AG 371 Phil Rec; South Luzon Force Report, pp. 16, 19, copy in OCMH.

[29] QM Rpt of Opns, pp. 20-21.

[30] Interv with Gen R. J. Marshall, 7 Apr 48; Carlos Romulo, *I Saw the Fall of the Philippines* (New York: Doubleday, Doran), 1942, pp. 68-90.

[31] Hart, Narrative of Events, Asiatic Fleet, p. 41, ONR&L.

[32] *Ibid.,* pp. 45-46; Rad, Hart to Stark, 241225, Dec 41, and Ltr, Hart to MacArthur, 25 Dec 41, sub: Move of Comd Post, both in War Diary 16th Nav Dist; Rockwell, Naval Activities in Luzon Area, pp. 6-8, ONR&L.

[33] Lieutenant General Lewis H. Brereton, *The Brereton Diaries* (New York: Morrow, 1946), pp. 55-59; Wesley Frank Craven and James Lea Cate, eds., *The Army Air Forces in World War II,* Vol. I: *Plans and Early Operations: January 1939 to August 1942* (Chicago: University of Chicago Press, 1948), pp. 221-22.

[34] Clark Lee, *They Call It Pacific* (New York: Viking Press, 1943), pp. 125-27.

[35] Romulo, *I Saw the Fall of the Philippines,* pp. 73-74.

[36] The following pages were prepared by Robert Ross Smith and are based on Chapters V, XIII, and XVII and the Conclusion of a forthcoming volume by him, *Triumph in the Philippines,* in *United States Army in World War II.*

CHAPTER 6

[1] George F. Howe, *Northwest Africa: Seizing the Initiative in the West,* in *United States Army in World War II* (Washington, 1957), covers in detail the operations that led to victory in Tunisia in May 1943. The Navy story is related by Samuel Eliot Morison, *History of United States Naval Operations in World War II,* Vol. I: *The Battle of the Atlantic, September 1939-May 1943* (Boston: Little, Brown, 1950), and Vol. II: *Operations in North*

African Waters, October 1942-June 1943 (Boston: Little, Brown, 1950). Books that deal with the TORCH decision are: Maurice Matloff and Edwin M. Snell, *Strategic Planning for Coalition Warfare 1941-1942* (Washington, 1953), and Richard M. Leighton and Robert W. Coakley, *Global Logistics and Strategy, 1940-1943,* in *United States Army in World War II;* Robert E. Sherwood, *Roosevelt and Hopkins: An Intimate History* (New York: Harper, 1948); Henry L. Stimson and McGeorge Bundy, *On Active Service in Peace and War* (New York: Harper, 1948); Winston S. Churchill, *The Hinge of Fate* (Boston: Houghton Mifflin, 1950); Arthur Bryant, *The Turn of the Tide* (Garden City, N.Y.: Doubleday, 1957).

[2] For a full discussion of the views presented at ARCADIA, see Matloff and Snell, *Strategic Planning, 1941-1942.*

[3] Memo, COS (for CofS), 22 Dec 41; sub: American-British Strategy, Operations Division (OPD) files ABC 337 ARCADIA (24 Dec 41).

[4] Joint Board (JB) 355 Ser. 707, 11 Sep 41, sub: Brief of Strategic Concept of Operations Required to Defeat Our Potential Enemies. Before TORCH there were a number of plans for the invasion of North Africa. As early as the spring of 1941 the U.S. Joint Board had begun work on plans to seize Dakar. The code name for this operation was BLACK, later changed to BARRISTER. GYMNAST and SUPER-GYMNAST contemplated joint operations with the British in the Casablanca area in French Morocco. The British also had a plan for a landing in Tunisia. For additional details on GYMNAST and SUPER-GYMNAST, see Matloff and Snell, *Strategic Planning for Coalition Warfare, 1941-1942,* Chapters XI and XII.

[5] Memo, WPD for CofS, 28 Feb 42, sub: Strategic Conceptions and Their Application to SWPA, OPD files, Exec 4, Envelope 35; Notation by Eisenhower, 22 Jan 42 entry, Item 3, OPD Hist Unit File.

[6] Notes, GCM [George C. Marshall], 23 Dec 41, sub: Notes on Mtg at White House With President and Prime Minister Presiding, War Plans Division (WPD) 4402-136.

[7] Interv with Brig Gen Paul M. Robinett, USA (Ret.), 29 Jun 56, OCMH.

[8] Morison, *The Battle of the Atlantic,* Chs. VI, VII.

[9] Ltr, Secy War and Secy Navy to President, 2 Jun 41, copy filed in JB 325, Ser. 642-5.

[10] Stimson and Bundy, *On Active Service,* pp. 415-16.

[11] *Ibid.,* pp. 418-19; Matloff and Snell, *Strategic Planning, 1941-1942,* pp. 183-85; Bryant, *The Turn of the Tide,* p. 280.

[12] Min of Mtg, U.S.-British Planning Staffs, London, 11 Apr 42, Tab N, ABC 381 BOLERO (3-16-42), 5. For a fuller treatment of these discussions, see Gordon A. Harrison, *Cross-Channel Attack* in *United States Army in World War II* (Washington, 1951), pp. 13-18.

[13] Ltr atchd to Min of Mtg, U.S. Representatives-Br War Cabinet, 14 Apr 42, Chief of Staff 1942-43 files, WDCSA 381.1.

[14] Msg, Marshall to McNarney, 13 Apr 42, CM-IN 3457.

[15] Churchill, *The Hinge of Fate,* pp. 323-24.

[16] Paper, COS, 13 Apr 42, title: Comments on Gen Marshall's Memo, COS (42)97(0) Tab F, ABC 381 BOLERO (3-16-42), 5; Churchill, *The Hinge of Fate,* pp. 181-85; Bryant, *The Turn of the Tide,* pp. 286-87.

[17] Stimson and Bundy, *On Active Service,* pp. 418-19.

[18] Bryant, *The Turn of the Tide,* pp. 300-01.

[19] Leighton and Coakley, *Global Logistics 1940-1943,* p. 377.

[20] *Ibid.*

[21] *Ibid.,* pp. 379-80.

22 Quoted in W. K. Hancock and M. M. Gowing, *British War Economy, History of the Second World War, United Kingdom Civil Series* (London: H.M. Stationery Office, 1949), pp. 406-07.

23 Matloff and Snell, *Strategic Planning, 1941-1942*, pp. 231-32; Sherwood, *Roosevelt and Hopkins*, pp. 568-70.

24 Matloff and Snell, *Strategic Planning, 1941-1942*, pp. 231-32.

25 Memo, COS for War Cabinet, 2 Jul 42, sub: Future Operations WP (42) 278 (COS 42) 195(0), ABC 381 (7-25-42) Sec. 4-B, 19; Matloff and Snell, *Strategic Planning, 1941-1942*, p. 266.

26 Stimson and Bundy, *On Active Service*, p. 419.

27 Churchill, *The Hinge of Fate*, pp. 334-35.

28 See JCS 24th Mtg, 10 Jul 42; Msg, Churchill to Field Marshal Dill, 12 Jul 42, ABC 381 (7-25-42) Sec. 4-B; Bryant, *The Turn of the Tide*, pp. 301-02, 318.

29 How serious the British considered this latter threat to their vital oil resources is clearly indicated in the many references to it in Brooke's diary; see Bryant, *The Turn of the Tide*, Chs. 8, 9.

30 Memo, COS for War Cabinet, 2 Jul 42, sub: Future Opns WP (42) 278 (COS 42), ABC 381 (7-25-42) Sec. 4-B, 19.

31 Msg, War Cabinet Offs to Joint Staff Mission, 8 Jul 42; Leighton and Coakley, *Global Logistics, 1940-1943*, p. 384.

32 Leighton and Coakley, *Global Logistics, 1940-1943*, p. 382.

33 *Ibid.*

34 Memo, King and Marshall for President, 10 Jul 42, WDCSA file BOLERO.

35 Draft Cable in CofS file ABC 381 (7-25-42) Sec. 1.

36 Msg, Roosevelt to Marshall, 14 Jul 42, WDCSA file BOLERO; Sherwood, *Roosevelt and Hopkins*, p. 602.

37 Stimson and Bundy, *On Active Service*, p. 425.

38 Memos, Roosevelt for Hopkins, Marshall, and King, 16 Jul 42, sub: Instructions for London Conf, Jul 42, signed original in WDCSA 381, Sec. 1; Sherwood, *Roosevelt and Hopkins*, pp. 603-05; Matloff and Snell, *Strategic Planning, 1941-1942*, p. 273.

39 Combined Staff Conf, 20 Jul 42, WDCSA 319.1; Matloff and Snell, *Strategic Planning, 1941-1942*, p. 278.

40 Memo, Conclusions as to Practicability of SLEDGEHAMMER, 17 Jul 42; Diary of Commander in Chief, OPD Hist Unit file. This memorandum was prepared by General Eisenhower after consultation with Maj. Gen. Mark W. Clark, Maj. Gen. John C. H. Lee, and Col. Ray W. Barker.

41 Quotation from Brooke's diary, 23 July entry, in Bryant, *The Turn of the Tide*, p. 344.

42 Msg, President to Hopkins, Marshall, and King, 23 Jul 42, WDCSA 381, Sec. 1; Matloff and Snell, *Strategic Planning, 1941-1942*, p. 278; Howe, *Northwest Africa*, p. 13.

43 For War Department views on Middle East operations, see OPD study 15 Jul 42, sub: Comparison of Opn GYMNAST With Opns Involving Reinforcements of Middle East, Exec 5, Item 1, 4 Feb 42.

44 CCS 34th Mtg, 30 Jul, ABC 381 (7-25-42), Sec. 1.

45 Memo by CCS, 24 Jul 42, sub: Opns in 42-43, circulated as CCS 94, ABC 381 (25 Jul 42). For details, see the treatment of CCS 94 and its interpretation in Matloff and Snell, *Strategic Planning, 1941-1942*.

46 Sherwood, *Roosevelt and Hopkins*, p. 611.

47 Msg, President to Hopkins, Marshall, and King, 25 Jul 42, WDCSA 381, Sec. 1.

[48] This view is also expressed in a personal letter, Marshall to Eisenhower, 30 Jul 42, GCM file under Eisenhower, D. D.

[49] Min, 34th Mtg CCS, 30 Jul 42, ABC 381 (7-25-42), Sec. 1.

[50] Memo, Maj Gen Walter B. Smith for JCS, 1 Aug 42, sub: Notes of Conf Held at the White House at 8:30 P.M., 30 Jul 42, OPD Exec 5, Item 1, Tab 14.

[51] For an extended account of this subject, see Leighton and Coakley, *Global Logistics, 1940-1943*, pp. 427-35.

[52] Ltr, Prime Minister to Harry Hopkins, 4 Sep 42, as quoted in Churchill, *The Hinge of Fate*, p. 539; Bryant, *The Turn of the Tide*, pp. 401-02.

[53] For an extended account, see Leighton and Coakley, *Global Logistics, 1940-1943*, pp. 417-24.

[54] Draft Outline Plan (Partial) Opn TORCH, Hq ETOUSA, 9 Aug 42, ABC 381 (7-25-42), 4A.

[55] Bryant, *The Turn of the Tide*, p. 400.

[56] Msg, Eisenhower to AGWAR, 22 Aug 42, copy in ABC 381 (7-25-42) Sec. 4-B.

[57] Msg, King to Marshall, 22 Aug 42, sub: Sp Opns, OPD Exec 5, Item 1; Msg 236, COS to Jt Staff Mission, 4 Aug 42, Exec 5, Item 2.

[58] Matloff and Snell, *Strategic Planning, 1941-1942*, p. 289.

[59] Bryant, *The Turn of the Tide*, p. 403.

[60] Churchill, *The Hinge of Fate*, pp. 484-86; Bryant, *The Turn of the Tide*, pp. 373-74.

[61] Churchill, *The Hinge of Fate*, p. 528.

[62] *Ibid.*, p. 530.

[63] Msg 1511, London to AGWAR, 26 Aug 42, ABC 381 (7-25-42) Sec. 4-B.

[64] Churchill, *The Hinge of Fate*, p. 531.

[65] Msg, Roosevelt to Churchill, 30 Aug 42, Exec 5, Item 1; Churchill, *The Hinge of Fate*, p. 532.

[66] AFHQ Commander in Chief Despatch, North African Campaign, p. 4.

[67] These views of Churchill are not in accord with the reports from British intelligence agents that Churchill showed Harry Hopkins in July when he was urging the United States to accept a North African offensive. Nor are they the same as those expressed in his message of 12 July to Dill. Sherwood, *Roosevelt and Hopkins*, pp. 610-11; Msg, Churchill to Field Marshal Dill, 12 Jul 42, ABC 381 (7-25-42) Sec. 4.

[68] Churchill, *The Hinge of Fate*, p. 534.

[69] Msg 144, Prime Minister to Roosevelt, 5 Sep 42, Exec 5, Item 1; Churchill, *The Hinge of Fate*, Ch. VII; Bryant, *The Turn of the Tide*, p. 403.

[70] CCS 103/3, 26 Sep 42, sub: Outline Plan Opn TORCH.

[71] Leighton and Coakley, *Global Logistics, 1940-1943*, p. 424.

[72] Memo, Col Hughes, DCAO AFHQ, to Gen Clark, 14 Sep 42, sub: Estimate of the Supply and Administrative Aspects of Proposed Operations; original in European Theater of Operations file, USFET AG 400, Supplies and Equipment, Vol. V.

CHAPTER 7

[1] The present study is based primarily on Richard M. Leighton and Robert W. Coakley, *Global Logistics and Strategy, 1940-1943* (Washington, 1956), and T. H. Vail Motter, *The Persian Corridor and Aid to Russia* (Washington, 1952), both in *United States Army in World War II*. Some use has also been made of two other volumes in the same series: Joseph Bykofsky and Harold Larson, *The Transportation Corps: Operations Overseas* (Washington, 1957),

for certain details relating to the transportation problem in Iran; and Maurice Matloff and Edwin M. Snell, *Strategic Planning for Coalition Warfare, 1941-1942* (Washington, 1953), for the story of the development of Anglo-American strategy. On the convoys to North Russia, Samuel Eliot Morison, *History of U.S. Naval Operations in World War II,* Vol. I: *The Battle of the Atlantic, September 1939-May 1943* (Boston: Little, Brown, 1947) and Winston S. Churchill, *The Hinge of Fate* (Boston: Houghton Mifflin, 1950) contain useful information. Guides to the original source material beyond those cited herein may be found in the footnotes and bibliographies of *United States Army in World War II.*

2 For the text of the Soviet protocols, see U.S. Dept. of State, *Wartime International Agreements: Soviet Supply Protocols,* Publication 2759, European Ser. 22 (Washington, no date).

3 On these early developments see Motter, *The Persian Corridor,* pp. 13-15, 28-100; Leighton and Coakley, *Global Logistics,* pp. 108-14, 503-07, 552-56, 567-69.

4 Rpt on War Aid Furnished by the United States to the USSR, prepared by the Protocol and Area Information Staff, USSR Br, and the Div of Research and Rpts, Dept of State, 28 Nov 45 (hereinafter cited as Rpt on War Aid to USSR, 28 Nov 45); Leighton and Coakley, *Global Logistics,* pp. 555-56, 567-68.

5 Churchill, *The Hinge of Fate,* pp. 256-66; Morison, *The Battle of the Atlantic,* pp. 158-71; Leighton and Coakley, *Global Logistics,* pp. 557-58.

6 Ltr, President to SW, 24 Mar 42, AG 400.3295 (8-14-41) Sec. 1.

7 Leighton and Coakley, *Global Logistics,* pp. 560-69.

8 Msg 100, AGWAR to AMSIR, 10 Apr 42; Msg 177, 9 May 42; and Msg 208, 20 May 42, all in AG 400.3295 (8-9-41), Secs. 4 and 5.

9 Motter, *The Persian Corridor,* pp. 59-64.

10 Bykofsky and Larson, *Transportation Corps: Operations Overseas,* pp. 379-82, 403-04.

11 *Ibid.,* pp. 380-81; Motter, *The Persian Corridor,* p. 84.

12 Leighton and Coakley, *Global Logistics,* pp. 569-70.

13 *Ibid.,* pp. 570-73; Motter, *The Persian Corridor,* pp. 85, 101-55, and App. A, Table 5.

14 Churchill, *The Hinge of Fate,* pp. 262-71; Morison, *The Battle of the Atlantic,* pp. 179-92.

15 On the strategic developments of this period, see Matloff and Snell, *Strategic Planning,* particularly pp. 233-84.

16 Msg 151, Prime Minister to President, 22 Sep 42, ABC 381 (7-25-42), Sec. 4-B.

17 Leighton and Coakley, *Global Logistics,* pp. 564-66.

18 Memo, President for Hopkins, Marshall, and King, 16 Jul 42, quoted in Robert E. Sherwood, *Roosevelt and Hopkins: An Intimate History,* rev. ed. (New York: Harper, 1950), pp. 603-05. See also Matloff and Snell, *Strategic Planning,* pp. 273-78.

19 Motter, *The Persian Corridor,* pp. 177-78, 190 n.; Sherwood, *Roosevelt and Hopkins,* pp. 544, 600; Leighton and Coakley, *Global Logistics,* p. 574.

20 Motter, *The Persian Corridor,* pp. 180-90; Leighton and Coakley, *Global Logistics,* pp. 574-75.

21 Msg, Churchill to Roosevelt, 22 Aug 42, quoted in Motter, *The Persian Corridor,* p. 190.

22 Msg, Harriman (signed Maxwell) to President, 22 Aug 42, CM-IN 8657, 23 Aug 42.

23 Memo, Somervell for Lutes, 29 Aug 42, Hq Army Service Forces (ASF) Folder Operations. (ASF records have been retired to National Archives.) MS Index to Hopkins Papers, V, Aid to Russia, Item 69; a copy of this index to Hopkins papers in the Hyde Park Library is in OCMH. Motter, *The Persian Corridor,* pp. 191-92.

24 (1) Plan for the Operation of Certain Iranian Communications Facilities Between Persian Gulf Ports and Tehran by U.S. Army Forces, 3 Sep 42, Persian Gulf Command Folder 235 (hereafter cited as SOS Plan). The Persian Gulf Command folders (PGF), at present with Army records in Federal Records Center, Alexandria, Va., consist of some of the documents used by Motter in preparation of the volume *The Persian Corridor and Aid to Russia.* (2) Control Division, ASF, folder of same title as above contains most of the papers used by Col. Elliot in preparation of the plan, including memorandums from various persons who rendered advice and from chiefs of technical services. It is to be found with the rest of the ASF records in the National Archives.

25 Memo, Maj Gen C. P. Gross, CofT, for Gen Somervell, 30 Aug 42, sub: Transportation Service for Persian Gulf; Control Div, ASF, folder on SOS Plan.

26 SOS Plan, par. 4. Memo, Spalding for Somervell, 4 Sep 42, sub: Target Estimates of Persian Gulf Supply Routes; and Memo, Spalding for Elliot, 5 Sep 42, with Incl, Comments by Lt Col W. E. V. Abraham of British Middle East Command on American Estimates, both in Control Div, ASF, folder on SOS Plan.

27 SOS Plan, Synopsis, pars. 7, 8.

28 CCS 109/1, Rpt by CPS, 22 Sep 42, title: Development of Persian Transportation Facilities.

29 *Ibid.*

30 Msg 151, Prime Minister to President, 22 Sep 42, ABC 381 (7-25-42), Sec. 4-B; Leighton and Coakley, *Global Logistics,* p. 583.

31 CCS 109/1, 22 Sep 42.

32 All quotations above from CCS 109/1. See also Memo, Elliot for Lutes, 4 Sep 42, OPD 334.8, CCS, Case 16; CCS 109, 2 Sep 42, title: Development of Persian Transportation Facilities; Research Draft prepared by OPD Hist Unit, USSR in U.S.-British Plans and Operations in 1942, pp. 83-95, MS, OCMH.

33 Memo, President for SW, 2 Oct 42, AG 400.3295 Sec. 12; Motter, *The Persian Corridor,* p. 180; Leighton and Coakley, *Global Logistics,* pp. 578, 584.

34 Estimate for August 1942 is based on Msg, AMSIR to AGWAR, 12 Oct 42, CM-IN 05027; all other figures are from Motter, *The Persian Corridor,* App. A, Tables 4, 5. See also Leighton and Coakley, *Global Logistics,* pp. 577-83.

35 State Dept Rpt on War Aid to USSR, 28 Nov 45; Leighton and Coakley, *Global Logistics,* pp. 583-97.

CHAPTER 8

1 The present essay is condensed from several chapters of Richard M. Leighton and Robert W. Coakley, *Global Logistics and Strategy, 1943-1945,* a forthcoming volume in *United States Army in World War II,* based on original research in the records of the Joint and Combined Chiefs of Staff, including the official minutes and papers of the Cairo-Tehran Conferences, and Army records in the custody of the Deputy Chief of Staff for Operations, G-3,

filed in the Federal Records Center of the National Archives. A contrasting interpretation of the Cairo-Tehran Conferences will be found in another volume in this series, Maurice Matloff, *Strategic Planning for Coalition Warfare, 1943-1944* (Washington, 1959). The conferences are also described from various points of view in a number of other works in the series: Gordon A. Harrison, *Cross-Channel Attack* (Washington, 1951); Charles F. Romanus and Riley Sunderland, *Stilwell's Command Problems* (Washington, 1956); Forrest C. Pogue, *The Supreme Command* (Washington, 1954); and Louis Morton and Henry Morgan, *The Pacific War: Strategy and Command, The Road to Victory* (in preparation). Three other American studies deal with the Cairo-Tehran Conferences at some length: Herbert Feis, *Churchill, Roosevelt, and Stalin* (Princeton: Princeton University Press, 1957); William Hardy McNeill, *America, Britain, and Russia: Their Co-Operation and Conflict, 1941-1946* (London: Oxford University Press, 1953); and Robert Sherwood, *Roosevelt and Hopkins: An Intimate History* (New York: Harper, 1948). The outstanding British interpretation is John Ehrman, *Grand Strategy,* Vol. V: *August 1943-September 1944* (London: H.M. Stationery Office, 1956), in the official British *History of the Second World War.* Of the large memoir literature, Winston S. Churchill's *Closing the Ring* (Boston: Houghton Mifflin, 1951) contains the most detailed and valuable account. The published memoirs of Admiral William D. Leahy, Admiral Ernest J. King, General Dwight D. Eisenhower, and Major General John R. Deane are also useful, though sketchy on the conferences themselves. Unfortunately, the memoirs for this period of two of the chief participants, Lord Alanbrooke (General Sir Alan Brooke) and General George C. Marshall, have not yet been published, but Arthur Bryant's memoir-biography of the former, *The Turn of the Tide* (Garden City, N.Y.: Doubleday, 1957), is valuable for the background of the British position. Three American studies, recently published, contain brief provocative analyses, from the American point of view, of the Anglo-American debate on European strategy in World War II: Kent Roberts Greenfield, *The Historian and the Army* (New Brunswick, N. J.: Rutgers University Press, 1954); Samuel Eliot Morison, *Strategy and Compromise* (Boston: Little, Brown, 1958); and Trumbull Higgins, *Winston Churchill and the Second Front* (New York: Oxford University Press, 1957).

[2] Frederick C. Lane, *Ships for Victory: A History of Shipbuilding Under the U.S. Maritime Commission in World War II* (Baltimore: Johns Hopkins Press, 1951), pp. 601-05; Gerald J. Fischer, *A Statistical Summary of Shipbuilding Under the U.S. Maritime Commission During World War II* (Washington, 1949), Table A-4; Leighton and Coakley, *Global Logistics, 1943-1945,* Ch. VII.

[3] For figures on distribution of LST's in November 1943, see CCS Memo for Info 175, 23 Nov 43, Landing Craft Reports, 1 Nov 43.

[4] Richard M. Leighton and Robert W. Coakley, *Global Logistics and Strategy, 1940-1943, United States Army in World War II* (Washington, 1955), pp. 376-82, 602-03, 682-83; George Mowry, *Landing Craft and the War Production Board* (WPB Study No. 11, July 1944), Ch. II; Jeter A. Isley and Philip A. Crowl, *The U.S. Marines and Amphibious War* (Princeton: Princeton University Press, 1951), pp. 1-4, 47-48; Harrison, *Cross-Channel Attack,* pp. 60-61. For a description of the various types of landing ships and craft, see *ONI 226, Allied Landing Craft and Ships* (Office, Chief of Naval Operations, April 1944).

[5] JPS 152/1, 3 Apr 43, title: Production of Landing Craft.

⁶ Leighton and Coakley, *Global Logistics, 1943-1945,* Chs. I and III.

⁷ *Ibid.,* Ch. VII.

⁸ *Ibid.*

⁹ This section is condensed from Leighton and Coakley, *Global Logistics, 1943-1945,* Chs. VI, VIII, and IX. For a good summary, see Harrison, *Cross-Channel Attack,* Ch. II.

¹⁰ Henry L. Stimson and McGeorge Bundy, *On Active Service in Peace and War* (New York: Harper, 1948), pp. 435-38; Bryant, *The Turn of the Tide,* pp. 573-76.

¹¹ OPD paper [about 12 Nov 43], U.S. Courses of Action in Case SEXTANT Decisions Do Not Guarantee OVERLORD, Exec 5, Item 12a. See also various staff studies in ABC 381 Strategy Section Papers (7 January 1943), Numbers 131-95.

¹² Memo, Representatives COS, in CCS 379, 26 Oct 43, Opns in Mediterranean.

¹³ Msg 51, Deane to JCS, 9 Nov 43, with related papers in Exec 5, Item 15, Env 3; John R. Deane, *The Strange Alliance* (New York: Viking Press, 1947), p. 35; Churchill, *Closing the Ring,* pp. 286-89; Cordell Hull, *Memoirs of Cordell Hull* (New York: Macmillan, 1948), Vol. II, p. 1301; Ehrman, *Grand Strategy,* Vol. V, pp. 100-01, 156-57.

¹⁴ Leighton and Coakley, *Global Logistics, 1943-1945,* Ch. VIII.

¹⁵ Quoted in Churchill, *Closing the Ring,* pp. 329-33. See also Matloff *Strategic Planning for Coalition Warfare, 1943-1944,* Ch. XVI.

¹⁶ CCS 409, Note by COS, 25 Nov 43, OVERLORD and the Mediterranean; Ehrman, *Grand Strategy,* Vol. V, pp. 109-12.

¹⁷ CCS 409, cited N.16(1); Ehrman, *Grand Strategy,* Vol. V, pp. 104-21, 165-67; Min, 2d Plenary Mtg, SEXTANT, 24 Nov 43.

¹⁸ The discussion of these points is described in detail in Leighton and Coakley, *Global Logistics, 1943-1945,* Ch. VIII.

¹⁹ Ehrman, *Grand Strategy,* Vol. V, pp. 148-53; Romanus and Sunderland, *Stilwell's Command Problems,* Ch. II; [Mountbatten] *Report to CCS by Supreme Allied Commander Southeast Asia, 1943-45* (London: H.M. Stationery Office, 1951), p. 27; Matloff, *Strategic Planning for Coalition Warfare, 1943-1944,* Chs. XIV and XVI, pp. 2-3.

²⁰ [Mountbatten] *Report,* p. 27; Romanus and Sunderland, *Stilwell's Command Problems,* p. 51; Ernest J. King and Walter Muir Whitehill, *Fleet Admiral King: A Naval Record* (New York: Norton, 1952), pp. 509-10; Ehrman, *Grand Strategy,* Vol. V, p. 162; Min, CCS 129th Mtg, 24 Nov 43.

²¹ Msg, PM for CofS Com, 21 Nov 43, quoted in Churchill, *Closing the Ring,* p. 686; Ehrman, *Grand Strategy,* Vol. V, pp. 114, 159; Min, 2d Plenary Mtg, SEXTANT, 24 Nov 43; Romanus and Sunderland, *Stilwell's Command Problems,* p. 66.

²² See Marshall's outburst quoted in Joseph W. Stilwell (Theodore H. White, ed.), *The Stilwell Papers* (New York, Sloane, 1948), p. 255; Min, 129th Mtg CCS, 24 Nov 43; Min, 130th Mtg JCS, 25 Nov 43.

²³ Churchill, *Closing the Ring,* p. 328; Ehrman, *Grand Strategy,* Vol. V, pp. 162, 164-65, 571; Min, CCS 128th Mtg, 23 Nov 43; Romanus and Sunderland, *Stilwell's Command Problems,* p. 65; Min, 1st Plenary Mtg, SEXTANT, 23 Nov 43.

²⁴ See Marshall's remark at the JCS meeting earlier in the day. Min, JCS 130th Mtg, 25 Nov 43.

²⁵ The evidence on this last point is strong but not conclusive. Churchill asserts unequivocally that the pledge was given (*Closing the Ring,* page 328), and Ehrman accepts this as fact (*Grand Strategy,* Vol. V, p. 165). Matloff

(*Strategic Planning for Coalition Warfare, 1943-1944,* Ch. XVI) regards it as at least highly probable. Romanus and Sunderland, who give little attention to the amphibious phases of the war in Burma, do not mention the pledge, though they do mention the promise to equip more Chinese divisions. It may be significant that the President, in the interview with Stilwell and Marshall mentioned above, seemed from his remarks to have the Andamans operation on his mind. But the most convincing evidence is to be found, as shown below, in the abrupt change in the attitude and position of the JCS on the morning of November 26.

26 Min, JCS 131st Mtg, 26 Nov 43.

27 Msg, FDR to Byrnes, Dir OWM, 23 Nov 43, Exec 5, Item 14; Msg, Byrnes to President, 25 Nov 43, in JCS Memo for Info 171, 27 Nov 43, ABC 561 (30 Aug 43); Mowry, *Landing Craft and the WPB,* pp. 30-32.

28 Min, CCS 131st Mtg, 26 Nov 43; Ehrman, *Grand Strategy,* Vol. V, pp. 166-67.

29 Min, 1st Plenary Mtg, EUREKA, 28 Nov 43.

30 *Ibid.;* Ehrman, *Grand Strategy,* Vol. V, pp. 174-76.

31 Min, 132d Mtg JCS, 28 Nov 43.

32 Ehrman, *Grand Strategy,* Vol. V, p. 175; Churchill, *Closing the Ring,* p. 355.

33 Min, 1st Plenary Mtg, EUREKA, 28 Nov 43; Ehrman, *Grand Strategy,* Vol. V, p. 176. Italics supplied.

34 Min, 1st Plenary Mtg, EUREKA, 28 Nov 43; Ehrman, *Grand Strategy,* Vol. V, p. 176.

35 Min, Military Mtg, EUREKA, 29 Nov 43; Min, 2d Plenary Mtg, EUREKA, 29 Nov 43; see also Churchill's account of Stalin's attack on General Brooke at the banquet on the evening of November 30, *Closing the Ring,* pp. 386-88.

36 Min, Military Mtg, EUREKA, 29 Nov 43.

37 Quoted in Mowry, *Landing Craft and the WPB,* p. 31; see also pp. 32-33. Actually, the program had already been accelerated, in response to Roosevelt's message of November 23, since certain measures had to be set in train immediately, without waiting for the President's order. See Leighton and Coakley, *Global Logistics, 1943-1945,* Ch. VII.

38 Min, 2d Plenary Mtg, EUREKA, 29 Nov 43. This was hardly a compelling argument for a May OVERLORD since the Russians, as the British pointed out, had never launched a summer offensive in that month. According to Churchill, Stalin told him at lunch on November 30 that he wanted OVERLORD in May or in June in order for it to synchronize with the Soviet offensive. In the event, the latter jumped off on June 23, two and a half weeks after OVERLORD. See Churchill, *Closing the Ring,* pp. 380, 383.

39 Min, 2d Plenary Mtg, EUREKA, 29 Nov 43; Churchill, *Closing the Ring,* p. 371; Ehrman, *Grand Strategy,* Vol. V, p. 179.

40 Min, 2d Plenary Mtg, EUREKA, 29 Nov 43; Churchill, *Closing the Ring,* p. 370; Ehrman, *Grand Strategy,* Vol. V, p. 180; Sherwood, *Roosevelt and Hopkins,* p. 788. The British accounts indicate that both Roosevelt and Stalin gave the OVERLORD date as "in May," or words to that effect.

41 Churchill, *Closing the Ring,* p. 376; Ehrman, *Grand Strategy,* Vol. V, p. 181.

42 Ehrman, *Grand Strategy,* Vol. V, p. 181.

43 Min, 132d Mtg CCS, 30 Nov 43; Harrison, *Cross-Channel Attack,* p. 125; James D. Hamilton, *Threat to Southern France* (in draft MS), on the southern France operations, OCMH. The Americans had little reliable data on the southern France operation with them at Tehran.

44 Min, 132d Mtg CCS, 30 Nov 43; Msg WAF 492, Eisenhower to CCS, 29 Oct 43, quoted in Ehrman, *Grand Strategy,* Vol. V, pp. 188-89.

45 Min, 132d Mtg CCS, 30 Nov 43; Ehrman, *Grand Strategy*, Vol. V, p. 182; Msg FAN 281, CCS to Eisenhower, 1 Dec 43, Exec 3, Item 13.

46 Min, 3d Plenary Mtg EUREKA, 30 Nov 43.

47 Min, JCS 131st Mtg, 26 Nov 43; see Hopkins' strong statement in Sherwood, *Roosevelt and Hopkins*, pp. 793-96.

48 CCS Memo for Info 165, 2 Dec 43, Military Conclusions of the EUREKA Conference. It was also noted that Stalin had undertaken to attack Bulgaria if the latter attacked Turkey.

49 Min, CCS 135th Mtg, 5 Dec 43; Ehrman, *Grand Strategy*, Vol. V, pp. 185-86; Romanus and Sunderland, *Stilwell's Command Problems*, pp. 65-67; Morton and Morgan, *The Pacific War: Strategy and Command, The Road to Victory*, Ch. I.

50 Min, CCS 133d Mtg, 3 Dec 43; Min, 3d Plenary Mtg, SEXTANT, 4 Dec 43; CPS 131/1, 3 Dec 43, Amph Opns Against South of France; Msg 10131, Adm Badger to VCNO, 5 Dec 43, Exec 5, Item 13; CCS 424, Rpt by CPS and CAdC, 5 Dec 43, Amph Opns Against South of France; Ehrman, *Grand Strategy*, Vol. V, pp. 184, 187, 195.

King's offer was accompanied by a warning that it might result in setting back the operation against Truk, the main Japanese base in the Caroline Islands. He did not mention that the JCS had already decided, some three weeks earlier, to suspend the attack on Truk pending the results of carrier raids to test whether it might be feasible to bypass the fortress. See Min, JCS 123d Mtg, 15 Nov, and 124th Mtg, 17 Nov 43, and Robert Ross Smith, *The Approach to the Philippines*, in *United States Army in World War II* (Washington, 1953), p. 6.

51 The total extra lift required was figured at 3 XAP's (modified assault transports), 12 MT ships (freighters fitted for vehicle carriage), 26 LST's, and 31 LCT's. King promised to provide the XAP's, the LST's, and 26 of the LCT's. The MT ships were, or would be, available in the area; the five LCT's could be taken from craft earmarked for OVERLORD, to be replaced by others in the contingent promised for OVERLORD on November 5. See CCS 424, 5 Dec 43, cited n. 50.

52 Min, 4th Plenary Mtg, SEXTANT, 5 Dec 43.

53 Churchill, *Closing the Ring*, p. 411; Min, 4th Plenary Mtg, SEXTANT, 5 Dec 43; Ehrman, *Grand Strategy*, Vol. V, pp. 190-92; King and Whitehill, *Fleet Admiral King*, p. 425; William D. Leahy, *I Was There* (New York: Whittlesey House, 1950), p. 213; Sherwood, *Roosevelt and Hopkins*, p. 801.

54 Min, 136th Mtg JCS, 6 Dec 43; Min, 136th Mtg CCS, 5 Dec 43; Min, 137th Mtg CCS, 6 Dec 43; CCS 427, Rpt by CPS, 5 Dec 43, title: Amph Opns in Southeast Asia Alternative to BUCCANEER; Romanus and Sunderland, *Stilwell's Command Problems*, p. 70; Ehrman, *Grand Strategy*, Vol. V, pp. 192-93.

55 Msg, President to Chiang, 5 Dec, Exec 10, Item 70; Min, 5th Plenary Mtg, SEXTANT, 6 Dec 43. Since the CCS recommendations were those approved by the JCS and had been drafted by General Marshall, it is possible that Marshall had earlier shown this draft to the President and that the latter used it, but without informing Marshall. At all events, it seems unlikely that the Chiefs of Staff could have known on the morning of December 6 that the President had already cabled Chiang, since they were discussing their own draft with a view to submitting it to the President. See Matloff, *Strategic Planning for Coalition Warfare, 1943-1944*, Ch. XVI, p. 60.

56 Ehrman, *Grand Strategy*, Vol. V, pp. 193, 211-12; [Mountbatten] *Report*, p. 29; Romanus and Sunderland, *Stilwell's Command Problems*, pp. 75ff.

57 For example, Sherwood (*Roosevelt and Hopkins,* p. 788) states that Churchill at the plenary meeting on November 29 "bowed to the inevitable" —*i.e.,* accepted OVERLORD—by promising Stalin that "Britain would hurl every ounce of her strength across the Channel at the Germans." Admiral Leahy in his memoirs (*I Was There,* p. 209) speaks of the decision on a May OVERLORD (which he represents as a capitulation by the British, not a compromise) in the same sense—*e.g.,* the British "fell into line." See also Harrison, *Cross-Channel Attack,* pp. 125-26; Ray S. Cline, *Washington Command Post: The Operations Division,* in *United States Army in World War II* (Washington, 1951), p. 229; Matloff, *Strategic Planning for Coalition Warfare, 1943-1944,* Ch. XIII, pp. 71-72, and *The Decision to Invade Southern France* (in Ms), pp. 8-9; Greenfield, *The Historian and the Army,* p. 54; Higgins, *Winston Churchill and the Second Front,* pp. 212-13, 244.

58 Churchill, *Closing the Ring,* p. 380.

59 The additional lift was listed as follows:

| | OVERLORD | | ANVIL | |
	U.S.	British	U.S.	British
LST's	23	3	36	5
LCI(L)'s	24			
LCT's	19	45	31	
Assault Transports			3	6

See CCS 428 (Rev.), 15 Dec 43, Annex V.

60 CCS 426/1, 6 Dec 43, Rpt to President and Prime Minister.

61 CCS 428 (Rev.), 15 Dec 43, Annex V; CCS 426/1, 6 Dec 43, Rpt to President and Prime Minister. A summary of the Cairo-Tehran decisions prepared for the Army Service Forces on December 15 stated that Turkish intervention and surrender of Bulgaria were considered "probable," and that in this event it would be necessary "to mount such operations as may be practicable in the Eastern Mediterranean. . . ." See Memo, Gen Wood for various addressees, 15 Dec 43, sub: SEXTANT Decisions, ASF Planning Div Folder SEXTANT Decisions.

62 Churchill, *Closing the Ring,* p. 376.

CHAPTER 9

1 This study is based on John Miller, Jr., *Cartwheel: The Reduction of Rabaul* (in press), in *United States Army in World War II.*

2 These campaigns are treated in the following volumes of *United States Army in World War II:* John Miller, Jr., *Guadalcanal: The First Offensive* (Washington, 1949); Samuel Milner, *Victory in Papua* (Washington, 1957); Robert Ross Smith, *The Approach to the Philippines* (Washington, 1953). *Cartwheel: The Reduction of Rabaul* treats the campaigns from June 30, 1943, through March 1944 and includes the Admiralties operations. In the *American Forces in Action* series, by the Historical Division, War Department Special Staff, *The Admiralties: Operations of the 1st Cavalry Division (29 February-18 May 1944)* (Washington, 1943), treats the Admiralties fighting in detail. General Walter Krueger devotes Chapter V of his *From Down Under to Nippon: The Story of Sixth Army in World War II* (Washington: Combat Forces Press, 1953) to the Admiralties.

3 See, for example, Encl B, JWPC 58/D, 24 Jun 43, Memo for RAINBOW Team, in Operations Division (OPD) File 384 Marshall Islands Sec. 1 (10 Jun 43).

[4] JCS Min, 92d Mtg, 15 Jun 43; Rad, JCS to MacArthur, CM-OUT 6093, 15 Jun 43, in Gen Marshall's OUT Log.

[5] Rad, MacArthur to Marshall, CM-IN 13149, 20 Jun 43; Rad, MacArthur to Marshall, CM-OUT 13605, 22 Jun 43, both in Gen Marshall's IN Log. Halsey sent his views to MacArthur who relayed them to the JCS.

[6] JCS Min, 20 Jul 43; JCS 386/1, 19 Jul 43, Strategy in the Pacific; JPS 205/3, 10 Jul 43, Opns Against Marshall Islands; Draft Memo, JPS for JCS, 12 Jul 43, sub: Strategy in the Pacific, and OPD Draft Memo, 14 Jul 43, both in OPD File 381 Security 195; JPS Draft, 19 Jul 43, sub: Strategy in the Pacific, and attached papers, with JPS 219/D, in OPD File ABC 384 Pacific (28 Jun 43); OPD Brief, Notes on JWPC 58/2, in OPD File 384 Marshall Islands Sec. 1 (10 Jun 43).

[7] Rads, Marshall to MacArthur, No. 8604, 21 Jun 43, and MacArthur to Marshall, No. 16419, 23 Jun 43, in Gen Marshall's IN and OUT Logs.

[8] Smith, *Approach to the Philippines*, Ch. I; CCS 319/5, 24 Aug 43, Final Rpt to the President and Prime Minister; CCS 301/3, 27 Aug 43, Specific Opns in Pacific and Far East, 1943-44; Rad, Marshall to MacArthur, No. 8679, 2 Oct 43, in Gen Marshall's OUT Log.

[9] GHQ Warning Instructions 3, 23 Nov 43, in ALAMO Force ANCHORAGE Jnl, 1, 23 Nov 43-12 Feb 44.

[10] File on Manus-Kavieng Base Development in GHQ SWPA G-3 Jnl, 5 Nov 43.

[11] Memo, SJC [Maj Gen Stephen J. Chamberlin, AC of S G-3, GHW SWPA] for Jnl, 21 Dec 43, sub: Conf at GHQ, 20 Dec 43, in GHQ SWPA G-3 Jnl, 21 Dec 43.

[12] Fleet Admiral William F. Halsey and Lt. Comdr. J. Bryan, III, *Admiral Halsey's Story* (New York: Whittlesey House, 1947), pp. 186-87; Fleet Admiral Ernest J. King and Walter Muir Whitehill, *Fleet Admiral King, A Naval Record* (New York: Norton, 1952), pp. 533-34.

[13] Philip A. Crowl and Edmund G. Love, *Seizure of the Gilberts and Marshalls,* in *United States Army in World War II* (Washington, 1955).

[14] Rad, CINCPOA (Nimitz) to CINCSWPA (MacArthur), CNO (King), COMSOPAC (Halsey), 7 Jan 44, CM-IN 8330, in Gen Marshall's IN Log.

[15] Memo, Carney for Halsey, 12 Dec 43, sub: CINCPOA-SOPAC Stf Conf, 9-12 Dec 43, in GHQ SWPA G-3 Jnl, 21 Dec 43; Memo, B. F. (Brig Gen Bonner Fellers, G-3 Sec GHQ SWPA), no addressee, 22 Dec 43, sub: Conf G-3 Plng Sec, in GHQ SWPA G-3 Jnl, 22 Dec 43.

[16] Rad, CINCPAC (Nimitz) to COMINCH (King), 22 Dec 43, in GHQ SWPA G-3 Jnl, 24 Dec 43; Rad, Halsey to MacArthur, 5 Jan 44; Rad, MacArthur to Marshall and Halsey, 6 Jan 44; Rad, COMSOPAC to COMSOPAC ADMIN, 9 Jan 44; Rad, CINCPAC to CINCSWPA, CNO; and COMSOPAC, 7 Jan 44, CM-IN 8330, all in Gen Marshall's IN Log.

[17] JCS 679, 24 Jan 44, Dirs for Seizure of Bismarck Archipelago; Rads, JCS to CINCPAC and CINCSWPA, 23 Jan 44, with JCS 679.

[18] Forces involved were: 3 CVs, 3 CVLs, 7 CRUs, and 18 DDs. In addition 4 OBBs, 7 CRUs, 4 CVEs, 1 AGC, 19 APAs, 3 LSDs, 5 DMSs, 36 LSTs, and 36 LCIs would be assigned to Halsey's Third Fleet for Kavieng, while, for Manus, Kinkaid's Seventh Fleet was to receive 3 CLs, 4 CVEs, 35 DDs, 8 PFs, 1 AGC, 1 APA, 1 AKA, 2 DMSs, 1 LSD, 13 APDs, 30 LSTs, 30 LCIs, 70 LCTs, and 30 SSs. Halsey and Bryan, *Admiral Halsey's Story,* p. 188; George C. Kenney, *General Kenney Reports: A Personal History of the Pacific War* (New York: Duell, Sloan & Pearce, 1949), p. 346; Smith, *Approach to the Philippines,* pp. 7-8; Halsey, Narrative Account of the South Pacific Campaign, copy in OCMH; Rad, CINCPAC to COMINCH-CNO,

29 Jan 44, in GHQ SWPA G-3 Jnl, 30 Jan 44; Ltr, CINCPOA to CO-MINCH, 30 Jan 44, sub: Assignment Naval Forces and Assault Shipping to Third and Seventh Fleets for Opns Bismarck Archipelago, ABC 384 Pac (17 Jan 44) Sec. 3-A.

19 Southeast Area Naval Operations, III, Japanese Monograph 50, p. 6, OCMH.

20 GHQ SWPA Warning Instructions 3, 23 Nov 43, in ALAMO ANCHORAGE Jnl, 1, 23 Nov 43-12 Feb 44; Memo, Chamberlin for CINC, 9 Feb 44, sub: Outline Plan—Hansa Bay, and Memo, Chamberlin for Comdrs, 9 Feb 44, sub: Hansa Bay, SWPA Forces, both in GHQ SWPA G-3 Jnl, 9 Feb 44; Note SJC to CINC, 12 Feb 44, in GHQ SWPA G-3 Jnl, 13 Feb 44.

21 Wesley Frank Craven and James Lea Cate, eds., *The Army Air Forces in World War II,* Vol. IV: *The Pacific: Guadalcanal to Saipan* (Chicago: University of Chicago Press, 1950), p. 559; Kenney, *General Kenney Reports,* p. 358.

22 GHQ SWPA G-2 Daily Summary of Enemy Intel and GHQ SWPA G-2 Est Enemy Sit 700, 20-21 Feb 44, in GHQ SWPA G-3 Jnl, 21 Feb 44.

23 Rad, Comdr AdVon Fifth AF to Comdr Allied Air Forces SWPA, 23 Feb 44, in GHQ SWPA G-3 Jnl, 23 Feb 44.

24 Kenney, *General Kenney Reports,* p. 359.

25 Rad, MacArthur to Comdr ALAMO, CG AdVon Fifth AF, and Comdr VII Amphib Force, 24 Feb 44, in GHQ SWPA G-3 Jnl, 24 Feb 44; Rad, MacArthur to same addressees, 25 Feb 44, in GHQ SWPA G-3 Jnl, 25 Feb 44.

26 Rad, Comdr AdVon Fifth AF to Comdr Allied Air Forces SWPA, 26 Feb 44, in GHQ SWPA G-3 Jnl, 26 Feb 44.

27 Note, G-2 to G-3, 25 Feb 44, in GHQ SWPA G-3 Jnl, 25 Feb 44; GHQ SWPA Monthly Summary of Enemy Dispositions, 29 Feb 44, in GHQ SWPA G-3 Jnl, 29 Feb 44. In a book published ten years after these events, Gen. Willoughby stated that 3,250 Japanese were estimated as holding the Admiralties. See Charles A. Willoughby and John Chamberlain, *MacArthur: 1941-1951* (New York: McGraw-Hill, 1954), p. 151.

28 Cf. par. 1a (2) of BREWER TF FO 2, 25 Feb 44, with Annex I, Intel, in ALAMO ANCHORAGE Jnl, 3, 24-26 Feb 44. ALAMO FO 9 and BREWER TF FO 1 are orders prepared for the one-division invasion of the Admiralties scheduled for April 1.

29 8th Area Army Operations, Japanese Monograph 110, p. 133, OCMH; Southeast Area Naval Operations, III, Japanese Monograph 50, pp. 35-36, OCMH. The 1st Cavalry Division, losing 326 men killed, 1,189 wounded, and 4 missing, reported that it buried a total counted dead of 3,280 and captured 75. Krueger estimated that the Japanese had disposed of 1,100 additional bodies. ALAMO Rpt BREWER Opn, p. 26.

30 Admiral Kinkaid's statement to author, Nov. 16, 1953.

31 Kenney, *General Kenney Reports,* p. 361.

32 Rad, Chase to Krueger, Serial 7, 0900, 1st Cav Brig Jnl, 29 Feb 44, Vol. III of 1st Cav Brig Hist Rpt Admiralty Islands Campaign. (The 1st Cavalry Division, which fought as infantry in World War II, was square at that time.)

33 Quoted in 1st Cav Brig Hist Rpt Admiralty Islands Campaign, I, 3. There are other versions of MacArthur's statement in existence, all to the same effect.

34 Comment by the force G-2, Lt Col Julio Chiaramonte, attached to Ltr, Chase to the Chief of Military History, 6 Nov 53, OCMH files; Rad, CINCSWPA to CTF 76, CGs ALAMO and Fifth AF, 29 Feb 44, in GHQ SWPA G-3 Jnl, 1 Mar 44.

[35] 8th Area Army Opns, Japanese Monograph 110, p. 135, OCMH.

[36] *Building the Navy's Bases in World War II: History of the Bureau of Yards and Docks and the Civil Engineer Corps, 1940-1946,* Vol. II (Washington, 1947), pp. 295-302; Office of the Chief Engineer, GHQ AFPAC, *Engineers of the Southwest Pacific, 1941-1945,* Vol. VI, *Airfield and Base Development* (Washington, 1951), pp. 208-22, and Vol. VIII, *Critique* (Washington, 1951), pp. 145-53.

[37] Min of Conf, 1700, 3 Mar 44, at GHQ SWPA, in GHQ SWPA G-3 Jnl, 3 Mar 44; Smith, *Approach to the Philippines,* p. 9.

[38] Rad, MacArthur to C of S USA for JCS, 5 Mar 44, in GHQ SWPA G-3 Jnl, 5 Mar 44.

[39] JCS 713/4, Future Opns in Pac, 12 Mar 44; Rad, JCS to MacArthur, 12 Mar 44, in Gen Marshall's OUT Log.

CHAPTER 10

[1] The main sources for this study have been the captured documents of the German Army, copies of which are on file at the National Archives in Washington. The most important single source was the War Diary of the German Armed Forces High Command, Operations Section (OKW/WFSt, KTB). Extensive use was also made of manuscript chapters by Howard McGaw Smyth which will be published in a volume of *United States Army in World War II* entitled *Sicily and the Surrender of Italy.* Other sources found useful and informative were the postwar manuscripts written by high-ranking German participants in the Italian campaign, including Field Marshal Albert Kesselring and his former Chief of Staff, General Siegfried Westphal, and the commander of Tenth Army, General von Vietinghoff (OCMH files). A translation of the notes of Hitler's conferences with Admiral Karl Doenitz, published by the Office of Naval Intelligence, and taken from the War Diary of the German Naval Operations Staff, provided important information on Hitler's thoughts and decisions and supplemented the War Diary of the Armed Forces Operations Section of the High Command.

[2] Quoted by Smyth, *Sicily and the Surrender of Italy,* Ch. VII.

[3] German Foreign Office Document: *"Aufzeichnung über die Unterredung zwischen dem RAM und dem Staatssekretär Bastiani im Schloss Klessheim,"* 9 April 1943 (OCMH files).

[4] For a detailed discussion of German-Italian relations during 1943 and for German plans relating to the possibility of Italian defection, see Smyth, *Sicily and the Surrender of Italy,* Chs. III, VII, and IX.

[5] *OKW/WFSt/Op Nr. 661138/43,* 22 May 1943, in *Westl. Mittelmeer, Chefsachen* (CRS H 22/290).

[6] Walter Warlimont, *"Die Strategie der deutschen obersten Fuehrung im zweiten Vierteljahr 1943,"* OCMH, MS P-049, p. 149.

[7] *Führer Conferences on Matters Dealing with the German Navy, 1943,* translation (Washington: Office of Naval Intelligence, 1947) (hereafter referred to as *Führer Conferences, 1943*).

[8] Siegfried Westphal et al., *Der Feldzug in Italien,* Part I, Ch. IV, *"Die Verstärkung der deutschen Heereskräfte und die Entwicklung der Erdlage in Italien bis zum Abfall des Bundesgenossen,"* OCMH MS # Tla.

[9] Albert Kesselring, *Soldat bis zum Letzten Tag* (Bonn, 1953); Siegfried Westphal et al., *Der Feldzug in Italien,* Part I, *"Abschliessende Bemerkungen"* by Albert Kesselring, OCMH MS # Tla-K1.

[10] *Führer Conferences, 1943,* pp. 102-06; Hitler's Conferences (fragments of

stenographic notes taken at Führer Hq), Nr. 14 (1), 25 Jul 43 and Nr. 16 (1), 26 Jul 43 (OCMH files); Smyth, *Sicily and the Surrender of Italy,* Ch. VII.

11 *OKW/WFSt/Op Nr. 661763/43,* 1 Aug 43, in *Westl. Mittelmeer, Chefsachen* (CRS H 22/290).

12 Siegfried Westphal *et al., Der Feldzug in Italien,* Part I, Ch. IV, *"Die Verstärkung der deutschen Heereskräfte und die Entwicklung der Erdlage in Italien bis zum Abfall des Bundesgenossen,"* OCMH MS # Tla.

13 *Führer Conferences, 1943,* p. 94.

14 *OKW/WFSt, KTB 1.VII.-30.IX.43,* entry of 9 Jul 43; *Führer Conferences, 1943,* p. 117.

15 Warlimont, *"Die Strategie der deutschen obersten Führung,"* MS # P-049, p. 135.

16 *OKW/WFSt, KTB 1.VII.-30.IX.43,* entry of 1 Aug 43.

17 *OKW/WFSt, KTB 1.VII.-30.IX.43,* entry of 5 and 19 Aug 43.

18 Smyth, *Sicily and the Surrender of Italy,* Ch. IX.

19 *OKW/WFSt, KTB 1.VII.-30.IX.43,* entry of 5 and 19 Aug 43.

20 *OKW/WFSt, KTB 1.VII.-30.IX.43,* entry of 14 Aug 43.

21 *OKW/WFSt, KTB 1.VII.-30.IX.43,* entry of 16 Aug 43.

22 Smyth, *Sicily and the Surrender of Italy,* Ch. IX.

23 Westphal *et al., Der Feldzug in Italien,* Ch. VI, *"Die Kämpfe der 10. Armee in Süd- und Mittelitalien"* (written by Vietinghoff), p. 13.

24 Westphal *et al., Der Feldzug in Italien,* Ch. VI, Memo, *"Vermerk über Besprechung beim Führer am 17.8.43,"* in *Tenth Army KTB, Anlagen X.VIII.-12.9.43* (CRS, AOK 10, 42803/2).

25 Smyth, *Sicily and the Surrender of Italy,* Ch. VIII.

26 *OKW/WFSt, KTB 1.VII.-30.IX.43,* entry of 13 Aug 43.

27 Order, *OKW/WFSt* Nr. 661966/43, 18 Aug 43, in *Westliches Mittelmeer, Chefsachen* (CRS H 22/290).

28 *OKW/WFSt, KTB 1.VII.-30.IX.43,* entry of 29 and 30 Aug 43.

29 Order, Tenth Army, *"Armeebefehl Nr 2,"* 4 Sep 43, in *Tenth Army KTB, Anlagen 8.VIII.-12.IX.43* (CRS AOK 10, 42803/2).

30 *OKW/WFSt, KTB 1.VII.-30.IX.43,* entry of 8 and 9 Sep 43.

31 Smyth, *Sicily and the Surrender of Italy,* Ch. IX.

32 *OKW/WFSt, KTB 1.VII.-30.IX.43,* entry of 7 and 8 Sep 43.

33 Smyth, *Sicily and the Surrender of Italy,* Ch. VII, p. 16.

34 *OKW/WFSt, KTB 1.VII.-30.IX.43,* entry of 12 Sep 43.

35 Tel, Commander-in-Chief South to Tenth Army, Nr. 6159/43, 14 Sep 43, in *Tenth Army KTB, Anlagen 12.IX.-20.IX.43* (CRS AOK 10, 42803/3).

36 In postwar accounts, General Siegfried Westphal, Kesselring's former Chief of Staff, and Kesselring himself claim to have requested the transfer of two Panzer divisions from Army Group B to Salerno. Available records do not indicate that such a request was made by Commander-in-Chief South. Westphal *et al., Der Feldzug in Italien,* Chs. VII and Kl.

37 Westphal *et al., Der Feldzug in Italien,* Tla-Kl.

38 Westphal *et al., Der Feldzug in Italien,* Tla-Kl.

39 *OKW/WFSt, KTB 1.VII.-30.IX.43,* entry of 15 Sep 43.

40 *OKW/WFSt, KTB 1.VII.-30.IX.43,* entry of 8 Sep 43.

41 *LI Mtn Corps, Ia Nr. 579/43,* 4 Nov 43, in *Italien-Verschiedenes-Allgemein* (CRS H 22/145); Westphal *et al., Der Feldzug in Italien,* Ch. VII.

42 Westphal *et al., Der Feldzug in Italien,* Ch. VII, *"Die Auffassung der Heeresgruppe";* B. H. Liddell Hart, ed., *The Rommel Papers* (New York: Harcourt, Brace, 1953), p. 446.

[43] Siegfried Westphal, *Heer in Fesseln* (Bonn, 1950), p. 237; Liddell Hart, *The Rommel Papers*, p. 446.

[44] *OKW/WFSt, KTB 1.VII.-30.IX.43* and *1.X.-31.XII.43*, entries of 8 Sep and 4 Oct 43.

[45] *OKW/WFSt, KTB 1.VII.-30.IX.43*, entry of 17 Sep 43.

[46] Hitler's Conferences (fragments) Nr. 46, 31 Aug 44.

[47] *Führer Conferences, 1943*, p. 140.

[48] *OKW/WFSt, KTB 1.X.-31.XII.43*, entry of 1 Oct 43; Liddell Hart, *The Rommel Papers*, p. 446.

[49] *OKW/WFSt, KTB 1.X.-31.XII.43*, entry of 1 Oct 43.

[50] Order, *OKW/WFSt/Op Nr. 662409/43*, 4 Oct 43, in *Westl. Mittelmeer, Chefsachen* (CRS H 22/290).

[51] *OKW/WFSt, KTB 1.VII.-30.IX.43*, entry of 25 Sep 43.

[52] Tel, *OKW/WFSt/Op Nr. 66274/43*, 10 Oct 43, in *Westl. Mittelmeer, Chefsachen* (CRS H 22/290).

[53] Westphal, *Heer in Fesseln*, p. 236; Liddell Hart, *The Rommel Papers*, p. 446.

[54] Order, *OKW/WFSt/Op Nr. 6123/43*, 6 Nov 43, in *H.Gr.C, Grundsätzliche Befehle* (CRS HGr C 75138/12).

[55] For further details concerning Kesselring's appointment, see Lucian Heichler, "Kesselring's Appointment as Commander in Chief Southwest," OCMH MS # R-3.

CHAPTER 11

[1] The Italian campaign, from the autumn of 1943 to the spring of 1944, is covered in the author's forthcoming *Salerno to Cassino,* a volume in the series *United States Army in World War II.* Accessible secondary sources on the Anzio landing include: Mark W. Clark, *Calculated Risk* (New York: Harper, 1950); Lt. Col. Chester G. Starr, ed., *From Salerno to the Alps: A History of the Fifth Army, 1943-1945* (Washington: Infantry Journal Press, 1948); Lt. General L. K. Truscott, Jr., *Command Missions* (New York: Dutton, 1954); [Capt. John Bowditch, III, and 1st Lt. Robert W. Komer] *Anzio Beachhead,* in *American Forces in Action* (Washington, 1947).

[2] Summary Minutes of Meeting, Eisenhower's Villa, Algiers, 29 May-3 June 1943, in ABC 384. Accounts of the Algiers conference may be found in Maurice Matloff, *Strategic Planning for Coalition Warfare, 1943-1944, United States Army in World War II* (Washington, 1959), Ch. VI; and Dwight D. Eisenhower, *Crusade in Europe* (Garden City, N.Y.: Doubleday, 1948), pp. 193-95.

[3] Clark, *Calculated Risk,* p. 245.

[4] Planning papers on the Italian invasion during the first nine months of 1943 refer often to the need not only for amphibious hooks but also for Rome. See Allied Force Headquarters (AFHQ) Microfilms.

[5] An excellent discussion of the early Anzio planning may be found in [Capt. Harris G. Warren and Capt. John Bowditch, III] *Fifth Army History,* Part IV, 16 January 1944-31 March 1944, *Cassino and Anzio* (Florence, Italy: L'Impronto Press, n.d.), pp. 10-24.

[6] 15 Army Group Operations Instruction 31, 8 Nov 43.

[7] *Fifth Army History,* Part IV, p. 15; Richard M. Leighton and Robert W. Coakley, *Global Logistics and Strategy, 1943-1945,* a volume in preparation for *United States Army in World War II,* Ms Chapter "Scratch HERCULES and PIGSTICK—Enter SHINGLE"; *Report by the Supreme Allied Commander,*

Mediterranean [General Sir H. Maitland Wilson] *to the Combined Chiefs of Staff on the Italian Campaign, 8 January 1944 to 10 May 1944* (Washington, 1946), p. 6; Field Marshal the Viscount Alexander of Tunis, *Despatch,* 19 Apr 47 (published as "The Allied Armies in Italy from 3rd September, 1943, to 12th December, 1944," in the *Supplement to the London Gazette* of Tuesday, June 6, 1950), p. 2909 (referred to hereafter as Alexander *Despatch*); Interv., Dr. Sidney T. Mathews with Brig. Gen. K. W. D. Strong (formerly AFHQ G-2), 30 Oct 47, OCMH files.

[8] Alexander *Despatch,* p. 2910. The U.S. Joint Chiefs of Staff believed an Anzio landing essential for a drive on Rome and a line north of Rome essential for an invasion of southern France later in 1944. Leighton and Coakley, *Global Logistics,* chapter cited in footnote 7.

[9] Cable, Clark to Alexander, 2 Jan 44, quoted in *Fifth Army History,* Part IV, p. 17.

[10] 15 Army Group Operations Instruction 32, 2 Jan 44.

[11] 15 Army Group Operation Instruction 34, The Battle for Rome, 12 Jan 44.

[12] Fifth Army FO 5, 12 Jan 44. See also Annex 1, G-2 Plan, Outline Plan Operation SHINGLE, and overprinted maps.

[13] Fifth Army SHINGLE Intelligence Summary 4, 30 Dec 43.

[14] *Ibid.*

[15] Lucas Diary (photostat copy in OCMH files), Part I, Sicily, and Part II, Italy.

[16] Lucas Diary, Part III, Anzio, entry 14 Jan 44.

[17] *Ibid.,* 15 Jan 44.

[18] Lucas Diary, Part II, entries 27 and 29 Dec 43.

[19] Lucas Diary, Part III, entry 4 Jan 44. Unless otherwise noted, all quotations from General Lucas are taken from his diary. After the war General Lucas added to his diary to fill in certain details, but he carefully distinguished between these later entries and his original remarks. Where later entries rather than the contemporary record have been used in this study, that fact is specifically noted.

[20] Clark, *Calculated Risk,* pp. 268-69.

[21] Lucas Diary, later addition to entry of 12 Jan 44.

[22] Sun Force (504th Para Inf Regt) Outline Plan for Operation SHINGLE, n.d., and 504th Combat Team Arty Outline Plan, 8 Jan 44, both in SHINGLE Correspondence File, Kansas City Records Center.

[23] Ralph S. Mavrogordato, *The Battle for the Anzio Beachhead,* OCMH MS #X-113.

[24] Albert Kesselring, *A Soldier's Record* (New York: Morrow, 1954), pp. 230-31.

[25] The German Operation at Anzio (German Military Documents Section, Military Intelligence Division, Camp Ritchie, Md., 1946), p. 9.

[26] *Ibid.,* pp. 12-13.

[27] Ralph S. Mavrogordato, *XIV Panzer Corps Defensive Operations Along the Garigliano, Liri, and Rapido Rivers,* OCMH MS #R-78.

[28] OCMH MS #X-113; see also Magna M. Bauer, Shifting of German Units . . . , OCMH MS #R-75.

[29] The German Operation at Anzio, p. 14.

[30] *Ibid.*

[31] Lucas Diary, later addition to entry of 24 Jan 44.

[32] Clark, *Calculated Risk,* p. 296.

[33] Kesselring, *A Soldier's Record,* p. 233.

[34] *Ibid.;* OCMH MS #X-113.

[35] Lucas Diary, later addition to entry of 2 Feb 44.

[36] ACMF [15th Army Group] Operations Instruction 37, 2 Feb 44. The 15th Army Group headquarters had been renamed "Allied Central Mediterranean Forces."

[37] Lucas Diary, entry of 3 Feb 44. For the text of the Fifth Army message, see later addition to entry of 3 February.

[38] Lucas Diary, later addition to entry of 22 Feb 44; see also Interv, Mathews with Clark, 20 May 48, OCMH files.

[39] Interv, Mathews with Clark.

[40] Clark, *Calculated Risk,* p. 296.

[41] Interv, Mathews and others with Marshall, 25 Jul 49, OCMH files.

[42] Interv, Mathews with Strong.

[43] Interv, Mathews with Lemnitzer, 16 Jan 48, OCMH files.

[44] Lucas Diary, later addition to entry of 27 Jan 44.

[45] Lucas Diary, later addition to entry of 29 Jan 44.

[46] Cunningham to Rear Adm. F. J. Lowry, Directive to the Naval Commander, Operation SHINGLE, 29 Dec 43, in SHINGLE Correspondence File, Kansas City Records Center.

[47] Interv, Mathews with Lucas, 24 May 48, OCMH files.

[48] Fifth Army Tactical Study of the Terrain Anzio-Nettuno-Colli Laziali-Rome, 17 Nov 43; Fifth Army G-2 Estimate, App. 1 to Annex 1 to Outline Plan SHINGLE, 22 Nov 43.

[49] See Britt Bailey, *The German Situation in Italy,* OCMH MS #R-50.

[50] CSDIC/CMF/M296, n.d. [c. Aug 45], Intelligence Activities, in File 383.4, Kansas City Records Center.

[51] Siegfried Westphal, *The German Army in the West* (London: Cassell, 1951), p. 158.

[52] Intervs, Mathews with Alexander, 10-15 Jan 49, OCMH files; see also Alexander *Despatch,* pp. 2909-10.

CHAPTER 12

[1] Details of this and earlier fighting in Italy may be found in Sidney T. Mathews, *The Drive on Rome,* and Martin Blumenson, *Salerno to Cassino,* volumes being prepared for publication in *United States Army in World War II.* For the story of Anzio, see [Capt. John Bowditch and 1st Lt. Robert W. Komer] *Anzio Beachhead,* in *American Forces in Action Series* (Washington, 1947). Other published works bearing on the subject include Mark W. Clark, *Calculated Risk* (New York: Harper, 1950); Lt. General L. K. Truscott, *Command Missions* (New York: Dutton, 1954); and Lt. Col. Chester G. Starr, ed., *From Salerno to the Alps: A History of the Fifth Army, 1943-1945* (Washington: Infantry Journal Press, 1948).

[2] Allied Armies in Italy (AAI) Operation Order 1, 5 May 44, in *Fifth Army History,* Part V.

[3] See Min, AAI Conference of Army Commanders, 2 Apr 44, in Fifth Army files, Kansas City Records Center.

[4] Fifth Army FO 6, 20 Apr 44, in *Fifth Army History,* Part V.

[5] Intervs, Mathews with Clark, 10-21 May 48 (hereafter cited as Clark Intervs), OCMH files; Clark Diary, 11 May-5 Jun 44, loaned to the author by General Clark; Clark, *Calculated Risk,* p. 356.

[6] Fifth Army FO 6.

[7] AAI FO 1.

8 Truscott, *Command Missions,* p. 369; Truscott Diary, 6-7 May 44, loaned to the author by General Truscott.

9 Clark Diary, 17 May 44; Clark, *Calculated Risk,* pp. 350-51.

10 Clark Diary, 19, 27 May 44; Truscott Diary, 18 May 44; Clark to Truscott, 18 May 44 (radio), in Truscott Papers; Truscott, *Command Missions,* p. 370.

11 Clark Diary, 19, 27 May 44; Clark Intervs.

12 Fifth Army G-3 Jnl, 25 May 44; Wood File, Fifth Army Messages, May-Jun 44; and Fifth Army Message file, May 44, all in Fifth Army files; Clark Diary, 25 May 44.

13 Clark Diary; Clark Intervs; Wood File, May-Jun 44; Fifth Army G-3 Jnl, 25 May 44; VI Corps War Room Jnl, 24-25 May 44.

14 Fourteenth Army and 76th Panzer Corps War Diaries, text volumes, 24-27 May 44, in German Military Documents Section, Federal Records Center; Telephone Conversations, VI Corps War Room Jnl, 23-25 May 44; Fifth Army G-2 Periodic Report and G-3 Jnl file, 23-26 May 44; VI Corps G-2 Periodic Reports, 24-26 May 44; VI Corps War Room Jnl, 24-27 May 44; Truscott Comments at Division Commanders' Conference, 25 May 44, in VI Corps files.

15 Clark Diary, 17 May 44; Clark Intervs; Clark, *Calculated Risk,* pp. 350-51.

16 Clark Intervs; Clark Diary, 15 May-5 Jun 44; Clark, *Calculated Risk,* pp. 337-66, *passim.*

17 Clark Diary, 17-22 May 44; Clark Intervs.

18 Clark Intervs; Clark Diary, 25, 27-30 May 44.

19 VI Corps War Room Jnl, 24-28 May 44.

20 *Ibid.*

21 Fourteenth Army and 76th Panzer Corps War Diaries, May 44.

22 Clark to Gruenther, 25 May 44, in Clark Diary, 25 May 44; Truscott's Comments at Division Commanders' Conference, 25 May 44; VI Corps War Room Jnl, 25 May 44; Clark Intervs.

23 Clark Diary, 25-27 May 44; Clark Intervs; VI Corps War Room Jnl, 25 May 44; Wood File, May-Jun 44.

24 Clark Intervs; Clark, *Calculated Risk,* pp. 356-57.

25 Clark Intervs; Clark, *Calculated Risk,* pp. 335-66, *passim.*

26 Truscott, *Command Missions,* p. 369.

27 Clark Intervs; Clark Diary, 14 May-5 Jun 44.

28 Clark Intervs; Clark Diary, 24 May-5 Jun 44; Clark, *Calculated Risk,* pp. 336-40, 352ff.

29 Clark Diary, 24-25 May 44; Clark Intervs; Clark, *Calculated Risk,* pp. 356-57.

30 Clark Diary, 25-27 May 44; Clark Intervs; Wood File, May-Jun 44.

31 Clark Diary, 25 May 44; Wood File, May-Jun 44.

32 Brann to Clark, 25 May 44 (radio), Wood File, May-Jun 44.

33 Telephone Conversation, Truscott to Brann, VI Corps War Room Jnl, 25 May 44. That Truscott might have had reservations about the plan, or that he might have openly objected to it, does not appear in any contemporary record, though after the war he recalled that he was "dumfounded" by it and "protested that the conditions were not right." See Truscott, *Command Missions,* p. 375; Intervs, Mathews with Truscott, 3 and 10 Apr 48, OCMH files.

34 Clark Diary; Fifth Army Advance CP G-3 Jnl, 25 May 44; Fifth Army G-2 and Air Support Jnls, 25 May 44; VI Corps War Room Jnl, 25 May 44.

35 Clark Diary, 25-26 May 44; Truscott Diary, 25 May 44; VI Corps War Room Jnl, 25 May 44.

36 Report of Division Commanders' Meeting at VI Corps CP, 24 May 44, VI Corps War Room Jnl, 25 May 44.

37 Alexander Intervs; Memo, Gruenther for Clark, 26 May 44, Clark Diary, 26 May 44.

38 Clark Diary, 25-26 May 44.

39 Memo, Gruenther for Clark, 26 May 44, cited in footnote 37.

40 Alexander Intervs.

41 VI Corps War Room Jnl, 26 May-5 Jun 44; II Corps After Action Reports, May, Jun 44, Federal Records Center; Clark Diary, 26 May-5 Jun 44; War Diaries, Tenth and Fourteenth Armies and XIV Panzer Corps, May-Jun 44; Alexander Intervs. See also various accounts in *Der Feldzug in Italien,* a collection of postwar manuscripts prepared by German officers, OCMH files; and G. W. C. Nicholson, *The Canadians in Italy: 1943-45* (Ottawa, Canada: 1956), *passim.*

CHAPTER 13

1 An undocumented and somewhat abbreviated version of the following essay, which grew out of a talk given by the author at the Army War College, appeared in *United States Naval Institute Proceedings* (July, 1958), under the title "Was the Invasion of Southern France a Blunder?" The Institute has kindly granted permission to reproduce portions of the article here. The subject is developed fully in the context of the story of Allied strategy in mid-war in Maurice Matloff, *Strategic Planning for Coalition Warfare, 1943-1944,* in *United States Army in World War II* (Washington, 1959). Various aspects of it may be pursued further in the publications cited below.

2 For a description of wartime relations with the Soviet Union as seen from his post as head of the American Military Mission in Moscow, see John R. Deane, *The Strange Alliance* (New York: Viking Press, 1947).

3 The debate on strategy within the Grand Alliance may be traced in Maurice Matloff and Edwin M. Snell, *Strategic Planning for Coalition Warfare, 1941-1942,* in *United States Army in World War II* (Washington, 1953); Maurice Matloff, *Strategic Planning for Coalition Warfare, 1943-1944,* in *United States Army in World War II* (Washington, 1959); John Ehrman, *Grand Strategy,* Vol. V: *August 1943-September 1944* (London: H.M. Stationery Office, 1956); Robert E. Sherwood, *Roosevelt and Hopkins: An Intimate History,* rev. ed. (New York: Harper, 1950); Winston S. Churchill, *The Grand Alliance* (Boston: Houghton Mifflin, 1950), *The Hinge of Fate* (Boston: Houghton Mifflin, 1950), and *Closing the Ring* (Boston: Houghton Mifflin, 1951).

4 Msg, Deane to Joint Chiefs of Staff (JCS), 9 Nov 43, CM-IN 5951; Msg, Deane to Marshall, 11 Nov 43, CM-IN 7461; see also Gordon A. Harrison, *Cross-Channel Attack,* in *United States Army in World War II* (Washington, 1951), p. 121.

5 Operations Division (OPD) Draft Memo, CofS for President, 8 Nov 43, sub: Conduct of the European War, with Tab 90 in ABC 381 Strategy Sec Papers, Nos. 2-95 (7 Jan 43); Henry L. Stimson and McGeorge Bundy, *On Active Service in Peace and War* (New York: Harper, 1948), p. 439; Matloff, *Strategic Planning for Coalition Warfare, 1943-1944,* Ch. XIII.

6 The following discussion on the Tehran Conference is based on Sherwood, *Roosevelt and Hopkins,* Ch. XXIII; Churchill, *Closing the Ring,* Chs. 4, 5, 6; Matloff, *Strategic Planning for Coalition Warfare, 1943-1944,* Ch. XVI. The

minutes of the meetings are contained in the official SEXTANT Conference Book.

7 For interpretations of the President's role at Tehran, see Sherwood, *Roosevelt and Hopkins,* pp. 780, 789; Deane, *The Strange Alliance,* pp. 41-43; and William D. Leahy, *I Was There* (New York: Whittlesey House, 1950), pp. 204ff.

8 Churchill, *Closing the Ring,* p. 346.

9 Min, 132nd Mtg Combined Chiefs of Staff (CCS), 30 Nov 43.

10 Joint Planning Staff (JPS) 249, 9 Aug 43, title: Plan for Invasion of Southern France; Study, 29 Nov 43, title: Operation Against Southern France, ABC 384 Europe (5 Aug 43), 9a; Harrison, *Cross-Channel Attack,* pp. 123-25.

11 CCS 426/1, 6 Dec 43, title: Report to the President and Prime Minister.

12 Details of the debate are traced in Matloff, *Strategic Planning for Coalition Warfare, 1943-1944,* Chs. XVIII, XXI; Harrison, *Cross-Channel Attack,* Ch. V; Forrest C. Pogue, *The Supreme Command,* in *United States Army in World War II* (Washington, 1954), Chs. VI, XII; Ehrman, *Grand Strategy,* Vol. V, Chs. VI, VII, IX; Churchill, *Closing the Ring,* Ch. 11, and *Triumph and Tragedy* (Boston: Houghton Mifflin, 1953), Ch. 4.

13 For the War Department views, see especially Memo, Hull for Handy, 15 Feb 44, no sub, Paper 253, Book 15, Exec 9; Memo, Hull for CofS, 14 Mar 44, sub: Anvil, Book 16, Exec 9; Ltr [Handy] to Devers, 15 Mar 44, Paper 403, Book 16, Exec 9.

14 Memo, Marshall for Leahy and King, 9 Feb 44, sub: Overlord-Anvil, with Min, 132d Mtg CCS, in ABC 384 Europe (5 Aug 43), 1-A; Msg, Marshall to Eisenhower, 9 Feb 44, CM-OUT 3919.

15 Copy of Msg, Leahy to President, 24 Feb 44, Incl to Memo, Col A. J. McFarland, JCS, for OPD, and for Aide to COMINCH [US Fleet], 24 Feb 44, sub: Msg From British Chiefs of Staff on Conclusions Agreed This Morning at Meeting Held Between British Chiefs of Staff and General Eisenhower, with Paper 17, Item 55, Exec 10.

16 Msg, Eisenhower to Marshall, 21 Mar 44, CM-IN 15429; CCS 465/12, 23 Mar 44, title: Firm Recommendations with Regard to OVERLORD and ANVIL; CCS 465/14, 24 Mar 44, title: OVERLORD and ANVIL; Churchill, *Closing the Ring,* pp. 512-13.

17 Memo, Roberts for Handy, 23 Mar 44, sub: What Shall We Do About ANVIL? Book 16, Exec 9.

18 Msg, COS to Jt Stf Mission, 16 Apr 44, COS (W) 1284, Item 68, Exec 10; Msg, COS to Jt Stf Mission, 16 Apr 44, COS (W) 1285, Item 16, Exec 3; CCS 465/22, 18 Apr 44, title: OVERLORD and ANVIL.

19 Msg, CCS to Wilson and Eisenhower, 14 Jun 44, CM-IN 11530.

20 Msg 718, Prime Minister to President, 28 Jun 44, Item 63c, Exec 10; James D. T. Hamilton, *Southern France and Alsace,* Ms, Ch. IV, OCMH files; Churchill, *Triumph and Tragedy,* pp. 63ff; Msg 573, President to Prime Minister, 28 Jun 44, Item 63c, Exec 10; Msg, Marshall to Eisenhower, 27 Jun 44, CM-OUT 57012.

21 Churchill, *Triumph and Tragedy,* p. 63.

22 *Ibid.,* p. 716.

23 Msg, President to Prime Minister, 29 Jun 44, quoted in Churchill, *Triumph and Tragedy,* p. 723.

24 Churchill, *Triumph and Tragedy,* p. 65.

25 *Ibid.* The italics are Churchill's.

[26] Quoted in Churchill, *Triumph and Tragedy*, p. 66.

[27] Msg, CCS to Wilson and Eisenhower, 2 Jul 44, CM-IN 1613.

[28] Msg 742, Prime Minister to President, 4 Aug 44, Item 63c, Exec 10; Dwight D. Eisenhower, *Crusade in Europe* (Garden City, N.Y.: Doubleday, 1948), pp. 281-84; Hamilton, *Southern France and Alsace,* Ch. IX.

[29] Msg 596, President to Prime Minister, 7 Aug 44, Item 63c, Exec 10; Eisenhower, *Crusade in Europe,* pp. 281-84; Churchill, *Triumph and Tragedy,* pp. 71, 99-101.

[30] Hanson W. Baldwin, *Great Mistakes of the War* (New York: Harper, 1950); Captain W. D. Puleston (USN, Ret.), "Revealed—Blunders of World War II," *US News & World Report,* February 4, 1955.

[31] Eisenhower, *Crusade in Europe,* p. 294.

[32] Churchill, *Closing the Ring,* p. 426.

[33] J. F. C. Fuller, *The Second World War, 1939-45* (New York: Duell, Sloan & Pearce, 1949), pp. 250, 266, 385.

[34] Chester Wilmot, *The Struggle for Europe* (London: Collins, 1952), p. 128.

[35] Gordon Harrison, "Operation OVERLORD," transcript of an address delivered at the Army War College, 19 November 1951, OCMH files.

[36] The most recent examination of the Prime Minister's position is contained in Ehrman, *Grand Strategy,* Vol. V; for Churchill's position on the Balkans in 1943, see Vol. V, pp. 112-13, and Appendix, pp. 554-56.

CHAPTER 14

[1] The events described in this paper are covered in detail in the author's *Breakout and Pursuit,* a volume in preparation for *United States Army in World War II.*

[2] See, for example, Supreme Headquarters, Allied Expeditionary Force (SHAEF) /17100/35/Ops, NEPTUNE, Summary of Revised Joint Operations Plan—U.S. Forces for Phase II of Operation OVERLORD, 20 May 44, in EUCOM Files, Box 3. See also Forrest C. Pogue, *The Supreme Command,* in *United States Army in World War II* (Washington, 1954).

[3] 12th A Gp Ltr of Instrs 2, 3 Aug 44. The 12th Army Group letters of instruction and directives are conveniently reproduced in an appendix of the Third U.S. Army (TUSA), After Action Reports (AAR), Vol. I.

[4] 21 A Gp General Operational Situation and Directive, 4 Aug 44. Scattered through SHAEF and 12th Army Group files, the 21st Army Group directives are most conveniently found in Pogue, where they are extensively quoted and paraphrased. See also Field Marshal Viscount Montgomery, *Normandy to the Baltic* (Boston: Houghton Mifflin, 1948).

[5] TUSA Ltr, Directive, 5 Aug 44 (confirming fragmentary orders issued 4 Aug), and Directive, 5 Aug (confirming telephone orders issued 1640, 5 Aug); 12th A Gp Ltr of Instrs 3, 6 Aug. Third Army directives are conveniently reproduced in an appendix of the TUSA AAR, Vol. I.

[6] 21 A Gp Operational Situation and Directive, 4 Aug; see also Montgomery, *Normandy to the Baltic,* pp. 118-19.

[7] 21 A Gp General Operational Situation and Directive, 6 Aug.

[8] Omar N. Bradley, *A Soldier's Story* (New York: Holt, 1951), pp. 372, 374-75; Montgomery, *Normandy to the Baltic,* pp. 157-58; Dwight D. Eisenhower, *Crusade in Europe* (Garden City, N.Y.: Doubleday, 1948), p. 275; Capt. Harry C. Butcher, USNR, *My Three Years with Eisenhower* (New York: Simon & Schuster, 1946), p. 636.

[9] The details of the Canadian attack may be found in Col. C. P. Stacey, *The*

Canadian Army, 1939-1945: An Official Historical Summary (Ottawa: King's Printer, 1948), pp. 201-03.

[10] 21 A Gp General Operational Situation and Directive, 11 Aug.

[11] 12th A Gp Ltr of Instrs 4, 8 Aug.

[12] 21 A Gp Operational Situation and Directive, 11 Aug.

[13] Memo, Patton for Gaffey, 8 Aug; TUSA Ltr of Instrs, Patton to Haislip, 8 Aug; TUSA Directive, 10 Aug (confirming fragmentary orders issued 8 Aug); XV Corps Operations Instructions issued 2200, 11 Aug; XV Corps Chief of Staff's Notes of Meeting, 0730, 12 Aug. Important XV Corps papers are to be found in the XV Corps Chief of Staff's Journal and File.

[14] Haislip to Patton, 2130, 12 Aug.

[15] Gaffey to Haislip, 0040, 13 Aug.

[16] Gaffey to Haislip, received at XV Corps 1415, 13 Aug; see also Memo, Patton for Haislip, 13 Aug, and TUSA Directive, 13 Aug.

[17] Chester Wilmot, *The Struggle for Europe* (New York: Harper, 1952), pp. 424-25.

[18] Eisenhower to Marshall, 17 Aug, OCMH files.

[19] See, for example, George S. Patton, Jr., *War As I Knew It* (Boston: Houghton Mifflin, 1947), p. 105, and MS # B-807 (Kuntzen), the latter (in English translation) in OCMH files.

[20] Sources cited footnote 13, above.

[21] See 12th A Gp Ltrs of Instrs 4, 8 Aug.

[22] Hitler Order, *WFSt/Op. Nr. 772830/44.g.Kdos. Chefs,* 11 Aug, quoted in *AGp B* to the armies, 0030, 12 Aug, in *AGp B Fuehrer Befehle;* Telecons, Blumentritt and Speidel, 0200, 11 Aug, Kluge and Eberbach, 0315, 11 Aug, in *AGp B KTB;* Msg, Kluge to *OKW/WFSt* (information to subordinate commands), 1745, 11 Aug, in *AGp B Lagebeurteilungen, Wochenmeldungen.* Copies of the captured German Army records are on file at the National Archives. See also *OB WEST, A Study in Command,* pp. 57, 129, OCMH.

[23] Bradley, *A Soldier's Story,* p. 377; Eisenhower, *Crusade in Europe,* pp. 278-79. See also Butcher, *My Three Years with Eisenhower,* p. 641.

[24] Bradley, *A Soldier's Story,* p. 377.

[25] Wesley Frank Craven and James Lea Cate, eds., *The Army Air Forces in World War II,* Vol. III: *ARGUMENT to V-E Day, January 1944 to May 1945* (Chicago: University of Chicago Press, 1951), pp. 253-54; 12th A Gp Memo for Record, 18 Aug.

[26] Bradley, *A Soldier's Story,* p. 377.

[27] Stacey, *The Canadian Army,* p. 204; Patton, *War As I Knew It,* p. 105; Craven and Cate, *ARGUMENT to V-E Day,* pp. 257-58.

[28] Answers by Generals Walter Bedell Smith and Harold R. Bull to questions by Historical Section, European Theater of Operations, U.S. Army (ETOUSA), 14-15 Sep 45, OCMH files.

[29] Bradley, *A Soldier's Story,* p. 376.

[30] *Ibid.,* p. 377.

[31] Lt. Gen. Josef Dietrich, commander of the Fifth Panzer Army, stated this in a telephone conversation with Lt. Gen. Hans Speidel, Lt. Gen. Friedrich Wiese, and Lt. Gen. Alfred Gause, 1035, 13 Aug, in *AGp B KTB.*

[32] Hitler Order, quoted in Msg, *OB WEST* to *AGp B,* 0445, 14 Aug, in *AGp B Fuehrer Befehle;* Telecon, Kluge and Jodl, 1245, 16 Aug, in *AGp B KTB.* See *OB WEST* and *AGp B KTBs* for 16 Aug.

[33] Eisenhower, *Crusade in Europe,* pp. 278-79; see Pogue, *Supreme Command,* p. 214.

[34] Major General Sir Francis de Guingand, *Operation Victory* (New York: Scribner's, 1947), p. 407.

[35] 12th A Gp Directive for Current Operations, 15 Aug; Bradley, *A Soldier's Story*, pp. 378-79; see also 21 A Gp Directive, 11 Aug.

[36] TUSA Directive to XV Corps, 14 Aug, and Directive, 15 Aug (confirming oral orders, 14 Aug); Telecon, Gaffey and Menoher, 2145, 14 Aug.

[37] See, for example, XV Corps G-2 Periodic Rpt 12, 0300, 15 Aug; see also Magna E. Bauer, Major Shifts of Divisions Made by Germans to and Within the German Normandy Front Between 30 July and 25 August 1944, and the Significance of These Movements in View of Allied Strategy, OCMH MS # R-33.

[38] Royce L. Thompson, A Statistical Study of Artillery Battalions at the Argentan-Falaise Pocket, MS, OCMH files.

[39] Bradley, *A Soldier's Story*, p. 379.

[40] Capitaine Even, "La 2d D.B. de son Débarquement en Normandie à la Libération de Paris," *Revue Historique de l'Armée,* I (March, 1952), pp. 107-32; Capitaine Jean Maigne, "Les Forces Françaises et la Jonction 'OVERLORD-DRAGOON,'" *Revue d'Histoire de la Deuxième Guerre Mondiale,* No. 19 (July, 1955), pp. 17-33; Msgs, Haislip to Leclerc and Oliver, 1845, 12 Aug, and Haislip to Patton, 12 Aug; XV Corps and 5th Armd Div AARs, Aug 44; XV Corps FO 3, 9 Aug; Telecon, Speidel, Wiese, Gause, and Dietrich, 1035, 13 Aug, and Friedel Telecons, 1230 and 2140, 13 Aug, in *AGp B KTB.*

[41] MS # A-922 (Eberbach), in OCMH files.

[42] V Corps G-2 Estimate of Enemy Situation 7, 23 Aug; FUSA ARR, Aug 44; see B. H. Liddell Hart, *Strategy, The Indirect Approach* (New York: Praeger, 1954), p. 317.

[43] Fifth Panzer Army Report, 1650, 28 Aug, in *AGp B KTB.*

CHAPTER 15

[1] The present article was first published, in a similar form, in *Military Review,* XXXI, No. 5 (August, 1951), under the title "Logistic Limitations on Tactical Decisions." A full account of the logistical story in the European theater may be found in Roland G. Ruppenthal, *Logistical Support of the Armies,* Vol. I, in *United States Army in World War II* (Washington, 1953), and Volume II (in preparation), specifically Ch. I. See also Forrest C. Pogue, *The Supreme Command* (Washington, 1954), in the same series; and Field Marshal Viscount Montgomery, *Normandy to the Baltic* (Boston: Houghton Mifflin, 1948); Chester Wilmot, *The Struggle for Europe* (New York: Harper, 1952); George S. Patton, Jr., *War As I Knew It* (Boston: Houghton Mifflin, 1947); Dwight D. Eisenhower, *Crusade in Europe* (Garden City, N.Y.: Doubleday, 1948); and Omar N. Bradley, *A Soldier's Story* (New York: Holt, 1951).

[2] Ruppenthal, *Logistical Support of the Armies,* Vol. I, Chs. IV, VII; Vol. II, Ch. I.

[3] See Supreme Headquarters, Allied Expeditionary Forces (SHAEF) Planning Staff Studies, Post-NEPTUNE, 17 Jun and 17 Aug 44, in SHAEF G-3 SHAEF/18008/Plans 44; Administrative Staff Study 14, The Logistical Implications of a Rapid Advance by AEF Beyond the Seine, 23 Aug 44, in SHAEF G-4 381 War Plans General, I, 44; Planning Paper, Logistical Implications of a Rapid Thrust to Berlin, Sep 44, SHAEF G-4 Logistical Forecasts, Folder 13.

4 Cbl, Eisenhower to Marshall, 24 Aug 44, Operations Division Executive Office File 9; see also Eisenhower to Montgomery, 24 Aug 44, and Eisenhower to CCS, 9 Sep, both in SHAEF SGS 381 Post OVERLORD Planning, I.

5 Tedder's (Air Chief Marshal Sir Arthur Tedder) Notes on Meeting at Brussels, 10 Sep 44, OCMH files.

6 Bradley Ltr of Instr to Comdrs, 10 Sep 44, in SHAEF SGS 381 Post OVERLORD Planning, I; see also Ltr, Whipple to CAO, US Troop Flow to Support a Maximum Effort [early Sep 44], SHAEF G-4 Logistical Forecasts, Folder 13.

7 Whipple Ltr, cited n. 6; Memo, Moses for CofC 12th A Gp, Use of Divisions on Line of Comms, 5 Sep 44, 12th A Gp G-4 Memos 1944, Folder 56, Drawer 11.

8 Ltr, Eisenhower to Marshall, 14 Sep 44, OPD Exec Office File 9; see also Cbl, Eisenhower to Marshall, 4 Sep 44, OPD Cable Files.

9 Cbl, Eisenhower to Marshall, 24 Aug 44.

10 A detailed discussion is found in Pogue, *Supreme Command,* pp. 249ff., 288-98.

11 Eisenhower to Army Comdrs, 13 Sep, and Eisenhower to A Gp Comdrs, 15 Sep, in SHAEF SGS 381 Post OVERLORD Planning, I; Eisenhower to Montgomery, 20 Sep, in OCMH files.

12 Min, Mtg SHAEF War Room, 22 Sep 44, and Ltr, Eisenhower to Montgomery, 24 Sep 44, SHAEF SGS 381 Post OVERLORD Planning.

13 See Ltr, Eisenhower to Marshall, 14 Sep 44.

14 Ltr, Bradley to Patton, 23 Sep 44, 12th A Gp 371.3, Mil Objs, I; Memo, Moses for Barringer, Confirmation of Telephone Conversation This Date, 9 Sep 44, 12th A Gp G-4 Memos 1944, Folder 56.

15 SHAEF G-3 Appreciation, Factors Affecting Advance into Germany After Occupation of the Ruhr, 24 Sep 44; Memo by Planning Staff, 24 Sep 44, SHAEF SGS 381 Post OVERLORD Planning; Memos, Moses for Stratton, Supply Estimate, 25 Sep 44 and 1 Oct 44; SHAEF G-4 Allocation of Tonnages, 1, 8 Oct 44—SHAEF G-4 400 Supplies General 44, IV; Memo, Ravenhill for G-4 10 Oct 44, SHAEF G-4 Maintenance of British and U.S. Forces 153/2/GDP-1, Box 1, Folder 42; Cable, SHAEF to Bradley, 11 Oct 44, SHAEF AG 381-3 SHAEF to AGWAR Rpts on OVERLORD.

CHAPTER 16

1 This operation is covered in detail in Charles B. MacDonald, *The Siegfried Line Campaign,* a forthcoming volume in *United States Army in World War II.* See also Forrest C. Pogue, *The Supreme Command* (Washington, 1954), in the same series; Chester Wilmot, *The Struggle for Europe* (New York: Harper, 1952); Dwight D. Eisenhower, *Crusade in Europe* (New York: Doubleday, 1948); and Field Marshal Viscount Montgomery, *Normandy to the Baltic* (Boston: Houghton Mifflin, 1948).

2 These events are covered in Martin Blumenson, *Breakout and Pursuit,* a forthcoming volume in *United States Army in World War II.* For the cross-Channel invasion, see Gordon A. Harrison, *Cross-Channel Attack* (Washington, 1951), in the same series.

3 SHAEF Weekly Intelligence Summary 23, 26 Aug 44, in SHAEF G-2 files.

4 The logistical story is covered in Roland G. Ruppenthal, *Logistical Support of the Armies,* Volume I, in *United States Army in World War II* (Washington, 1953), and Volume II (in preparation).

[5] George S. Patton, Jr., *War as I Knew It* (Boston: Houghton Mifflin, 1947), pp. 114, 117, 132; First Army After Action Report, Sep 44.

[6] Montgomery, *Normandy to the Baltic*, p. 214.

[7] Eisenhower to Montgomery, 13 Sep 44, in SHAEF Secretary of the General Staff (SGS) File 381, Vol. I.

[8] 12th A Gp Administrative Instructions 13, 27 Aug; Ltr of Instr 8, 10 Sep; Memo, Future Operations, 25 Aug; Ltr of Instr 6, 25 Aug; see also Ltrs, Bradley to Eisenhower, 26 Aug, and Eisenhower to Bradley, 29 Aug, all in 12th A Gp Military Objectives File 371.3, Vol. I.

[9] For a detailed discussion, see Pogue, *Supreme Command*, pp. 261ff.

[10] SHAEF Planning Drafts, 3 and 30 May 44, in SHAEF SGS File 381, I; Eisenhower to Marshall, 22 Aug 44, in SHAEF Cable Logs; Ltr, Eisenhower to Montgomery, 24 Aug 44, in SHAEF SGS File 381, I; Eisenhower to Marshall, 5 Sep 44, copy in OCMH files; see also Eisenhower, *Crusade in Europe*, p. 345.

[11] Eisenhower correspondence cited in footnote 10.

[12] For details on the formation of the First Allied Airborne Army, see James A. Huston, Airborne Operations, Ms, in OCMH files.

[13] Pogue, *Supreme Command*, pp. 119, 269-71, 279ff.

[14] The fledgling plans had embraced a variety of objectives, among them the city of Boulogne; the city of Tournai, with the aim of blocking German retreat from the Channel coast; the vicinity of Liége, in order to get the First Army across the Meuse river; the Aachen-Maastricht Gap, to facilitate Allied passage through the West Wall; and Operation COMET, to put British forces across the Lower Rhine. See Hq, First Allied Airborne Army (FAAA) History of Headquarters First Allied Airborne Army, 2 Aug 44-20 May 45; see also John C. Warren, *Airborne Operations in World War II, European Theater*, USAF Historical Studies: No. 97, USAF Historical Division, 1956, pp. 80, 88-100; see also Huston Ms.

[15] Quoted in Pogue, *Supreme Command*, p. 279.

[16] Omar N. Bradley, *A Soldier's Story* (New York: Holt, 1951), pp. 401-03.

[17] *Ibid.*, p. 403.

[18] FAAA, Operations in Holland; see also The Climate of the Rhine Valley, Germany, in XIX Corps After Action Report (AAR), Oct 44, and The Climate of Central and Western Germany, Annex 1 to First U.S. Army (FUSA) G-2 Periodic Report 92, 10 Sep 44, in FUSA G-2 Files.

[19] FUSA G-2 Estimate 24, 3 Sep 44, in FUSA Operations Reports.

[20] See, for example, Third U.S. Army (TUSA) G-2 Estimate 9, 28 Aug 44, in TUSA AAR, Vol. II.

[21] SHAEF Weekly Intelligence Summary 26, week ending 16 Sep 44, in SHAEF G-2 File.

[22] *Ibid.*

[23] Hq Air Troops Operational Instruction 1, 13 Sep 44, in 1st Airborne Division AAR on Operation MARKET, Parts 1-3, SHAEF FAAA.

[24] Intelligence Summary 26 cited in footnote 21.

[25] Air Chief Marshal Sir Arthur W. Tedder's Notes on Eisenhower-Montgomery Meeting at Brussels, 10 Sep 44, copy in OCMH files; see Eisenhower, *Crusade in Europe*, pp. 306-07.

[26] Ltr, Eisenhower to Montgomery, 20 Sep 44, copy in OCMH files; Montgomery, *Normandy to the Baltic*, pp. 196, 213.

[27] See, for example, Eisenhower to Army Group Commanders, 15 Sep 44, in SHAEF SGS File 381, I; Eisenhower to Montgomery, 22 Sep 44, copy in OCMH files.

28 Report by the Supreme Commander to the Combined Chiefs of Staff on the Operations in Europe of the Allied Expeditionary Force, 6 June 1944 to 8 May 1945, p. 67.

29 SHAEF Planning Draft, 30 May 44, in SHAEF SGS File 381, I.

30 On the Canadian task, see Col. C. P. Stacey, *The Canadian Army, 1939-1945: An Official Historical Summary* (Ottawa: King's Printer, 1948), pp. 210ff.

31 Wilmot, *The Struggle for Europe,* p. 488.

32 See, for example, Montgomery to army commanders, 26 Aug 44, in SHAEF SGS File 381, I; see also par. 6 of 21 A Gp Operational Situation and Directive, 3 Sep, and Ltr, Bradley to Eisenhower, 14 Sep 44, both in 12th A Gp Military Objectives File 371.3, I.

33 Wilmot, *Struggle for Europe,* p. 488.

34 Pogue, *Supreme Command,* pp. 281-82.

CHAPTER 17

1 The planning and preparations of the German Ardennes offensive are described in detail in Hugh M. Cole, *The Ardennes,* a volume in preparation for *United States Army in World War II.* Other volumes in this series covering related operations and events are: Forrest C. Pogue, *The Supreme Command* (Washington, 1954), especially Chapter XX; Martin Blumenson, *Breakout and Pursuit,* and Charles B. MacDonald, *The Siegfried Line Campaign* (both in preparation); Hugh M. Cole, *The Lorraine Campaign* (Washington, 1950).

Reference is made below to monographs (in the R-Series) dealing with special aspects of German operations in World War II. The R-Series monographs are historical studies based on German captured documents and additional information obtained from high-ranking German participants in the events described. These manuscripts are written in support of volumes in *United States Army in World War II* and are in OCMH files.

2 Minutes of Conference of 31 July 1944: *Besprechung des Führers mit Generaloberst Jodl am 31. 7. 1944 in der Wolfsschanze* (near Rastenburg, East Prussia). *OKW/WFSt (Oberkommando der Wehrmacht/Wehrmachtführungsstab—Armed Forces High Command/Armed Forces Operations Staff), KTB (Kriegstagebuch—War Diary), Ausarbeitung, Der Westen, 1.IV.-16.XII.44,* referred to hereafter as *Der Westen* (Schramm); Maj. Percy E. Schramm, keeper of the *WFSt* War Diary, wrote this draft war diary from records and daily notes made at OKW headquarters.

3 The exact date when Hitler made his startling announcement was Sunday, September 16, during a situation conference with his top advisers. A detailed account of the meeting is contained in the personal diary of the Chief of Staff of the *Luftwaffe,* General Werner Kreipe, in OCMH files as MS #P-069 (Kreipe). See also Hitler-Jodl Conference, 31 Jul 44, cited above in footnote 2. Measures taken to implement the decision to launch a large-scale counteroffensive were, among others, the constitution of the Sixth Panzer Army (Sepp Dietrich) ordered on September 6, 44. For details on the origin of the idea and the course of events leading up to the Ardennes offensive, see MS # R-9, The Idea for the German Ardennes Offensive in 1944, by Magna E. Bauer.

4 MS # R-19, Germany's Situation in the Fall of 1944, Part III, The Military Situation, by Charles V. P. von Luttichau.

5 U.S. Strategic Bombing Survey (USSBS), "The Over-all Report (European

War), September 30, 1945," and "The Effects of Strategic Bombing on the German War Economy, October 31, 1945"; for additional information, see MS # R-25, Germany's Situation in the Fall of 1944, Part II, The Economic Situation, by Charles V. P. von Luttichau.

[6] *The Rise and Fall of the German Air Force (1933-1945)*, issued by the Air Ministry (London, 1948), pp. 370-73; Adolf Galland, *Die Ersten und die Letzten* (Darmstadt: Franz Schneekluth, 1953); Chester Wilmot, *The Struggle for Europe* (New York: Harper, 1952), pp. 442-44.

[7] Minutes of Conferences of the Commander in Chief, Navy, with Hitler, 1-3 Jan 44, 9 Jul 44, 19 Jan 45, in Führer Conferences on Matters Dealing with the German Navy 1944 and 1945, in OCMH files; Wilmot, *The Struggle for Europe*, pp. 147, 151-52, 617-20; Heinz Guderian, *Erinnerungen eines Soldaten* (Heidelberg: Kurt Vowinckel, 1951), pp. 320, 322, and 341ff. (English language edition, *Panzer Leader*, New York: Dutton, 1952. Subsequent references are to the German edition).

[8] USSBS sources cited in footnote 5; Guderian, *op. cit.*, pp. 341ff; for more detail see MS # R-25.

[9] *KTB, GenStdH/Org Abt (General Staff of the Army/Organization Division)*, 13 Jun-31 Aug 44; for more detail, see MS # R-12, The Ardennes Offensive, Planning and Preparations, Ch. I, The Preliminary Planning, by Charles V. P. von Luttichau; *Der Westen* (Schramm), chapter entitled *Die Vorbereitungen einer eigenen Offensive zwischen Monschau und Echternach.*

[10] Cordell Hull, *The Memoirs of Cordell Hull*, 2 vols. (New York: Macmillan, 1948), Vol. II, pp. 1573-74; Franz von Papen, *Der Wahrheit eine Gasse* (München: Paul List, 1952), p. 585 (English edition published by Andre Deutsch, London, 1952); for additional information see MS # R-27, Germany's Situation in the Fall of 1944, Part I, The Political Situation, by Charles V. P. von Luttichau.

[11] Hitler addressing commanding generals before the Operation NORDWIND, 28 Dec 44, Fragment No. 27, in collection known as *Conferences Between Hitler and Members of the German Armed Forces High Command, December 1942-March 1945*, referred to hereafter as *Minutes of Hitler Conferences.*

[12] Conference Between Hitler and Generalleutnant Siegfried Westphal and Generalleutnant Hans Krebs, 31 Aug 44, Fragment No. 46, in *Minutes of Hitler Conferences.*

[13] *Trial of the Major War Criminals Before the International Military Tribunal, Nuremberg, 14 November 1945-1 October 1946* (Nuremberg, 1948), Vol. XVI, p. 498.

[14] *ETHINT* 50 (Jodl), in OCMH files; Fragment No. 27, cited in footnote 11; Hitler addressing commanding generals before the Ardennes offensive, 12 Dec 44, Fragment No. 28, in *Minutes of Hitler Conferences.*

[15] MS # T-122, The History of OB WEST (Commander in Chief West) (Generalleutnant Bodo Zimmermann *et al.*), Section D, pp. 329ff; this section was written by General von Buttlar and gives an account of the development of the plan for the Ardennes offensive. MS # P-32i, Ardennes Project, Questionnaire No. 1 (General der Infanterie Hans von Greiffenberg *et al.*).

[16] See sources cited in footnote 6.

[17] Hitler conference, 31 Jul 44, cited in footnote 2.

[18] MS # T-122, cited in footnote 15; *Der Westen* (Schramm).

[19] MS # R-19, cited in footnote 4.

[20] See sources cited in footnote 15.

[21] *ETHINT* 50 (Jodl).

22 See sources cited in footnote 15.

23 MS # R-12, cited in footnote 9.

24 *Ibid.*

25 *Ibid.* See also *Der Westen* (Schramm), p. 259; sources cited in footnote 15.

26 For a fuller discussion of Hitler's reasoning, see MS # R-12, cited in footnote 9, and MS # R-13, The Ardennes Offensive, Planning and Preparations, Ch. II, The Framework for the Operation WACHT AM RHEIN, by Charles V. P. von Luttichau.

27 Operation Directive, WACHT AM RHEIN, 10 Nov 44, by Hitler, in *OB WEST, KTB Anlage 50,* 1 Jul-31 Dec 44, Vol. I, pp. 95-104; *ETHINT* 50 (Jodl).

28 *Ibid.*

29 *ETHINT* 50 (Jodl); MS # P-032i (Greiffenberg *et al.*). The comments by Albert Speer bear out the fact that Hitler was fully aware of the desperate gamble he had undertaken.

30 See sources cited in footnote 27.

31 For the various dates when the Ardennes offensive was considered to have failed, see MSS # R-11 and R-15, Key Dates During the Ardennes Offensive 1944, Parts I and II, by Magna E. Bauer and Charles V. P. von Luttichau.

32 Pogue, *Supreme Command,* pp. 396-97.

33 Fragment No. 27, 28 Dec 44, in *Minutes of Hitler Conferences.*

34 *Ibid.*

35 For discussion of German losses, see MS # R-60, The Cost of the Ardennes Offensive, by Magna E. Bauer.

36 MS # T-122 (Zimmermann *et al.*).

CHAPTER 18

1 This essay is essentially Chapter 1 of *Triumph in the Philippines,* by Robert Ross Smith, a forthcoming volume in *United States Army in World War II.* Additional background information is to be found in *The Approach to the Philippines* (Washington, 1953), by the same author; M. Hamlin Cannon, *Leyte: The Return to the Philippines* (Washington, 1954); and Philip A. Crowl and Edmund G. Love, *Seizure of the Gilberts and Marshalls* (Washington, 1953), all in *United States Army in World War II.* Maurice Matloff, *Strategic Planning for Coalition Warfare, 1943-1944* (Washington, 1959), in that series, deals with the broader strategic aspects of the decision.

2 See Louis Morton, *The Fall of the Philippines* (Washington, 1953), in *United States Army in World War II,* for the opening phases of Japan's attack in the Pacific and a description of prewar plans with especial reference to the Philippines. Morton's general volume on the Pacific theaters, *Strategy and Command: Turning the Tide, 1941-1943,* will cover prewar plans in more detail.

3 See JCS 287/1, 8 May 43, and JPS 67/4, 29 Apr 43, both entitled Strategic Plan for the Defeat of Japan, and associated papers in OPD ABC 381 Japan (8-27-42) Secs. 1 and 2.

4 See the sources cited in footnote 1, above, and also JCS 713, 16 Feb 44, Strategy in the Pacific; JCS 713/1, 10 Mar 44, Future Opns in the Pacific, and associated sources in OPD ABC 384 Pacific (1-17-43).

5 Memo, King for Marshall, 8 Feb 44, sub: CINCSWPA Despatch [*sic*] C-121702 Feb 44, and other documents in OPD ABC 384 Pacific (28 Jun 43); JCS Memo for Info No. 200, 7 Mar 44, sub: Sequence and Timing of Opns CenPac Campaign [a rpt by Nimitz], and associated sources in OPD ABC 384 Pacific (1-17-43) Secs. 3-A and 4; Supplementary Minutes, JCS

145th and 150th Mtgs, 8 Feb and 7 Mar 44; Minutes, JCS 151st Mtg, 11 Mar 44; Minutes, JPS 125th Mtg, 2 Feb 44; Rad, Nimitz to King and Mac-Arthur, 4 Jul 44, CM-IN 2926.

6 Memo, Marshall for King, 10 Feb 44, no sub, in OPD ABC 384 Pacific (28 Jun 43); Memo, Col Charles K. Gailey, Jr. (Exec O OPD) for Maj Gen Thomas T. Handy (ACofS OPD), 22 Feb 44, no sub [reporting Mc-Narney remarks], and associated materials in OPD ABC 384 Pacific (1-17-43) Sec. 3-A; JPS 418/1, 23 Mar 44, Basic Decision Which Will Give Strategic Guidance for . . . the War in the Pacific, in OPD ABC 384 Pacific (8 Mar 44); Rad, Marshall to MacArthur, 23 Jun 44, CM-OUT 55718; Supplementary Minutes, JCS 150th Mtg, 7 Mar 44.

7 Memo, Somervell for Handy, 15 Jul 44, sub: JCS 924, and associated papers in OPD ABC 384 Pacific (1-17-43) Sec. 3-A; Rad, MacArthur to Marshall, C-3302, 20 Jun 43, CM-IN 13149; GHQ SWPA, Estimates of the Situation and Rough Draft RENO Plan [RENO I], 25 Feb 43, photostat copy in OCMH files; Minutes, JPS 134th, 157th, and 159th Mtgs, 8 Mar, 28 Jun, and 26 Jul 44.

8 JCS 713/4, 12 Mar 44, Future Opns in the Pacific, in OPS ABC 384 Pacific (1-17-43) Sec. 3-A; see also Smith, *Approach to the Philippines*, Ch. I.

9 JCS 713/8, 13 Jun 44, Future Opns in the Pacific, in OPD ABC 384 Formosa (8 Sep 43) Sec. 1-C; Rad, JCS to MacArthur and Nimitz, 13 Jun 44, CM-OUT 50007; Rad, Marshall to MacArthur, 23 Jun 44, CM-OUT 55718.

10 Rad, JCS to MacArthur and Nimitz, 13 Jun 44, CM-OUT 50007.

11 Rad, MacArthur to Marshall, CX-13891, 18 Jun 44, CM-IN 15058; Rad, Nimitz to King and MacArthur, 4 Jul 44, CM-IN 2926; Rad, Marshall to MacArthur, 23 Jun 44, CM-OUT 55718; Minutes, JPS 157th, 158th, and 159th Mtgs, 28 Jun and 12 and 21 Jul 44; JPS 404/5, 23 Jun 44, Future Opns in the Pacific, and related papers in OPD ABC 384 Formosa (8 Sep 43) Sec. 1-C and ABC 384 Pacific (1-17-43) Sec. 4; see also Smith, *Approach to the Philippines*, pp. 451-52.

12 No evidence that strategic decisions were reached at Pearl Harbor is to be found in contemporary sources. See Rad, MacArthur to Marshall, C-15589, 1 Aug 44, CM-IN 496; Memo, King for Marshall and Arnold, 9 Aug 44, no sub [quoting parts of a letter on the Pearl Harbor Conference from Nimitz to King, dated 31 Jul 44], in OPD ABC 384 Pacific (1-17-43) Sec. 4; Ltr, Lt Gen Robert C. Richardson, COMGENPOA, to Marshall, 1 Aug 44, no sub, in OPD Personal File on Gen Marshall. See also Fleet Admiral William D. Leahy, *I Was There* (New York: Whittlesey House, 1950), pp. 247-52. Leahy also participated in the conferences, and Richardson was MacArthur's host in Hawaii.

13 See, for example, Minutes, JPS 160th Mtg, 2 Aug 44.

14 Rad, MacArthur to Marshall, C-3302, 20 Jun 43, CM-IN 13139; Rad, Mac-Arthur to Marshall, CX-13891, 18 Jun 44, CM-IN 15058; Rad, MacArthur to Marshall, C-15689, 3 Aug 44, CM-IN 2479; RENO I, 25 Feb 43; GHQ SWPA, Basic Outline Plan for MUSKETEER (Philippine) Opns [MUS-KETEER I], 10 Jul 44.

15 MUSKETEER I, 10 Jul 44; MUSKETEER II, 29 Aug 44; MUSKETEER III, 26 Sep 44.

16 See the sources cited in note 6, above, and also JCS 713/10, 4 Sep 44 [memo from King for the JCS], and associated papers in OPD ABC 384 Pacific (1-17-43) Sec. 5; Minutes, JCS 171st and 172d Mtg, 1 and 5 Sep 44.

17 Rad, MacArthur to Marshall, C-15689, 3 Aug 44, CM-IN 2479.

18 JPS 414/10, 29 Jun 44, Future Opns in the Pacific, and associated sources in OPD ABC 384 Formosa (8 Sep 43) Sec. 1-C; JCS 713/14, 7 Sep 44, Pro-

posed Directive, and connected materials in OPD ABC 384 Pacific (1-17-43) Sec. 5; Minutes, JCS 171st-173d Mtgs, 1, 5, and 8 Sep 44; Minutes, JPS 160th, 162d, 163d, 165th, and 167th Mtgs, 2, 10, 16, and 28 Aug and 2 Sep 44.

[19] Rads, Nimitz to King, 18 and 24 Aug 44, CM-IN 16755 and CM-IN 22182; Rad, Nimitz to Arnold, 5 Sep 44, CM-IN 4996; Memo [unsigned, but prepared by Col. William L. Ritchie of OPD, who had just returned to Washington after talking with most of the ranking Army and Navy commanders in the Pacific], n.d. [*circa* 15 Aug 44], sub: Notes for Discussion With General Marshall [hereafter cited as Ritchie Notes for Marshall], and related sources in OPD 384 Pacific (1-17-43) Sec. 5; Fleet Admiral William F. Halsey, USN, and Lieutenant Commander J. Bryan, III, USNR, *Admiral Halsey's Story* (New York: McGraw-Hill, 1947), p. 195.

[20] Halsey and Bryan, *Admiral Halsey's Story,* p. 195.

[21] Ritchie Notes for Marshall; George C. Kenney, *General Kenney Reports: A Personal History of the Pacific War* (New York: Duell, Sloan & Pearce, 1949), p. 371; Leahy, *I Was There,* p. 259; Rad, Richardson to Marshall, R-28617, 22 Aug 44, CM-IN 19958.

[22] For the events leading up to this change in plans, see Cannon, *Leyte: The Return to the Philippines,* Ch. I.

[23] Rad, MacArthur to Marshall, C-18103, 21 Sep 44, CM-IN 19803.

[24] The following discussion of tactical and logistical problems (to footnote reference 25) is based generally upon: Minutes, JPS 162d, 165th, and 167th Mtgs, 10 and 28 Aug and 2 Sep 44; OPD, Draft Appreciation of a Plan of Campaign, n.d. [*circa* 1 Sep 44], and associated sources in OPD 381 Strategy Section Papers (4 Sep 44); Memo, Handy for Marshall, n.d. [*circa* 5 Sep 44], sub: Opns in the Western Pacific, and related documents in OPD ABC 384 Pacific (1-17-43) Sec. 5; Minutes, JCS 171st and 172d Mtgs, 1 and 5 Sep 44.

[25] Rad, Stilwell to Marshall and MacArthur, CFBX-22674, 16 Sep 44, CM-IN 15768. See also Charles F. Romanus and Riley Sunderland, *Time Runs Out in CBI* (Washington, 1959), in *United States Army in World War II.*

[26] Memo, Hull for Handy, 2 Sep 44, sub: Pacific Strategy; OPD, Draft Appreciation of a Plan of Campaign, n.d. [*circa* 1 Sep 44], both, with associated sources, in OPD 384 Pacific (1-17-43) Sec. 5; Minutes, JCS 172d Mtg, 5 Sep 44.

[27] Memo, King for Marshall, 23 Sep 44, no sub, in OPD ABC 384 Pacific (1-17-43) Sec. 5.

[28] Rads, R. J. Marshall to MacArthur, 26 Sep 44, CM-OUT 37000 and 37001. The first radio informed MacArthur of the nature of King's arguments, told MacArthur what Army planners needed to counter King's objections, and cautioned MacArthur to make no reference to the first radio in replying to the second. The second radio, signed by R. J. Marshall, was actually a formal request for information sent by the Joint Chiefs of Staff to MacArthur.

[29] Rad, MacArthur to Marshall, C-18496, 28 Sep 44, CM-IN 26358.

[30] Conf Notes, Rear Adm Forrest P. Sherman (Nimitz' planning chief) and Rear Adm Charles M. Cooke (King's deputy chief of staff), 27 Sep 44, in OPD Exec Files 17, Binder 3; JCS 713/18, 2 Oct 44, Future Opns in the Pacific [a memo by King to the JCS], in OPD 384 Pacific (1-17-43), Sec. 5. Nimitz personally presented his views to King at a secret conference in San Francisco over the week end of 29 September-1 October 1944.

[31] JCS 713/18, 2 Oct 44; Rad, JCS to MacArthur, Nimitz, and Stilwell, 3 Oct 44, CM-OUT 40782.

[32] *Ibid.* The B-29's operated under the direct control of the JCS, with General Arnold acting as the JCS executive agent.

CHAPTER 19

[1] This study in substantially its present form was published with the title, "Why Eisenhower's Forces Stopped at the Elbe," in *World Politics*, IV, No. 3 (April, 1952), 356-68. It is based on Chapters XXIII and XXIV of the author's volume *The Supreme Command* (Washington, 1954), in *United States Army in World War II*, with additions based on subsequent publications. Other published works valuable for a study of the subject are: Dwight D. Eisenhower, *Crusade in Europe* (Garden City, N.Y.: Doubleday, 1948); Omar N. Bradley, *A Soldier's Story* (New York: Holt, 1951); William D. Leahy, *I Was There* (New York: Whittlesey House, 1950); Winston S. Churchill, *Triumph and Tragedy* (Boston: Houghton Mifflin, 1952); John Ehrman, *Grand Strategy*, Vol. VI (London: H.M. Stationery Office, 1956) in the British official *History of the Second World War;* U.S. State Department, *Foreign Relations of the United States: The Conferences at Malta and Yalta, 1945* (Washington, 1955).

[2] Philip E. Mosely [adviser to the U.S. delegation to the European Advisory Commission in London], "The Occupation of Germany: New Light on How the Zones Were Drawn," *Foreign Affairs*, XXVIII, No. 4 (July, 1950), 580-604; U.S. Dept of State, *The Conferences at Malta and Yalta, 1945*, pp. 110-23, 131, 498-99, 511-12, 514-15, 570, 592-93, 639, 970; Churchill, *Triumph and Tragedy*, p. 510.

[3] Roosevelt obviously assumed that Berlin would fall to the Russians if one may judge by his statement to Stalin that he had made several bets en route to Yalta as to whether the Americans would capture Manila before the Russians took Berlin. Stalin said he felt the Americans would win their prize first because of the heavy resistance which the Russians were meeting on the Oder. U.S. Dept of State, *Conferences at Malta and Yalta, 1945*, pp. 510, 727.

[4] In mid-April 1945, officials of the European and Russian Affairs Divisions of the Department of State were reported to believe "that for governments to direct movements of troops definitely indicated *political* action and that *such movements should remain a military consideration* at least until SHAEF is dissolved and the ACC (Allied Control Commission) is set up" [italics in the original]. Members of the War Department in noting this view concluded that the State Department preferred "a straight military solution" to the problem of moving Allied troops out of areas which they might seize in the Russian zone of occupation. Memo by G. A. L. [Brig Gen G. A. Lincoln] to Gen Hull, Military Contacts with the Russians, 13 Apr 45, CCS 805/7 and CCS 805/8, OPD 381, Sec. V.

[5] Eisenhower, *Crusade in Europe*, p. 396.

[6] SHAEF Planning Draft of Post-NEPTUNE Courses of Action after the Capture of the Lodgment Area, Main Objectives and Axes of Advance, I, 3 May 44, SHAEF SGS Post OVERLORD Planning, 381, I.

[7] Eisenhower to Bradley, Montgomery and Devers, 15 Sep 44, SHAEF SGS Post OVERLORD Planning, 381, I.

[8] This concept appears in several of General Eisenhower's letters. The particular figure of speech is that of Lt. Gen. Walter Bedell Smith, SHAEF Chief of Staff, who used it in explaining the Supreme Commander's viewpoint. Interv, author with Smith, 1 Nov 51, OCMH files.

9 Churchill recognized the importance of this disproportion of strength in his statement to the British Chiefs of Staff during the March and April debate over strategy: "I hope . . . we shall realise that we have only a quarter of the forces invading Germany, and that the situation has thus changed remarkably from the days of June 1944. . . ." Churchill, *Triumph and Tragedy,* p. 460. See also Pogue, *Supreme Command,* pp. 409-13.

10 Bradley, *A Soldier's Story,* pp. 531-37, 544.

11 Eisenhower to Mil Mission, Personal to Marshal Stalin, SCAF-252, 28 Mar 45, SHAEF SGS 373.5 Bomb-Line, Liaison, and Co-ordination of Fronts, I.

12 Marshall to Eisenhower, W-61337, 31 Mar 45, Eisenhower personal file; Churchill, *Triumph and Tragedy,* pp. 460-61.

13 Churchill, *Triumph and Tragedy,* pp. 46-62; Marshall to Eisenhower, W-61337, 31 Mar 45, Eisenhower personal file.

14 Churchill to Roosevelt, 931, 1 Apr 45, Incl to CCS 805, 29 Mar 45, ABC 384 Europe (5 Aug 43), Sec. 1-D; Churchill, *Triumph and Tragedy,* pp. 464-66; Eisenhower, *Crusade in Europe,* p. 399.

15 Draft of message for the President to the Prime Minister (with notation "dispatched as is per White House") in reply to message of 1 Apr 45, Operations Division (War Department) files ABC-384, Europe (5 Aug 43), Sec. 1-D.

16 Eisenhower to Churchill, FWD-18428, 1 Apr 45, Eisenhower personal file.

17 Churchill to Roosevelt, 933, 5 Apr 45; Marshall to Eisenhower, W-64244, 6 Apr 45, Eisenhower personal file.

18 Paraphrase of U.S. views given in Marshall to Eisenhower, W-64349, 6 Apr 45, Eisenhower personal file; Churchill, *Triumph and Tragedy,* pp. 511-12.

19 Eisenhower to Marshall, FWD-18710, 7 Apr 45, Eisenhower personal file.

20 Eisenhower to Montgomery, 8 Apr 45, Eisenhower personal file.

21 Eisenhower to Marshall, 15 Apr 45, Eisenhower personal file; Bradley, *A Soldier's Story,* pp. 537-39.

22 Churchill, *Triumph and Tragedy,* pp. 515-16.

23 Churchill, *Triumph and Tragedy,* pp. 514-15; Harry S. Truman, *Memoirs,* Vol. I: *Year of Decisions* (Garden City, N.Y.: Doubleday, 1955), pp. 61-62, 83; Leahy, *I Was There,* pp. 350-51.

24 WD Memo, with covering note by Maj Gen Clayton L. Bissell, G-2, German Line of Demarcation Between Anglo-American and Soviet Operations, 22 Mar 45, OPD 381; Marshall to Eisenhower, 26 Mar 45, Eisenhower personal file; U.S. Dept of State, *The Conferences at Malta and Yalta, 1945,* pp. 603-05, 640ff.

25 Eisenhower to War Dept, 5 Apr 45; War Dept to SHAEF, 12 Apr 45; Mil Mission Moscow to Eisenhower, MX-23875, 14 Apr 45; and Eisenhower to Mil Mission Moscow, SCAF 282, 15 Apr 45—all in SHAEF SGS 373.5 Bomb-Line, Liaison, and Co-ordination of Fronts, I.

26 Eisenhower to Mil Mission Moscow, 21 Apr 45, and Eisenhower to Mil Mission Moscow, 22 Apr 45, both in SHAEF SGS 373.5, Bomb-Line, Liaison, and Co-ordination of Fronts, I.

27 Mil Mission Moscow to Eisenhower, MX-24032, 24 Apr 45, and Mil Mission Moscow to Eisenhower, MX-24055, 25 Apr 45, both in SHAEF SGS 373.5, Bomb-Line, Liaison, and Co-ordination of Fronts, I.

28 Marshall to Eisenhower, W-74256, 28 Apr 45, SHAEF Cable Log. (This also contains a statement of the British position.)

29 Eisenhower to Marshall, FWD-20225, 29 Apr 45, SHAEF Cable Log. In a letter to the author dated Feb 20, 1952, General Eisenhower said that no

political directive was ever given him to stop at the Elbe *or* to go to Berlin or Prague.

30 Eisenhower to Mil Mission Moscow, SCAF-323, 30 Apr 45, SHAEF SGS 373.5, Bomb-Line, Liaison, and Co-ordination of Fronts, II.

31 Eisenhower to Mil Mission Moscow, 4 May 45; Mil Mission Moscow, MX-24166, 4 May 45, and Mil Mission Moscow, MX-24193, 5 May 45—all in SHAEF SGS 373.5, Bomb-Line, Liaison, and Co-ordination of Fronts, II.

32 Series of messages, 6, 7, and 8 May 45, SHAEF EACS SH/9 Czechoslovakia.

33 Churchill to Eisenhower, 2920, 7 May 45, Eisenhower personal file.

34 Note on transmittal slip of request from Czech Mil Mission, 9 May 45, SHAEF EACS SH/9 Czechoslovakia.

35 Czech Mil Mission to SHAEF, 6 May 45; 12th Army Group to SHAEF, 7 May 45; and SHAEF to Mil Mission Moscow, FWD-21001, 8 May 45—all in SHAEF SGS 370.64 Czechoslovakian Resistance Groups; Eisenhower to Mil Mission Moscow, 8 May 45, Eisenhower personal file.

36 Report of Col. Wilhelm Meyer-Detring [OKW officer who was sent by Doenitz to Schoerner, 10 May 45], OKW, *Einsatzabteilung Heer 2.V.-22.V.45*. The broad details of the report are confirmed by *V Corps Operations in the ETO*, p. 454; Eisenhower to OKW, 10 May 45, and Eisenhower to Mil Mission Moscow, 10 May 45, both in Eisenhower personal file.

37 The British official historian on the strategy of this period says that the strategy which the British wished to adopt in Germany was designed "not for reasons of defence or attack against Russia . . . but with the object, which they recognized must remain subsidiary to the immediate military task, of negotiating from strength." Ehrman, *Grand Strategy,* Vol. VI, p. 150.

CHAPTER 20

1 The study that follows was published in substantially its present form in *Foreign Affairs,* Vol. XXV, No. 2 (January, 1957). It is republished here with the kind permission of *Foreign Affairs*.

2 James Phinney Baxter, 3rd, *Scientists Against Time* (Boston: Little, Brown, 1946), p. 419.

3 Henry L. Stimson, "The Decision to Use the Atomic Bomb," *Harper's* Magazine (February, 1947). The article is reproduced with additional comments in Henry L. Stimson and McGeorge Bundy, *On Active Service in Peace and War* (New York: Harper, 1948), Chapter XIII, and in *Bulletin of the Atomic Scientists,* Vol. III, No. 2 (February, 1947).

4 The best semitechnical account of the development of the bomb is by H. D. Smyth, *A General Account of the Development of Methods of Using Atomic Energy for Military Purposes . . .* (Washington, 1945). An excellent short account is in Baxter, *Scientists Against Time,* pp. 419-50. The best popular accounts are W. L. Laurence, *Dawn Over Zero* (New York: Knopf, 1946), J. W. Campbell, *The Atomic Story* (New York: Holt, 1947), and R. Jungk, *Brighter Than a Thousand Suns* (New York: Harcourt, Brace, 1958). For a graphic account of the establishment of the Los Alamos Laboratory, see the testimony of Dr. J. Robert Oppenheimer in U.S. Atomic Energy Commission, *Transcript of Hearings Before Personnel Security Board in the Matter of Dr. J. Robert Oppenheimer, 12 April-6 May 1954* (Washington, 1954), pp. 12-15, 28-29 (cited hereafter as *Oppenheimer Hearings*). For a vivid account of the bombing, see Merle Miller and Abe Spitzer, *We Dropped*

the A-Bomb (New York: Crowell, 1946), and Laurence, *Dawn Over Zero,* pp. 207-11.

[5] The one exception was the Navy's work in the field of atomic energy as a source of power for naval vessels. *Hearings Before the Special Committee on Atomic Energy,* 79th Cong., 1st Sess., Senate, S.R. 179, Part 3, pp. 364-89, testimony of Dr. Ross Gunn.

[6] Stimson, "The Decision to Use the Atomic Bomb," *Harper's,* p. 98; *Oppenheimer Hearings,* p. 33.

[7] *Hearings Before the Special Committee on Atomic Energy,* Part 2, p. 302, testimony of Dr. John A. Simpson.

[8] *Ibid.,* p. 303; *Oppenheimer Hearings,* p. 33; Leo Szilard, "A Personal History of the Bomb," *The Atlantic Community Faces the Bomb,* University of Chicago Roundtable 601, September 25, 1949, p. 14.

[9] Wesley Frank Craven and James Lea Cate, eds., *The Army Air Forces in World War II,* Vol. V: *The Pacific: Matterhorn to Nagasaki* (Chicago: University of Chicago Press, 1953), pp. 705-08.

[10] Memo, Groves for CofS, 30 Dec 44, sub: Atomic Fission Bombs, printed in U.S. Dept of State, *Foreign Relations of the United States: The Conferences at Malta and Yalta, 1945* (Washington, 1955) (hereafter cited as *Malta-Yalta Conferences*).

[11] Fleet Admiral William D. Leahy, *I Was There* (New York: Whittlesey House, 1950), p. 434.

[12] Ray S. Cline, *Washington Command Post: The Operations Division,* in *United States Army in World War II* (Washington, 1951), pp. 347, 348n.

[13] John J. McCloy, *The Challenge to American Foreign Policy* (Cambridge: Harvard University Press, 1953), p. 42. See also Fleet Admiral Ernest J. King and Walter Muir Whitehill, *Fleet Admiral King* (New York: Norton, 1952), pp. 620-21; James F. Byrnes, *Speaking Frankly* (New York: Harper, 1947), p. 257.

[14] Stimson, "The Decision to Use the Atomic Bomb," *Harper's,* p. 98, prints the memorandum Stimson prepared on this conversation; King and Whitehill, *Fleet Admiral King,* p. 621, indicates the status of the project and the optimism of the period. See also Byrnes, *Speaking Frankly,* p. 258.

[15] *Hearings Before the Special Committee on Atomic Energy,* Part 2, p. 303ff, testimony of Dr. Simpson.

[16] His memorandum of this meeting is printed in Stimson, "The Decision to Use the Atomic Bomb," *Harper's,* pp. 99-100.

[17] *Ibid.;* Harry S. Truman, *Memoirs,* Vol. I: *Year of Decisions* (Garden City, N.Y.: Doubleday, 1955), pp. 10-11; William Hillman, ed., *Mr. President* (New York: Farrar, Straus, 1952), p. 249; Byrnes, *Speaking Frankly,* p. 259. President Truman actually first learned about the bomb from Byrnes.

[18] Stimson, "The Decision to Use the Atomic Bomb," *Harper's,* p. 100; Byrnes, *Speaking Frankly,* p. 259; *Oppenheimer Hearings,* p. 34.

[19] Stimson, "The Decision to Use the Atomic Bomb," *Harper's,* p. 100.

[20] *Oppenheimer Hearings,* pp. 34, 257, testimony of Drs. Oppenheimer and Compton; Byrnes, *Speaking Frankly,* pp. 260-61; Stimson, "The Decision to Use the Atomic Bomb," *Harper's,* pp. 100-101.

[21] Stimson, "The Decision to Use the Atomic Bomb," *Harper's,* p. 101; Truman, *Year of Decisions,* p. 419. Byrnes mistakenly states that the Interim Committee made its recommendations on July 1; see Byrnes, *Speaking Frankly.*

[22] Stimson, "The Decision to Use the Atomic Bomb," *Harper's,* p. 101. The same idea is expressed by Winston Churchill, *Triumph and Tragedy* (Boston: Houghton Mifflin, 1953), pp. 638-39.

[23] "Report of the Committee on Social and Political Implications," signed by Professor James Franck of the University of Chicago and submitted to the Secretary of War, 11 June 1945, *Bulletin of Atomic Scientists*, Vol. I, No. 10 (May 1, 1946), p. 3.

[24] *Ibid.*, pp. 3-4.

[25] *Ibid.*, p. 1; Leo Szilard, "A Personal History of the Bomb," University of Chicago Roundtable 601, p. 15. See also P. M. S. Blackett, *Fear, War, and the Bomb* (New York: Whittlesey House, 1949), pp. 114-16.

[26] *Oppenheimer Hearings*, p. 34.

[27] Quoted in Stimson, "The Decision to Use the Atomic Bomb," *Harper's*, p. 101. The Scientific Panel was established to advise the Interim Committee and its report was made to that body.

[28] *Ibid.;* Byrnes, *Speaking Frankly*, p. 261.

[29] Stimson, *op. cit.; Oppenheimer Hearings*, p. 163, testimony of General Groves.

[30] Truman, *Year of Decisions*, p. 11. Leahy in his memoirs frankly admits having said this.

[31] For an account of the strategic plans evolved for the defeat of Japan, see *The Entry of the Soviet Union into the War Against Japan: Military Plans, 1941-1945* (Department of Defense Press Release, September 1955), pp. 28, 62-67, and *passim;* Cline, *Washington Command Post*, Ch. XVII; Leahy, *I Was There*, pp. 383-385; Craven and Cate, *The Army Air Forces in World War II*, Vol. V, p. 702 and *passim.*

[32] The alternatives to invasion were outlined by General Marshall for MacArthur in a message of April 12, 1945, reproduced in *The Entry of the Soviet Union into the War Against Japan*, pp. 54-55.

[33] Leahy, *I Was There*, pp. 384-85; King and Whitehill, *Fleet Admiral King*, p. 598. See also H. H. Arnold, *Global Mission* (New York: Harper, 1949), pp. 595-96; Major General Charles A. Willoughby and John Chamberlain, *MacArthur, 1941-1951* (New York: McGraw-Hill, 1954), pp. 287-88.

[34] This message is reproduced in *The Entry of the Soviet Union into the War Against Japan*, pp. 55-57.

[35] For a summary of this meeting, see *The Entry of the Soviet Union into the War Against Japan*, pp. 77-85. See also McCloy, *Challenge to American Foreign Policy*, pp. 42-43; Walter Millis, ed., *The Forrestal Diaries* (New York: Viking Press, 1951), pp. 70-71; Leahy, *I Was There*, pp. 383-85; King and Whitehill, *Fleet Admiral King*, pp. 598, 605-06.

[36] McCloy, *Challenge to American Foreign Policy*, p. 41. See also sources cited in footnote 35.

[37] *The Entry of the Soviet Union into the War Against Japan*, p. 90; Leahy, *I Was There*, p. 385; King and Whitehill, *Fleet Admiral King*, p. 606; *Malta-Yalta Conferences*, pp. 288-400, 827-32.

[38] *The Entry of the Soviet Union into the War Against Japan*, p. 83; Joseph C. Grew, *The Turbulent Era*, ed. by Walter Johnson, 2 vols. (Boston: Houghton Mifflin, 1952), Ch. XXXVI; McCloy, *Challenge to American Foreign Policy*, pp. 42-43; Ltr, McCloy to Hamilton Fish Armstrong, editor of *Foreign Affairs*, 18 Jun 56.

[39] McCloy, *Challenge to American Foreign Policy*, p. 43. See also Millis, *The Forrestal Diaries*, pp. 70-71.

[40] An excellent official summary of this subject which reproduces the most important documents is *The Entry of the Soviet Union into the War Against Japan*. The subject is also well covered in Ernest R. May, "The United States, the Soviet Union, and the Far Eastern War, 1941-1945," *Pacific His-*

torical Review (May, 1955), pp. 153-74. See also, John R. Deane, *The Strange Alliance* (New York: Viking Press, 1947); Statement of W. Averell Harriman in *MacArthur Hearings*, 82d Cong., 1st Sess. (Washington, 1951), Part 5, pp. 3328-42; William H. McNeill, *America, Britain, and Russia, Their Cooperation and Conflict, 1941-1946* (New York: Oxford University Press, 1953).

41 Ltr, Stimson to Grew, 21 May 45, reproduced in Grew, *The Turbulent Era*, Vol. II, p. 1458, and in *The Entry of the Soviet Union into the War Against Japan*, pp. 70-71.

42 For expressions of this view, see Deane, *The Strange Alliance*, pp. 263-65; Leahy, *I Was There*, pp. 318, 339; Byrnes, *Speaking Frankly*, pp. 207-09; Millis, *The Forrestal Diaries*, p. 78; King and Whitehill, *Fleet Admiral King*, p. 606.

43 Millis, *The Forrestal Diaries*, p. 50, minute by Charles E. Bohlen dated 23 April 1945; Truman, *Year of Decisions*, p. 72.

44 *The Entry of the Soviet Union into the War Against Japan*, p. 85.

45 Statement to Leahy quoted in *I Was There*, p. 369. See also Harriman's statement, *MacArthur Hearings*, Part 5, p. 3341; War Department memorandum of 21 May 1945, quoted in Grew, *The Turbulent Era*, Vol. II, p. 1458.

46 *The Entry of the Soviet Union into the War Against Japan*, pp. 85-88; OPD Study by Brig. Gen. George A. Lincoln, dated 4 June 1945, quoted in Cline, *Washington Command Post*, p. 344. See also, Leahy, *I Was There*, pp. 343, 346-47; Stimson, "The Decision to Use the Atomic Bomb," *Harper's*, pp. 101-02; Willoughby and Chamberlain, *MacArthur, 1941-1951*, p. 286; *Allied Operations in Southwest Pacific Area*, GHQ SWPA, I, pp. 397-404.

47 G-2 Memorandum prepared for OPD and quoted in Cline, *Washington Command Post*, p. 347. The same study was presented to the Combined Chiefs and is reproduced in part in *The Entry of the Soviet Union into the War Against Japan*, pp. 85-88.

48 *Ibid.* This view is presented by Karl T. Compton in an article entitled, "If the Atomic Bomb Had Not Been Dropped," *Atlantic Monthly* (December, 1946), pp. 54-60.

49 Robert J. C. Butow, *Japan's Decision to Surrender* (Stanford: Stanford University Press, 1954), pp. 40, 54-57. Other accounts of the situation in Japan are Toshikazu Kase, *Journey to the "Missouri"* (New Haven: Yale University Press, 1950); U.S. Strategic Bombing Survey (USSBS), *Japan's Struggle to End the War* (Washington, 1946); Takuhiro Hattori, *Complete History of the Greater East Asia War* (Japan: Masu Shobo Co., 1953), Vol. IV.

50 Butow, *Japan's Decision to Surrender*, pp. 90-91, 125-131; Hattori, *Complete History of the Greater East Asia War*, Vol. IV, pp. 274, 312-16; USSBS, *Japan's Struggle to End the War*, pp. 6-7; Kase, *Journey to the "Missouri,"* pp. 193-94.

51 Stimson, "The Decision to Use the Atomic Bomb," *Harper's*, p. 102; Cline, *Washington Command Post*, p. 345; Millis, *The Forrestal Diaries*, pp. 68-70.

52 Millis, *The Forrestal Diaries*, pp. 74-77; Ellis M. Zacharias, *Secret Missions* (New York: Putnam, 1946), p. 335.

53 OPD Compilation for the Potsdam Conference, quoted in Cline, *Washington Command Post*, p. 345.

54 *Ibid.*, pp. 345-46.

55 Truman, *Year of Decisions*, pp. 416-17. A detailed account of Grew's efforts can be found in Grew, *The Turbulent Era*, Vol. II, Chapter XXXVI.

56 The memorandum is reproduced in Stimson, "The Decision to Use the Atomic Bomb," *Harper's*, pp. 102-04. For the background of the memo-

random, see Grew, *The Turbulent Era*, Ch. XXXVI; Millis, *The Forrestal Diaries*, pp. 68-70; Byrnes, *Speaking Frankly*, pp. 206, 262; McCloy, *Challenge to American Foreign Policy*, pp. 42-43; Stimson and Bundy, *On Active Service*, p. 624.

[57] In his diary, under the date June 19 Stimson wrote: "The last-chance warning . . . must be given before an actual landing of the ground forces in Japan, and fortunately the plans provide for enough time to bring in the sanctions to our warning in the shape of heavy ordinary bombing attack and an attack of S-1 [the atomic bomb]." Stimson and Bundy, *On Active Service*, p. 624.

[58] Stimson, "The Decision to Use the Atomic Bomb," *Harper's*, pp. 101, 104.

[59] *Ibid.*, p. 105.

[60] Quoted in Cline, *Washington Command Post*, p. 344.

[61] For an exposition of this view, see Blackett, *Fear, War, and the Bomb*, p. 136; Hanson W. Baldwin, *Great Mistakes of the War* (New York: Harper, 1950), pp. 100-101.

[62] See, for example, Byrnes, *Speaking Frankly*, p. 208; Stimson and Bundy, *On Active Service*, p. 637; Leahy, *I Was There*, p. 419; Blackett, *Fear, War, and the Bomb*, Ch. X; Norman Cousins and Thomas K. Finletter, "A Beginning for Sanity," *Saturday Review of Literature*, XXIX, No. 4 (June 15, 1946), pp. 5-8.

[63] Szilard, "A Personal History of the Atomic Bomb," pp. 14-15.

[64] Byrnes, *Speaking Frankly*, pp. 257-58; Hillman, *Mr. President*, p. 247. The Truman Committee had already made inquiries, but its investigators were called off at the request of Mr. Stimson. Truman, *Year of Decisions*, p. 10.

[65] Leahy, *I Was There*, p. 441. For a statement of the same argument, but with a refutation, see "Report of the Committee on Social and Political Implications," 11 June 1945, *Bulletin of Atomic Scientists* (May 1, 1946), Vol. I, No. 10, p. 4.

[66] Blackett, *Fear, War, and the Bomb*, p. 138.

[67] Churchill, *Triumph and Tragedy*, p. 639. For the coordination between the British and Americans on the development of the atomic bomb, see Smyth, *Atomic Energy for Military Purposes, passim;* Winston Churchill, *The Hinge of Fate* (Boston: Houghton Mifflin, 1950), pp. 377-81; Truman, *Year of Decisions*, p. 418; Leahy, *I Was There*, pp. 265, 432. General Groves opposed this coordination and testified so later; see *Oppenheimer Hearings*, p. 175.

[68] Churchill, *Triumph and Tragedy*, p. 638.

[69] Hillman, *Mr. President*, p. 248; Truman, *Year of Decisions*, p. 415. General Eisenhower was at Potsdam and his advice, Truman says, was asked. The various participants differ in their recollections of this meeting. See also King and Whitehill, *Fleet Admiral King*, p. 621; Arnold, *Global Mission*, p. 585.

[70] Truman, *Year of Decisions*, p. 416. See also Byrnes, *Speaking Frankly*, p. 263.

[71] Combined Chiefs of Staff Report to the President and Prime Minister, 24 July 1945, quoted in Cline, *Washington Command Post*, p. 346, and reproduced in *The Entry of the Soviet Union into the War Against Japan*, pp. 89-91.

[72] Truman, *Year of Decisions*, p. 306; Churchill, *Triumph and Tragedy*, p. 642. See also Byrnes, *Speaking Frankly*, p. 205; Leahy, *I Was There*, p. 420.

[73] Robert E. Sherwood, *Roosevelt and Hopkins: An Intimate History* (New York: Harper, 1948), p. 902, Leahy, *I Was There*, p. 383.

[74] Cordell Hull, *The Memoirs of Cordell Hull*, 2 vols. (New York: Macmillan, 1948), Vol. II, pp. 1591-94; Byrnes, *Speaking Frankly*, pp. 205-07; Stimson

and Bundy, *On Active Service*, pp. 626-27; Grew, *The Turbulent Era*, Vol. II, pp. 1424-27.

[75] Hull, *Memoirs*, Vol. II, p. 1593.

[76] The text of the declaration is printed in Stimson and Bundy, *On Active Service*, and in Butow, *Japan's Decision to Surrender*, Appendix C.

[77] For expressions of this view, see Baldwin, *Great Mistakes of the War*, pp. 91-92; McCloy, *Challenge to American Foreign Policy*, p. 43.

[78] This incident has given rise to a controversy best understood by a linguist. It is covered in detail in Kazuo Kawaii, "Mokusatsu," *Pacific Historical Review* (November, 1950), pp. 409-414; and William J. Coughlin, "The Great Mokusatsu," *Harper's* Magazine (March, 1953), pp. 31-40.

[79] Kase, *Journey to the "Missouri,"* p. 222.

[80] For an account of these preparations, see Craven and Cate, *The Army Air Forces in World War II*, Vol. V, pp. 713-25.

[81] *Ibid.*, p. 714. The relevant documents, including a letter from President Truman to Professor Cate, are reproduced on pages 696-97, 712-13. See also Leahy, *I Was There*, pp. 430-31, and Truman's letter to Dr. Karl T. Compton, published in *Atlantic Monthly* (February, 1947), p. 27.

[82] Truman, *Year of Decisions*, pp. 420-21.

[83] For a vivid account of the bombing, see Miller and Spitzer, *We Dropped the A-Bomb*, and Laurence, *Dawn Over Zero*, pp. 207-211. The statement is published in the New York *Times*, August 7, 1945. See also Leahy, *I Was There*, p. 430, and Byrnes, *Speaking Frankly*, p. 209.

[84] Butow, *Japan's Decision to Surrender*, pp. 153-54; the New York *Times*, August 9, 1945.

[85] Craven and Cate, *The Army Air Forces in World War II*, Vol. V, pp. 714-23; Laurence, *Dawn Over Zero*, pp. 228-43; Miller and Spitzer, *We Dropped the A-Bomb*, pp. 89-124.

[86] Blackett, *Fear, War, and the Bomb*, p. 137. Norman Cousins and Thomas K. Finletter take the same position in the article, "A Beginning for Sanity," cited in footnote 62.

[87] Sherwood, *Roosevelt and Hopkins*, p. 902; Edward R. Stettinius, *Roosevelt and the Russians* (Garden City, N.Y.: Doubleday, 1949), p. 91.

[88] The story of the last few days of the war in Japan is told in considerable detail in Butow, *Japan's Decision to Surrender;* USSBS, *Japan's Struggle to End the War;* USAAF, *Mission Accomplished* (Washington, 1946). On the American side, the chief sources are Byrnes, *Speaking Frankly*, pp. 209-11; Leahy, *I Was There*, pp. 434-45; Millis, *The Forrestal Diaries*, pp. 82-85; Stimson and Bundy, *On Active Service*, pp. 626-67; Deane, *The Strange Alliance*, pp. 277-78.

[89] USSBS, *Japan's Struggle to End the War*, p. 13. See also Arnold, *Global Mission*, p. 598.

[90] Dr. Karl T. Compton, "If the Atomic Bomb Had Not Been Dropped," *Atlantic Monthly* (December, 1946), p. 54.

[91] Arnold, *Global Mission*, p. 598. Nimitz' statement is quoted in Baldwin, *Great Mistakes of the War*, p. 93.

[92] The New York *Times*, August 15, 1945, quoting an interview with Chennault.

A Note on the Office of
the Chief of Military History
and Its Publications

Early in World War II President Franklin D. Roosevelt urged the executive departments to begin compiling their war record with the main purpose of "preserving for those who come after us . . . an accurate and objective account of our present experience." To consolidate its historical activities, the Army in August 1943 established a Historical Branch in the G-2 Division of its General Staff. After the war, the Branch became the Office, Chief of Military History, a separate staff division with the principal task of preparing a detailed narrative history of the Army's participation in the greatest war of modern times. The series *United States Army in World War II,* on which the chapters of this book are based, is the impressive result.

The Army is no novice in the field of history. In the nineteenth century, it enriched libraries in this country and abroad with its massive compilation of Civil War documents known as *The War of the Rebellion.* After World War I, its historical efforts produced seventeen volumes of documents recording the experience of the American Expeditionary Forces. The enormous quantities of records amassed by the Army during World War II made comprehensive publication of documents impracticable, and the Army turned its hand to narrative histories. The first such official writings on the World War II experience were inspired by General George C. Marshall, who wanted published accounts of combat operations made available to the soldiers who had fought in them. Between 1943 and 1948, the Army prepared and published fourteen narratives in its *American Forces in Action* series. After the series became available to the public, more than 200,000 of these pamphlets were sold.

The general and more comprehensive *United States Army in World War II* began to appear in 1947, and since then more than fifty volumes of this series have been published or are now in press. A number of additional volumes, as indicated in the following list, are still in preparation. This vast undertaking—the largest co-operative effort in the writing of narrative history ever attempted in the United States—has been possible only because the Army really wanted to know the truth about its wartime record. In 1947, President Dwight D. Eisenhower, then the Army's Chief of Staff, insisted that the big history "must, without reservation, tell the complete story of the Army's participation," and tell it "with no reservations as to whether or not the evidence of history places the Army in a favorable light." No contemporary history can be perfect or definitive, but both scholars and professional soldiers have acknowledged that the volumes of the World War II series maintain the highest standards of scholarship, objectivity, and readability. They are the product of a team effort:

of enthusiastic and effective leadership by the distinguished officers who have served as Chief of Military History; of unsparing dedication on the part of a group of professional historians, who have worked with assurance that their integrity and responsibility as scholars would be respected; and of guidance from an advisory committee composed of members of the academic world and the Army's own school system.

Today the work of the Office of the Chief of Military History encompasses much more than writing the World War II volumes, which are now nearing completion. Besides preparing and publishing many other historical works of particular interest to the Army, the Office is presently engaged in preparing volumes on the Cold War, the Korean War, and other post-World War II developments. In addition, it helps to stimulate *esprit de corps* and pride of the soldier in his unit. And it provides the historical information required to support current Army plans and operations.

Space does not permit listing all the works published by the Army in recent years, but a brochure describing them will be sent in response to a request to the Office of the Chief of Military History, Department of the Army, Washington 25, D.C.

European Theater of Operations

Cross-Channel Attack	6.75
The Lorraine Campaign	11.00
The Supreme Command	6.50
Logistical Support of the Armies, Vol. I	4.50
Logistical Support of the Armies, Vol. II	
The Siegfried Line Campaign	
The Ardennes Campaign	
Breakout and Pursuit	
Southern France and Alsace	
The Last Offensive	

The War in the Pacific

The Fall of the Philippines	5.25
Guadalcanal: The First Offensive	4.00
Okinawa: The Last Battle	8.50
The Approach to the Philippines	6.25
Leyte: Return to the Philippines	6.75
Gilberts and Marshalls	5.75
Cartwheel: Reduction of Rabaul	
Victory in Papua	6.00
Triumph in the Philippines	
Campaign in the Marianas	
Strategy and Command, Vols. I and II	

China-Burma-India Theater

Stilwell's Mission to China	5.50
Stilwell's Command Problems	6.25
Time Runs Out in CBI	

The Middle East Theater

The Persian Corridor and Aid to Russia	4.00

Ordnance Department

Planning Munitions for War	4.25
From Factory to Fighting Front	
Ordnance Overseas	

Corps of Engineers

Troops and Equipment
Construction in the United States
Operations Against Germany
Operations Against Japan

Medical Department

Hospitalization and Evacuation: ZI	4.00

Chemical Warfare Service

Organizing for War
From Laboratory to Field
Chemicals in Combat

Finance Corps

Finance Corps in WWII

Civil Affairs

Soldiers Become Governors

Special Projects

Master Index: Reader's Guide	.50
Military Relations Between the U.S. and Canada, 1939-45	
History of the Women's Army Corps	6.25
Three Battles: Arnaville, Altuzzo, and Schmidt	4.50
The War Against Germany and Italy: Mediterranean and Adjacent Areas (Pictorial Record)	4.00
The War Against Germany: Europe and Adjacent Areas (Pictorial Record)	3.75
The War Against Japan (Pictorial Record)	4.00
The Employment of Negro Troops	
Statistics	
Chronology	
Rearming the French	4.25

Index

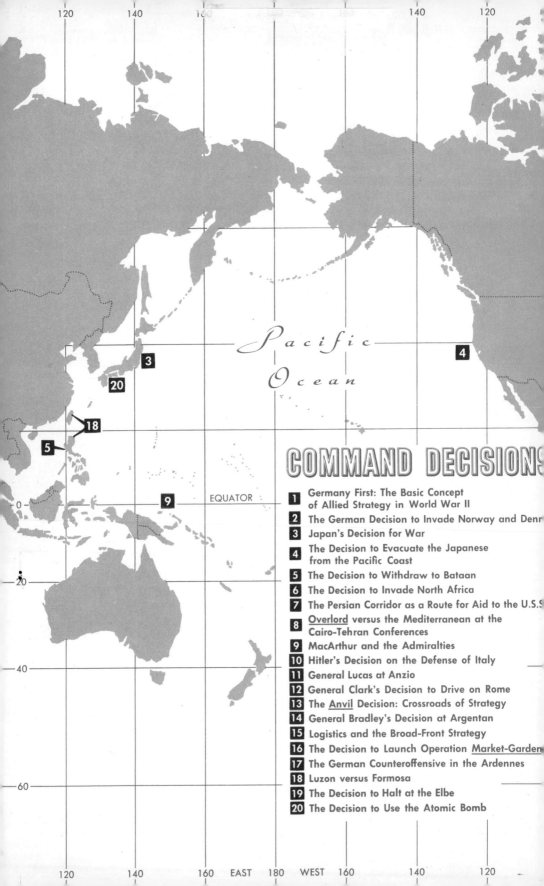

120 140 160 140 120

Pacific

3

20

Ocean

4

18

5

9 EQUATOR

COMMAND DECISIONS

120 140 160 EAST 180 WEST 160 140 120